This book is to be returned on or before
the last date stamped below

The Duchess of Windsor

THE DUCHESS OF WINDSOR

The Uncommon Life of Wallis Simpson

Greg King

AURUM PRESS

In memory of
Diana, Princess of Wales

Contents

Preface

I DON'T WANT PEOPLE referring back to inaccuracies after I am dead."[1] So said Wallis, Duchess of Windsor, in an interview in 1956, prior to the publication of her memoirs, *The Heart Has Its Reasons*. In spite of her wishes, however, Wallis had the dual misfortune of having inaccuracies written and spread about her not only after her death but during her lifetime as well.

Wallis had always fascinated me, and through my interest in the British Royal Family, I had casually studied the lives of the Duke and Duchess of Windsor. Like most people, I was prepared to believe the worst: tales of ambition, humiliation, treason, and sexual escapades. Certainly, the vast majority of those who have chronicled the Royal Family have expressed little sympathy for the Windsors. After twenty years of reading the worst that authors and historians had to offer on Wallis Windsor, I felt her portrait seemed set, and it was an unflattering one at that.

It would be difficult to imagine a woman more vilified in the twentieth century than the Duchess of Windsor. Beyond the intimate circle of those still alive who knew the Duchess well, she has been all but lost to myth. From the middle of the 1930s, when she first became a public figure, to the present day, Wallis has been condemned as common and vulgar, a scheming adventuress, a frivolous woman whose fierce determination to become Queen of the United Kingdom of Great Britain and Northern Ireland provoked the abdication of King Edward VIII. Thereafter, her ambitions thwarted, she married the former King and embarked on one of the most self-indulgent and extravagant lives in recorded history. Popular legend has it that Wallis never loved the man who had given up the throne to marry her and did little more than nag him to his grave.

There is much more. Wallis, it is suggested, was a Russian spy, an American spy, a German spy, an Italian spy; she was mistress to both Hitler's and Mussolini's diplomats; she dealt illegal drugs; she prosti-

tuted herself in Chinese brothels; had illicit affairs before and after her
marriage to the Duke; and was in reality a hermaphrodite. The sheer
breadth of the accusations is staggering. Was this woman really as
despicable as most historians have led us to believe?

The few voices raised in defense of the Duchess of Windsor,
therefore, struck me as rather apologetic, almost dismissive of the
apparently overwhelming evidence of her sordid life and shameful
character. Ralph G. Martin's biography *The Woman He Loved* presented
a portrait of Wallis Windsor so contrary to the public image that it
seemed impossible to treat it seriously. Lady Mosley's 1980 biography,
coming from a close friend of the Duchess's, seemed far from impar-
tial. And Michael Bloch, who authored six books on the Duke and
Duchess of Windsor between 1983 to 1996, had done so at the request
of their French lawyer, Maître Suzanne Blum, and could therefore be
considered partisan. Surely, I thought, the Windsors cannot have been
the couple presented in these books: a rather human man and woman,
both somewhat stubborn at times but neither one the unsympathetic
nuisance of whom I had often read.

History is rarely composed of those with black or white characters. Undoubtedly, the Duchess of Windsor was neither a villain nor a
saint. Somewhere between these polar views had to be the truth. Over
the years, I toyed with the idea of writing a biography of the Duchess if
only because it seemed to me that here was a woman—like the subject
of my first book, Empress Alexandra Feodorovna of Russia—whose vile
public image concealed what was undoubtedly something rather more
mundane. Still, the territory was abundant with memoirs and biographies. What more could be said? Unlike Empress Alexandra, Wallis
failed to strike an emotional chord in me; as far as I was concerned,
whatever favorable qualities I was ready to allow her by virtue of sheer
logic failed to outweigh what I continued to perceive as her hard
character, faulty judgment, and aimless life. Then, too, the Duchess of
Windsor was a little outside my favored realm of research—nineteenth-
century European Royals and the Russian Imperial Family. Without
completely dismissing the thought, I moved on to other projects.

I admit that most of my antipathy toward the Duchess of Windsor was based on esteem for the British Royal Family. If the much-
loved and revered Queen Mother despised her, she must have had
good reason. But this naive view changed when I, like millions of
others around the world, witnessed—through publication of authorized and semiauthorized memoirs, stolen love letters and indiscreet
photographs, televised admissions of adultery and taped telephone
conversations, divorces and haggles over paying taxes—the unraveling
of the beatific myth surrounding the House of Windsor. With the
monarchy under increasing pressure, certain incidents over the last

seventy years began to take on a new perspective, and assume definite shades of gray. As they did, I often thought about Wallis; realizing that the present Royal Family was quite capable of ruthless behavior and self-preservation, I wondered if the pattern would have been all that different where the Duke and Duchess of Windsor were concerned. Indeed, the same powerful matriarchy which had largely been responsible for the Windsors' ostracism, headed by Queen Elizabeth, the Queen Mother, remains firmly in place. If the Royal Family were not the bastions of virtue and selflessness, an image they had themselves promoted, was it also possible that Wallis was not necessarily the evil adventuress they had always made her out to be?

With growing interest, I began to view the Duchess of Windsor in this light: someone who had blundered into a system she did not understand and which refused to change; who came under the influence of a man more stubborn than she, whose petulant determination to wed her would, ironically, be viewed as her own ambitious plan; and whose continued existence was a much-resented and painful reminder to the Royal Family of the crisis through which they had passed. For the rest of her life, the Duchess of Windsor was to be punished—denied her rightful style of Royal Highness, her efforts in the Second World War completely ignored by King George VI, and, at the side of her husband, condemned to an exile which kept her in perpetual disgrace. With each new crack in the Royal Family's image, the Duchess became more sympathetic to me. It was rather obvious that she, like Diana, Princess of Wales, had suffered at the hands of the family into which she had married and their attendant court and been the subject of a carefully orchestrated whispering campaign.

In the spring of 1996, I was living in London, researching a future work on the court of Tsar Nicholas II and doing publicity for the U.K. editions of my first two books. During a visit to Hatchard's, one of London's premier book stores, I had a conversation with Robin Piguet of the Biography Department about my possible subsequent projects. I casually mentioned Wallis, but Robin told me that Michael Bloch would shortly be publishing a new biography of the Duchess of Windsor. Hearing this, I thought, Well, that's that, then. Bloch, I reasoned, had years of unprecedented access to the Windsors' private papers in Paris and was surely the best-informed man on the subject. His biography would undoubtedly be the final word, answering the many charges made against her.

A few weeks later, Robin rang my flat and told me that Bloch's new book, *The Duchess of Windsor*, had just arrived. Curious, I ran down to Hatchard's and picked up a copy. I was somewhat surprised to find that it was a mixture of text and photographs, running to just over two hundred pages. I bought the book, walked up Piccadilly to

Green Park, and sat down in the sunshine to read. This was not the massive biography which I had been expecting: Bloch had produced a clear, concise account of her life for the curious but admitted in a preface that he had made no attempt to write a definitive work. I left Green Park that evening and rounded onto the Mall as the floodlights were being turned on at Buckingham Palace. I paused, as I always did, to sit for a few minutes on the steps of the Queen Victoria Monument and look up at the palace's rather grim stone façade. Now, however, I saw it as a powerful symbol of all that Wallis Windsor had fought for in her life—dignity, respect, tradition, solidity—and also of her rejection by the aristocracy, court, and the Royal Family. Sitting before the palace, I knew I would write about the Duchess of Windsor.

My decision was reinforced when I happened to watch the British television premiere of a documentary called *Edward on Edward*, produced by Prince Edward, Queen Elizabeth II's youngest son. This seemed to me little more than another attempt by the Royal Family to depict the Duke and Duchess of Windsor as a rather sad, puerile couple leading profligate and self-indulgent lives. I, on the other hand, was becoming increasingly sympathetic to the Windsors, believing that the Duke—and especially the Duchess—had been grossly and unfairly subjected to years of wild rumor and innuendo. Out of this grew a desire to write a favorable but accurate biography of the Duchess, something no one had really attempted since Ralph G. Martin's *Woman He Loved* some twenty years earlier.

This proved to be more of an undertaking than I had anticipated. I faced over sixty years of largely negative press concerning the Duchess, from allegations of her sexual liaisons to accusations of collaboration with the Nazi regime. Above and beyond the actual assertions concerning Wallis were the hundreds of open questions surrounding her life: Had she loved the Duke? Why had she and the former King not had any children? Had they really treated their servants badly? What were the true circumstances of her last years?

Aside from memoirs, diaries, letters, and published works, the best hope of getting at the truth lay with those who knew the Windsors most intimately: their family members, friends, and those who had formed their household and staff. Understandably, they were reluctant to speak of the Duke and Duchess. Some feared reprisals from the Royal Family and court, while others, having suffered through inaccurate quotations and previous scandal-plagued biographies, had little reason to trust anyone writing about the Windsors. Eventually, I managed to convince most of those I approached to cooperate; while quite a few still requested anonymity, which I have honored, others went on record for the first time. All have my sincere thanks.

What has emerged from my research is a portrait of the Duchess of Windsor that is vastly different from that of popular conception. I make no apologies that the Duchess of Windsor, herein described, is a generally sympathetic character, in contrast to the usual depiction of a scheming, vulgar, and flamboyant woman so often featured in previous works. In part, this is intentional: I have focused largely on those aspects of her life that have been ignored—such as her war work in the Bahamas or her charity work in the later part of her life—because they not only illuminate her character but have also been all but neglected by most other writers. Nor do I feel it necessary to repeat each and every unfavorable story concerning the Windsors. When some detail of her life seemed particularly important, I have, of course, examined the circumstances. Wallis was not an extraordinary woman; she undoubtedly had faults as well as strengths. If I have focused less on the former and more on the latter, it is not because I do not believe they ever existed, rather, that most other writers have taken great pains to point out her human failings. Anyone can pick up a book and read about the Duchess's alleged intrigues, her rumored affairs, and her supposed unhappy marriage to the Duke. I am no apologist for the Duchess of Windsor: While some of these tales are undoubtedly true, it seems to me counterproductive in a biography whose declared aim is to present an accurate and sympathetic portrait of the Duchess to endlessly repeat them here. Rather, I have tried to examine the allegations and gossip, place them in context, answer charges made against the Duchess, and refute or acknowledge them accordingly.

I also freely admit that the picture of the British Royal Family contained within is not a very flattering one. I do not, however, feel that it is in any way distorted. My focus is on the way in which the Royal Family responded to and treated Wallis. If there is nothing of the Queen Mother's benevolent public smile or Elizabeth II's dedication to duty here, it is because these qualities are irrelevant to their private relations with the Duke and Duchess of Windsor. As with the Duchess of Windsor, I have examined the other side of the myth. Whereas in previous biographies Wallis's favorable qualities and sympathetic character have largely remained hidden, the Royal Family's often callous and calculating actions have been glossed over. In reconciling these two myths, I know I shall be accused of partiality. I can only say that any honest and accurate portrayal of the Royal Family's dealings with the Duke and Duchess of Windsor has, of necessity, to reflect their less-than-admirable behavior; in an admittedly sympathetic biography of the Duchess, this is even more true. At the same time, I have tried to examine the reasons why the Royal Family behaved as they did, even when I am highly critical of their actions.

Of necessity, a number of subjects—allegations of Nazi sympathies, questionable relationships, and most principally, the abdication crisis—have been dealt with at length, even when it may appear that their relevance veers more toward the Duke than the Duchess. I would ask my readers, however, to remember that the events of King Edward VIII's brief reign and his life thereafter in exile, along with his friendships and associations, have long been used against the Duchess in an attempt to paint her with the same brush of traitorous behavior as has been used against the Duke. I have kept the discussion of the actual abdication crisis to a minimum, but obviously, even in an episode in which Wallis herself played little direct part, it is necessary to reexamine the details in any biography of the woman the King of England gave up his throne to marry. In their life following the abdication, the Duke and Duchess operated as a team; slights against her were taken as direct insults against them both; his behavior was perceived to be influenced by her; and their actions often reflected decisions made together. Therefore, I have dealt at some length with important incidents in the Duke's life when they have affected Wallis's reputation. At times, it has been possible to examine the Duke's behavior in a new light, and I think his portrait, like that of his wife, is likewise largely a sympathetic one.

This book is an attempt to write a fair and favorable biography of the Duchess of Windsor. I do not claim to have produced the definitive work; it still needs writing. But I think that with the assistance of the Windsors' friends I have managed to correct many of the misconceptions about the Duchess—and, by extension, the Duke—and answer the years of rumor and innuendo which have plagued Wallis. There remain outstanding questions, and some answers may never be found. But I believe that enough of the pieces have come together to form an accurate picture of her memorable life.

And it was, indeed, a memorable life. Wallis may not have been very different from most women, but she lived through astonishing events and managed to transcend her circumstances and create one of the most remarkable lives of the twentieth century. She had few talents, but those which she mastered—the decoration of her homes, her fashion sense, her entertainments, and her care of the Duke—ensured her a place in the public eye for most of her life. And while she famously created brilliant houses and presided over grand parties, perhaps her most unsung and important accomplishments were those she made during the Second World War, when she transformed the struggling relief agencies in the Bahamas into efficient care centers and funded and opened canteens for the thousands of soldiers who never failed to succumb to her charm.

In a life which has largely been condemned as shallow and frivolous, Wallis achieved a rare balance: forced to live in the glare of an unceasing spotlight of publicity, she remained, against all odds, very much the same woman with whom the Duke had fallen in love. It is arguable that, with her proven abilities in the Bahamas and natural ease, she would have made an admirable addition to the British Royal Family had they welcomed her after her marriage. But, condemned for her past and blamed for the feelings of the man who loved her, Wallis was doomed to remain forever anathema in the eyes of her husband's family. Her contributions, therefore, must be measured against the circumstances which were imposed upon her and the times in which she lived; in this, Wallis rarely failed.

"Mine is a simple story—or so I like to think," the Duchess of Windsor wrote in her memoirs. "It is the story of an ordinary life that became extraordinary."[2] That story—of the aristocratic but poor girl from Baltimore who inadvertently found herself at the center of the century's greatest romance—is indeed one which needs a fresh telling.

Prologue

Paris sweltered in the hot afternoon sun as the car pulled to a stop before the tall iron gates at 4, route du Champ d'Entraine-ment. Within a few seconds, they parted, and the automobile swept along the drive, beneath the shade of the old chestnut and oak trees, and came to a stop before the portico of the Windsor villa. The glass-and-wrought-iron doors of the house were opened by Martin Gregory, the tall, distinguished-looking man who for many years had worked as assistant butler to the Duke and Duchess of Windsor and who now looked after the property for its current resident, Egyptian-born mil-lionaire Mohammed al Fayed. Al Fayed's forty-one-year-old son, Dodi, escorted Diana, Princess of Wales, up the steps and into the welcome cool of the villa's entrance hall.

This was thirty-six-year-old Diana's second visit to the former home of the Duke and Duchess of Windsor. Five weeks earlier, on July 25, she and Dodi Fayed had spent an afternoon wandering through its magnificent rooms, restored at great cost by his father to their former glory. Now, on this last Saturday in August 1997, the villa stood empty, its chambers stripped of furniture, carpets, curtains, and paintings. In three weeks, Sotheby's, at the request of Mohammed al Fayed, would auction off the contents of the house in New York City.

Sunlight spilled through the three tall windows of the drawing room, washing the honey-colored parquet floor with a brilliant sheen, as Diana and Dodi entered. Here the world's most famous royal out-cast, Wallis Simpson, Duchess of Windsor, had entertained, presiding over sparkling parties attended by the elite of European aristocracy, writers, actors, artists, and authors. Now the only sound came from Diana's low-heeled shoes as they clicked across the bare floor.

Like the Duchess of Windsor, Diana, Princess of Wales, stood beyond the bounds of royal convention, having been cast adrift fol-lowing her divorce from Prince Charles almost exactly a year earlier. She had lost the style of Her Royal Highness; her name as the spouse of the Prince of Wales had been removed from the regular prayers for members of the Royal Family; her foreign tours were downgraded at the request of Buckingham Palace; and, perhaps most significant, she was the victim of a subtle yet persistent campaign to marginalize her role in public life.

Wallis, Duchess of Windsor, had suffered years of deliberate humiliation at the hands of the British Royal Family and the court. Her position as a twice-divorced American commoner made her anathema to many, and she was widely blamed for Edward VIII's abdication. The abdication was nothing if not a moral crisis—a battle waged between the new King's modern approach to life and the traditional attitudes of the aristocracy. That the stigma of Wallis's divorce made her unsuitable as a queen consort in 1936 is without question; that in exile, married to the Duke of Windsor for thirty-five years, she warranted the continued punishment is open to debate. For the very presence of Diana, Princess of Wales, in the Windsor villa that Saturday afternoon proved nothing if not how much values and circumstances had changed in the family of Queen Elizabeth II.

The first cracks in Elizabeth II's reign came in 1967, when her cousin the Earl of Harewood left his wife to live openly with his mistress, whom he later married. His brother also later divorced his wife. The Queen's sister, Princess Margaret, following a very public renunciation of her divorced paramour in the 1950s, found her marriage to Antony Armstrong-Jones, the Earl of Snowdon, crumbling amid intense media scrutiny. Their marriage was dissolved in 1978.

The painful collapse of the marriage of the Prince and Princess of Wales, played out in front pages of newspapers around the world and on television programs, where both partners confessed their affairs, was surely as much a crisis as the abdication, if in a different way. Whereas the abdication had pitted Edward VIII against his government, the disintegration of the Waleses' marriage seemed destined to tear at the loyalties of those faithful to Elizabeth II and tradition and those who championed the Princess of Wales, arguably the most popular woman of the twentieth century.

Divorce also reared its head in the marriages of Elizabeth II's other children: in 1992, the same year in which the Waleses' marriage ended, the Duke and Duchess of York separated; and Princess Anne, the Princess Royal, not only divorced her husband, Capt. Mark Phillips, but remarried in a quiet ceremony in Scotland. This last occasion aptly demonstrated how much the monarchy had changed since the days of the abdication crisis. Not only did Anne marry a man with whom stolen and published letters indicated she had had an affair while still wed to her first husband, but the union was celebrated in the presence of both the Queen and the Queen Mother, the two women who had, for the last forty years, steadfastly refused to accept the Duchess of Windsor. The mounting criticism of the Royal Family, the behavior of its members, the shouts of "Ernest Simpson!" which greeted Andrew Parker-Bowles, husband of Prince Charles's mistress, when he appeared at the Turf Club, all built into pressures that seemed as threatening to the continued survival of the monarchy as the relationship between Wallis Simpson and Edward VIII nearly sixty years earlier.[1]

Sarah Ferguson, the estranged Duchess of York, for one, was left pondering her future in a family whose rejection and indifference she had come to know well. Like her sister-in-law, the Duchess of York felt trapped by the machinations of court officials, those same forces whom the Duchess of Windsor had long ago blamed for much of the abdication crisis. "I thought quite a bit about the most famous female outcast of them all," wrote the Duchess of York of the winter of 1991, "the one who had led a king to abdicate and ultimately brought Elizabeth to her throne. There were yellow roses strangely growing in my garden at Sunninghill at the time, defying the cold. I picked a bunch and took them to Frogmore, the royal mausoleum. And I laid those stubborn flowers on the sparsely kept grave of Mrs. Wallis Warfield Simpson, another woman who could never fit in."[2]

As they had done with Wallis Windsor, the Royal Family closed ranks against Diana. Her isolation, her troubled private life, her quest for a meaningful life of her own, had led her to this elegant stone palace. Over the last few weeks, media around the world had reported her relationship with Dodi Fayed, a sometime film producer and rather genial man who both clearly adored her and also undoubtedly relished the idea of a liaison with her. Although the relationship appears to have been little more than a summer romance, there was ample speculation that Diana might find refuge in these regal rooms. The irony that the world's most famous divorcée might discover peace in the miniature palace created by the subject of the twentieth century's most famous romance was not lost on the press. That same week, in fact, author Hugo Vickers, in the British magazine *Hello!* had written of the possible benefits Diana might enjoy were she to abandon life in England for the sheltering walls of the Windsor villa.[3]

Just before five, Diana and Dodi left the villa. Diana had looked around carefully, examining the rooms, asking questions about the kitchen and bathrooms. According to one close friend, Diana was considering the idea of dividing her time between London and Paris and the Windsor villa had been proposed as a suitable residence. It seems likely that this—and not a future relationship with Dodi Fayed—was responsible for her interest.[4] The couple left 4, route du Champ d'Entrainement. Their car carried them to Dodi Fayed's apartment and then to his father's Ritz Hotel, where they shared a late supper. Just after midnight, they left the Ritz in a new car, a sleek black Mercedes, chased by a contingent of paparazzi and driven by a man with over three times the legal limit of alcohol in his blood. Twelve hours after wandering through the hushed, tomblike villa in the Bois de Boulogne, Diana, Princess of Wales, would be dead.

The Duchess of Windsor

"Mortality for others, immortality for oneself."

—Wallis, Commonplace Book

1

Romeo and Juliet in Baltimore

SIXTY YEARS after the fact, writing her memoirs from the comfort of her great nineteenth-century Parisian villa and pondering her place in history, Wallis, Duchess of Windsor, deliberately altered the date of her parents' wedding. Records indicate that the marriage was solemnized on November 19, 1895. Wallis Windsor, however, would insist that it had taken place in June, a difference of five months. Like so many aspects of her life, this discrepancy would lead to years of insinuation.

There was nothing extraordinary in the glum little ceremony that united Teackle Wallis Warfield and Alice Montague in marriage that late November afternoon. The circumstances, however, belied the peculiar nature of the event. The Reverend Dr. C. Ernest Smith faced the couple not before the altar of his Church of St. Michael and All Angels in Baltimore but in the dimly lit drawing room of the adjacent rectory. The customary trappings of a happy society wedding were notably absent: No congregation looked on in support as their vows were exchanged; no organ thundered in celebration; no voices were raised in joyous song; no fragrant scent of flowers filled the air.

It cannot have been the wedding that twenty-four-year-old Alice Montague had envisioned for herself. Tall and slender, with golden hair worn plaited or loosely coiled atop her head, Alice was the product of a proud, aristocratic heritage. In the waning November light, wide deep blue eyes gazed out from the chiseled lines of her ivory face. She possessed other charms as well: In an era when most young women remained carefully sheltered and prided themselves on their domestic skills and comprehension of social expectations, she happily dominated conversations with her biting wit. Her mind was exceptionally quick, and her charm impressed even the most staid of companions.[1]

Quiet, thoughtful Teackle Wallis Warfield had been attracted to the vivacious and magnetic woman who now stood at his side.

3

T. Wallis, as the groom chose to call himself, looked much older than his bride, an unwelcome illusion aided by his receding hairline and slight, almost-stooped figure. But he was also handsome, with light blue eyes and a dashing little mustache that lent him an air of dignity. Half-hidden in the shadows was the pallor of his skin, the hollowed cheeks, the red-rimmed eyes that spoke of his inability to sleep. His loud coughs, however, interrupting the short, sad service, were an uncomfortable reminder of not only just how ill the groom had become but of the uncertainties the young couple would face in the future. For T. Wallis Warfield, at the age of twenty-five, was already dying.

The nature of his illness, the troubling circumstances surrounding the union, and the absolute hush that descended over the marriage taking place that November afternoon in Baltimore would forever haunt the little girl born to the couple seven months later. It is but one of the many ironies in the life of Wallis, Duchess of Windsor, that she, party to perhaps the twentieth century's most celebrated and publicized marriage, should have been the product of one of the nineteenth century's most private.

In the fading years of the nineteenth century, the city of Baltimore was a place of great contrasts. Its heritage was firmly rooted in the distant days of the eighteenth century, but the city also reflected the changing times: telephone and electric lines formed aerial lattices over colonial squares, and factory smokestacks spewed forth clouds of industrial waste into the Atlantic sky. The city, like the great mass of America itself, filled with immigrants and tycoons, great wealth and appalling poverty, and the still-bleeding wounds from the devastating Civil War, hovered uneasily between the old century and the new.

Baltimore remained a bastion of the defeated Confederacy, a city that prided itself on its unique, carefully cultivated charm. Although it lay less than fifty miles from the nation's capital, Baltimore regarded itself not as a northern town but as a refined southern outpost. When the Civil War had come, the city's sympathies were expressed in lively demonstrations, street parades, and a rebellious state legislature that had argued the benefits of secession from the United States. As a result, it was occupied by Union troops throughout the hostilities, leaving divisive scars which lasted well into the twentieth century.

Mingled with these southern influences was a distinctly English flavor. Baltimore had modeled itself not only on the great cities to the south but also along the more genteel lines of English towns, a holdover from the days before the American Revolution, when an imported British aristocracy ruled the New World and transplanted the ideas of Georgian London to the wild shores of the Americas. Many of the town's illustrious families were descendants of the first English settlers along the eastern seaboard; in time they had formed into a carefully knit community which believed itself superior to later settlers. Here position and breeding counted for a great deal, and the offspring of these families were raised with high expectations and imbued with a sense of their own social heritage and unique obligations.

The charm of Baltimore lay in its picturesque atmosphere. Cobbled streets, shaded by rows of linden and oak trees, were lined with Georgian and Italianate mansions. Endless rows of upright brick town houses skirted narrow side streets and circled small parks whose stretches of grass were guarded by wrought-iron fences. The smell of salt air wafting in on ocean breezes, the squawking of gulls, clatter of carriages, chiming of clocks, and tolling of church bells filled the senses. Chesapeake Bay brought commerce and trade, and the waterfront was lined with the swaying masts of dozens of ships. When night came, sidewalks were illuminated by flickering gaslights.

Here, in a quiet, dignified house on 34 East Preston Street, an indomitable widow, Anna Emory Warfield, presided over one of the city's noble old families. The house, like its owner, was austere, solid, and unobtrusive. The Warfields were socially prominent, respectable, and comfortable, if not wealthy. For generations they had acted as civil servants, bankers, businessmen, and public officials. They knew the importance of their place in Baltimore society, and each generation was raised with a careful understanding not only of their position but of their impressive inheritance and breeding.

In the midst of the abdication crisis, Wallis was often dismissed as a common, vulgar American of little breeding and no heritage. In truth, the Duchess of Windsor was born of privileged ancestry, and the number of kings, earls, dukes, and aristocrats in her family tree rivaled those of her most vehement enemy, Queen Elizabeth, the Queen Mother. Like her future husband, she counted William the Conqueror among her forebears. Indeed, one of her ancestors, Pagan de Warfield, had accompanied William from France and fought beside him in the Battle of Hastings.[2] For his service, he was rewarded with a grant of land near Windsor Castle in Berkshire, named Warfield's Walk in his honor. Thereafter, the Warfield name appeared frequently in British history, and the family could proudly boast of their mention in the famous *Domesday Book*.[3]

During the reign of King Edward III, Robert de Warfield was made a Knight of the Order of the Garter, the highest honor in the kingdom.[4] The King himself, through one of those murky liaisons that litter royal history, was thought to have been an ancestor.[5] Throughout the centuries, Warfields served prominently at the English court, enjoying both close ties with the Royal Family and impressive financial and titular rewards for their loyal sacrifices.

The American history of the family was just as illustrious. In

1662, Richard Warfield left his native Berkshire and sailed to the colonies, where he became a prosperous gentleman farmer. He purchased hundreds of acres of fertile land along the Severn River, near what was to become Baltimore, and his wealth ensured his lasting influence in the colony. When he died, he left his six sons an impressive inheritance of land, money, and power.[6] In the centuries that followed, Warfields fought in George Washington's army during the Revolution and became successful bankers, lawyers, and civil servants; several held positions of great political power, including Edwin Warfield, who became governor of Maryland.

True to the sentiments of their Baltimore neighbors, the nineteenth-century Warfields remained staunch supporters of the Confederacy. Anna Emory Warfield's late husband, Henry Mactier Warfield, had been one of those local heroes who had proudly upheld the tradition. A prominent member of the Maryland legislature when the Civil War erupted, he had been one of the first officials to call for the secession of his state from the Union. Although there was widespread support for such a drastic measure, the forces of the Union won the day. On September 12, 1861, the night before the scheduled vote, Gen. John A. Dix, Baltimore's federal department commander, ordered the arrest of the rebel legislators, Warfield included.

For fourteen months, Henry Mactier Warfield and nine of his fellow legislators languished in Union bonds. At first, he was imprisoned within the thick, menacing bastions of Baltimore's Fort McHenry. From the tiny windows of his dank cell he could gaze upon the same impressive ramparts above which, fifty years earlier, Francis Scott Key had spied the fluttering remnants of an American flag and been moved to write *The Star-Spangled Banner*. Warfield was later taken to Fort Lafayette, thence to Fort Warren, located in Boston Harbor. The damp, musty cells, the meager diet, and the ferocity of life in a Union prison took their toll on Warfield's body, but his spirit remained as independent as ever. He refused repeated offers of freedom, on the condition that he take a public oath of allegiance to the Union and was moved to write to Abraham Lincoln's secretary of war, Edwin Stanton: "Sir, as I am confined without charges, I renew my claim to be discharged without conditions." Such stubborn resolve eventually paid off, and it was a point of family pride that Warfield was released without ever having taken a Union oath.[7]

Upon his release from prison, Henry Mactier Warfield resumed his business life with great success. His eventual position as one of the directors of the Baltimore and Ohio Railroad provided ample prestige and financial security for his growing family. He invested large sums of his sizable income in grain and flour exports and further increased his holdings. His success and popularity eventually won him the first presidency of the Baltimore Chamber of Commerce.

Warfield was not a man obsessed with the outward trappings of wealth. The family's comfortable town house on Baltimore's East Preston Street, home to the generation of Warfields who would shepherd the family into the twentieth century, was a perfect expression of his solemn character. Here he and his wife, Anna Emory, raised their seven children according to strict Victorian standards. Along with two daughters, Ann and Elizabeth, Anna had given birth to five sons, including Daniel, who died while still a child; Solomon Davies; Richard Emory; and Henry Mactier Jr.

The youngest son, Teackle Wallis, had been named after his father's great friend Severn Teackle Wallis, a fellow legislator who had been imprisoned at the outbreak of the Civil War for supporting Henry Mactier Warfield's call for secession. Wallis, like his friend, had been released from prison and gone on to great personal and financial success. His credits included distinguished author and lawyer; in time he became a provost of the University of Maryland, immortalized in a statue that dominated Baltimore's Mount Vernon Place.[8]

Teackle Wallis, however, proved unequal to the aspirations implicit in his prestigious name. Although he grew into a rather handsome young man, he never managed to match either the considerable accomplishments of his famous namesake or even those of his successful brothers. Fathered when Henry Mactier was already in his early sixties, T. Wallis was charming and extremely thoughtful; but he was also weak and suffered from chronic illness. Whereas his brothers had been noted for their robust health and physical presence, T. Wallis had never expressed more than a passing interest in athletic pursuits, and whatever intellectual promise he had shown had been cut short when he fell ill with consumption and had to withdraw from the university. The greater part of his life was passed in isolation, alone in his room, with hours spent either in bed or brooding over his future.

Within the sheltered, privileged world inhabited by the Warfields, illness was regarded not so much as a personal misfortune as it was a weakness of character and private disgrace. At the time, America was consumed with a new appetite for healthy living and outdoor exercise, led by future president Theodore Roosevelt; summer camps and rustic hotels had sprung up to accommodate the taste for rural holidays filled with vigorous activity. Weakness and physical frailty were abhorred. A young man such as T. Wallis, therefore, had quickly become a disappointment to his family, and it appears that little attempt was made to disguise these feelings. Rather than acknowledge their son's illness, the family made a fateful decision: The Warfields deliberately ignored it. T. Wallis was not, as might have been expected, dispatched to some distant health resort in a warmer climate, but instead put to work as a clerk at his uncle's Continental Trust in Baltimore, to learn the business by starting at the lowest level.

The job at the Continental Trust was scarcely glamorous, and T. Wallis seems not to have much cared for the career chosen by his family. But his continuing financial dependence ensured his silent cooperation. In these gloomy, routine surroundings, the young man's romantic inclinations remained carefully cloistered. Then, at the age of twenty-five, he fell in love.

The object of his affections was twenty-four-year-old Alice Montague, daughter of insurance salesman William Montague and his wife, Mary Anne. In later years Alice left no record of her first meeting with her future husband, nor did her daughter seem too inquisitive. We know nothing, therefore, of their first acquaintance and very little of their courtship.

Alice Montague, like her future husband, was the product of distinguished stock. The family was an old and respected one in their native England. They could lay claim to at least one king, Sir Simon Montecute, who was head of the House of Montague in the fourteenth century and married Aufrica, daughter of the King of the Isle of Man, in the Irish Sea. When Aufrica's father died, Simon inherited his throne and reigned as king for over fifty years. Ties with the British aristocracy were equally close. The Montagues were not only nobles in their own right but were also related to the Dukes of Manchester and the Earls of Sandwich.[9]

In 1621, some forty-one years before the first Warfield arrived, Peter Montague (Wallis's first U.S. ancestor) left Buckinghamshire and took up residence in the New World, settling in Virginia on a land grant, which, under King Charles II, was further expanded. He became a successful farmer, took a seat in the House of Burgesses, and married the daughter of the Virginia colony's governor.[10] Like the Warfields, the Montagues fought valiantly in the American Revolution, and one even threw himself in the path of a charging soldier, taking a saber cut meant for Gen. George Washington.[11]

"Beyond the fact that the Warfields and the Montagues shared the Mason-Dixon line as a common frontier," the Duchess later wrote, "they had almost nothing in common."[12] Unlike the staid Warfields, with their indomitable sense of duty, the Montagues placed more emphasis on enjoyment of life. Their magnetic personalities captivated and bewitched, and their slightly bohemian habits gave them a reputation as true southern eccentrics. Whereas solemnity and dignity were hallmarks of the Warfields, the Montagues were frivolous and carefree. As the years passed, the lands, prestige, and wealth faded. By the end of the nineteenth century, they were still regarded as one of Virginia's most distinguished families, although reduced circumstances meant that they no longer lived in the style to which their ancestors had become accustomed. According to the Duchess, her family's money had all but disappeared: "It had been a painfully long time since any except the most venerable of them could remember having enough to support themselves in the style they considered traditionally their own."[13] Although their once-great houses crumbled from lack of funds, they continued to live in them like relics of some vanished civilization, holding fast to a heritage peppered with notable names and cultivated charms.

Whatever the attraction that initially drew these two diverse personalities together, T. Wallis and Alice fell in love. The Montagues were themselves none too pleased that their lovely, energetic daughter had seemingly fallen in love with a melancholy young man who was already beginning to show the first signs of the tuberculosis that would eventually kill him. They felt that Alice, with her great beauty and charm, deserved a better match. Nor, despite their slightly cavalier attitude toward money, were the financial implications of the proposed marriage lost on the Montagues. T. Wallis, as the youngest son, possessed only fairly good prospects for the future, and there seemed little promise, with three older brothers, that this situation would be remedied with any estate settlement.

Nor were the Warfields any more enthused about the proposed match: The Montagues could scarcely be regarded, whatever their past glories, as a prosperous, socially prominent family, and Alice herself, with her buoyant good nature and free laughter, struck a discordant note in the serious, closeted world the Warfields inhabited. T. Wallis's family was also acutely aware of his illness, and the odds that he would be able to support a wife and family seemed dismal. Later, the Duchess would only half-jokingly refer to her parents' romance by relating it to the warring Montague and Capulet families in Shakespeare's tragedy *Romeo and Juliet*.[14]

Family conclaves were held; arguments were presented and voices raised, but no one seemed able to convince the young lovers that their marriage would be a disaster. Alice seemed oblivious of her future husband's illness, and he himself saw no reason, given his uncertain future, to forestall whatever happiness might temporarily be granted him.

When the couple married in a quiet service on November 19, 1895, no member of the Warfield or Montague families attended. Given the expressed reservations of both the Warfields and Montagues, it is entirely possible that neither T. Wallis nor Alice bothered to inform either their friends or their families until after the union had taken place. Such an attitude of opposition, adopted by both families, helps account for the complete silence surrounding the union, for no announcement ever appeared in any Baltimore newspaper.

This, at any rate, is the most favorable explanation. But more than one author has suggested that the quiet wedding and lack of family attendance indicated another reason: that Alice learned she was pregnant and that the couple wed privately to avoid any public scandal.

Since the future Duchess of Windsor was born a mere seven months after her parents' wedding, this idea is not without merit. Even in the morally rigid Victorian era, it may be that because of Alice's impetuous and carefree character and the weight of T. Wallis's illness a heavy portent, the Duchess's parents consummated their relationship prior to their wedding. This is almost certainly what the Duchess herself believed and helps account for her deliberate ambiguity and revision when writing her memoirs. Having herself been born in June 1896, she apparently feared, not unreasonably, that the date of her arrival in the world would cast a shadow over her conception.

The evidence that Wallis arrived prematurely, however, is equally strong. Thus, it is impossible to say a hundred years after the fact what forces—family disapproval or unexpected pregnancy—drew T. Wallis and Alice into the rectory drawing room that cold November day. For all of the Duchess's well-intentioned plans, her fearful alteration would result only in even more outrageous claims a century after her birth.

The newly married couple first lived quietly in T. Wallis's former bachelor apartment at 28 Hopkins Place, a small, dreary flat in a less than fashionable section of Baltimore. Whatever family tensions existed apparently remained unspoken, if not forgiven. T. Wallis returned to his job at the Continental Trust, and by the end of 1895, Alice was expecting a child.

Baltimore could be miserable in the summer, especially for one suffering from tuberculosis. The stale, still, humid air did nothing for T. Wallis's health, and he and Alice decided to spend the season elsewhere.

They chose Blue Ridge Summit, a small resort town nestled high in the mountains of Monterey County, along the Pennsylvania-Maryland border. The Warfields took up residence in a two-story cabin known as Square Cottage. Owned and operated by the town's Monterey Inn, their new home offered the couple two benefits: a long, wide veranda from which to take the air and, perhaps more important, privacy.[15]

On June 19, 1896, Alice went into labor. No preparations had been made; Alice's own doctor was unavailable; instead, one of his newly graduated students, Dr. Lewis Allen, was hurriedly dispatched, arriving in Blue Ridge Summit with scarcely enough time to supervise the delivery. On that day, T. Wallis and Alice's only child, Bessie Wallis Warfield, was born.

Like the wedding that had united her parents, a curious silence accompanied Wallis's birth. No formal announcement was made, and this newest addition to the illustrious Warfield clan was all but ignored. Nor was the birth registered.

Such circumstances have led at least one of the Duchess's biographers to speculate that she was not born in 1896 at all. Charles Higham declared that not only was the Duchess born a full year earlier than has always been assumed but that her parents did not bother to marry until November 1896, seventeen months after the event. To bolster his argument, he relies not only on the circumstantial evidence that no mention of the Duchess's birth was made at the time she was born but also quotes a census report of 1900 in which a birth date of 1895 is given.[16]

However much this scandalous assertion of illegitimacy enlivens the telling of the Duchess's life, the evidence to support it is slim indeed. T. Wallis Warfield and Alice Montague certainly married under a dark cloud, but it seems likely to have been imposed as much by the strong disapproval of their respective families as by a possible out-of-wedlock pregnancy. The very fact that the Warfields and Montagues opposed the match seems to have led the couple to take such secretive measures; after the fact, they certainly would not publicize such a controversial union. If a general announcement was made, almost certainly questions as to why the families had opposed the match—not to mention why the couple had felt compelled to marry secretly—would have become fodder for Baltimore gossips. The most reasonable step, therefore, seems to have been the one selected by T. Wallis and Alice: a private marriage, unpublicized, followed by their discreetly notifying family and friends.

Even if we are to assume, for the sake of argument, that Alice conceived her child out of wedlock, it strains credulity to believe that she and T. Wallis would wait seventeen months after discovering this fact to legitimize their union. Higham rightly points out the scandal and stigma which would attach itself, in the Victorian era, to birth out of wedlock but seems not to make the logical progression that learning of this alleged pregnancy, then not only giving birth to the child but waiting seventeen months to marry, could only have threatened even further scandal. That Alice had conceived the child out of wedlock would certainly have been discovered shortly thereafter. If the parents—with their staid, religious, proper upbringing—were worried about such a scandal, would they really have waited so long to make their union legal? Such a scenario utterly contradicts everything known of upper-middle-class Victorian values. A quick, private marriage would at least guarantee the child's legitimacy and thus prevent further scandal.

The suggestion that Bessie Wallis was born in June 1895 rather than a year later rests entirely on a 1900 census report. Given the weight of the available evidence, it seems likely that the year of birth was simply mistranscribed by the census taker or that whoever supplied the details accidentally wrote down the wrong year.

The lack of a birth certificate and failure to register the baby's arrival have assumed sinister proportions in recent years. Not only have these facts been held up as evidence that the Duchess might have been born a year earlier or was conceived out of wedlock, but most recently author Michael Bloch has questioned whether they might have indicated that the future Duchess of Windsor was born gender confused, with both male and female genitalia.[17] Happily, this last theory can be definitely put to rest by the physician who treated the Duchess until her death in 1986. According to Dr. Jean Thin, "her genitalia were simply normal, female genitalia, and you can quote me on this issue."[18]

Although it is possible that the child was conceived out of wedlock, the circumstances of her birth actually argue in favor of a premature arrival. Had the marriage followed an unexpected pregnancy and the time frame cut short, it should scarcely have come as a shock that Alice was expecting while they were in residence at Blue Ridge Summit. As it was, the parents were apparently surprised when the child was born. They were some distance away from their regular doctor, no arrangements had been made in advance, and a physician had to be hastily called in from Baltimore to assist in the delivery. All of this argues heavily for a premature birth.

Nor is there anything particularly sinister in the fact that the birth was not registered. As Michael Thornton points out, there was no legal requirement in Pennsylvania to do so, nor was it always done as a matter of course.[19] That the parents were themselves residents of Maryland rather than Pennsylvania might also help explain the lack of action; neither T. Wallis nor Alice were particularly well versed in the ways of the world, and it is possible that they simply assumed the birth should be registered in their usual place of residence. Upon their return, when T. Wallis fell very ill, such a legal nicety may well have been forgotten. It is also possible that the couple believed that it was the doctor's duty to register the birth, while the doctor assumed that the parents would do so.

Little should be read into the lack of registration: another famous and formidable lady, born five years after the future Duchess of Windsor, likewise seems to have arrived unexpectedly. The parents of the Honorable Elizabeth Bowes-Lyon waited a considerable time before reporting her birth to the proper authorities and paid a fine for having neglected the law. This, in turn, has led to speculation as to the exact time and place of birth of the woman who was to become Queen Elizabeth, the Queen Mother.

The new baby soon captivated her adoring parents. She had her mother's piercing blue eyes and fine features, crowned with her father's dark hair. They called her Bessie, after her mother's older sister, and Wallis in honor of her father. Both names were run together, according to southern custom, and as she grew older, the child soon came to despise the name. "So many cows are called Bessie," she once complained, somewhat undiplomatically, to her aunt of the same name.[20] Eventually, the Bessie would be dropped and the child referred to simply as Wallis.

The birth of his only child brought a welcome joy to T. Wallis's otherwise bleak existence. By the time he took his new family back to Baltimore at the end of summer, he was becoming increasingly ill. He and Alice moved from his old bachelor apartment to a slightly run-down establishment called the Brexton Residential Hotel, located on Baltimore's Park Avenue. This shabby hotel, with its worn carpet, faded paint, and rooms that inevitably smelled of food, was to become T. Wallis's last home.

As summer faded into autumn, even the ever-cheerful and optimistic Alice must have realized that the end was near. Her husband's painful coughs and gasps for breath filled their dingy rooms; in his condition it became dangerous to expose the baby to her father, and little Wallis remained carefully cloistered in an adjoining room.

By the beginning of November, T. Wallis realized that he was dying. Although the family physician was called in, he could do nothing; T. Wallis was in far too delicate a state to be moved to a more healthful climate. Anticipating the inevitable, he summoned his wife to his bedside and asked her to have their baby daughter photographed for the first time; he had been forbidden any contact for fear of passing on his illness, and he wished to see her one last time. Alice duly complied. When she presented the photographs to her dying husband, T. Wallis gazed at them thoughtfully. Alice would later tell Wallis that her father's only comment had been a sad one: "I'm afraid, Alice, she has the Warfield look. Let us hope that in spirit she'll be like you—a Montague."[21] On November 15, 1896, only four days short of his first wedding anniversary, T. Wallis Warfield was dead.

2

Childhood

At twenty-five, Alice Montague Warfield found herself a penniless, widowed single mother. Her prospects were bleak. As the fourth son, T. Wallis had had little opportunity to either acquire inherited wealth or devote his life to amassing it through his own devices. No matter what feelings she had expressed in the past, it must have come as an immense relief when Anna Emory Warfield invited her bereaved daughter-in-law and baby granddaughter to live with her. Whatever Alice's own inclinations, she was in no position to refuse. She duly packed her few belongings and vacated her rooms at the Brexton Residential Hotel for the more dignified surroundings of her husband's family home.

The Warfield home, at 34 East Preston Street, stood in a quiet, solidly upper middle class neighborhood near the old center of Baltimore. It was one of more than a dozen identical narrow, red-brick town houses along the tree-shaded streets, with a simple four-story façade enlivened by generous white-stone cornices. There was no garden or lawn before the house; a set of white marble steps led from the sidewalk straight to the heavy front door.

Here, in this rather unremarkable house, the future Duchess of Windsor—renowned for her skills in interior arrangement—was first exposed to domestic decoration. Her grandmother's taste ran to massive, ornately carved mahogany pieces, marble-topped tables, and a forest of potted palms. Fringed lamps, Oriental rugs draped over consoles, marble busts, and dozens of framed photographs added to the Victorian clutter. Candlesticks, urns, a tea set, and serving dishes from Baltimore's famous Kirk Silverworks lined the sideboard in the dining room, bearing witness to the Warfields' prosperity. It was all very rich and comfortable, redolent of the upper-middle-class values espoused by Mrs. Warfield.

Sixty years old when Alice and Wallis first came to stay, Anna was tall and thin, with refined features and a thick head of gray hair, which she wore parted in the middle and pulled tightly back. Her stature and manner were both impeccable: When she sat, according to her granddaughter, she was "so erect that her back never seemed to touch the chair," a posture Wallis carefully copied.[1] Anna habitually dressed in black, and even after a decade had passed, she refused to forgo what she considered proper mourning for her late husband. Her stiff black-satin dresses, with high collars of white lace, were austere, and Anna refused to enliven them with any jewels beyond a small pearl brooch and black-enamel mourning bracelet.[2]

The other imposing presence in the house was Anna's eldest son, Solomon Davies Warfield, an older, heavier, and less handsome version of Wallis's father, with a receding hairline, narrow eyes, and carefully groomed mustache. Solomon was in his thirties when Alice and Wallis took up residence at East Preston Street. Unlike his brothers and sisters, Solomon had never married; although he possessed several large country estates just outside Baltimore, he preferred to reside with his mother when in the city. Their relationship was exceptionally close, and Anna depended on her eldest son to look after her financial interests.

Solomon was the most successful of the Warfield sons. He began his career as a simple clerk but in his spare time managed to develop and patent a number of inventions. By his thirtieth birthday, he had formed the Warfield Manufacturing Company to distribute them across America. He served on a number of corporate boards, and at the time Alice and her daughter moved into the house on East Preston Street, he had recently been appointed to the prestigious position of Baltimore's postmaster general.

Solomon struck many as humorless, cold, and intolerant. Young Wallis, upon whom he was to have a formidable influence, later wrote: "For a long and impressionable period he was the nearest thing to a father in my uncertain world, but an odd kind of father—reserved, unbending, silent. Uncle Sol was destined to return again and again to my life—or, more accurately, it was my fate to be obliged to turn again and again to him, usually at some new point of crisis for me, and one seldom to his liking. I was always a little afraid of Uncle Sol."[3]

Wallis was a healthy, happy child. Warfields and Montagues alike were duly impressed with her luxuriant golden curls and deep blue, almost lilac-colored, eyes. Each morning, she was taken from the small third-floor room which served as her nursery, washed, and fed by an elderly Irish governess who had looked after several generations of Warfields. In the afternoon, she was proudly pushed in her perambulator along the tree-shaded avenues of Baltimore.[4]

One of her cousins, Elizabeth Gordon, later recalled: "While rambling up Charles Street one sunny afternoon, I noticed in a go-cart a very attractive child dressed in white, with a large pink bow on her cap. When asked who she was, the nurse replied, 'This is Wallis, Mrs. Warfield's little girl.' It was not that she was so pretty, but she had individuality and charm, and she possessed, even then, the most entrancing little glance out of the corner of her eye, with head tilted to one side. I had hardly gone a block when I met her mother. 'Alice,' I said, 'I've just seen your little girl; I feel that some day she will do something wonderful; she already has so much personality."[5]

Wallis was raised without a father, living on the charity of relatives, but she lacked for nothing. She was dressed in crisp white frocks covered with lace or fashionable sailor-suit dresses; her hair was bound with silk ribbons and tied with satin bows; she played with expensive toys and was coddled and cosseted by both her Irish nurse and her fawning mother. Under such circumstances, it is not surprising that she became precocious. In what may well be an apocryphal tale, her first words, according to author Cleveland Amory, were not "Mama" but "Me-Me."[6] She named her paper dolls "Mrs. Astor" and "Mrs. Vanderbilt," after the leading society hostesses of the day, indicating an early awareness of society which would later dominate her life.[7] Young Wallis enjoyed being noticed. For her first children's party, her mother selected a white dress with a blue sash; but when Wallis caught sight of it, she stomped her feet in an unruly fit, demanding that she be allowed to wear a red sash so that—she later wrote—the boys would notice her.[8]

Daily life in the house on East Preston Street revolved around Anna Emory Warfield. "She ruled the world from a series of rocking chairs," Wallis later declared.[9] Each morning, promptly at eight, the entire family, along with their servants—cook, maids, butler, nurse, and valet—assembled for prayers in the parlor. Following breakfast, the dowager received her servants and gave them their daily orders. At all times of the day, she held a set of keys; all closets, pantries, and cellars were kept locked, and when one of the servants wished to fetch something, they had to request permission from the mistress of the house to use the requisite key. Young Wallis watched and learned the way her grandmother maintained strict control over all aspects of the running of her household.

Occasionally, there were exciting excursions. Within the proper, cloistered confines of the Warfield household, Wallis discovered one of the friendliest faces of her childhood: her Uncle Solomon's valet-footman, Eddie. A soft-spoken, elderly descendant of former slaves, Eddie had formerly worked for Teackle Wallis, Wallis's father's namesake, before joining Solomon Warfield's household.

Baltimore remained a southern outpost, with prevailing attitudes about race, and Eddie, along with a day nurse, were the first blacks young Wallis encountered. Although she later held true to the conventions of both her day and place of birth, it is interesting that her first real friendship was formed with the elderly black man who had spent most of his life working for her family. Wallis followed him as he trod up and down the flights of stairs, clad in his frock coat, striped gray trousers, and a stiffly starched shirt with a wing collar. Occasionally, she would be allowed to visit his family, riding the trolley with him to his nearby house, where she happily sipped tea and ate sweets.[10]

Alice Warfield made the best of her situation at East Preston Street, but it is doubtful that she was very happy. Her only joy was her young daughter, but she constantly battled with her strong-willed mother-in-law, who had her own ideas as to how the child should be raised. Each lady tried her best to imbue Wallis with her own character, inevitably leading to confusion and desperation to please on the part of the young girl. "It may seem strange to say but one of my early impressions is that I was somehow the product of two family strains so dramatically opposed in temperament and outlook as to confront each other with impenetrable mysteries," Wallis wrote.[11] She felt as if she were composed of "two alternating sides, one grave, the other gay. If the Montagues were innately French in character and the Warfields British, then I was a new continent for which they contended."[12]

The relationship between grandmother and granddaughter was not conventionally close, for Anna was never one to display much affection or betray emotion. Instead, she drew Wallis to her, demonstrating her feeling by filling her with a sense of family pride and social obligation. Wallis was taught early to respect her heritage, behave properly, and never forget that she was a lady. If she slid and bounced around on a favorite slippery leather couch, her grandmother scolded loudly: "Bessiewallis, can't you be still for just a minute?" And if she failed to emulate her grandmother's impeccable posture, Anna would ask in her throaty southern drawl: "Bessiewallis, how will you ever grow up to be a lady unless you learn to keep your back straight?"[13]

Sitting firmly in her rosewood and mahogany rocker, her fingers constantly busy with needlework as she spoke and the black silk of her dress rustling as she moved back and forth, Anna Emory Warfield imparted to Wallis nothing short of an education in life, politics, religion, and deportment. Her grandmother raised Wallis to respect her southern roots. "I doubt whether she ever knowingly invited a Northerner into her house," she later declared. "Never marry a Yankee," Anna Warfield would implore young Wallis, reminding her of her grandfather's imprisonment at the outbreak of the Civil War.[14]

This southern heritage was reflected in the care Wallis took with her clothes and appearance. Her concepts of hospitality and entertaining also formed around southern ideals that all should be made to feel welcome and important. Her charm and conversational wit stemmed from these talks, with her grandmother constantly reminding her that southern women should be decorative, pretty, and amusing at table. She learned that she must never be boring, that she should always watch others, listen to them, draw them into conversation, and smile as they spoke. It was her job, as a southern woman, to entertain, to pull her own weight, and to cater to the needs of her guests.

On Saturdays, Wallis accompanied her grandmother as she did the week's shopping. At eight in the morning, a polished black victoria rolled up before the white marble steps where Wallis, carefully attired in a white dress and blue overcoat, waited impatiently at the door for her grandmother, who was garbed in her most formal widow's weeds, complete with black bonnet and crepe veil.[15] Assisted by the driver and a footman, the pair climbed into the waiting carriage and, drawn by Anna's big mare Gadfly, set off through the streets of Baltimore to the Richmond Market, where rows of stalls spread beneath canvas awnings. At the end of the day's shopping, if Wallis had behaved, Anna Warfield led her granddaughter to the candy stand, where she was rewarded with a bag of yellow taffy.[16]

Sundays were reserved for services at Baltimore's Episcopalian Christ Church, embellished with all the refinements of clerical robes, glistening silver, and glorious litanies. On the rare occasions when, due to illness, Anna Emory Warfield could not lead her family to their regular pew, she expected young Wallis to return to the house on East Preston Street immediately following the service and repeat the details of the day's sermon and Bible lessons. She followed along in the leather-bound family Bible, her place marked with a purple satin ribbon; if Wallis misquoted, her grandmother would promptly correct her.[17]

Eventually—and perhaps inevitably—tensions between Alice Warfield and her late husband's family rose to a fever pitch. Each month, Alice received an allowance from her brother-in-law Solomon; this charity was humiliating enough, but Alice was often questioned about her expenditures, which were frequently extravagant, and made to feel like a naughty schoolgirl. For a proud, sensitive woman, this was unbearable. Even worse, no matter what she did, no matter whom she befriended, how she spent her days, how she dressed, or how she raised her daughter, nothing Alice did seemed to meet with the approval of her censorious relatives. When a suitable period had passed, the still-young and attractive Alice cast aside her widow's weeds and escaped the oppressive mourning by discreetly allowing suitable young men to escort her to evening dinners and other entertainments. Anna, who had never ceased mourning her husband or worn anything other than black, was horrified at what she believed to be her daughter-in-law's fast morals and lack of respect for the memory of her dead son.

Alice was also distinctly uncomfortable at East Preston Street for another reason. For some time she had been aware of Solomon's growing interest in her life. Increasingly, the naive young woman understood that he had fallen in love with her; Alice did not share his feelings, and the tension soon became unbearable. Long silences at the dinner table continued in the parlor as evenings wore on. Anna also quickly realized her son's feelings and blamed her daughter-in-law for the change in Solomon's affections. Jealous, the dowager became openly hostile toward Alice, criticizing her incessantly for any perceived shortcoming. In the end, Alice could no longer stand the pressure, scrutiny, unwelcome advances, and condemnation. In 1901 she packed her bags and moved both herself and her five-year-old daughter out.[18]

To Alice, the situation was desperate. She had no money of her own and no reason to believe that her circumstances would change. She could not turn to her own family for assistance, for they had so strongly disapproved of her marriage that nearly all contact had been severed between her and the Montagues. In the end, Alice was forced to return to the run-down Brexton Residential Hotel, where she and Wallis would live in a double room. Her independence was an illusion, for her life was still controlled from East Preston Street.

Solomon did not abandon his sister-in-law, but his resentment over her rejection spilled into his financial arrangements. Without fail, Solomon dispatched a check each month to Alice to help cover her expenses, but the amounts varied each month, and Alice never knew for certain if she would receive just enough to cover the rent at the hotel or enough to place some in her meager bank account. Some months, she could not meet the bills and had to beg for more. Years later, Wallis surmised that this constantly changing allowance might very well have been her uncle Solomon's way of both reminding Alice of her continuing dependence on the Warfield largesse and also of the danger of not living frugally.[19]

Alice had not been raised to work. "She lived for laughter," Wallis later recalled; "the gay quip was the only currency she really valued."[20] There were few employment opportunities then available to young women, and those that were required skills Alice did not possess. Women of her station were not accustomed to labor—which was regarded as a disgrace—and, in any case, Alice was temperamentally unsuited to regular work. She could engage in sparkling conversation, preside over dinner parties, and charm those around her. The two skills she did possess were sewing and cooking. Using the first of these, she joined the Women's Exchange in Baltimore, a charitable organization that made clothing for the poor. Alice spent hours carefully crafting and altering these clothes, for which she received a small weekly salary.[21]

Thus, from her earliest days, Wallis was painfully reminded of both the necessity of money in her life as well as the lack of it in her mother's bank account. These were days spent scraping for funds, watching her mother make her clothes, while other girls played in the latest store-bought dresses. More than most, Wallis knew the power of money not only for the material comfort it provided but, perhaps more important, for the peace of mind it brought.

Wallis had her toys from Preston Street and wore the clothes which had filled her closets there. But clearly nothing was the same. She was too young to understand the reasons for their move to the Brexton; in place of explanations there was only uncomfortable silence on the part of her mother. Alice attempted to make out of this dreary existence a happy life for her child, but it was all a charade. Their lonely meals, their tension-filled visits to see the Warfields at Preston Street, and their humble new surroundings made a deep impression on young Wallis.

Nothing seemed certain or secure. Wallis was terrified of quiet, of being alone in darkened rooms filled with shadows. Above all, she dreaded the idea of loss, of being abandoned, of having no one left to care for her. "A shivery feeling comes," Wallis later wrote, "as when on a crisp fall day the sun is momentarily obscured; and the tenuous apprehensions that now assailed me took the form of a dread of being left alone, even for a few hours, as if my mother, too, might vanish."[22]

Even with the extra income earned from her clothing, Alice continued to struggle. A year after she moved out of the Warfield house on East Preston Street, she swallowed her pride and accepted an invitation to live with her widowed sister, Bessie Merryman, in her gray-stone house at 9 West Chase Street.

Wallis's aunt Bessie was to become the third formidable and influential woman in her life. Alice and her sister were utterly unalike in character; whereas Alice was carefree, Bessie was serious. Her concern for young Wallis, as much as sympathy for her sister, had led her to issue the invitation. Wallis adored her mother, but she also longed for the stability which her kind aunt offered. Bessie, in turn, understood Wallis, and the two became inseparable. Wallis came to rely on her aunt's common sense, a trait notably lacking in her mother. Nor was her influence confined to more practical concerns. Bessie was not yet the matronly figure she was later to become; she cultivated a love of fashionable clothes, elegant surroundings, and the finer things in life, all traits passed along to her impressionable niece. If at times Alice seemed preoccupied with her own pursuits, Bessie more than compensated with a love and affection which helped reassure Wallis.

In 1902, Wallis was sent off to school. Appealing to whatever familial instincts Solomon Davies Warfield possessed, Alice managed to convince him to pay for the education of his brother's only child.[23] With his money behind her, Alice selected a prestigious private institution on 2812 Elliott Street, run by Miss Ada O'Donnell; her pupils were a mixture of boys and girls drawn from upper-class districts around the school. Wallis did well there, impressing both teachers and fellow students with her wit, energy, and enthusiasm for learning. She became a star pupil, priding herself on her position within the class, and enjoyed the attention and acceptance it brought. Wallis was quickly angered when denied either. Once, when one of her classmates beat her in raising a hand and shouting an answer, she was so incensed that she smacked him over the head with her pencil box.[24]

Years later, Ada O'Donnell remembered Wallis as "an attractive, lively six-year-old who was full of fun and pep, and was well-liked by all the children."[25] Alice ensured that if Wallis could not have the best of everything, she at least would be immaculate and dressed as well as possible.

In 1906, Wallis left Miss O'Donnell's. Baltimore possessed several excellent girls' schools, and both Alice and her daughter fully expected that, whatever their reduced financial circumstances, the scion of the Warfield and Montague families deserved the best. Luckily, Solomon agreed to continue paying the fees, and Alice set about selecting her daughter's new school. The most fashionable girls' school, Bryn Mawr, proved too expensive for Solomon's taste, and so Wallis was forced to settle for Arundell, only slightly less prestigious.

The Arundell School for Girls was an entirely new experience for Wallis, allowing her to meet a wider range of girls, many from distinguished and socially prominent families. The curriculum was a challenge, but Wallis, who was rapidly developing into a scholar, appreciated the difficulty and soon proved more than up to the task. Still, her lingering insecurities—from moving around so much, her fatherless childhood, and the strained relations between her mother and her relatives—took their toll. She was desperate to fit in, to be accepted. When she learned that all of the other girls regularly wore blue or white pleated skirts with white sailor-suit blouses, she quickly begged her mother—who could not afford to purchase the clothes in a regular store—to make them for her. Soon enough, Wallis sported the same fashions as her fellow students, and only her closest friends knew that they were made by her mother.[26]

Wallis was popular at Arundell. Teachers and classmates alike remembered that she was cheerful without fail, always courteous to others, intelligent, kind, and despite her academic ability, not a show-off. If this sounds too good to be true, it was at least tempered by her appearance, which both Wallis and her mother considered a disappointment. As a baby and young child, she had been engaging; as she grew older, Wallis developed into an angular, almost masculine looking young woman. But her hair was thick and full, and her piercing lavender eyes accentuated the chiseled lines of her face. She took great pride in those aspects of her appearance which she could control: Her dresses were always clean and pressed, her hair was swept back and tied with pretty ribbons or bows, and her shoes were carefully polished. Even if she was not traditionally pretty, at least her clothing and appearance would be above reproach. She also began to develop considerable charm, which she worked to great effect on both her fellow students and her teachers.

Wallis joined nearly all of the teams at Arundell. She did not particularly care for sports but enjoyed being accepted as part of the group. On three afternoons a week, she and the other girls trooped off to a small building at the corner of Charles Street and Mount Vernon Avenue known as the Gymnasium. This was a private establishment run by Miss Charlotte Noland, who would later found the famous Foxcroft School.

Wallis did well at the Gymnasium and managed to play lead positions in several sports.[27] Her time there appears to have been happy, although she was not averse to using the odd feigned illness to sit out the more tiring games. Years later, recalling her penchant for suddenly appearing with a sprained ankle, jammed finger, or terrible cramps, Miss Noland declared, "I have never known anyone who could so consistently for so many years so successfully evade the truth."[28]

Wallis was a surprisingly diligent student. Each day after school she joined her friends as they played jacks, jump rope, and dolls but was careful to be at her desk every night to do her homework.[29] She worked hard at her lessons, determined to remain near the top of her class. She loved English and history but did less well in mathematics, much to the chagrin of her uncle Solomon.[30]

Although Wallis continued to pay regular visits to her grandmother Warfield and Uncle Sol, her mother—for understandable reasons—did not often accompany her. These occasions were often painful reminders of what Wallis and Alice had left behind: At East Preston Street there were servants and a dozen rooms and shining silver on the dining table. One Sunday evening each month, Wallis had to take her report cards from Arundell and submit them to Solomon for his inspection and approval. Solomon, a man of little imagination, had no taste or understanding of Wallis's interests or achievements in history or English; a businessman to his very core, he preferred success with practical courses and liked to quiz her with impromptu mathematics questions between mouthfuls of food. Unfortunately for Wallis, Solomon's stern lectures seldom made much sense, and she invariably gave the wrong answers. One evening, knowing that she was about to face a similar inquisition, Wallis carefully prepared to get the better of her demanding uncle. As he stood up at the head of the table to carve the roast, Wallis, unprompted and unquestioned, shouted out: "The square of the hypotenuse of a right-angled triangle is equal to the sum of the squares of the other two sides. The area of a circle is equal to pi-r squared." Solomon was so shocked, according to Wallis, that the carving knife fell from his hand and clattered to the table. Then, with a slight smile, he congratulated her and sat down to his dinner, having forgone his usual inquisition for the evening.[31]

By 1908, Alice's finances were once again under control, and she was on the move again. This time, she took Wallis and left her sister Bessie's town house for a suite of rooms in the Preston Apartment House. She had longed for her independence, and this was certainly a step up from the time she had spent at the Brexton Residential Hotel. The Preston Apartment House, just a few blocks down the same street from where the Warfields lived, was a respectable, solidly upper middle class establishment.

But money still ran short on occasion, and Alice improvised. She sometimes temporarily let extra rooms to relatives. This, however, was not Alice's only financial endeavor. When she discovered that many of her fellow residents regularly dined out, Alice hit upon a new scheme. Since one of her few skills was an ability to cook, she determined that she would utilize this talent to supplement her income. She hired a cook and quickly lined up a dozen residents who agreed to become her paying guests. But Alice never knew how to temper her extravagant tastes with practicality. She cooked prime rib and squab, and served soft-shell crabs, terrapin, and delicate pastries. The guests loved the overwhelming, elaborate dinners; but soon enough the grocers' bills arrived, and Alice was unable to pay them. Once again, Aunt Bessie stepped in and arranged for her sister's debts to be settled. Thus ended what, in the words of her daughter Wallis, "had undoubtedly been the finest dining club in Baltimore history."[32]

Charles F. Bove, who lived in the apartment block and occasionally dined at Alice's table, recalled: "I was particularly fascinated by the young girl who helped her mother serve the meals I took with the family. She was an exuberant child of twelve with ... hair parted in braids, high cheekbones and a prominent nose that made one think of an Indian squaw. I teasingly called her Minnehaha and she responded with a wide grin."[33]

One of the stories which would most disturb Wallis in her later life and one she would always vehemently deny was that her mother ran a boardinghouse. These allegations presumably arose from the arrangements at the Preston Apartment House. But as Frances Donaldson has pointed out, "One cannot imagine that Mrs. Warfield had the resources to become 'the landlady' of the Preston Apartment House," nor do any business or title documents bear out this assertion.[34]

The relationship between mother and daughter was a curious one, rather more like that of sisters than parent and child. Alice continued to indulge Wallis, although as she grew older and the two grew more alike in character, there were often extended battles of will, with each stubbornly refusing to give way. Wallis later recalled being spanked, when she misbehaved, with a heavy silver hairbrush or having her tongue scrubbed with a nailbrush if she swore. Still, Alice doted on her only child; worried that she might somehow inherit her late father's tuberculosis, Alice insisted that Wallis drink a tumbler of blood squeezed from a raw steak upon her return from school each day.[35]

Shortly after Wallis began her term at Arundell, Alice managed to move into their first house, at 212 Biddle Street, using money from Solomon. It was a typical Baltimore brownstone, with three floors and a front door reached from the sidewalk by six marble steps. The first floor held a parlor, library, dining room, pantry, and kitchen; Wallis occupied a room on the third floor, while her mother took a large bedroom on the second. Behind this was another bedroom, which Wallis thought was reserved for guests.[36] But Alice had something quite different in mind, which was to shock her daughter.

For a number of months, Alice, still young and vibrant at thirty-six, had been quietly seeing a man one year her senior named John Freeman Rasin. Rasin, the eldest son of the head of the Baltimore Democratic Party, Carroll Rasin, was sociable, intelligent, kind, and perhaps most important, wealthy. He had little ambition, a fact borne out by his rather portly figure, and seemed to spend the majority of his time indulging his passion for alcohol and smoking; indeed, Wallis would later recall that he seemed to do little else.[37] But he was also very kind both to Alice and her daughter, always showering Wallis with little gifts which did much to endear him to her, including her first pet, a French bulldog called "Bully." "He had an infectious laugh," Wallis recalled, "and I had liked him until my mother told me of her intention to marry him."[38]

Alice's decision to remarry was understandable, especially since a union with Rasin promised financial security and freedom from the powerful influence of her brother-in-law and his money. But Wallis felt otherwise. On the verge of enjoying her first real home with her mother, her first taste of independence from relatives and others, her illusions were shattered. She had no wish to share either the house or her mother with a stranger who, however nice he might be, was still an intruder in her world.[39]

Upon learning of her mother's intentions, Wallis immediately threatened to run away. Alice pleaded with her stubborn daughter, but the young girl would not give way. She spent hours and hours alone in her room crying, declaring that she would not attend the wedding. Alice, completely overwhelmed, felt helpless and called in her sister Bessie and cousin Lelia Barnett to calm her daughter and try to reason with her. They carefully explained that Alice loved Mr. Rasin and that it was wrong of Wallis to hurt her mother by not attending a ceremony that should be a joyful celebration and would bring Alice much happiness.[40]

Wallis was stubborn, but she reluctantly agreed that she would watch as her mother wed Mr. Rasin. The wedding took place on June 20, 1908. Shortly before three that afternoon, a number of guests, including members of both the Warfield and Montague families, arrived to witness the small, private wedding that was to take place in the parlor of the house on 212 Biddle Street.

Wallis duly appeared as promised, wearing a gown of embroidered batiste laced with blue ribbons, and watched in silence as her mother and her new stepfather recited their vows. However, halfway through the ceremony, she slipped out of the parlor and disappeared into the adjoining dining room, where the wedding cake stood waiting for the reception. Hidden within its layers were a number of small, symbolic tokens of good luck, including a new dime and a thimble. Whether out of boredom, as a subtle act of vengeance against her mother and new stepfather, or simple childhood curiosity, Wallis reached into the cake with her hands, tearing it apart. As she continued to dig through the layers for the good-luck symbols, the doors to the dining room swung open, and suddenly she was confronted with the quizzical stares of the new Mr. and Mrs. Rasin. For a moment, no one spoke; then, clearly saving what might have turned the day into a disaster, Wallis's new stepfather stepped forward, held out his arms, and grabbed her, twirling her around in the air and laughing out loud. This act of forgiveness won Wallis over; thereafter, although she refused to call him anything but Mr. Rasin, she made no trouble for her mother and her new husband.[41]

3

Youth

LIFE AT 212 BIDDLE STREET slowly settled into a quiet, relaxed pattern. Although Wallis became fond of her new stepfather, their relations remained marked with a certain distance and formality. Rasin was a curious, almost-minimal presence within the household; he was always disappearing behind the library doors, where he spent his days reading newspapers and smoking cigarettes. He had no need to work and drew his monthly income from a sizable trust fund.[1]

Rasin's money allowed Alice to entertain again, and she filled the rooms of 212 Biddle with attractive new furniture, carpets, and a piano. Alice also tried to provide some of the finer things for her daughter and hired an elderly lady called Miss Jackson to give Wallis piano lessons. Miss Jackson came one afternoon a week and supervised as Wallis sat pounding away at the keyboard. Not surprisingly, the young girl hated these lessons, for she was tone deaf. She begged her mother to be allowed to quit, but Alice refused, and Wallis stuck it out until her first recital. When she had finished, the audience duly applauded; "not exactly an ovation—a kind of gratitude that the thing didn't last any longer," Wallis later wrote. This disaster was enough to convince Alice to heed her daughter's pleas, and Wallis was allowed to stop her lessons.[2]

Two months before her fourteenth birthday, Wallis was confirmed into the Episcopal church. Neither Alice nor Rasin was particularly religious, but the influence of her grandmother remained strong, and Wallis's religious instruction was not neglected. Wallis learned her catechism, and on April 17, 1910, dressed in a plain white dress, she joined the rest of her class at an elaborate ceremony held at Christ Church in Baltimore.

With Rasin's money, Wallis attended the fashionable Burrlands Summer Camp, run by her athletic instructor at Baltimore's Gymnasium, Miss Charlotte Noland. Her previous summer holidays had always been spent with wealthy Warfield relatives in their country estates outside Baltimore, surroundings in which Wallis inevitably felt very much a poor cousin. Burrlands, therefore, was a welcome relief. Situated deep in the lush countryside near Middleburg, Virginia, Burrlands offered a taste of life in the old South, with its white-columned, Greek-revival plantation house, afternoons spent riding, playing lawn tennis and croquet, and concentration on good manners. Rough edges were polished through elaborate afternoon teas, carefully chaperoned parties, and formal Sunday dinners.

In this environment Wallis blossomed—and developed her first real crush. The object of her affection, Lloyd Tabb, was a handsome seventeen-year-old whose family lived at the nearby Glen Ora estate, which would later be used by John F. Kennedy as a weekend retreat from the White House. Lloyd Tabb was a tall, athletic young man with a passion for football, swimming, and riding. Wallis did not particularly care for such pursuits, but she was canny and managed to quickly endear herself to Lloyd by learning all she could about his tastes and flattering him no end. With Miss Noland's permission, she visited the Tabb estate, sitting for hours with Lloyd on the veranda, reading aloud from books of poetry or listening (though rarely joining in) as the family sang together.

"Being full of romance and poetry at that age," Lloyd recalled, "we would maneuver around and find a secluded spot in which to 'speak of love' and 'give the direct gaze.'" His impressions form the first real, independent picture of Wallis as a young woman. He recalled "a touch of pathos and sweetness bordering on wistfulness" in her character. "No one who really knew Wallis well ever said anything against her," he declared. She never acted "silly" around boys, he said.

> She was always very feminine but clever, and at times shrewd. . . . She was not impulsive; on the contrary, she seemed rather studied or thoughtful in determining on a course of action. We used to have close harmony parties on the porch, or down in the garden of our house. Curiously enough, Wallis rarely joined in the singing, though she obviously enjoyed the efforts of others, and was one of the best at thinking up new numbers. Having made suggestions, she would lean back on her slender arms. Her head would be cocked appreciatively, and by her earnest attention she made us feel that we were really a rather gifted group of youngsters.[3]

In 1911, Wallis left Arundell. She could have remained and completed her education, but for a girl of her social background, it was considered obligatory to attend one of the local finishing schools. Both Alice and her sister Bessie suggested Oldfields, at Glencoe, Maryland, some distance from Baltimore. That it was also the most expensive and fashionable school for girls did not escape Wallis's attention, and she eagerly agreed to the idea.

Oldfields had been founded in 1867 by Rev. Duncan McCulloch and his sister, Anna, on her family estate along the Gunpowder River. A large white clapboard-and-brick mansion, set in the middle of several hundred acres of woodlands, formed the center of the school. Students were housed in a large wing, added onto the main house; several other buildings, including a gymnasium and an infirmary, stood nearby. The old mansion still retained a touch of its former grandeur, with a magnificent grand staircase, drawing rooms hung with silk, and a ballroom, with crystal chandeliers, in which the girls practiced their dancing lessons. Through the trees Wallis could catch a glimpse of the local parish church where students attended services each Sunday.

Anna McCulloch struck Wallis as "a replica of my grandmother."[4] In her early sixties, Anna, called Miss Nan by the students, was tall and thin, draped in black silk dresses with white collars. She was careful to instill in the girls a sense of gentility and grace. Signs reading Gentleness and Courtesy Are Expected of the Girls at All Times, were posted on the doors of the dormitories, and the school's two basketball teams were also called Gentleness and Courtesy.[5]

Boarding school was a new experience for Wallis. Inevitably, her new friends were wealthy, privileged girls whose settled lives contrasted sharply with the uncertainties and struggles she had faced. Her most valued friend at Oldfields, Mary Kirk, was a dark-haired, blue-eyed girl whose family owned the Kirk Silverworks in Baltimore. Mary would remain a friend for many years to come and play a pivotal role in Wallis's later life. Two other close friends were young heiress Renée du Pont and Ellen Yuille of North Carolina, whose father worked for Duke Tobacco.

Days at Oldfields were strictly organized and followed religious principles. Each morning, a bell summoned the girls to prayers, said according to the Episcopalian church's *Book of Common Prayer*. There were few privileges: only two at-home weekends, in addition to regular holidays, were allowed each girl during the entire school year, and before leaving for Christmas break, each student had to memorize and recite a chapter from the Old Testament before the ever-vigilant Miss Nan. The girls could not write letters to boys and were not allowed to receive letters from any men other than relatives. In the evening, before dinner, students gathered to sing hymns. On Sundays, all students had to memorize the collect and gospel before joining the congregation in the nearby parish church; at half-past five on Sunday afternoons, there was an Evensong service and, following dinner, further hymns. By ten o'clock, lights were extinguished; there were severe penalties for breaking curfew.[6]

Wallis enjoyed her first months at Oldfields. She liked most of the other girls, studied hard, and thrived. However, with her growing streak of independence and headstrong nature, she soon resented the tight discipline. To escape the strict daily regimen, she began to complain of ill health: one week it was a cold; the next, a headache, followed by stomach flu or weakness. She enjoyed being coddled and indulged, although the other girls seemed to have quickly realized that most of Wallis's infirmities were an act. Still, she managed to manipulate those around her through uniquely creative means. She even went so far as to have her mother write a note asking that she be excused from taking algebra classes, asserting that prolonged exposure to mathematics gave her hives.[7] Somehow her charming craftiness overcame all objections, and she usually won in the end.

Undoubtedly, Wallis was a unique presence at Oldfields. The other girls were either pretty or plain, but Wallis managed to comfortably embrace her assets and make the most of her shortcomings. "My endowments were definitely on the scanty side," she later recalled. "Nobody ever called me beautiful or even pretty."[8] Of medium height, thin, and slightly flat-chested, Wallis was not conventionally pretty: Her jawline was a bit too square, her eyebrows were thick, and a very prominent mole distracted from her face. But her hair continued to be a special pride, and, above all, it was her blue-violet eyes which captivated. Adela Rogers St. John recalled that "she had the most beautiful eyes I ever saw."[9]

As she grew older, Wallis began to experiment with fashion. The lacy gowns and hobble skirts of the era were not at all to her taste. Instead, she liked to wear men's shirts and bow ties with her long skirts, wrapping tight belts around her waist to emphasize its slenderness. At one time, she took to wearing a monocle, in what one must conclude was an effort to both challenge convention and attract attention to herself.

In manner, she was generally charming and good-natured. Her high-pitched voice, a curious mixture of eastern accent and southern drawl, could often be heard when she was laughing and joking with fellow students. And yet she seemed somehow different from the other girls, more mature, sophisticated if not cultured, with a certain weariness which she masked behind an ebullient façade. In part, this was owing to her childhood experiences, but it also reflected a growing consciousness on her part. All around her—in the country estates of her relatives, in her grandmother's solid house, in the lifestyle of the girls who attended school with her—was money, an asset Wallis lacked. She craved excitement, acceptance, and prestige and realized that if society were to deliver these things to her, she, in turn, had to compensate for what she did not possess. Most twelve-year-old girls entering Oldfields were not at all concerned about wealth or power or position, but Wallis was extremely aware of their importance. Her carefully crafted sense of style, the ease of her conversation, her slightly theatrical quality, were all meant to attract attention and open doors.

Wallis was serious when necessary but was known among her friends for her love of excitement and slightly dangerous adventures, characteristics which only enhanced the exotic quality she cultivated. She knew this would entice the girls, but it had the added benefit of making her terribly attractive to young men as well. "She tended to be interested in boys," one man later recalled. "Girls were just people who happened to be around . . . and some of the young ladies were critical of her because she cut in on their preserves a bit."[10] Wallis was known for her independence: "In those days," recalled a friend, "that was considered forward for a young lady."[11] Several girls at Oldfields later described the Wallis they had known as "fast." But this designation meant something quite different then. No one ever indicated that Wallis was promiscuous, or that she chased after boys. She seems to have enjoyed flirting, which made her friends uneasy, but had she been aggressive in her pursuits, Wallis would undoubtedly have been cut dead by her fellow students.

One of Wallis's first serious boyfriends was Carter Osborne, son of a Baltimore bank president. Osborne was an attractive, athletic young man who shared Wallis's love of laughter and fun. Theirs was an almost charmingly innocent relationship, fraught with danger on both sides, as Osborne later recalled: "I used to take my father's car and drive down a dirt road. I wasn't allowed to have the car, but I took care of that. At a certain point in the road, I'd stop, and Wally could see the car from her dormitory window. The moment she spotted it, she'd slip out. I don't know yet how she managed it, but as far as I know, she never got caught. She not only got out, but she also got back in without being observed. She was very independent in spirit, adhering to the conventions only for what they were worth and not for their own sake. Those dates were all the more exciting for being forbidden."[12]

It was during Wallis's senior year at Oldfields that tragedy once again struck her family. Her stepfather had not been well for some time; when doctors were eventually called in, they diagnosed Bright's disease, an unfortunate, and ultimately fatal, effect of Rasin's frequent drinking binges. Hoping that the sea air would somehow revive his health and postpone the inevitable, doctors advised Rasin to take a cottage at Atlantic City, New Jersey. He and Alice moved there in the spring, but his condition worsened. On April 4, 1913, Wallis was called out of class at Oldfields and asked to go to Miss Nan's office. There she learned that her stepfather had died. Wallis immediately packed a suit-case and returned to Baltimore.

The next day, Wallis stood waiting on the railway platform, watching as the train carrying her mother and her stepfather's body slowly steamed into the station at Baltimore. Wallis spotted her mother as soon as she climbed down the steps of her carriage. Wrapped in black, she stumbled across the platform and collapsed in her daugh-ter's arms. The loss of her second husband left Alice inconsolable. Her near hysterics tore at Wallis; although she had grown fond of Rasin, she had not realized the extent of her mother's devotion until his death. Throughout these days, Wallis dealt with the funeral arrange-ments, looking after her mother and easing tensions between Warfield and Rasin relatives, a measure of her maturity.

After Rasin's death, the monthly checks from his trust fund stopped, and Alice was once again left to the mercy of her wealthier relatives. Much to Wallis's humiliation, she found that her mother was forced to move out of 212 Biddle Street and take an apartment at 16 Earl's Court, at the corner of St. Paul and Preston Streets, not far from the Warfield household. These difficult circumstances changed Alice greatly; on school holidays, Wallis found that she had aged, and was less certain of herself and often depressed.[13]

Oldfields had no graduation ceremony; at the end of her senior year, Wallis joined her fellow graduates in attending a great May Day festival at which the girls sported white dresses, wore flowers in their hair, and danced around Renée du Pont, who had been selected queen. This was followed by an award dinner and farewell dance. As they left the festivities, the girls signed their comments in a large visi-tors' book. Most remarks were commonplace, about school or friend-ships, but Wallis was different: in a bold hand, she recorded: "All is Love."[14]

Wallis was just shy of her eighteenth birthday when she left Old-fields. Despite her proven academic prowess in those subjects which she enjoyed, she gave no thought to pursuing her education. None of her friends went off to a university, and Oldfields had been designed not so much to provide academic qualifications as to mold its pupils into genteel young ladies, proficient in social arts, conversation, charm, and deportment. Nor was any emphasis given to the idea of pursuing a career; young ladies of suitable birth from well-to-do families were simply expected to marry and raise a family of their own.

That summer of 1914, Archduke Franz Ferdinand of Austria and his morganatic wife were shot and killed by a Serbian nationalist during a visit to Sarajevo. As Austria began shelling Belgrade, Ger-many invaded Belgium, and the Great War erupted in Europe, the heads of the young girls in Baltimore were filled with one thought: their debuts. Alice, having been denied the social benefits she felt belonged to her by dint of her privileged background, was determined that her daughter not suffer the same fate. She had made certain that Wallis attended the best schools, and mixed with the most important girls from Baltimore's most prestigious families, and she had carefully groomed her daughter to sparkle and charm in public. A successful debut, leading to an important marriage—and the accompanying social prestige and economic well-being—was, Alice declared, no more than Wallis's birthright, her chance to restore the faded Montagues to their proper glory.

Before Wallis could even contemplate a debut, she had to undergo what must have been a rather unpleasant, though necessary, task: a special visit to her uncle Solomon to explain her financial needs. By this time, Solomon was the president of the Continental Trust Company, a prosperous bank housed in a new fifteen-story brick building at the corner of Baltimore and Calvert Streets. At the appointed day and hour, Wallis, seated in the rear of her grandmother's new Pierce-Arrow, was chauffeured through Baltimore to her uncle's office. Solomon listened as she explained that she could not possibly make her debut unless she had new gowns to wear, along with day dresses for luncheons and tea gowns for afternoon dances. Eventually, much to her great surprise and delight, he presented her with two ten-dollar bills.[15]

With her financial freedom guaranteed—at least for several months—Wallis launched herself into a frenzy of engagements. She attended the Princeton Prom, dressed in a lacy blue gown of her own design. November was a particularly busy month. On November 5 she attended a football dance at the Cantonsville Country Club; the following day, Wallis was invited to a luncheon at the Stafford Hotel, given in honor of her fellow debutante Augusta Eareckson. A week later, on November 13, she joined friends at an oyster roast given by Albert Graham Ober for his debutante-niece, Rebecca Ober, at his country estate in Green Spring Valley; that same evening, Wallis assisted receiving guests at a party at Lehmann Hall given for her friend Priscilla Beacham. On November 17, she attended a luncheon at the Baltimore Country Club for friend Carolyn McCoy; on November 19, she was back at the country club, this time for Mary Kirk's debutante luncheon. On November 25, there was a luncheon for Rena Alverda Sawyer. Three days later, Wallis and Priscilla Beacham took a weekend trip to Philadelphia for a football game followed by a dance. Wallis returned to the Baltimore Country Club on December 2 for a luncheon given in honor of her friend Eleanor Nosley; and on the following day she attended a luncheon for fellow debutante Jessie Van Rensselaer Bond.[16]

Each of these occasions required new dresses, outfits, and gowns. Wallis, in common with her fellow debutantes, would not have dared appear in public during her season wearing the same outfit twice. However, whereas most debutantes had the money to invest in an ample wardrobe, Wallis did not. Rather than spend the entire twenty dollars she had received from her uncle Sol, she instead bought only two or three different outfits; with the help of her skilled mother, she worked feverishly between engagements to alter style, design, dress length, trim, collars, necklines, and sleeves. By adding overlays of lace and tulle, they successfully managed to disguise their economies.

The highlight of the debutante year in Baltimore, and the biggest social hurdle, was the Bachelors' Cotillon. (The misspelling was a deliberate affectation.) The Bachelors' Club, formed in the nineteenth century as a bastion of the city's privileged males, was one of Baltimore's most prestigious institutions. Each autumn, their board of governors met and together reviewed a list of the year's debutantes. Unlike other events during the debutante season, the Bachelors' Cotillon remained inaccessible: only a lucky forty-seven debutantes, of the hundreds whose names were submitted, received invitations, and this selectively marked out the event—and its eventual invitees—as the most socially prestigious in Baltimore.

Along with other hopeful debutantes, Wallis eagerly awaited news of the invitation list. She later recalled that she spent many restless nights worrying whether she would receive the all-important piece of paper. Finally, she was rewarded: Wallis's name appeared on the list. In truth, she had little reason to worry. Her father had been a member of the Bachelor's Cotillon; her uncle was one of the city's most important businessmen; the Warfields were greatly respected; and she herself had gone to the best schools.

Wallis could not afford to purchase one of the new, fashionable frocks which filled the store windows of Baltimore's smart shops. Instead, she impatiently sat through numerous fittings with a local seamstress, who designed a gown according to the young debutante's specifications. Wallis had admired a dress worn by fashionable dancer Irene Castle during an appearance on Broadway, and it was this dress that was so faithfully copied. She was less pleased at the result of the new white gown against her already pale features, however, and it took some considerable effort on her mother's part, along with the new and calming influences of face powder and rouge, to appease Wallis's fears.[17]

Each debutante was allowed to invite several male escorts, along with family members, to accompany her to the cotillion. It was common practice for the girls to choose older relatives rather than current boyfriends. Wallis was to have two dates: her mother's cousin

Lelia Gordon's husband, George Barnett, was a major general in the U.S. Marine Corps and promised to present a gallant figure in his sleek uniform; and her cousin Henry Warfield, who, at twenty-seven years of age, was guaranteed to turn heads with his dashing good looks.[18]

The Bachelors' Cotillon took place on December 7, 1914. Wallis spent the afternoon carefully preparing for the event, dressing in her new gown and letting her mother fuss over her hair and daub her cheeks with rouge. Her gown, of white satin with chiffon, fell loosely to her knees in a series of folds. The low-cut shoulders were covered with a light chiffon wrap, and the front panels of the gown had been finely embroidered and sewn with seed pearls.[19]

Once ready, Wallis waited expectantly in the parlor. Finally, the doorbell rang and her cousin Henry Warfield confidently strode into the room, attired in white tie and tails. He bowed low before Wallis, presented her with a massive bouquet of American Beauty roses, and declared, "Kiddo, I can assure you that you will be the most enchanting, most ravishing, most exquisite creature at the Cotillon." Satisfied, Wallis allowed him to escort her to the waiting Warfield Pierce-Arrow, which Henry had borrowed for the evening from Uncle Sol, and together with Alice and General and Mrs. Barnett, they set off through the streets of Baltimore to the Lyric Theatre, where the cotillion would be held.[20]

The Warfield Pierce-Arrow pulled up along the curb outside, and Wallis and her party made their way across the crimson carpet that had been stretched over the sidewalk and toward the glowing lights of the theater. As they entered, the strains of a distant orchestra could be heard floating above the excited voices and nervous laughter of the girls and their families.

The theater's interior had been completely transformed. Shimmering golden curtains draped the crimson-and-gilt boxes, columns, arches, and candelabra, which had been twisted with garlands of out-of-season flowers. A polished wooden dance floor stretched from the rear of the stalls to the edge of the stage, where an ivy-covered trellis enclosed a dozen white-and-gold-draped tables for the midnight supper. Each debutante had been given one of the boxes circling the dance floor to decorate before the cotillion. Wallis arranged for her box to be festooned with dozens of American Beauty roses to match her bouquet, along with trailing vines of ivy laced with pale ribbons.[21]

For her first dance, Wallis took to the floor with General Barnett. Dances with her cousin Henry and then with several other eligible young escorts followed. At eleven, the excited crowd fell silent as the board of governors of the Bachelors' Club appeared. The forty-seven debutantes all stood silently in a long, straight line, their escorts at their sides, and slowly marched around the perimeter of the room as their names were called out.[22]

At half-past one in the morning, following hours of dancing and a rushed supper, Wallis, accompanied by Henry and an immense group of fellow debutantes, left the cotillion. While the parents, relatives, and older escorts cooperatively retired for the evening, the young revelers set off in their racing motorcars for the Baltimore Country Club, where the party included Wallis's friend Mary Kirk. The young couples tangoed, dined, and partied until sunrise called an end to their festivities. Wallis returned home exhausted but exuberantly triumphant.

Her debut marked Wallis's recognized entry into womanhood. It was also intended to launch her into polite society and prepare her for marriage. The round of dinners and receptions increased with a frenzied pace as young women and men mixed and mingled under the watchful eyes of suitable chaperones. Wallis never failed to make a favorable impression. One fellow debutante recalled that she "was superlatively smart, without being beautiful, and she had poise and a knack for finding her way around that made most of us feel like clumsy children."[23] Wallis encouraged the flirtatious boys who competed for her attentions and had a number of handsome, though not altogether serious, boyfriends. These dates, in Baltimore, at Princeton, or at the nearby Naval Academy in Annapolis, were, in keeping with the southern tradition, regarded as "engagements."[24]

Wallis "had more beaux than any other girl in town," a friend would later recall.[25] But of these only one—Carter Osborne—was rather serious. A friend remembered how the young man "was always waiting to take Wallis home, to tea, or wherever she might want to go. He would jump and obey her every wish. He was wildly in love with her and, although no one really knew, the general inference was that Wallis rather liked Carter. To our girlish minds, it seemed it would be a 'go.'"[26]

Osborne himself recalled Wallis fondly: "For her time, she was very sophisticated. You know, there are stories about how she used to insist the young men in Baltimore take her out to places that were so expensive they could hardly afford to pay the bill afterwards. All I can say is I don't recall anything like that happening during the three years I went around with her."[27]

The relationship burned with the intensity of a first love. "I think for a while we were in love with each other," he remembered.[28] The pair were careful, however, to keep their feelings private. Still, there was much passionate talk: "Between ourselves, we said we were engaged," he said. "We thought we were serious and planned to marry."[29]

The one thing Wallis desperately wanted—her own debutante ball—eluded her, for she and Alice were far too poor to undertake the enormous expense involved. Although it was common practice for each young lady to host her own ball, if only to reciprocate the hospitality she had been shown by her fellow debutantes, Wallis was unable to convince her uncle Solomon to foot the bill. Instead, he had a special notice published in the society column of Baltimore's paper, using the outbreak of the Great War as a convenient excuse: "The report that I will give a large ball for my debutante niece, Miss Wallis Warfield, is without foundation in that I do not consider the present a proper time for such festivities, when thousands of men are being slaughtered and their families left destitute in the appalling catastrophe now devastating Europe."[30]

Wallis was devastated by this announcement, but she did not suffer for long: Lelia Barnett soon arranged for an elaborate tea dance to be given in her honor. For the occasion, Lelia transformed the Band Hall of the Marine Barracks in Washington, D.C., with bunting, flags, and immense bowers of flowers. Debutante friends came down from Baltimore, and Wallis was greeted at the front door by a guard of honor, dressed in smart blue uniforms covered in gold braid. Within, Lelia had arranged for the sixty-man-strong presidential marine band, attired in their blue and red coats, to provide the music. It made for an impressive afternoon, with a touch of institutional grandeur which the other debutantes envied.[31]

Along with Wallis's triumph came sadness. Anna Emory Warfield had not been well for some time. She had fallen and broken her hip earlier that year, and her injury confined her to her house. In the chill Baltimore winter, she grew weaker; when she caught pneumonia, she was too weak to battle its debilitating effects. In December she died.

The funeral was an elaborate one, and Baltimore society turned out in force to drape itself in black and watch as one of the city's last great dowagers was buried. Afterward, Wallis was surprised to learn that her grandmother had left her four thousand dollars in her will—an enormous sum for a nineteen-year-old girl in 1916. But she was not to be allowed the sum until her twenty-first birthday and was reliant on her uncle Solomon even then for its distribution.

Even though she had loved her grandmother, Wallis found the prolonged mourning a stifling experience. She had just taken her first, heady plunge into the exciting social world of the debutante and had no wish to alter her taste for entertainment. She longed, more and more, to escape from the closeted, shrouded atmosphere of her relatives in Baltimore.

Once again, Wallis was rescued by understanding relatives. Lelia Barnett's younger sister, Corinne, had, in 1907, married a handsome

U.S. Navy aviator named Henry Mustin, and the pair lived in Florida, where Captain Mustin had recently been appointed commander of the Pensacola Naval Air Station. In the midst of family mourning, Corinne asked Wallis to join them for a holiday. The Warfields were horrified at the idea, considering a vacation both improper and disrespectful to the memory of her recently deceased grandmother. But after many scenes Wallis prevailed. In April 1916, she left Baltimore for Florida, a momentous trip on which she would meet her first husband.

4

Win

WALLIS WAS HAPPY to escape both her mourning family and the cool Baltimore spring. She had always been fond of her cousin Corinne, whom she treated like an older sister, and she greatly admired Corinne's accomplished husband, Lt. Comdr. Henry C. Mustin. Mustin, some years older than his wife, was a distinguished member of the U.S. Navy. He was master of the battleship USS *Mississippi* and had been appointed to help establish the new U.S. Naval Air Station at Pensacola.

Pensacola was a new experience for Wallis. She was captivated by the tall palm trees, miles of white sandy beaches, exotic Spanish architecture, and blue skies filled with the burning sun. The Mustins lived on the naval base in a modest white frame cottage perched along a sloping street lined with similar bungalows. At the end was the base itself, with its long hangars and constant roar of airplanes; in the sheltered bay beyond, rows of battleships lay at anchor. Wallis spent long, lazy mornings sitting in the sunshine, reading, watching the ocean, or visiting shops, old Spanish missions, and museums with Corinne.

Several times a week, Henry Mustin brought his fellow officers home for luncheon; although she never admitted complicity, Wallis later suspected that Corinne had, in fact, secretly asked her husband to invite the men to entertain and amuse her.[1] One balmy day, Wallis was standing on a corner of the front porch, looking down at the bay, when Henry, accompanied by three officers, rounded the corner. Wallis immediately noticed their regal bearing, their sleek figures in crisp white uniforms, and their golden tans from hours in the Florida sunshine.[2]

Wallis was introduced to all three men, but she only recalled one, Earl Winfield Spencer Jr. Known to his friends as Win, the twenty-seven-year-old was a junior-grade lieutenant. His quick smile and dashing uniform worked their magic. Wallis saw only the gold stripes on his shoulder boards, the dark hair, closely cropped mustache, and shining eyes. That Spencer was short, a bit thick round the middle, and had a dissipated look in his dark-circled eyes was completely lost on her.

Wallis knew nothing about airplanes, which seemed to be the chief topic at the luncheon table, but she forced herself to participate when she could. She repeatedly turned to Spencer, asking him questions about his work and the dangers of flying; the effect was immensely flattering. As he spoke, Wallis continued to size up Win Spencer. "I gained an impression of resolution and courage," she later wrote. "I felt here was a man you could rely on in a tight place."[3]

The luncheon party eventually broke up. As Win Spencer stepped through the Mustins' door, he turned around to face Wallis, and asked if he could call on her the following afternoon. She was startled at this direct approach and haltingly suggested that her cousin might have other plans for her. But Win seemed not to care as long as he was included in them. With that, he was off, leaving a slightly stunned Wallis standing at the door.[4]

If Win Spencer had hoped to provoke an interest from Wallis, his calculations proved successful. She had never before encountered a man so confident, so sure of himself, so commanding, as Win Spencer. His strength was intoxicating. True to his word, Spencer appeared the following afternoon clad in another striking uniform. He greeted Wallis warmly but did not fawn over her as the evening progressed. This peculiar mixture of fascination and disinterest on his part was utterly different from anything Wallis had experienced. The young men she had known back in Baltimore were eager for her attentions; Spencer seemed to pride himself on studied indifference. "By the end of the evening," Wallis later wrote, "I knew I was in love—in love at first sight, yes, but nonetheless completely, totally, and helplessly."[5] To her mother, she happily wrote, "I have just met the world's most fascinating aviator. . . ."[6]

He had been born on September 20, 1888, in a small Kansas town, one of six children in a comfortable, though scarcely wealthy, family. His father, Winfield Spencer Sr., eventually went on to become a Chicago stockbroker, although he had once dabbled in big-game hunting; the walls of the family home, in fashionable Highland Park, Illinois, were hung with his trophies. His British wife, Agnes, was a quiet, reserved woman, subject to bouts of depression and sudden changes of mood.

In 1905, Win entered the U.S. Naval Academy at Annapolis, near Baltimore. His career was checkered with petty misdemeanors and demerits, from unpolished shoes and unclean laundry to dirty quarters and high-spirited rebellion. However, ordinary incidents aside, Win Spencer did well and was popular with his fellow cadets. Following his graduation in 1910, he went to sea aboard the battleship USS

Nebraska and first became fascinated by the idea of flight. After returning to shore, Win Spencer actively threw himself into the navy's flight-
training program. He received his wings and in November 1914 was
posted, along with a small group of fliers, at that time just twenty-five,
to the U.S. Naval Air Station at Pensacola. Among the men, Win was
commonly believed to be one of the best fliers in the field.

Win Spencer was a novelty. Not only was he confident, mature,
and distinguished; his position was a unique, privileged, and glamorous one to the impressionable young woman from Baltimore. The
American military was still less than certain about the merits of flying;
the U.S. Naval Air Station at Pensacola was the only one in the nation,
and Win was one of only a handful of trained and recognized aviators.[7]

Pensacola, at heart, remained a quiet little southern town, and
there were not many activities to keep Wallis enthralled. Each morning,
she and Corinne walked through the officers' compound to the long
white beaches and watched the fighters take off on their daily assign-
ments. The distant chugging of a motor broke the silence over the
placid bay, and one after another, a string of fragile-looking biplanes,
their fabric-covered wings crisscrossed with wire struts, soared into
the sky. Wallis witnessed firsthand the dangers involved in this daring,
new defense field; after several crashes killed some of Win's fellow aviators, Wallis developed a fear of flying, one which would last all of
her life.[8]

Win, who enjoyed golf, spent long afternoons at the scrubby little
course, its green lawns dried brown from the hot southern sun, trying
to impart both a love of the sport and a knowledge of its play to Wallis.
She found golf boring but continued the lessons, for it was one of the
few occasions on which she could be alone with Win.[9] Suitably chaperoned by Henry and Corinne Mustin, Wallis frequently joined Win
for Saturday evening dinners at the San Carlos Hotel, where they
danced together on the terrace beneath the waving palm fronds in the
light of the low orange moon.[10]

During the week, when evening came and Win escaped his
duties at the station, he collected Wallis, and the two strolled along the
beach, watching the sun set in a fiery burst of crimson as they stooped
to pick up shells. Once night fell, they set off in Win's Ford for the local
cinema, watching silent comedies in the flickering light after quietly
slipping into seats in the back row and holding hands in the dark
along with the other young lovers. Dances at the Pensacola Country
Club ended on the long, dark veranda. There, in the blackness of night
and the warm air perfumed with the semitropical flowers and alive
with the soft chirping of crickets and dancing of fireflies, Win first
kissed Wallis.[11]

Wallis was only nineteen, little more than a high-spirited schoolgirl, still uncertain of both herself and her feelings but enjoying the relatively innocent thrill of her new relationship with an older, more mature man. She knew little of the facts of life "beyond the whispered conjecture" of her former schoolmates. She had never before been drawn so quickly to a member of the opposite sex, and her confusion over the situation into which she had unexpectedly plunged mounted with each passing day. Wallis knew she had rushed into the romance. She suffered occasional pangs of doubt and halfheartedly tried several times to slow the progress of the relationship. Nevertheless, she later recalled her impatience with the hovering presence of a chaperone and her longing to break free of the constraints preventing her relationship with Win from progressing. That he was also something of a mystery was not lost on Wallis, who, with stubborn determination, believed she would somehow single-handedly crack through his veneer of reserve and discover the man she assumed was hidden beneath. Wallis would tame his rugged spirit.[12]

Her determination seemed to be matched by both Win's affection and his desire to possess her. If she spent the evenings with other young officers, Win was quick to express his jealousy.[13] With no experience in such affairs, Wallis failed to recognize Win's darker side, but the clues were clearly visible. She was surprised at his sudden bursts of anger, his penchant for brooding, and the speed with which he often turned against her over the most minor misunderstanding. Sometimes the mood passed, and he returned to his carefree manner; but, she began to learn, just as often he would persist in his gloomy silence, his anger unspoken but barely contained.

As a young, eligible officer, Win Spencer suffered no shortage of beautiful female admirers and must have had something of a reputation at the air station. One wonders what, if any, objections Henry and Corinne Mustin, who had known Spencer for some time and had therefore been aware of some of his less pleasant traits, expressed to Wallis; on this issue, Wallis's memoirs are utterly silent.

With a promising career and success at his important post, Win could have attracted any number of potential wives. The demands that went with the position were daunting and certainly required great skill and an easy spirit. On the surface, at least, there was little to recommend Wallis as the perfect mate. She was young, immature, and self-centered. Nor could she be called beautiful: Corinne jokingly referred to her cousin as "Skinny."[14] But Wallis was also from a good, if not wealthy, family. Her brash and adventurous spirit, so unlike that of the women Win Spencer usually encountered, attracted him immensely. In addition, she possessed an important measure of breeding and was clearly cultured, considerations not to be underestimated in an officer's wife.

There was also another consideration. Win Spencer, for all his flattering attentions, was a dominant man. Little given to intense contemplation, he needed a partner who would bow to his authority. Although he valued Wallis's independent spirit, her youth and inexperience suggested that she might suitably be molded to fit Win's own version of an ideal wife.

One evening, Win collected Wallis from the Mustins' and took her to the movies. To Wallis's surprise, as soon as the lights began to dim, Win stood up, took her hand, and led her from the theater. He seemed suddenly overcome with some unspoken determination. In silence, he drove Wallis to the Pensacola Country Club and led her through the crowded rooms to the darkened veranda. There, in the warm spring night, with the flames of the gas torches dancing on the distant terrace, he asked Wallis to marry him.[15]

If Wallis was stunned at this development, she did nothing to let on. She told Win that although she loved him, she needed to be certain of her feelings. In any case, she declared, she would have to receive the permission of both her mother and her uncle Solomon.[16]

"I never expected you to say yes right away," he answered with a smile, "but don't keep me waiting too long."[17]

After nearly two months, Wallis was finally due to leave Pensacola; during the few short days leading up to her departure, she and Win were nearly inseparable. On the day she left, Win escorted her to the train station and helped her climb aboard her carriage, telling her that he would come to Baltimore on his summer leave and expect a final answer when he arrived. He reached up, took her in his arms, and kissed her goodbye. He stood, watching and waiting, as her train slowly steamed north.[18]

Before leaving Pensacola, Wallis had dispatched two letters to her mother describing her whirlwind romance with Spencer. When Wallis arrived home, Alice had prepared her arguments carefully. Wallis had only known Win for two months, she declared. His career was a dangerous one, and Wallis might easily end up a young widow, and with growing tensions in Europe, there was every chance that Win might be posted overseas and killed in action. The navy had high expectations for its officers' wives, and Wallis's streak of independence would not be appreciated, Alice warned. Moreover, she and Win would have to move frequently and would have little money and few permanent friends. Nor was this the grand society match Alice had anticipated for her daughter: The years of ensuring that Wallis attended the best schools, made the right friends, and had a proper debut would all go for naught if she married a simple lieutenant who had no money of his own and none coming from a wealthy family.[19]

But Wallis was also prepared. To counter her mother's arguments, she declared that the adventure of life with Win as a navy wife was what appealed to her most. She did not, she said, want to end her days as a dull Baltimore matron. Unspoken, but also in her thoughts, was the idea that her marriage would relieve her mother of the burden of financial support. With resignation, Alice told Wallis that it was just another example of her stubborn determination to get whatever she wanted.[20]

When Win arrived in Baltimore, Wallis happily informed him that she would marry him. Whatever doubts Alice might have harbored were quickly set aside once she met Win, whose easy charm and rugged good looks captivated her. Aunt Bessie also liked the young aviator, and even staid Uncle Solomon heartily approved, declaring that Win Spencer was clearly a man who had his feet on the ground.[21] In August, it was Wallis's turn, and she accompanied Win to Chicago to meet his family. His father and mother greeted Wallis warmly but seemed a bit puzzled by the unexpected announcement.[22]

Before the engagement was announced, Wallis wrote a long letter to Carter Osborne, who had gone to Mexico with the U.S. Cavalry in pursuit of Pancho Villa. She informed him of her intended marriage and wished him well in the future. Although Wallis later dismissed her romance with Carter as merely casual, it was a bit more serious than she herself liked to admit. The very fact that she wrote this letter indicates that their feelings for each other were at one time strong.[23]

The engagement of Bessie Wallis Warfield and Earl Winfield Spencer Jr. was announced in the Baltimore papers on September 16, 1916. Wallis had the distinction of being one of the first debutantes of her season to become engaged, and she delighted her friends by flashing her diamond ring, which had cost Win several months' pay.[24] The *Baltimore News-Post* wrote that the engagement was "of unusual interest to Society in Maryland, as well as in Virginia" and described Wallis as "one of the most popular girls in Society since she made her debut."[25]

The wedding was set for November 8, 1916 in Baltimore. The two-month interval left Wallis with little time to organize what she hoped would be an extravaganza. There was no trousseau, and she spent frantic days shopping for clothing and housewares. These activities had to be sandwiched between family luncheons and dinners in her honor: Wallis was a member of one of the city's most socially prominent families, and the wedding and its attendant festivities received a fair amount of publicity in the local newspapers. There was a luncheon hosted by Emily McLane Merryman at Gerar, her house near Cockeysville; Aubrey Edmunds King gave another at the Baltimore Country Club; Mrs. Barnett and her daughter Lelia Gordon gave a tea at their house in Washington, D.C.; and Wallis's great friend Mary

Kirk and her mother, Mrs. Henry C. Kirk Jr., hosted a lavish tea at the Baltimore Country Club.[26]

With the passing weeks, wedding gifts began to pour in: Wallis's uncle Solomon gave the engaged couple a large silver bowl, while Win's family sent an elaborate silver cutlery service and a matching silver tea service made by Kirk Silverworks. There were china settings and crystal; linens and picture frames; furniture and housewares, all destined for the newly married couple's first home in Pensacola.[27]

The day before the wedding was filled with frantic activity. Wallis had last-minute fittings for her gown and continually fretted over the smallest details. That evening, Win attended a bachelor party given in his honor at the Belvedere Hotel in Baltimore; his fiancée and her friends went to the theater to see a performance of the popular comedy *His Bridal Night*.[28]

The wedding took place at six o'clock the following evening. The interior of Baltimore's Christ Church had been filled with flowers: annunciation lilies stood at either side of the altar, while bowers and sprays of white chrysanthemums decorated the aisles and pews. Shortly after five, the doors of the church were opened, and the ushers, all Win's fellow naval flight officers, began escorting the guests down the aisles. By six, Win stood at the steps to the altar, carefully attired in his full-dress uniform as a junior-grade lieutenant, exchanging whispers with the Reverend Edwin Barnes Niver, who was to conduct the ceremony. At Win's side stood his brother Dumaresque Spencer, who served as best man.[29]

The thunder of the church organ signaled the approach of the bride. First came her six bridesmaids: her cousins Lelia Gordon and Emily McLane Merryman; Win's sister, Ethel Spencer; and Wallis's schoolfriends Mary Kirk, Mary Graham, and Mercer Taliaferro. Wallis had helped design their gowns herself. They wore orchid-colored faille dresses, with full skirts and tight bodices covered in blue velvet, and large picture hats of blue velvet with orchid-colored faille silk decorated with a single silver rose. Each lady carried a bouquet of yellow snapdragons. Wallis had selected her former schoolmate Ellen Yuille as maid of honor, and she wore a similiar gown in blue, with silver stitching, and a large picture hat of blue satin decorated with a single orchid-colored plume. As maid of honor, she carried a bouquet of orchids.[30]

Finally, Wallis appeared on the arm of her uncle Solomon. She wore a gown of white panne velvet, its pointed bodice intricately embroidered with pearls.[31] Her full skirt opened up to reveal a petticoat of heirloom lace, and a long court train fell from her shoulders. Around her neck she wore a single strand of perfectly matched pearls that had belonged to her grandmother Anna Emory Warfield. A bouquet of white orchids and lilies of the valley was tied with white silk ribbons, while a spray of orange blossoms circled her hair in a coronet, holding her veil of tulle edged with old lace around the sides and back of her head.[32]

The wedding service was short, and both bride and groom exchanged their vows in loud, clear voices. Immediately afterward, they exited the church beneath the crossed swords of Win's fellow officers and drove to the Stafford Hotel, where the reception took place. To bursts of applause, the newlyweds entered the hotel's ballroom, and Win led Wallis to the middle of the room, where the pair opened the reception with a dance. As the orchestra continued to play, they circled the room, receiving the congratulations of their friends and family and much good-natured chiding from Win's fellow officers. Wallis, holding a sword with Win, sliced through her multitiered wedding cake, and the pair enthusiastically joined in the seemingly endless champagne toasts. Finally, flushed and exhausted, Wallis changed clothes, and the newly married Spencers left the hotel, showered in a cascade of rose petals, for the first night of their honeymoon, at the Shoreham Hotel in nearby Washington, D.C.[33]

After their first night together, they traveled by train to White Sulphur Springs, West Virginia, to stay at the Greenbrier Hotel. The West Virginia countryside was dappled with flames of brilliant red and orange foliage as they arrived, and the air was cold, a wind rushing through the valley in which the hotel stood. It was here that Wallis had her first real hint of trouble. As they were dressing for dinner that first evening, Win suddenly declared, "Imagine this happening to a man on his honeymoon." He pointed to a notice atop the table declaring West Virginia a dry state and explaining that no alcoholic beverages would be served at the hotel. "That's hospitality for you," he continued. "We certainly can't stay here."[34]

Although he said this with a smile on his face, Wallis realized that Win was annoyed. However, he quickly solved the problem by pulling a flask filled with gin from his suitcase and settled down to his drinking. When Wallis tried to question him, Win cut her off with a dismissive laugh. She said nothing more and convinced herself that her hardworking husband deserved to be left alone. But a troubling suggestion had planted itself in her mind; and as the honeymoon progressed, she would learn that Win and his precious flask were inseparable.[35]

5

Marriage

AT THE END OF TWO WEEKS, the Spencers returned to Pensacola. Wallis was delighted to find that their new house, at 6 Admiralty Row, was on the same street as that of her cousin Corinne. From the main gate to the U.S. Naval Air Station, Admiralty Row gently descended past the commanding officer's mansion down to the long white beach. The house itself, like the Mustins', was a single-story frame bungalow, painted white and faced with a large veranda. Aromatic and colorful oleander and roses bloomed in the neat yard, and it commanded a lovely view of Pensacola Bay.[1]

The house was fairly large, with a living room, dining room, kitchen, three bedrooms, and two bathrooms. This was the first opportunity Wallis had had to decorate a home of her own, and she filled the house's rooms with white-painted furniture, plants and potted palms, wicker chairs, and chintz curtains, which helped enliven the somewhat stark Craftsman-style interiors. The crates of wedding gifts were carefully unpacked: Family photographs topped tables, china filled the shelves, and the Kirk silver service glistened on the dining-room sideboard. Carefully arranged vases of flowers added color. Although Win's salary was tight, they found money to hire a maid and a cook, the latter a necessity, for Wallis had not yet learned the culinary arts.[2]

At first, life in Pensacola was easy and comfortable for Wallis. The weather was usually good for late-afternoon walks, and Win's pay was enough to keep Wallis in the latest fashionable, if slightly practical, clothes. She had security previously unknown in her life. Corinne escorted her to luncheons, where she met the officers' wives. Wallis was sociable but found she had little in common with these rather quiet, reserved women who spent their afternoons discussing children, gardening, and needlework—all topics which held absolutely no interest for Wallis. The wives, in turn, found Wallis unconventional: She was bold, she spoke her mind freely, and she laughed easily. Perhaps inevitably, Wallis got on better with their husbands, whom she and Win frequently hosted for evenings of bridge or poker.

On Saturday evenings, they often drove to the San Carlos Hotel for dinner and dancing. It was only after dinner on Saturday nights that officers were allowed to drink, but Win and his comrades circumvented this by sneaking martinis at dinner in soup bowls. On occasion, the alcohol got the better of Win, who once grabbed a neighbor's cane and hat and danced around the dining room, pretending he was George M. Cohan. Wallis said nothing; her husband's performance was slightly embarrassing but harmless enough.[3]

Each morning, Wallis saw Win off to his daily flights. A gong was stationed at the edge of the airfield and was rung to alert the entire station whenever an accident occurred. "Whatever else we might be doing on our own account," Wallis recalled, "our subconscious was always waiting for it to sound. Then, once it had sounded, the first frightening thought was 'Has it sounded for me?'" Telephone use was forbidden on the base during an emergency, and Wallis, along with the rest of the wives, could only sit and wait. The minutes and hours of uncertainty seared themselves into her consciousness, leaving a fear so intense that she would refuse to fly for the rest of her life except in cases of the utmost emergency.[4]

For all of her worry, however, Wallis could not prevent the inevitable. One day, she learned that Win had crashed; although he had somehow managed to escape unharmed, the danger was a terrifying jolt to Wallis. She began to loathe his hours in the air, the tenor of the times leading to war, and the dreaded anticipation underlying life at Pensacola.

The regularity of life at Pensacola soon proved monotonous to the young woman who had so craved her freedom. To relieve the pressure of worry over Win's safety as well as her increasing boredom, Wallis often sat through repeated showings of the same films at the local cinema, happy for whatever distraction she could find.

But the hostilities in Europe were soon to take their toll. As war fever increased, so did the population of the air station; every week, trains deposited new recruits, whom Win supervised in their flight training. His hours at work grew longer, and he returned home exhausted. Inevitably, he began to drink more and more; not sociably, with Wallis, but alone, with his flask. Some nights, he would return home already drunk; other evenings, he would disappear to the beach or lock himself in the bathroom, only to stumble out a few hours later, intoxicated. Wallis's despair was coupled with loneliness: in January 1917, Henry Mustin was transferred to Washington, D.C., and with Corinne gone, she found herself alone except for Win.[5]

Finally, on April 6, President Woodrow Wilson went before the

U.S. Congress to declare war on Germany, news which those at Pensacola greeted with relief. Win was promoted to full lieutenant and in May received orders to go to Squantum, Massachusetts, near Boston, to help organize a new naval air station. He had hoped to be posted to active duty in Europe and was disappointed with his new assignment. His brother Dumaresque had joined the famous Lafayette Escadrille; his two youngest brothers, Egbert and Frederick, were members of the U.S. Army's Expeditionary Forces and were on their way to Europe to join in the combat. For a man who prided himself on his abilities, having to remain behind in the United States while others had the excitement of fighting the war was a blow to his considerable and increasingly fragile ego.

The Spencers took a small apartment in a residential hotel in Boston's Back Bay. Each morning, Wallis was up at six to cook Win's breakfast; by seven, he was on his way to work. He rarely returned before eight at night, often later. He was frequently too tired to do anything but join Wallis in the hotel's dining room for dinner and go straight to bed.[6]

Their time in Boston was lonely for Wallis. There was no established base and therefore no opportunity to mix with other navy wives. She knew no one, and even had she made friends, their apartment was too small to entertain properly; the only alternative was the hotel's dining room. Instead, she spent her days sight-seeing, touring the various monuments and historical landmarks connected with the American Revolution. When this diversion wore thin, she discovered a rather surprising new activity: attending trials. Wallis found that she could sit in courtroom galleries for hours on end, watching the latest cases; this soon became an obsession. Entire weeks were lost attending one murder trial, and she later sheepishly admitted that she had been fascinated by the grisly proceedings.[7]

Win ushered his new recruits through an advanced eight-week course in seamanship, navigation, gunnery, meteorology, signaling, aerodynamics, and aviation basics. Once they had successfully completed their initial training, he supervised their flight instruction. He had only been given a handful of petty officers to assist him, none of whom knew much about flying. Through his sheer energy, Win toiled and managed to create the Squantum Naval Air Station.[8]

His accomplishments were clearly recognized, for in October 1917, Win received orders to transfer to California, where he was to organize a new naval air station on North Island, near San Diego. Once again, he was not happy, having campaigned for an overseas combat assignment. He felt worthless and despondent and questioned his abilities; he seemed unable to comprehend that he was more important as an instructor to thousands than as a single combat airman. But the transfer, as Wallis repeatedly pointed out, was an immense promotion: at San Diego, he was to supervise hundreds of others and once again be responsible for the establishment of a station.[9]

After a long train ride, the Spencers arrived in San Diego on November 8. San Diego was a prosperous town at the time, with a population of nearly 100,000, and Wallis was enchanted with the palm trees, semitropical flowers, and warm climate. Their first home was a furnished, two-room ground-floor flat in the Palomar Apartments. Although the rent was slightly higher than in Boston, the management provided a Japanese houseboy to look after tasks, and Wallis fell in love with the views to adjacent Balboa Park, the tiled patio bordered with flowers, and the inviting atmosphere.[10]

The extra expense of their new apartment meant that Wallis had to do without a cook. She bought a copy of *Fannie Farmer's Boston Cooking School Cook Book* and read it from cover to cover. When she felt sufficiently prepared, she sent out invitations to a young army couple for her first dinner party. The menu was carefully planned: Campbell's cream of tomato soup, roast beef and gravy, roast potatoes, artichokes with hollandaise sauce, and ice cream with chocolate sauce.[11] By the time Win arrived home, however, he found Wallis a nervous wreck. He made her a double martini, which she quickly downed. Within a few minutes, she recalled, her worries had disappeared, and she was utterly unconcerned as she watched the hollandaise fly off her spoon and slide down the walls as she stirred wildly. From that moment on, Wallis was convinced of the benefits of a daily cocktail hour.[12]

Although she was the wife of the commanding officer of the North Island Naval Air Station, Wallis found that there was little to occupy her time. When Win was working, she visited newly made friends, did the shopping, practiced cooking, and toured the California sights. She longed for a social life and eagerly accepted invitations to luncheons in Santa Barbara, polo matches in Del Monte, or afternoon picnics along the beach in La Jolla. But Win, under considerable pressure, had no wish to socialize after work; the only company he sought was his own, and his drinking increased dramatically. Within a year, the first cracks in the marriage were already beginning to show.[13]

Win poured all his effort and energy into his job; there was little left to give to the marriage. He made conscientious attempts to reform his behavior, but as the strain increased, his moods became darker; he was more withdrawn, and Wallis noted that he rarely spoke when home. Then, in the middle of January 1918, he learned that his beloved brother Dumaresque had been killed in an aerial battle in the war in Europe; grief, along with the shame that he felt at not serving his country in the trenches, inevitably led him again and again to the solace of the bottle. Win's drinking also began to change him physically: he was no longer the young, handsome aviator who had captivated Wallis, but a thicker, prematurely aged man, with growing circles under his eyes, speckled, graying hair, and a rapidly increasing waistline.

On November 11, 1918 the Armistice was signed, ending the Great War in Europe. There were wild celebrations in San Diego, and Wallis and Win joined the crowds, dancing in the streets at midnight to the light of exploding fireworks.[14] The sounds of gunfire, whistles, honking horns, and bells filled the air; on the following day, Win proudly led his men through the streets in a parade, loudly cheered by Wallis. She dared hope that now the pressures on her husband, both from his work and from his own guilt at not fighting, would disappear.

But the happy times were soon over. Now that the war had ended, and the North Island Naval Air Station was successfully up and running, he felt worthless. Before, the pressure had driven him to drink; now it was frustration and irritation that poisoned him. Although their own private lives were strained, as a commanding officer, Win could not avoid the usual round of social functions with Wallis at his side. However, once at parties or receptions, the gloves came off. He had always been jealous of the attentions other men paid to his wife; now these feelings turned to suspicion. He became unaccountably sadistic. "At parties," Wallis later wrote, "he would go out of his way to direct at me a running barrage of subtle innuendoes and veiled insults. Outsiders were not supposed to understand these clever thrusts, but I certainly did, and they made my evenings terribly uncomfortable."[15] Win sat silent at a table, slowly sipping on drink after drink, while his lively wife circulated, her boisterous gaiety gradually working away at his morose character. He refused to mix with the crowds and more often than not disappeared entirely, leaving Wallis alone, with no idea of his whereabouts. Embarrassed, she would quickly make excuses, and finding a friend with a motorcar, set out in search of her missing husband. On occasion, Win went missing for several days before finally turning up, looking much worse for wear and without any explanation. Everyone at the naval air station knew of this behavior, and the state of the Spencer marriage became fodder for base gossips.[16]

Wallis was a private person, not given to living her personal life under such a microscope. Although she was aware that her marital difficulties were being discussed openly, she was determined not to complain, not to show any evidence that the union was less than perfect. For comfort, she became great friends with Katherine Bigelow, a charming, vivacious woman whose husband had recently been killed while on duty in France. The two women quickly became inseparable and formed a friendship which would last many decades. In December 1919, Henry Mustin was posted to San Diego, where he assumed command of the air detachment of the Pacific Fleet; a month later, his wife, Corinne, followed, increasing Wallis's circle of intimates.

But her cousin and new friend could not prevent the inevitable, and life for Wallis soon became a nearly unbearable nightmare. Win spent entire days sulking in silence. When he did talk, it was most often to accuse Wallis of flirting with his fellow officers or of deliberately ignoring him. His tirades, induced by his increasing intake of alcohol, soon became violent. He often locked Wallis in the bathroom for hours at a time, leaving her trapped in a room from which she could not escape while he disappeared to drink. Sometimes this punishment stretched into the evening and night, and Wallis, terrified and without food, could do nothing. She grew to fear being left alone with him.[17] During one terrifying outburst, he left her lying on the bed and forced her to watch while he proceeded to smash all the photographs of her family on the floor.[18]

At first, Wallis excused her husband's increasingly erratic behavior: He was under too much pressure at his job; he felt guilty over the death of his brother in the war; he felt that his talents were wasted as an instructor; she herself had done something wrong, paid too much attention to one of his friends or not enough to Win. When Win was sober and in good humor, he was the same man Wallis had been infatuated with in Pensacola: still dashing, if a bit aged; still sleek in his uniform, if a bit fuller around the middle. But as incident followed upon incident, it became more difficult for Wallis to rationalize her discomfort and growing fear.

In February 1920, Win was placed in charge of a detachment of aviators training at March Field in Riverside, California. He duly packed up his bags and set off, leaving Wallis behind by mutual agreement. She had grown weary of her life; the petty annoyances which might have ordinarily faded into the background in happier times haunted her. She longed to break free of the incessant moves, military housing, and tiresome struggles. More than anything else, she was overwhelmed by the uncertainty, the terrible dread, which filled her days and nights as she wondered if Win would come home and if he did, what punishment might be meted out to her for some presumed infraction.[19]

He returned on April 7, 1920, when Edward, Prince of Wales, visited San Diego. The Prince arrived with his cousin, Lord Louis Mountbatten, aboard the cruiser HMS *Renown*, on their way to Australia. William E. Stephens, governor of California, L. J. Wilde, mayor of San Diego, and dozens of local and military officials headed the welcoming party. There was an official navy luncheon aboard the battleship *New Mexico*, and although Corinne and Henry Mustin were on the guest list, neither Win nor Wallis was included due to limited space. The Prince spent the afternoon greeting people and being paraded through the streets of the city to San Diego Stadium, where he gave a speech before some twenty-five thousand people. But Wallis and Win, along with a thousand others, did receive invitations to the Mayoral Ball at Hotel del Coronado that evening. The great redwood-paneled ballroom was hung with American, British, and California state flags, and the band from the USS *New Mexico* played current hits as the men in their tuxedos and uniforms and the ladies in filmy, shapeless gowns danced the night away. The Spencers did not attend the banquet with the Prince that followed, however, and the royal party left San Diego that evening, Wallis having only glimpsed from a distance the man who would one day become her third husband.

Throughout that spring, Win occasionally returned to San Diego. There were momentary flashes of happiness, followed inevitably by drinking binges and psychological violence against his wife. Wallis was confused, wondering what she herself had done to warrant such treatment. Still, she continued to pretend that all was well when her mother came to visit. Alice seemed to sense that something was terribly wrong in the Spencer household, but she did not say a word to her daughter or son-in-law.[20]

Even if she had wanted to leave Win, Wallis had nowhere to run. She had no money, no prospects, no marketable abilities. She was all too aware of the fate suffered by her mother, abandoned by her family and left to beg for monthly stipends. With some relief, she learned in November 1920 that Win had received orders calling him back to Pensacola for a tour of duty as senior flight instructor. After discussing the situation, both Wallis and Win agreed that she would stay in San Diego. Wallis was not at all convinced that she was making the right decision, but she needed more time away from Win to consider their future together.

Six months passed before Win received word that he had been promoted assistant to Rear Adm. William Moffett in the U.S. Department of the Navy in Washington, D.C. He soon wrote to her saying he had stopped drinking and asked her to join him. Wallis pondered her decision. She had no money and nowhere to go. This was perhaps the last chance to save her marriage, and she knew how her family would turn on her if she admitted failure. Convinced at last that she had no other choice, Wallis packed her luggage and boarded a train for the nation's capital.[21]

The Spencers took a small flat in a residential hotel called the Brighton on California Street. At first, everything went smoothly, and Wallis was certain that Win had finally overcome his personal demons. Soon enough, however, the new job in Washington, D.C., did not work out as well as Wallis had hoped. Win grew bored with his responsibilities and again began to drink heavily. Feeling himself powerless to change his position at work, Win became a tyrant at home.

If San Diego had been a time of uncomfortable silences, periodic embarrassments, and emotional abuse, Washington, D.C., reached entirely new levels of mistreatment. Win would arrive home late in the evening and begin to drink; by midnight, when the hotel's other residents had retired for the evening, the nightly war between the Spencers would begin. Wallis tried to hide away in a corner, reading or writing, hoping that her husband would ignore her. But Win would inevitably charge through the flat, screaming at the top of his lungs, accusing his wife of not supporting him, of being unfaithful, of conspiring with officials in the navy to keep him from being promoted. She later confessed to a friend that the abuse turned physical, with frequent kicks and blows.[22] As she cowered, Wallis could hear the sounds of doors opening and closing down the corridors as people were roused from their sleep. By the time Win began to smash furniture, a representative of the management would usually show up.[23]

One Sunday afternoon, without any warning, he grabbed her, dragged her screaming through the apartment, roughly pushed her into the bathroom, and locked the door. Nothing but silence filled the following hours, and Wallis had absolutely no idea if Win lay beyond the door, simply passed out from too much drink, or if he had left the apartment altogether. She tried working loose the screws on the bathroom door with a nail file but could not get them to budge. As night fell, her sense of panic increased. "I wanted desperately to call for help," she later wrote, "but held myself in check. Our situation was already distressing enough without my drawing attention to so sordid an episode." Finally, she heard the key in the lock turn, followed by further silence. After several hours, she got up enough courage to open the door herself and found Win passed out on their bed. Wallis lay down on the sofa in the living room, "endlessly reviewing the events that had led to my personal catastrophe. Of only one thing I was certain: I had somehow become the symbol of Win's frustrations and to leave matters as they were going could only result in the final destruction of his career and of my life along with his. There was no solution but to leave him."[24]

The next morning, Win left for work without a word, and Wallis slipped from the apartment, hurrying to her mother's house across town.[25] Without divulging too many intimate details, Wallis carefully broke the news of her decision to her mother. Alice was visibly upset by the troubles in her daughter's marriage but absolutely horrified when Wallis suggested divorce. Never before had there been a divorce among the Warfields or Montagues, and Alice was not about to let her daughter become the first member of either family to make what she considered a shameful and terrible mistake.[26]

Alice was adamant, warning that divorce might appear to be the easiest solution but would likely lead to unforeseen difficulties in the future. None of the family, she reminded Wallis, would support her decision, nor would they be willing to help her financially. The meeting with Wallis's aunt Bessie went no better. She urged Wallis to try again; to take a holiday by herself or, if she was determined, to settle for a legal separation.[27] No one in her family was very sympathetic to Wallis's plight. "You know perfectly well you just married him out of curiosity," her cousin Lelia declared at one point.[28]

Wallis, however, could not be so easily dissuaded. Although she returned to Win that evening, they did not speak, and he had gone again by the time she woke the next morning. She made the inevitable call upon her uncle Solomon at his office in Baltimore, confessing the humiliation she had endured and her own fear of her husband. As soon as she mentioned the purpose of her visit, however, he exploded. "I won't let you bring this disgrace upon us!" he bellowed. "What will the people of Baltimore think?" Although his attitude softened as the interview progressed, Solomon was still a formidable influence; by the end of the visit, Wallis had reluctantly agreed to return to Win.[29]

For several weeks, Wallis lived an eerie charade, and Win, finally aware that his marriage was breaking apart, made a halfhearted attempt at altering his behavior. Inevitably, though, he could not control his frustration and anger and began the cycle of verbal and physical abuse once again. This time, Wallis, genuinely fearing for her safety, made up her mind and fled.[30]

Wallis left Win that evening, moving in temporarily with her mother. She spent the next few days reluctantly informing her relatives, apologizing for any pain caused by her actions. Uncle Solomon wrote her a letter, saying that if she proceeded, no financial assistance would be forthcoming from the Warfields should she fall upon hard times.[31]

Wallis knew only too well the realities she faced. Alice, working as a paid hostess at the Chevy Chase Club in Washington, D.C., had no money and could offer her daughter little except a sofa on which to sleep. The shock of her announcement had driven an instant wedge between Wallis and her family; not even Aunt Bessie approved of her decision. But Wallis had made up her mind: she would not return to Win. Her decision was made a little easier in February 1922 when Win was commissioned captain of a gunboat and sent to Hong Kong. From this distance, he wrote Wallis constantly, thoughtfully enclosing each month $225 from his pay.[32]

In an effort to forget her troubles, Wallis flung herself into the

social life of Washington, D.C. She found the capital filled with exciting, vibrant men and women: diplomats, reporters, politicians and
their wives, lawyers, and officials in the armed forces. Fortunately for
Wallis, it was the Roaring Twenties, and the bathtub gin, reckless jazz,
and thirst for pleasure provided exactly the escape for which she was
searching. Her wit and charm made her extremely popular, and she
was invited to join the famous Soixante Gourmets, an exclusive private club led by Wilmont Lewis, correspondent for the *Times* (London)
and responsible for some of the capital's most sought after invitations.

At one embassy reception, Wallis encountered a thirty-five-year-
old Latin American diplomat named Felipe Espil. He had come to
America nearly a decade earlier as an attorney attached to the Argentine embassy and risen quickly through the ranks to become first secretary to the ambassador, an indication of his not inconsiderable
talents. Espil was tall and slender, with chiseled features, jet black hair,
and dark, piercing eyes. He had perfect manners, was impeccably
dressed, and was charming and cultured—all the things Win had not
been.

Without deliberation, Wallis fell quickly and deeply in love.
Although she and Win were only separated, she allowed herself to
drift closer to Espil—in complete contrast to the love which she had
felt for Win. In Pensacola she had been captivated by an older, more
mature man, by his dashing uniform, and above all else, by her thirst
for freedom. Espil was an altogether different matter. Here was a man
who represented all of the things to which Wallis aspired: education,
power, money, and respect. If her feelings for Win had been somewhat
girlish and immature, those she harbored for Espil were based on
deeper qualities.

Soon enough, they were regularly seen together at the city's most
fashionable receptions and parties. Espil slowly began to reshape
Wallis. He taught her to feel at ease in the company of important dig-
nitaries and, under his guidance, master the art of social conversation.
Together they read several newspapers each day, Espil providing background information to the stories and filling in Wallis's educational
gaps. Under his influence, she cultivated a knowledge and appreciation of fine food and wine. They visited antique stores, where Espil
pointed out the most valuable pieces, and spent evenings at the theater,
at concerts, or at the ballet. Above all, Espil taught Wallis how to enjoy
life and make an art of it; the results of their time together would last
her entire life.

Espil, a rising young diplomat, also had *entrée* to the capital's
most exclusive functions. He escorted Wallis to elaborate diplomatic
receptions and balls where, clad in expensive, sleek gowns, she
whirled across the parquet floors of embassy ballrooms doing the fox-

trot, cocktail in hand. Often, she would not return home until two in the morning. Such a ceaseless pursuit of pleasure troubled Alice, who made no secret of her disapproval. Eventually, Wallis moved into the Georgetown house of Dorothy McNamee, the wife of another naval officer stationed abroad; now, for the first time, she had money, a house in which to entertain, a happy relationship, and above all, her independence.

But Wallis, plunged headlong into her own version of a schoolgirl fantasy, was too unrealistic to recognize that Espil's affections were transitory in nature. She managed to delude herself into believing that Espil would one day, when she was free of Win, marry her. Espil, however, was not as captivated. That he was genuinely fond of her is certain; but he was also keenly aware of his diplomatic career, and in the most frank terms, Wallis was a liability rather than an asset. He was Roman Catholic; she was Protestant. She had no fortune in her own right or any prospect of inheriting wealth; and perhaps most important, she was married. For a rising young Catholic diplomat, a divorced Protestant wife would never do.

The liaison might have lasted comfortably for several years were it not for Wallis's sheer determination to marry Espil. In his position, Espil had to spend time at embassy receptions with important women, and Wallis grew intensely jealous. Her attentions soon became too much for Espil's tastes. Ironically, as had Win with her, she found herself believing the worst of Espil, accusing him of flirting behind her back. Heated arguments, followed by romantic reconciliations, proved a considerable nightmare for the young diplomat, and he brought the affair to an end. Ironically, he eventually married a twice-divorced woman, a move which apparently did little to harm his career. He served as Argentine ambassador to the United States from 1931 to 1943 and died in his native land in 1972.

Wallis was inconsolable. She had been utterly convinced that Espil shared her feelings. Now, for the first time, she was confronted with an ugly truth: Just as her family had warned, she would forever be viewed as tarnished. The realization that she herself could do nothing to alter such perceptions preyed on her mind. She had given her heart, and in the end, those feelings had been rejected. In her mind, she had become a victim—of circumstances and, above all, of the men in her life. She had wanted love from these men—acceptance, protection, friendship—and instead found that somehow she was unable to meet their needs. From this point on, she carefully guarded her emotions. Her relationships with men would never again be outwardly warm ones, and even her friendships would possess more than a note of distance and formality. The passion which she might have felt was tempered with practicality, and she was more than a little reluctant to ever let herself fall in love again or reveal her true feelings except in the most intimate of circumstances.

In 1923, Henry Mustin died unexpectedly. After a suitable period of mourning had passed, Corinne, still young and vibrant, cast aside her widow's weeds and asked Wallis to accompany her on a trip to Paris. Wallis herself did not have enough money to go, so, bracing herself, she decided to visit her uncle Solomon and ask for a grant. Solomon Davies Warfield kept an apartment at the Plaza Hotel in New York City; Wallis had never before been there, but it was widely whispered within the family that it was to this enclave that he brought numerous actresses and singers for discreet romantic trysts. Wallis was shocked at the suggestive photographs which lined the apartment walls, but they gave her the emotional and moral ammunition she needed to press her request. Her uncle, mortified that a relative was staring at evidence of his other life, did not even bother to put up a fight and gave her five hundred dollars for the trip.[33]

Wallis and her cousin left the United States in January 1924. They crossed the Atlantic on a small American ocean liner that pitched and rolled in the heavy seas. The seemingly endless movement left Corinne sick and confined to their cabin for most of the voyage, but the two women still managed to work themselves into a state of excitement by planning their itinerary in their stateroom.[34]

On their first night in Paris, the two cousins, traveling without reservations, ended up in a small, decrepit hotel in an unfashionable section of the city. A few days later, they managed to book better accommodations at a hotel on the rue Pierre Charron. They spent their days sight-seeing, sitting along the sidewalk cafés sipping coffee, week-ending in the Loire Valley and visiting the old châteaus, and exploring the twisting alleys and ancient churches of Paris. Wallis came to love the city, with its thrilling sounds and smells, its cosmopolitan sophistication, and its studied elegance.[35] When Corinne returned to America, Wallis remained behind, sharing a flat with two friends for several months before reluctantly abandoning her European idyll.[36]

When Wallis returned home, she found a stack of letters from her estranged husband, all begging her to reconsider their arrangement and come live with him in China. He was lonely, unhappy, and missing her. Wallis, too, began to view the past nostalgically, glossing over the abuse she had suffered. She and Win were separated, but their emotions were still woven together in, as she later wrote, "a tangled skein of threads too stubborn to be broken."[37] With the relationship with Espil over and her money gone, there was little to tie her to America. Eventually, Wallis was worn down. On July 17, 1924 she boarded the USS *Chaumont* at Norfolk, Virginia, and, along with a dozen other navy wives, set off for the Orient.

6

China

ACCORDING TO WALLIS, the USS *Chaumont* was "the original slow boat to China."[1] The voyage, down the east coast of the United States, through the Panama Canal, and across the Pacific Ocean, seemed to take forever. Wallis became ill early on and suffered throughout the voyage from a terrible cold.

The trip was apparently uneventful. Author Charles Higham alleges that Wallis provided sexual favors to members of the ship's crew in the presence of several children and their mother, with whom she shared her cabin. This is fairly typical of the sort of unsubstantiated gossip which has been repeated about Wallis; Higham declares that his information comes from a nephew of the ship's captain, who in turn is said to have drawn on the reminiscences of the captain himself, who presumably learned details from his crew. (An odd source, surely, for what crew member would inform his captain that he had copulated in front of other passengers?) No evidence for this story, third-hand at best, has ever surfaced. Needless to say, Wallis would have had to have been not only a woman of exceptionally loose morals but also an incredibly stupid one to have behaved in the manner alleged. The evidence clearly suggests she was neither and that the story is just another rumor, like the infamous "China Dossier" (discussed later in this chapter), which has managed to work itself into her story.[2]

After six weeks and stops along the way in Hawaii and Guam, the ship finally reached Manila. Here Wallis boarded the *Empress of Canada* for the voyage to Hong Kong. At the end of the second day, September 8, Wallis stood on deck, watching as Hong Kong came into view, its harbor filled with hundreds of bobbing junks and sampans, the sloping hillsides above littered with wooden huts and the mansions of British officials. Win waited at the crowded dock to greet her, nearly lost amid the cacophony of vendors and shouted welcomes. "He looked better than I had ever seen him since our first meeting in

Pensacola—tanned, clear eyed, and charming," Wallis later recalled. As they drove to his small apartment in Kowloon, on the Chinese mainland, he declared that he had not taken a drink since receiving word that Wallis was to rejoin him.[3]

Wallis arrived at a dangerous time. China was poised on the verge of chaos. Indeed, the very week that the *Empress of Canada* docked at the Royal Naval Anchorage, civil war finally erupted on the Chinese mainland. Hong Kong itself, although a British crown colony under the protection of the Royal Navy and other British forces, had a similiarly volatile atmosphere. There was much resentment over colonial imperialism and foreign domination, not only English but European and American, and street demonstrations, assassinations, and other violent outbursts were common. The natural beauty of the city was lost on Wallis, who suffered in the intense heat as well as from having to avoid an outbreak of typhoid ravaging the city. The humid apartment always smelled of food; opening the windows brought the odor of raw sewage. This was not the exotic Orient she had expected but a gritty collection of diverse nationalities existing side by side in the most cramped quarters imaginable.

For a few weeks, all was well, and Wallis was convinced that she had made the correct decision. Then, one evening, the inevitable happened. Win had agreed to join Wallis for a prearranged dinner after his workday ended. When he failed to appear, she became worried. It was after midnight when he finally staggered home, dead drunk. He said nothing, and Wallis, without comment, put him to bed. The next morning, he was off to work without any explanation.[4]

Wallis was convinced that she had done something wrong. But when she tearfully asked Win, he denied that she had been to blame. Little more was said about the incident, and in the middle of October, Win left for Canton. This was a dangerous assignment, for the city lay at the very heart of the burgeoning civil war. The Red Army, composed of disenfranchised workers as well as professional mercenaries, had invaded the city, murdering, raping, and burning their way through the streets. Over a thousand people had been killed in heavy fighting, many of them women and children.

Win was dispatched as master of the *Pampanga*, an old gunboat whose hull was shattered with holes from shells fired at it from the Chinese mainland. This vessel was an ex-Spanish gunboat, commissioned in 1888, stretching 121 feet and armed with 4 three-pound and 2 one-pound guns to defend herself. She was the only ship in the South China patrol able to regularly cruise the estuaries of the Canton Delta.[5] Win's job was an important one, for river patrols were a regular and visible feature of the navy presence, an immense asset in the preservation of Western interests.[6]

Wallis, unwilling to lose whatever chance she might have at saving her marriage, followed him a few days later. The harbor was filled with gunboats when she arrived, their guns trained on the docks in case of trouble. Above the city, the acrid stench of burning buildings and bodies still hung in the air. She and Win moved into quarters in the Foreign Concession, which was at least regularly patrolled and protected. It was now that the Spencer marriage began to completely unravel.

Win began drinking again and accused Wallis of having affairs with his fellow officers. Wallis never knew if pressure from his job, dislike of his position, depression, or merely her presence pushed him once again to the bottle. But when it occurred, all of the ferocity of Washington, D.C., was again unleashed.

In her memoirs, Wallis wrote that doctors had diagnosed a kidney infection at this time.[7] But according to one intimate friend, the Duchess confessed that her first husband had beaten and kicked her so severely in the stomach that she had bled internally. Battered and bruised, Wallis became violently ill, and Win, fearful, begged for her forgiveness. He accompanied her back to Hong Kong, where she received further treatment.

Win continued to express guilt and regret over his actions and declared that he loved Wallis as he had no other woman; but Wallis had been through this cycle before: the violence followed by repentance, which lasted only as long as Win's ability to steer clear of his flask. Previously, she had remained with Win out of fear: She had nowhere to go, no money and little hope that she would be able to succeed in life if she broke her marital bonds. But her time in Washington, D.C., her trip to Europe, and her romance with Espil had taught her perhaps the most valuable lesson she would ever learn, that of independence. When her stubborn determination set in, Wallis knew that she could be surprisingly strong and take care of herself. Now she made up her mind.

As soon as she had recovered, Wallis told her husband that she no longer wished to live with him and would seek a divorce. Something snapped within Win; previously, he had at least kept his abuse a private matter, or so he thought; now, however, he seemed intent on deliberately humiliating his wife and subjecting her to his abuse in public. His sadistic streak increased; he forcibly dragged Wallis along with him on excursions to local brothels, openly flirting with whores, kissing and caressing them, while he made his wife watch. If she protested, he warned, he would kill her.[8]

The malicious rumors that Wallis was somehow connected with these infamous Chinese brothels undoubtedly stem from these forced visits. In 1935 a dossier is said to have been compiled at the request of

British prime minister Stanley Baldwin. Baldwin charged the British Intelligence Service, known as MI6, with the task of investigating Wallis, who was then at the height of her relationship with Edward, Prince of Wales. The result, the so-called China Dossier, supposedly made its way into Buckingham Palace, where it was read with horror by King George V and Queen Mary.

The dossier supposedly claimed that she not only visited these Chinese brothels with her husband but that she was trained in certain sexual practices within their walls. According to these stories, Wallis was said to have learned various lesbian techniques as well as a form of erotic massage said to be particularly helpful with men suffering from premature ejaculation and, her most famous secret, the "Chinese grip," which allegedly enabled her during intercourse to contract the walls of her vagina to an extraordinary degree. Not only did Wallis allegedly learn these techniques, but according to this dossier, she quickly and enthusiastically put them into practice not only on Win but on any number of men who frequented the brothels. In effect, according to the dossier, she became a prostitute.[9]

Much has been made of these unsavory allegations. The simple truth is that the document never existed: There is not one shred of reputable evidence to support it. "Absolutely preposterous, absolutely no truth in that whatsoever," Wallis's friend Aline, Countess of Romanones, declared, having discussed the stories with her.[10] Not only has no one ever been able to produce the China Dossier, but in the twenty years in which the document has been widely discussed, not one single person has actually ever claimed to have seen it. Kenneth de Courcy, the Duc de Grantmesnil, heard contemporary rumors about the dossier and once asked Major the Honorable Sir John Coke, an equerry to Queen Mary, if it indeed existed. Coke, although he had not seen the document himself, apparently told de Courcy that he had heard it did, in fact, exist.[11] On such slender allegations have the tales of the China Dossier been built. There is no record of its having been passed to King George V and no reference to its existence in the Royal Archives at Windsor Castle. Nor do official government records contain any mention of the document. The most reliable expert on the subject, Edward VIII's official biographer Philip Ziegler, has gone as far as to declare what must be accepted as the final word: that it was the figment of several vindictive imaginations.[12]

Nor does there appear to be any evidence that Wallis was acting as an intelligence agent on behalf of the U.S. government during this time period. Charles Higham makes much of the fact that, while in Washington, D.C., Wallis apparently was friendly with the wife of the head of naval intelligence and surmises that Wallis was dispatched to the Far East as some form of special courier.[13] But the fact that Wallis associated with men who were either in navy intelligence or in diplomatic circles is scarcely surprising. She was still a navy wife, her friends came from these same ranks, and her husband, after all, had been a fairly important member of various naval circles as well.

Higham also recounts tales that Wallis may have acted as a Soviet spy during her time in China, that she fronted drugs on behalf of illegal Chinese gangs, and that she participated in illicit gambling practices. "It is all a fascinating subject of conjecture," he writes, "impossible to authenticate at this stage."[14] Nor has any evidence ever come to light to support any of these allegations.

Wallis had come to China hoping to salvage her marriage. Now it was painfully obvious that nothing remained to be saved. Win's brutality finally drove her to leave him, this time for good. "There was no scene," Wallis wrote; "the final unraveling was singularly without emotion; not even the capacity for anger remained."[15] According to what the Duchess later told a friend, however, there had been no scene for a simple reason: One day, when Win was at work, she quickly packed her things, wrote him a letter saying she was going to divorce him, and left before he could return to confront her again.[16] Given Win's unpredictable nature and brutish behavior, this indeed seems to have been the sensible choice.

Mary Sadler, a friend from Washington, D.C., happened to be traveling from Hong Kong to Shanghai. With nothing to keep her in the city and no plans for the future, Wallis decided to accompany her. The two women took a small overnight liner, arriving in the port city on November 22.

Fifty thousand foreigners lived in the international settlement in Shanghai, protected by stone walls and a police force culled from various national militias.[17] The Palace Hotel, where Wallis and her friend took rooms, lay just inside these encircling walls; from her windows Wallis could gaze out upon the ancient, decaying remnants of the Imperial Palace. The panoply of sights, smells, and sounds filled her senses: animals wandered loose in the streets, rickshas clattered across the uneven cobblestones, and garbage rotted in forgotten doorways. The city pulsed with refugees: not only Chinese but Russians as well, caught in a permanent, uneasy exile after the civil war in their homeland. Thieves and murderers wandered about, seeking victims; prostitution and drugs flourished, and venturing into the streets beyond dusk was considered extremely dangerous.

But Shanghai was also a cosmopolitan, sophisticated place. Wallis looked up a British diplomat, Harold Robinson, to whom she had been given a letter of introduction while still in Washington, D.C. He recognized her loneliness and quickly swept Wallis away from her troubles, giving her flowers and baskets of exotic fruit, escorting her to cocktail parties, and taking her to horse races at the Shanghai Race Club. One suspects that his efforts were not necessarily humanitarian, and he seems to have been quite taken with Wallis. They spent evenings dancing in the sunken courtyard of the Majestic Hotel amid bowers of exotic flowers, the sounds of chirping birds, and the scent of jasmine in the air, the entire scene illuminated by the soft lights of the hanging Chinese lanterns.[18] But beyond the hotel walls the distant sounds of machine-gun fire could be heard as street gangs strolled past brothels and opium dens.

Wallis eventually decided to go to Peking, where a friend, Col. Louis Little, a Marine Corps officer from Washington, D.C., served as commander of the U.S. Legation Guard. It would be easier, with Little's help, for her to return to America on her own, without having to rely on her status as Win's wife. After much argument, she persuaded Mary Sadler to accompany her on the long rail journey, which was fraught with danger. A coastal steamer, creaking, rusty, and tossing about in a terrible storm, took them to Tientsin. When they landed, they learned that a regional civil war had broken out, and travelers were advised of the danger, but they continued on at their own risk. Wallis prevailed, and the two women climbed aboard the battered old carriage as the train set off, its aisles crowded with Chinese passengers. They passed tiny villages left in smoking ruins by bands of raiders and long lines of peasants struggling to flee the onslaught of the hostilities. At one point on the journey, rebel bandits raided the train, climbing aboard the carriages and storming through the aisles brandishing rifles. Wallis pretended not to care, displaying a surprising streak of courage she did not really feel, and the rebels eventually left the train without further incident.[19]

All around them, the carriage was filled with crying refugees: women and children, victims of famine, typhoid, and starvation. Several of the windows were nothing but shattered glass, and the cold winter wind howled miserably through them as the train chugged along. The journey took almost two full days, complicated by the frequent breakdowns of the steam engine, which left the carriages stranded in abandoned, muddy fields for hours at a time. Colonel Little came out to meet the two women, and ushered them through the dangerous city.

Wallis took up residence at the Grand Hotel de Pekin, near the legation quarters in Peking. The city, beyond the carefully protected and sheltered confines of the legation, was a smoldering mass of uncertainty, anxiously fearing the imminent seizure by Sun Yat-sen's army. This surreal atmosphere was made even more unbelievable by the character of life which went on around the legation and in the hotel, with its marble lobby and playing fountains. Wallis intended to stay merely for a fortnight, shopping for perfumes, porcelains, and silks. Then, one evening, she attended a dance at the hotel and spotted Katherine Bigelow, a friend from her days at San Diego.

Katherine and Wallis immediately renewed their friendship. Katherine had been widowed young and spent her days working on a Red Cross train in Europe. In 1920 she had married Herman Rogers. Herman had attended Groton and gone on to Yale, where he was a member of the crew team and the prestigious Skull and Bones Society and was a Phi Beta Kappa scholar. He had grown up in great wealth: His father, millionaire railroad tycoon Archibald Rogers, had been a neighbor and a trusted confidant of Franklin D. Roosevelt's, and the two families were neighbors at Hyde Park, New York. Herman himself was able to retire by the time he was thirty-five, and he and Katherine enjoyed a leisurely life of roving the world.

With his handsome looks, intellect, love of polo, and political interests, Rogers greatly reminded Wallis of Espil. For nearly two decades Wallis, Katherine, and Herman would be inseparable companions, which inevitably gave rise to all sorts of gossip. Wallis was certainly fond of Herman, and he adopted a fatherly, protective attitude toward her. Years later, Herman's second wife, Lucy (whom he married after Katherine died), said, "Wallis was the great love of his life. But it was purely a platonic relationship. He was such a straightforward man that he would not have had it any other way—and he would never have divorced Katherine, who knew how he felt about Wallis but put up with it. But if Herman had become a widower earlier, before Wallis met the Duke, I'm sure he would have married her. In fact, he told me so."[20]

Katherine and Herman asked Wallis to stay at their house in Tartar City, near the Hatamen, one of the old gates that ringed the city. The Rogers's house was set on a small, narrow lane hidden behind a very plain and unassuming, high gray-stone wall pierced by a door opening to the courtyard. Inside, however, was a hidden paradise. The courtyard was paved with gray stones, filled with carefully pruned trees, and crossed by a quiet reflecting pool. The interior was suitably exotic and eclectic, with moon-shaped doors, Oriental carpets spread across floors and furniture, tapestries hung on the walls, and beautiful porcelain and works of art scattered throughout, mingled with fringed lampshades and framed photographs. Wallis insisted on paying rent and helping with the food bills; she also discovered that for fifteen dollars a month she could have her own rickshaw, complete with boy.[21]

The Rogers often entertained, and Wallis put her poker skills to use. Although they played for small stakes, on the first evening she won over two hundred dollars. In spite of this, she quickly became a popular addition to the Rogers's set and accompanied them everywhere. "There now began for me," she later recalled, "without conscious plan or foreknowledge, what was beyond doubt the most delightful, the most carefree, the most lyrical interval of my youth."[22]

If Hong Kong and Shanghai had been disappointments, Peking was a place of enchantment. The skyline, low and gray, was dotted with brilliant red and golden roofs, guarded by vicious dragons that lay curled at the corners. Pagodas and temples, markets and restaurants, snaked their way around cobbled squares, enclosing hidden alleys and tiny warrens leading to the massive gates that studded the walls around the city. Peking seemed isolated, broken into compartments, a cloistered world filled with foreigners, spies, diplomats, and secrets. Its ancient face glimpsed through dirty streetcar windows and from the plush rear seats of imported limousines, and the gentle sound of its tinkling temple bells were pierced by shrill cries of hawkers in their stalls, screams of children, honking horns, and shouted warnings from rickshaw boys as they raced their passengers along narrow lanes.

The cost of living in Peking was modest, and Wallis found that she could buy recently imported fashion magazines at a news agent, take them to a local seamstress, and for a few dollars have a quality reproduction in whichever glittering Oriental silk she chose.[23] She managed to collect an impressive assortment of carved jades, elegant porcelains, and a few lacquer boxes exquisitely painted with scenes of the city. Wandering about the walled city, she visited the Imperial City, pagodas, street markets, and the old palace. Each night, the gates were closed, locking in the inhabitants and underscoring the unique feeling of isolation. The small foreign community in the city banded together, and all of its members knew one another. Single men—new young diplomats, bankers, and merchant representatives being posted at regular intervals—were also plentiful.[24]

"The social life in Perking of those days has probably never been duplicated," one journalist recalled, "and will certainly never be restored. Aside from the Legation Guards there were only an average of 2,600 Americans and Europeans in the huge city. Foreign money went very far, and much of the entertaining was on a lavish scale. The Peking Club, the French Club, the German Club, and the Golf Club out on the Hill of the Eight Sacred Treasures, were all delightful places. The Race Club, with its track a few miles outside the city walls, was gay. . . . In the fall the duck and goose hunting was superb, and the pheasants and quail were so thick they damaged the grain crops. Every winter there was about three months of ice skating."[25]

Wallis's days were lazy. Each morning, if the weather was mild, she took breakfast in the open courtyard. Mornings and afternoons were spent shopping, visiting friends, riding horses, playing tennis at the British legation, or swimming in the pool at the U.S. legation.

Together with Katherine and Herman Rogers, she often attended matches at the Polo Club and dined out in the evenings, riding to restaurants through the crowded streets in rickshaws, enveloped in the scents of night air, thick with the perfume of flowers and smells of cooking and spices.[26]

The trio spent weekends in the country. Katherine and Herman had rented the old Black Dragon Temple in the Western Hills as a summer house. On Friday afternoons, they would set off in a car, driving from the city to the surrounding forests, before the roads eventually ceased. There servants would be waiting with donkeys on which they continued their climb into the foothills. Abandoned, crumbling temples dotted the landscape. The Rogerses had selected a well-preserved example, with a multicolored, tiled roof, bells hanging from the eaves, and a large central hall surrounded by several smaller rooms, all brightly decorated with old murals. An enormous Buddha, its gilt peeling away, surveyed the main chamber. There was no electricity: Servants had come before their arrival, bringing candles and lamps and hampers of food. They picnicked at twilight in the open courtyard, with its old fountain and clusters of plants and trees, watching the neighboring hillsides grow pink and blue, the flashing fires from the open braziers around them shining upon the old faded colors and gilding of the temple.[27]

After a year spent with the Rogerses, Wallis left Peking in early spring and went to Shanghai. During her brief stay there, she fell violently ill and spent several weeks in a hospital. This incident, in the hands of gossips, quickly turned against her. It was whispered that Wallis had had a love affair with a young Italian count, Galeazzo Ciano, by whom she is said to have become pregnant, and that an abortion was performed which went tragically wrong, leaving Wallis permanently unable to have children. This is theoretically possible, but there is simply no evidence to support it. Contrary to this, it is known that Wallis had already suffered the ill effects of one of Win's tantrums; therefore, it is entirely possible that she suffered a relapse of the injuries or infection while in Shanghai.

She was still ill when she sailed for America on the liner *President McKinley;* upon docking in Seattle, she had to have emergency surgery for an intestinal blockage. Alone in this strange city, she telephoned Win, who happened to be back in the United States. He met her in Chicago and accompanied her on her train trip back to Washington, D.C. It was to be the last time they would ever meet.[28]

Wallis spent several months with her mother, who, by this time, had married again, her third husband, Charles Gordon Allen, a legal clerk in the Veteran's Administration. Wallis discovered that she could obtain a decree of desertion after three years' separation from Win if

she had a year's residency in Virginia. She eventually moved to War-
renton, in Fauquier County, near the edge of the Blue Ridge Mountains, a slightly faded, small southern town with dusty streets and little
excitement.[29]

Her new home was the Warren Green Hotel, an old brick inn
where she took a second-floor single room measuring fifteen by twelve
feet, at a cost of seventy dollars a month.[30] Here, amid the faded, peeling wallpaper, battered furniture, and lingering aromas, Wallis was to
spend the next year. She decorated her room with Chinese jades and a
lacquer screen she had brought back from the Orient, but the effect
was still somewhat shabby. She spent long hours sitting on the hotel's
second floor veranda, reading Sinclair Lewis, John Galsworthy, Somerset Maugham, and Will Durant's *Story of Philosophy*.[31] There was
nothing for her to do but wait.

7

Ernest

In 1926, WALLIS ACCEPTED an invitation from her old friend Mary Kirk to spend Christmas with her and her husband, Jacques Raffray, in New York City. The Raffrays lived in an elegant flat facing Washington Square, and Wallis and Mary happily spent long days sight-seeing and shopping. Mary was bright and vivacious, and she and Wallis got on well together, for both loved gossip, parties, conversation, and mischief.

It was Mary who introduced her friend to Mr. and Mrs. Ernest Simpson. Ernest Aldrich Simpson had been born in New York City twenty-nine years earlier, the son of an English businessman and his American wife. His father had opened a ship brokerage firm, Simpson, Spence and Young, with offices in New York and London, and made a great success of it. Their position enabled them to send Ernest to Harvard, and he enjoyed summer holidays in England, where he often stayed with his older sister, Maud Kerr-Smiley, in London. During his last year at Harvard, he quit school, went to London, joined the Coldstream Guards as a second lieutenant, and became a British subject.[1]

Tall, of comfortable build, with a dark mustache and brown hair, Ernest seemed calm and reasonable and affected an air of studious interest in the finer things in life. Barbara Cartland, a friend of Maud's, would later describe him as "good-looking, with a very square chin," although his somewhat serious appearance "gave the impression his collar was too tight."[2] He was sophisticated and intelligent, slightly reserved but with an impressively quick, droll wit which Wallis found enchanting. He dressed in the finest English suits from the best tailors on Jermyn and Bond Streets, spoke well, and enjoyed theater, dancing, and dining. His peculiar half-English, half-American accent set him slightly apart, as did his indulgence in Havana cigars and his somewhat arrogant manner.

In 1923, Ernest had married Dorothea Dechert, daughter of a

Massachusetts Supreme Court judge, and the couple had one child, a daughter, Audrey. By the time Wallis and Ernest first met, however, the Simpson marriage was in deep trouble. While Ernest was clearly drawn to Wallis, his wife, not unreasonably, felt quite differently. Dorothea later said, "From the moment I met her, I never liked her at all . . . she moved in and helped herself to my house and my clothes and, finally, to everything."[3]

At first, Wallis continued to meet the Simpsons at the Raffrays' apartment. Gradually, however, as he and Dorothea drifted apart, Ernest began to see Wallis alone. She was impressed with the depth of his knowledge. They visited art galleries and museums, and Wallis eagerly listened as he pointed out favorite paintings, spoke about artists and writers, and then escorted her to lunches and dinners at the city's fashionable restaurants.

Eventually, Ernest and his wife began divorce proceedings. His growing attraction to Wallis most likely accelerated the decay of a relationship that was already doomed and had hung together simply because of convention and their daughter. During one of their evenings together, Ernest asked Wallis to marry him when they were both free. Although she had grown closer to him and fallen under his stabilizing influence, she was uncertain of her own feelings and told him she must wait despite her fondness for him.[4]

In the midst of her developing relationship with Ernest, Wallis received a welcome invitation from Aunt Bessie asking that she accompany her on an extended trip to Europe. Wallis agreed, and in the summer of 1927 she and her aunt sailed from New York for the Mediterranean. They visited Naples, Palermo, and the Dalmatian coast before leaving their ship at Trieste, where they had booked a car for a trip across the Continent.[5] After stays in Monte Carlo, Nice, Avignon, and Paris, Wallis chose to remain in a small hotel there after her aunt returned to America that fall.

On October 25, Wallis happened to be strolling through the streets of Paris when she stopped at a news agent to buy a paper. Turning it over, she was startled to read that her uncle Solomon had died the previous day; a cable from her mother informing her of the details awaited her at the hotel. Wallis returned to America for the funeral, but the reading of his will which followed proved a disappointment. Solomon Warfield had left most of his estate, estimated at roughly $5 million, for the formation of a home for impoverished ladies, in memory of his mother.[6] This was a blow to Wallis, who had almost certainly been his favorite niece; she had failed to recognize that her divorce had poisoned Solomon's mind against her. She was mentioned once: "If my niece, Bessiewallis Spencer, wife of Winfield Spencer, shall survive me, I give to the Continental Trust Company the sum of

$15,000 in trust, to collect and receive the income arising therefrom, and to pay over the income to my niece in quarterly installments, so long as she shall live and not remarry."[7] This infuriated Wallis, and she, along with several other relatives who had been all but ignored, hired an attorney to contest the will. Eventually, the suit was settled in their favor, but by then the Great Depression had all but decimated the money which had been left.[8]

Her divorce from Win was finally granted on December 10, 1927, by the circuit court of Fauquier County, Virginia, after four days of proceedings heard by Judge George Latham Fletcher. Wallis was represented by her attorney, State Senator Aubrey Weaver.[9] Weaver entered into evidence a letter Win had written to Wallis: "I have come to the definite conclusion that I can never live with you again. During the past two years, since I have been away from you, I have been happier than ever before."[10] There can be little doubt that both Wallis and Win obviated a bit where the rules of the divorce proceedings were concerned, for this letter was almost certainly backdated to help fulfill the necessary three-year separation required. Thus, it is likely that Win's attesting to his intention of living apart from Wallis and her own deposition that they had not seen each other for several years thereafter amounted to perjury. However, at the end of the day, both parties had what they wanted: freedom.

Wallis returned to the Warren Green Hotel, for she had no other option except to move in with her mother. During her stay there she mixed and mingled with quite a few eligible suitors. One of her friends, a young banker named Hugh Spilman, recalled: "She must have had thirty different proposals while she was here. I know I proposed to her regularly once a day."[11]

Now that she was free, Ernest again asked her to marry him. After some thought, Wallis agreed. For her, however, the marriage was not so much romantic fulfillment as a sort of fatalistic realization that an opportunity had presented itself which might not be bettered. If her approach appears cold, it should be remembered that Wallis had, by this time, been seared by two very unpleasant relationships: an abusive, humiliating marriage with Win and an unfulfilled passion for Espil that had been sacrificed on the altar of his ambition. As to Ernest, Wallis explained to her mother: "I am very fond of him, and he is kind, which will be a contrast. . . . I can't go wandering on the rest of my life, and I really feel so tired of fighting the world all alone and with no money. Also, 32 doesn't seem so young when you see all the really fresh youthful faces one has to compete against."[12]

Ernest had to return to London, and Wallis accepted an invitation from Katherine and Herman Rogers to stay with them at their new villa in the South of France. Villa Lou Viei stood high on the hillside above Cannes and overlooked the sparkling blue waters of the Mediterranean. From the stone terrace, staircases descended to a lush and fragrant garden filled with jasmine and roses and shaded by palm and cypress trees.

Wallis and Ernest were married on July 21, 1928, at the Chelsea Registry Office in London. "The setting," she recalled, "was more appropriate for a trial than for the culmination of a romance; and an uninvited sudden surge of memory took me back to Christ Church at Baltimore, and the odor of lilies and the bridesmaids in lilac and the organ playing softly."[13] She wore a bright yellow dress with a blue coat made in Paris for the occasion as she stood next to Ernest and his father in the small, cluttered office while a bored official conducted the civil service. "A cold little job" was how Ernest later recalled the occasion.[14] He was described on the marriage certificate as "the divorced husband of Dorothea Parsons Simpson, formerly Parsons, Spinster," while she was "formerly the wife of Earle [sic] Winfield Spencer from whom she obtained a divorce."

After a quick champagne wedding brunch at the Grosvenor Hotel, Wallis and Ernest climbed into his new Lagonda touring car and, driven by a chauffeur named Hughes, set off for the Channel ferry. They spent a week in Paris at the Hotel St. Regis on the rue Jean Goujon visiting churches and museums and dining in small, hidden restaurants. Wherever they went, Ernest continued to instruct Wallis in his two loves: architecture and the arts.

Returning to London, Wallis and Ernest took up temporary residence in a small hotel. While Ernest spent his days at work, Wallis began to hunt for a house, assisted by Ernest's sister, Maud. Eventually they found a house in the West End, at No. 12 Upper Berkeley Street, near Portman Square and Marble Arch. The house was owned by Lady Chesham, and Wallis managed to secure a year's lease, which included the furniture.[15]

The house stood on a short street. An iron balcony crossed the first floor of the tall, red-brick building, which blended easily with those of its neighbors. From the sidewalk, a short flight of steps led to the front door, painted a bright green. There was a dining room with walls of pale wood on the first floor; up a flight of stairs was a large drawing room painted green and filled with Chippendale furniture. A large bedroom with a bathroom and dressing room, occupied the third floor. The kitchen, as well as rooms for servants, was in the basement. Although they were not rich, the Simpsons managed to keep a fairly large staff for such a modest house: They had a butler, a cook, a personal maid for Wallis, a Scottish parlor maid, a housemaid named Agnes, and the chauffeur, Hughes.[16]

Wallis found her new country a rather curious place. England was only beginning to recover from the devastating effects of the 1926 General Strike and was still in the midst of a severe economic depression. The second Labour government, headed by Ramsay MacDonald, faced rising unemployment and dissatisfaction. Unrest filled the air, a powerful remnant of the suffering and shock left from the war.

In the midst of these hardships and doubts, society thrived with a vibrance unequaled before or since. The great houses of London, shuttered during the long years of the war, now pulsed with the gathered royals, politicians, and literary and artistic stars of the era. At the very apex of society stood the Royal Family, headed by King George V and his consort, Queen Mary. The monarchy was above reproach, staid, formal, and even dull but was ultimately held in awe by the majority of the old King's subjects. This was the age of cafe society, of flappers and "Bright Young Things." Every night, the young and privileged packed the smoke-filled rooms of the most fashionable nightclubs: the Night Light, the Kit-Kat, and the Embassy. It was a society patrolled and reported on by *Vogue* and the *Tatler*—set against glittering art-deco backdrops, peopled with the svelte figures of shapeless women in shimmering silver lamé gowns, with their bobbed hair and bright red lipstick and nail polish, and gentlemen in white ties and cutaways—filled with the sounds of jazz and the clink of martinis, all viewed through the haze of cigarette smoke.

Wallis entered this new and strange world with reluctance. She knew no one and often felt awkward. She particularly stuck out as an American and was determined to do all she could to learn British manners and customs; she began by devouring the daily papers and reading the Court Circular, which listed the activities of the Royal Family. She had learned, as a navy wife, to be witty and entertaining, but what worked in America did not necessarily translate to London. She soon discovered that her independence and outspokenness were both a subject of amusement as well as condemnation.[17]

As much as she tried, however, Wallis could not hide her heritage. Eventually, she began to feel a bit too conspicuous and spent more and more of her evenings at home. Her stubborn streak was still intact: Deciding that she could never truly fit in, Wallis began to emphasize her American roots, speech, and habits.

Barbara Cartland, who happened to meet Wallis soon after her marriage to Ernest, recalled her unfavorable impressions: "I was frankly disappointed. . . . Wallis wore a dowdy black dress and a shapeless hat which accentuated her very bad complexion. She had large hands and used them too much. She was however very vivacious, but was too obviously determined to be aggressively American."[18]

Wallis was often lonely in London. She was accustomed to phoning her friends, dropping in unannounced for tea, and spending afternoons shopping. None of this ease seemed to have settled upon London, where she found that most relationships were conducted with a stiff formality. She often kept to herself. She loved to stroll around London and adored the thick fogs and mists and gray rain which enveloped the city during her first winter.[19] As she had in Boston while married to Win, Wallis played tourist while Ernest was at work and visited the Tower of London, Westminster Abbey, St. Paul's Cathedral, and the Houses of Parliament. She was eventually taken under the wing of her sister-in-law, a slightly older woman who was separated from her husband. Maud often invited Wallis to the parties and luncheons at her big house near Berkeley Square; in the evenings, Wallis and Ernest would join dinner parties and stay until the early morning, playing bridge or poker.

Most afternoons, Wallis climbed into their car and had Hughes drive her through the city to collect Ernest at his office. One day, the car came to a halt before St. James's Palace, and Wallis watched as the sentries standing at the entrance stiffened and presented arms. A gate opened, and out came a sleek black motorcar; she caught a slight glimpse of a boyish-looking figure inside. When she asked the chauffeur, she was told that it had been the Prince of Wales.[20]

Ernest was not wealthy, but Wallis was comfortable. Each week, he gave her an allowance for food, household expenses, clothing, and personal shopping. Wallis never overspent and never complained or wanted for anything. She even managed to save money and often went to Fortnum and Mason to splurge on caviar or other exotic foods as a treat for Ernest.[21] With the money she herself was able to save, she sent her mother small but welcome checks.[22]

Wallis enjoyed doing the household shopping. Several mornings each week, she would journey to nearby Paddington and stroll from the butcher to the fishmonger, the greengrocers, the bakery, and the confectioner's. Her skills as a hostess ensured that she took particular care on these expeditions, and she often took along her battered copy of *Fannie Farmer* to show the butcher how to cut a T-bone steak or another cut of meat. She was also careful to ensure that each guest received the same-sized portion so that no one would be embarrassed at taking too much or too little.[23]

The Simpsons regularly entertained, but because Ernest often had to work the next morning, he preferred to spend evenings at home either alone with his wife or with friends. Occasionally, the couple did take in the latest play or go to the cinema, followed by a late dinner at the Savoy. Most of their dinner guests were business acquaintances of Ernest; he seemed to have few real friends. Wallis noted that Ernest, like herself, was curiously out of place in London, not really American like her but not quite English, either.[24]

It was around this time, according to Barbara Cartland, that Wallis had a tubal ligation. "It was fashionable at the time," she said. "Contraception was difficult in those days as the 'Pill' had not been invented, and the methods suggested by doctors were not always successful. Quite a number of women disappeared mysteriously to Paris, where it was possible to have an abortion."[25]

Barbara Cartland was a friend of Maud's and was therefore sufficiently well placed to be included in the latest news. There is therefore no reason to doubt the accuracy of her story. Wallis was never a particularly maternalistic woman, and as Ernest already had a daughter, it seems likely that they made a decision jointly not to have any children. Then, too, Wallis, having been dependent for so long on the financial kindness of others, no doubt disliked the idea of bearing such an obligation to another. Her life had settled down to a comfortable existence, she was making friends, and their money and freedom allowed her and Ernest to entertain and enjoy the hospitality of others. With her love of pleasure, it is unlikely that Wallis would have wished to take on the burden of raising a child.

The following spring, Wallis received a cable from her aunt Bessie, summoning her home; her mother had become seriously ill. She and Ernest boarded the RMS *Mauritania* and sailed from Southampton to New York in May. Wallis was shocked at her mother's decline: The once-vibrant Alice was now bedridden, her hair gray, her proud figure emaciated. Wallis's stepfather explained that she had also lost sight in one of her eyes and was suffering from thrombosis. Even so, there remained much of the old Montague spark. On seeing her daughter, Alice exclaimed: "Oh, Wallis, why did they bring you so far? Have you come to see me die?" She immediately followed this by chastising her daughter for wearing what she considered an ugly brown dress.[26]

It was the first time that Alice had met Ernest. Luckily, she liked him and told Wallis how happy she was that she had finally settled down. It soon became clear that although she was ill, Alice was not about to die and that Aunt Bessie had overreacted. After a week Ernest had to return to London, but Wallis stayed on, chatting with her mother and describing her life with Ernest in London. After consulting with doctors, who informed her that Alice could remain in this condition for years, Wallis decided to return to London, saying that she could be summoned if necessary.[27]

Wallis was depressed upon her return to London. To cheer her, Ernest began taking her on weekend excursions around England. They spent the summer of 1929 touring ruined castles and churches, cathedrals and country houses. Ernest enjoyed history and loved explaining the importance of these attractions as they wandered over the crumbling stones. Wallis was fascinated by these monuments to power and privilege. At night, they stopped at charming country inns in the Cotswolds or Kent.[28]

In October 1929 another cable came from Aunt Bessie. Wallis rushed back to America alone, for Ernest was tied up with business concerns. Mary Raffray met her in New York and informed her that her mother had lapsed into a coma. Wallis stayed at her bedside, but Alice never regained consciousness. On November 2, 1929, she died.[29] Wallis had adored her mother, but the last decade had kept them apart, and as she matured, she grew less tolerant of Alice's more peculiar qualities. In the end, the loss was made easier by the continued presence of Aunt Bessie, who, for many years, had functioned as a second mother.

Back in England, Wallis busied herself in searching for a new home. Eventually, they found a first-floor flat in a modern building at 5 Bryanston Court, on George Street, not far from Marble Arch. From the second-floor landing, glass-and-iron-grille doors opened onto a small entrance hall. The flat was spacious, with a drawing room, a dining room, kitchen, three bedrooms, three bathrooms, and four servants' rooms in another portion of the building. "I had a wonderful time furnishing the flat," Wallis recalled. "For the first time in my life I had the means and the opportunity to create the kind of setting I had always wanted, a place where good things out of the past would intermingle gracefully with good things of the present, with the accent on color and a pleasing symmetry."[30]

She consulted with Syrie Maugham, former wife of novelist Somerset Maugham and a fashionable decorator whose vogue for white, cream, and beige rooms had captivated London. Wallis had been collecting a few antiques and now put them to use. She painted the walls of the drawing room pale green to provide a contrast to the soft beige of the carpet and curtains. One wall was lined with shelves filled with Ernest's books and his collection of first editions and original manuscripts by Charles Dickens and A. A. Milne. Wallis added two sleek, comfortable sofas and chairs, a William and Mary chest, a Dutch secretary, and an Italian long table on which stood an old gilt Buddha from her days in Peking.[31] The surfaces of the tables were covered with photographs, jade, porcelain, and lacquer boxes she had purchased in the Orient.

The dining room was small, and Wallis could only seat ten people. She covered the walls with French toile de Jouy depicting pastoral scenes to help enliven the limited space. Syrie Maugham helped her select the sideboard and console by the Adamses, the large table, and the twelve matching chairs upholstered in white leather.[32] The corner master bedroom overlooked Upper George Street. Wallis painted the walls aquamarine and covered the bed and windows in aquamarine and pink. Ernest made an adjoining room into a dressing room for himself. Although she was never fully satisfied with the results, Wallis had found an outlet for her creative energies which she was to pursue with vigor for the rest of her life.[33]

Wallis soon had a full staff working at Bryanston Court. Her cook, Mrs. Ralph, had formerly worked under Lady Curzon's French chef. She quickly adapted herself to her new mistress's American ways.[34] The staff also included the Scottish maid, Mary Cain, the housemaid Agnes, and Mary Burke, the part-time ladies' maid, all having followed the Simpsons from their house on Upper Berkeley Street.

Safely ensconced in her new home, Wallis set about cultivating a social set. From the first she determined that her dinners and parties would be different; any hostess in London could entertain in the usual way, and there was no shortage of formal, staid receptions. Wallis would not bore: instead, she would invite only the most brilliant guests; feed them the most interesting dishes; serve them the latest cocktails; and pamper them with personal attentions. No one before had used the cocktail hour as a social occasion, and this new and intriguing opportunity was not lost on her. As her reputation for interesting evenings grew, she slowly expanded her guest lists, from friends and Ernest's business acquaintances to minor politicians, writers, artists, and diplomats. In time, members of society and the aristocracy, curious, began to accept invitations as well. The Simpsons' flat soon became known for its lively, intelligent occasions, and Wallis happily watched as her star began its ascent.[35]

Still, Wallis did not win everyone over so easily. Cecil Beaton, who happened to be a distant relation of Ernest Simpson through marriage, recalled his first meeting with her in unfavorable terms: "Mrs. Simpson seemed somewhat brawny and raw-boned in her sapphire-blue velvet. Her voice had a high nasal twang."[36]

In time the Simpsons became friends with the second Marquess and Marchioness of Milford Haven. George Milford Haven, brother of Lord Louis Mountbatten, was closely related to the Royal Family: His mother, Victoria, had been a granddaughter of Queen Victoria's, and one of his aunts, Alexandra, was married to the last Emperor of Russia, Nicholas II. In 1916, George had married Nada, Countess Torby, the daughter of Grand Duke Michael Michailovich of Russia and his morganatic wife, Sophie Merenberg. The Milford Havens were a curious pair. Nada was a lively, dark beauty whose sense of fun and adventure endeared her to Wallis. George, on the other hand, was a rather quiet, reserved man whose great interest in life was amassing a large collection of pornography.[37] Wallis and Ernest often visited the Milford

Havens at their country estate, Lynden Manor, near Maidenhead. Another frequent visitor was George's young nephew, Prince Philip of Greece, who would marry the future Queen Elizabeth II in 1947. "It is nice for us to meet all these swell people," Wallis wrote to Aunt Bessie, "even if we can't keep up their pace!"[38]

Another friend was Benjamin Thaw, the first secretary of the U.S. embassy in London. The Thaws were one of America's most socially prominent families. During her period in New York, Wallis had spent several long weekends with Benjamin's wealthy, elderly cousin, Mary Copley Thaw, in her decaying Gothic mansion. This experience was made even more surreal for Wallis by the presence of Mrs. Thaw's son, Harry. In 1906, Harry K. Thaw, a decadent and insane man, had shot and killed Stanford White in a quarrel over the architect's affair with his wife, Evelyn Nesbit. During Wallis's visits to the Thaw mansion, Harry would thunder through his mother's house, bellowing at the top of his lungs, breaking china, and then disappearing as suddenly as he had appeared. Not surprisingly, such experiences unnerved Wallis greatly, and after one such evening she quickly packed her bags and never returned.[39]

In 1923, Benjamin Thaw had married the former Consuelo Morgan. She was one of three famous Morgan sisters: Consuelo, eldest by two years, and twins Gloria and Thelma. They were daughters of Harry Hays Morgan, an American diplomat, and their exotic Latin American mother, Laura Kilpatrick. Their father had been consul at Lucerne, and their grandfather, Gen. Judson Kilpatrick, had been an American minister in Chile. Laura Morgan, who fancied herself a descendant of the grandees of Spain, was absolutely determined to make the most brilliant marriages for her daughters. She first arranged a union between Consuelo and the French count Jean Marie Emmanuel de Maupas du Juglart during her husband's tenure as consul general in Brussels. This marriage lasted but two years, until the nineteen-year-old Consuelo was charged with adultery and divorced by her husband.

Consuelo's sisters were celebrated society beauties. Gloria made a grand match with Reginald Vanderbilt, while her sister Thelma, after a failed marriage to James Vale Converse, eventually married Viscount Furness. This relationship proved a rather curious arrangement, with both Lord and Lady Furness freely indulging in various affairs, Marmaduke with a series of beautiful French women and Thelma with Edward, Prince of Wales.

Thelma later described Wallis as she recalled her at their first meeting: "At that time she did not have the chic she has since cultivated. She was not beautiful; in fact, she was not even pretty. But she has a distinct charm and a sharp sense of humour. Her dark hair was parted in the middle. Her eyes, alert and eloquent, were her best feature. She was not as thin then as in later years—not that she could be called fat even then; she was merely less angular. Her hands were large; they did not move gracefully, and I thought she used them too much when she attempted to emphasize a point."[40]

The friendship between Lady Thelma Furness, and Wallis Simpson was a casual one. They met infrequently at parties or luncheons given by mutual friends. But it was this slim connection which was to lead Wallis straight into the orbit of her future husband.

8

The Prince of Wales

I N THE SUMMER OF 1894, Queen Victoria was at the height of her glory. She had occupied the British throne for fifty-seven years, presiding over an England which had led the Industrial Revolution and an empire that embraced a quarter of the world's population. At no other time had England's influence been so pervasive, her reach so vast, her navy so powerful, and her position so respected.

Victoria dominated her family as she dominated her empire. Even as an elderly widow, wrapped in the comforting blanket of incessant mourning for her long-dead husband, Prince Albert, she was formidable. Her children were as intimidated by her forceful nature as politicians and princes.

Her son Albert Edward had been Prince of Wales for half a century. His mother persistently refused to allow him any real responsibilities, and as a consequence, the Prince grew bored, indolent, and somewhat promiscuous. He could only wait for his seemingly indefatigable mother to die before he could ascend the throne himself. Bertie, as he was known within the family, had always been something of a disappointment to his parents. The strict and censorious Prince Consort had expected much of his first son, but Bertie had few intellectual capabilities, and whatever talents he may have possessed were stifled under the unbelievably strict educational regimen imposed by his parents. Knowing that he was a disappointment, Bertie instead focused his efforts on pleasure.

By 1894 the Prince of Wales was a bearded gentleman whose enormous appetite for life was matched by his immense stomach. His main pleasures were food, which he managed to consume in astonishing quantities; cigars, which he smoked incessantly; and a string of personable, beautiful, though somewhat vapid, mistresses, including Lillie Langtry and Alice Keppel. He was not without his talents: He possessed a keen understanding of international politics, and his skill as a diplomat would earn him the epitaph of Edward the Peacemaker.

But his accomplishments were largely overshadowed by the scandals that constantly plagued both him and his Marlborough House set, culminating in his two courtroom appearances: the first when he was called as a witness in a divorce case and the second after a friend had been caught cheating at baccarat during a house party attended by the Prince.

In 1863, two years after his father's death, Bertie married Princess Alexandra of Denmark, a beautiful woman whose natural charm and style endeared her to the British public. Her education had been largely neglected, and as a result, she remained at heart simple and rather childlike, a quality that enhanced her vulnerability and made her seem all the more sympathetic. As a result of otosclerosis, inherited from her mother, she rapidly lost her hearing, a condition accelerated by a case of rheumatic fever in 1867. Increasingly unable to communicate freely with her husband's sophisticated friends, Alix, as she was called, retreated to a small circle of family and friends. Above all, she possessed an extraordinary understanding and patience, qualities necessary in a woman well aware of her husband's repeated and flagrant infidelities. Together, Bertie and Alix had three sons, Albert Victor, George, and Alexander, who only lived for a few hours, and three daughters, Louise, Victoria, and Maud.

Their eldest son, Prince Albert Victor, known as Eddy, was a disappointment. Born two months premature in 1864, he grew up curiously devoid of any intellect or interest in anything beyond his army regiment, shooting, and pleasure. Throughout his education, his tutors agonized over their inability to instill in him even the slightest affinity for learning. He grew into a pleasant, if aimless, young man, charming, handsome in a slightly epicine way, but utterly unsuited to inherit the British throne. He was notoriously dissipated, probably bisexual, and was involved in a scandal surrounding the police raid on a homosexual brothel. He may very well have been infected with syphilis during one of his many amorous adventures.[1] His family repeatedly tried to find a strong-willed wife to guide him. He himself fell in love with his cousin Princess Alix of Hesse and by Rhine, but she refused him, only to later marry the last Tsar of Russia. Another woman with whom he fell in love was Helene de Orleans, daughter of the Comte de Paris, but her Catholicism prevented the relationship from progressing.

Finally, his family decided on Princess Victoria Mary, the only daughter of the Duke and Duchess of Teck. Her father, Prince Franz, was haunted by the fact that his father, Duke Alexander of Württemberg, had married morganatically, a union which deprived him of his claim to the throne of Württemberg and entitled him and his children only to the style of "Serene" rather than the more important "Royal"

Highness. All of his life he attached great importance to rank and precedence, a trait he passed on to his daughter. His wife, Mary Adelaide, was a granddaughter of King George III. She was so large—250 pounds was the estimate of the American minister to the Court of St. James's—that she was known in the family as "Fat Mary."[2] Her daughter, called May in the family, dreaded dance recitals, at which her mother was forced to sit on two gilt chairs pushed together to accommodate her bulk, a sight which provided the other girls in the class with no end of humiliating jokes and stories.[3] Her frivolous habits and uncontrolled spending finally forced the family to temporarily flee England to avoid creditors; they took up residence in Florence, and it was here that young May cultivated a love of art and collecting.

Back in England, the Tecks were allowed to occupy rooms in Kensington Palace and enjoy the grace and favor of White Lodge in Richmond Park. The Princess of Wales was fond of the Duchess, and thus May's name was raised as a possible bride for the wayward Eddy. The Tecks were thrilled at the idea that their daughter might one day become Queen. Romantic feeling mattered little: She was certainly not in love with Eddy; indeed, she scarcely knew him, and the prospect cannot have been a terribly happy one for May. But she was shrewd enough to recognize the golden opportunity at hand, and propelled by her family's slightly mercenary attitude, as well as her own, she accepted his proposal.

May was saved from whatever trauma a marriage to Eddy might have caused when, in January 1882, he contracted pneumonia and died at Sandringham in Norfolk. But all was not lost: Eddy's brother George took his place in the line of succession, and soon plans were afoot to marry May off to the new heir to the throne. May's father spent the greater part of his time wandering about muttering loudly, "It must be a Tsarevich, it must be a Tsarevich!"[4] (This was a reference to the marriage of Alix's younger sister Dagmar, who, some thirty years earlier, had been engaged to Tsarevich Nicholas, heir to the Russian throne. When Nicholas died before the wedding could take place, his younger brother Alexander inherited both his position as future emperor and his fiancée.)

George, like his brother, was no intellectual; however, unlike Eddy, he was conscientious and devoted to the idea of duty. His only real education came from his tenure in the Royal Navy; here he learned that it was best to conform. He was bored with most music, cared little for art, regarded most reading as a waste of time, and was highly suspicious of new ideas. George's first son, David, had written of his father: "He had the Victorian's sense of probity, moral responsibility, and love of domesticity. He believed in God, in the invincibility of the

Royal Navy, and the essential rightness of whatever was British. At the same time, he had the Edwardian flair for clothes and fondness for sport—from partridge to tiger shooting, from deer-stalking to fishing."[5]

Although George and May had almost nothing in common, he understood what his family expected and duly proposed. May, much fonder of George than she had been of Eddy and certain that a third chance to become future Queen would not come her way, accepted. When one relative protested the proposed match, Queen Victoria replied indignantly, "Well, you know May never was in love with poor Eddy!"[6] George was created Duke of York, and they were married in July 1893.

George and May undoubtedly loved each other, but it was a curious sort of love: He adored her from a safe distance, and she, in turn, treated him with an almost Oriental subservience. Whatever passions they felt were kept strictly confined to paper. Just before their wedding, May wrote to him: "I am very sorry that I am still so shy with you, I tried not to be so the other day, but alas failed, I was angry with myself! It is so stupid to be so stiff together & really there is nothing I would not tell you, except that I *love* you more than anybody in the world, & this I cannot tell you myself so I write it to relieve my feelings."[7] George himself replied: "Thank God we both understand each other, & I think it really unnecessary for me to tell you how deep my love for you my darling is & I feel it growing stronger & stronger every time I see you; although I may appear shy & cold. But this worry & busy time is most annoying & when we do meet it is only [to] talk business. . . ."[8] Not that this remarkable set of circumstances was the result of simple shyness, for it continued on throughout their forty-two years of marriage. As a middle-aged woman, May could still be found writing sadly to her husband: "What a pity it is you cannot *tell* me what you write for I should appreciate it so enormously. . . ."[9]

On June 23, 1894, their first child was born at White Lodge, Richmond. He was christened Edward Albert Christian George Andrew Patrick David, the last four names after the patron saints of England, Scotland, Ireland, and Wales. His family called him David. Among his godparents were Queen Victoria, King Christian IX of Denmark, King William of Württemberg, the future Tsar Nicholas II and his fiancée, Princess Alix of Hesse and by Rhine, and the Queen of the Hellenes. The contrast with the humble world into which Wallis would be born could not have been greater.

The occasion of the new Prince's birth was greeted with much enthusiasm. But one lone voice rose out in protest at the adulation, leaving remarks forever destined to be quoted in relation to the Duke of Windsor, so prescient do they seem. The Scottish socialist leader Kier Hardie declared in the House of Commons: "From his childhood onwards this boy will be surrounded by sycophants and flatterers by the score and will be taught to believe himself as of a superior creation. A line will be drawn between him and the people he is to be called upon some day to reign over. In due course, following the precedent which has already been set he will be sent round the world, and probably rumours of a morganatic alliance will follow and the end of it all will be the country will be called upon to pay the bill."[10]

David was followed by a brother, Albert (called Bertie) in 1895; a sister, Mary, in 1897; and three more brothers: Henry (called Harry) in 1900; George in 1902; and the youngest son, John, born in 1905. When it was discovered that John suffered from epilepsy—a still-somewhat mysterious and disgraceful illness—he was hastily dispatched to Sandringham, to spend his life in isolation from his family.

It would be difficult to imagine a more disastrous set of parents than George and May. Both were essentially good people and certainly loved their offspring, but they had absolutely no understanding of, or sympathy for, their own children. As parents, they were distant, aloof, unemotional, and very often intimidating.

May, in the words of historian David Duff, "was out of touch with the human side of life."[11] She harbored an intense dislike of both pregnancy and childbirth, which she once described as "the penalty of being a woman."[12] With such an attitude, it is not surprising that her husband's aunt, Empress Frederick of Germany, described her as "very cold and stiff and very unmaternal."[13]

There can be little doubt, as Frances Donaldson has written, that this "almost total estrangement from their mother, the coldness with which she rejected them," greatly affected her children.[14] May found it extraordinarily difficult to express any normal love, affection, or warmth toward them. It was not merely a question of simple Victorian reserve at work; even by the standards of the day, she was, in the words of Kenneth Rose, "an uncommonly detached mother."[15] Years later, David himself was to declare, "My mother was a cold woman, a cold woman."[16]

George was just as uncomfortable with his children. "I have often felt," David later wrote, "that despite his undoubted affection for all of us, my father preferred children in the abstract, and that his notion of a small boy's place in a grown up world was summed up in the phrase 'Children should be seen, not heard.'"[17] To David, it seemed as if he and his brothers and sister were "young nuisances in constant need of correction."[18]

To George belongs one of the most infamous quotes in royal history: "My father was frightened of his mother, I was frightened by my father, and I am damned well going to see to it that my children are frightened of me."[19] Whether George actually uttered these words is in some dispute; but it certainly expressed his sentiment and without a doubt what his children felt.[20] Even Alexander Hardinge, who served George as a loyal private secretary, mused upon the "mystery" of why his master, "who was such a kind man, was such a brute to his children."[21]

That George and May were royal did not help deepen the bond between parents and children. Not only did the customs of the day leave the children in the care of nurses, nannies, and tutors, but public obligations ensured that both mother and father were often absent not only for the frequent ribbon cuttings, factory inspections, and garden parties but also for extended foreign visits, which meant months of separation. Nevertheless, it would be wrong to ascribe the strained relations between parents and children simply to royal circumstance: Any number of other contemporary European sovereigns, most notably Tsar Nicholas II and his wife, Alexandra, managed to enjoy happy and loving, close-knit ties with their children.

"My father had a most horrible temper," David later recalled. "He was foully rude to my mother. Why, I've seen her leave the table because he was so rude to her, and we children would all follow her out; not when the staff were present of course, but when we were alone."[22] It was this temper which did much to alienate George from his children. "Since he was impetuous by nature," wrote John Gore, "he gave vent to his feelings instantly and without reserve."[23]

All of the children dreaded being punished. "No words that I was ever to hear could be so disconcerting to the spirit as the summons, usually delivered by a footman, that "His Royal Highness wishes to see you in the Library," David recalled.[24] And although May eventually came to represent a soothing—if not altogether maternal—presence in their lives, she positively refused to intercede between her husband and her children. "I have always to remember that their father is also their King," she said.[25]

This lack of parental warmth was to have a devastating and lasting effect on George and May's children. They found it exceptionally difficult to have any but the most ordinary of conversations with their parents; personal matters were rarely discussed, and unpleasant subjects were fervently avoided. The children found it impossible to confide in their parents, and neither George nor May could bring themselves to speak freely with them. An emotional gulf stretched between children and parents which neither side was able to bridge.

David had few memories of his formidable great-grandmother. He was occasionally taken to visit Gangan, as he called Queen Victoria, and recalled her crisp black silk dresses, white tulle caps, and enormous girth.[26] Her death in 1901 was to him a time of "piercing cold, the interminable wails, and of feeling very lost among scores of sorrowing grown-up relatives—solemn Princes in varied uniforms and Princesses sobbing behind heavy crepe veils."[27] His grandparents, Bertie and Alix, became King Edward VII and Queen Alexandra, and his parents, after several months as Duke and Duchess of Cornwall, became Prince and Princess of Wales, traditional title of the heir apparent to the British throne.

Increased royal obligations meant that George and May were often forced to leave their children for even longer periods of time. David and his brothers and sister inevitably stayed with the King and Queen, both of whom indulged their grandchildren and provided them with an affection they never received from their parents. David dreaded the thought of leaving this warm and loving atmosphere and returning to his parents' care. When one courtier asked him, "Aren't you delighted because you are going to see your mother and father again?" he replied, "Oh, yes." Then, after a moment's thought, he added, "Only you know mother is a little difficult sometimes."[28]

The children spent much of their time at York Cottage, Sandringham. Harold Nicolson described it as "a glum little villa, encompassed by thickets of laurel and rhododendrons ... separated by an abrupt rim of lawn from a pond at the edge of which a leaden pelican gazes in dejection upon the water lilies and bamboos."[29] An imitation Tudor-style conglomeration of gables and bay windows and turrets, York Cottage had been built to house the overflow of guests from the main house at Sandringham, and over the years, rooms had been tacked on here and there as needed. May found the place dreadful, but her husband loved its small, low-ceilinged rooms, which reminded him of a ship's cabins.

David's nurses and minders were a mixed lot. One, Mary Peters, so resented turning him over to his parents for his daily visit that she inevitably twisted his arms or pinched him as she sent him off into the drawing room, ensuring terrified sobs and a quick return to her care. Both George and May were left confused at what they took for their son's willfulness and fear of them, and such was their alienation from their children's daily lives that three years passed before they learned of Peters's behavior and dismissed her from her post.[30]

David and Bertie were especially close as children. The older brother developed an intensely protective feeling for the younger, who already suffered from a nervous disposition and the beginnings of stomach ulcers. More so than David, Bertie had good reason to dislike his father, who made Bertie learn to write with his right hand upon finding that he was left-handed; made him wear heavy iron braces on his knocked knees; and even worse, deliberately humiliated him. Bertie had a terrible stammer, and in the words of one of George's friends, his father "thought the best way of dealing with it was by mimicking him and laughing at him, and he always did this."[31]

When David was six, his father engaged a tutor, Henry Hansell, to begin the boy's instruction. Because George himself was poorly educated, he gave little importance to education beyond the most basic of classes, and Hansell was utterly unsuited to the task of helping form the future King of England. "He never taught us anything at all," David was to say later. "I am completely self-educated."[32]

David was a bright child with an inquisitive mind. His memory for history, faces, and places was excellent, a trait which was to serve him well in royal life. He had a natural sympathy for others less fortunate than himself and questioned Hansell about how situations could be improved. But he never developed a love of music, art, or reading and remained surprisingly ignorant of even the most basic literary achievements.

At the age of twelve, David was sent to the Royal Naval College at Osborne, located at his grandmother's former summer house on the Isle of Wight. It was an ironic decision, for his father, having entered the navy, realized that he himself was handicapped by his lack of understanding of international affairs, his inadequate knowledge of society and politics, and his inability to speak any foreign languages. And yet, when it came time to educate his two oldest sons, he sent them along the same path he knew was responsible for his own shortcomings as future monarch. Only after he himself came to the throne and began to realize how deficient his own education had been did George try to make amends, insisting that David study languages in France and Germany and be allowed to go to Oxford. Later, he sent David's brothers Harry and George to private preparatory schools as well.

David later expressed that at Osborne he felt like "rather a lost dog."[33] Like other students, he shared a dormitory, lived according to a difficult schedule, and went through the agonies of being tortured by senior classmates—having ink dumped on him and being dragged around and punished by senior cadets.[34] His father studied his rather meager academic achievements in the regular reports sent home and usually accepted his shortcomings. David's two years at Osborne made him more secure, and he managed to get on with others and gain confidence, which would serve him well as a prince. At the end of his term, he moved on to Dartmouth to prepare for his stint in the Royal Navy.

In May 1910, Edward VII died, and David's parents became King George V and Queen Mary. The young boy automatically became Duke of Cornwall, and on his sixteenth birthday, he received the title Prince of Wales. He was also proclaimed Prince of Wales in a ceremony at Caernarvon Castle in Wales. David hated the white satin breeches and the mantle and surcoat of purple velvet edged with ermine that he was required to wear and complained to his mother. But Queen Mary told him, "You mustn't take a mere ceremony so seriously. Your friends will understand that as a Prince you are obliged to do certain things that may seem a little silly."[35]

After a training mission on the battleship *Hindustan* in the fall of 1911, David entered Magdalan College, in Oxford. The last future king who had been sent to Oxford was David's grandfather, the future Edward VII. His time there, initiated and regulated by a series of tutors and minders handpicked by Prince Albert, was designed to turn him into a studious young man, even if previous attempts had failed. He was separated from the general student body and was told what to read and whom to befriend.

David's time at Oxford was thankfully different. He lived in college, chose his own friends, and seems to have done well. "He is alleged to have thrown his weight about at Oxford, demanding to be addressed as 'Sir,'" recalled his friend and fellow student J. Paul Getty. "I never witnessed—nor even heard of—any incidents to support such a claim and, needless to say, they would have been much discussed by other students if they had occurred."[36]

In 1912, David was sent to France to improve his grasp of the language and spent his holiday the following year in Germany with numerous relatives. As a boy, he had been raised to respect his Teutonic heritage; indeed, his ancestry was almost entirely German. King George I, who could not even speak English, had come from the German kingdom of Hanover. Three successive Georges followed him to the throne, all of whom married German princesses, further strengthening the Teutonic line. George IV's brother Edward, Duke of Kent, married a German princess, and their daughter, Queen Victoria, married a German prince from the Duchy of Saxe-Coburg and Gotha. The future Edward VII's wife, although a princess of Denmark, was the daughter of a German prince and princess to whom the throne had passed, and David's own mother was a German princess by blood.

On his trip, David stayed with a host of titled relatives: King Wilhelm and Queen Charlotte of Württemberg at Stuttgart; Grand Duke Adolphus of Mecklenburg-Strelitz and his mother, the old Grand Duchess, who was his own mother's favorite aunt and a granddaughter of George III; Prince Heinrich of Prussia and his wife, Irene, at their estate Hemmelmark; and with his second cousin, Carl Eduard, Duke of Saxe-Coburg and Gotha, before moving on to Berlin to visit Kaiser Wilhelm II and his family. David had been raised by his mother not only to respect his heritage but to speak the language from an early age. Much of his later sympathy for Germany stemmed from this holiday along with other early influences.

In 1914, David celebrated his twentieth birthday. He was a rather slight young man, handsome in a boyish way, with light brown hair and pale blue eyes. He was a curious mixture of regal manners and common delights. Although he appreciated the luxuries which his royal life ensured, he was keenly aware of the misfortunes of others, even if his concern was somewhat shallow and short-lived. His intellectual achievements had been adequate, if not impressive, but he was certainly capable of applying himself when the subject was of interest. His friendships tended to be without depth, for he remained essentially shy. He preferred to spend his time in solitary pursuits: riding, jumping, shooting, and golf.

Just before the outbreak of the First World War, David joined the Grenadier Guards. Eventually, he went to France, where he was assigned a job working for the general staff. But he was haunted by the thought that while his fellow soldiers were allowed to fight and die, he was trapped behind the front line. "I do hate being a Prince and not allowed to fight!!" he wrote.[37] When his father and other officials protested that the heir to the Throne could not possibly fight, David insisted, "What does it matter if I am killed? I have four brothers."[38] He was allowed to conduct inspections and visits as long as he himself was in no danger, and these often left unforgettable impressions. He once visited a field hospital and noticed that one patient had been hidden away behind some curtains. When told that the man had been so terribly disfigured that it was thought better to keep him out of royal sight, he immediately pulled the curtains aside, bent down, and kissed what remained of the man's forehead.[39]

Such shows of sympathy did much to endear David to his father's subjects. They saw in him a champion, someone who recognized their problems and expressed a determination to do something to change intolerable conditions. He was a prince, but he also managed to combine his status with a human touch, to communicate freely and sincerely in ways which no member of the Royal Family had done before. The end of the war brought immense desire for change, and David seemed to understand the hopes and needs of the common man. "The young Prince of Wales," wrote James Pope-Hennessy, "was swiftly coming to personify for millions the longings and the aims of the new post-war generation, with its driving wish for freedom from tradition and convention, whatever the costs. This was, to say the least of it, an unusual role for any member of the British Royal Family, and it was one which, naturally enough, Queen Mary could not altogether understand."[40]

Indeed, David's instincts stood in stark contrast to those of his parents. Throughout the war, the King and Queen had fulfilled their roles admirably, but always in a rather stiff, detached manner. They had little understanding of their subjects' lives or daily concerns. Once, during a tour of run-down lodging houses in London's East End, Queen Mary, rather embarrassingly, reacted with great horror and thoughtlessly asked the huddled family whose room she was surveying, "Why, why do you live here?"[41]

There had been times during the war when the future of the monarchy seemed doubtful. Fear for his own position led George V to campaign actively against the invitation of asylum his government had extended to his cousins Tsar Nicholas II and Empress Alexandra, a rather shameful effort which undoubtedly condemned his Russian relatives to a Bolshevik firing squad just over a year later. But George, by blood almost entirely German himself, knew that voices were being raised against his throne.[42]

In reaction to this anti-German sentiment, George V made a bold decision. On July 17, 1917, after a meeting of the Privy Council, the King relinquished all his German titles. He also changed the name of the family and the dynasty. At first, no one knew with any certainty what the family surname was. Any of the answers—"Whipper" or "Guelph" or "Wettin"—were distinctly Teutonic.[43] Finally, at the suggestion of his private secretary, George V proclaimed the Royal House of Windsor.[44]

Following the war, David was sent on a series of tours around the empire which were to intermittently keep him away from England for six years. In August 1919 he boarded HMS *Renown*, sailed to Canada, and began an extended journey that would take him from one side of the country to the other. It was during his visit to Alberta that he purchased a four-thousand-acre ranch forty miles south of Calgary. After the Canadian tour, he visited America for the first time, with stays in Washington, D.C., and New York, where he was given a ticker-tape parade.

After a break of several months in England, he set sail again on the *Renown*, this time headed for Australia and New Zealand. He was accompanied on this journey by a favorite cousin, twenty-year-old Lord Louis Mountbatten. Lively and boisterous, Dickie, as Mountbatten was called, joined David in boyish pranks which, though utterly harmless, caused great distress to the staid George V and Queen Mary.

Further tours followed. In 1920, David traveled to India and Asia; over the next few years, he paid two extended visits to the United States, returned to Canada and his ranch in Alberta, and toured South America and Africa. During his September 1923 visit to New York, the Prince indulged his love of pleasure. He attended several nightclubs, watched polo matches, and frequently disappeared for hours at a time, much to the dismay of his bodyguards. However, there can be no denying that David worked hard during these years. He had visited forty-five countries within the Empire and racked up over 150,000 miles of travel. "I could have qualified as a self-contained encyclopedia on railroad gauges, national anthems, statistics, local customs and dishes, and the political affiliations of a hundred mayors," he recalled. "I knew the gold output of the Rand, the storage capacity of the grain elevators at Winnipeg, and the wool export of Australia; and I even held my own on the subject of the chilled-beef trade of the Argentine."[45]

The impact of these tours was enormous. For the first time, many people in the Empire came face-to-face with royalty, and what they saw was indeed a surprise. This was Prince Charming, smiling, jovial, handsome—a complete contradiction of what they had expected. Except for his noble birth, he seemed absolutely no different from those who turned out to see him. To David, too, travel was a revelation. As he visited country after country, he was amazed at the thousands of people who stood waiting for hours on end just to catch a glimpse of him. He was hailed in every city and town, feted, toasted, cheered, and photographed. So many hundreds of people shook his hand that doctors bandaged it and the Prince was forced to use his left, so enthusiastic was his reception.

The Prince's hard work impressed his parents, and he received letters expressing their pride. However, this rare praise was mitigated by more numerous letters from his father and mother, which criticized much of what he had done, how he had dressed, and how he had acted. His parents made no secret of their disapproval. "I've seen all his letters from home," Mountbatten wrote. "His father's might be the letters of a Director of some business to his Assistant Manager and even his mother seems so stiff and unnatural. . . ."[46]

There was a clear clash of beliefs between David and his parents. Unlike King George and Queen Mary, the Prince did not believe that the monarchy must remain aloof and mysterious. Sir Frederick Ponsonby, keeper of the privy purse, once lectured the Prince on his duties: "If I may say so, Sir, I think there is risk in your making yourself too accessible." "What do you mean?" David asked. "The monarchy must always retain an element of mystery," Ponsonby replied. "A Prince should not show himself too much. The Monarchy must remain on a pedestal." David disagreed strenuously with this reasoning, but Ponsonby warned, "If you bring it down to the people, it will lose its mystery and influence."[47]

David was less concerned with the magic of the monarchy than with utilizing his power and position to help others. As Duke of Cornwall he had inherited the Duchy of Cornwall estates, including land in South London which housed low-income residents. One of his first concerns was improving their housing conditions, and he reduced rents to ease the strain. Although not always successful, he tried to remain sensitive to the impression he gave. He once arrived at a local train station to embark on a tour of working-class neighborhoods only to find a Rolls-Royce waiting to carry him and his party. Seeing the car, he shook his head and said with determination, "I'm sorry, I'm not going to ride in that."[48]

His commitment was genuine enough. His cousin Prince Christopher of Greece recalled a conversation he had with David after the latter's return from one visit to a working-class neighborhood in the north of England: "I can't get those poor fellows out of my mind," he told Christopher. "It's terrible to see the despair in their eyes. I can imagine what I would feel in their place. So many of them have been through the War. What have they come back to? How can one tell them to go on hoping?"[49]

"From the time of his return to England the Prince of Wales chose an independent way," wrote Hector Bolitho. "It led him far from the traditions of his father's Court. He resented the old order, and conventional society did not amuse him. Like his grandfather, he found pleasure in a small coterie of friends, chosen for their amusing qualities rather than for their position or their intellectual gifts. In time, the dwindling ranks of society resented the originality of his choice of friends. He seldom went to stay in great country houses, where he might have met and known his contemporaries, and, as independence increased, he was almost stubborn in his habit of turning his back upon the conventions of polite society."[50]

Bolitho was correct in saying that the Prince was fairly isolated. He had few friends and possibly no close male relationships. But the fact that David kept to himself was not, as Bolitho suggests, due to some conscious decision or character flaw on his part. He and his brothers had been raised to be suspicious of close friendships, for royalty, unlike their subjects, could never be entirely certain of discretion on the part of confidants; his brother Bertie, the future King George VI, also had few close male friendships.[51]

David enjoyed a measure of independence. He moved into York House, a suite of apartments, corridors, and labyrinthine staircases occupying a portion of St. James's Palace, just down the Mall from Buckingham Palace. He also acquired a household of his own, presided over by Godfrey Thomas, who acted as his private secretary. In 1920 a man who was to play a crucial role in the drama of the abdication joined the Prince's staff: Alan "Tommy" Lascelles, who served as assistant private secretary under Thomas.

Lascelles, nephew of the fifth Earl of Harewood, was born in 1887 and was educated at Trinity College, Oxford. He twice failed the Foreign Office exam to become a civil servant, became a stockbroker instead, and enlisted in the army at the outbreak of the war in 1914. "It could be said," writes Duff Hart-Davis, "that Tommy was the wrong person for the Prince of Wales: that his moral outlook was too severe, his idea of duty too rigid, his code of conduct too unbending, for him to be compatible with such a high-spirited employer. Yet it could equally be said that he was exactly the *right* person for the Prince, and that someone of precisely his calibre, with his powerful intellect and high principles, was needed to shape the future King for his role."[52] Lascelles himself was to have a mixed relationship with his royal master. He apparently thought little of him. He later said, "For some hereditary or physiological reason his mental and spiritual growth stopped dead in his adolescence, thereby affecting his whole consequent behaviour."[53]

In 1917, King George V had announced to his Privy Council that he and Queen Mary had decided to allow their children to marry suitable spouses of noble birth. No longer were David, his brothers, and his sister required to make political matches with foreign princesses or princes. In November 1921, David's sister, twenty-four-year-old Princess Mary, became the first of the children to take advantage of this by becoming engaged to a man nearly forty, Viscount Lascelles, son of the Earl of Harewood. Both shared a love of horses and country life, although unfavorable gossip held that he had proposed after losing a bet. In February 1922 they were married.

Bertie was the next child to marry. He had fallen in love with Lady Elizabeth Bowes-Lyon, daughter of the Earl of Strathmore. Elizabeth, who was to play a pivotal role in Wallis's life, was known for her good sense, concern for others, and rather carefree approach to the problems of everyday life. She was not exactly beautiful: Short, she had a tendency to stoutness, which would increase with the passing years, but her face was pleasant, and she used her sparkling blue eyes, warm smile, and genuine charm to win over those whom she encountered. Beneath this exterior there lurked another woman, however: overly protective, filled with steely determination, stubborn, and unforgiving. Elizabeth came to be the dominant partner in her relationship with Bertie. Chips Channon later wrote of Bertie, "He had few friends and was almost entirely dependent on her, whom he worshipped. She was his will power, his all."[54]

On April 26, 1923, Bertie and Elizabeth were married in Westminster Abbey in London and received the titles of Duke and Duchess of York. Elizabeth easily won over her new relatives. The King was utterly under her spell, writing, "She is a pretty and charming girl, and Bertie is a very lucky fellow."[55] And she succeeded with Queen Mary through sheer subservience. The Queen's lady-in-waiting, Mabell, Countess of Airlie, recalled: "She was very unlike the cocktail-drinking, chain-smoking girls who came to be regarded as typical of the nineteen twenties."[56]

David himself, however, was less successful in his serious romantic endeavors. His first real love affair seems to have been with Lady Rosemary Leveson-Gower, daughter of the fourth Duke of Sutherland. They had first met when she was working as a Red Cross nurse in a field hospital he toured in France during the war. Like Elizabeth Bowes-Lyon with his brother Bertie, Rosemary Leveson-Gower at first refused the Prince's proposal, not wishing to subject herself to the public scrutiny life as a royal would entail. When she finally seemed on the verge of relenting, David was informed by his parents that he would not be allowed to marry her.

The King and Queen seemed to object to the proposed match for several reasons, all relating to Rosemary's family background. Five years earlier, her father had died, and within twelve months, her mother, Millicent, Duchess of Sutherland, had married Brig. Gen. Percy Desmond Fitzgerald. This marriage soon failed, and Millicent instigated divorce proceedings. As soon as she was free, the Duchess immediately married Lt. Col. George Hawes. She soon discovered, however, that Hawes kept a male lover, and they were divorced almost immediately thereafter.[57] Such marital antecedents were deemed too controversial for the mother of the would-be Queen of England.

David's isolation from his parents increased dramatically as he entered his thirties. George V, deeply suspicious of the changing world around him, became even more reactionary. He had no understanding of, or sympathy for, the emerging generation of which his eldest son was an idol. To the King, flappers, bathtub gin, jazz, and nightclubs reeked of indolence and moral irresponsibility. Instead, George and his queen carefully began to cultivate the idea of the Royal Family as a representation of all that was good in England and the Empire. In fairness, it cannot be said that the idea originated during George V's reign, for certainly Queen Victoria and her large family had been held as moral examples to the nation. But it was during George V's tenure that the news media were first called into action to support the notion of the nation's ideal family. Books and newspapers hailed the virtues embodied by the King, Queen, and their children; here was a true picture of domestic happiness and moral rectitude with which the lower and middle classes could identify. The arrival of the Duke and Duchess of York's first daughter, Princess Elizabeth, was cause for national celebration. Neither the Duke nor the Duchess was slow to recognize the value of their happy family life, and photographs and accounts of their domestic bliss soon flooded the burgeoning media. This idea of perfect family life was promoted to such an extent that authorized books were produced, and the rapidly growing public appetite for news about the Royal Family's private life was encouraged, decisions which would come to have fatal results a generation later.

While the press and public were fed this idyllic view, life within the Royal Family was far different. The King was so suspicious of his sons and fearful that they would somehow fall prey to corruption that he had them followed by agents who would report to Buckingham Palace any indiscretions. His sons continued to live in fear of his frequent outbursts. One morning, David and his brothers were all expected, as usual, to breakfast with their parents. According to rigid custom, all were to be standing at the table when the King entered. Harry, however, happened to be detained; he rushed through the door just as his father entered the room. The King fixed him with a deadly stare, and Harry, terrified, fell away in a dead faint.[58]

David, as heir to the Throne, was subject to even more intense criticism. His father was particularly concerned about his appearance and would dispatch hastily written warnings if his son dared wear the wrong kilt, a pair of cuffed pants, or suede shoes. Once, when David entered his study to ask a favor, his father looked at him and thundered, "You dress like a cad. You act like a cad. You are a cad. Get out!"[59]

Not surprisingly, such occurrences did little to endear David to his temperamental parent. "My Father doesn't *like* me," he once said to a friend. "Not at all sure I particularly like *him.* "[60] And, perhaps more tellingly, when Lord Louis Mountbatten's father, the Marquess of Milford Haven, died, David told his cousin Dickie, "I envy you a father whom you could love. If my father had died, we should have felt nothing but relief."[61]

The isolation of life at court did little to strengthen the bond between the King and Queen and their children. "This resistance to change and rejection of gaiety puzzled the sons of the King and Queen," noted James Pope-Hennessy. "They became restive, and seized upon or manufactured opportunities to avoid family evenings which ended at ten or ten-thirty, and during which the King would interrogate one or other of them as to what he had been doing latterly and why he had been doing it."[62] Even the staid and dutiful Bertie once complained to Lady Airlie about Ascot weekend house parties at Windsor Castle: "No new blood is ever introduced, and as the members of the party grow older every year there's no spring in it, and no originality in the talk—nothing but a dreary acquiescence in the order of the day. No one has the exciting feeling that if they shine they will be asked again next summer—they know they will be automatically, as long as they are alive. Traditionalism is all very well, but too much of it leads to dry rot."[63] Such apathy inspired Max Beerbohm to compose a one-act play, in the form of a poem, called *Ballade Tragique a Double*

Refrain, in which a lady- and lord-in-waiting exchanged complaints in verse detailing their boredom, each example ending with the alternating lines "The Queen is duller than the King" and "The King is duller than the Queen." Finally, unable to suffer their dilemma any longer, they agree to a murder-suicide pact to escape service at court.[64]

In November 1928, while David was on safari in Africa, an incident occurred which has repeatedly been used to tarnish his reputation. The only account we have comes from David's assistant private secretary, Alan Lascelles, who was admittedly prejudiced and who bore a grudge against his master. Interestingly, just before the occurrence, Lascelles wrote to his wife: "A good private secretary ought to be wholeheartedly devoted both to his man and to his aims. I'm very far from being either, I fear, and the result is I'm always having to be deceitful, which is very bad for one. Even if I were red-heatedly convinced that Monarchy is a flawless and indispensable institution (which I'm not), his interpretation of the duties and aims of royalty is utterly discrepant from mine."[65]

One day during the safari, the Prince received word from Prime Minister Stanley Baldwin that his father was terribly ill. "I don't believe a word of it," David is reported to have said. "It's just some election dodge of old Baldwin's. It doesn't mean a thing." But Lascelles declared, "Sir, the King of England is dying, and if that means nothing to you, it means a great deal to us." The Prince looked at him, said nothing, and spent the night seducing the wife of a local British official.[66] The next day, however, David duly returned to England.

Whatever hesitation David showed in returning to England is indicative of two factors in his life. First, it clearly shows the breach that had developed between him and his father. Relations had become so strained that as David had earlier told his cousin Dickie Mountbatten, the thought of his father's death brought not sorrow but a sense of relief. Second, this incident, in whatever form it occurred, undoubtedly shows what undeniably existed: a darker side to the Prince, a self-indulgent preoccupation with his own interests. It was this last trait which so grated on Lascelles. When they returned, he resigned, telling the Prince exactly what he thought of him. Typically, David accepted the scolding good-naturedly and even gave Lascelles a car as a thank-you gift for his years of service.

David increasingly turned to his own pursuit of pleasure. He had first met Freda Dudley Ward in an air-raid shelter during a dance in March 1918; ironically, the dance was given by Maud Kerr-Smiley, sister of Ernest Simpson. Freda (née Winifred Birkin) was the daughter of a wealthy lace manufacturer from Nottingham; she was the wife of the Right Honorable William Dudley Ward, a member of Parliament and vice chamberlain of the royal household. By 1918 the Wards were largely living separate lives. Everyone who knew Freda liked her. Lady Cynthia Asquith described her dismissively as "a pretty little fluff," but she was rather more substantial.[67] She had a quick sense of humor and was good-natured, intelligent, and charming.

The relationship between David and Freda soon became, at least for the Prince, a sustaining passion in life. She cheered him when he was depressed, and within her house, surrounded by her small daughters and Freda's motherly attentions, he even managed to experience something which had thus far been denied him: a happy family life. She cared for him, nurtured him, and convinced him to drink and smoke less and to be more attentive to his responsibilities. As a mistress, Freda was entirely safe: a married woman, discreet, and perhaps more important to David, sympathetic to his emotional needs.

Although David's feelings for Freda ran deep, they were not exclusive, and he let himself wander into less binding liaisons as well. A mutual love of London's vibrant nightlife drew David and Lady Thelma Furness together. "We talked a great deal," she wrote, "but mostly about trivialities. The Prince was not a man for abstract ideas or ponderous thought; nor was he interested to any extent in the theatre, books, or art. Our talk was mostly about people we knew or had known, and about places we knew and liked. And this was enough. There was a special rapport that seemed to exist between us, and this rapport was intuitive; we did not have to build it slowly through a discovery together of complex issues."[68]

Together David and Thelma went on safari in Africa. "This was our Eden, and we were alone in it. His arms about me were the only reality; his words of love my only bridge to life. Borne along on the mounting tide of his ardor, I felt myself being inexorably swept from the accustomed moorings of caution. Every night I felt more completely possessed by our love, carried ever more swiftly into uncharted seas of feeling, content to let the Prince chart the course, heedless of where the voyage would end."[69]

Thelma's Eden would end on the day she introduced the Prince to her friend Wallis Simpson.

9

A Fateful Weekend

I N THE FIRST WEEK of January 1931, Wallis received a telephone call which would change the course of not only her life but also British history. Benjamin Thaw's wife, Consuelo, rang Wallis and explained that her sister Thelma, Lady Furness, was having the Prince of Wales and a small party up for a weekend of hunting at Burrough Court, her husband's estate at Melton Mowbray in Leicestershire, on the weekend of January 10, 1931. The Thaws were to have acted as chaperones, but Benjamin's mother had unexpectedly fallen ill, and Consuelo was forced to go to Paris to look after her. Although Benjamin would attend, Thelma still needed a married couple, and Consuelo asked Wallis if she and Ernest would agree to attend in Consuelo's stead.[1]

Wallis later wrote that she was not overly enthusiastic at the prospect. All of the guests except Benjamin would be strangers, and although she was interested in meeting the Prince of Wales, she was also extremely nervous. The entire weekend would center around riding, hunting, and royalty, topics about which Wallis knew next to nothing. She did not even know Thelma Furness particularly well. At first, Wallis declined, but Consuelo persisted, promising that the weekend would go smoothly and that the Prince adored Americans.[2]

Wallis telephoned Ernest at his office and discussed the proposal with him. Excited, he immediately told her to ring Consuelo back and say that they would attend. Wallis, still nervous at the thought of the weekend, dutifully did as he requested. A few hours later, Thelma herself rang to thank her, and she, too, insisted that all would go well.[3]

In the days leading up to the weekend, Wallis caught a cold, which quickly worsened. Her temperature rose and fell, her body ached, and she could scarcely breathe. Nevertheless, there was no pulling out. On Saturday afternoon, she and Ernest met Benjamin Thaw at St. Pancras Station in London, and together the three boarded a train for Melton Mowbray. As they sat in their compartment, Wallis asked Benjamin to show her how to curtsy to the Prince; her only previous attempt had been seventeen years before, during her presentation at the Bachelors' Cotillon in Baltimore. Benjamin replied that as an American she would not be obliged to curtsy, but Wallis, terrified of giving offense, threatened to get off the train at the next stop. Finally, he rose and attempted to lead her through the procedure.[4]

They arrived at the siding at Melton Mowbray just after six and immediately began the drive to the house. The rich Leicestershire countryside was shrouded in a veil of thick fog swirling about the leafless trees like a specter. Eventually, Burrough Court, a long, low brick mansion set in a groomed garden, appeared. Averill Converse, Thelma's stepdaughter, waited on the doorstep to greet them. She explained that the royal party had been delayed by the fog but were expected to arrive shortly.

Wallis wanted to disappear upstairs to rest; her cold was worse, and her head ached. Not knowing when the Prince and his party might arrive, she waited in the drawing room with Ernest and Benjamin. They sat before a roaring fire, taking tea and trying to warm themselves. Eventually, servants appeared, drawing the curtains across the dark windows, then clearing the table of its used china and replacing it. Still, there was no word from the expected guests.[5]

Finally, at half-past seven, Wallis heard the sound of a motorcar in the court outside; voices followed in the hall. The thick curtains separating the drawing room from the hall parted, and Thelma appeared, accompanied by the Prince of Wales and his younger brother, Prince George. Wallis, Ernest, and Benjamin stood as the brothers were presented; Wallis successfully executed her curtsy to the Prince of Wales and followed it with another to his brother. Everyone then took tea, Wallis and the others for the second time in less than two hours.[6]

Here, standing before Wallis, face-to-face, was the most famous man in the world, a man whom, until now, she had only seen in photographs or in brief glimpses from a distance. She was struck by how boyish he appeared for a thirty-seven-year-old man, how much the Prince of Wales resembled his photographs, with his rumpled golden hair and sad eyes. George, much taller than the Prince of Wales, had inherited most of the family's physical beauty and was the best looking of the brothers. Wallis felt immediately at ease as the two Princes questioned her about life as an American, and she was surprised at how natural they appeared.[7]

Prince George was collected by some friends with whom he was to spend the weekend and said goodbye. Dinner was to be served at nine, and Wallis and Ernest disappeared upstairs to dress. She felt even more ill and soaked herself in a hot tub, wishing she could curl up in bed and fall asleep. She took two aspirins and girded herself for a lengthy ordeal. Ernest, however, clearly awed by his encounter with royalty, was filled with excited anticipation. "I have come to the conclusion that you Americans lost something that is very good and quite irreplaceable when you decided to dispense with the British monarchy," he declared as he dressed.[8]

That fall, Wallis had gone to Paris and purchased several new dresses, one of which now made its appearance. More unknown faces greeted her as she and Ernest descended the staircase to partake of dinner with the Prince of Wales. Talk at the table centered on hunting—a subject which Wallis knew of only from tales of her ancestors. Years later, the Duke recalled turning to Wallis and asking if, as an American living in England, she missed central heating. "I am sorry, Sir," he remembered her saying, "but you have disappointed me." "In what way?" he asked. "Every American woman who comes to your country is always asked the same question. I had hoped for something more original from the Prince of Wales."[9]

Wallis herself, writing her memoirs after the Duke wrote his, declared that she could not recall or imagine any such conversation, while Thelma Furness, who was present, wrote, "This meeting has been the subject of an enormous amount of fiction." She declared that the conversation about central heating almost certainly never took place, a conclusion bolstered by Wallis's memoirs. "It would have been not only bad taste," wrote Thelma, "but bad manners. At that moment Wallis Simpson was as nervous and as impressed as any woman would have been on first meeting the Prince of Wales."[10] After dinner, the guests broke into small groups, playing bridge or poker, or chatting; Wallis, unused to the high stakes, grew nervous and ended up losing eight pounds before the Prince said good night and the guests could retire.[11]

The next morning, she slept late and took breakfast in her room. She felt much better by the time she again encountered the Prince of Wales, who was accompanied by his equerry, Brig. Gen. Gerald F. Trotter, a slightly older gentleman who had lost his right arm in the Boer War.[12] At luncheon, Wallis sat next to the Prince; she could not later recall the conversation, only that she was careful and conscious of trying to put her best foot forward.

After bidding goodbye to the Prince of Wales, Wallis and Ernest left for London. The weekend had been an exciting adventure, a privileged glimpse of a world of wealth, power, and royalty. But it was an anomaly; neither Wallis nor Ernest expected to meet the Prince of Wales again. Still, following the weekend party at Melton Mowbray, she began to follow accounts of his life as reported in the London papers "with," as she recalled, "more than a casual interest."[13]

However, they soon met again by accident. After the Prince of Wales returned from a tour of South America, Thelma gave a party in his honor at her house on 21 Grosvenor Square and invited Wallis and Ernest. As Wallis stood chatting with fellow guests, Thelma arrived with the Prince. As he made his way through the crowd, he stopped before Wallis and Ernest and said how delighted he was to see them again before moving along. Wallis thought he looked exhausted, but both she and Ernest were immensely flattered that he had recalled their encounter.[14]

Wallis began to deliberately nurse her relationship with Thelma. She managed, through her charm and wit, to ingratiate herself into her privileged circle. She came to know Thelma's twin sister, Gloria Vanderbilt, who was, at the time, living in England with her young daughter, known as Little Gloria and soon to be the subject of one of America's greatest custody battles.

Wallis genuinely liked Thelma and enjoyed the social whirl in which she moved. For several years, Wallis had had to content herself with small dinner parties at the flat or evenings out at cafés and nightclubs. Thelma's invitations offered a world of titles and grand houses, of dinners at the best restaurants and private boxes at the theater. Wallis's head had been turned, and she was determined to enjoy whatever benefits her acquaintance could reap. It does not seem likely, however, that her relationship with Thelma was cultivated expressly for the purpose of striking a closer bond with the Prince of Wales. At this time, Wallis had no indication that there was any crack in the liaison between Thelma and the Prince, nor was she confident enough to assume that she could rise to such dizzying heights. It is also of interest to note that Ernest, fully aware of the liaison between Thelma and the Prince, expressed no moral objection; he understood both the honor of being selected as the Prince's favorite and the European tolerance for such affairs.

On June 3, 1931, Wallis and Ernest attended the derby at Epsom Downs; a week later, she was formally presented at the Court of St. James's. This event had been in the works for several months, however, and was not related to her meeting with the Prince. For the once-impoverished girl from Baltimore, this was truly a surreal experience. Maud Kerr-Smiley, Ernest's sister, had just presented her own daughter as a debutante and thus had to wait, according to the heavy protocol of the court, three years before she could sponsor another lady. Wallis had to be presented as an Englishwoman, since the court considered her British by marriage, not American. Eventually, one of her American friends, Mildred Anderson, who had also married an Englishman, agreed to present her at court.[15]

King George V, with his prim Victorian morals, presided over a court which had refused to countenance such things as divorce. For many years, no divorced person could be presented at court; when this was finally altered, the applicant had to prove that she was the injured, blameless party in a divorce action and provide legal proof to the office of the Lord Chamberlain. Wallis therefore had to obtain copies of her divorce decree from the United States and forward them to St. James's Palace.

In an effort to save money, she borrowed Consuelo Thaw's presentation dress and Thelma's presentation train, feathers, and fan.[16] She bought a large, imitation aquamarine cross to wear around her neck and regulation elbow-length white gloves. The ceremony at Buckingham Palace was impressive. She and Ernest, handsomely attired in his Grenadier Guards uniform, arrived at the palace among a long line of cars stretching down the Mall. Inside, officials in scarlet tunics covered with gold braid and medals directed guests up the grand staircase, lined with plumed gentlemen-at-arms standing rigidly at attention. Wallis joined the other women who waited for their presentations. She followed as they slowly snaked their way through the corridors, listening eagerly for the loud announcement of her name which signaled that it was time. Wallis entered the white-and-gold ballroom, following the crimson carpet to the massive, scarlet-draped dais where the King and Queen sat on their thrones. George V, attired in full dress uniform, and Queen Mary, in a beaded evening gown with the blue sash of the Order of the Garter across the bodice, nodded politely as Wallis swept a deep curtsy before them. There was no verbal exchange; behind her, far above the heads of the audience, an orchestra was playing. She rose from her curtsy, backed away and turned, exiting the ballroom and entering the state apartments of the palace. It was all over in thirty seconds. Afterward, the King, Queen, and other members of the Royal Family circulated among the guests. As the Prince of Wales passed, Wallis overheard him say to his uncle Arthur, Duke of Connaught, "Something ought to be done about the lights. They make all the women look ghastly."[17]

After the presentation, Wallis and Ernest attended a small party given by Thelma. Inevitably, the Prince of Wales soon arrived. He greeted Wallis and complimented her on her gown.

"But, sir, " she replied with a rather bold playfulness, "I understood that you thought we all looked ghastly." The Prince of Wales was speechless for a moment; undoubtedly, he was unused to this sort of pointed humor. Then he gave Wallis an apologetic smile and declared, "I had no idea my voice carried so far."[18]

The Prince left the party before Wallis and Ernest; but as they walked down the stairs, they spotted him and Gerald Trotter, his equerry, standing at the curb by his motorcar. The Prince offered them a ride, and they eagerly accepted. On the way to Bryanston Court, the Prince explained that he was on his way to his country house, Fort

Belvedere, in Windsor Great Park in Berkshire. He described for them how he had found and fallen in love with the Gothic structure and was busy restoring both the house and its gardens. When the car came to a halt, Wallis asked the Prince if he would like to see their flat; he declined, then added that he was eager to do so one day, hoping that he might be inspired with ideas for his own house.[19] Months would pass before they met again.

At the end of June 1931, Wallis traveled to France to spend a weekend with Consuelo at Cannes. They were joined by Consuelo's sister Gloria and Nada, Lady Milford Haven. During this weekend, Wallis apparently discovered what had only been whispered in polite society: that Gloria was involved in a lesbian liaison with Lady Milford Haven. One morning, Gloria's maid, Maria Caillot, walked in on her mistress and Lady Milford Haven together in bed, engaged in a passionate kiss. This incident would loom large in the custody case over her daughter, Little Gloria.[20]

With her slightly masculine appearance, Wallis may well have been the object of some desire on this trip. Her memoirs are silent, although she did later tell one friend, without further elaboration, that it had been an uncomfortable time.[21] One can only assume that this discovery shocked her, for she abruptly packed her bags and fled back to London. Thereafter, although she continued to see Thelma, her relations with Gloria, Consuelo, and Lady Milford Haven were infrequent and finally ceased altogether.

She returned from Cannes to another stark dose of reality. In the midst of her privileged friendships, meetings with royalty, and grand parties, she discovered that Ernest's business was suffering from the Depression. Money was tight. They spoke of giving up their car if the situation did not improve and of letting servants go. Ernest's father, with whom Wallis did not get on particularly well, was cautious with his money, so she and Ernest were increasingly grateful for the welcome checks Aunt Bessie often dispatched.

The financial worries took a physical toll on Wallis. She suffered from terrible stomach ulcers, which left her violently ill and unable to leave her bed for days at a time. In the midst of this struggle, she developed a high fever and sore throat; doctors diagnosed inflammation of the tonsils, and Wallis had to enter the hospital to have them removed.

In January 1932 she and Ernest suddenly, and rather unexpectedly, received an invitation to spend the weekend of the thirtieth with the Prince of Wales at Fort Belvedere. Thelma would be acting as hostess, and Consuelo and Benjamin Thaw would be present as well.[22]

On the appointed afternoon, Wallis and Ernest left London and drove the thirty or so miles to Windsor Great Park. In the darkness, they followed the road across the countryside before finally coming to a set of gates, where they presented their invitation to a sentry on duty. Their car then swept along a winding gravel drive, through thick clusters of beech and evergreen trees, before rounding a bend and arriving at the top of a low hill. There, before them, stood Fort Belvedere, its towers and chimneys rising in sharp outline against the black night, the arched, Gothic windows flooded with warm light.[23]

Fort Belvedere had been built by William, Duke of Cumberland, the third son of King George II. After his occupancy, it was abandoned for some years before George IV hired architect Jeffrey Wyattville to enlarge the existing structure and enhance it with Gothic details. Following George IV, however, no one lived in the Fort, and it was largely abandoned until the Prince of Wales happened to spot it one day in 1929 and decided to make it his country house. When the Prince had asked for it, his father had implored, "What could you possibly want that queer old place for? Those damn weekends, I suppose."[24] Wallis thought it "the most beautiful house I have ever known," even though she did find it a bit odd that the thoroughly modern Prince chose to live in such a distinctly old-fashioned place. A number of towers, ringed with crenellations, rose from the flat roofs. There was little of the castle left in the Fort; wide, mullioned windows were clearly meant to let the light in rather than keep attackers out. The light stone walls were covered with creeping ivy and flowering wisteria.[25] "The house is an enchanting folly," wrote Lady Diana Cooper, "and only needs fifty red soldiers stood between the battlements to make it into a Walt Disney coloured symphony toy."[26]

As their car ground to a halt in the circular gravel court before the hulking Fort, Wallis spied the Prince of Wales standing silhouetted in the light streaming through the open door. As a servant unloaded their luggage, Wallis and Ernest followed the Prince through a small hallway and into an octagonal hall with a black-and-white-marble floor. Eight chairs, upholstered in yellow leather, stood against the plain white plaster walls.[27]

Thelma waited in the drawing room to greet them. Wallis quickly took in the octagonal room, paneled in natural pine, its tall, arched windows shrouded in yellow velvet curtains. A fire burned in the grate; one wall was lined with a full bookshelf; the expensive, though comfortable, furniture was Chippendale; a baby grand piano stood in one corner; and several Canalettos hung on the walls. It seemed elegant, yet hospitable.[28]

Wallis and Ernest were shown to their room to dress for dinner. When they reappeared for cocktails, Wallis was surprised to find the Prince busily working at a large needlepoint picture. When she asked him about it, he explained that his mother, Queen Mary, had taught all of her children how to do needlework. "This is my secret vice, the only one, in any case, I am at pains to conceal," he said.[29]

During the entire evening, two small cairn terriors named Jaggs and Cora raced about the rooms, nipping at unsuspecting guests. The Prince of Wales, dressed in a kilt, led his guests to the dining room, also paneled in natural pine and hung with several paintings by George Stubbs. They dined on oysters from the Prince of Wales's own oyster beds in Cornwall, roast beef, salad, and dessert.[30]

They spent the evening playing cards or putting together jigsaw puzzles. Wallis joined a card game with the Prince of Wales, although she warned him that she had not played for years. He offered to coach her, but after she began to win, he smiled and left her to her own devices.[31]

Thelma put the record "Tea for Two" on the gramophone and began to dance with the Prince. Everyone joined in, and the Prince made the rounds of the women present, including Wallis. As they danced, he explained to Wallis that she must consider herself absolutely at home at the Fort. He excused himself, saying that he wished to get up early to work in the garden, but insisted that his guests sleep as late as they wished.[32]

Wallis and Ernest retired shortly after midnight. The next morning, breakfast was brought to their room. When she and Ernest eventually entered the drawing room, they walked to the French doors and watched the Prince, clad in baggy plus fours and a thick sweater, swinging a machete at the shrubbery surrounding the garden. He spied them and strode up the slope to the terrace, explaining that he was at war with the laurel, which was threatening to overtake his carefully planned garden.[33]

The Prince disappeared back to his garden, telling Ernest he was free to join in if he wished. His equerry, Gerald Trotter, explained to Ernest that he could, of course, remain at the Fort but that no other guest had ever done so. Ernest wisely said he would be delighted to join in the gardening and went back to fetch a sweater.[34]

The view from the terrace was exceptional. The land sloped away to Virginia Water, a long, languid lake half-hidden by the groves of trees. The Cedar Walk, lined with ancient trees, led away into the thick rhododendron and azalea dells. Descending terraces surrounding the Fort were ringed with stone battlements and eighteenth-century Belgian cannons; below the battlements, to one side, was a swimming pool; to the other, a tennis court. Small, twisting paths, lined by thick, herbaceous borders, wound from the green lawns, through old cedars, to hidden rock gardens.

The Prince led his male guests away into the forests to cut down the flowering laurel, and Wallis returned to the Fort along with the rest of the women. A few hours later, the men returned for lunch, after which the Prince took Wallis and Ernest on a tour of the house. The small library was filled with Queen Anne furniture; the Prince's own bedroom, off the octagonal hall on the ground floor, was a larger room whose chintz-curtained windows overlooked the garden. The walls were covered with photographs, and the Prince's bed stood beneath an immense British Order of the Garter banner hung as a tapestry on the wall.[35]

Upstairs there were six bedrooms, including Prince George's Room, named for the Prince of Wales's brother, and the Yellow, Pink, Green, and Blue Bedrooms. The largest bedroom, the Queen's Room, was a unique hexagonal space with wide bay windows, an intricate cornice, and a large draped bed towering in a shallow alcove.[36] When the Prince remodeled the Fort, he had tried to fit in as many modern bathrooms as possible, an unusual feature in an eighteenth-century house. He also managed to install a steambath in the basement, a luxury he indulged in each evening.[37]

The Simpsons do not seem to have seen the Prince again until October 1932, when they were asked to the Fort, once for tea and again for a weekend house party. Then, in 1933, their Fortunes took an upswing. They were invited to spend the weekend at the Fort with the Prince in January, then twice in February, and again in March. In January, Wallis reported that during a weekend at the Fort, she, Thelma, and the Prince had been out ice-skating with the Duke and Duchess of York at Virginia Water. "Isn't it a scream!" she wrote to Aunt Bessie.[38] They had clearly impressed the Prince of Wales and broken into the charmed circle of his intimates. Yet, looking back, Wallis was to write: "If the Prince was in any way drawn to me I was unaware of his interest."[39]

10

"Wallis in Wonderland"

IF WALLIS WAS UNAWARE of the Prince's growing interest in her, this illusion was soon shattered. Aunt Bessie had sent her some money, and in March 1933 she sailed to New York aboard RMS *Mauritania*. Ernest, owing to business concerns, was unable to join her. As the ship left its berth in Southampton, a messenger knocked on her stateroom door, delivering a cable from the Prince of Wales wishing her a pleasant voyage. Word of this royal greeting quickly spread among the ship's crew. During the crossing, she was showered with extra attention by the staff, a bonus of being a royal favorite she did nothing to protest.[1] Wallis returned on RMS *Olympic*, sister ship of the ill-fated *Titanic*, made friends with the purser, and was moved to an enormous cabin in exchange for acting as hostess at his table.[2]

Once she had returned to London, the Prince's attentions became more direct. He began to visit the Simpsons at their Bryanston Court flat with increasing frequency, dropping in unannounced for cocktails and occasionally remaining for dinner. Often these impromptu evenings lasted until three or four in the morning. The Prince reciprocated their hospitality. The first weekend of June 1933, Wallis and Ernest stayed at the Fort with the Prince. Among the other guests were Grand Duke Dimitri Pavlovich of Russia and his morganatic wife, Audrey Emery. Before the weekend, Wallis was carefully briefed not to mention the subject of Rasputin, the Russian mystic whose hold over Tsar Nicholas II and his family had come to an abrupt end when he was murdered in a conspiracy led by Prince Felix Youssoupov and the Grand Duke. "It was fun, but a touch too royal," Wallis wrote to Aunt Bessie.[3] On June 19, Wallis received further evidence of the Prince's increasing interest: He gave her a surprise birthday party at Quaglino's and presented her with orchids when she arrived.[4]

On July 4, Wallis gave a small party at the flat to celebrate Independence Day in America. The Prince of Wales was invited and was delighted to join in this patriotic spectacle celebrating his great-great-

great-grandfather King George III's loss of the American colonies. Wallis had decided that a typical American meal of black bean soup, grilled lobster, fried chicken, and raspberry soufflé would do, and the Prince enjoyed every minute of it. There were ten guests that evening, including Thelma Furness and Consuelo and Benjamin Thaw.[5]

There were evening visits with the Prince and his friends to the Embassy Club or Sartori's, and more often than not Wallis and Ernest spent their weekends at the Fort. Here Wallis encountered many members of the Prince's household. His equerry, Maj. Gen. John Aird, was a former member of the Grenadier Guards Regiment. Tall and thin, he was known affectionately as Jack and was prized for his loyalty. Another important member of the household was Maj. Edward Metcalfe, the Prince's aide-de-camp. Known as Fruity, he had been the Prince's aide-de-camp during his tour of India, when, as a member of the Indian cavalry, he had succeeded in winning the prize appointment. The Prince liked him, and Metcalfe eventually followed him back to England, where, in 1925, he married the Hon. Alexandra Curzon, daughter of the famed George, Marquess Curzon of Kedelston, viceroy of India. Fruity Metcalfe was the closest thing the Prince ever had to a lifelong friend.

Wallis also befriended George, the Prince's youngest brother. George was a handsome, intelligent, slightly dilettantish young man, the favorite of his mother, whose tastes in art and collecting he had inherited. There was much talk about his private life. Kaiser Wilhelm II's grandson, Prince Louis Ferdinand, described him as "artistic and effeminate" and noted his use of strong perfume.[6] Stories circulated about an alleged affair George had supposedly had with a black actress, but this was nothing compared to the scandal which arose when one of his young male lovers apparently tried to blackmail him. The Prince of Wales had to journey to Paris to try to smooth over the situation and retrieve several expensive Tiffany and Cartier cigarette boxes and lighters that had been personally inscribed by the Prince to his boyfriend.[7] Worse still for the Royal Family, George was known to have a problem with drugs, especially cocaine and morphine, an addiction which the Prince of Wales eventually helped him overcome. All of these scandals made him introspective, and Wallis grew very fond of him.

At the beginning of 1934, Wallis had a fateful meeting with Thelma Furness. Although the two had occasionally lunched together, they most often saw each other at the Fort. Now Thelma was being summoned back home to America, where her sister, Gloria Vanderbilt, was embroiled in a nasty legal battle over custody of her only child. The day before Thelma sailed, she asked Wallis to lunch at the Ritz.

There is some disagreement as to what next took place and, with both women dead, no way of ever knowing whose version is correct.

In her memoirs, Wallis recalled that over coffee Thelma casually remarked, "I'm afraid the Prince is going to be lonely. Wallis, won't you look after him?"[8]

Thelma, however, remembered the conversation a bit differently. According to her account, Wallis said, "Oh, Thelma, the little man is going to be so lonely."

"Well, dear," she replied, "you look after him for me while I'm away. See that he does not get into any mischief."[9] "It was later evident," Thelma wrote, "that Wallis took my advice all too literally. Whether or not she kept him out of mischief is a question whose answer hinges on the fine points of semantics."[10] No matter who first raised the issue, both accounts agree that Thelma indeed asked Wallis to look after the Prince. Wallis agreed, and on Thursday, January 25, Thelma sailed for America.

Thelma had previously taken center stage in the Prince's days, evenings, and weekends. Now, in the words of Michael Thornton, "the ill-advised departure of Thelma Furness had opened up a temporary vacuum in the life of a lonely and inadequate personality, and Wallis was the woman immediately on hand to fill that vacuum."[11] The day after Thelma left, Wallis and Ernest returned to the Fort to spend the weekend as the Prince's guests. In return, Wallis asked him to dine at Bryanston Court the following week. Then, on Tuesday, January 30, the Prince invited them both to a party he was giving at the Dorchester Hotel, an evening which marked a turning point in the relationship between him and Wallis. While the other guests danced, Wallis and the Prince sat alone at the table, talking quietly. She began to question him about his royal duties, his plans for future reform, and his hopes for his own reign. The Prince was charmed, declaring, "Wallis, you're the only woman who's ever been interested in my job." When they eventually took to the dance floor to join the others, he whispered a request to be allowed to stop by each week, as his schedule permitted, and join her and Ernest at Bryanston Court for cocktails.[12]

The Prince now began to visit the Simpsons on a regular basis. He remained "Sir" to them, and neither Wallis nor Ernest ever thought of crossing the clearly defined but unspoken line which separated ordinary people like them from royals. On occasion, the Prince stayed unexpectedly for dinner, which caused untold anxieties for the staff at Bryanston Court. The Prince would spend hours discussing life, his plans for the Fort, or his interest in housing projects and desire to help the less fortunate who would one day become his subjects as King.[13] Neither Wallis nor Ernest was entirely comfortable with the situation, but neither felt like sending the Prince away. At first, Ernest and the Prince engaged in long intellectual and political chats, but eventually these dwindled as the Prince's interest turned more and more toward

Wallis. Inevitably, Ernest began to excuse himself from the after-dinner conversations, explaining that he had work to do for the next day's business.

Occasionally, Wallis summoned others to these intimate evenings. She was quite careful, however, about the company she chose, inviting only those known for their social connections and ability to tell witty stories. Some of her friends criticized her for not asking a more astute mixture of politicians, bankers, and other important leaders, but she explained, "He spends his days in the company of stuffed shirts. He comes here to be amused." The Prince thus encountered people of interest whom he would likely not otherwise have met and was able to relax at Bryanston Court.[14] After a month, his language became peppered with American slang, and members of his father's court were taken aback to hear the occasional "Okey-doke" escape his lips.

Ernest was not a stupid man. He realized that the Prince was not visiting, not coming around, not telephoning, to see or speak to him. But he also realized that his wife was too stubborn to be ordered out of the friendship. For Ernest, half British, there was also an element of both honor that the attentions of his future monarch should fall upon his wife and of humble service to the Crown. Wallis herself was utterly lost, seduced by her sudden importance in the life of the Prince of Wales; she had never been terribly introspective and had always let her emotions carry her along without thought, often until the situation had reached a crisis.

On the second week of February 1934, Wallis wrote to Aunt Bessie: "We have inherited the 'young man' from Thelma. He misses her so that he is always calling us up and the result is one late night after another—and by late I mean 4 A.M. Ernest has cried off a few but I have had to go on. I am sure the gossip will now be that I am the latest."[15] A few days later she wrote: "It's all gossip about the Prince. I'm not in the habit of taking my girl friends' beaux. ... I'm the comedy relief and we like to dance together—but I always have Ernest hanging around my neck so all is safe."[16]

Thelma returned to London on March 22. Unfortunately for her, gossip about a liaison she had enjoyed with Prince Aly Khan, the only son of the millionaire Aga Khan, had preceded her. Her reunion with the Prince of Wales was distinctly uncomfortable. "I hear Aly Khan has been very attentive to you," he said upon greeting her. She asked lightly, "Are you jealous, darling?"[17] But he did not reply, and an awkward silence hung between them.

Thelma wrote that the Prince, "although formally cordial, was personally distant. He seemed to want to avoid me. I knew that something was wrong. But what? What had happened in those short weeks while I was away?"[18] Soon thereafter, she arrived at Bryanston Court, clearly upset. She told Wallis that the Prince was now avoiding her, that he would not even take her telephone calls, and she had no idea what she herself had done. When she had gone to America, she feared that he would return to Freda Dudley Ward or somehow grow less fond of herself; she had not expected that his attentions might be directed somewhere entirely different. However, having returned to London and been exposed to a steady stream of gossip about Wallis and the Prince, she wondered if her friend had somehow managed to assume her place in his affections. Finally, pointedly, she asked Wallis directly if the Prince was "keen" on her.[19]

"Thelma," Wallis replied, "I think he likes me. He may be fond of me. But, if you mean by 'keen' that he is in love with me, the answer is definitely no." Whether this was a clever bit of prevarication or Wallis actually believed it was true, it failed to fool Thelma Furness.[20]

Unfortunately, during this conversation, the telephone rang, and the maid answered. When she came into the drawing room and announced the call, Wallis was perturbed, declaring, "I told you I did not want to be disturbed. . . ."

"But madam," the maid said, "it's His Royal Highness." Wallis excused herself, but she could be heard whispering, "Thelma is here." Nothing further was said of the conversation.[21] But Thelma left Bryanston Court suspecting that she had lost the Prince to her American friend.

The following weekend, Thelma had her confirmation. During a tense house party at the Fort, the Prince treated Thelma coldly while at the same time showering great affection on Wallis. Then, at dinner, when the Prince began to pick up a leaf of lettuce with his fingers, Thelma watched in horror as Wallis reached out and playfully slapped his hand with a sharp gesture, telling him to mind his manners and use a fork. He only smiled at her, blushing, and did as he was told. Thelma stared at this scene with wide-eyed disbelief. "Wallis looked straight back at me. . . ." Thelma recalled. "I knew then that she had looked after him exceedingly well. That one cold, defiant glance had told me the entire story."[22] Thelma said nothing, retired early, and without saying goodbye to anyone, left the Fort the next morning.

Wallis also was witness to the elimination of another rival: Mrs. Freda Dudley Ward, whose relationship with the Prince of Wales had lasted some sixteen years. When one of her daughters fell ill, Freda tried to call the Prince but was unable to reach him. When, finally, a few weeks later, she rang the switchboard at York House, St. James's Palace, the operator declared, "I have something so terrible to tell you that I don't know how to say it." When pressed, she confided, "I have orders not to put you through."[23] Thus did Freda Dudley Ward learn of her fall from grace. Philip Ziegler has suggested that Wallis may have pushed the Prince to this extreme, but there seems little reason to doubt that he, in fact, acted of his own accord, especially since, at this early stage, Wallis had no idea if her relationship with the Prince would last.[24]

Freda Dudley Ward, like Wallis, had also taken an interest in the work of the Prince of Wales, but the difference between the approaches of these two women could not have been greater. As an English-woman, Freda Dudley Ward had been raised in a country accustomed to ceremony; there was therefore little in the Prince of Wales's ritual of royal engagements which provoked interest or question. Wallis, on the other hand, was completely drawn into this unknown royal world, and her enthusiasm for the public side of the Prince's life undoubtedly appealed to him. Then, too, being from a prosperous background, Freda had little personal knowledge of the difficulties of the working class; Wallis, on the other hand, could question the Prince about housing, labor conditions, and education.

On April 15, Wallis reported to Aunt Bessie, "Thelma is still in Paris. I'm afraid her rule is over and I'm trying to keep an even keel with my relations with him by avoiding seeing him alone as he is very attentive at the moment. And of course I'm flattered."[25] Wallis felt she could reasonably dismiss the Prince's attentions as mere infatuation. She realized that since she was scarcely young and could not be con-sidered conventionally beautiful, the Prince must be interested in something else entirely. Perhaps it was her American heritage, her independent spirit, or her sense of humor. Then, too, she realized that he was a man of great paradox: the most famous bachelor in the world was also a very lonely man, and she had been one of the few around him to have expressed any interest in his royal duties.[26]

Wallis, too, had a singular gift which neither Freda nor Thelma possessed. As a southern woman, she had been raised to nurture a man and devote herself to making him happy. The sort of attention and affection with which she showered the Prince happened to fit in exactly with what he himself wanted. Wallis was no fool; she earnestly studied newspapers and questioned others so that she could speak knowledgeably with the Prince. This, however, was not quite as mer-cenary as has often been suggested. She was simply acting as she always had by making the man she was talking to feel that he was the most important person in the world. And though his royal trappings made him fascinating, she was forthright and natural with him, and he had seldom come across a woman so independent of spirit. Lord Castlerosse, who knew the Prince well, said that he had "an inferiority complex. Mrs. Simpson has built up her man. . . ." He added, "The attraction between them is NOT sex."[27]

David, in turn, felt he could freely confide in Wallis about certain matters; he had never been able to do so with either Freda or Thelma. Freda, having been raised in England, could never forget his position as Prince of Wales; this invisible wall in many ways prevented David from sharing himself completely. And Thelma, for all her charm and sophistication, was not a woman who seemed to care greatly for thoughtful conversation. Wallis, however, treated David "as a man first, as a Prince second," in the words of his future equerry Dudley Forwood.[28] He was able to speak freely to Wallis of his hopes and fears for the future, his family life, his relationships with his parents, and she listened, expressing interest and offering advice and comfort. The deeper the bond this created between them, the more impossible it became for David to consider giving up Wallis.

Things were moving quickly. The Simpsons were still dazzled by the royal favor, even if friendship with the Prince of Wales entailed certain sacrifices neither had anticipated. The first of these to make itself known was money: Ernest's family business was already in trouble, and now his limited income had to stretch to cover a host of expenses neither he nor Wallis had ever expected. There were parties to attend and to be given, new clothes to buy and wear, and tips to be dispersed.[29]

As yet, the friendship of the Prince of Wales still encompassed both Simpsons. Nothing untoward had taken place. Society gossips had begun a whispering campaign against Wallis, but the truth was that in the spring of 1934 her relationship with the Prince amounted to no more than a slightly flirtatious friendship. Certainly her feelings for the Prince were ambiguous, and she was always careful to pay attention to Ernest lest he feel slighted in any way. When her aunt Bessie warned that she was treading into dangerous territory, Wallis agreed, saying that she was willing to give up the Prince if Ernest in any way objected.[30]

At the same time, Wallis began, at the Prince's request, to insinuate herself, and her influence, into his households, at both Fort Belvedere and at York House, St. James's Palace. Although her informal style greatly appealed to the Prince, it was an altogether different matter where his staff was concerned. When the Simpsons and the Prince were out evenings, they would sometimes return to the Fort or York House at three or four in the morning, then expect the entire staff to fix them cocktails and late-night suppers and wait on them until they chose to retire, forgetting that these same servants had duties to attend to in the early morning. Wallis soon became accepted as the natural hostess at the Fort and expected that weekend menus be regularly submitted for her approval. This did not sit at all well with Osborne, the head butler at Fort Belvedere, who had been with the Prince's staff during the war and was accustomed to receiving orders only from his master. Things were more dire at York House, where the butler, Finch, was fired when he refused to take orders from this American commoner.

The remaining staff quickly learned to accept Wallis without question. She once rang society florist Constance Spry to give her some instructions on arrangements for a party. Spry, who had previously had a free hand in her floral work for the Prince, promptly called the comptroller at St. James's Palace: "Look, have you by any chance got a new housekeeper called Mrs. Simpson?" There was a long pause before she received the answer: "Mrs. Spry, any orders that come from Mrs. Simpson should be instantly complied with."[31]

That year, the Prince secured passes to the Royal Enclosure at Ascot for the Simpsons, a rather serious move in view of the fact that both had been divorced and no divorced person was allowed in the Royal Enclosure. The Prince smiled at her as he drove past in the royal carriage procession, and immediately afterward both she and Ernest returned to the Fort for a house party.[32]

In August, the Prince went on holiday to Biarritz, where he had taken a house, the Villa Meretmont, overlooking the ocean. He asked the Simpsons to join him, but Ernest had business in the United States, and Wallis excused herself by explaining that her aunt Bessie had already made arrangements to come visit her in London. But the Prince would not be put off and insisted that Wallis and her aunt accompany him.[33]

The Prince had accepted an invitation from Lord Moyne to join him on his yacht *Rosaura* as he cruised along the coast. This vessel proved to be something of a letdown: an old, converted Channel steamer, rather decrepit and unsteady. Unfortunately for the royal party, they encountered heavy seas, and Wallis fell terribly ill.

Once the weather cleared, however, the mood lightened considerably. The Prince and Wallis often took the yacht's launch and went ashore at secluded coves to picnic and swim. In the afternoons, they played poker and bridge or explored the nearby towns. Royal ceremony was carefully excluded. The Prince, insisting he was on holiday, refused to wear anything but shorts and sandals; when he went ashore, it took some clever arm-twisting to get him to wear a shirt and linen slacks. "I get very bored with all this dressing up," he declared.[34] Wallis followed his example: Clad in her bathing suit, with a pair of sunglasses perched on her head, she spent hours reading in the sunshine. When ashore, she wore simple linen-and-cotton sleeveless summer dresses. At night, they often dined together at small cafes and restaurants.

For three days, the yacht anchored in the quiet waters off Formentera, on the island of Majorca. "Perhaps it was during these evenings off the Spanish coast," Wallis later wrote, "that we crossed the line that marks the indefinable boundary between friendship and love."[35] Something had clearly changed between the pair. When they returned to Cannes, the Prince, unwilling to end this make-believe life with Wallis, decided to stay for several extra days. On their first evening in Cannes, the Prince and Wallis slipped ashore, and accompanied by John Taylor, the local British vice-consul, and his wife, they visited the Palm Beach Club, where they danced with each other until dawn. Wallis's friends Herman and Katherine Rogers, who lived nearby, entertained the pair the following evening with a midnight supper and a moonlight cruise on a friend's yacht. By the third day at Cannes, the Prince was so taken with Wallis that he dangerously booked the two of them into a suite at the Hotel Miramar. While Wallis slept, the Prince rang the night manager of the hotel and asked him to, in turn, summon to work the staff of the local branch of the Cartier store; he then disappeared into the night to do some private jewelry shopping.

Upon his return, he awakened Wallis and told her that they should leave immediately. The entire party, sleepy and not quite certain of what was happening, duly packed and returned to the yacht, which steamed out to sea. There, standing on deck under the moonlight, the Prince presented Wallis with a diamond-and-emerald charm for her bracelet.[36] After another two weeks of visiting Nice, Genoa, Lake Como—where Wallis and the Prince rowed in the deep blue waters—and other southern cities, the party reluctantly returned to France. From there, the Prince flew back to England, thence to Scotland, so that he could see the launch of the new RMS *Queen Mary*, and Wallis and the others sailed from Cherbourg.

For her part, Wallis would recall, she harbored strong feelings for the Prince but somehow managed to convince herself that it was a passing infatuation on his part.[37] She acted nonplussed, but Aunt Bessie was more forthright, suggesting that Wallis was indeed treading into dangerous territory. "If you let yourself enjoy this kind of life," she warned, "it will make you very restless and dissatisfied with everything you've ever known before." But Wallis had dismissed her concerns, saying that she knew exactly what she was doing.[38]

However, Wallis was keenly aware of the delicate balancing act her life had become. She had no reason to believe that her relationship with the Prince, as increasingly serious as it was, would lead to anything more than fond memories. Ernest was her husband; she cared for him and had no intention of losing him. In November she confided to Aunt Bessie that she had spoken at length separately with both her husband and with the Prince about this curious situation. Apparently, Ernest, reassured that she had no desire to leave the security and comfort of her marriage, expressed no objection to her continuing friendship with the Prince. While he cannot have been terribly happy with the growing public perception that he was a cuckold, Ernest genuinely liked the Prince. In addition, he was not averse to the aura of importance and prestige which surrounded both him and his wife in their favored position. "I shall try and be clever enough to keep them both," Wallis wrote to her aunt.[39]

The true measure of their new status came in November, when they received an invitation to the wedding of the Prince of Wales's brother Prince George to Princess Marina of Greece at Westminster Abbey on the twenty-ninth. Two days before the wedding, the Simpsons attended a state ball for the bride and groom given by King George V and Queen Mary at Buckingham Palace. The King and Queen by this time knew of their son's new American interest, and when they saw her name on the guest list, they allegedly ordered the Lord Chamberlain to cross it off. The Prince of Wales forced a confrontation. Marie Belloc Lowndes wrote: "The Prince, hearing of this, went to his parents and said that if he were not allowed to invite these friends of his, he would not go to the ball. He pointed out that the Simpsons were remarkably nice Americans, that it was important England and America should be on cordial terms, and that he himself had been most kindly entertained in the States. His parents gave way and the Simpsons duly came to the ball."[40]

Wallis and Ernest made quite a picture on this their second appearance at Buckingham Palace. Ernest had to wear black knee breeches, according to court custom; Wallis, in a violet lamé dress with a green sash, borrowed a tiara from Cartier for the evening. She was quickly sought out by the Prince of Wales, who presented her to Prince Paul of Yugoslavia. He then took Wallis over to where the King and Queen were standing. "I want to introduce a great friend of mine," he said.[41] Wallis stepped forward and sank into a deep curtsy before the King, who had taken her hand in his. She turned to Queen Mary, who wore a long blue gown and glittered with jewels, and curtsied once again. Like her husband, Queen Mary reached out and shook her hand. Later, she would tell one of her ladies-in-waiting, Mabell, Lady Airlie, that she had done so without thought.[42]

Two days later, the magnificent wedding took place at Westminster Abbey. Wallis was delighted to find that she and Ernest had been given very prominent positions in the transept, from which they could view the entire proceedings. All around her life was changing, and she was captivated. "It seemed unbelievable that I, Wallis Warfield of Baltimore, Maryland, could be part of this enchanted world," she later wrote. "It seemed so incredible that it produced in me a dreamy state of happy and unheeding acceptance." From now on, she would describe her existence to Ernest as being like "Wallis in Wonderland."[43]

11

The Relationship Deepens

THE YEAR 1935 was to mark the major turning point in Wallis's life. Her relationship with the Prince accelerated at the same time as her marriage to Ernest began to fade away. Her position as the Prince's new favorite was fast being recognized by members of society; no word as yet leaked out in the British press, but those in the Royal Family, the court, and the aristocracy were aware. That Christmas, the Prince had asked Wallis to help select the hundreds of presents his staff would receive for the holidays. When word of this got back to them, many of these retainers were openly resentful that this American upstart should be exercising such intimate control over the household of the heir to the throne. But the Prince himself was pleased and rewarded Wallis with a cairn terrier puppy she called Slipper; in time, due to her inability to house-train him, Wallis would also call him Mr. Loo.[1]

The Prince had grown so fond of Wallis that he now telephoned every day if he could not visit her in person. The deeper the friendship between her and the Prince grew, the less Ernest seemed to be included. However, with Wallis's assurances, he had felt confident that there was no threat to the marriage. Indeed, Wallis had no plans at all to end it. Ernest represented emotional and financial security, while the Prince was simply a glamorous and exciting interlude.

Ernest continued to be just as enthusiastic over the royal favor and enjoyed the social doors which had opened to him and Wallis. The Prince was free with both his money and his entertainments, and for Ernest, conscious of class and position, spending weekends with the heir to the throne and his titled friends in the intimate surroundings of the fort was itself a reward for whatever dignity may have been lost in the process. Among the upper class, there had always been a certain amount of social cachet to be found in complacent acceptance of such royal favor, and Ernest, bound by convention, made little fuss. Soon enough, however, he began to find excuses to disappear when the

Prince called or reasons to remain behind at Bryanston Court, working on business, when Wallis went to the fort. Increasingly, he referred to the Prince, somewhat bitterly, as "Peter Pan."[2] Jokes began to be made at his expense. One of the most popular alleged that he was to write a play called *The Unimportance of Being Ernest*, in which the hero cries out, "My only regret is that I have but one wife to lay down for my King."[3]

At the beginning of February, the Prince invited the Simpsons to join him on a ski holiday in Kitzbühel, Austria. Wallis eagerly accepted the invitation in both of their names. But when she told Ernest, he declared that he had absolutely no interest in skiing. Over dinner he asked Wallis if she would still accompany the Prince.

"Why not?" she replied. "I wouldn't dream of missing it."

Ernest stood up, pushed his chair in, and said quietly, "I rather thought that we might have gone to New York together. I see now that I was wrong." He walked out of the dining room and disappeared into his dressing room, slamming the door loudly behind him.[4]

Wallis had no intention of giving up the trip. Although Ernest was clearly upset at the prospect, she refused to reconsider. Her stubborn determination to do as she wished, coupled with an undeniable selfishness, would increasingly drive a wedge between her and her husband. Wallis felt there was no reason why she should deprive herself of such an opportunity or why her husband might feel differently. Throughout 1935 the Simpson marriage disintegrated.

In contrast, the holiday in Kitzbühel proved idyllic. She and the Prince took the *Simplon Express* from Paris to Kitzbühel, arriving in the midst of a terrible storm on February 5. They were greeted by the mayor and a host of officials, and the Prince responded warmly to their welcome in fluent German. Wallis had never before been on skis and could progress no further than the simplest of slopes. She enjoyed the Grand Hotel, where the royal party stayed, sitting before a blazing fire in the afternoon and sipping hot cocoa or dining in the small local cafes to the music of mountain folk songs played on an accordion or zither.[5]

Among their party was Dudley Forwood, who would later play an important role in their lives. This handsome, dark-haired, and mustachioed twenty-three-year-old former Guards officer was junior attaché to Sir Walford Selby, the British envoy in Vienna, and had been dispatched by his office to attend the Prince. He was immediately struck by the Prince's "incredible charisma. When His Royal Highness came into a room, all conversation stopped. His presence was overwhelming." He also got to know Wallis rather well. He found her "riveting. She was a very nice, very American, aristocratic woman. She was prepared to treat me very well."[6]

Forwood had never before been in attendance to a member of the Royal Family and was uncertain of his duties. He recalls one afternoon particularly well:

> His Royal Highness was never great physically at sports. His Royal Highness loved to play golf, but he was not a great golfer. He loved to ride point-to-points, but he wasn't a great horseman. He wasn't a great skier. So he was on the nursery slopes, and there were two very smart, very typically French, ladies there, who everytime they saw him said in loud voices, "O, c'est le Prince de Galles, comme ils elegant, comme ils charmant, O, Mon Dieu!," at the top of their voices. His Royal Highness was embarrassed and irritated. He suddenly, on the nursery slopes, in the midst of these ladies, lost control of his skis and rushed headlong into a kind of pile of snow at the base of the slope. And the two French ladies, I'm afraid, saw their chance and aimed their skis at the snow drift. So that we had the Prince of Wales, and two French ladies of great elegance, floundering about in the snow drift. I wasn't sure what my duties were, but I realized I had to get my Prince out of the drift. I ran there and extricated His Royal Highness and took off his skis. He was not pleased with himself, and infuriated with the French ladies, who were making foolish noises in the snowdrift. I was young, and amazed that I was so bold and presumptuous, but I said, "Oh, Sir, is that the first time Great Britain has been raped by France?" Fortunately, His Royal Highness thought that this was funny, and he called over to Mrs. Simpson, who was not a great sportswoman, and who was standing at the side of the snowdrift, and shouted, "Oh, Wallis! Dudley says I've been raped by France! Isn't that fine?"[7]

At the end of their stay, the Prince suddenly decided that he would like to visit Vienna, declaring that he wished to waltz.[8] "This," recalls Forwood, "caused all sorts of problems. The Prince of Wales simply couldn't go anywhere he wished on the spur of the moment. We had to make telephone calls, talk to embassies, speak to the Foreign Office, ring local officials—all in a matter of hours."[9]

They left on the midnight express on February 16, traveled through the snowy Alps, and ensconced themselves in the Bristol Hotel, where they took over an entire floor. They spent their evenings dancing and visiting the local coffeehouses. While Wallis shopped, the Prince garnered favorable attention among the locals by visiting several housing projects and mixing with their inhabitants. Waltzing in Vienna, however, was soon displaced by the Prince's sudden desire to hear Hungarian Gypsies; the next morning, they were off on a train to

Budapest, where they wandered up and down the old, cobbled back-streets in search of the most authentic nightspots.

When Wallis had left for Austria, the tension between her and Ernest had been real. He had not wanted her to go and was upset that she had apparently made a decision to choose both the Prince and her own interests over his clearly expressed feelings. Wallis, in turn, had left England angered over what she believed to be his unreasonable stance. Having repeatedly told Ernest that there was no threat to their marriage, she found it impossible to reconcile his natural jealousy and humiliation with what she, in her own mind, knew to be only a passing attachment.

These circumstances colored the Austrian trip. Until this time, it is doubtful that Wallis and David were lovers. Certainly the Prince himself had expressed strong feelings for her, but Wallis—whatever her feelings—had been reluctant to jeopardize her marriage. Now, however, alone with David in the romantic surroundings of Kitzbühel, Vienna, and Budapest, it seems likely that Wallis made a decision which would seal her fate.

Several years later, after the abdication, the Duke repeatedly and vehemently denied that he and Wallis had been lovers before their marriage. He successfully sued author Geoffrey Dennis for suggesting in his book *Coronation Commentary* that Wallis had been his mistress. Indeed, for the rest of their lives, neither the Duke nor the Duchess would ever admit that their relations had been anything but absolutely proper.

It is impossible to say precisely when the pair crossed the fine line defining their unique romantic friendship and became lovers. There has been endless speculation as to the exact nature of the sexual relationship between Wallis and David. All manner of peculiar rumor and innuendo has, in the absence of hard fact, effaced truth, leaving a tangle of sexual flotsam which is nearly impenetrable. However, somewhere beyond the unsubstantiated gossip lies the source of Wallis's seemingly inexplicable hold over David.

Among the most persistent of all rumors is that David was homosexual. Twenty years after the abdication, an obscure little book was published called *Lese Majesty* in which much space was devoted to a discussion of the Duke's sexual preference. Although the author produced little in the way of evidence, the allegations stuck.

A more thoughtful analysis was put forth by author Christopher Warwick in his book *Abdication*. Warwick argues that David might have spent his life living as a repressed homosexual, only vaguely understanding the latent tendencies within.[10] To this end, he mentions David's desire to be dominated; his vehement declarations against homosexuality; and the possibility that he drove himself so hard in his sports activities as a young man in an attempt to prove his manhood. In the somewhat masculine Wallis, Warwick suggests, he may have found not only a mother figure but also an acceptable substitute for a male lover.[11]

David's sexual appetites, however, were well known. He maintained a rather successful record of conquests, all female. There never seemed to be any doubt whatsoever as to his own inclinations among those who knew him well. Certainly no member of his household or staff—those best in a position to learn his intimate secrets—ever suggested that he enjoyed anything other than heterosexual affairs.

In complete contradiction to this, it has long been rumored that David was impotent. According to this theory, it was only on bedding Wallis that he managed to find sexual fulfillment. But this is a curious charge to make. As Frances Donaldson rightly notes: "It might be true to say that during the whole of his youth the Prince was criticized for over-indulgence in the sexual act, while ever since he was believed incapable of it until he met his wife."[12]

Thelma Furness would later claim that the Prince was an inadequate lover.[13] According to at least one source, she declared that he suffered from premature ejaculation.[14] It has long been assumed that Wallis, having allegedly mastered various sexual arts during her time in China, was able to put them into practice on David, controlling their lovemaking with a skill which managed to bring him to orgasm.

The idea that only Wallis was able to finally provide David with the sexual satisfaction thus far missing in his life is rather difficult to accept. Not only do allegations of her alleged sexual techniques rest on the infamous China Dossier—a document which almost certainly never existed—but the Prince had enjoyed numerous relationships with various women before Wallis came along. He had never been unable to fulfill his sexual urges.

There have also been suggestions that David was a masochist who took sexual pleasure in being beaten and whipped.[15] Author Anne Edwards has alluded to these stories and even speculated that such desires might have stemmed from his experiences in childhood with Mary Peters, his abusive nanny.[16] This has been an appealing explanation to many, including Philip Ziegler. "That Wallis Simpson provoked in him profound sexual excitement is self-evident," Ziegler writes. "That such excitement may have had some kind of sadomasochistic trimmings is possible, even likely."[17] Not only is this an incredibly simplistic view of the relationship between Wallis and David, it is also entirely speculative. This, in spite of Ziegler's own warning in his book two pages earlier: "No one knows what happens behind a bedroom door except those who are inside."[18]

Finally, completely contrary to such speculation is the proposal that Wallis never had sexual relations with any of her husbands, the Duke of Windsor included. Such an assumption rests entirely on several offhand statements Wallis is alleged to have made. According to one source, she told Jack Aird in 1936, "I have had two husbands and I never went to bed with either of them."[19] Maître Suzanne Blum, who would act as the lawyer for the Duchess during her last years, more than once expressed the idea that Wallis remained a virgin until her death, a belief apparently passed on to her protégé, Michael Bloch, who repeated it in his last book on the Duchess.[20]

Such an idea, however, strains credulity. Win Spencer was a virile, sexually charged man, given to drunken rages and abusive displays of his power over Wallis. It seems highly unlikely that such a man would have been content to remain married to a woman for five years and fail to take possession of her, whether consensually or not. Indeed, Wallis later confessed to a friend that when drunk, Win Spencer had often forced himself upon her.[21] Nor was Ernest Simpson any more likely to have been ambivalent about ordinary sexual relations with a wife whom he loved and clearly found attractive.

Fortunately, the idea that the Duchess of Windsor remained a virgin until her death can be dismissed. Dr. Jean Thin, who treated Wallis for the last fourteen years of her life, was clearly astounded at Bloch's assertion. "How, I wonder, could he know if the Duchess remained a virgin or not until the day she died?" he says. "I, on the contrary, am qualified to certify that she was not a virgin."[22]

The truth of the sexual relationship between Wallis and David is undoubtedly much less shocking than the years of rumor would have it. No one can be said to have been in a reliable position to speak with authority on what went on in their bedroom except for the Duke and Duchess. As Ralph G. Martin pointed out, "These were not two people who would ever discuss such things with anyone."[23]

The simple truth is that those who look to the bedroom in an attempt to explain the strength of the bond between Wallis and David have overlooked entirely the emotions that drove them together. If the Prince simply wanted to possess Wallis sexually, surely his need for her would have waned with the passage of time. Nor is any speculative examination of their sexual bond likely to yield the answer. It was not the act of lovemaking—or any exotic techniques or practices on Wallis's part—which drew the pair together; rather, the love itself.

Other women could supply the Prince with sex, but Wallis was the first woman who managed to combine intimacy with a true emotional understanding and indulgence of him. She provided reassurance. She paid attention when he spoke in a way which no one had before her. Courtiers, Freda Dudley Ward, Thelma Furness listened, but through ears which heard a prince speaking; Wallis heard the man first and answered not with sycophantic assurances but thoughtful replies. She took an interest in his work and responded to his needs in exactly the way she had always been taught. He adored her gaiety and sense of fun, her independence and compassion for him.

Above all, she recognized his need to be loved and accepted unconditionally. David had continually sought out support and reassurance from older women who served not only as lovers but as slightly maternal figures as well. Having been denied close parental bonds in his childhood, he wanted nothing more than that which he had never had in his life: affection and protection. The relationship between him and Wallis was overwhelmingly based on her intuitive understanding of his desires. He sought to give affection, to have it received openly, to be protected and guided, and to establish, with her, in whatever fashion he could, the one thing he had never known: a happy family life.

Perceptively, Wallis indulged his desires. Although others would look on in horror as she openly chastised him or spoke to him sharply, the truth is that this treatment was no more than what David himself wished. All of his life David had been subject to the sterile criticism of his parents and court officials, rebukes which did not appear to be based on anything more than tradition and concern for appearances. Wallis, on the other hand, provided criticism based on love. In her authoritarian role, he knew, Wallis demonstrated her feeling for him. It cannot have been easy for her to have assumed such a peculiar role, which often became matron, mother, lover, and friend at once, but this only made her all the more valuable to the Prince. David was left with little doubt that in her comforting words, her reproachful tone as she corrected him, and her sympathetic encouragement of his duties, he had found in Wallis the one woman who not only understood his needs but loved him enough to indulge them as well.

Wallis noted a change in Ernest upon her return to London. Not surprisingly, he chose not to question her about her adventures with the Prince. Nor did he seem to have much interest in discussing what both of them knew was quickly becoming a serious threat to their marriage. Instead, he became withdrawn and silent and spent more and more of his time at his office.

The trip had also changed Wallis. She had previously been cautious, protective of her marriage, careful of her actions. Now her carefully maintained emotional distance from the Prince had faded. She was far too enraptured with both him and his enchanted style of life to consider at all the dangerous territory into which she had ventured.

Her relationship with David now took on a slightly reckless quality. They spent long evenings together at the Embassy Club without

Ernest, in full view of London society, and together attended parties and receptions given by the great hostesses of the era. David also began to shower her with expensive jewels. Finally, they were photographed together, as a couple, in formal portraits by society photographer Hugh Cecil, the surest sign that their relationship had indeed reached a new, deeper stage during their winter holiday.

In time, London society opened its doors to the Prince's new favorite. She and Ernest were often entertained by Sir Philip Sassoon, a tall, thin homosexual with dark hair and eyes and pale skin. Sassoon hosted elaborate parties in his luxurious flat at 25 Park Lane, decorated with Lalique chandeliers and art-deco motifs, or at his country estates of Trent Park and Port Lympe. Lady Portarlington hosted receptions in Wallis's honor; Helen Fitzgerald, former sister-in-law of Lord Beaverbrook's, became a fast friend; and Margot Asquith, widow of Prime Minister Herbert Henry Asquith, also issued frequent invitations to the Simpsons. The guest lists at these parties staggered the imagination: the most brilliant politicians of the day—from Ramsay MacDonald to Winston Churchill—could often be found chatting in the drawing rooms, along with famed artists like Rex Whistler; members of the Bloomsbury circle; society photographer Cecil Beaton; playwright Noël Coward; and aesthetes, such as Harold Acton and Stephen Tennant.

Wallis realized that most of these invitations were issued out of curiosity, and also in the hope that her presence might ensure that of the Prince of Wales. Ernest, still disgruntled but silently complacent, was usually at her side. No matter what his personal feelings might have been, he was always charming and genial in public.

This was a different world entirely, and at first Wallis moved carefully. She tried, unsuccessfully, to contain her enthusiasm, but her rapid-fire talk—"like the tack-tack-tack of a machine gun," in the words of one fellow guest—often left unfavorable impressions of brash and bold behavior.[24] Finally, several women, in particular Margot Asquith, took Wallis under their wing, warning her that she must guard her actions as well as her words, as they were now certain to be taken as representative of the Prince of Wales.[25]

At first, Wallis often failed to find favor. Sir Steven Runciman recalls a luncheon with the Aga Khan and Wallis, at which David was not present, in May 1935. "I can't say I was favorably impressed. She was very elegantly dressed, but had a very hard face. It was a small lunch party, and she was hardly allowed to say a word by the old Aga Khan, who clearly disliked her and interrupted her every time she opened her mouth—indeed he behaved very badly but what he said was full of interest."[26]

Three particular members of these social circles were to prove important friends of Wallis's, especially during the abdication crisis. The first was a fellow American, Henry Channon III, who went by the nickname Chips. He had been born in Chicago, the son of wealthy parents, and had come to England to live. There he had married Lady Honor Guinness, eldest daughter of the second earl of Iveagh; in 1935 he was elected as a Member of Parliament.[27]

Chips was a great snob. He did as much as possible to forget his hated American background and deliberately cultivated his aristocratic connections in England. He was renowned for his biting wit, his unbridled social ambition, and his eye for detail, this last characteristic brought fully to fruition in his famous diary. Invitations to the Channons' London house, with its glittering blue-and-silver rococo dining room, were particularly sought after by members of society.

He first met Wallis in the beginning of 1935. "She is a nice, quiet, well-bred mouse of a woman with large startled eyes and a huge mole," he wrote of his first impressions. "I think she is surprised and rather conscience-stricken by her present position and the limelight which consequently falls upon her."[28] Two months later, he noted, Wallis had already begun to change: "We had a luncheon party here, and the plot was to do a 'politesse' to Mrs. Simpson. She is a jolly, plain, intelligent, quiet, unpretentious and unprepossessing little woman, but . . . she has already the air of a personage who walks into a room as though she almost expected to be curtsied to."[29]

The other two important friends were Duff and Diana Cooper. Lady Diana, one of the daughters of the eighth Duke of Rutland, was known for her vibrant personality and her "fog-horn voice," in the words of Chips Channon.[30] In 1919 she had married Duff Cooper, a poor but rising clerk in the Foreign Office whose mother was a sister of the first Duke of Fife. Their married life together was an endless string of torrid affairs. "Both had passion to spare," writes Kenneth Rose, "and there have been more eternal triangles in their joint lives than in the whole of Euclid."[31] Duff himself was a rather calm, quiet, astute man, thoughtful and diligent about politics. It was Diana, with an amazing, almost ethereal beauty, brilliant wit, and great charm, who sparkled.[32]

This was the age of the great social hostesses in London, and theirs was the world which Wallis now entered. These women fell into roughly two groups—the political and the social hostesses. The political arena was dominated by the Marchioness of Londonderry, whom Wallis came to know quite well. She had been born Edith Chaplin, a granddaughter of the third Duke of Sutherland; in 1899 she married Charles Henry Vane-Tempest-Stewart, the seventh Marquess of Londonderry, and became chatelaine of the immense and grand Londonderry House. During her famous parties, Lady Londonderry would stand on the landing of her sweeping grand staircase, receiving a long line of important visitors.

Her chief rival was Mrs. Ronald Greville, who presided over a glittering London house in Charles Street and an immense country estate, Polesden Lacey, in Surrey. She was born the illegitimate daughter of a Scottish millionaire brewer, John McEwen, and did as much as possible to put her less-than-aristocratic beginnings behind her.[33] In time, she came to believe herself immensely powerful and influential; although the Prince of Wales found her sycophantic fawning distasteful, other members of the Royal Family adored her. She was particularly beloved by Queen Mary and by the Duke and Duchess of York, who had spent a part of their honeymoon with her at Polesden Lacey. Aside from these royals and those with social ambition who sought out her favor, however, Mrs. Greville was roundly despised in London circles. Those who frequented the great London houses in the 1930s—Harold Nicolson, Chips Channon, the Coopers, and Cecil Beaton—disliked her intensely. Her wit was nonexistent; her tongue, bitter and biting. In the words of Brian Masters, she was "quite simply malevolent."[34] In time, Mrs. Greville would become one of Wallis's most vehement enemies in society.

Another of the great hostesses to befriend Wallis was fellow American Laura Corrigan, daughter of a Wisconsin carpenter. She was perhaps most eccentric and bizarre of the great hostesses and also the most beloved. She was married when, in 1913, she met steel heir James Corrigan; he was so taken with her that he paid her current husband an immense sum of money to divorce her so that he could take Laura as his wife. He died a few years later, leaving his young widow with millions of dollars to spend on parties and balls. She moved to London and tried to infiltrate society but found its doors closed. Determined to succeed, she rented a house on Grosvenor Street from Mrs. George Keppel, former mistress to King Edward VII, on condition that Mrs. Keppel's guest list accompany the house. Once ensconced, she dispatched hundreds of invitations to dinner parties and balls; at first, London society declined. Then she brilliantly struck on the idea of offering great prizes to those who attended. Curious guests accepted and were showered with Cartier watches, gold cuff links, and uncut gemstones. Word soon spread, and thereafter society flocked to her entertainments.

Laura had gone bald and was known for her number of bizarre wigs: a stock of party wigs arranged in different styles; windswept wigs for yachting parties; rain-dampened wigs for outdoor excursions; and disheveled wigs for the unexpected appearance of sudden guests. Anyone who arrived at her door—whether an invited guest or the postman—was instantly presented with a cocktail. She once received

the Duke of Kent standing on her head. Her malapropisms were legendary: Speaking of a great cathedral she had visited, she startled her
guests by announcing, "The flying buttocks were magnificent." On
another occasion, upon returning from a trip to Turkey, she was asked
if she had seen the Dardanelles. "I did have a letter of introduction to
them," she said, "but I haven't sent it."[35]

Lady Sibyl Colefax became another important friend. From
Argyll House on King's Road, she presided over a circle of artistic
friends, which included Ivor Novello, Kenneth Clark, and John Giel-
gud. It had been Sibyl, almost single-handedly, who had promoted the
talents of Noël Coward to her society friends. The daughter of a civil
servant, she was married to Sir Arthur Colefax, a patent lawyer and a
man generally regarded as one of London's greatest bores. Chips
Channon described Lady Colefax as "obsidian or onyx—shiny and
metallic."[36] He also added that she was "garrulous, gracious and
absurd."[37] It was Sibyl, along with business partner John Fowler, who
pioneered and made popular the vogue for chintzes and the interior-
decoration style which would come to be known as English country.[38]

Syrie Maugham was another London decorator who had a profound influence on Wallis. Syrie had left her husband, author Somerset
Maugham, for his secretary and soon became renowned for her white-
on-white interior designs as well as the use of browns, beiges, and mirrors. Another woman, society florist Constance Spry, taught Wallis how
to arrange masses of banked flowers and passed along her love of all-
white floral displays.

The exotic Elsie de Wolfe, wife of Sir Charles Mendl, virtually
transformed Wallis during this period. An American who had come to
Europe, she was known for her eccentricities, which ranged from her
blue-tinted hair to her flair for memorable parties. Elsie took Wallis
under her wing. She taught her how to host a large dinner party, how
to select a guest list which ensured a successful and interesting
evening, and how to plan menus and ease conversation along. She
worked with those skills Wallis already possessed, sharpening her
innate ability to take charge of a situation and dedicate herself to
ensuring the enjoyment of others.

Lady Mendl also introduced Wallis to new fashion designers. She
advised Wallis to dress in simple gowns, with straight lines which
accentuated her boyish figure. Elsie took Wallis to Molyneux, Schiaparelli, and above all, Mainbocher. Born Main Rousseau Bocher in
Chicago, the young designer had run his first and last names together,
settled in Paris, and took up work in the couture houses there before
finally coming into his own. His clothes—angular, stark, and luxurious—suited Wallis and formed the perfect backdrop to the impressive
collection of jewels with which the Prince had begun to shower her.

Cecil Beaton, who had first encountered Wallis a few years earlier, noted that she had now changed considerably. "I liked her immensely," he wrote. "I found her bright and witty, improved in looks and chic."[39]

Perhaps the most important of these new friends was Emerald, Lady Cunard, the greatest of London's hostesses. Born in San Francisco, the former Maud Burke had married Sir Bache Cunard, grandson of the founder of the Cunard Line, after which she changed her name to the more evocative Emerald. A slight woman, she was constantly on the move through the great rooms of her mansion at the corner of Grosvenor Square. It was, in the words of Oswald Mosley, a place where one could find "the cleverest men, together with the most beautiful women."[40]

Oswald Mosley later described Lady Cunard as "a bright little bird of paradise." Her dinner parties were legendary. She orchestrated conversations like a conductor, although she herself rarely participated. Her role was to provoke discussion, and in this she had no equal. A few words, dropped in the middle of a silence at her dinner table would guarantee an entertaining and often passionate discourse.[41]

"I was constantly struck by Lady Cunard's faculty of producing, in a theatrical sense, the people who entered her orbit," said Harold Acton. "It was like the action of sunshine on a garden. Not that she could make Lytton Strachey garrulous, but whatever he said was intensely characteristic."[42]

Emerald Cunard was to have a great influence on Wallis and her life. It was at her house, for better or for worse, that Wallis was first introduced to the political topics then currently making the rounds of London intellectual society. Germany and Adolf Hitler; Mussolini and his Fascist government in Italy; and the Labour government in the United Kingdom and its leader, Ramsay MacDonald, were all topics of conversation in Lady Cunard's house. Emerald cultivated these talks and encouraged controversial, diverse opinions, welcoming powerful and influential proponents to her table. Many of them were exiled Russian aristocrats, who, understandably, saw in Hitler not a bigoted madman but a rabid anti-Communist whose expressed ambitions would save their former country.

It was Lady Cunard who first introduced Wallis to German diplomat Joachim von Ribbentrop, who had come to London as Hitler's special envoy. Emerald enjoyed these encounters with Ribbentrop and loved nothing more than watching him squirm under her relentless grilling at the dinner table. True to form, she was forthright. "What does *Herr* Hitler truly think about *God*?" she once inquired. More famously, she stopped Ribbentrop dead in his conversational tracks by asking, "We all want to know, dearest Excellency, why does Herr Hitler dislike the *Jews*?"[43]

It has frequently been reported that Ribbentrop, having met Wallis and understanding the important position which she held in the life of the heir to the throne, carefully cultivated a special relationship with her. This is said to have included his regular dispatch of long-stemmed red roses to her flat at Bryanston Court in an apparent effort to curry her favor. In fact, Ribbentrop was but one of many who sought out Wallis in these months, believing she had access to the Prince of Wales.

It has also been speculated that Wallis and Ribbentrop became lovers. This is a highly doubtful scenario. Wallis was undeniably involved with the Prince of Wales; perhaps more important, having seen an admirable demonstration of David's jealousy over the relationship of Thelma Furness with Aly Khan, she would be unlikely to risk her privileged position by having an affair with a German diplomat. Wallis herself would later recall only two meetings with Ribbentrop, although they undoubtedly attended the same social occasions from time to time.[44] But the rumors of this alleged liaison with the German diplomat so unnerved Wallis that in May 1937 she granted an interview to American journalist Helena Normanton in which she again declared that she had only met Ribbentrop twice and denied that she had in any way been used as a tool by the Nazis in London.[45]

Ribbentrop was but one of a number of Wallis's highly controversial friends and acquaintances in London. Often these friendships were initiated by the Prince himself. One such example was Sir Oswald Mosley. Mosley was a dapper man with a small mustache and a slightly receding hairline. He was head of the British Union of Fascists and had founded the New Party to combat what he perceived as the unfair unemployment policies of the Labour government. In 1932, he had founded the British Union of Fascists, an organization largely composed of ultraconservative monarchists. They, like Mosley himself, were virulently anti-Communist. The Blackshirts, as Mosley's organization came to be called, impressed a great many people in the first years of its inception. Along with Lady Cunard, supporters included the Sitwells, George Bernard Shaw, and most famously, two of the daughters of Lord and Lady Redesdale.

Mosley's first wife had been Lady Cynthia Curzon, daughter of Lord Curzon. (Cynthia's sister Alexandra was married to Fruity Metcalfe.) In 1932, when Lady Cynthia died after a short illness, Mosley received much sympathy, including a supportive message from the King and Queen.[46]

Mosley soon became romantically involved with the stunningly beautiful former Honorable Diana Mitford (daughter of Lord Redesdale), who was at the time married to the Honorable Bryan Guinness. Diana was a member of the immensely charming and talented Mitford clan, one of the most fabled aristocratic families, whose brilliant members included authors Nancy and Jessica Mitford, as well as Deborah, the present Duchess of Devonshire. Diana divorced Guinness and in 1936 she and Mosley were married in a secret ceremony which took place in the drawing room of the Berlin house of German minister of propaganda Josef Goebbels and his wife, Magda. Among other guests, Hitler attended the wedding to honor Mosley. It was through this connection that Diana's sister Unity came into the orbit of the Führer and became one of his most devoted admirers.

Wallis and the Prince were also guests in the home of the German ambassador Leopold von Hoesch, who, on Hitler's orders, lavishly entertained the pair and tried to press German interests and policies. His house in Carlton House Terrace had been completely redesigned by Nazi architect Albert Speer to impress those who walked through its doors. There has been much speculation that the Germans made overtures to the Prince through Wallis and that she became a paid conduit to ensure that Hitler's policies and proposals were given an audience with the heir to the throne. But there is no evidence that Wallis was used by these men to try to influence the Prince in any pro-German stances; in truth, she had no need to do so, because the Prince of Wales was almost completely sympathetic to the German cause.

In May 1933, Hitler had launched his campaign for German renewal. He gave a celebrated speech in which he frequently quoted from the Versailles Treaty's own tenets of national self-determination and a just peace in an effort to make his case for the rebuilding of the German state. "So great was the general gratification at Hitler's moderation that no one detected the warning contained within his speech," writes Joachim Fest. "Along with the London *Times* many influential voices throughout the world supported Hitler's demand that Germany be treated on a footing of equality with the other powers.[47]

Hitler then boldly withdrew from both the League of Nations and the Disarmament Conference. In June 1934, he consolidated his power in the Night of the Long Knives, the bloody massacre of Ernest Röhm's storm troopers. He followed this in March 1935 with a plebiscite in the Saarland, then administered by the League of Nations; the results indicated overwhelming support for incorporation into the Reich. On the strength of this vote, Hitler repudiated the arms provision of the Treaty of Versailles and reintroduced German conscription.

He was moving cautiously, step by step, carefully watching and waiting to see how each of his decisions was accepted by the rest of the world. Above all, he was concerned with British reaction. Hitler hoped to reach an understanding with England and was willing to do whatever was necessary to achieve it. He was determined not to go to war with England. Hermann Goering's second wife later recalled a remark

Hitler made at a private dinner party given for several English guests: "I am so happy because I believe that we shall come to an understanding with the English, which is what I want above anything else."[48]

Hitler was convinced that in the Prince of Wales he had found his best guarantee for British support. In June 1935, David gave a speech at the Annual Conference of the British Legion. He declared that the best way to ensure the future peace of the world was for the British veterans of the Great War to "stretch forth the hand of friendship to the Germans." Afterward, public opinion had it that this speech was "the seal of the friendship agreement between the two countries."[49] But the reaction was far from favorable. In a memo to the U.S. State Department, Ambassador William E. Dodd wrote: "It is difficult to conceive of any announcement better calculated to appeal to the prevalent German conception than the announcement by the Prince of Wales. ... Hardly had the news been published in Berlin than statements in support were elicited from Goering, Hess, and Ribbentrop. All the press, on June 12th, seized up the statements of the Prince of Wales with the greatest avidity."[50]

King George V was livid when he learned of the speech. Not only had the Prince failed to seek prior authorization from the Foreign Office for what he undoubtedly knew were controversial remarks, but he had willfully crossed the line separating the Royal Family from political questions. Although his son's speech was not very different from his own personal views, the King warned the Prince that he was never to discuss political questions again.

But David, having witnessed firsthand the destruction of war and the random loss of life among the men who formed the fighting ranks, was determined to do all he could to prevent such carnage again. His sensibilities hinged far more on this desire to maintain the peace and not on any real support for Hitler, even if he did see—as did many others—a welcome opportunity to finally stop the Communist threat. But to Hitler the Prince's remarks had indicated something more: He was utterly convinced that here, at least, was one man who would prove pliable when it came to reaching an understanding with Germany. Such delusions were to play havoc forever with the reputations of both the Duke and Duchess of Windsor.

12

The Passing of the King

In May 1935, King George V celebrated his silver jubilee, marking twenty-five years on the British throne. The Prince of Wales was desperate to include Wallis on the guest lists for official functions. So great was this desire that he sought out an audience with his father and raised the subject of invitations for the Simpsons himself. At first, the old King was adamant, declaring that he could not possibly invite his son's mistress to any official affairs. But David would not be put off so easily. He insisted that relations between himself and Wallis were absolutely proper. Unwilling to argue the point, George V relented.

Hearing of this decision, the King's private secretary, Clive, Lord Wigram, wrote that he himself had learned of Mrs. Simpson's adultery with the Prince from members of the staff at Fort Belvedere. "Apart from actually seeing H.R.H. and Mrs. S. in bed together," he declared, "they had positive proof that H.R.H. lived with her."[1] But Wigram could do little; the King had agreed, and the invitation was duly dispatched.

The Jubilee Ball took place at Buckingham Palace on May 14. Wallis and Ernest joined the other well-turned-out guests as they ascended the grand staircase to the state apartments. By tradition, the Prince of Wales opened the ball by dancing with his mother. As soon as this dance had come to an end, however, he quickly sought out Wallis and led her to the middle of the ballroom. They waltzed past the enthroned King and Queen, sitting silent and curious on the crimson dais at one end of the room. As they danced, the magnificent diamond clips on Wallis's gown—a gift from David—sparkled in the soft light. "I thought I felt the King's eyes rest searchingly on me," Wallis recalled. "Something in his look made me feel that all this graciousness and pageantry were but the glittering tip of an iceberg that extended down into unseen depths I could never plumb, depths filled with an icy menace for such as me. . . . In that moment I knew that between David's world and mine lay an abyss that I could never cross, one he could never bridge for me."[2]

Like a besotted schoolboy, David was determined to show off Wallis to his family and friends. He cornered his cousin Prince Christopher of Greece, saying, "I want you to meet Mrs. Simpson."

"Mrs. Simpson, who is she?" Christopher asked.

"An American," David said with a wide smile. "She's wonderful." The impression was immediate. "Those two words," Christopher recalled, "told me everything. It was as though he had said: 'She is the only woman in the world.'" After meeting Wallis and observing his cousin, Christopher knew without a doubt that the Prince of Wales was lost to Thelma. "He was in love as it is given to men and women to love only once in a lifetime," he said.[3]

The closer David drew to Wallis, the more alienated he became from his family. One of the great myths of the abdication crisis, however, is that the then king, Edward VIII, sprang Wallis on a completely unsuspecting Royal Family, which was suddenly confronted with what they considered a highly unsuitable relationship. The truth is that not only was the Royal Family aware of Wallis and her position for several years before the abdication but that there was much talk among themselves and with officials concerning the possible outcome of the relationship.

King George V, though rarely a man to share his private thoughts, spoke at length with Cosmo Lang, the Archbishop of Canterbury, in the spring of 1935 about his eldest son's liaison. One of Queen Mary's ladies-in-waiting, Mabell, Lady Airlie, also confided to the Archbishop that the Prince's mother had discussed the affair with her. "I said," Lady Airlie told Lang, "that the Prince had had previous friendships, like most young men, especially those who had grown up during the war years."

"That is what I told His Majesty," the Archbishop answered. "But he believes that this affair is much more serious than the others. That is what worries him."[4]

The Royal Family came to view Wallis as an adventuress. They believed that she dominated David, acted purposely to keep him away from his family and old friends, and deliberately schemed for power and prestige. That she was also an American—and, by extension, unfamiliar with the traditional role of a mistress—was a source of constant worry. Freda Dudley Ward, for instance, had known better than to appear with David in public or covered with his expensive gifts of jewelry; Wallis, on the other hand, seemed to positively delight in her newfound fame. The family could not see beyond these limited views and refused to believe that Wallis's influence was anything but pernicious. By blaming Wallis for David's own actions, they ignored his own streak of stubborn determination, a characteristic which was becoming increasingly obvious.

Wallis's meetings with members of the Royal Family had been, with the exception of Prince George and his wife, Marina, rather infrequent and, in the case of David's parents, formal. She had met the Duke and Duchess of York from time to time, usually at the Fort; at first, relations had been casual, and Bertie and Elizabeth had treated Wallis in the same accepting and jovial fashion in which they had welcomed Thelma Furness. But the deeper David's relationship with Wallis became, the colder their thoughts and actions toward his mistress.

An incident early in 1935 did little to endear Wallis to the Duchess. One day, as Wallis stood in the drawing room of the Fort, she decided to entertain the guests gathered there with a mocking rendition of the high-pitched, clipped voice of the Duchess of York. She was in the midst of this comedic impersonation when suddenly the faces before her went blank. She turned around, only to discover the real Duchess standing silently in the doorway, staring at her. Before Wallis could say a word, Elizabeth turned on her heels and left the Fort.[5]

If the incident described actually took place, it is doubtful that Wallis was acting maliciously. Unfortunately, her biting sense of humor often expressed itself in the most inopportune ways and at the worst possible times. No matter her intention, she succeeded not only in making her room of guests laugh but also in making of the Duchess of York her implacable enemy. Not that Elizabeth herself was above such behavior. "Mrs. Simpson did not go down well with the Duchess of York," writes Anne Morrow, "who to this day makes jokes at her expense, doing her excellent imitation of an American accent."[6]

The Royal Family refused to recognize the favorable effect of Wallis's influence on David. He was a changed man with Wallis around, happier than he had ever been before. Winston Churchill wrote: "He delighted in her company, and found in her qualities as necessary to his happiness as the air he breathed. Those who knew him well and watched him closely noticed that many little tricks and fidgetings of nervousness fell away from him. He was a completed being instead of a sick and harassed soul. This experience which happens to a great many people in the flower of their youth came late in life to him, and was all the more precious and compulsive for that fact."[7] And Chips Channon recorded: "Mrs. Simpson has enormously improved the Prince."[8]

Caught in the middle and unable and unwilling to make a choice, Wallis quickly found herself under considerable strain. Increasingly, Ernest absented himself completely, preferring business trips to America to weekends at the Fort. For a year, Wallis had sincerely believed—

and repeatedly reassured Ernest—that their marriage was in no danger because of her relationship with the Prince; now, for the first time, she came to accept the possibility that by pursuing whatever brief happiness she might have with the heir to the throne at the expense of her bond with Ernest, she might lose both men. And yet, propelled by her taste for these royal holidays, ceremonial occasions, showers of jewels, and it must be said, by a steadily growing feeling of love for David, she plunged ahead into the unknown.

That summer, the Prince of Wales decided to go to Cannes for his holiday. Although he issued an invitation to both the Simpsons, Ernest conveniently excused himself by saying that he had to conduct business in America. David rented a villa from the Marquess of Cholmondeley and, accompanied by Wallis, Lord Perry and Lady Brownlow, Helen Fitzgerald, Lord Sefton, the Buists, and John Aird, set off for the South of France. They managed to commandeer the Duke of Westminster's yacht *Cutty Sark* for a cruise to Corsica, followed by another cruise on a yacht belonging to Daisy Fellowes, which took them along the coast, stopping at secluded coves and small resorts, where they dined ashore each evening.

David again wished to visit Vienna and Budapest, and so the royal party made a detour from Cannes to Austria and Hungary. Before returning to England, they spent four days in the remote Alpine village of St. Wolfgang, near Salzburg. Later, the Prince would commemorate this brief stay with gifts of jewelry, and it seems likely— whether or not he discussed the idea with Wallis—that it was during the visit to St. Wolfgang that he firmly made up his mind that he would one day marry Wallis. "The hope formed," he later wrote, "that one day I might be able to share my life with her. . . . It was all quite vague but none the less vivid, the dream of being able to bring into my life what for so long had been lacking, without which my service to the State would seem an empty thing. . . . I could not discount the possibility of having to withdraw altogether from the line of succession if my hope were ever to be fulfilled. However, I took comfort from the fact that my brother Bertie, to whom the succession would pass, was in outlook and temperament very like my father. . . ."[9] If nothing else, this seems to indicate that David had thought of abdication, even before the beginning of his reign, as a possible solution to the alternative of life without Wallis.

He would later confide to Walter Monckton that his decision to marry Wallis had indeed been reached during this trip. "To him," Monckton wrote, "she was the perfect woman. She insisted that he should be at his best and do his best at all times, and he regarded her as his inspiration. It is a great mistake to assume that he was merely in love with her in the ordinary physical sense of the term. There was an intellectual companionship, and there is no doubt that his lonely nature found in her a spiritual comradeship. . . . He felt that he and Mrs. Simpson were made for one another and there was no other honest way of meeting the situation than marrying her. The easy view is that she should have made him give her up. But I never knew any man whom it would have been harder to get rid of."[10]

When Wallis returned to London in early October, Ernest was still in New York. "I had the feeling that more than business was now drawing him back to America," Wallis wrote. "We were both going our separate ways; the core of our marriage had dissolved; only a shell remained—a façade to show the outer world."[11] The marriage was indeed over in all but name. During this trip, Ernest had an affair with Wallis's friend Mary Kirk Raffray; whether he told Wallis of this or not upon his return is not known.

"Though nothing about Mrs. Simpson appears in the English papers," wrote Cecil Beaton in the autumn of 1935, "her name seems never to be off people's lips. For those who enjoy gossip she is a particular treat. The sound of her name implies secrecy, royalty, and being in the know. As a topic she has become a mania, so much so that her name is banned in many houses to allow breathing space for other topics."[12] The one exception to this came in November, when Paris dressmakers named Wallis one of the twenty best-dressed women in the world. The accompanying story cautiously noted that she was "often seen with the Prince of Wales."[13]

David continued to shower Wallis with jewels, often engraved with little messages of love and marked by their joint initials, WE. After one evening at the Fort, Diana Cooper telephoned Chips Channon and promptly reported, "Mrs. Simpson was glittering, and dripped in new jewels and clothes."[14] This jewel collection caused a riot of interest among these social circles. Marie Belloc Lowndes recalled one weekend house party given by Sir Philip Sassoon at Trent Park in January 1936. She was sitting with the rest of the party in the drawing room when Mr. and Mrs. Simpson were announced. "Most of the people . . . did not know them and we all felt a very real sense of thrill, of interest and of curiosity. I was at once impressed by Mrs. Simpson's perfect figure. She was of medium height, and beautifully dressed in the French way, that is, very unobtrusively. I did not think her in the least pretty. She was very much made up with what I would call a Red Indian colouring, that is, yellow and brick-red. Her hair appeared at night very dark, and was cut much shorter than was just then the fashion among Englishwomen. She had an intelligent but in no sense remarkable face." At dinner, Marie was placed next to Ernest and across the table from Wallis. On Wallis's ensemble, she reported: "She was wearing a plain dress, high at the throat, but with bare arms.

She wore a very great deal of jewelry, which I thought must be what is called 'dressmaker's' jewels, so large were the emeralds in her bracelets and so striking and peculiar a necklace." After the party had broken up and the Simpsons left, Mrs. Lowndes sat talking with some of the other guests. She commented that Mrs. Simpson had surprised her by wearing so many obviously fake jewels. "At that," she remembered, "they all screamed with laughter, explaining that all the jewels were real, that the then Prince of Wales had given her fifty thousand pounds' worth at Christmas, following it up with sixty thousand pounds' worth of jewels a week later at the New Year."[15]

January 1936 was exceptionally cold in England. For several months, snow had swept across the land. At Sandringham in Norfolk, the King, during his usual Christmas holiday stay, had gone out shooting and caught a chill. Within a few days, undoubtedly aggravated by his incessant smoking, it had developed into bronchitis. Greatly weakened, the frail monarch took to his bed.

The last months of 1935 had not been kind to the King. His health, already uncertain, caused endless worry, and his thoughts repeatedly turned to his heir. On November 6, his third son, Prince Harry, Duke of Gloucester, had married Lady Alice Montagu-Douglas-Scott, a daughter of the recently deceased Duke of Buccleuch. "Now all the children are married but David," the old King noted ominously in his diary.[16]

Occasionally, he expressed his doubts as to his eldest son's capabilities. "When I am dead, the boy will ruin himself in twelve months," he predicted to the new prime minister, Stanley Baldwin. And, more famously, speaking of his second son, the Duke of York, and *his* eldest daughter, Elizabeth, he declared, "I pray to God that my eldest son will never marry and have children, and that nothing will come between Bertie and Lilibet and the Throne."[17] Such hesitation, later taken as a signal of the King's distress over his son's affair with Wallis, seems in actuality to have reflected more a growing apprehension at David's capacity to deal with the throne's many burdens than with his personal life. At this point, no one—least of all George V—had any idea that the Prince of Wales would even consider the idea of attempting to marry his mistress.

There has been much speculation that David intended to flee England before his accession and take Wallis with him. Several historians have discussed this theory. Two days after the abdication, Lascelles told Harold Nicolson that "from 'internal evidence' they suspect that he had decided to run away with Mrs. Simpson before the King died. They were to do a bunk in February."[18]

The problem with this theory is that David could certainly not have run away with Wallis in February 1936 to marry her. First, she was not free to remarry; indeed, no mention had been made of divorce proceedings. All reliable sources agree that the issue of divorce was first raised and discussed after the King's accession to the throne. Wallis herself, whatever she may or may not have privately discussed, as yet had made no move to divorce Ernest. Because of this, any decision she might have made to flee with David would have been provable adultery and collusion in any divorce case according to British law. All indications show that this scenario was carefully avoided six months later, and there is no reason to believe that such considerations would not have been equally valid in the fall of 1935. Above all, from what is known of David and his love for Wallis, he would not have wished to have her if she had to disgrace herself publicly.

One January afternoon, as Wallis stood in the drawing room of the Fort, a footman announced a message for the Prince from Sandringham. When he reappeared, he clutched in his hand a cable informing him that his father was very ill. Without a word, he handed it to Wallis and immediately rang his private pilot to arrange for an airplane to fly him to Norfolk.[19] The following day, Wallis was back at Bryanston Court when she received a telephone call from David. When he had arrived that day at Sandringham, Norfolk, he had quickly been informed that his father had no more than a few days left to live.

The situation at Sandringham was grim. When David entered his father's room, he found the King sitting by a blazing fire, wrapped in a dressing gown, barely able to recognize him. Over the next few days, Lord Wigram, the King's private secretary, held discussions with the Prince of Wales and his brother the Duke of York in which ownership of Sandringham and Balmoral was discussed. Queen Mary was also greatly worried over the distribution of the royal jewels in the King's will. She confided to Wigram that she was dividing up the jewels of the King's sister Victoria, who had died a month before, among the Duchesses of York, Kent, and Gloucester, fearing that her eldest son would somehow manage to get hold of them and that he "might pass them on to Mrs. Simpson."[20]

On Monday afternoon, January 20, Lord Dawson of Penn, the King's physician, declared that the King had but a few hours to live. A coffin was ordered, Wigram began to make arrangements for the funeral ceremonies, and the entire Royal Family, led by the Prince of Wales, gathered in the King's bedroom to await the end. Lord Dawson, who had the responsibility of issuing bulletins with proper times attached, kept entering and leaving the sickroom; all of the clocks in the house were set to Sandringham time, a half hour ahead of regular time—an invention originally intended to create more daylight hours for shooting. David was irritated at this constant interruption, which resulted in several mistakes concerning his father's decline. Finally, when he had had enough, he stormed out of the bedroom, muttering angrily, "I'll fix those bloody clocks."[21] He immediately ordered all of the clocks at Sandringham set to the proper time, an act which many took as callous indifference to his father, but which he meant with no disrespect.

But the King lingered on, contrary to Dawson's expectations, and seeing that his coma might last for hours or even days, the doctor decided to end his patient's life with an injection of morphine and cocaine. Queen Mary declared that she had no wish to prolong her husband's life, and Dawson pointed out that if the King should die before midnight, his death would then first be reported in the "quality" newspapers; if he happened to die after this, in the middle of the night, it would first be published in less reliable journals. With such media concerns, the lethal dose was administered, and the King was pronounced dead at 11:55 P.M.[22]

Previously, Wallis had accepted an invitation that Monday to attend a charity cinema premiere, and despite the crisis, she felt honor-bound to make an appearance. The showing of the film, however, was interrupted dramatically at half-past nine that evening when the manager appeared to read a bulletin which Lord Dawson had just issued: "The King's life is moving peacefully toward its close." The audience rose, sang "God Save the King," and disappeared into the night.[23]

Wallis had returned to a late dinner with her friends the Lawson-Johnstons after the cinema; just after midnight, the telephone rang. After a few words, the butler summoned her to the receiver, saying that the call came from Sandringham. In a few words, she learned the shattering news from David. "I am so very sorry" was all she could say. He quickly told her that he would return to London the following morning and telephone her as soon as he could. "It was only as I hung up," she recalled, "that I realized that David was now King."[24]

Alice Montague Warfield with her daughter, Wallis, the future Duchess of Windsor, 1896

Baby Wallis, about one year old URBAN ARCHIVES, TEMPLE UNIVERSITY, PHILADELPHIA, PENNSYLVANIA

Aunt Bessie Merryman and Wallis about 1905 URBAN ARCHIVES, TEMPLE UNIVERSITY, PHILADELPHIA, PENNSYLVANIA

The future Duchess at age ten CORBIS/UPI

Wallis Warfield, left, with her cousin Anita Warfield and her uncle Solomon Davies Warfield, 1907 URBAN ARCHIVES, TEMPLE UNIVERSITY, PHILADELPHIA, PENNSYLVANIA

Nineteen-year-old Wallis Warfield as a Baltimore debutante   CORBIS/UPI

Wallis with her first husband, Lieutenant Win Spencer, at the Mexican border, July 1918   URBAN ARCHIVES, TEMPLE UNIVERSITY, PHILADELPHIA, PENNSYLVANIA

Wallis, San Diego, about 1920 UNDERWOOD & UNDERWOOD/CORBIS

Wallis with her second husband, Ernest Simpson, and her aunt Bessie Merryman, on holiday at Baden-Baden in Germany, 1930 URBAN ARCHIVES, TEMPLE UNIVERSITY, PHILADELPHIA, PENNSYLVANIA

Wallis and her aunt
Bessie Merryman,
on holiday in
Europe, about 1930
URBAN ARCHIVES,
TEMPLE UNIVERSITY,
PHILADELPHIA,
PENNSYLVANIA

Queen Victoria,
with her son the
Prince of Wales (the
future King Edward
VII), his daughter
Princess Victoria of
Wales, and his
grandson, Prince
Edward of York
(David, the future
King Edward VIII
and the Duke of
Windsor), Balmoral,
1898 URBAN
ARCHIVES, TEMPLE
UNIVERSITY,
PHILADELPHIA,
PENNSYLVANIA

Mary (May), the Princess of Wales and future queen, with her eldest son, David, at Abergeldie Castle in Scotland, August 1903 URBAN ARCHIVES, TEMPLE UNIVERSITY, PHILADELPHIA, PENNSYLVANIA

(*Below*) The visit of the Russian Imperial Family to the British Royal Family, Cowes, August, 4, 1909. *Standing, left to right*: David; Queen Alexandra; Princess Mary of Wales; Princess Victoria (daughter of King Edward VII and Queen Alexandra); Grand Duchess Olga Nicholaievna; and Grand Duchess Tatiana Nicholaievna. *Seated, left to right*: the Princess of Wales (Mary); Tsar Nicholas II; King Edward VII; Empress Alexandra Feodorovna; the Prince of Wales (the future King George V); and Grand Duchess Marie Nicholaievna. *Seated on the carpet in front* are Tsarevich Alexei Nicholaievich and his sister Grand Duchess Anastasia Nicholaievna.
URBAN ARCHIVES, TEMPLE UNIVERSITY, PHILADELPHIA, PENNSYLVANIA

David as Prince of Wales,
about 1912

David's parents, King
George V and Queen Mary,
about 1911

13

The New Reign

THE NEXT DAY, the King's Accession Council met at St. James's Palace in London. Many of those who gathered—even at this early hour in the new King's reign—were filled with growing doubts. Clement Attlee recalled: "As a Privy Councillor I attended the meeting in St. James's Palace of the Accession Council. . . . I thought King Edward looked very nervous and ill-at-ease. I remember Baldwin expressing to me his anxiety for the future and his doubts as to whether the new King would stay the course."[1]

As soon as he had returned to his own apartments at York House within the palace, David telephoned Wallis. Although he sounded tired, he asked if she would like to attend his proclamation by the Garter King-of-Arms at St. James's Palace; when she agreed, he said he would dispatch a car to collect her.[2]

The proclamation took place in Friary Court at St. James's Palace. Four state trumpeters, dressed in tabards covered with gold lace, slowly walked onto the low balcony, followed by sergeants at arms holding aloft their gold maces. A fanfare of trumpets announced the Garter King, Sir Gerald Wollaston, along with the heralds and pursuivants, dressed in flashing gold braid and scarlet uniforms. Wollaston stepped to the edge of the balcony and proclaimed the accession of King Edward VIII.[3] Wallis stood shielded behind a window, watching, when the door to the room opened and the King appeared. Everyone bowed or curtsied, Wallis included, as he swept in. He turned to his private secretary, Godfrey Thomas, and declared, "This may strike you as somewhat unusual, but the thought came to me that I'd like to see myself proclaimed King."[4] As he and Wallis stood together at the window, newsreel cameras captured their staring faces, flashing them around the world.

When the ceremony had ended, the regimental band in the courtyard struck up "God Save the King"; Wallis stood by the window, crying softly. Suddenly, she seemed to have grasped the immensity of the change occurring. Turning to David, she whispered that she understood that from now on things would be different.[5] But he only smiled and assured her that nothing could change his feelings toward her.[6] She left the palace in a large black car which belonged to the King, its blinds pulled half down. Chips Channon, who was also watching, saw the gathered crowd bowing, under the impression that it carried the Duchess of Kent.[7]

That afternoon, David disappeared to attend the reading of his father's will. This proved a less than pleasurable experience. To his amazement, he had not been included in George V's will; every few sentences, he interrupted the late King's solicitor, Sir Halsey Bircham, saying, "Where do I come in?" It was left to Lord Wigram to explain that although he inherited a life tenancy in Balmoral and Sandringham, he had not been left any sum because the late King had assumed that, as Prince of Wales, he would have saved a substantial amount of his income from the Duchy of Cornwall, estimated at upward of a million pounds a year. In truth, he was far from poor, with revenues from lands and estates, but he was haunted by the thought that he had little cash. In addition, he had just inherited hundreds of officials and staff, along with their pensions, yearly gifts, and other expenses. Although his reaction could be understood, his vehemence did not sit well with members of his father's court.[8]

As she had feared, Wallis saw little of David over the next few days. She watched as he led the mourners in his father's funeral procession, a long, grim line of soldiers and carriages passing through the London streets. Anne Morrow Lindbergh, wife of the famous aviator, recalled the "black and purple banners marking the route of the procession. . . . The draped shop windows, the flags at half-mast, everyone in black on the street. . . . The bands in the distance, the different regiments. . . . It seemed very quiet—just that slow moving line of men in somber colours and the muffled drums. . . . The sound of pipers— unmistakable and rather eerie—in the distance and then, with a startling suddenness, below us around the corner those even lines of sailors, white collars all in line and the white ropes, taut like a woven pattern. . . . They pulled evenly that little bare gun carriage—the coffin, terribly small, covered in the rich gold of the flag."[9] The new King and his brothers followed the coffin toward Westminster Hall, the imperial state crown, orb, and scepter balanced gingerly atop its lid as it rumbled through the streets. Suddenly, the jeweled Maltese cross atop the imperial state crown tumbled loose and fell into the gutter, from where it was quickly retrieved. David saw the glint out of the corner of his eye. "Christ! What's going to happen next?" he muttered loudly. "That," MP Walter Elliot noted, "will be the motto of the new reign."[10]

While Wallis remained secluded at Bryanston Court, David was busy moving his offices into Buckingham Palace. He continued to live at York House, however, for the foreseeable future, not wishing to dislodge his mother from her apartments at the palace. Everything temporarily remained as it had been under his father. A slight air of formality was introduced at the Fort once David was able to return; the moment he set foot inside, the royal standard was raised over the turret, but this was the only outward sign that his position had changed.[11]

King Edward VIII acceded to the throne with a range of expectation and goodwill that was almost unprecedented. As Prince of Wales, he had attracted much favorable press and was the most famous and idolized young man of the age. He had admirably shown his courage in war and in sport and tirelessly dedicated himself to his future subjects. He was largely adored throughout the empire for his fresh approach and open character and promised to be a different sort of monarch than was his father. At forty-one, he looked at least ten years younger, and his youth and vigor seemed to hint at the exciting possibilities opening to the world.

Other opinion, however, was divided. Sir Samuel Hoare wrote that the King's "fatal weakness, more serious than his personal affections, was that he did not like being King. The ritual and tradition of a historic office made no appeal to him. . . . Even without the affair of the marriage, whilst I hoped against hope that the interests of a King's life would gradually reconcile him to kingship, I doubted whether he would ever like the part sufficiently to make a success of it."[12]

David spoke frankly to his friend Walter Monckton of the new duties which accompanied the throne. While he intended, he said, to conduct all royal business expected of him, he considered that his private life was utterly private. What went on behind the walls of Buckingham Palace or Fort Belvedere was no one's concern but his. "He never spoke to me of any doubt or hesitation about accepting his position as King," Monckton recalled. "It was only later on in the year, when the controversy was upon him, that he would sometimes say that if they were wanting someone exactly reproducing his father, there was the Duke of York."[13]

He clearly felt constricted by some of the trappings and expectations with which he was now surrounded. "Being a Monarch," he later wrote, "whether man or woman in these egalitarian times can surely be one of the most confining, the most frustrating, and over the duller stretches, the least stimulating jobs open to an educated, independent-minded person. Even a saint would on occasion find himself driven to exasperation by the taboos which invisibly and silently envelop a constitutional monarchy."[14]

David later refuted the suggestion that he had not wanted the throne. Left to his own choice and without his birthright, he explained, it is true he might well have chosen some other field of activity for his work. "But not to wish to be King was something else. Only my death or some precipitous action on my part could have prevented my becoming King when my father died. Now that he was dead I *was* the King. And what was more, I wanted to be a successful King, but a King in a modern way."[15]

Wallis was to insist that David had been filled with plans to modernize the monarchy. "This was extremely important to him, and he talked about little else." But, Wallis thought, certain members of the court felt quite differently, and she noted the "cold, serried resentment" that was rippling beneath the surface.[16]

His plans were not quite as radical as some have suggested. "I brought to the Throne," he later wrote, "no ambitious blueprints for reform—no Royal counter-parts of the Five-Year-Plan. I had no desire to go down in history as Edward the reformer." His intention was "to throw open the windows a little and to let into the venerable institution some of the fresh air that I had become accustomed to breathe as Prince of Wales. My modest ambition was to broaden the base of the Monarchy a little: to make it a little more responsive to the changed circumstances of my times."[17]

Since the abdication, speculation has thrived as to what sort of King Edward VIII would have made had he remained on the throne. The popular view that in leaving he did Britain and the world the greatest favor is rather too simplistic to be accepted. During his reign as king he was to carry out rather successfully a majority of those duties expected of him. He had always tried to make himself useful, to use his position as Prince of Wales for the greater good of the country and empire, even if his concerns—unemployment, housing for the poor, rehabilitation of wounded soldiers—seemed a touch too controversial for officials in his father's court. He was certainly not lazy and had proved himself, in his years of service as Prince of Wales, capable of exhausting engagements. As Frances Donaldson writes: "It may be true that he had no taste for paper work and could never have spent the necessary hours . . . but surely some means could have been found to alter the procedure so that he was presented with precis of only the most important documents. . . . Surely in different circumstances it would not have been beyond the wits of Edward VIII's secretaries to supplement his good qualities and overcome his bad."[18]

But of those who surrounded the new King, few could be regarded as supporters, and several had even expressed outright disloyalty to him. The most important official was his private secretary, a post occupied by Lord Wigram. Wigram had served George V as private secretary for many years and had agreed to stay on in his post until the new King could replace him. The private secretary was a privileged position, the most senior ranking official in the King's staff. It was he who directed the flow of papers between the King and Whitehall and kept track of all correspondence related to the business of government. He also presented opinions and frequently acted as intermediary between monarch and those who sought to influence the throne. Wigram was sixty-three when David became king. A man of traditional ideas and conservative tastes, Wigram was firmly convinced that the new king was headed for disaster.

Within a few months, Wigram had had enough and tendered his resignation. The obvious candidate to replace him was Godfrey Thomas, who had served as private secretary to the Prince of Wales. But Thomas felt unequal to the task, and David appointed Maj. Alexander Hardinge.

Hardinge was a rather humorless sort of man, the product of a proud and noble family. His great-grandfather had been the governor-general of India, and his father was first Lord Hardinge of Penshurst. In 1921, Hardinge had joined the royal household, and eventually he became an assistant private secretary to George V. With Hardinge, tradition was everything; he had no tolerance for innovation. Although he was the same age as David, they seemed worlds apart. A few months before Edward VIII came to the throne, Chips Channon wrote: "Emerald told us how she had lunched today with Alec Hardinge who, though quite young, has already taken on the Court 'colour.' He very much criticized the Prince of Wales and his entourage. It is high time such dreary narrow-minded fogies were sacked, as, indeed, they will be, in the next reign."[19]

Thus, there can be little doubt that Hardinge, from the beginning, took a dim view of his new master. He and his wife, Helen, were also outraged over David's affair with Wallis. "We did not *seek* her company, ourselves," Helen Hardinge later recalled.[20]

Godfrey Thomas decided that he wished to share his duties as assistant private secretary. David reluctantly asked Alan "Tommy" Lascelles to act as fellow assistant private secretary. Since leaving the service of the Prince of Wales in 1929, Lascelles had taken several years off from royal service, only rejoining the royal household at the request of King George V the year before.

Lascelles, who would remain in royal service for many years after the abdication, is usually remembered as a valuable courtier, with great knowledge of his duties and unswerving loyalty to the throne. But in his relationship with King Edward VIII his role and tactics were nothing short of Machiavellian. He almost certainly feared for the continued stability of the throne, but in his quest to preserve the monarchy, he was increasingly disloyal to the monarch. Many of the sentiments he expressed bordered on treason. In August 1927, when he was still the Prince's assistant private secretary, he asked for an interview with Prime Minister Stanley Baldwin. He told Baldwin that in his opinion "the Heir Apparent, in his unbridled pursuit of wine and women, and whatever selfish whim occupied him at the moment, was rapidly going to the devil, and unless he mended his ways, would soon become no fit wearer of the British Crown." When Baldwin agreed with him, Lascelles added that when the Prince was riding in his point-to-point races, he "couldn't help thinking that the best thing that could happen to him, and to the country, would be for him to break his neck." Baldwin's reply was equally startling: "God forgive me, I have often thought the same thing."[21]

The King also asked Rowland Thomas Baring, second Earl of Cromer, to remain in his position as Lord Chamberlain. The Earl of Crawford recorded in his diary: "Cromer did not quite take it as a compliment; for he knows that war was in effect declared against the old gang; but it is possible that H. M. is beginning to realize the paucity and meagreness of his own entourage—perhaps he now sees how small is their fund of experience and *savoir-faire*—hence a reaction in favour of King George's staff."[22]

The older aristocracy that filled the ranks of Court officials had never been terribly fond of the new King. Even in his days as Prince of Wales he had seemed too liberal, too impatient to suit their tastes. In truth, there was little danger that David would do any serious damage to the British throne or its traditions. He believed in the idea of the monarchy, supported by a privileged aristocracy. To these men, however, the King's determination to reform the monarchy and the court seemed to threaten their very way of life.

There were dramatic, if somewhat harmless, instances of the King's desire to break with the past. With each reign, royal coins depicting the new monarch's profile were minted; it was tradition that with each reign the monarch face in the opposite direction from his or her predecessor. George V had been depicted in left profile, and so, according to custom, Edward VIII should be seen from the right. But David, who had to sit for both left- and right-profile portraits, disliked his right profile so much that he insisted that Sir Robert Johnson, the deputy master of the Royal Mint, alter tradition and depict him in left profile on the coins and stamps.

Another of his first acts as king provoked untold resentment. He instituted a 10 percent wage cut for all of those in the royal household and staff. This simply seemed further indication of David's parsimony, and most suspected that it had been done in order that he could shower his mistress with even more luxurious jewels. In fact, as

Michael Bloch points out, British civil servants had been required to take a similiar cut in pay due to the depression four years earlier, and David was now simply trying to bring the royal household in line with other official institutions.[23] This was standard practice at the beginning of each new reign. "He was doing no more than follow precedent," wrote Marguerite Peacocke, "for both his father and grandfather had taken advantage of the opportunity afforded by a new reign for a certain amount of reform."[24]

David's day was now filled with duties. He had a steady stream of ceremonies, inspections, visits, and appointments, along with his daily job of "doing the Boxes," the specially locked red-leather cases filled with Foreign Office dispatches, ministerial reports, telegrams, and empire communications, all of which he had to read, understand, approve, and sign. One of the boxes contained the secret minutes of the cabinet meetings, to keep him updated on all that was happening with the government. The King also automatically became the admiral of the fleet as well as field marshal of the army and marshal of the Royal Air Force, each of which required specific duties. In addition, he had his own household and staff to supervise, with its administrative detail, along with the complexities of the court and the management of the royal estates.

Perhaps no one was more uncomfortable with the new King than his prime minister, Stanley Baldwin. Baldwin's father had been chairman of the Great Western Railway and head of Baldwins, Ltd., an iron-and-steel works. He had also served as a member of Parliament, and his son succeeded him in all three endeavors. Baldwin entered civil service as private parliamentary secretary to Andrew Bonar Law; when Bonar Law retired in 1923 owing to illness, King George V selected Baldwin as his successor over fellow Conservative Lord Curzon. His first term as prime minister lasted less than a year, and he was replaced by the Labour government of Ramsay MacDonald. Baldwin returned in 1924 with a tremendous majority, struggled through the general strike of 1926, ran for reelection in 1929, and lost. By 1935 he was back again as prime minister.

At the time Edward VIII acceded to the throne, Baldwin was seventy years old, tired, and nearing the end of his political career. His critics thought him humorless and without personality, and Baldwin himself took pride in his traditional views and unobtrusive character. Such a man was undoubtedly destined to clash sooner or later with Edward VIII, and Baldwin had the additional difficulties of being high-strung, nervous, and suspicious. "Within him storms a chaos," his secretary once declared.[25] Those who knew him well agreed that he had little sense of proportion and a diminished ability to deal with stress.

"Every burden becomes a nightmare," his secretary noted.[26] At the beginning of the new reign, he was close to a nervous breakdown, and his doctors insisted that he take a rest for several months.

Together, these two men—king and prime minister—would face growing international pressures. Edward VIII has often been accused of harboring Fascist tendencies, but in this he was largely in accord with the mood of his subjects at the time of his accession. Even with the increasing tensions surrounding Italian and German aggression in Europe, few supported active intervention. Isolationist policies, along with a growing call for disarmament, had even led Baldwin to deliberately ignore the European question in his political campaign of a year before. He later admitted that had he raised the issue of preparing England for a possible European confrontation, the mood of the voters was such that he would undoubtedly have lost the election.

Nor were the new King's views too terribly different from those of his father. In 1935, Italy had invaded Abyssinia. George V was not prepared to confront Mussolini and vehemently declared: "I will not have another war. *I will not.* The last one was none of my doing and if there is another one and we are threatened with being brought into it, I will go to Trafalgar Square and wave a red flag myself sooner than allow this country to be brought in."[27]

It was to be Edward VIII's dealings with Nazi Germany which were to cause so much controversy and be the subject of later accusations of treachery. His German heritage played a natural part in his sympathies, as did his fear of the spread of communism. But there was also a very real admiration for what Hitler had managed to accomplish as well as his expressed aims. Hitler had managed to restore in large measure the respect which Germany had lost in the years following the Treaty of Versailles. Through his national socialist programs, unemployment had been reduced, youth and sports festivals were shaping a future generation of leaders, and government-sponsored works were constructing autobahns and an admirable infrastructure. The Nazi agenda still professed respect for borders and the sovereignty of other nations, and Hitler repeatedly denied that Germany sought anything more than her due. The King was attracted to this orderly regime and the manner in which Hitler had succeeded against such vast odds. As yet there was but little hint of the brutal horrors still to come.

Such views as the King possessed toward Nazi Germany were largely shared by many others. Baldwin's government, through the Foreign Office, was quietly pursuing warmer relations with Berlin, and many influential members of the government and the aristocracy—faced with an efficient German Fascist state, which continually sought improved relations with the United Kingdom, and Communist Russia, which appeared to threaten the world order—clearly sided with the Nazis. Historian Sir John Wheeler-Bennett has rightfully termed these "the 'respectable years' of the Nazi Revolution, and Hitler took full advantage of them. He indulged in no more outbursts of international violence but confined himself to activities of diplomacy."[28]

Edward VIII also suffered from an inflated German perception of his own favorability to their ideas and aims. After he became king, the German ambassador in London, von Hoesch, reported to the Foreign Ministry in Berlin: "You are aware from my reports that King Edward, quite generally, feels warm sympathy for Germany. I have become convinced during frequent, often lengthy, talks with him that these sympathies are deep-rooted and strong enough to withstand the contrary influences to which they are not seldom exposed. . . . I am convinced that his friendly attitude toward Germany might in time come to exercise a certain amount of influence on the shaping of British foreign policy. At any rate, we should be able to rely upon having on the British Throne a ruler who is not lacking in understanding for Germany, and in the desire to see good relations established between Germany and Britain."[29]

Hitler was clearly anxious to continue cultivating the sympathies of Britain's new King. He knew little of Edward VIII's actual power, but reports from his agents in London did nothing to lessen his belief that the key to securing his position in Europe lay in the actions of the British monarch. Such ideas were commonly expressed, as evidenced by a dispatch from Ribbentrop to the Führer: "If the King were to give his support to the idea of Anglo-German friendship, his great popularity might well help to bring about an understanding."[30]

This attempt to win over the new King began with the death of his father. Hitler himself planned and attended an elaborate memorial service for George V in Berlin, at which he sat alongside Crown Princess Cecilie, Heinrich Himmler, Josef Goebbels, and Hermann Goering.

To represent his interests in England, he dispatched Edward VIII's second cousin Carl Eduard, Duke of Saxe-Coburg-Gotha. The Duke, born in Britain and educated at Eton, had inherited his German title at the age of sixteen. He quickly became enamored of Hitler's Nazi Party and joined the SS; at George V's funeral, he proudly wore his SS uniform as he walked behind the coffin through the streets of London.

Coburg had several talks with his cousin the King, the subjects of which would inspire controversy. The Duke claimed that the King had declared that a British-German alliance was of the utmost urgency and a necessity for maintaining a lasting European peace; that the League of Nations was a farce and that he wished to curb England's participation in it in the future; and that he wished to concentrate the business of British government more on himself and away from the Prime Minister and the Foreign Office. "To my question whether a discussion between Baldwin and Adolf Hitler would be desirable for future German-British relations, he replied in the following words: 'Who is King here? Baldwin or I? I myself wish to talk to Hitler, and will do so, here or in Germany.' "[31]

When this report was made public a generation later, Harold Nicolson commented: "Coburg was an awful snob who was very concerned to impress Hitler with his high connections. Edward certainly felt his role in life was to help his country to reach an understanding with Germany, and I often argued with him about the practicability of this, considering the nature of the regime. What he dreaded was war. Perhaps he believed more than he should have in German integrity, and perhaps he exaggerated his chances of influencing the course of events. But so did many other people. He was always perfectly frank with everyone about his views, and there was nothing discreditable or unconstitutional about it."[32]

The first test of Edward VIII's reaction came on March 7, 1936, when German troops marched into the demilitarized Rhineland, an open breach of the Locarno Treaty that might have meant Allied military intervention. The King's role in what happened next comes, it must be admitted, from the report of a source whose credibility is suspect. Fritz Hesse, press attaché of the German embassy in London, later claimed to have eavesdropped on a conversation between Ambassador von Hoesch and the King. Hesse declared: "I was with von Hoesch when the telephone rang. Von Hoesch whispered to me: 'The King!' and handed the second receiver to me, so that I could listen to the conversation.

"'Hallo,' a voice called, 'is that Leo? David speaking. Do you know who's speaking?'

"'Of course I do,' replied von Hoesch.

"'I sent for the Prime Minister and gave him a piece of my mind. I told the old so-and-so that I would abdicate if he made war. There was a frightful scene. But you needn't worry. There won't be a war.'

"Von Hoesch put down the receiver. He jumped up and danced round the room. 'I've done it, I've outwitted them all, there won't be a war! Herr Hesse, we've done it! It's magnificent, I must inform Berlin immediately.' "[33]

Although this version has been widely repeated, its veracity is open to doubt. In particular, Frances Donaldson points out that it is unlikely the King would have spoken in such strong terms and that he would have referred to himself as "David" when speaking with an ambassador.[34] Von Hoesch himself later declared that he had only had indirect contact with the King over the Rhineland question, although certainly the two men discussed the situation. Ribbentrop reported on March 11 that the King had issued "a directive to the Government . . . that no matter how the details of the affair are dealt with, complications of a serious nature are in no circumstances to be allowed to develop."[35]

This was exactly the news for which Hitler had been waiting. Albert Speer, who happened to be with him, recalled that on receiving the cable, Hitler "sighed with relief." "At last!" Hitler declared jubilantly. "The King of England will not intervene. He is keeping his promise.' "[36]

In hindsight, of course, the decision proved disastrous, opening a path of opportunism which Hitler would follow to the outbreak of the Second World War. But the King's desire for peace and his government's policy of appeasement happened to coincide—a fact conveniently ignored by Edward VIII's critics. Nor did the King interfere in diplomatic matters in any way out of the ordinary: He did nothing where the Rhineland crisis was concerned, nor did his father previously when Mussolini had invaded Abyssinia. And yet no one has accused George V of improper conduct over the Italian incident.

In the midst of such German overtures toward the King, it is only natural that allegations should have been leveled against Wallis. There were rumors, which have only gained currency with time, that she was supplying the German government with British state secrets. It is said that Sir Robert Vansittart, who unofficially headed up the British Intelligence Service MI6, had proof of her complicity. The source of this allegation, however, was not Vansittart himself but a second party, who claimed that the intelligence chief received his information from a Russian secret agent; the Russian agent, in turn, is said to have received his information from Wallis's dressmaker in London, Anna Wolkoff.

The sheer logistics of such a circle tend to militate against its existence; are we really to believe that Wallis would be so indiscreet as to confide state secrets to her dressmaker, who just happened to be friendly with a Russian double agent, who in turn was feeding secrets to the British government? It has also been suggested that Wallis was channeling information through the Italian embassy in London, another peculiar theory in view of the fact that Hitler and Mussolini were still at odds over issues of European supremacy and it is known that the King, as well as his government, had been playing very real negotiating games over the struggle for power. It seems most unlikely that the Italian embassy would have featured passing any British state secrets to the Germans by way of a Russian spy. But it is typical of the sort of unsubstantiated rumor which has managed to attach itself to both Wallis and the King.[37]

14

The King's Mistress

As WALLIS HAD FORESEEN, life had seemingly changed overnight. David's new position and responsibilities threatened to overwhelm what little time he could now manage to spend with her, and she felt increasingly isolated. "As I watched David becoming absorbed in his duties, it seemed to me there was little left of Peter Pan; he had become the prisoner of his heritage."[1] She saw no reason to believe that her privileged position would last. Inevitably, she thought, now that David was King, he must marry and provide an heir.

But David's feelings for her only intensified with the passage of time. The strain of his new office and the increasing duties which consumed him made him long all the more for company, Wallis's in particular. The more deeply he plunged into the duties of the throne, the more he prized his private life. Wallis was at the center of his emotional well-being; she was the only person with whom he could relax and in whom he felt able to confide.

The last British king to keep a mistress so openly had been David's grandfather Edward VII, who had indulged his passions with a string of paramours drawn from the ranks of the aristocracy and the stage. His most famous mistress had been Alice Keppel, wife of the Honorable George Keppel, a younger son of the Earl of Albemarle. She first met Edward in 1898, when he was still Prince of Wales: he was fifty-six, portly, and prematurely aged; she was twenty-nine, vibrant, and beautiful. Although her physical charms had initially drawn to her the Prince of Wales, it was her understanding, affection, and companionship which he came to value most. She was kind, charming, and discreet—"the most perfect mistress in history," as Anita Leslie has called her.[2] Their relationship was to last for twelve years, until his death in 1910. As Edward VII lay dying, his long-suffering wife, Queen Alexandra, had summoned Mrs. Keppel to his bedside so that her husband might bid farewell to his favorite.

Inevitably, Mrs. Keppel and nearly all of those who came before her had shared certain qualities as royal mistresses: discretion, unobtrusiveness, and social position. With Wallis, however, polite society was confronted with the complete antithesis of previous royal mistresses. As yet, no one had any idea that the King was contemplating marriage, and little concern was expressed over her marital record. Wallis was judged on visible factors. She was not particularly beautiful, and many wondered what the new King saw in her. Her American outspokenness differed greatly from the retiring manners the court expected. Above all, Wallis was far too brash not only in behavior but in appearance as well. Her now carefully cultivated and modern glamour stood in complete contrast to, in the words of Valerie Cumming, "the bourgeois domesticity of family life which George V and Queen Mary, and the Duke and Duchess of York and their two daughters had represented for nearly ten years."[3]

When the aged Alice Keppel said of Edward VIII's liaison, "Things were done differently in my day," she spoke for a majority of the old-guard aristocracy and members of the court.[4] Against this mounting disapproval were the voices of those confidants who had first embraced Wallis: Duff and Diana Cooper, Emerald Cunard, Sibyl Colefax, and Chips Channon. She received numerous letters praising her influence on the King and imploring her not to abandon him. "Of course I am very fond of him," she confided to Aunt Bessie, "and proud, and want him to do his job well and he is so lonely and needs companionship and affection, otherwise he goes all wrong. Ernest has of course been marvelous about it all."[5]

At the same time, Chips noted, there was increasing pressure from certain elements of the court to isolate Wallis. "We are concerned that some of our friends should be trying to poison the Kents against Mrs. Simpson and hence the King, and are attempting to drive a wedge between the Royal brothers," he noted early in the King's reign.[6]

In some circles, there was indeed a growing dissatisfaction with both Wallis and the King. On February 2, the Earl of Crawford wrote: "The King again spends the weekend at Belvedere and one assumes that Mrs. Simpson is there. If the emotions of the past fortnight have not been strong enough to bring that liaison to an end, we must contemplate its continuance until she is supplanted by some younger rival. . . . Criticism may become insistent, bitter; then he may do something fatuous by talking of abdication: he had done so *en famille* before now."[7]

David himself was under constant pressure from his mother and family to marry and provide an heir, but he managed to ward off such concerns. "Oh, Mama, let's not bother with that now," he would tell Queen Mary. "You know that I'll get around to it at the proper time."[8]

Queen Mary was greatly upset at such developments. In February

1936 she said to Lady Airlie, "Your sons are about the age of mine, Mabell, and you have had to bring them up without a father. Tell me, have they ever disappointed you?"

"I answered," Lady Airlie wrote, "that I thought all sons—and daughters too—disappointed their parents at some time or other, and that when this had happened in the case of my children I had always tried not to be possessive, and to remember that their lives were their own and not mine."

"Yes, one can apply that to individuals, but not to a Sovereign," Queen Mary answered slowly, "He is not responsible to himself alone." She turned once again to her needlework, then said quietly, "I have not liked to talk to David about this affair with Mrs. Simpson, in the first place because I don't want to give the impression of interfering in his private life, and also because he is the most obstinate of all my sons. To oppose him over anything is only to make him more determined to do it. At present he is utterly infatuated, but my great hope is that violent infatuations usually wear off."[9]

Queen Mary was well aware of the progress of her eldest son's relationship. Although David and his brother Bertie were no longer very close, the King did maintain frequent contacts with his favorite brother, George, the Duke of Kent, and his wife, Princess Marina, whom he and Wallis often visited in London and at their country house, Coppins. David's other brother, Harry, Duke of Gloucester, and his wife, Alice, occasionally visited the Fort, but neither were enthralled to inevitably discover Wallis in residence as well. "This was awkward," Alice recalled, "as we were unhappy with the liaison as the rest of the family, but as a brother Prince Henry felt obliged to go."[10]

Increasingly, these weekends at the Fort were provoking much gossip and dissatisfaction. David's behavior left little doubt that he was absolutely enamored of his mistress, and his behavior was often distressing to those unprepared for such devotion. Lady Diana Cooper said of one weekend in February 1936: "Wallis tore her nail and said, 'Oh!' but forgot about it, but he needs must disappear and arrive back in two minutes, panting, with two little emery-boards for her to file the offending nail."[11] A footman, asked by a prospective employer why he had left the King's employ at the Fort, replied, "Well, Madam, the butler, Mr. Osborne, sent me down to the swimming pool with two drinks. When I got there what did I see but His Majesty painting Mrs. Simpson's toenails. My Sovereign painting a woman's toenails. It was a bit much, Madam. I gave notice at once."[12]

By the end of February 1936, the delicate balancing act which Wallis had been performing between Ernest and David had taken its toll on her health and nerves. Hoping to have time to consider her situation, she told both men that she wished to leave England for a week.

She traveled alone to Paris, where she had booked a room at the Hotel Meurice. Although she could not have known it, this was the worst possible decision Wallis could have made, for while she was gone, Ernest and David, acting without her knowledge, came together to decide her fate.[13]

In the fall of 1935, Ernest had gone to New York alone on business, and Wallis, in a curious twist on the actions of Thelma Furness, had asked her friend Mary Kirk Raffray to look after him. Mary had recently left her husband, Jacques, and was now living in an uptown New York apartment. What began as quiet evenings together quickly blossomed into a romance. There is no reason to believe that they were not intimate, for Ernest was apparently spied creeping out of her flat early one morning, and they are known to have spent a weekend together in Atlantic City.[14]

It is doubtful that this affair with Mary Kirk Raffray was more than just a casual liaison, but it was to become the impetus for the dissolution of the Simpsons' marriage. Previously, Ernest had listened to his wife's repeated assurances that she had no interest in, or desire to seek, a divorce. The deeper her relationship with David had become, however, the less inclined Ernest had been to believe her. He thought Wallis was deluding herself about the strength of her feelings for David and that given the opportunity, she would be far more willing to abandon her husband than her lover.

It was while Wallis was away that Ernest and David met at York House. Ernest told the King that Wallis would have to make a choice between them and asked what he intended to do about it. Without hesitation, David declared that he was going to marry Wallis, saying, "Do you really think I would be crowned without Wallis by my side?"[15]

Ernest apparently made his decision. After this talk, Ernest joined Wallis in Paris, where he informed her that he and the King had reached an understanding. He finally told her of his feelings for Mary Kirk Raffray, a piece of news which cannot have come as a complete shock to Wallis. It is impossible, however, to know if she realized the full extent of their affair; her written memoirs indicate that she did not, while her published private correspondence seems to suggest that she had at least some idea as to what had been taking place.

According to their agreement, Ernest would agree to a divorce. The King had assured Ernest that he would take care of her. Wallis was devastated by this news. "She was completely taken by surprise," a friend later recalled. "Can you imagine? Her whole future, decided by these two men, and both without even discussing it with her! It left her absolutely shaken. And the terrible thing was, she hadn't any intention of divorcing Simpson—and there it was."[16]

But neither Ernest nor David was prepared for Wallis's reaction.

Not only was she outraged that these two men would attempt to manipulate her future in such a manner without previously discussing their plans with her, but such a course of action ran absolutely counter to what she herself wanted. For a year, Wallis had insisted that she had no wish to divorce Ernest, and there is no reason to doubt her sincerity. The Simpsons returned to London, she angry and upset and their marriage in a shambles. But she stubbornly clung to the illusion that everything could continue as it had been before.

Ironically, on their return to London, Mary Kirk Raffray came to stay with Wallis and Ernest on a previously arranged visit. Her time with the Simpsons at Bryanston Court was strained; Wallis seems to have had at least some idea as to the liaison between her friend and husband, and Mary left rather quickly, moving on to France. From here, she dispatched two letters, the first, a thank-you note to Wallis, the second, a love letter to Ernest. Unbelievably, she placed the two letters in the wrong envelopes and had dropped them in the post before she finally realized what she had done. Quickly, she sent Wallis a cable, warning her that a letter addressed to her was not written for her and saying that she should not open it. Needless to say, Wallis opened both letters when they arrived at Bryanston Court.[17] Here, for apparently the first time, she had conclusive evidence not only of Ernest's feelings for Mary Kirk but also of their affair.

For the moment, however, Wallis refused to act. Stubbornly, she clung to the delusion that things could continue on exactly as they had in the past. Ernest was still willing enough to maintain the deception, and Wallis honestly believed that she could remain the King's mistress until such time as she should be supplanted in his affections either by a new, younger lover or, more likely, by a suitable bride who would become his queen.

But such an arrangement was not what David had in mind. Now, for the first time, she learned the extent of his plans. He wanted nothing less than Wallis as his bride; she would become his queen. If he could not marry her and remain king, he would abdicate the throne. Although Wallis would later claim that the question of marriage was not raised until several months later, it is apparent from her letters that both the marriage and the idea of his abdication were discussed shortly after her return from Paris.

David was impetuous and simply refused to accept any option other than marriage to Wallis. Her protests went unheeded. In his own mind, David had already begun to plan their future together. He continued to shower her with gifts of jewelry, although now they bore inscriptions which spoke of the stress of their relationship. On March 27, he gave Wallis an extravagant piece ordered from Van Cleef & Arpels: an exquisite ruby-and-diamond bracelet with the words "Hold

Tight" inscribed on the clasp. He also bestowed on Wallis a substantial amount of money, drawn from his private fortune, so that, no matter what happened, she should always be financially comfortable.

Wallis, however, continued—at least for the time being—to stand her ground. She reciprocated his sentimental gifts, but hers were marked with a certain sadness, which undoubtedly reflected the pressures which were overwhelming them both. In April she presented him with a gold memorandum case mounted with his monogram; inside the cover, engraved in a copy of her own handwriting, was a children's poem by Eleanor Farjeon:

> King's Cross! What shall we do?
> His Purple robe is rent in two.
> Out of his crown he's torn the gems.
> He's thrown his sceptre into the Thames.
> The Court is quaking in every shoe.
> King's Cross! What shall we do?
> Leave him alone for a minute or two.
> April 1936 WE.[18]

On March 28, David gave a party at Windsor Castle, to which he invited the Hardinges and Lord and Lady Wigram. These courtiers were waiting at the sovereign's entrance to the castle when the King arrived from Fort Belvedere. He was accompanied by his other guests, including the Simpsons (Ernest still, for appearance' sake, at the side of his wife), and Colin and Gladys Buist.

The King and his guests went to the White Drawing Room, where a projector had been set up, and watched a newsreel of the Grand National Race, followed by an Eddie Cantor film. When the film was over, they walked down the grand corridor. "Mrs. Simpson was very agreeable to everyone, and she admired the Victorian settings of my jewelry," Lady Hardinge noted.[19]

"Gradually, from desultory talk," Lady Hardinge recalled, "the story of George IV and Mrs. Fitzherbert seemed to detach itself and as a theme made its way into the conversation. And as we wandered among the paintings that night, perhaps because of the hints and talk about them, their presence became very real, and George IV and Mrs. Fitzherbert seemed to emerge and join us. They seemed more solid, less brittle, than ourselves. Our little group bristled with unspoken confidences about the present, as we discussed the personal affairs of George IV."[20]

A few weeks later, Wallis was staying with David at the Fort when a new station wagon he had ordered from America arrived. After inspecting the vehicle, he said to Wallis: "Let's drive over to Royal

Lodge. I want to show Bertie the car." He and Wallis, along with some other guests, drove through Windsor Great Park to the Royal Lodge, where his brother the Duke of York and his family were staying.[21]

The Duke and Duchess of York met the King at the door of the Royal Lodge. David took his brother over to see the new station wagon. Wallis noted that the Duke seemed "quiet, shy, obviously dubious of this newfangled American contrivance." Wallis had previously met the Duke and Duchess of York at both York House and at the Fort.[22]

Wallis and David stayed to take tea in the saloon of the Royal Lodge, where the Duke and Duchess's two daughters, Princess Elizabeth, then aged ten, and Princess Margaret, six, joined them, brought in by their governess, Marion Crawford. "They were both so blonde, so beautifully mannered, so brightly scrubbed," Wallis wrote, "that they might have stepped straight from the pages of a picture book."[23]

Marion Crawford later recalled her meeting with Wallis: "She was a smart, attractive woman, already middle-aged but with that immediate friendliness American women have. She appeared to be entirely at her ease; if anything, rather too much so. . . . She had a distinctly proprietary way of speaking to the new King. I remember she drew him to the window and suggested how certain trees might be moved, and a part of a hill taken away to improve the view." This seemingly innocent action caused great distress to both the Duke and Duchess of York; the Duke had himself helped plan the garden at Royal Lodge and taken particular care in the placement of the trees and lawns. Wallis's comments were met with stony silence. "The atmosphere was not a comfortable one," Marion Crawford later wrote.[24]

The Duchess of York eventually turned to the governess and said, "Crawfie, would you like to take Lilibet and Margaret into the woods for a while?" As they left, Princess Elizabeth, having encountered the woman whose love affair would one day place her on the British throne, turned to her governess and asked, "Crawfie, who is she?"[25]

The afternoon had been anything but a success. If the Duchess of York had previously harbored a dislike of Wallis, her ill-conceived gardening suggestions and easy treatment of the King only intensified Elizabeth's feelings. "I left," Wallis wrote, "with a distinct impression that while the Duke of York was sold on the American station wagon, the Duchess was not sold on David's other American interest."[26]

Wallis continued to operate under considerable strain. Although she and Ernest appeared to have reached something of an understanding, David remained insistent. This was terribly wearing on Wallis, who found the strain almost unbearable. By the beginning of May, it was apparent even to Wallis that things could no longer continue as they had in the past. In a letter to her aunt Bessie, she explained that her former life with Ernest at Bryanston Court had now slipped away forever; Ernest might be content to let the situation continue, but she was not. "I've outgrown it and Ernest," she admitted candidly. She knew there was no going back. If she gave up the King, she would always be haunted by a string of what-ifs; at the same time, she realized that one day it would all come to an end. "Should HM fall in love with someone else I would cease to be as powerful or have all I have today . . ." she wrote. "I should be comfortably off and have had a most interesting experience. . . ."[27]

On May 10, Chips Channon wrote: "It appears that the King is Mrs. Simpson's absolute slave, and will go nowhere where she is not invited, and she, clever woman, with her high pitched voice, chic clothes, moles and sense of humour is behaving well. She encourages the King to meet people of importance and to be polite; above all she makes him happy. The Empire ought to be grateful."[28]

Two days later, Wallis and David attended a party given by Col. Mike Scanlon, assistant military attaché for air at the U.S. embassy, and his wife. Among the guests were Col. Charles Lindbergh and his wife, Anne, who left a detailed account of her meeting with Wallis: "Mrs. Simpson beautifully dressed with the poise and ease of knowing that whatever she does is right and that she is the person in the room that people will turn to. . . . She at least is honest and playing her own part, not someone else's. She is one of the few authentic characters in a social world—one of those who *start* fashions, not one of those who follow them. . . . She is not beautiful and yet vital and real to watch. Her vitality invests her movements with charm or a kind of beauty. I like watching her."[29]

One day in May, David told Wallis he was inviting the prime minister, Stanley Baldwin, to join him for dinner at the Fort. He asked Wallis to act as hostess. "It's got to be done," he said with a smile. "Sooner or later my Prime Minister must meet my future wife."[30]

Wallis later wrote that she was startled at this piece of information and protested that such a marriage could never take place. But her letters make quite clear that the issue had already been discussed between them, at least in some cursory fashion, and so, at least on this count, her memoirs must be dismissed.[31] From this point forward, irrespective of what she would later claim, Wallis was fully aware of David's designs to make her his queen. Whether she herself wished this or thought there was any likelihood of this happening is another matter entirely.

The dinner took place at York House on May 27. The guests included not only the prime minister and his wife but Lord and Lady Louis Mountbatten; Lord and Lady Wigram; Duff and Lady Diana

Cooper; Emerald Cunard; the King's equerry, Sir Piers Legh, and his wife, Sarah; Admiral of the Fleet Sir Chatfield; and Col. and Mrs. Charles Lindbergh. Ernest also attended. During the dinner, Lindbergh, who had just returned from Germany, reported on the state of affairs under Hitler. Both Baldwins seemed curious about Wallis, and she noted that they seemed to exchange meaningful glances as the evening wore on.[32] Afterward, Lucy Baldwin commented sadly, "Mrs. Simpson had stolen the Fairy Prince."[33]

The dinner, having been an official function, was duly noted—along with the names of those present—in the court circular the following day. "It was ironic," wrote Lady Hardinge, "that the Press which had steadfastly restrained itself from linking HM's name with Mrs. Simpson was now obliged to do so at his insistence. Great efforts were made to stop the King from doing this, by those members of his staff who were trying to protect him. . . . If Mayfair society had shown any self-restraint before in speculating about King Edward's private life, it had no cause to do so now."[34]

Queen Mary showed the court circular to Mabell Airlie. "He gives Mrs. Simpson the most beautiful jewels," she said quietly. Then, after a pause, she continued: "I am so afraid that he may ask me to receive her." Lady Airlie recalled: "Bright spots of crimson were burning on her cheek bones. It was easy to imagine what such a demand would represent to her all-pervading loyalty to the Monarchy."[35]

Nancy Astor, born in America and the first woman to sit in the House of Commons, was horrified when she read the court circular. Harold Nicolson found her

> terribly indignant at the King for having invited to his first official dinner Lady Cunard and Mr. and Mrs. Simpson. She says that the effect in Canada and America will be deplorable. She considers Lady Cunard and Chips Channon as "disintegrating influences," and she deplores the fact that any but the best Virginian families should be received at Court. I stick up for both Emerald Cunard and Mrs. Simpson, but I refrain from saying that, after all, every American is more or less as vulgar as any other American. Nancy Astor herself, by her vain and self-conscious behaviour in the House, cannot claim to be a model of propriety. In any case, she is determined to tell the King that although Mrs. Simpson may appear at Court, she must not appear in the Court Circular. I suggest to her that any such intimation would be regarded by HM as a gross impertinence. She says that when the dignity of the United States and the British Empire is involved, it is her duty to make such sacrifices.[36]

By the beginning of June, not even Wallis was able to withstand the constant pressure from David, and she agreed to seek a divorce from Ernest. The King himself was working against the calendar: he wished to marry Wallis before his coronation, which had just been announced for May 12, 1937. If she began proceedings immediately, the case would most likely be heard in the fall. There was, according to British law, a six-month waiting period between the decree and its formalization, a span of time which would mean that Wallis would be free to marry again by April.

Once she had made her decision, Wallis asked David if he could recommend a lawyer. He arranged for her to see his solicitor, Sir George Allen. Allen himself sought out another lawyer to handle the case; eventually, he settled on Theodore Goddard, a specialist in divorce.

Throughout the proceedings, David consulted his friend Walter Monckton, solicitor for the duchy of Cornwall, and one of his few intimates. Monckton, the son of a family from Kent, had made a great success of his time at Balliol College when he was president of the Oxford Union. A man of medium height, with thinning hair and thick glasses, Monckton resembled nothing so much as an Oxford don. A brilliant barrister, he had also advised the nizam of Hyderabad. That summer, he came to know Wallis particularly well. She told Monckton that she wished to pursue a divorce. The King himself complained to Walter that he in no way wanted his friendship with Mrs. Simpson to bring unwanted publicity to her divorce. "I was convinced that it was the King who was really the party anxious for the divorce," Monckton noted, "and I suspected that he felt some jealousy that there should be a husband in the background."[37]

On Wednesday, June 10, David and Mrs. Simpson attended a dinner given by Lady Colefax at Argyll House. Among those present were Kitty and Perry Brownlow; the Duchess of Buccleuch; Lady Diana Cooper; Lord and Lady Vansittart; Mr. and Mrs. Artur Rubinstein, Harold Nicolson, and Robert Bruce Lockhart. Lockhart noted that Edward "looks older and harder—a little stiffer perhaps since he became King, definitely more confidence in himself since he met Mrs. Simpson." He continued: "Afterwards Artur Rubinstein played to us. King sat down on little stool beside Mrs. Simpson. Seemed rather bored, but stayed on." At half-past twelve, Winston Churchill, Noël Coward, Daisy Fellowes, and the Kenneth Clarks arrived. Rubinstein had been playing classical pieces on the piano for nearly an hour, and the King had had enough. As he prepared to play another, Edward stood up, walked across to the piano, and said loudly, "We enjoyed that very much, Mr. Rubinstein."[38] Instead, the King asked Noël

Coward to entertain, and for the next half hour, Edward, Wallis, and the other guests sang along while Coward thumped out such tunes as "Oh, Mrs. Worthington, Don't Put Your Daughter on the Stage" and "Mad Dogs and Englishmen."[39] Lockhart recalled that the "King bucked up and looked quite amused."[40]

By the first week of July, Chips Channon reported, "The Simpson scandal is growing, and she, poor Wallis, looks unhappy. The world is closing in around her, the flatterers, the sycophants, and the malice. It is a curious social juxtaposition that casts me in the role of Defender of the King. But I do, and very strongly in society, not for loyalty so much as for admiration and affection for Wallis, and in indignation against those who attack her."[41]

Wallis was just beginning to learn that her private life had become the subject of great interest in the American press. She wrote to her cousin Corinne Murray: "Darling Rinny—Please don't believe all you read. I am still the same nut you have always known—and it makes me pretty damn sick that it is my country and my countrymen and especially women who take the trouble to talk so shabbily about me—the English have been too kind and lovely to me. . . ."[42]

On July 9 the King gave another controversial dinner party at York House, presided over and planned by Wallis. Several members of Parliament attended: Winston Churchill and his wife, Clementine; David Margesson, Conservative chief whip; Sir Samuel Hoare, newly appointed First Lord of the Admiralty, and his wife, Maud Hoare; and Sir Philip Sassoon, undersecretary of state for air. The Duke and Duchess were also present. During the conversation after dinner, Churchill—one suspects with a certain amount of gleeful deliberation—introduced the topic of George IV's mistress, Mrs. Maria Fitzherbert. Hearing this, the Duchess of York replied cautiously, "Well, that was a *long* time ago."[43]

Churchill did not notice the disapproving look on the Duchess's face, for he next launched into a pointed conversation about the wars between the houses of Lancaster and York and the War of the Roses. The Duchess, with more determination in her voice, said strongly, "That was a very, very long time ago."[44]

On July 16 the King participated in a military review at Hyde Park. Wallis sat in a special stand with Emerald and the Fitzgeralds; a royal box held Queen Mary and the two York princesses. As he reviewed the gathered members of the Guards regiments, he spoke movingly of the horrors of war and expressed his sincere sentiments that the world would never again engage in such devastating conflict. As the King, riding on his horse behind a contingent of guards, returned to Buckingham Palace, he passed Hyde Park Corner and beneath Wellington Arch. At just this moment, a man standing in the crowd raised a gun and aimed at the King. Before he could fire, however, a horse came between him and the King, and he threw the revolver; David saw what had happened and, keeping charge of his horse, yelled for the police to grab the would-be assassin. David, calm, continued his ride to the palace. There he learned that police had indeed apprehended the suspect, George McMahon, an Irishman living in Glasgow. After a trial, he was sentenced to twelve months in jail.[45]

On July 20, Wallis attended the Kemsleys' ball at Chandos House; nearly all London society was present. Chips recorded that Wallis "was in a rage, as she had just received a letter from an MP signed by a well-known name, which she was clever enough not to reveal, in which he warned Mrs. Simpson against Lady Astor and her campaign. Wallis asked Honor [Chips' wife] for her advice, and soon Honor had spilt the beans about Nancy Astor's various attacks on me in regard to Wallis at the House of Commons. I fear that there may be a proper scandal and 'bust up' as Wallis will, and in fact, already has, told the King."[46]

A week later, Sir Robert Bruce Lockhart noted: "Emerald told me . . . that Lady Astor has been attacking Mrs. Simpson very violently— and by implication the King—in the House of Commons and elsewhere and that a Member of Parliament had written to Mrs. Simpson and Mrs. Simpson had shown the letter to the King."[47]

The scandal was indeed growing and at times threatened to overwhelm society. As Michael Thornton points out, "By constantly appearing in public covered in costly jewels bought for her by the adoring King, Wallis Simpson proclaimed herself *maîtresse en titre* to society at large. It was on the grounds of vulgar display, rather than alleged immorality, that the criticism of her, and of him, was justified."[48]

On July 21 the King hosted his first garden party at Buckingham Palace, which he also managed to make into a formal court presentation of debutantes. Formerly, George V had held four presentation courts in May and June, and they were generally regarded as the highlight of the season. This year, however, George V's death had pushed the courts into July, the end of the six-month mourning period. As a result, six hundred debutantes waited for their formal presentations at court.

Lord Cromer, the Lord Chamberlain, suggested to the King that he expedite the situation by holding two massive garden parties at Buckingham Palace and using them as an opportunity for presentations. A special dais had been erected in the garden to make the occasion more impressive: The King sat beneath the huge red-and-gold Shamiana canopy, used by his parents at the 1911 Delhi durbar in India.[49] The Yorks, the Kents, and several other members of the Royal Family sat beside him, waiting to greet the debutantes; Wallis occupied a discreet seat near the rear of the pavilion.

Three hundred girls, all dressed in their summer finery, stood waiting in a long line which stretched around the lawns and back into the palace. As the Lord Chamberlain called out a name, the debutante stepped forward, curtsied to the King, and moved on. Throughout the ceremony, David appeared bored, tugging nervously at his collar and occasionally glancing down the line to see how many more girls waited. Unfortunately, midway through this ceremony, London's notorious weather struck, and the skies opened up, pelting everyone with a violent rainstorm. David, sitting in his covered pavilion, was safe, but the debutantes were rapidly becoming drenched and their dresses ruined. Eventually, the King summoned the Lord Chamberlain to his throne and said, "We can't let this go on." Cromer agreed, and the remaining presentations were canceled.[50]

The following afternoon, the second garden-party presentation took place, but those debutantes who had not been presented the previous day were not asked to return. The Lord Chamberlain issued a statement that was carried in the *Times* the following morning: "Those ladies summoned to the afternoon's reception who, owing to the interruption of the ceremony by the weather, were unable to pass the King's presence, would be considered as having been officially presented at Court."[51] Many of the debutantes and their families were angry, and court officials quickly pointed out the occasion as another example of David's inability to cope with the burdens of the throne. Indeed, David himself later admitted that he had made a mistake and underestimated the importance of the presentation. In retrospect, he said, he should have walked down the line of remaining debutantes and wished each girl well. But it was too late; his distaste for the ceremony had led him to seek the easiest way out, and the damage had been done.[52]

As the summer wore on, so did the preparations for the Simpson divorce. Although both Wallis and Ernest wished to divorce, according to British law such desire was not itself sufficient to dissolve a marriage. Nor was the wish of one party to marry another a circumstance which was regarded in divorce cases as collusion. The only circumstances in which divorces were ordinarily permitted were those where the petitioner—in this case Wallis—could show that the respondent had grievously damaged the marriage through improper conduct. In short, Ernest had to agree to accept total blame for the failure of the marriage and provide evidence sufficient to the court to prove his wife's claim. Thus, Ernest agreed to go through a ludicrous charade in which he would theatrically flaunt his adultery with another woman in order to provide Wallis with a motive to seek a divorce.

On July 21 he booked himself into the Hotel de Paris at Bray under the name Ernest A. Simmons. He was accompanied by a lady who gave her name as "Buttercup" Kennedy. They took breakfast in bed together the following morning and were thus observed by the hotel staff. This was all the evidence needed for Wallis to begin proceedings, and she had in fact hired a detective to follow them. It cannot have been an accident that this was done, and one can only assume that she must have known what was to take place. Within a day, Wallis wrote a letter to Ernest informing him that she knew he had been at the hotel with a lady other than herself and that she was beginning proceedings to end their marriage.

15

The Nahlin *Cruise*

In the summer of 1936, King Edward VIII once again left England to take his holiday on the European continent. There was a great deal of criticism over this decision. For twenty-five years, his father, George V, had followed a careful schedule of summer engagements and migrations and had never felt the need to go abroad for the holidays. Yachting at Cowes on the Isle of Wight was followed by stays at Windsor Castle and Holyrood House in Edinburgh and then an extended vacation at Balmoral Castle in Scotland. To many members of the court, Edward VIII's European holiday was clearly another example of his disregard for tradition and determination to do exactly as he pleased. They conveniently forgot that the King's grandfather, Edward VII, as well as his great-grandmother Queen Victoria had both regularly taken holidays in Europe.

Originally, David had wished to rent a villa in Cannes, but complications arose. In France, the Laval government had collapsed, and now the left-wing Léon Blum was premier; certain elements in the British government feared that if the King summered in France, radical left-wingers close to Blum might attempt an assassination of the monarch.

Instead, David decided to charter a yacht and cruise along the Dalmatian coast, through the Bosporus and the Greek Isles. He had wished to embark on the voyage from Venice; but this news sent members of the Foreign Office into a frenzy. Mussolini had recently invaded Abyssinia, and his intervention in the Spanish Civil War caused much unease among members of the British government. The Foreign Office eventually insisted that the King avoid Italy altogether, and reluctantly he agreed.

From Calais, Wallis and the King took a private car coupled to the Orient Express through Austria to Yugoslavia. Here they were met at the frontier by Prince Paul of Yugoslavia and took tea with him and his wife, Princess Olga, sister of Princess Marina, Duchess of Kent.

A crowd of some twenty thousand people, dressed in their colorful native costumes, waited in the Dalmatian port of Sibenik to see the royal group off at the pier. Here, where there had been no news blackout over the King's romance, there was great curiosity over Wallis. As she strolled down the pier, she felt the inquisitive eyes of the gathered thousands upon her.

The King had the old royal yacht *Victoria and Albert* at his disposal, but for this voyage he decided that a more modern ship was in order. He had chartered a 1,391-ton yacht called the *Nahlin*, a 250-foot-long shining white beauty crowned with two tall masts and a low white funnel. Large awnings sheltered the teak decks, which were scattered with wicker chairs and tables; below were eight main staterooms, each with its own bathroom.[1] Everywhere the yacht went, it was shadowed by an escort of two British destroyers, HMS *Grafton* and HMS *Glowworm*, whose presence ensured that the voyage would not remain a secret.

A number of friends joined David and Wallis on the cruise. This group included Herman and Katherine Rogers; Duff and Lady Diana Cooper, Lord Sefton; Mrs. Josephine Gwynne (an American friend of Wallis's); Helen Fitzgerald; Colin and Gladys Buist; the Duke of Kent's equerry, Humphrey Butler, and his wife; the King's favorite golf partner, Archie Compston; John Aird, the King's equerry; and the King's two assistant private secretaries, Godfrey Thomas and Tommy Lascelles.[2] Lady Cunard and Lord and Lady Brownlow later joined the yachting party as well.

For a month, the yacht cruised up and down the coast; occasionally, it steamed into a deserted cove, and David, Wallis, and others would take a launch or paddle boat ashore, where they would swim and picnic on the beaches. There were also frequent visits ashore to small coastal towns where Wallis and David dined in sidewalk cafes and haunted the local shops for souvenirs.

Lady Diana Cooper recalled one of these visits on shore: "The King walks a little ahead talking to the Consul or Mayor, and we follow, adoring it. He waves his hand half-saluting. He is utterly himself and unselfconscious. That I think is the reason why he does some things (that he likes) superlatively well. He does not *act*. In the middle of the procession he stopped for a good two minutes to tie his shoes. There was a knot and it took time. We were all left staring at his behind. You or I would have risen above the lace, wouldn't we, until the procession was over? But it did not occur to him to wait, and so the people said: 'Isn't he human! Isn't he natural! He stopped to do up his shoe like any of us!' "[3]

In Corfu, Wallis and David dined with King George II of the Hellenes, only recently restored to the Greek throne after a forced exile.

Also present was the King's mistress, Mrs. Britten-Jones, an English-woman who had just been divorced from her husband. This peculiar situation, with the two cousins who reigned over their respective countries sitting side by side with their respective mistresses, did not go unreported, and news of the luncheon caused a riot of gossip among London society.

The group spent a day visiting different sights on Corfu. The group toured Mon Repos, the royal villa which Queen Olga had copied from one where she had spent her summers in Russia at the imperial estate of Alexandra, Peterhof. There was also a visit to the empty white marble palace originally built by Empress Elizabeth of Austria and last inhabited by Kaiser Wilhelm II. They found the iron gates locked, and David happily climbed atop them and broke the lock so that his group could explore the gardens.[4]

They returned to the yacht at the end of a long day. Lady Diana Cooper, who was unwell and suffering from a violent bout of flu, recalled that a chair was accidentally placed atop the hem of Wallis's gown, ripping it. David got down on his hands and knees to pull it clear, but Wallis seemed more irritated at the loss of the dress than pleased at the display of gallantry. She had not particularly enjoyed her day and began to complain of the way in which David had treated Mrs. Britten-Jones, perhaps overly sensitive about her paramour's behavior toward another royal mistress.[5]

By this point, Diana was rapidly becoming disenchanted with both her own ill health and the trip itself. Something of her disillusion is reflected in the cutting comments she made about the King's mistress. She reported: "Wallis is wearing very, very badly. Her commonness and Becky Sharpishness irritate. . . . The truth is she's bored stiff by him, and her picking on him and her coldness towards him, far from policy, are irritation and boredom."[6]

Many years later, when asked to reflect on the cruise, Diana declared: "I have constantly been asked if I thought they went to bed together on the *Nahlin* and so on. I tell them all, 'I haven't the least idea. How should I know?' Though I'm perfectly sure they did."[7]

One memorable evening, as the *Nahlin* lay anchored off the small fishing village of Cetinje, Wallis and David stood on deck, watching the sun set. Suddenly, hundreds of people appeared along the shore and climbed down the winding hillside paths leading to the beach, all carrying flaming torches. As they stood silhouetted against the night sky, they sang folk songs to the distant yacht, the sounds of their voices floating over the quiet waters. David assured Wallis, "It's all for you—because these simple people believe a King is in love with you."[8]

At the request of the Foreign Office in London, the royal party made its way to Istanbul. Britain had recently concluded a commercial trade agreement with Turkey, and the government was anxious to reinforce its willingness to forge stronger ties with the dictator there, Mustafa Kemal Atatürk. Atatürk treated Wallis as if she were a queen, seating her beside David during a celebratory parade and, later, at a magnificent state dinner. As evening fell, Atatürk ordered hundreds of small boats, covered with flickering lights which sparkled as they bobbed in the waters, into the harbor.

The royal party returned by train through Bulgaria, Yugoslavia, and on to Vienna. Here they visited old friends, stayed at their favorite hotel, the Bristol, attended a performance of Wagner's *Götterdämmerung* in the company of Winifred Wagner, the composer's daughter-in-law, and dined at the famous Three Hussars Restaurant. Society hostess Elsa Maxwell happened to be in the lobby of the Bristol when the royal party arrived. She recalled: "The clicking of heels by the manager and his staff sounded like castanets and a crew of porters scurried through the door with mountains of luggage. Then the King's entourage entered, led by a small, beautifully dressed woman. Her sullen expression and the purposeful way she walked gave me the impression that she would brush aside anyone who had the temerity to get in her path. I took a second, startled look at her when I saw the King following a few paces behind. I had never seen Mrs. Simpson, but from pictures of her it was no feat of deduction to guess her identity."[9]

After a short visit to Zurich, the King returned to London; Wallis went on to Paris to spend a few days alone. It was then that she began to learn just how much controversy her recent holiday with David had caused. This should scarcely have come as a surprise, given the very public manner in which David and Wallis had conducted themselves; they seemed oblivious of the crowds of curious onlookers and hordes of photographers that followed them around from place to place. Naively, they assumed that they would be left alone. Now no one could seemingly hear enough about this extraordinary voyage, which Michael Thornton has called "the most bizarre royal odyssey since the Prince Regent's wife, Caroline of Brunswick, cavorted through Europe with her Italian chamberlain, Bartolomeo Bergami."[10]

The reaction in English society was decidedly unfavorable. Osbert Sitwell, a typical aristocrat with strong anti-American views, wrote disparagingly of those who had accompanied the King on the cruise: "They were, for the most part, a wise-cracking team of smartish, middle-aged, semi-millionaire Americans, with the usual interchangeable names and over-life-size faces, customarily to be seen in bars and in hotels in Paris and the South of France—the rootless spawn of New York, Cracow, Antwerp, and the Mile End Road, with loud voices, never a doubt except of their own position and continual loud laughs bottled in alcohol and always on tap."[11] Sitwell, however—in common with a great many like-minded critics—seemed to have conveniently ignored the fact that more than half of the guests were, like himself, members of the English aristocracy.

The only mention made in the British press came in the London weekly magazine *Cavalcade,* which printed a front-page picture of the King, with Wallis, and captioned it: "The Duke of Lancaster and a Guest."[12] All American magazines and newspapers shipped to Britain had any references snipped by censors. But now, in Paris, Wallis read for the first time mail forwarded from her friends and family in the United States which informed her of the press she and the cruise were receiving in American newspapers. She was shocked; when she informed David, however, he assured her that the British press had agreed to maintain their silence.[13]

The *Nahlin* cruise, which Wallis had hoped would be a time for private romance, had instead turned into something of a string of strained appearances, culminating in the barrage of press attention around the world. Although her memoirs do not mention the fact, Wallis—weary of living her life in the public eye and fearful that she was damaging David's position on the throne—now tried to sever her relationship with David. Ernest was living with Mary Kirk, and divorce proceedings had begun, but she believed that if she told him that the only way in which to save the monarchy was to return to her, he would comply and agree. With this thought in mind, she awoke from the dream into which she had happily allowed herself to sink and faced what could only be the unpleasant reality of her situation. Now she only wanted to escape her royal entanglement.

From the Hotel Meurice in Paris, she wrote what was intended to be a farewell letter to David: "I must really return to Ernest. . . . We are so awfully congenial and understand getting on together *very* well. . . . I know Ernest and have the deepest affection and respect for him. I feel I am better with him than with you—and so you must understand. I am sure dear David that in a few months your life will run again as it did before and without my nagging. . . . I am sure you and I would only create disaster together. I shall always read all about you . . . and you will know I want you to be happy. I feel sure I can't make you so and I honestly don't think you can me."[14]

But David refused to listen to Wallis. He pleaded with her, begged her not to give him up. She was too fond of him to hurt him by pressing her case. Things were moving too quickly for her, and she found herself dazzled by rapidly moving circumstances. Years later, she would tell author Gore Vidal: "I never wanted to get married. This was all *his* idea. They act as if I were some sort of idiot, not knowing the rules about who can be queen and who can't. But he insisted."[15]

When she returned to England, Wallis was forced to deal directly with her divorce. In July, her solicitor, Theodore Goddard, had lodged the case against Ernest. On Goddard's advice, the divorce would be heard outside London and thus away from the press. He selected Ipswich, in Suffolk, as a likely spot; this required Wallis to take up temporary residence there, and she let a cottage called Beech House near Felixstowe. She had agreed to let the flat at Bryanston Court go and had to make the arrangements on her way to Ipswich.

Before taking up residence in Felixstowe, Wallis joined David at Balmoral in Scotland. Queen Mary had been delighted to hear that David was going to Balmoral, as his father had, and dared to hope that this marked at least some return to tradition; but then she discovered that Wallis was also to stay at Balmoral, a move which seemed to indicate the worst.

Herman and Katherine Rogers accompanied Wallis on the train north to Aberdeen; David met them at the station. This caused something of an incident. Previously, the lord provost of Aberdeen, on behalf of the authorities at a local hospital, had asked the King to dedicate the new Royal Infirmary buildings in the town. The King, however, had refused, saying he was still in mourning for his father, and he asked the Duke of York, who was staying at Birkhall, on the Balmoral estate, with his family, to perform the task in his place. But on the very day that the Duke was across town dedicating the hospital in his mourning brother's place, David was seen as he greeted Wallis and her friends at the railway station and escorted them to Balmoral. On his orders, Wallis had not even gone as far as the royal station at Ballater, which would have offered more privacy than the very public railway siding in Aberdeen.

David naively thought that such an action would go unnoticed. That evening, the headline of the *Aberdeen Evening Express* read: "His Majesty in Aberdeen—Surprise Visit in Car to Meet Guests." The article that followed was a masterpiece of understatement and made no comment on the invitation which the King had refused: "The King made an unexpected visit to Aberdeen today to welcome some of his guests who travelled from London by train. ... His Majesty did not enter the station but received his guests at the entrance. Only a few people, mostly railway employees, were at the station entrance at the time but they immediately recognized His Majesty as he stepped from his car. They doffed their hats and caps, and their greeting was acknowledged by a salute from the King who was in Highland dress. He again saluted as the car drove off."[16]

When the Duke and Duchess of York learned of that afternoon's events, they were exceptionally angry, feeling—quite rightly—that David had used them.[17] More to the point, no one was fooled by the King's actions; court mourning had come to an official end in July. If the Duke of York could be expected to perform his duties, there was no reason for his brother to remain in seclusion.

Wallis spent a week at Balmoral. At the King's request, those guests traditionally invited to the castle—the prime minister, the Archbishop of Canterbury, and cabinet ministers—were excluded. It would not be correct, however, to say that David had abandoned established society entirely, for he filled Balmoral with guests that represented the cream of the British aristocracy. Among those present were the Duke and Duchess of Kent; Lord and Lady Louis Mountbatten; the Duke and Duchess of Marlborough; the Duke and Duchess of Buccleuch; the Duke and Duchess of Sutherland; and the Earl and Countess of Rosebery.

David's decision to eliminate what had formerly been at least a semiofficial guest list caused much distress among both his family, who felt he was ignoring tradition, and certain members of the government, who saw it as evidence of his growing disinterest in the political side of his position. But David felt differently. His time at Balmoral formed the last few weeks of his holiday, and he had no desire to fill his leisure time with official meetings. Any necessary business, he declared, could be transacted through official channels via the red-leather dispatch boxes, which continued to arrive daily or by cable or telephone.[18]

He also had more personal reasons for excluding Cosmo Lang, Archbishop of Canterbury. For several months, he had been keenly aware of Lang's disapproval over his relationship with Wallis. The Archbishop, an elderly, conservative, and narrow-minded man, made no secret of his feelings; rather than discuss the growing problem with the King himself, he preferred to confide his doubts in others in the Royal Family—particularly Queen Mary and the Yorks—as well as government officials and members of society. Not surprisingly, David had little patience for the Archbishop and no desire to spend the last week of his holiday under his inquisitive eye.[19]

Wallis enjoyed Balmoral and took long walks along the River Dee and through the surrounding forests. Wallis and Edwina Mountbatten accompanied the men on their shoots for grouse and pheasant, joining in the picnic lunches set up beside waterfalls and in forest clearings. Lord Louis Mountbatten's new valet, Charles Smith, recalled: "Mrs. Simpson dressed smartly for the shoot. She changed into a warm tweed costume and boots. I found her very friendly and considerate, far from the dominating type of woman the public was led to believe she was."[20] Others, however, found her presence less welcome. In the evenings, there were games of cards in the drawing room or motion pictures in the castle's ballroom. Afterward, Wallis arranged for triple-decker toasted sandwiches to be served, an unusual meal which the guests enjoyed but which the servants, who were thoughtlessly kept up quite late working in the kitchens, found intolerable.[21]

While Wallis entertained at Balmoral, the Duke and Duchess of York remained in disapproving isolation at nearby Birkhall. Their irritation with the King over the Royal Infirmary dedication kept them away from Balmoral except for the occasional afternoon tea. They were also busy entertaining their houseguest, the Archbishop of Canterbury. Their decision to invite the primate has always been explained away as an act of kindness intended to maintain something of the tradition which the King seemed determined to ignore.

David, however, having had his own reasons for not inviting the Archbishop to Balmoral, was greatly angered that his brother had ignored his decision and seen fit to play host to Lang. Wallis would later tell a friend that David was upset over Lang's presence not only because the Duke of York had seemingly gone against his wishes but also because he took it as a not-so-subtle declaration of war against his authority. In effect, she explained, the Yorks had chosen to follow the traditions established by the sovereign and in doing so appeared to be setting up a rival court to that of the King.[22]

On Saturday, September 26, the King gave a fateful dinner at Balmoral. With great reluctance, the Duke and Duchess of York had agreed to attend. The rest of the dinner guests were already assembled when the Yorks arrived. What happened next has been the subject of endless controversy. Wallis stepped forward to greet the Duke and Duchess as they entered the drawing room. She smiled and extended her hand, but Elizabeth, walking ahead of her husband, refused to greet Wallis. Instead, as Michael Thornton discovered, she walked straight past Wallis and said in a loud voice, "I came to dine with the King."[23]

The Duchess of York made no further attempt at conversation with Wallis; in fact, she pointedly ignored her all evening. After an uncomfortable dinner, the guests assembled in the ballroom to watch a screening of the movie *Swing Time,* starring Fred Astaire and Ginger Rogers. As soon as the movie had ended, the Duke and Duchess of York were the first to leave.[24]

Elizabeth's defenders have claimed that her reaction had been entirely justified. David had placed Wallis, a very nonroyal interloper at Balmoral, in the difficult position of appearing to receive a member of the Royal Family in a house in which Elizabeth herself had often lived. Elizabeth was horrified at this and was no longer willing to continue the polite charade. She and her husband both believed that David, by ignoring tradition and inviting his mistress to preside in Queen Victoria's favorite house, had irreparably damaged the prestige of the monarchy.[25]

But what had Wallis done, exactly, to provoke such a response? There is no indication that she behaved in a presumptuous manner at Balmoral or that she was anything less than friendly toward the Duchess. The Yorks had taken her simple gesture of greeting for something which it almost certainly was not: an unpardonable breach of royal etiquette and good manners. Wallis had indeed been in a tricky situation: David had asked her to act as hostess, and her duty, as such, was to greet the arriving guests. If anyone was to blame for the incident, it was certainly the King.

Elizabeth's reaction would cause an immense gulf between the royal brothers at a time when neither could afford to alienate the other. Inevitably, most writers have squarely placed the blame for this deterioration on the shoulders of the King. Sarah Bradford, for example, writes that after this, David "excluded the Yorks entirely."[26] This represents only half the story. The Yorks also chose not to involve themselves in David's life after this episode. Whether their actions were justified or not is irrelevant in assessing blame, for they surely must bear, along with the King himself, an equal share in the breakdown of the brothers' relationship. Previously, Elizabeth had managed to behave in a friendly fashion with Thelma Furness, so she cannot have had any great objection on moral grounds to David's having a mistress.

It must also be said that David was greatly angered over what had transpired during his time at Balmoral. His brother and sister-in-law had deliberately chosen to ignore his wishes and invited one of his most bitter and vocal critics to spend the holiday with them, a move that he cannot have looked upon with favor. Above all, however, David could not forget how rudely his sister-in-law had treated the woman he loved. The break—long in coming—would never be healed. These two strong, dominant women—Wallis Simpson and Elizabeth of York—would remain bitter and powerful enemies for the rest of their lives.

16

The Divorce

O<small>N</small> O<small>CTOBER</small> 1, <small>THE</small> K<small>ING'S</small> <small>MOTHER</small>, Queen Mary, vacated her apartments at Buckingham Palace and moved down the Mall to Marlborough House. Four days later, Edward VIII formally took up residence at Buckingham Palace. He refused, however, to occupy the private apartments on the first floor where the sovereign normally lived; instead, he selected the ground-floor Belgian Suite, a series of rooms overlooking the terrace and gardens beyond. He managed to engage, after much negotiation by the British ambassador, Sir George Clerk, the principal chef from Maxim's in Paris, M. Legros. David's only other additions to the palace were a squash court and a modern innovation much more in character: television.[1]

When Wallis returned to London, she supervised the moving of her furniture and possessions into a four-story house she had let at 16 Cumberland Terrace, on Outer Circle Drive in Regent's Park. The house formed a portion of what has been called "the grandest and most spectacular building in Regent's Park."[2] A long white building dominated by a massive central portico whose Ionic columns supported a pediment filled with Wedgewood-style motifs and crowned with classical statuary, Cumberland Terrace had been designed in the early nineteenth century by architect John Nash. Ironically, the property was owned by the Crown, and Wallis sublet it. When crowds of curious people would stop and stare at its black windows, policemen would say, "This is Crown property, move along, move along . . . ordinary people don't live here, y'know."[3]

Public interest in Wallis was fanned by the incessant attention given her every move in the American press. Although her name did not appear in British papers and American publications were censored in England to remove all references to her existence, inevitably word of mouth and smuggled copies of forbidden journals aroused great excitement. In the United States, newspaper tycoon William Randolph Hearst had single-handedly engaged in an effort to promote Wallis as a suitable bride for the King. Hearst himself had, for many years, lived openly with his actress-mistress at his magnificent castle above the Pacific Ocean.

Wallis was a good story, and Hearst wanted to nurture it along. In March 1936 he had telephoned one of his top reporters in New York, Adela Rogers St. John, and told her that she was to leave for England immediately to work on the story. He said he wanted the truth about Mrs. Simpson. "Let us see if we can make her Queen of England."[4]

St. John spent a considerable amount of time interviewing Wallis's friends and poking around London, but in the end she reported back to Hearst that there was no real story and that the King was not going to marry Mrs. Simpson. Hearst, however, was not satisfied by this, and wanted Wallis presented in the most enticing and favorable light. He felt that if a war came, it would be important for Britain to have an American queen. At his insistence, the articles eventually appeared, but they did little to promote the truth behind the story.

Clearly, the intense coverage of her every move was beginning to get to Wallis. She had arranged to sit for society photographer Cecil Beaton. When she entered his studio, he greeted her warmly, but she cut him off with a laugh: "I don't want you to call me by that name of Mrs. Simpson, which the American yellow press has made me loathe."[5]

London Observer fashion editor Alison Settle happened to be at Beaton's studio as well. The photographer had asked to borrow marble busts of the young Queen Victoria and the Prince Consort, which Settle had brought with her. As she helped place the busts on their pedestals, Settle noted a woman waiting for her portrait. "Now let me think, where have I seen her? she wondered. I know she has her nails done next to me at Elizabeth Arden. But she did notice that the woman's makeup was all wrong for a black-and-white photograph.

"I'm awfully afraid you'll have to have your face washed and redone," Settle matter-of-factly told Wallis. "The make-up girl will be here in a minute or two." Settle quickly turned around and examined the setting; she noted several other royal busts, including one of Queen Alexandra. "My, we have gone royal today, haven't we?" she said loudly. Wallis said nothing, but her disapproval was clear. Only when she had returned to her own office did Settle realize the identity of Beaton's sitter.[6]

Beaton suggested using draped ermine as a background for the portraits, but Wallis immediately objected. "Don't do anything connected with the Coronation with me," she warned. "I want none of that now." Beaton noted, "Whatever fantastic changes have taken place in Mrs. Simpson's life, she has obviously suffered. There is a sad look to be seen in her eyes."[7]

When the proofs were ready, Beaton took them to Cumberland Terrace. "This day," he recalled, "Mrs. Simpson looked immaculate, soignée and fresh as a young girl. Her skin was as bright and smooth as the inside of a shell, her hair so sleek she might have been Chinese. . . . She spoke amusingly, in staccato sentences punctuated by explosive bursts of laughter that lit up her face with great gaiety and made her eyebrows look attractively surprised."[8]

The Simpson divorce was scheduled to be heard in the Ipswich assizes on October 27. Hoping to escape the press, Wallis rented a small cottage in the Suffolk town of Felixstowe. A week after arriving back in London, Wallis—accompanied by George and Kitty Hunter—took up residence at Felixstowe. The King had also dispatched Chief Inspector David Storrier from Scotland Yard to watch over her and guard against any unwelcome intrusion.

The night they arrived at the cottage, the Hunters told Wallis they wished to speak with her. Until four in the morning, they warned her against going through with her divorce, saying that it could only end in disaster. The King was becoming increasingly unpopular, they said, due to his relationship with her. Wallis was clearly not prepared for their vehemence. The following morning, plagued with doubt, she wrote to David: "Really David darling if I hurt you to this extent isn't it best for me to steal quietly away. . . . I can't help but feel you will have trouble in the House of Commons etc. and may be forced to go. I can't put you in that position. . . . Do please say what you think best for all concerned when you call me after reading this. Together I suppose we are strong enough to face this mean world. . . . Hold me tight please David."[9]

But David, as always, was full of reassurances, and by now Wallis had begun to believe them. She knew nothing at all about British politics, next to nothing of the constitutional position of the monarchy, and very little of public opinion. And yet the King, who would, of course, have known the intricate details, never failed to tell her that everything would somehow work itself out. To the end, she saw no reason to doubt him.

There was a fair amount of wishful thinking at work here; Wallis, after all, could not have failed to be entranced at the idea that she could somehow rise above all the obstacles and become Queen of England. David's overwhelming, obsessive need for her, at times frustrating in its totality, was also undoubtedly flattering. Here was one of the richest and most powerful men in the world, who could transport her to exotic places and shower her with extravagant gifts, and yet only she had it in her power to give him the one thing he most desired: herself.

As entrenched as David's need for her appeared to be, there was another consideration: Wallis loved him. Her feelings had grown stronger, more assured. Her traumatic relationships with Win and Felipe Espil had taught her to guard her heart, and her emotions remained largely private. Wallis was far too cautious to simply fall in love with David; her practical, pragmatic approach was deliberately unhindered by sentiment. Hers was a love founded on his need for her, on the friendship they shared, on his tender care and concern for her welfare. "She loves him, though I feel she is not *in* love with him," Cecil Beaton summed up accurately.[10]

It was this love—this desire to remain in David's life—which blinded Wallis to the realities of her situation. She would have been content to continue as the King's mistress; her practical side told her that anything else would be impossible. Undeniably, she allowed herself to envision another resolution, one which ended with their marriage and coronation. In this context, Wallis truly believed that she and David would form a thoroughly modern partnership, in keeping with his desire to reshape the monarchy, together forming a visible break with the past, "an impossibly chic king and queen, a royal version of William Powell and Myrna Loy in *The Thin Man* films," as one writer noted.[11] These conflicting visions of her future were to torment Wallis throughout the abdication.

The date for the Simpson divorce had been carefully calculated by the King. After a decree *nisi* was granted, English law required a wait of six months before the divorce was made final. The delay was originally provided in the event that a child was born in the interval, in which case the divorce might be rescinded. This six-month lapse meant that Wallis would first be free to marry on April 27, 1937. The coronation ceremony had been announced for May 12; this gave David adequate time, if he intended, to marry Wallis and then have her crowned at his side as queen.

The night before her divorce was to be heard, Wallis was so nervous that she could not sleep. She spent the long hours pacing the floor, wondering if she was doing the right thing.[12]

The international press had assembled in force at Ipswich, but only a few British journalists were there. This was due more to a peculiarity of British law than respect for the King. In 1926, Parliament had passed an act restricting reports of divorce cases; in truth, there was little they could say about the Simpson case. Special arrangements within the courtroom had also been made. Access to the public seats had been restricted; those that faced the witness box were left vacant. Only thirty tickets had been issued to the press, and their seats were placed so that they could only see the backs of the witnesses's heads.

Theodore Goddard and his partner collected Wallis at Felixstowe and accompanied her to the Ipswich court. Wallis, dressed in a navy blue double-breasted coat with matching skirt and a navy blue felt hat with veil, kept her head lowered as Goddard ran her through the crowd of journalists that lined the sidewalk from the street to the assizes door. Once inside, she was quickly led to the courtroom. She sat in the barrister's well, with a man on either side of her, surrounded by seven police, four plainclothes detectives, facing the spectators. One reporter described Wallis's behavior as "queenly." However, another mentioned her nervous "spasms of coughing."[13]

A guardsman, dressed in a scarlet tunic, entered the room and heralded the arrival of the judge with a blast on his silver trumpet. His lordship, Mr. Justice Sir John Hawke, entered the room, coughing and repeatedly blowing his nose. He was a short, elderly man, almost completely hidden behind his crimson-and-ermine robes and long white wig. He took his place beneath the red-velvet canopy and glanced about his courtroom. He seemed clearly perturbed at the unusual circumstances, and Wallis later recalled that he appeared to spend most of the proceedings staring directly at her. Uncomfortable, she herself kept her head bowed during most of the hearings.

Wallis's case was presented by Norman Birkett, K. C. Birkett was accompanied by his assistant, Walter Frampton, who sat to one side of Wallis. Ernest was not present; he was instead represented by his lawyer, North Lewis. Hawke did not hesitate to express his irritation with the entire business. He continued to look Wallis up and down, noting the empty courtroom, and asked, "How did the case come here?" After some whispering from the clerk of assize, he muttered to himself, "Yes, yes, I see."

Wallis took the stand, removing her right glove to raise her hand and take the oath. Justice Hawke questioned Wallis at length, coughing and sneezing and blowing his nose throughout, often mumbling to himself, then shouting his questions at her. A chair had been placed for her in which to sit, although it was customary that a witness stand. She told of her happy marriage to Ernest, insisting that all had been well until the autumn of 1934, when he had begun to disappear on long weekends.

Birkett asked, "Did you live happily with the respondent until the autumn of 1934?"

"Yes."

"Was it at that time the respondent's manner changed toward you?"

"Yes."

"What was the change?"

"He was indifferent and often went away for weekends alone."

"Did you complain about this?"

"Yes, I did."

"Did he continue to do what you complain of—going away alone and staying away weekends?"

"Yes."

"On Christmas Day, 1934, did you find a note lying on your dressing table?"

"Yes."

The note was passed to the judge, and the barrister suggested it was in a woman's handwriting.

Justice Hawke read it, then declared, "It may be in a woman's handwriting, but it's not very legible." He was then given a typewritten transcript of the letter. "This is evidence against nobody," he said loudly, clearly annoyed. "I do not understand it."

Birkett ignored the judge's consternation and continued to question Wallis.

"Did the finding of the note cause you considerable distress?"

"It did."

"Did you complain to your husband at that time?"

"No, I thought I better not, in the hope conditions would improve."

"Did they improve?"

"I'm afraid they did not."

This note remains a great mystery, for it was never entered into evidence. It is possible it was a note from Mary Kirk Raffray, although, at the time, it seems unlikely that she and Ernest had begun their liaison.

Wallis then testified that she had received another letter, addressed to her but intended for her husband, a letter thanking Ernest in a warm, loving way for a gift of some roses. After this, she had sought counsel and hired detectives. Birkett then submitted a letter she had written afterward to her husband:

Dear Ernest:

I have just learned that while you have been away, instead of being on business, as you have led me to believe, you have been staying at the Hotel Bray with a lady. I am sure you realize this is conduct which I cannot possibly overlook and must insist you do not continue to live here with me. This only confirms the suspicions I have had for a long time. I am therefore instructing my solicitors to take proceedings for divorce.

With this letter, Wallis finished her time on the witness stand and quietly slipped back into her seat alongside Birkett and Frampton.

Birkett next called two employees who worked at the Hotel de Paris in Bray. Each testified that on July 28, 1936 they had served breakfast in bed to a man they identified as Ernest Simpson and a woman called Buttercup Kennedy—almost certainly Mary Kirk.

With this, the plaintiff's case was over. No one questioned precisely how Wallis had managed to ascertain her need for a detective on the same day that Ernest would conveniently commit a public act of adultery. Hawke seemed suspicious. For several minutes, he said nothing. Finally, he began to question Birkett about the incident at the Hotel de Paris.

Without waiting for Hawke to finish his question, Birkett interrupted him by saying, "I assume that what your Lordship has in mind—"

But Hawke would not let him complete his sentence. "How do you know what is in my mind?" he asked angrily. "What is it that I have in mind, Mr. Birkett?"

"I think, with great deference," replied Birkett gently, "that Your Lordship may have in mind what is known as 'ordinary hotel evidence,' where the name of the lady is not disclosed. I thought that might have been in Your Lordship's mind."

Hawke was silent for several moments. He eyed Wallis suspiciously, then declared, "That is what it must have been, Mr. Birkett. I am glad of your help."

"The lady's name," Birkett said, "was mentioned in the petition, my Lord, so now I ask for a decree *nisi* with costs against the respondent."

"Yes, costs against the respondent, I am afraid," Hawke agreed with great hesitation. "I suppose I must in these unusual circumstances. So you may have it, with costs."

"Decree *nisi* with costs?" asked Birkett.

"Yes," Hawke replied, "I suppose so."[14]

With this, it was all over. Wallis crept out of the courtroom, but she paused long enough to speak to a reporter from United Press International, who had asked her if she was planning to return to America now. "I will never return to the United States," Wallis said directly. "After all the nasty things said about me I could never show my face there again. I have never experienced anything like it in my life. I don't know why they should talk about me that way. I certainly am not that important. . . . The things that have been said about me are almost beyond belief. I have never seen or heard anything like it. I feel terribly hurt and humiliated."[15]

Ironically, on the same day, Win Spencer was divorced from his second wife, Miriam, in San Diego, California. She had charged him with desertion, drunkenness, cruelty, and physical violence in breaking up their furniture in his drunken rages. Some enterprising reporters tracked him down a few weeks later; while he refused to comment on either of his two divorces, he was gracious where his first wife was concerned: "Wallis was one of the finest women I ever knew. My work did not allow me to partake of the social life which Wallis loved so dearly. Gradually we drifted apart. I suppose that is the price we pay for a career. . . . I wish her nothing but the best."[16]

The American press gave the Simpson divorce enormous play. On October 26, the day before the divorce, the *New York Journal-American* wrote: "In all probability, in June 1937, one month after the ceremonies of the coronation, will follow the festivities of the marriage (of King Edward VIII) to the very charming and intelligent Mrs. Ernest Simpson, of Baltimore, Maryland, USA."[17] Another American newspaper headlined the event famously, "KING'S MOLL RENO'D IN WOLSEY'S HOME TOWN."[18]

In England reaction was far more subdued, but critics were virulent and vocal. One man remarked, "The courts of law are open to all—like the Ritz Hotel." Few acquainted with the facts of the case believed that there had been no collusion. George Buchanan, an MP from Glasgow, declared: "The whole law courts were set at defiance for this one man. A divorce case was heard when every one of you knows it was a breaking of the law. The law is desecrated. The courts are thrust aside."[19]

"Uncensored copies of *Time*, the first publication to take notice of the scandal," wrote Jessica Mitford, "were hard to come by. Only those lucky enough to know someone who received a subscription direct, from America, were able to follow the progress of the shocking affair week by week. All reference to it had been neatly scissored out of the news-stand copies."[20]

The British Royal Family, especially the Duke and Duchess of York and Queen Mary, were highly suspicious of the Simpson divorce. All believed that there had been collusion. However, a subsequent investigation by Thomas Barnes, the King's proctor, and Sir Donald Somervell, the attorney general, found that "the divorce—even if it had some collusive fact—e.g. the willingness of Mrs. S. that her husband should be unfaithful—was not a collusive divorce in the ordinary or any provable sense."[21]

The day after the divorce, Harold Nicolson wrote: "There are very serious rumours that the King will make her Duchess of Edinburgh and marry. The point is whether he is so infatuated as to insist on her becoming Queen or whether the marriage will be purely morganatic. . . . I gather from other people that there is considerable danger."[22]

17

Growing Troubles

O N OCTOBER 16, while Wallis was away at Felixstowe, the King held an important meeting at Buckingham Palace with William Maxwell Aitken, First Lord Beaverbrook. Beaverbrook, a confident, crafty Canadian, had made his fortune in industrial construction; in 1918 he had joined the British cabinet as minister of information in charge of propaganda. With his fortune, he bought control of the *London Evening Standard* and the *Daily Express*, and founded the *Sunday Express*.

The King did not know Beaverbrook particularly well, but he recognized that the press baron could become a powerful ally in any coming war over his relationship with Wallis. Beaverbrook recalled what took place that evening at Buckingham Palace:

> The King asked me to help in suppressing all advance news of the Simpson divorce, and in limiting publicity after the event. He stated his case calmly and with great cogency and force.
>
> The reasons he gave for his wish were that Mrs. Simpson was ill, unhappy and distressed by the thought of notoriety. Notoriety would attach to her only because she had been his guest on the *Nahlin* and at Balmoral. As the publicity would be due to association with himself, he felt it his duty to protect her.
>
> These reasons appeared satisfactory to me, and so I took part in a negotiation to confine publication of the news to a report of Mrs. Simpson's divorce, making no mention of her friendship with the King.[1]

At the same time, the King also met with Esmond Harmsworth, son of Lord Rothermere, the press baron who owned London's *Daily Mail* and the *Evening News*. Harmsworth supervised his father's newspapers, and as with Beaverbrook, the King appealed to his sense of loyalty to the throne and asked that he refrain from mentioning Mrs. Simpson in his publications. Like Beaverbrook, Harmsworth agreed. This gentlemen's agreement was to last for nearly the entire abdication crisis. Having satisfied himself that disaster had been averted, David left that same Friday evening and went to Sandringham, where he was to spend the weekend.

The day before this meeting took place, Alexander Hardinge had first learned that the Simpson divorce case was to be heard at Ipswich in two weeks. Hardinge at once wrote to Prime Minister Baldwin, begging him "to see the King and ask if these proceedings could not be stopped, for the danger in which they placed him [HM] was becoming every day greater."[2]

Hardinge was quick to seize upon the issue. In the past, he had made little secret of his disapproval of the King, and it seems unlikely that his motivation that October was a personal concern over Edward VIII's well-being. The traditional analysis of the situation would suggest that Hardinge acted in good faith, fearful of the effect that the relationship between the King and Wallis was having on the prestige of the throne. On the other hand, it has been suggested more than once that the King's liaison simply provided a convenient excuse upon which his enemies at court were able to act in an effort to force his removal from the throne.

Technically, David was free to marry whenever and whomever he wished. It would be unconstitutional, however, as Sir Donald Somervell, the attorney general, informed Baldwin that October, for the King to marry against the advice of his ministers. Knowing this, Hardinge worked tirelessly. His dual strategy was to persuade Baldwin to make it quite clear that the King's marriage to Wallis was unacceptable, therefore putting the King in the position in which in order to marry her he would have to reject his prime minister's advice. His second plan was to gather evidence demonstrating that such a marriage was unacceptable to the people of the empire.

Hardinge owed his loyalty to the King, but this did not stop him from conducting secret meetings with Baldwin. On October 17 he arranged to meet the prime minister at Cumberland Lodge, a grace-and-favor residence rented to Lord Fitzalan in Windsor Great Park. Also present were Lord Cranborne, undersecretary of state for foreign affairs and later to succeed as fifth Marquess of Salisbury; the Duke of Norfolk, the nation's senior peer and the Earl Marshal of the kingdom; and Lord Kemsley, who, with his brother Lord Camrose, was the proprietor of the *Sunday Times*, the *Daily Telegraph,* and the *Financial Times*. Hardinge pressed the prime minister to urge the King to ask Mrs. Simpson to drop her divorce action and to make their relationship less conspicuous.[3] Hardinge also met with Theodore Goddard and warned him that a crisis threatened unless the King could be convinced to stop the Simpson divorce. Goddard conveyed this news to Walter Monckton, David's friend and adviser, who, in turn, informed the King of Hardinge's visit to Goddard.

At the same time, Hardinge left an urgent message at Sandringham for the King saying that the prime minister wished to meet with him on important business as soon as possible. David declared that he would return to the Fort on Tuesday, October 20, and meet the prime minister at that time. Over the weekend, David, knowing that Hardinge had approached Goddard and that he had also been in touch with the prime minister, determined that the government was about to push for a declaration of his intentions.

Baldwin arrived at the Fort at ten on Tuesday morning as scheduled and was shown into the drawing room. The prime minister was clearly nervous; he asked for a whiskey and soda, much to David's surprise. Nevertheless, the King rang for a servant and asked for whiskey to be brought. Baldwin began to mix the drink himself, then turned to the King and asked if he would like one as well. "No, thank you, Mr. Baldwin," he replied. "I never take a drink before seven o'clock in the evening."[4]

Finally, Baldwin asked about Wallis's upcoming divorce action. "Must this case really go on?" Baldwin inquired.

"Mr. Baldwin," David answered, "I have no right to interfere with the affairs of an individual. It would be wrong were I to attempt to influence Mrs. Simpson just because she happens to be a friend of the King's."[5]

True to his word and indeed his inclinations, David refused to interfere. During the whole time Wallis was at Felixstowe, he was lonely and restless, unable to concentrate. Winston Churchill recalled the effect of separation from Wallis on the King: "I saw him when she'd gone away for a fortnight. He was miserable, haggard, dejected, not knowing what to do. Then I saw him when she'd been back a day or two, and he was a different man—gay, debonair, self-confident. Make no mistake, he can't live without her. . . ."[6]

Wallis returned to London immediately after her divorce case was heard. It took two hours for her to drive from Ipswich to her new house at Cumberland Terrace; she was scarcely through the door before her maid, Mary Cain, announced that the King was on the telephone. He was absolutely overcome with joy and relief, for he had feared, until the last, that some circumstance would arise which would cancel the proceedings in Ipswich.

Later that afternoon, David kept a number of appointments, including a meeting with Prime Minister Mackenzie King of Canada.

"It had been hoped," noted Geoffrey Dawson, proprietor of the *Times*, in his diary, "that the P.M. of Canada might have said something on this occasion about the growing anxiety in his own country. He was in a strong position to give such a warning; but it was quite clear from his conversation with me that he had done nothing of the kind—had indeed, if anything, made matters worse by discoursing on the King's popularity in the Dominions."[7]

That same evening, Wallis and David were reunited when he came to her house at Cumberland Terrace to dine. Reluctantly, he told her of Baldwin's visit the week before but again reassured her that all would be well. For David, the evening was one of celebration, and nothing would dampen his happiness that the woman he loved was now on her way to divorce. He pulled from his pocket a box from Cartier and presented it to her: inside was the massive Mogul emerald, set in a platinum ring. It was to be Wallis's engagement ring, and was engraved on the back: "WE are ours now, 27 X 36. [October 27, 1936]"

On November 3 the King presided at the state opening of Parliament. Traditionally, the sovereign rode in state in a magnificent carriage procession, escorted by members of the household cavalry; a violent storm, however, caused David to cancel these plans, and instead he arrived at the Palace of Westminster in the royal Daimler. Within the House of Lords, every available space had been filled with inquisitive peers and peeresses. The King's speech included references to the strengthening of defense forces; concern over the growing tensions in Europe, China, and Japan; and, ironically, discussion of preparations for the upcoming coronation as well as his intention to go to India to repeat the Delhi durbar, which his parents had undertaken in 1911.

That evening, Wallis dined with Chips and Honor Channon at their home in Belgrave Square. According to Chips, she was "gay and amusing. We discussed her divorce, which she says was at Ernest's instigation, and at no wish of hers."[8] From her comments, it is apparent that Wallis still believed that she would be able to avoid a crisis. "I am lying here making all sorts of *wise* decisions," she told Edwina Mountbatten. She explained that she was determined to leave England and that "soon the charming people, the man in the street and the lunatics will forget me, and all will be well once more."[9]

Two days later, Wallis joined David for a dinner party given by the King's lord-in-waiting, Perry Brownlow, and his wife, Kitty, at their London house. Also present was Lord Beaverbrook, who met Wallis for the first time. "She appeared to me to be a simple woman," he recalled. "Her smile was kindly and pleasing, and her conversation interspersed with protestations of ignorance of politics and with declarations of simplicity of character and outlook. ... I was greatly impressed by the way the other women greeted her. . . . All but one of them greeted Mrs. Simpson with a kiss. She received it with appropriate dignity, but in no case did she return it. . . ."[10]

On Friday, November 6, Wallis attended a party given by Emerald Cunard. During the evening, Edith, Lady Londonderry, cornered Wallis and told her that "if the King had any idea of marrying her, he ought to be quickly disabused of the notion, since the English people would never stand for a Queen or King's Consort who had been twice divorced and whose previous husbands were both still living."[11]

For Wallis, this simply confirmed her own growing fears. Three days later, Wallis's aunt Bessie arrived aboard RMS *Queen Mary*, filled with disgust at the coverage her niece, and her relationship with the King, were receiving in the American press. The papers back in the United States, she told Wallis, were filled with mocking stories about the Warfields and the Montagues, their finances and lack thereof, and even allegations that her mother had run a boardinghouse in a poor part of Baltimore. "You'd think that we'd all come right out of Tobacco Road!" she exclaimed with disgust.[12]

That same evening, David finally confessed to Walter Monckton in the Empire Drawing Room at Buckingham Palace that he intended to marry Wallis once she was free. This came as no great surprise to Monckton, but he advised that the King should keep his intentions private; there was no point, he declared, in announcing the plan now, because Mrs. Simpson would not possibly be free to marry until the spring. "I could see at once," Monckton recalled, "that he did not agree with this advice because he felt that he could not go forward to the Coronation on 12 May 1937 meaning in his heart to make the marriage whatever happened and, as he felt, deceiving the government and the people into imagining that he had dropped the association or, at any rate, did not intend to marry."[13] Monckton, well aware of the King's character and determination, realized that there was little he could do to dissuade David from his stated course of action. "The trouble," wrote Monckton, "was that on this matter his mind was made up by himself long before he knew it, and this is the explanation of what must have seemed to many a strange and obtuse obstinancy."[14]

On November 11, the King performed what was to become his last public engagement in London by attending Remembrance Day ceremonies in Whitehall and laying a wreath at the Cenotaph, which served as a monument to the war dead. As soon as this duty had been completed, David left London for a tour of the home fleet at the Portland Naval Base. This proved a triumphant success. "No one could deny his surpassing talent for inspiring enthusiasm and managing great crowds," noted Sir Samuel Hoare, then First Lord of the Admiralty. "He seemed to know personally every officer and seaman in the

Fleet. . . . In my long experience of mass meetings I never saw one so completely dominated by a single personality. . . . Elbowing his way through the crowd, he walked to the end of the hall and started community singing to the accompaniment of a seaman's mouth organ. When he came back to the platform, he made an impromptu speech that brought the house down. Then a seaman in the crowd proposed three cheers for him, and there followed an unforgettable scene of the wildest and most spontaneous enthusiasm."[15]

During the two days the King was away, events moved quickly. A week earlier, Helen Hardinge had noted ominously in her diary, "Government are not prepared to carry on."[16] She could have only received such a serious piece of news from her husband, the King's private secretary. The inescapable conclusion, therefore, is that on November 6, Alexander Hardinge had private information that the British government, led by Prime Minister Stanley Baldwin, was willing to resign if the issue of the King's affair with Mrs. Simpson was not resolved to its satisfaction.

Rather than immediately inform his master of this vital piece of news, however, Hardinge would wait a week, during which time he conducted numerous meetings with the very same officials who apparently had proclaimed their willingness to force the issue of the King's private life. On November 12 he dined with Baldwin to discuss the situation and what could be done next.

For several months, certain Conservative politicians, clerics, and members of the court had been trying to convince Baldwin to take a more aggressive stance where the King's affair with Mrs. Simpson was concerned. Until now, the prime minister had always been loath to interfere in the private affairs of the King. He had no wish to stir up trouble. And yet he himself was greatly worried over the liaison.

Now, Hardinge warned Baldwin, the situation was fast becoming a crisis, and the private secretary felt he could no longer maintain his silence. He showed the prime minister the draft of a letter he intended to send to the King informing him that his relationship with Mrs. Simpson was about to lead to a confrontation with the government. It was written on Buckingham Palace stationery and was dated November 13:

> Sir,
>   With my humble duty.
>   As Your Majesty's Private Secretary, I feel it is my duty to bring to your notice the following facts which have come to my knowledge, and which I know to be accurate:
>   (1) The silence of the British Press on the subject of your majesty's friendship with Mrs. Simpson is *not* going to be maintained. It is probably only a matter of days before the outburst

begins. Judging by the letters from British subjects living in foreign countries where the Press has been outspoken, the effect will be calamitous.

(2) The Prime Minister and senior members of the Government are meeting to-day to discuss what action should be taken to deal with the serious situation which is developing. As Your Majesty no doubt knows, the resignation of the government—an eventuality which can by no means be excluded—would result in Your Majesty having to find someone else capable of forming a government which would receive the support of the present House of Commons. I have reason to know that, in view of the feeling prevalent among members of the House of Commons of all parties, this is hardly within the bounds of possibility. The only alternative remaining is a dissolution and a general election, in which Your Majesty's personal affairs would be the chief issue—and I cannot help feeling that even those who sympathize with Your Majesty as an individual would deeply resent the damage which would inevitably be done to the Crown, the corner-stone on which the whole Empire rests.

If Your Majesty will permit me to say so, there is only one step which holds out any prospect of avoiding this dangerous situation, and that is for Mrs. Simpson to go abroad *without further delay*, and I would *beg* Your Majesty to give this proposal your earnest consideration before the position has become irretrievable. Owing to the changing attitude of the press, the matter has become one of great urgency.

I have the honour etc. etc.

Alexander Hardinge.[17]

Baldwin read through the letter and did nothing to stop Hardinge, although he—like the private secretary himself—must have known that the King's reaction to this intrusion into his relationship with Wallis was likely to be immediate and unfavorable.

The following day, Friday, November 13, Hardinge asked Geoffrey Dawson, to come to Buckingham Palace. Dawson was a conservative man of traditional views. He took a dim view of Edward VIII; personally, he was highly critical of both the King's passion for modernization as well as his relationship with Mrs. Simpson, and the *Times* was not shy in subtly pointing out what Dawson perceived to be the King's weaknesses.

Dawson had previously confided his doubts about the King to Hardinge. In his position as editor of the *Times*, Dawson had received several letters expressing displeasure with the King; none of these letters was ever printed, and Dawson himself paid little attention until one day in October 1936 when a letter arrived from America. Signed "Britannicus," the letter consisted of nine pages in which were delineated "a perfect avalanche of muck and slime" in the American press about the King.[18] According to the writer, the King's relationship with Mrs. Simpson had made England appear to be "a dizzy Balkan musical comedy. . . ."[19] "Britannicus" repeated stories he claimed were prevelant in the American media: that Queen Mary had been forcibly evicted from Buckingham Palace to make room for the King's mistress; that Wallis was being used to act as an official agent to help collect the outstanding war debt Britain still owed to the United States; and that the King had screamed and ranted at Baldwin for trying to interfere in his relationship. "I cannot refrain," the writer concluded, "from saying that nothing would please me more than to hear that Edward VIII had abdicated his rights in favour of the heir presumptive. In my view, it would be well to have such a change take place while it is still a matter of individuals, and before the disquiet has progressed to the point of calling in question the institution of monarchy itself."[20]

This letter represented no more than the view of one expatriate living in the United States and subject to a stream of demonstrably false allegations about the King. Nevertheless, Dawson trumpeted it as evidence that the public mood was about to turn against the King. Not only did he show the letter to the prime minister; he also took a copy to Buckingham Palace and gave it to Alexander Hardinge. To the private secretary, of course—already prejudiced against his master— this was simply further proof that the monarch was causing untold damage to the prestige of the British throne.

Now it was Hardinge's turn to confide in Dawson. On that Friday afternoon, he showed him the draft of his letter to the King. Although it is arguable that Hardinge was within his rights to consult the prime minister, such reasoning cannot be successfully advanced in his decision to consult the King's most vocal critic in the press. "The King's Private Secretary is a solitary figure," Hardinge weakly tried to explain in his own defense. "At this moment of anxiety and distress I desperately needed an outside opinion as to the general wisdom and propriety of my letter, as well as its accuracy; and, it seemed to me, no one could help me more over this than a man with the discretion, experience and integrity of Geoffrey Dawson, who was at the same time 'very much in the know.'. . ."[21]

"What," Lord Beaverbrook would later ask, "can be said of a Private Secretary who discussed his master's affairs with the editor of an opposition newspaper and even disclosed the contents of a letter of severe criticism that he meant to send to his employer? Bad. Worse still when the master is a King, and the servant is a public official."[22] But Hardinge, driven by his conservatism and his dislike of the King, was determined to do everything within his power to break the relationship between his master and Mrs. Simpson.

On the morning of Friday, November 13, Baldwin met with several senior politicians, including former Labour Party prime minister Ramsay MacDonald and Neville Chamberlain of the Conservative Party. Chamberlain produced two letters which he proposed that Baldwin should send to the King. The first, written by Chamberlain for Baldwin, read:

> I have before me an official communication in which the advice of Your Majesty's Government is formally tendered, to the effect that in view of the grave dangers to which, in their opinion, this country is being exposed, your association with Mrs. Simpson should be terminated forthwith. It is hardly necessary for me to point out that should this advice he tendered and refused by Your Majesty, only one result could follow in accordance with the requirements of constitutional monarchy, that is, resignation of myself and the National Government. If Mrs. Simpson left the country forthwith, this distasteful matter could be settled in a less formal manner.

The second letter had been drafted a week earlier by a group of senior civil servants led by Warren Fisher, permanent secretary to the treasury:

> Unless steps are promptly taken to allay the widespread and growing misgivings among the people, the feelings of respect, esteem and affection which Your Majesty has evoked among them, will disappear in a revulsion of so grave and perilous a character as possibly to threaten the stability of the nation and of the Empire. The dangers to the people of this country of such a shock, the disunity and loss of confidence which would ensue at a time when so much of the world is looking to the United Kingdom for guidance and leadership, through a sea of troubles, cannot but be obvious to Your Majesty. In Mr. Baldwin's opinion there is but one course which he can advise you to take, namely to put an end to Your Majesty's association with Mrs. Simpson.[23]

Baldwin had not read either letter until that morning. According to his biographers, Middlemas and Barnes, he "was deeply shocked by their tone. He knew he could not send either to the King; if they were made public, they would inevitably rally the country in the cause of a popular monarch, whom the Government were apparently blackmailing."[24]

The prime minister, however, agreed to take the letters with him to Chequers, his country estate, for consideration over the weekend. On Sunday, the Australian high commissioner in London lunched with Baldwin at Chequers, during which time the prime minister informed him of the King's relationship with Mrs. Simpson. Whether Baldwin was seeking counsel or not, what he had done was, in effect, to place himself in the position where he was subject to the advice of empire officials. There can only be two explanations for this behavior: Either Baldwin was seriously inept and did not realize that in raising official objection to the King's relationship he was likely to force the monarch's abdication; or he did so precisely for those reasons. When he returned to London, the commissioner wrote to Baldwin: "I think you have to advise the King ... that the people of this country and of the Dominions would not accept this woman as Queen ... and that because of the perils both to the Throne and the Empire the King's conduct has created, there would be a demand for his abdication that you would find impossible to resist. ... You would have to tell him that unless he was prepared to abandon any idea of marriage ... you would be compelled to advise him to abdicate, and unless he accepted such advice you would be unable to continue as his adviser and would tender the resignation of Government."[25]

Late Friday afternoon, David returned to Fort Belvedere from his tour of the home fleet. Wallis and Aunt Bessie had already gone out to the Fort and were waiting to welcome him. He greeted them warmly, but hurried away to take a long, hot bath; waiting for him were the usual red-leather dispatch boxes from Whitehall. In one, he found an envelope marked "Urgent and Confidential." He opened it and found inside the letter from Alexander Hardinge, which he read. David himself was shocked at the letter; he felt that Hardinge had betrayed him and perceived the letter as a challenge to both himself and to his continued relationship with Wallis. For the moment, he did nothing. Within an hour, David reappeared in the drawing room at the Fort for drinks with Wallis and her aunt. Wallis noticed that he seemed distant and preoccupied, but when she tried to ask him if anything was wrong, he simply replied that he was tired. She thought that the trip to review the home fleet must have worn him out.

Saturday passed quietly at the Fort, but on Sunday, Sibyl Colefax, who had come for lunch, managed to corner Wallis and speak to her frankly about the growing controversy over her relationship with the King. Harold Nicolson wrote that Sibyl had found Wallis "really miserable. All sorts of people had come to her reminding her of her duty and begging her to leave the country. 'They do not understand,' she said, 'that if I did so, the King would come after me regardless of anything. They would then get their scandal in a far worse form than they are getting it now.' "[26] Wallis went as far as to tell Sibyl that she "wanted to leave him and clear out, but the King threatened to quit, to follow her, even to commit suicide."[27]

Sibyl asked Wallis bluntly if the King and she planned to marry; Wallis, taken aback, quickly answered, "Of course not." If this was true, Sibyl told her, then it might be a good idea for certain restless members of the cabinet to be informed that there was no danger. Wallis agreed and even authorized Sibyl to see Neville Chamberlain and deny that marriage was in the works.[28]

There is no clearer indication of Wallis's continued conflicting views of her future than this discussion, which appears, on the surface at least, duplicitous at best. However, it is more than likely that she, realizing the potential crisis, was desperately seeking a way in which to prevent a catastrophe. Her own protests had been worthless against David; perhaps, she believed, if others interceded, he might be put off his plans, at least temporarily. Years later, she confided to a friend: "In the weeks before the Abdication I was willing to do anything—*anything*—to prevent his going. I lied to our friends, I lied to the King—all in the hope that someone would put a stop to it."[29]

That Sunday afternoon, Wallis and David were scheduled to take tea with the Duke and Duchess of Kent at their country house, Coppins, in Buckinghamshire. As they were preparing to leave the Fort, however, David told Wallis to go without him, saying that he had to stop at Windsor Castle and attend to some business and would join her later.

David had arranged to meet Walter Monckton at the castle. He wasted no time in expressing his anger over the incident; it was all Monckton could do to prevent him from firing Hardinge that afternoon. He warned David that such an action would only be likely to provoke unfavorable comment as to the cause of Hardinge's termination and inevitably to talk about Mrs. Simpson herself.

Late that afternoon, David duly appeared at Coppins. He greeted his brother warmly and settled in for tea. Wallis thought he appeared relaxed enough when he arrived. It was only later, once they had returned to Fort Belvedere, that she learned the truth. David pulled her aside, opened a red-leather dispatch box, withdrew Hardinge's letter, and without a word, handed it to Wallis to read.

Although to some extent Hardinge had manufactured the crisis, Wallis had no reason to question his loyalty and read the letter at face value. She was horrified. "This was the end I had always known in the back of my mind was bound to come," she later wrote. "Such a letter, emanating as it did from a man whose duty it was to maintain the closest contact with the King's Ministers, could mean only that the Government was preparing for a crisis with the King."[30] She had dared to believe David when he assured her that everything would work out; now he no longer could control his ministers or government, and the relationship threatened to spiral out of control. He had been keeping the truth of the brewing crisis from her, trying to spare her; now it was too late, and all she could do was watch helplessly, unable to escape without tragic results.

Her first reaction was to flee; she told David that she would do as Hardinge suggested and leave at once, but he refused to allow her to do so. For the next hour she tried to convince him that there was simply no alternative but for her to disappear; each time she suggested a solution, he refused to listen. Finally, he declared flatly, "They can't stop me. On the Throne or off, I'm going to marry you."[31]

Wallis continued to beg David to let her go, saying that if the government was opposed, it was a hopeless situation. He took her hand in his and calmly said, "I'm going to send for Mr. Baldwin to see me at the Palace tomorrow. I'm going to tell him that if the country won't approve our marrying, I'm ready to go."[32]

This came as a shock to Wallis. Until now, David had never mentioned the idea of abdication. She burst into tears. "David, it is madness to think, let alone talk, of such a thing," she cried.[33]

He declared that he was not about to give up, that there were certain things which he could do. He explained to Wallis that he wanted to consult certain friends who held positions in the cabinet, to sound them out on the idea of his marriage, including Sir Samuel Hoare, the First Lord of the Admiralty, and Duff Cooper, secretary of state for war.[34] Constitutionally, the King was required to seek the prime minister's permission before independently approaching any member of the cabinet, but he assured Wallis that he did not believe this would be a problem.[35] Thus, the wheels were set in motion for the King's private relationship with Wallis to become an official matter of government interest.

18

"A Pretty Kettle of Fish"

T HE HISTORY OF THE ABDICATION," wrote Frances Donaldson in her biography of Edward VIII, "seems to prove that the sovereign is free to choose his own consort providing his choice is approved by the Prime Minister and government of the day. If, on the other hand, he chooses someone generally regarded as unsuitable to be Queen, it in fact becomes a constitutional matter."[1]

In theory, David was free to marry whomever he wished. He was regulated not by written law but solely by tradition and accepted custom. Because England had no written constitution, many laws were only situational; a certain amount of governmental flexibility existed in the definition of what could or could not be done. This somewhat ambiguous allowance would not only serve the King but would work against him throughout the fall of 1936.

Members of the British Royal Family as well as those in direct line of succession to the throne were governed by two different legal statutes. The first, the Act of Settlement, had regulated the passage of the British Crown to the German House of Hanover and stipulated that potential heirs and successors could only marry a Roman Catholic on forefeiture of dynastic rights. The second statute was the Royal Marriages Act, which decreed that all members of the British Royal Family as well as potential heirs in the line of succession were required to obtain the sovereign's consent before contracting a marriage. Although the King, as sovereign, was obliged to follow the dictates of the Act of Settlement, he was himself exempt from the provisions of the Royal Marriages Act.

The ruling government of Great Britain had no legal authority to impose restrictions on the marriage of a king or regnant queen. Nor was there any constitutional requirement that the sovereign seek the permission of the prime minister or his cabinet. In short, there was nothing which allowed the government of the day to raise any objection to the marriage of the King.

Legally, the King was also perfectly free to marry a divorcée.

Once the British courts of justice had ruled in her case, as writer Stephen Birmingham has pointed out, Wallis was technically clear of any social or moral impediment to remarriage. The court, in the course of the divorce proceedings, had examined the evidence and advanced a judgment which had ruled for Wallis in the action; thus, according to British law, she was the injured party. For the court to have so ruled, they also had to conclude that her first divorce had been legal and without irregularity. Whatever doubts there might be as to collusion, according to centuries of British law at least, Wallis was blameless.[2]

Morally, however, the King was treading in dangerous waters where divorce was concerned. It was ironic that the traditions which defined the King's role as defender of the faith in the Church of England—which conflicted with his desire to marry Wallis—had been born out of another king's determination to divorce and remarry. When Henry VIII married his first wife, Catherine of Aragon, she was the widow of his brother, and he had been obliged to seek special papal dispensation. When the marriage soured due to Catherine's inability to provide the King with a male heir, Henry fell in love with Anne Boleyn and appealed to Pope Clement VII to annul his union with the Spanish princess. The Pope, however, refused; Henry VIII openly broke with Rome and created his own Church of England, of which he became defender of the faith. His new church was ruled by an archbishop of Canterbury, who promptly declared his marriage to Catherine invalid. As a result, the Pope excommunicated the British king.

In the years following Henry VIII's reign, however, the Church of England began to impose a strong prohibition on divorce. Only a few years before the abdication crisis, the Archbishop of Canterbury had declared that he was opposed to Anglican ministers performing marriages involving parties that had been divorced if the former spouse was still alive. Cosmo Lang, as Archbishop of Canterbury, was greatly worried about the King's relationship from a religious standpoint. Not only did he perceive Edward VIII as a corrupting, morally questionable influence, but he feared the forthcoming coronation, during which he would have to anoint the King with holy oil, an act which signified the church's blessing of a man openly living with his divorced mistress and who had now expressed his determination to marry her. "The thought of my having to consecrate *him* as King weighed on me as a heavy burden," Lang wrote in his diary. "Indeed I considered whether I could bring myself to do so." He added ominously: "But I had a sense that circumstances might change. . . ."[3]

On Monday, November 16, Wallis and Aunt Bessie returned to her house at Cumberland Terrace. That evening, David met with the prime minister at Buckingham Palace. He came straight to the point. "I understand," he said, "that you and several members of the Cabinet have some fear of a constitutional crisis developing over my friendship with Mrs. Simpson."

"Yes, Sir," Baldwin replied, "that is correct."[4]

The King explained that he had reached a private understanding with Lord Beaverbrook and Esmond Harmsworth, as the result of which the silence of their newspapers over the relationship would be guaranteed. But Baldwin, who maintained close ties with Geoffrey Dawson, knew that there was no such arrangement with the *Times,* and he warned the King that inevitably the silence of the press would be broken. Hearing this, David asked if a marriage between him and Wallis would meet with the prime minister's approval.[5]

Baldwin warned that this would not be likely. The prime minister later recalled: "That marriage would have involved the lady becoming Queen. I did tell His Majesty that I might be a remnant of the old Victorians, but that my worst enemy would not say of me that I did not know what the reaction of the English people would be to any particular course of action. ... I pointed out to him that the position of the King's wife was different from the position of the wife of any other citizen of the country. His wife becomes Queen; the Queen becomes the Queen of the country; and therefore, in the choice of a Queen the voice of the people must be heard."[6]

Instead, Baldwin emphasized that it was only marriage to which the government objected; the King could certainly keep Wallis as his mistress. But David protested that this was a hypocritical position. "There has always been," the prime minister replied, "a leniency regarding the private relations of Kings just because they are the only people subjected to strict regulation with regard to their marriages and wives."[7]

David considered this for a moment. Then, according to Baldwin, he declared: "I am going to marry Mrs. Simpson, and I am prepared to go."[8]

"Sir," Baldwin said, "that is most grievous news, and it is impossible for me to make any comment on it today."[9]

Although the prime minister tried to reason with the King, David refused to discuss the issue. "I have made up my mind," he said, "and I shall abdicate in favour of my brother, the Duke of York, and I mean to go and acquaint my mother this evening and my family. Please don't mention my decision to two or three trusted Privy Councillors until I give you permission."[10] David asked Baldwin if he might seek the advice of Hoare and Cooper, and the prime minister agreed. Baldwin returned to No. 10 Downing Street that evening, greatly shaken. He told his chief whip, Capt. David Margesson, "I have heard such things from my King tonight as I never thought to hear."[11]

Although David had told Baldwin that his decision had been made, it is also possible that he was simply testing the waters to determine what the prime minister's reaction would be to both a proposed marriage and an eventual abdication. Over the next three weeks, David would himself propose or investigate a number of options to abdication, so it is unlikely that he had come to a final decision on November 16. He knew, however, that there existed the distinct possibility that his dramatic threat would be forced into action.

From Buckingham Palace, David went to Marlborough House to dine with his mother. He found his sister Mary, the Princess Royal, already there, along with his brother Harry's wife, Alice, Duchess of Gloucester. "He was in a great state of agitation," Alice recalled, "and asked his mother if I could leave the room as he had a very serious family matter to discuss. Queen Mary was discernibly angered by this request, but with many apologies she asked me to go, which of course I did."[12]

Queen Mary led her eldest son and only daughter to her boudoir. There David informed his mother and sister that he intended to marry Wallis. He asked Queen Mary to receive her, but she refused. When he inquired why, Queen Mary replied, "Because she is an adventuress!"[13]

Of course, Wallis was far from being an adventuress. Queen Mary's strong, if understandable, condemnation rested on the false belief that Mrs. Simpson was actively campaigning to marry the King. The Queen made assumptions based on misinformation from court and political circles and the gossip she heard. It was unfortunate that she was prepared to believe the worst about the woman her son loved rather than listen to his version with an open mind.

"To my mother," David later wrote, "the Monarchy was something sacred and the Sovereign a personage apart. The word 'duty' fell between us. But there could be no question of my shirking my duty."[14] The Queen felt that her son had but two choices: marry Wallis and leave the country or not marry her and remain as King. Lady Airlie later admitted that her mistress believed strongly that her eldest son had absolutely no right to conduct a private life of his own choosing.[15] To the Queen, love for the throne came first; her feelings for her children, second. The majority of her life had been spent sacrificing personal desire for the sake of public duty. Her world was one of dignity and tradition; love was a personal emotion, completely separate from a royal marriage. She had been raised in a world in which one married for duty first; love, if it also existed, was to be appreciated, but the idea of disregarding one's sacred obligations for the sake of a frail human emotion was anathema to the elderly Queen. She could not even bring herself to consider such a union as her son now proposed; it was simply beyond her comprehension.

The Queen and her children were all aware not only of the King's relationship with Wallis but also of the threatening crisis. Queen Mary had discussed the situation with members of her own household, with the Archbishop of Canterbury, and with several members of the cabinet as well, urging them to take action to halt the Simpson divorce. But she had deliberately avoided the subject with the one person who most mattered: her eldest son. All her life, the Queen had found personal discussions and intimate talk difficult. Having erected an impenetrable wall around her emotions, she could not bring herself to abandon her reserve and speak frankly with David. She simply waited in silence, assuming, in the words of Michael Bloch, an "attitude of martyrdom," and hoped that somehow he might lose interest in his mistress.[16]

Nor did David feel able to confide his feelings to his family. All his life, he had been raised to suppress his emotions; his parents had trained him to avoid unpleasant subjects. Now, when he most needed his family as trusted confidants and advisers, he could only state his case and stubbornly declare that he had made up his mind.

David left Marlborough House knowing that he had failed to win his mother over. But he had certainly made an impression on her. "Really! This might be Romania!" she exclaimed in disgust.[17] And, on the following day, November 17, Queen Mary received the prime minister. As he entered her rooms, she greeted him with her hands held out in a gesture of despair and said, "Well, Mr. Baldwin, this is a pretty kettle of fish!"[18]

On November 17, David met with both Sir Samuel Hoare, First Lord of the Admiralty, and with Duff Cooper, secretary of state for war, at Buckingham Palace. Neither consultation went well. Hoare warned that Baldwin held control of the situation and that most members of the government seemed to support him. If the King pressed his cause, Hoare declared, he was likely to lose.[19]

The meeting with Cooper scarcely went better. David began the talk by declaring that he could not continue to reign unless he married Wallis. Cooper warned that if the King abdicated, all blame for such an action would fall squarely on Wallis. He advised that the King wait. "I also secretly thought that he might in the interval meet somebody whom he would love more," Cooper later wrote.[20]

That evening, David met with his brother the Duke of York. Like Queen Mary, the Duke had known of the serious nature of his brother's relationship. Disgruntled courtiers had for some time been secretly advising Bertie on the state of affairs, meeting with him behind the King's back at his London house, No. 145 Piccadilly. Alexander Hardinge, in particular, had spoken with the Duke about the King's relationship with Mrs. Simpson and a possible abdication several times, first on October 10 and then again on October 28, the day following the divorce hearing at Ipswich, when the Yorks dined with the King's private secretary and his wife.[21]

David told his brother that he had discussed the situation with Baldwin the previous evening. "It looks to me now, the way things are shaping up, that I shall probably have to go," he said.

"Oh, that's a dreadful thing to hear," the Duke replied. "None of us wants that, I least of all."

"I'm afraid," David said, "there's no other way. My mind is made up."[22] The King had indeed made up his mind: he would win the fight in his own way, or he would go.

Wallis, meanwhile, had only managed to see David briefly. He told her that the prime minister had approved his plan to seek the advice of certain members of the cabinet. But when she tried to question him, he told her, "I must work things out in my own way."[23]

While David was speaking with his brother, Wallis attended a dinner party given by Emerald Cunard. Prince and Princess Paul of Yugoslavia were also present. Chips Channon noted that Wallis "looked very well tonight, like a Vermeer, in a Dutch way. The conversation got on to tiaras, and Princess Olga said hers gave her a headache. Wallis Simpson laughingly added, 'Well, anyway, a tiara is one of the things I shall never have. . . .' There was an embarrassed pause. . . ."[24]

In the midst of these developments, the King made a scheduled journey to Wales to inspect impoverished mining towns. Increased oil consumption had resulted in mining layoffs and shutdowns, leaving the area economically depressed. David was startled at the poverty he saw. When he met one young man who said that he had never been able to find work, all David could say was a muttered "Terrible, terrible. . . ." A group of unemployed miners handed the King a letter: "This is a stricken valley. Slighted by the dead hand of poverty. . . . Our women grow prematurely old. . . . Our children are stunted. . . . Will an impoverished people be able to joyfully celebrate Your Majesty's Coronation?"[25] Touring the stricken households, seeing the grim faces and sad eyes, David was deeply moved. Spontaneously, he declared, "Something must be done to find them work."[26]

The King's offhand remarks made headlines the following day, spurring the government into action. The chancellor of the exchequer, Neville Chamberlain, ordered a new study on mining conditions and proposals to grant additional government funding to relieve the hardships of unemployment. Labour MPs in the House of Commons asked for quick legislation to attract new industrial development to South Wales. The *News Chronicle* declared: "The King is above and outside politics. What he has done is in the sole interest of truth and public service. . . . The man in the street feels that Whitehall stands condemned. . . ."[27]

But Baldwin feared political consequences. There was talk that the King had overstepped his bounds. Many Conservative politicians felt that the King had simply been trying to score popularity at the expense of the ruling government, and resentment against him continued to grow.

The visit to South Wales, however, had once again demonstrated in the most visible way possible the King's popularity with the working classes. This enthusiastic reception and support convinced him, it seems, that his case was not completely lost where Wallis was concerned. Whereas he had previously discussed abdication as being a necessary adjunct to a marriage with Wallis, after the Wales visit he seemed determined to marry her and retain the throne.

On November 19, the day he returned from Wales, David met with his brother. The change in his course of action soon became evident when he told George that he planned to marry Wallis.

The Duke was startled at this piece of news and stammered. "What will she call herself?"

"Call herself?" David asked. "What do you think—Queen of England of course."

"She is going to be Queen?" George asked incredulously.

"Yes, and Empress of India, the whole bag of tricks."[28]

19

The Morganatic Marriage Proposal

WHILE THE KING WAS AWAY on his tour of South Wales, Esmond Harmsworth asked Wallis to join him at Claridge's for lunch.[1] During the course of the afternoon, Harmsworth suggested that Wallis ask the King about the possibility of a morganatic marriage. Such a union, he explained, would allow the King to marry her, but she would not become queen. This, he believed, might end the rumblings in the government. "I realize, Wallis, that all this is not very flattering to you," he acknowledged. "But I am sure that you are one with us in desiring to keep the King on the Throne." He even suggested a possible title should she marry the King: Duchess of Lancaster, from one of the King's lesser titles.[2]

At first, Wallis had her doubts about a morganatic marriage. She felt that such a marriage would leave her in a peculiarly ambiguous position: not quite queen and yet undeniably the wife of the king. As she began to carefully consider the proposal, however, it seemed to offer a way out of a situation which was growing more impossible by the day.

Her feelings for David were deep and genuine. She had made her decision to remain at his side, no matter the consequences, trusting his assurances that he would somehow manage to work things out. At the same time, Wallis was increasingly aware of the obstacles facing any union. She remained utterly ignorant of the strength of feelings against the marriage, believing that the decision rested solely with certain members of the court and society. Nevertheless, she thought that such prejudice as existed was directed only at her assumption of the position of queen. As a twice-divorced American, even Wallis had to admit that her credentials for the post were doubtful. A morganatic marriage seemed to offer a hopeful solution to such opposition.

The idea of such a marriage also offered its own benefits. As the King's wife, she would become chatelaine of Buckingham Palace, Windsor Castle, Sandringham House, Holyrood House, and Balmoral

Castle; she would be responsible for acting as official hostess; she would holiday with David, enjoy the luxuries of the life he lived as monarch, and be treated with the greatest of respect. Moreover, she knew that a morganatic marriage also offered a degree of freedom which would have been impossible for the Queen. As a morganatic wife, her role would be largely private. She would not have to undertake public duties or even appear at the side of the King during official functions. To Wallis, never having been raised to live her life in the public eye and unaccustomed to the idea of royal duties, this aspect appealed greatly. She would have the King, the power and position of his wife, and the benefits of life as a royal, all without the encumbering obligations of service which went with the rank of Queen.

A day after her lunch at Claridge's, Wallis joined David at Fort Belvedere. She thought he looked tired and "harassed."[3] She told him of her talk with Harmsworth and suggested the idea of a morganatic marriage. At first, he greeted this proposal with skepticism, believing it would be an unacceptable and dishonorable position for Wallis. However, he listened to Wallis's arguments and duly agreed to examine the idea with care.

Wallis knew almost nothing of the history of morganatic marriages. The only recent association fresh in many people's minds was the case of King Carol II of Romania, whose morganatic marriage was annulled to allow him to marry a Greek princess; he had then left her for his mistress, Madame Lupescu. Such convoluted affairs were held to be highly dishonorable and intensely suspect. Most of Europe's royal houses had their own dynastic laws regulating marriages, and morganatic unions were often the refuge of those caught in scandal and illicit love affairs.

Morganatic marriages had been most prevalent among the German Kingdoms, principalities, and grand duchies. Most royal marriages were controlled by the principal of *Ebenbürtigkeit,* or equality of birth between partners. Should one partner contract a marriage with a spouse of unequal rank, such a union was considered to be morganatic.

Ironically, Queen Mary—that great upholder of tradition and unwavering opponent of her son's proposed union with Wallis—was herself descended from a morganatic marriage.[4] In 1835, His Royal Highness Prince Alexander of Württemberg attended a ball at the Imperial Palace of the Hofburg in Vienna. Here he met the beautiful and gifted Countess Claudine Rhedey, daughter of an ancient Hungarian noble family. In May 1835 the pair married morganatically. A few days later, the Emperor of Austria named her Countess Hohenstein. The pair had three children, the second of whom, His Serene Highness Franz, Duke of Teck, married Queen Victoria's first cousin, Her Royal Highness Princess Mary Adelaide of Cambridge, in 1866.

Their daughter became Queen Mary. Because she took her rank from her father, she was born a mere Serene Highness. Only when she married the future King George V did she become Her Royal Highness.[5]

There were other members of the British Royal Family with equally close ties to morganatic marriages. In 1851, Prince Alexander of Hesse, brother of Grand Duke Ludwig III of Hesse and by Rhine, broke dynastic protocol by marrying a commoner, Countess Julia Hauke, the daughter of a Polish general. "It is hard to conceive the enormity of the offense of a prince of royal blood marrying a commoner—and poor Julie was little better than that," writes Richard Hough. "It was regarded by the closely linked royal families of Europe as an act not just of disloyalty but of sedition. It threatened the whole delicately balanced and mutually inter-dependent dynastic structure built up over the centuries with the family-tree-like complexity of tall scaffolding."[6] She was created first Countess, then Princess, of Battenberg, named after the village close to the Rhine where the Hesse family owned a castle. Her husband, who was eventually forgiven by his elder brother and granted the title of His Serene Highness Prince Alexander of Battenberg, was grandfather of Edward VIII's great friend Lord Louis Mountbatten.

In Russia, where the Romanovs were bound by multiple marital laws requiring equal unions, morganatic marriages, ironically, were almost commonplace within the Imperial Family. In 1880, after the death of his wife, Emperor Alexander II had contracted a morganatic marriage with his longtime mistress Princess Catherine Dolgoruky, with whom he already had three children. The emperor was assassinated by terrorists before he had a chance to raise his wife, upon whom he had bestowed the courtesy title Princess Yourievskaia, to the rank of empress. One of Alexander's sons, Grand Duke Paul Alexandrovich, contracted a morganatic marriage with his mistress and was forced to live in exile until the outbreak of the First World War. Other grand Dukes, including Nicholas II's brother Grand Duke Michael Alexandrovich and his cousin Grand Duke Michael Michailovich, had likewise married morganatically.

Perhaps the most famous morganatic marriage was that of Archduke Franz Ferdinand, heir to the throne of Austria-Hungary, to Countess Sophie Chotek in 1900. Although she received the courtesy title of Duchess of Hohenberg from Emperor Franz Joseph, this was his only concession. In order to marry Sophie, Franz Ferdinand had been required to renounce the rights to the succession of any children born of the marriage. On public occasions, Sophie was forced to walk not with her husband but behind the least important female members of the imperial household. She could not attend official dinners given by her husband because her rank was not considered sufficient enough to be included. Even when she and Franz attended a private performance together at the theater, they were not allowed to sit in the same box.[7] Their assassination in Sarajevo in July 1914 precipitated the First World War.

In England, however, there were no recent precedents. Nearly a hundred years earlier, the Dukes of Sussex and Cambridge had contracted unequal marriages. Both, however, had married without seeking permission of the sovereign, as required by the Royal Marriages Act, so their unions were illegal and therefore not considered morganatic.

Nevertheless, only one potential legal impediment to a morganatic marriage stood in the King's way. In 1931, Parliament had passed the Statute of Westminster, which formally severed the sovereign authority of Great Britain over its dominions. While British political control over the dominions was thus weakened, the statute sought to strengthen their ties with the British Crown itself. Specifically, it allotted to the dominion heads and parliaments the right of consultation and assent where any alterations of the succession to the throne were made, as well as any changes in royal titles or styles. A morganatic wife of the king would indeed mean consultation with the dominions, a fact of which David was apparently unaware.

On Monday, November 23, David returned to London and sent for Esmond Harmsworth. After some discussion concerning the morganatic-marriage idea, he asked Harmsworth to raise the question with the prime minister. "From the moment the King proposed this," writes historian A. J. P. Taylor, "he put himself at the Government's mercy. He was now asking them for something, whereas previously they had been asking him."[8]

Harmsworth duly saw Baldwin that same evening. John Davidson, chancellor of the Duchy of Lancaster, later noted: "We discussed the matter, and tried to picture the scene in the House of Commons when SB [Baldwin] had to explain why Mrs. Simpson was good enough to be the King's wife but not good enough to be Queen. . . ."[9] Baldwin himself recalled: "I told him that he and his filthy paper did not really *know* the mind of the English people: whereas I *did*. And I explained to him that a morganatic marriage would mean a special Bill being passed in Parliament; and that Parliament would *never* pass it. Harmsworth said: 'Oh, I'm sure they would. The whole standard of morals is so much more broadminded since the War.' I replied: 'Yes, you are right: the ideal of morality . . . certainly *has* gone down since the War: but the ideal of Kingship has gone *up* . . .' "[10]

The entire meeting left Baldwin greatly upset. He believed the morganatic marriage was being promoted by Lord Rothermere and Winston Churchill, two men he regarded as his bitterest enemies. As soon as Harmsworth left, Davidson reappeared. The prime minister said with disgust: "He wants Mrs. Simpson to be a Duchess—not to be royal, but less than royal, but rather better than an ordinary Duchess."[11]

During this week, David continued to meet with Walter Monckton at Buckingham Palace. Although he had followed Monckton's advice and left Hardinge in his post, David believed—quite rightly—that his private secretary was secretly reporting to Baldwin. He took particular pains to disguise Monckton's visits, asking that the lawyer arrive at the visitor's entrance, in the southeast corner of the palace, rather than by the usual privy purse entrance, which would lead him past the household offices. Once inside, Monckton followed a circuitous path through the palace corridors to the Belgian Suite, where the King kept his private apartments. This exercise in avoiding Hardinge, however, was all for nothing: the private secretary managed to learn of each visit, and once he even dispatched a footman with a note asking if Monckton would like to join him for a drink before leaving.[12]

Monckton advised the King that "even in the unlikely event of the Cabinet approving a morganatic marriage, special legislation would be required, and the prospect of such a bill's ever passing Parliament was dubious."[13] Beyond this, he told the King, the approval of all eleven dominion cabinets would be required. David believed that his personal popularity in the dominions would help win opinion over to his side. However, he failed to understand that it was not the general population that would decide his future but politicians and individual cabinet members less well disposed to him.

On the morning of November 25, Baldwin met with Clement Attlee, Winston Churchill, and the leader of the Liberal Party, Archibald Sinclair, at No. 10 Downing Street. He discussed Harmsworth's visit and the idea of a morganatic marriage for the King. Although David had not yet asked Baldwin to consult any officials in the British cabinet, the prime minister wanted to assure himself that no surprises lay in store. Accordingly, he asked an important hypothetical question: If the King were to push for a morganatic marriage against the advice of his government and Baldwin resigned as a result, would any of these men be willing to form a replacement coalition government whose sole reason for existence was to push through legislation to allow the King to marry? Although Churchill declared that he would support the King, both Attlee and Sinclair assured Baldwin that they would not support a morganatic marriage and would refuse to participate in any new government if the King tried to form one under these conditions. Attlee declared that while most of his party members had no objection to an American becoming queen, "I was certain that they would not approve of Mrs. Simpson for that position."[14]

These answers largely satisfied the prime minister. Baldwin could now play from a position of strength. The King could marry whom he liked, but if it was Mrs. Simpson, the ruling government would resign, and no other party leader was willing to step into the breach and form a new government.

That evening, at half-past six, Baldwin arrived at Buckingham Palace for a meeting with the King. David asked the prime minister if he might marry Wallis morganatically, as an ordinary citizen rather than as king, under a special Act of Exclusion. Until this moment, David had largely been able to operate according to his own inclinations. The prime minister was empowered only to advise and warn. But David's impatience proved too much, and he suggested that Baldwin formally submit the idea to the cabinet for discussion. The prime minister explained that a formal examination meant that the dominion cabinets and prime ministers would also have to be consulted. "Sir," Baldwin asked, "would you like me to examine the proposal formally?"

"Yes," David replied, "please do so."[15]

These four words sealed the King's fate. David was thus precluded from seeking advice elsewhere until his prime minister and government had formally reported back to him on the issue of his marriage. More important, he was also bound to accept their advice as the formal recommendation of the government. If he ignored this advice and continued to pursue the marriage, the government would be within its rights to resign.

When Wallis learned of this development, she was shocked. She called his decision to consult the prime minister "inexplicable." She could not understand why the King would voluntarily let the cabinet debate the idea of their marriage. "David," she wrote, "was obviously allowing his better judgment to be swept aside by his impatience to break the deadlock. I began to suspect that the whole idea, however well meant, would turn out to be in reality a trap."[16]

The next day, Lord Beaverbrook called on the King, having cut short a trip to the United States at David's request. Beaverbrook was not particularly supportive of the monarchy in principle, but he greatly liked the King himself. His cooperation, however, rested on somewhat more malicious motives. Years later, when Randolph Churchill asked why, given his feelings about the monarchy, he had involved himself to such an extent in the abdication crisis, Beaverbrook answered, "To bugger Baldwin."[17]

Historian A. J. P. Taylor, however, has cast doubt on such a provocative revelation. "Despite his combative talk," he writes of Beaverbrook, "he was always a fixer when it came to the point, and what he wanted now was not a knock-out blow inflicted on Baldwin, but a compromise: the King secure on his Throne and the question of marriage with Mrs. Simpson postponed to a time when men had got used to the idea—or the King had lost interest."[18]

When the King told Beaverbrook of the morganatic proposal, the press baron was horrified. David explained that he was pursuing the option because Wallis preferred it to any other solution.[19] Beaverbrook strongly urged the King to withdraw his request that Baldwin formally examine the idea. David, however, hesitated, and Beaverbrook himself offered to consult several members of the cabinet to see what the likely decision would be. David reluctantly allowed that it might be possible to withdraw the idea from consideration if it seemed the cabinet would stand against it. The very next day, however, he rang Beaverbrook at his London residence, Stornoway House, and informed him that he had changed his mind: The formal consideration of the morganatic marriage proposal would be allowed to continue.

On November 26, Wallis attended a dinner party in Belgrave Square. Chips Channon wrote: "She was wearing new jewels—the King must give her new ones every day. . . . We talked of houses, and I suggested that she should move to Belgravia and she didn't reply. It is those occasional lapses which are mysterious. Why not say 'I'll look about' or something casual instead of leaving one with the feeling that she won't want a house in May as she'll be living in Buckingham Palace. I personally think that he'll marry her, and soon."[20]

The cabinet was set to meet in special session on Friday, November 27. The night before, Harold Nicolson recorded in his diary: "If the King insisted on marrying, the Privy Council would assemble in force and insist that he either abdicate or they resign. I do not understand the situation. On the one hand you have Mrs. Simpson saying that he has never suggested marriage, and on the other hand you have the Privy Council organised for revolt."[21]

The next morning, Baldwin formally briefed his cabinet for the first official time about the King's relationship with Mrs. Simpson and his desire to marry her. He explained that the King had asked that the cabinet formally examine a proposal to allow a morganatic marriage. Now Baldwin told them that he felt the idea was undesirable and that in his opinion the government must be prepared to choose: Either they must accept the King's choice of wife as their queen or allow for the possibility of his abdication. Neville Chamberlain believed that a morganatic marriage "would only be a prelude to the further step of making Mrs. S. queen with full rights."[22] Sir Donald Somervell recalled how he described the morganatic proposal to the cabinet: "I confirmed . . . that the wife of King is Queen, that it would require an Act of Parliament to prevent this result. I remember adding that it would have been an odd Act. If it had been an honest recital it would start 'Whereas the wife of the King is Queen & whereas the present King desires to marry a woman unfit to be Queen—be it hereby enacted etc.' "[23]

The following day, the red-leather dispatch boxes duly arrived for the King from Whitehall. But when he opened them, he found that the cabinet minutes on the morganatic discussion were missing: Baldwin had deliberately withheld them from the King. He learned the details of what had taken place from Lord Beaverbrook, who declared sadly, "Sir, you have put your head on the execution block. All that Baldwin has to do now is to swing the axe."[24] The next day, learning of the special meeting, Chips Channon noted ominously, "The Battle for the Throne has begun."[25]

The lines were indeed being drawn. Ramsay MacDonald, the former prime minister, summed up the situation for Harold Nicolson: "That man has done more harm to his country than any man in history." Nicolson pondered this and noted, "It seems that the Cabinet are determined that he shall abdicate. So are the Privy Council. But he imagines that the country, the great warm heart of the people, are with him. I do not think so. The upper classes mind her being an American more than they mind her being divorced. The lower classes do not mind her being an American but they loathe the idea that she has had two husbands already."[26]

Baldwin duly dispatched cables to the prime ministers of the dominions, offering three choices: that the King should remain and marry Mrs. Simpson as queen; that there should be a morganatic marriage; or that he should abdicate. Baldwin himself believed that the first two solutions were unacceptable; accordingly, he advanced no arguments in their favor. The cables were drawn up by the secretary of state for the dominions, Malcolm MacDonald, and his permanent undersecretary and were carefully worded to evoke a negative reply.[27] After explaining the morganatic marriage proposal, the cables read: "I feel convinced that neither the Parliament nor the great majority of the public here should or would accept such a plan." The cabinet further added: "Any more than they would accept the proposal that Mrs. Simpson should become Queen."[28]

The pressure was building from all sides, but the King continued to push ahead with his plans. A friend later wrote of Wallis and David: They "never acted like people who wanted to overthrow the Church of England. They acted like a couple in love who wanted to get married, and were plainly horrified by the momentous events this simple desire had set in motion. . . . You couldn't help loving them for it, they were honestly so damn naive."[29]

"I saw the King and Wallis during that time," one acquaintance would later recall, "and I never saw two people so *tired*. He was tired from his long battle to make Wallis Queen, which he was absolutely determined to do, and she was tired from trying to please him and please everybody else, too. They both acted like zombies when other people were around, and the only time they showed a spark of the old liveliness was when they were alone together. . . . I give you my word, they looked like kids."[30]

Wallis, aware only of what the King chose to tell her, was more isolated and alone than ever. She knew few details of his meetings with Baldwin and his family and continued to believe him when he assured her that everything would be worked out. David never told her the bad news; when the abdication crisis suddenly cascaded upon her, it was overwhelming.

Jack Beall of the *New York Herald Tribune* managed to get a rare interview with Wallis that November. "I think it is terrible the way the papers in America have been treating me," she said.

Beall asked her whether she thought her relationship with the King was going to interfere with the coronation. "No, I don't think it will." Then she added quickly, "No, I can't say anything about that, really."

"Did you know, Mrs. Simpson," Beall asked, "that they have organized in America a 'Simpson for Queen' movement?"

Hearing this, she burst into howls of laughter. "Oh, no!" she cried out. "Not really?"[31]

Wallis was so concerned about the way the American press was covering the relationship that she invited Newbold Noyes, then an associate editor of the *Washington Star,* to come and tell her story. Noyes had the benefit of being a member of the family: He had married her cousin Lelia Barnett and had known Wallis since she was eighteen.

Noyes reassured Wallis that at least 70 percent of the American press was favorable to her. She found this hard to believe, however. She explained that threatening letters from the United States had recently begun to appear in her post. "It isn't that I'm afraid of threats like that," she said, "but I'm sorry that people feel that way. If they knew the truth, I'm sure they'd feel differently."[32]

The noted author H. G. Wells wrote for the American press: "I never have yet heard one single word or suggestion that she was anything but a perfectly honourable, highly intelligent, and charmingly mannered woman. Why shouldn't the King marry her and make her his Queen? . . . Mrs. Simpson is far better fitted to be the King's wife than any possible bride that might be forced upon him to replace her." He continued about the King: "'Authorities' do not like him. People in privileged positions shiver slightly at the report of him. He flies about in airplanes, arrives unexpectedly, and looks at things, instead of traveling in a special train. . . . He betrays the possession of a highly modernized mind by his every act, he is unceremonious, he is unconventional, and he asks the most disconcerting questions about social conditions. . . . They know quite clearly within themselves that, if he cannot be humiliated and discredited into political impotence by forcing him to renounce, in most glaring publicity, his desire to marry this excellent consort, they would be happier without him."[33]

Wallis "could feel the mounting menace in the very atmosphere" around her. News was regularly leaking back to England from America and Europe, and those in the know now began to stare at her as she appeared in the streets. More disturbing, she continued to receive anonymous, threatening letters in the mail.[34]

One afternoon, Kenneth de Courcy came around to warn Wallis that her life was in danger. He was the honorary secretary to the Imperial Policy Group, a monarchist policy group dedicated to the promotion of the idea that Great Britain would maintain neutrality in any European conflict. De Courcy was also a close friend of George and Kitty Hunter's, early friends of Wallis when she had first come to London, with whom she had shared her cottage during her divorce proceedings at Felixstowe. The Hunters had heard of an alleged assassination plot against Wallis, and de Courcy approached Wallis's aunt Bessie to urge her to leave London.

When he learned of this, David moved quickly. He had also begun to hear of vague rumors threatening Wallis with assassination. Many years later, John Colville asked Churchill about the abdication. Churchill confessed that he had not thought it would happen and that he and Lord Beaverbrook had tried to scare Wallis out of the country. "When she was gone, he hoped the King would retire to Windsor and 'pull up the drawbridge, post Lord Dawson of Penn at the front gate and Lord Horder at the back gate,' and let it be announced that he was too ill to undertake public business. Winston said that great measures were taken to frighten Mrs. Simpson away. Bricks were thrown through her windows and letters written threatening her with vitriol. 'Do you mean that you did that,' I said, aghast. 'No,' he replied, 'but Max did.'" Beaverbrook, when confronted with this allegation years later, declared that he had done no such thing, but that some of his employees might have.[35]

David rang Wallis on the afternoon of Friday, November 27, and asked that she and her aunt Bessie leave London immediately and move into the Fort, where she could be protected. Wallis packed up her things, and at six that evening climbed into a car the King had sent to collect her. She and her aunt drove through the streets of London and out into the Berkshires to Windsor and the Fort. Wallis would not set foot in London again for nearly three years.[36]

20

Flight to France

WALLIS AND AUNT BESSIE arrived at Fort Belvedere just after seven that Friday evening. David arrived soon after. "The instant I entered the Fort," Wallis recalled, "I sensed the vast change that had come over its atmosphere in the short space of a week. The faces of the servants were drawn. No sooner had we entered the house than David was called to the telephone. There came to me the realization that this was no longer the enchanted Fort; it was the Fort beleaguered."[1]

Events that weekend bore out her worst fears. There was a constant stream of advisers calling from London to consult the King; the telephones rang ceaselessly; and David seemed to become even more withdrawn.[2] On Sunday he spent several hours discussing the situation privately with George Allen, his personal solicitor, and with Walter Monckton. At the end, David called Wallis into the library and delivered the bad news: Both Sir Samuel Hoare and Duff Cooper had advised that no option remained open to him where Wallis was concerned. He must, they declared, either give up the idea of marrying her or abdicate the throne. Both Hoare and Cooper advised that the King withdraw the idea of any potential marriage—whether morganatic or not—from the cabinet's consideration; proceed with his coronation in May 1937; and then, at some later date, after the crisis had passed, he might consider the idea of marrying Wallis.[3] But the King declared that going "through the Coronation ceremony while harbouring in my heart a secret intention to marry contrary to the Church's tenets would have meant being crowned with a lie on my lips."[4]

Although David assured Wallis that he was doing all he could and that he himself had not yet given up hope, she now understood the reality of the situation. He suggested that the people of the empire and dominions, if they understood the situation, might support him, and Wallis added that it might help if he made a speech to all concerned; David agreed, but explained that he would have to obtain the permission of the government in order to make such a broadcast.[5] She was aware of how Roosevelt had managed to captivate the American public with his broadcasts and was sure that the King could do likewise. David saw it as a perfect solution, for he believed the people, his people, would support him and his quest for happiness.

Over the next few days, David met with Monckton, Allen, and Maj. Ulick Alexander, the keeper of the privy purse. All suggested that if he remained determined to wed Wallis, he would be best served by temporarily handing over the royal power to a Council of State under the Privy Council, conduct whatever negotiations he needed in respect to his marriage, and then make his broadcast.[6] David had already begun to work on his speech. Eventually, however, he decided not to ask Baldwin's permission to broadcast until the prime minister had finally and formally received word from the heads of the dominion and Empire countries on the morganatic marriage proposal.

By the end of the weekend, it was all too much for Wallis, and she once again decided it would be best for everyone involved if she were simply to leave the country. She wrote to Sibyl Colefax: "I am planning quite by myself to go away for a while. I think everyone here would like that—except one person perhaps—but I am planning a clever means of escape. After a while my name will be forgotten by the people and only two people will suffer instead of a mass of people who aren't interested anyway in individual feelings but only the workings of a system."[7]

The following day, the Bishop of Bradford, the Right Reverend A. W. Blunt, made a speech at the annual diocesan conference that was to bring the crisis to a head. He had been in London and met the Archbishop of Canterbury as well as Baldwin, both of whom had expressed concern over the King's relationship with Mrs. Simpson. In his speech, he asked that God inspire the King to do what was necessary to fulfill his duty to the Crown and added that he hoped the monarch realized that he was in need of God's grace to do this. "Some of us," he added, "wish he gave more positive signs of such awareness." The Bishop of Birmingham had suggested that a wide range of clerics attend the coronation in the following year, and Blunt criticized this, saying that given the present circumstances, it scarcely mattered and that the religious aspects of the coronation service would be rendered nonexistent when it occurred. He would later explain that he had only meant to refer to the King's religious habits and not specifically to the King's relationship with Wallis. No one realized this, however, and the British press, assuming that the veil of silence about the King's relationship had now been broken, prepared to break the story of his romance with the twice-divorced American commoner.[8]

The Archbishop of Canterbury, although he later denied he had a hand in the speech, was presumably the driving force. He had recently met with Blunt and expressed grave concerns over the state of affairs.

Just before Blunt's speech, he had breakfast at Lambeth Palace, residence of the Archbishop of Canterbury, with Anne and Christopher Freemantle. An American paper on the side table bore the headline "Will David Wed Wally?" When he noticed the Freemantles looking at the paper, the Archbishop assured them that the marriage would be stopped. "It would be the end of the monarchy in England," he declared. He further told them that the following day the press silence would be broken.[9]

On Wednesday, December 2, David met with Baldwin at Buckingham Palace. Baldwin told him that although not all of the dominion reports had been received, those that had been were against the morganatic marriage. The King was thus left with the alternative of Wallis or abdication.[10] Baldwin begged and pleaded with him to change his mind, but David refused to listen. "I appealed to one thing after another. Nothing made the least impression. It was almost uncanny. . . . He seemed bewitched. . . ."[11]

That evening, David returned to the Fort for dinner. "One look at his face told me that the worst had happened," Wallis later recalled.[12] He did not speak, and along with Wallis's cousin Newbold Noyes and her aunt Bessie, they sat down to dinner as if nothing had happened. The menu consisted of clear turtle soup; a lobster mousse; roast pheasant with soufflé potatoes and a mixed green salad; frozen fresh pineapple and a toasted cheese savory. Footmen in scarlet coats handed around a light Bordeaux wine with dinner and a liqueur with coffee. During the dinner, Noyes noted, when the King and Wallis wished to speak only to each other, they did so in whispered German.[13]

After dinner, the conversation turned to marriage. Noyes asked: "If you marry, Sir, the woman you so honor will be one of three things. Correct me if I am wrong."

David asked him to name the three things.

"Your morganatic wife, the Queen of England, or shall we say, Mrs. Windsor, wife of the abdicated King of England."

"Nearly sixty-seven percent correct, but no more," David answered. "There is no such possibility as morganatic marriage for an English king."

This was startling news to Wallis, who had believed in, and hoped for, a morganatic solution until this moment.

"It would seem apparent then, Sir," Noyes continued, "that there are but three possible outcomes to this situation. Wallis becomes Queen. She becomes Mrs. Windsor, subsequent to your abdication. Or you renounce any intention of marrying her."

"Again, only sixty-seven percent correct, Mr. Noyes," he replied. "You should confine your possibilities to the first two—the only two that exist."[14]

Once they had finished, David led Wallis outside. As they strolled round the fog-wrapped garden, he finally told Wallis that it seemed as though there was no hope for the morganatic marriage proposal. He further declared that Baldwin, as prime minister, would not introduce the necessary legislation into Parliament required to pass a bill allowing a morganatic marriage. There was nothing further the King could do. "So it now comes to this," he declared. "Either I must give you up or abdicate. And I don't intend to give you up."[15]

Wallis now had news of her own for David. Earlier that day, Perry Brownlow had spoken with her, urging that she leave the country at once. She now told the King of her decision to leave. "David, I'm going to leave," she declared. "I've already stayed too long. I should have gone when you showed me Hardinge's letter. But now nothing you can say will hold me here any longer."[16]

David, for once, did not argue. Instead, he told her that on the following day the British press would break their silence and begin to print details of their relationship. There was nothing to be done, and David again declared that he must deal with the crisis on his own, in his own way.[17]

"I was braced for a blow," Wallis recalled; "but nothing had equipped me to deal with what faced me on my breakfast tray in the morning. There in big black type in paper after paper were the words 'Grave Constitutional Issue,' 'Grave Crisis,' and 'Constitutional Crisis.' The dam was broken."[18] She blamed herself for having allowed the situation to develop into a crisis and for not having left England earlier.

When she entered the drawing room that morning, David, who was standing over a table on which were arranged the morning papers, quickly tried to push them from her view. "Don't bother, David, I've seen them," she said sadly. In tears, she apologized for having put him into this terrible position.[19]

That day, the Earl of Crawford wrote:

Thursday. Sudden outbreak in the press—in the press united. After months, one might almost say years, the torrent is overwhelming—a cascade of articles, pictures, headlines, one would think that the relations of the King and Mrs. Simpson must exclude all other topics. Lots of portraits of the lady: posters about her, one says she is ill, another suggests that she has bolted. I went to Lancashire and kept picking up later editions of the evening papers and all alike break loose after the long period of self-suppression. The temptation to magnify the affair is irresistible—to propagate every possible rumour however absurd. In London I heard that the police are anxious as they think it possible some indignant person might fire a revolver at her, still more that the burglar confraternity might have a shot at her jewels.[20]

And Chips Channon sadly noted: "The Country and the Empire now know that their Monarch, their young King-Emperor, their adored Apollo, is in love with an American twice-divorced, whom they believe to be an adventuress."[21]

"For weeks," wrote Robert Bruce Lockhart, "MPs have been saying that [the] whole country is seething about [the] King's conduct and Mrs. Simpson and that they [the members] were being deluged with letters from their constituents. Probably true; but letters came from Mrs. Rector and Mr. Town Councillor. It is now quite clear that ninety percent of this country had never heard of Mrs. Simpson. . . . Gather that Whitehall wants King to abdicate in any case—altogether too irresponsible."[22]

The London papers quickly made their positions clear. Geoffrey Dawson, not surprisingly, was highly critical of the King in his editorial in the *Times*: "There are many daughters of America whom the King might have married with the approval and rejoicing of his people. It would have been an innovation, but by no means an unwelcome innovation in the history of the Royal House. . . . The one objection, and it is an overwhelming objection, is that the lady in question has already two former husbands living from whom in succession she has obtained divorce."[23]

The *Daily Telegraph* took much the same line: "Queen Mary, Queen Alexandra, Queen Victoria—these have been the Queens of England whom this country and Empire have known for a full century and they will not tolerate any other or different standard of Queenship."[24]

The Beaverbrook and Rothermere papers, however, took a different line. The *Daily Express* wrote: "Let the King speak. . . . Let the King give his decision to the people. . . . Are we to lose the King or are we to keep him? He knows the answer the people want to hear. But it must not be goodbye, for the citizens of these shores would hear him say it with their hearts loaded with grief and their heads bowed with sorrow."[25]

And the *Daily Mail* editorialized: "Abdication is out of the question because its possibilities of mischief are endless. The effect upon the Empire would be calamitous. It must never happen. The King and his Ministers must find a way out. . . . The people want their King."[26]

At the Fort that day, Wallis prepared for her departure. Immediately, she thought of her friends Herman and Katherine Rogers, who had settled in Cannes, and their Villa Lou Viei. Wallis considered that it would provide a safe haven and telephoned to ask the Rogerses if she might temporarily stay with them. Herman agreed at once, understanding her dilemma.[27]

David asked Lord Perry Brownlow to accompany Wallis to Cannes. Brownlow, a former officer in the Grenadier Guards and lord-in-waiting to the King, and his wife, Kitty, had spent a great deal of time with Wallis, and both liked her. In turn, she trusted Brownlow completely. Since the roads around the Fort were now under continual press surveillance, the King and Brownlow determined that George Ladbrook, the chauffeur, would drive Wallis's Buick to Newhaven on the coast, where he would lodge it aboard an overnight ferry to Dieppe. Ladbrook would be accompanied by Inspector Evans from Scotland Yard to ensure that there were no difficulties. Brownlow, meanwhile, would collect Wallis in his car at the Fort and drive her to the ferry, where they could then switch cars.[28]

Mary Burke, who had accompanied Wallis from London to the Fort, quickly packed her things. Wallis, meanwhile, spent the afternoon engaged in a less than pleasant task: Uncertain as to her future and well aware that threats were being made against her life, she drew up a new will on Fort Belvedere stationery. While Wallis packed, David continued to work on the speech he proposed to give to the nation; as soon as she left, he would return to London and meet with Baldwin at Buckingham Palace to formally seek his permission to broadcast to the country and empire.[29]

Late that afternoon, Walter Monckton arrived with his seventeen-year-old daughter, Valerie, and, together with David and Wallis, sat down to a late lunch at the Fort. Valerie would remember that Wallis, despite her earth-shattering troubles, had been immensely kind to her, making great efforts to include her in the conversation and asking questions about her life. Wallis, she remembered, carefully addressed the King as "sir" in her presence. From a previous visit, Valerie noted, the King had also remembered that she liked a particular kind of beverage and had himself made certain that it was placed on the dining table at Valerie's place.[30]

Perry Brownlow arrived late that afternoon, and Wallis's suitcases were quickly loaded in the two cars. "Hurried as were my last moments at the Fort," she later wrote, "they were nonetheless poignant. I think we all had a sense of tragedy, of irretrievable finality. As for me, this was the last hour of what had been for me the enchanted years. I was sure I would never see David again." Shortly after seven, Wallis walked through the octagonal hall and stood at the front door of the Fort. She hugged Aunt Bessie, then turned to David, who took her in his arms. "I don't know how it's all going to end," he said. "It will be some time before we can be together again. You must wait for me no matter how long it takes. I shall never give you up."[31]

Slowly, Wallis climbed into the waiting car. With tears running down his cheeks, David reached through the open window to touch her hand and whispered, "Bless you, my darling!"[32] As Ladbrooke eased the car down the gravel drive, Wallis turned to look back on the turrets of the Fort, the yellow lights of its windows burning against the dark sky.[33]

Wallis and Brownlow drove in silence through the thick fog for many minutes. Finally, however, Brownlow told Wallis that the previous evening he had been to Stornoway House, where he dined with Beaverbrook, Walter Monckton, George Allen, and Esmond Harmsworth. They had discussed the crisis at length and come to the conclusion that the only way to keep the King on his throne was for Wallis to publicly renounce him and disappear forever from his life.[34]

Now, as they drove through the quiet countryside, Brownlow went further. He explained to Wallis that if she left the country he felt certain that the King would almost assuredly abdicate the throne so that he could be at her side. Wallis was not entirely convinced, but Brownlow continued to argue persuasively until she finally asked what he thought she should do. He suggested that she come to his country house, Belton, at Grantham; by remaining in England, he hoped, Wallis would be able to influence the King not to abdicate. Ladbrooke pulled the car over to the side of the road while Wallis and Brownlow discussed the situation for several minutes.[35]

Wallis was quiet as she considered her options. She was convinced that David would be furious at this subterfuge. Brownlow agreed, but said he was willing to sacrifice his friendship with the King for the sake of keeping him on the throne.[36] Finally, Wallis made up her mind. "Knowing David as I did," she wrote, "I was more than doubtful that anyone, including me, could change his mind. If I stayed and my pleas failed, I should always be accused of secretly urging him to give up the Throne." She saw no option but to completely remove herself from the situation. "I am far from certain that I did the right thing in leaving Great Britain," she later wrote; "indeed, today, in the long view of hindsight, I am ready to concede that, in all likelihood, Perry was right and I was wrong. The instant I started across the Channel, I had ceased to exist, so far as my being able to influence the King's mind was concerned."[37]

At Newhaven, Wallis and Brownlow quickly boarded the ferry, where they took adjoining cabins under the name Mr. and Mrs. Harris. When they docked, they climbed into Wallis's Buick and left the ferry. However, they had neglected to change the paperwork, and customs' officials quickly learned that Mrs. Ernest Simpson was entering the country. "You've been found out, Mrs. Harris," Brownlow whispered to Wallis as they cleared customs. Within a matter of hours, word had reached the French press, and the hunt began.[38]

Thus began a drawn-out game of cat and mouse between Wallis and the press, played out across the 650 miles separating Dieppe and Cannes. At two in the morning, they stopped at Rouen, where they booked adjoining rooms under the name of Harris at the nearly deserted Hotel de la Poste. Wallis was too tired even to change out of her traveling clothes and simply collapsed on her bed.[39]

"Perry, will you please leave the door open between your room and mine?" she begged quietly. "I'm so frightened. I'm so nervous."

Brownlow heard her through the darkness, sobbing, an uncontrollable wail. Then she cried out, "Perry, will you please sleep in the bed next to me? I cannot be alone." "Sounds came out of her," Brownlow recalled, "that were absolutely without top, bottom . . . that were *primeval*. There was nothing I could do but lie down beside her, hold her hand, and make her feel that she was not alone."[40]

Eventually, Wallis stopped crying and fell asleep. The next morning, Brownlow woke her and said quickly that they had overslept and must leave at once. Wallis did not even have time to bathe or change clothes; she quickly ate a roll and downed a cup of tea before she joined Brownlow below. The hotel lobby was now filled with people, who, recognizing her, pointed and whispered loudly. She and Brownlow made a run for the car, but just as she entered, an altercation broke out, and Inspector Evans smashed a camera held by a girl trying to take Wallis's photograph. Once in the car, Wallis, visibly upset at the mob scene, asked Evans why he had taken the camera. He quickly explained that he was under strict orders from the King and had no way of knowing whether the girl had a concealed gun.[41]

They stopped at Evreux in Normandy so that Wallis could telephone the King. The connection was bad, and she had to shout through the receiver. Again, she begged David to do nothing rash, pleaded with him not to abdicate, and insisted that he meet with members of the government. There was little she could do, however, since David was even more distant and uncommunicative than ever before. Wallis left the booth in such a hurry that she forgot the rough notes on which she had scribbled her pleas and left them lying beside the telephone.[42]

During these conversations, and in the ones which followed once Wallis reached Cannes, she complained of a clicking noise. Perry Brownlow later discovered that the King's telephone lines were being tapped by the MI-5 British security force.[43] Brownlow recalled these conversations as agonized pleas: "You will never *ever* see me again," Wallis cried to David. "I will be lost in South America. *Never* leave your country! You *cannot* give in! You can *not*! You were *born* to this, it is your *heritage*, it is *demanded* of you by your country, by the traditions of nine hundred years."[44]

The incessant rain and fog made the drive difficult, and on the second night, the group stopped at Blois in the Loire Valley. Almost as soon as they had checked in to the local hotel, however, the lobby was filled with a mob of reporters. Brownlow appeared before them and in a loud voice informed Inspector Evans that they would be leaving at nine the following morning. He then ran upstairs and explained to Wallis that they must be ready to leave at dawn to avoid the press. Brownlow woke Wallis at three; she quickly dressed, took coffee, and silently crept out of the hotel, past the dozing reporters in the lobby.[45]

It was snowing as they continued their drive south. They stopped several times along the route, and Wallis was spotted by townspeople, who pointed at her and exclaimed, *"Voilà la dame!"* "This, I reflected bitterly, was what I had finally been brought to—no longer Wallis Simpson, no longer just another woman, but *the* woman. I was marked."[46]

By now, Wallis's Buick was being trailed by a long line of cars filled with members of the press. They stopped at a small cafe so that Wallis might ring the King, but the connection was bad, and she had to shout her pleas before the inquisitive eyes and ears of the gathered newsmen. To escape, she and Brownlow begged the restaurant manager to let them out by way of the kitchen. They had to climb from a first-floor window and drop onto the ground below. "It was a feat," Wallis recalled, "that would, I am sure, have brought a nod of approval from Miss Charlotte Noland, my girlhood gym instructor of Arundel days." As they drove away, Brownlow whispered with a smile, "Too bad Stanley Baldwin missed that little scene."[47]

Finally, at half-past two in the morning on December 6, the car reached Cannes. Wallis lay on the floor of the Buick, covered with a lap rug, as they passed through an immense mob of reporters, their cameras flashing as it drove through the gates of the Villa Lou Viei. Herman and Katherine Rogers waited at the door and quickly pulled Wallis inside. She had finally reached her safe haven.[48]

21

The Struggle
for the Throne

For Wallis, life had become intolerable. The press was encamped, "like a besieging army," all around the thick walls of the twelfth-century villa. Reporters crawled over the gates, tried to look into windows, and somehow, managed to tap the telephone lines. Finally, the French police had to be called in to clear the mob away.[1]

As soon as she had safely ensconced herself at Lou Viei, Wallis sat down and wrote an anguished plea to David: "I am so anxious for you not to *abdicate* and I think the fact that you do is going to put me in the wrong light to the entire world because they will say that I could have prevented it. . . . I feel so terrified of what the world will say. . . ."[2]

The storm had broken with a fury in America. Newspaper headlines screamed Wallis's name across their banners; reporters hinted that it was only a matter of days before the crisis reached its zenith. In Baltimore, crowds gathered on the sidewalk before her former house, staring at its blank windows. Souvenir hunters stormed Blue Ridge Summit and literally began ripping pieces of siding off the house where she had been born.

On December 3, the same day on which Wallis had left the country, Winston Churchill made a planned speech at Albert Hall in which he repeated his plea for rearmament and his defense of the League of Nations. He ended: "There is another grave matter that overshadows our minds tonight. In a few minutes we are going to sing 'God Save the King.' I shall sing it with more heartfelt fervour than I have ever sung it in my life. I hope and pray that no irrevocable decision will be taken in haste, but that time and public opinion will be allowed to play their part and that a cherished and unique personality may not be incontinently severed from the people he loves so well."[3] When Churchill sat down, the audience erupted into loud applause and shouted a resounding "Three cheers for the King."

As soon as Wallis left the Fort, David returned to London for a nine o'clock meeting with Baldwin at Buckingham Palace. The King raised the idea of possibly speaking to the country—something for which he needed to obtain the government's permission. Baldwin replied that he would consult his colleagues but that he thought the idea of the broadcast was itself unconstitutional.

"You want me to go, don't you?" David asked him bluntly. "And before I go, I think it is right, for her sake and mine, that I should speak."

"What I want, Sir," Baldwin replied, "is what you told me you wanted: to go with dignity, not dividing the country, and making things as smooth as possible for your successor. To broadcast would go over the heads of your Ministers and speak to the people. You will be telling millions throughout the world—among them a vast number of women—that you are determined to marry one who has a husband living. They will want to know all about her, and the press will ring with gossip, the very thing you want to avoid. . . ."[4]

As soon as the prime minister left Buckingham Palace, David drove down the Mall to visit his mother at Marlborough House. There he found that Queen Mary had also asked the Duke and Duchess of York and his sister Mary, the Princess Royal.

It is often repeated that the Duke and Duchess of York, who would inherit the throne should the King abdicate, were deliberately kept in the dark by Edward VIII during these crucial weeks. The Yorks certainly believed that David was avoiding them, and Elizabeth is said to have exclaimed in frustration, "Everyone knows more than we do; we know nothing. Nothing!"[5] But the abdication did not come without warning. On Monday, November 23, the Yorks had both written letters to David in which they indicated their support. "When you told me of your decision to marry Wallis the other evening," Bertie wrote, "I do hope you did not think that I was unsympathetic about it. Since then I have been thinking a great deal about you, as I do *so* long for you to be happy with the one person you adore. I, of all people, should understand your own personal feelings at this time, which I do indeed. I do realize all your great difficulties, & I feel sure that whatever you decide to do will be in the best interests of the Country & Empire." And the Duchess, aware of her husband's nervous disposition, implored David to treat Bertie with kindness, adding, "We want you to be happy more than anything else."[6]

Such letters were to cause great misunderstanding. David read them at their surface value: His brother and sister-in-law, knowing of his intention to marry Wallis or abdicate, had expressed their full support. They were aware of the consequences, and Bertie had even assured his brother that in following his heart, he was certain he would do what, in the end, was best for the country and the empire. On the very day after these letters were written, David again met with Bertie and told him that he would likely abdicate the throne. The Yorks were therefore as well informed as the King himself in the weeks preceding the crisis.

The Duchess of York was so angry at her brother-in-law that she declined to take part in the family discussions at Marlborough House that evening; she only learned the details later from her husband and from Queen Mary. David explained that he had refrained from seeing his family for the last week because he had been waiting for word from Baldwin and had been anxious to avoid any pain. "I have no desire to bring you and the family into all this," David declared. "This is something I must handle alone."[7]

Bertie, in an account of the abdication crisis written later, recalled: "Later [in Mary's and my presence] David said to Queen Mary that he could not live alone as King and must marry Mrs._____."[8] He could not even bring himself to write Wallis's name. After this, David asked his brother to come to the Fort on the following morning to meet with him.

On Friday, December 4, Baldwin was to speak in the House of Commons. Chips Channon recalled the anticipation as Baldwin entered the chamber: "The Cabinet, looking like a picture by Franz Hals, a lot of grim Elders of the Kirk, squirmed nervously. Then he rose, and in a stentorian voice, unsmiling and ungracious, I thought, announced flatly that there was no middle course. . . ."[9]

Baldwin declared:

Suggestions have appeared in certain organs of the Press yesterday, and again today, that if the King decided to marry, his wife need not become Queen. These ideas are without foundation. There is no such thing as what is called morganatic marriage known to our law.

The Royal Marriages Act of 1772 has no application to the Sovereign himself. Its only effect is that the marriage of any other member of the Royal Family is null and void unless the Sovereign's consent, declared under the Great Seal, is first obtained. The Act, therefore, has nothing to do with the present case. The King himself requires no consent from any other authority to make his marriage legal.

But, as I have said, the lady whom he marries, by the fact of her marriage to the King, necessarily becomes Queen. She herself therefore enjoys all the status, rights and privileges which both by positive law and by custom attach to that position, and with which we are familiar in the case of her late Majesty Queen Alexandra, and her Majesty Queen Mary, and her children would be in the direct succession to the Throne.

The only way in which this result could be avoided would be by legislation dealing with a particular case. His Majesty's Government are not prepared to introduce such legislation.

Moreover, the matters to be dealt with are of so common concern to the Commonwealth as a whole, and such a change could not be effected without the assent of all the Dominions. I am satisfied, from enquiries I have made, that this assent would not be forthcoming.[10]

Hearing this, Churchill stood up and shouted at Baldwin, "You won't be satisfied until you've broken him, will you?"[11]

That Friday evening, Baldwin was expected at the Fort for another meeting with the King. David, who had learned of the scene in the House of Commons, feared that a confrontation was inevitable. He knew that it was only the question of marriage that had caused the crisis: According to Perry Brownlow, the King told him "that the Archbishop of Canterbury had said to him, almost in so many words, that he should keep Wallis as his mistress, and in the background."[12] This somewhat hypocritical view is backed up by a letter written by Beaverbrook to his friend Roy Howard on December 8, 1936: "The opposition to the King's project of marriage to Mrs. Simpson is essentially religious in character. He is lay head of the Church of England, and the chief priests and the Sanhedrin say, in effect, that he may live in sin with her, but must not marry a woman who has been married twice before."[13] This option is almost certainly what Wallis herself would have preferred in light of the crisis. Although she may have harbored a desire to become his wife, she was more than willing to remain in the background as a mistress and stay at his side. Then, with the passage of time, her gradual introduction to society and the public through charity involvements and other appearances, and eventual acceptance, they might marry.[14]

When David had informed Monckton that he would likely be forced to abdicate, the latter was determined to do all he could to ensure that the King could marry Mrs. Simpson. "I was desperately afraid that the King might give up his Throne and yet be deprived of his chance to marry Mrs. Simpson." Until the decree was final, the King's proctor could claim collusion or illegalities in the Simpson divorce and stop the proceedings. The proctor could not cite David in the case, but once he ceased being King, he was as vulnerable to court action as any other subject. Monckton suggested that a special bill be coupled to the abdication which would make the decree *nisi* final immediately. "This would have cleared up a grave constitutional position affecting the whole world and left no ragged ends or possibilities for further scandal," he explained.[15] David readily agreed, since he did not want to wait until April to be with Wallis.

Baldwin arrived at the Fort and immediately delivered bad news: the cabinet would not allow the King to broadcast to the nation and Dominions. David was distressed at this, but he said nothing. The prime minister, realizing that he held the upper hand, then pushed the King to make a declaration of his intentions. When David put him off, Baldwin replied, "There is still time for you to change your mind, Sir. That is indeed the prayer of Your Majesty's servants."

"I studied the Prime Minister some time before answering. . . ." David later wrote. "For me to do what he asked would have meant my abandoning, in the full view of the watching world, the woman whom I had asked to marry me. If it were indeed Mr. Baldwin's prayer that I should save my Crown by so base a surrender, that noble ornament would have been laid upon a head forever bent in shame."[16]

The King then raised a sensitive political issue: Were he to abdicate, would it be possible to attach a special bill, as Monckton had suggested, to the abdication which immediately granted Mrs. Simpson's decree *nisi?* Hearing this, Baldwin must have realized that there would be no fight. David was more concerned with ensuring his eventual marriage to Mrs. Simpson than with keeping the throne. Knowing that the end was in sight, Baldwin told David that he would support the special bill, and if the House of Commons refused to pass the measure, he and the cabinet would resign.

David seemed relieved; he told Baldwin that he needed several days in which to sort through his affairs but that the prime minister would have a formal decision shortly. There was no doubt in Baldwin's mind that the King would leave. "Well, Sir," Baldwin is said to have declared, somewhat improbably, "whatever happens, my Mrs. and I wish you happiness from the depths of our souls." Hearing this, David was overwhelmed and began to cry; Baldwin soon joined him. "What a strange conversation piece, those two blubbering together on a sofa," wrote Harold Nicolson.[17]

An hour after Baldwin left, Churchill arrived at the Fort. Knowing that the King had previously pondered a decision to go abroad for the duration of the crisis, Churchill now advised David to remain in the country and drop the entire question of marriage until the decree absolute had been granted. If the government would not agree to the marriage after the coronation, the King could then accept their resignation rather than they his. But David said nothing, and Churchill left the Fort uncertain of his intentions.[18]

That night, pacing up and down his bedroom floor, David decided to abdicate. In truth, he now had little choice. If he persisted and attempted to marry Wallis before the coronation, as was his wish, the government would resign. David would then be forced to form a new government whose sole *raison d'être* would be justification and support of his controversial marriage. The two choices that might have allowed the King to remain on the throne, a morganatic marriage and a direct appeal to the people, had now both fallen through.

For all the criticism of the abdication, it must be admitted that given the circumstances, the King undoubtedly made the best choice. He loved Wallis too much to give her up; at the same time, he cared greatly about the empire he had inherited from his father and wished to maintain it. It would have been easy for him to force Wallis on the public; in doing so, however, he might have fractured the empire.

David later wrote:

> Even though I might have been able to recruit a commanding majority, I could not have persuaded the entire nation and all the Dominions. . . . By making a stand for myself, I should have left the scars of a civil war. . . . True, I should still be King. But I would no longer be King by the free and common consent of all. . . . The cherished conception of a Monarchy above politics would have been shattered. . . . I felt I had come to the limit of a man's power to shape events and fend off catastrophe. Were I to wait longer I might indeed reap the whirlwind. And so, in faith and calmness, not unmixed with sorrow, I resolved to end the constitutional crisis forthwith. I would close my reign with dignity, clear the succession for my brother with the least possible embarrassment and avoid all appearance of faction. . . . I reject the notion . . . that, faced with a choice between love and duty, I chose love. I certainly married because I chose the path of love. But I abdicated because I chose the path of duty. I did not value the Crown so lightly that I gave it away. I valued it so deeply that I surrendered it, rather than risk any impairment of its prestige."[19]

Having reached his decision, David was resolute; over the next few days, as he gradually told first one confidant, then another, that he would leave, he met arguments and objections with a stubborn silence. For the time being, he kept his decision to himself. That weekend, he continued to meet with his advisers, but he was more concerned now with details regarding a future off the throne with Wallis than with fighting against Baldwin.

On Sunday, December 6, the Earl of Crawford recorded: "In the press this morning there is a distinct tendency to scold the Church for butting into an affair which does not concern them. . . . They announce that Cantuar [the Archbishop of Canterbury] was mobbed and that ministers were hooted in Downing St.—merely the ebullitions of a score or two of rowdies; but it is evident that the gutter press has been enlisted to support the King in all he does and wishes to do with the object of overthrowing Baldwin."[20]

That same day, Churchill issued a strong statement that duly appeared in the papers:

I plead for time and patience. The nation must realize the character of the constitutional issue. There is no question of any conflict between the King and Parliament. Parliament has not been consulted in any way or allowed to express any opinion. The question is whether the King is to abdicate upon the advice of the Ministry of the Day. No such advice has ever before been tendered to a Sovereign in Parliamentary times. This is not a case where differences have arisen between the Sovereign and his Ministers on any particular measure. These could certainly be resolved by normal processes of Parliament or dissolution. In this case we are in the presence of a wish expressed by the Sovereign to perform an act which in no circumstances can be accomplished for nearly five months, and may conceivably, for various reasons, never be accomplished at all. That, on such a hypothetical and supposititious basis the supreme sacrifice of abdication and potential exile of the Sovereign should be demanded, finds no support whatever in the British Constitution. No Ministry has the authority to advise the abdication of the Sovereign. Only the most serious Parliamentary processes could even raise the issue in a decisive form. The Cabinet has no right to prejudge such a question without having previously ascertained at the very least the will of Parliament. This could, perhaps, be obtained by messages from the Sovereign to Parliament, and by addresses of both Houses after due consideration of these messages. For the Sovereign to abdicate incontinently in the present circumstances would inflict an injury upon the constitutional position of the monarchy which is measureless and cannot fail to be grievous to the institution itself, irrespective of the existing occupant of the Throne. Parliament would also fail entirely in its duty if it allowed such an event to occur as the signing of an abdication in response to the advice of Ministers without taking all precautions to make sure that these same processes may not be repeated with equal uncanny facility at no distant date in unforeseen circumstances. Clearly time is needed for searching constitutional debate. The next question is—What has the King done? If it be true, as is alleged, that the King has proposed to his Ministers legislation which they are not prepared to introduce, the answer of Ministers should be not to call for abdication, but to refuse to act upon the

King's request, which thereupon becomes inoperative. If the King refuses to take the advice of his Ministers they are, of course, free to resign. They have no right whatever to put pressure upon him to accept their advice by soliciting beforehand assurances from the Leader of the Opposition that he will not form an alternative Administration in the event of their resignation, and thus confronting the King with an ultimatum. Again, there is cause for time and patience. Why cannot time be granted? The fact that it is beyond the King's power to accomplish the purpose which Ministers oppose until the end of April surely strips the matter of constitutional urgency. There may be some inconvenience, but that inconvenience stands on a different plane altogether from the grave constitutional issues I have set forth. National and Imperial considerations alike require that before such a dread step as a demand for abdication is taken, not only should the constitutional position be newly defined by Parliament, but that every method should be exhausted which gives the hope of a happier solution. Lastly, but surely not least, there is the human and personal aspect. The King has been for many weeks under the greatest strain, moral and mental, that can fall upon a man. Not only has he been inevitably subjected to the supreme stress of his public duty, but also to the agony of his own personal feelings. Surely, if he asks for time to consider the advice of his Ministers, now that at length matters have been brought to this dire culmination, he should not be denied. Howsoever this matter may turn, it is pregnant with calamity and inseparable from inconvenience. But all the evil aspects will be aggravated beyond measure if the utmost chivalry and compassion are not shown, both by Ministers and by the British nation, towards a gifted and beloved King torn between private and public obligations of love and duty. The Churches stand for charity. They believe in the efficacy of prayer. Surely their influence must not oppose a period of reflection. I plead, I pray, that time and tolerance will not be denied. The King has no means of personal access to his Parliament or his people. Between him and them stand in their office the Ministers of the Crown. If they thought it their duty to engage all their power and influence against him, still he must remain silent. All the more must they be careful not to be the judge in their own case, and to show a loyal and Christian patience even at some political embarrassment to themselves. If an abdication were to be hastily extorted the outrage so committed would cast its shadow forward across many chapters of the history of the British Empire."[21]

However, Harold Laski, one of the Labour leaders, felt differently. He declared: "Out of this issue no precedent must be created that makes the royal authority once more a source of independent political power in the State. The Labour Party is a constitutional party. . . . Pivotal to that conception is the principle that a Labour government with a majority in the House of Commons is entitled to have its advice accepted by the Crown. . . . He may advise. He may encourage. He may warn. But if the Cabinet stands firm in its advice, the King must in our constitutional system necessarily give way."[22]

That weekend, hundreds took to the streets in London to demonstrate; large crowds gathered around the massive gates of Buckingham Palace day and night, singing, shouting, and cheering any vehicle that happened to appear. These supporters carried placards declaring their loyalty: "Hands off our King. Abdication means Revolution!" "We want Eddie and We want his Missus"; "Edward's right and Baldwin's wrong!";[23] and "Let the King know you are with him—you can't let him down. We want Edward. Perish all politicians!"[24] "The world is now divided into Cavaliers and Roundheads," Chips Channon noted on December 7.[25] Everyone seemed enthralled at the crisis, at the royal romance. "I think," says Dame Barbara Cartland, "that it was the first time the public had seen the inner feelings of royalty."[26]

Chief among these supporters was the King's friend Sir Oswald Mosley and his band of British Unionists. They stormed through the streets that weekend, shouting, "Stand by the King!"[27] Mosley himself clearly saw the crisis in political terms and lost no chance to state his case. "How would you like a Cabinet of old busybodies to pick *your* girl?" he was heard to ask.[28]

The weekend proved fatal to the King's popular support. While London, more sophisticated and tolerant, took to the streets to support their King in his wish, MPs returning home to their various ridings were often confronted not with support for the monarch but with shock. Their constituents could not see beyond the fact that their King wished to marry a woman with two previous husbands still living. This rural outrage filtered back to London; although David had privately made up his mind to go, his supporters continued to believe that through sheer effort they would win the day. Monday afternoon would see these last illusions shattered.

22

Abdication

ON MONDAY, DECEMBER 7, Baldwin informed the House of Commons during their regular session that the government was awaiting word from the King regarding the crisis. "In considering the whole matter," he stated, "it has always been, and remains, the earnest desire of the Government to afford to His Majesty the fullest opportunity of weighing a decision which involves so directly his own future happiness and the interests of all his subjects. At the same time they cannot but be aware that any considerable prolongation of the present state of suspense and uncertainty would involve risk of the gravest injury to national and imperial interests, and indeed no one is more insistent upon this aspect of the situation than His Majesty."[1]

As soon as Baldwin had finished, Churchill stood up and launched into an attack on the government, saying that it had no right to force the King to abdicate without allowing him to consult Parliament. It was now, however, that Churchill learned just how much the public mood had swung against the King. MPs, previously content to sit and watch the unfolding crisis from the backbenches, had been made fully aware of their constituents' disapproval of the King's relationship with Mrs. Simpson. As Churchill continued to speak, he was repeatedly interrupted with shouts, whistles, booing, and calls of "Sit down!" and "Shut up!" "Winston suffered an utter defeat. . . ." Harold Nicolson wrote. "First we had Baldwin—slow and measured. Then Winston rose to ask a supplementary question. He failed to do it in the right form and was twice called to order by the speaker. He hesitated and waved his spectacles vaguely in the air. 'Sit down!' they shouted. He waved his spectacles again and then collapsed. It was almost painful."[2] The next day, the *Times* described it as "the most striking rebuff in modern parliamentary history."[3]

After this scene, Churchill stormed out of the House in disgust. As soon as he had gone, an MP rose and asked the speaker, "Does the Prime Minister realize the deep sympathy which is felt for him in all sections of the House?"[4] The wild burst of applause which followed signaled the end of any idea for a King's Party. It was clear that such a course of action would tear the country apart.

That evening, as word began to filter back to the Fort of what had taken place in the House of Commons, David once again met with his brother the Duke of York. After their last meeting on Thursday, the King had asked the Duke to come to see him the following morning; however, David spent most of the next few days huddled with his advisers and repeatedly stalled Bertie's attempts to visit him at the Fort. This has always been interpreted as either cowardly or stubborn evasion on David's part; however, it must be said that at the time the Duke was certainly not being kept in the dark about anything. He had been informed by his brother that he would marry Wallis or abdicate. The King's weekend was consumed with important meetings, which were at the moment deciding his future. It is arguable, therefore, that Bertie was put off simply because David had no new news to tell him. David himself knew little of what was taking place within the government—the cabinet minutes outlining discussion on the issue were deliberately withheld from him. It seems reasonable to conclude, therefore, that in putting off his brother's meeting, David was simply waiting until he had definitive news to report. There was little to be gained in another painful talk during which both brothers would be nervous and uneasy, with no issues yet settled. Throughout the weekend, however, the Duke and Duchess of York waited at Royal Lodge, Windsor, hoping for word from David. The Duchess was confined to her bed with the flu, and her illness further worried her already nervous husband. Several times that weekend, though, the Duke secretly returned to London to meet privately with the prime minister at No. 10 Downing Street. Both men were almost positive by this time that the King would abdicate, and thus their talks centered on the Duke's eventual accession to the throne.[5]

The Duke of York arrived at Fort Belvedere at seven that Monday evening. "The awful and ghastly suspense of waiting was over," Bertie later wrote. "I found him pacing up and down the room, and he told me his decision that he would go."[6]

The next day, Tuesday, December 8, the *Times* carried several articles related to the crisis. Not surprisingly, these reflected the Conservative views of Geoffrey Dawson:

> It is contended again that there are precedents for a morganatic union of the kind contemplated. There are none. No British precedents exist and no Continental precedents apply. The analogy from them is both false and foolish. Some Continental monarchs have been constitutionally restricted to wives of certain

rank or birth. The morganatic marriage was a means whereby they could choose a wife outside the permitted circle, but without conferring upon her the status of a Royal Consort. In England this has never been necessary. The King of England—it needs to be repeated—is today, and throughout history has ever been, completely free in his choice of a wife, irrespective of rank and nationality, and is trammelled by no obligation to the Constitution or to his advisors. There has, as Lord Rothermere says, been no suggestion at any time from any quarter that the lady for whom the morganatic exception is recommended should become Queen. Yet in law—apart from the fact that she is not legally free to remarry—there is nothing to bar her from becoming Consort and Queen in the full sense. The disqualification here is not, as on the Continent, one of law, but of fact. What is demanded is statutory recognition of the fact that she is not fitted to be Queen. The Prime Ministers of the Empire are to be asked to propose, and the Parliaments to accept and ratify, a permanent statutory apology for the status of the lady whom the King desires to marry. The Constitution is to be amended in order that she may carry in solitary prominence the brand of unfitness for the Queen's Throne. Can anyone in possession of his faculties imagine any Prime Minister moving, or any Parliament undertaking to support, a proposition so indivious and so distressing?

This foolish and deplorable product of misguided ingenuity must be cleared away once and for all, and delicate and difficult grounds will be freed of at least one superfluous encumbrance.

Nor are its intrinsic embarrassments and absurdities the only reason for condemning its resurrection at this stage. Those who purport to be advancing it in His Majesty's interest are doing so in the face of the considered and unanimous decision of the five Empire Governments. In the form of advocacy which they have chosen, it is an unpleasantly significant recrudescence of the same movement—in the same quarter—which threatened not long ago to depict the Sovereign as in conflict with his elected and Ministerial advisers. It is also an attempt to force upon the King a decision which is his and his only, and which he may be trusted to make in his own time with full regard for the Coronation of which he is a custodian and for the hereditary trust, written and unwritten, that came into his hands from his father ten months ago.[7]

That Tuesday evening, David received Baldwin at the Fort and informed him of his decision to abdicate. After this staggering news, David quite calmly asked the prime minister if he would care to dine with him. Monckton, who was also present, later wrote in admiration of the King: "This dinner party was, I think, his *tour de force*. In that quiet panelled room he sat at the head of the table with his boyish face and smile, with a good fresh colour while the rest of us were pale as sheets, rippling over with bright conversations, and with a careful eye to see that his guests were being looked after. He wore his white kilt. On Mr. Baldwin's right was the Duke of York, and I was next to him, and as the dinner went on the Duke turned to me and said: 'Look at him. We simply cannot let him go.' But we both knew that there was nothing we could say or do to stop him."[8]

On Wednesday, Walter Monckton met with the Duke of York for several hours at his London residence, No. 145 Piccadilly. During this meeting, financial arrangements and other issues were discussed at some length. Monckton obtained the Duke's word that once the King abdicated the throne, he would remain a Royal Prince and retain his royal rank. David himself was particularly concerned about the future. He knew that he would have to absent himself from England for an undetermined period of time; Bertie, having consulted with members of the cabinet and with the prime minister, told Monckton that all concerned had now decided that this period of exile was likely to be at least two years, during which time the new King could comfortably settle into his role and win the confidence and affection of his subjects without the distracting presence of a rival former sovereign. But the Duke of York agreed that his brother could live at Fort Belvedere when the time came for the end of his exile. At this point, no one—least of all the Duke of York—believed that such an exile would last for the rest of his brother's life.[9]

The Duke of York returned to Royal Lodge, leaving his ill wife in London. That afternoon, Queen Mary, accompanied by her daughter Mary, the Princess Royal, drove from Marlborough House to Windsor and on to Royal Lodge, where they were to meet with David. Soon the King's black Daimler appeared through the rolling fog and mist, and David joined his mother and siblings in the saloon for tea. As gently as he could, he told them that he was to abdicate the following day. Walter Monckton happened to overhear Queen Mary exclaim in disgust, "To give up all that for this!"[10]

Late that evening, David gave his brother a draft of his proposed abdication. Bertie immediately took it back to London, where he arrived at Marlborough House shortly before midnight. He showed the draft to his mother, and as she read through it, he broke down and sobbed on her shoulder.[11] In her diary, the Queen wrote: "Bertie arrived very late from Fort Belvedere and Mr. W. Monckton brought him & me the paper drawn up for David's abdication of the Throne of this Empire because he wishes to marry Mrs. Simpson!!!!! The whole affair has lasted since Novr. 16th and has been very painful—It is a terrible blow to us all & particularly to poor Bertie."[12]

The Duke of York returned to his house late that evening knowing that on the following day he would become King. Throughout the previous week, the numerous visitors, secret meetings, and overheard tears had intrigued his two young daughters, ten-year-old Princess Elizabeth and six-year-old Princess Margaret. Their confusion was evident in a conversation a servant happened to hear that week."What's happening?" Margaret asked her sister. "I don't know really," the future Queen Elizabeth II replied, "but I believe Uncle David wishes to get married. I *think* he wants to marry Mrs. Baldwin—and Mr. Baldwin doesn't like it!"[13]

Meanwhile, in France, Wallis felt desperately cut off from the momentous events taking place in London. She repeatedly rang David at the Fort that weekend, urging him not to abdicate. The connections were almost always bad, and both had to shout at the tops of their lungs, over the crackling, hissing noises filling their receivers. David told Wallis that he hoped the situation was changing in his favor. Baldwin had agreed that he might consult Churchill, who could then present a constitutional argument to the House of Commons if he wished; meanwhile, Lord Beaverbrook had agreed to discuss the situation with members of the press.

"David, please listen to your friends," she begged him.

"I will," he replied.

"You must listen," she continued. "Nothing will be lost, nothing will be changed, by your waiting."

"You can trust me," he continued. "However, I must deal with this situation in my own way."[14]

David, shouting at his end, left others in the Fort well aware of what was taking place. Sir Edward Peacock, one of the directors of the Bank of England, later recalled "the insistence over the telephone of the lady that he should fight for his rights. She kept up that line until very near the end, maintaining that he was King and his popularity would carry everything. . . ."[15]

Such telephone calls began to take their toll on Wallis. She realized that there was no way she could remain in the situation and hope to win. Perry Brownlow told her frankly, "As I see it now, there is only one possible way of stopping this dreadful drift. It is for you to renounce the King." For once, Wallis did not argue. She knew such a powerful declaration would both hurt and humiliate David, but there seemed no other way.[16]

She discussed her decision with Brownlow, who agreed that only a strongly worded statement would be likely to avert an abdication.

Together with Brownlow and Herman Rogers, Wallis drafted a statement; she read it to David over the telephone. At first, he was upset
and hurt; he realized, however, that the statement would at least serve
to divert some of the public blame from Wallis. At seven o'clock that
Monday evening, the statement was released to the press: "Mrs. Simpson throughout the last few weeks has invariably wished to avoid any
action or proposal which would hurt or damage His Majesty or the
Throne. Today her attitude is unchanged, and she is willing, if such
action would solve the problem, to withdraw forthwith from a situation that has been rendered both unhappy and untenable."[17] That
night, Wallis slept soundly for the first time in days, believing that the
crisis would finally be averted by her statement.

Within an hour, Baldwin also had a copy of the press statement, which would be published in the newspapers the following
morning. This was not quite the categorical renunciation Baldwin had
hoped for; to find out what she intended, he dispatched her lawyer,
Theodore Goddard, to Cannes.[18] When David learned of this, he rang
Wallis and warned her not to listen to any threats or arguments he
might make.[19]

Vague rumors had reached the press that Goddard was accompanied by an anesthetist and a gynecologist; neither Wallis nor the
others encamped at the villa had any idea why the lawyer would be
accompanied by such men, and there were hints that Baldwin might
have ordered her drugged and seized. On Wednesday, when Goddard
arrived, Wallis learned the truth: He had come with his own doctor—
W. Douglas Kirkwood, formerly a surgeon at Queen Charlotte's Hospital for Women, one of London's largest maternity hospitals—not
with an emissary from Baldwin.[20] The current rumor was that Wallis
might be pregnant, and Kirkwood was there to make absolutely certain
that this was not so. If he could establish that she was not pregnant, it
would make the King's desire to push for a special bill to finalize her
decree absolute much easier.

Goddard urged Wallis to withdraw her divorce petition; if she
did, he explained, there could be no question of the King's marrying
her, and the crisis would be averted. "I will do anything within my
power to keep the King on the Throne," she declared. She asked if she
might advise Brownlow of her intended step and called him into the
room.[21] She knew Ernest would agree for the sake of the throne. If they
did this, they could have the King crowned, and the situation might
later resolve itself.

Brownlow, however, seemed less convinced. "If the King does
abdicate," he declared, "his object, as we all know, will be marriage;
and for you to scrap your divorce will produce a hopeless anticlimax
and an all-round tragedy."[22]

Instead, Brownlow advised Wallis that she should leave Europe at once. She agreed, thinking she might return to China, where she would be both fairly anonymous and out of reach of the King. She had decided to lie to him, to tell him that she was not in love with him, would never marry him, and did not want to spend her life with him. Hurtful as this would be to both her and David, it was her only hope that he might remain on the throne.[23] Goddard drew up an announcement and telephoned the text to Baldwin: "I have discussed the whole position with Mrs. Simpson—her own, the position of the King, the country, the Empire. Mrs. Simpson tells me she was, and still is, perfectly willing to instruct me to withdraw her petition for divorce and willing to do anything to prevent the King from abdicating. I am satisfied that this is Mrs. Simpson's genuine and honest desire. I read this note over to Mrs. Simpson who in every way confirmed it." The note was signed by Goddard and countersigned by Brownlow.[24]

In despair, Wallis put through a telephone call to David. Nerves were frayed, and the crisis had almost reached its climax. When she began to explain to him what she wanted to do, he cut her short. "I can't seem to make you understand the position," he said. "It's all over. The Instrument of Abdication is already prepared." Nothing Wallis might now do, he said, would change the situation.[25] So little did she know of the political situation and the King's power and status that she is said to have asked, "But, David, can't you remain Emperor of India even if you are no longer King of England?"[26]

Wallis was stunned. David had assured her that he would not abdicate; now he had done just that without bothering to inform her until it was too late. She had worried endlessly, tried to remove herself over and over again from the situation, been prepared to sacrifice her own desires and future happiness, to keep him on the throne. "I think ultimately she felt very, very betrayed by the abdication," a friend later declared. "She rarely spoke about that period of her life, but once, she did admit that the Duke's actions had hurt her terribly. I think, also, that she was more than a little put out at having her future essentially determined for her."[27]

Undoubtedly, too, there was a sense of dread at what inevitably must follow. Until now, Wallis had managed to remain out of the public eye, and the five days of press which had followed Blunt's speech had been relatively clear of criticism; but now she had little doubt that the entire world would hold her responsible for the abdication and that she would become the object of almost universal scorn. "I," Wallis recalled, "who had sought no place in history would now be assured of one—an appalling one, carved out by blind prejudice."[28]

Wallis hung up the telephone and collapsed in tears. Katherine Rogers rushed to her, saying, "You have done everything that could be expected of a woman in this situation. No one will blame you." The following afternoon, Wallis again spoke with the King on the telephone. He had announced his intention of going to Switzerland after he abdicated. Wallis, worried that he would be alone or surrounded by strangers, now recommended that he stay with their friends Baron Eugene de Rothschild and his wife at their country estate, Schloss Enzesfeld, near Vienna. He considered this and agreed.[29]

On Thursday, December 10, David, witnessed by his brothers, signed six copies of the Act of Abdication at ten in the morning in the octagonal drawing room at the Fort. The act, which would take effect at midnight, read:

> I, Edward the Eighth, of Great Britain, Ireland and the British Dominions beyond the Seas, King, Emperor of India, do hereby declare my irrevocable determination to renounce the Throne for Myself and My descendants, and My desire that effect should be given to this Instrument of Abdication immediately.
>
> In token whereof I have hereunto set My hand this tenth day of December, nineteen hundred and thirty six, in the presence of the witnesses whose signatures are subscribed.

That afternoon, Baldwin made the announcement in the House of Commons. Harold Nicolson wrote that the chamber was "nervous and noisy." Curious onlookers sat on the floor and in the gallery aisles, filling every conceivable space. Baldwin entered the House and fumbled with his papers. "The old man collects them hurriedly," wrote Nicolson, "and the next minute . . . walks hurriedly to the Bar, turns round, bows, and advances to the Chair. He stops and bows again. 'A message from the King,' he shouts, 'signed by His Majesty's own hand.' He then hands the papers to the Speaker. The latter rises and reads out the message of abdication in a quavering voice."[30] The message read:

> After long and anxious consideration, I have determined to renounce the Throne to which I succeeded on the death of my Father, and I am now communicating this my final and irrevocable decision. Realising as I do the gravity of this step, I can only hope that I shall have the understanding of my people in the decision I have taken and the reasons which had led me to take it.
>
> I will not enter now into my private feelings, but I would beg that it should be remembered that the burden which constantly rests upon the shoulders of a Sovereign is so heavy that it can only be borne in circumstances different from those in which I now find myself.

I conceive that I am not overlooking the duty that rests on me to place in the forefront the public interest when I declare that I am conscious that I can no longer discharge this heavy task with efficiency or with satisfaction to myself. I have accordingly this morning executed an Instrument of Abdication. . . .

I deeply appreciate the spirit which has actuated the appeals which have been made to me to take a different decision, and I have, before reaching my final determination, most fully pondered over them. But my mind is made up. Moreover, further delay cannot but be most injurious to the peoples whom I have tried to serve as Prince of Wales and as King and whose future happiness and prosperity are the constant wish of my heart.

I take my leave of them in the confident hope that the course which I have thought it right to follow is that which is best for the stability of the Throne and Empire and the happiness of my peoples. I am deeply sensible of the consideration which they have always extended to me, both before and after my accession to the Throne, and which I know they will extend in full measure to my successor.[31]

As soon as the speaker finished reading the King's message, Baldwin once again stood up and prepared to address the House. "The feeling," continues Nicolson, "that at any moment he may break down from emotion increases our own emotion. I have never known in any assemblage such accumulation of pity and terror."[32]

"No more grave message has ever been received by Parliament, and no more difficult, I may almost say repugnant, task has ever been imposed upon a Prime Minister," Baldwin began. He emphasized that he could only tell the story "truthfully, sincerely, and plainly, with no attempt to dress up or to adorn." He began by relating the good nature of his relations with the King, first as Prince of Wales and later as sovereign, and added curiously that "the discussions of this last week bound us more closely together than ever." He carefully outlined each of his meetings with the King and the course of the developing crisis. He spoke of the various ideas and the morganatic marriage proposal, explaining again how he had been forced to reject them, and how the dominions had also expressed their disapproval. He ended by saying, "My last words on that subject are that I am convinced that where I have failed no one could have succeeded. His mind was made up, and those who know His Majesty best will know what that means."[33]

Nicolson continues: "The 'Hear, Hears!' echo solemnly like Amens. His papers are in a confused state . . . and he hesitates somewhat. He confuses dates and turns to Simon, 'It was a Monday, was it not the 27th?' The artifice of such asides is so effective that one imagines it to be deliberate. There is no moment when he overstates emotion or indulges in oratory. There is intense silence broken only by the reporters in the gallery scuttling away to telephone the speech paragraph by paragraph. I suppose that in after-centuries men will read the words of that speech and exclaim, 'What an opportunity wasted!' They will never know the tragic force of its simplicity. 'I said, to the King . . .' 'The King told me. . . .' It was Sophoclean and almost unbearable. Attlee felt this. When it was over, he asked that the sitting might be adjourned until 6 P.M. We file out broken in body and soul, conscious that we have heard the best speech that we shall ever hear in our lives. There is no question of applause. It was the silence of Gettysburg."[34]

That evening, David consulted with Bertie at Fort Belvedere, a meeting which was to prove a source of great contention and resentment between the two brothers for the rest of their lives. Six other men, all financial and legal advisers, were also present: Sir Ulick Alexander, keeper of the privy purse under Edward VIII; Sir Edward Peacock, serving as the King's private financial adviser; Lord Wigram, the former private secretary to King George V, who was advising the Duke of York; Sir Bernard Bircham, the Duke of York's personal solicitor; George Allen, the King's solicitor; and Walter Monckton.

There were two principal issues discussed that evening: the dispersal of the private royal estates of Sandringham and Balmoral and their contents and what financial settlement the soon-to-be-former King could expect to receive after the abdication.

Both Sandringham and Balmoral were owned by the royal trustees; Edward VIII, according to the terms of his father's will, held a life tenancy in both properties. When he died, the properties would pass to any children he might have. Clearly, the Duke of York believed that the two estates were inalienable from the Crown even if, by law, they belonged to his brother. David had little interest in keeping them for himself; he only wished to return to the Fort. Therefore, an agreement was worked out whereby the two properties and their contents would be sold to the new monarch and thus remain within the Crown.[35]

Edward VIII possessed a large private fortune. From 1910 to 1936, he had received the revenues from the Duchy of Cornwall; these had been quite substantial, amounting to £70,941 in 1936. In his years as Prince of Wales, these had been increased through prudent investment, and by the time David came to the throne, they amounted to almost a million pounds.[36]

However, there were other financial considerations. As king, David had spent large sums from this private fortune buying jewels for Wallis and improving and restoring the Fort. He was actually in debt when he abdicated, as the annual revenues from the Duchy of Cornwall and Lancaster were not due until the middle of 1937. He had therefore borrowed money from Baring Brothers Bank in London in order to meet his routine household expenses, such as salaries and pensions. He had also given Wallis some £300,000 as a cash settlement to ensure that no matter what happened, she would have the means to remain comfortable. Although she would return nearly all of this money after the abdication, in December 1936 it remained an outstanding debt against the King's fortune.

In addition, as Prince of Wales and as sovereign, David had not paid income tax. If and when he returned to England, however, this would likely change. His tax then would be the standard rate of 22.5 percent, with an additional top rate of surtax due on any income over £20,000. In short, this would amount to an additional 47.5 percent, making any potential income-tax payments on his return nearly three-fourths of his entire income.[37]

An agreement in principle had already been reached whereby the King would surrender both Sandringham and Balmoral in return for £25,000 a year, payable for the duration of his life. No one knew who would pay this money, and there was some thought that indeed Parliament would vote it into consideration for the civil list for the new reign. Both Monckton and Allen had been assured by Sir John Simon, the home secretary, and the chancellor of the exchequer, Neville Chamberlain, that there did not seem to be any reason why Parliament would refuse to support the former King. This evening, however, the Duke of York promised to pay his brother the agreed upon sum if the government did not.

At midnight on Thursday, December 10, the Instrument of Abdication took effect, and Edward VIII ceased to be King, replaced by the Duke of York, who took the name George VI. On the eleventh, Monckton met the new King at No. 145 Piccadilly to again discuss the former King's titles. "I pointed out," Monckton recalled, "that the title 'His Royal Highness' was one which the Abdication did not take away, and one which would require an Act of Parliament for its removal. The King, for himself and his successors, was renouncing any right to the Throne but not to his Royal Birth which he shared with his brothers. The Duke saw the point and was ready to create his brother Duke of Windsor as the first act of the new reign."[38]

David had finally received permission to address his subjects that Friday evening. Before this, there was a family dinner at Royal Lodge with Queen Mary, the Princess Royal, the royal brothers, and Queen Mary's brother the Earl of Athlone and his wife, Princess Alice. David left at half-past nine to go to Windsor to make his speech. The dinner itself was fairly cheerful, Athlone recalled. Contrary to the popular myth that he was utterly confused and unprepared for his new role, the new King promptly took charge of the situation. He waited for his older brother to leave, then turned to his younger brothers and said, "If

You Two think that, now that I have taken this job on, you can go on behaving just as you like, in the same old way, you're very much mistaken! You Two have got to pull yourselves together."[39]

At Windsor Castle, David prepared himself for his speech. At ten o'clock, Sir John Reith, director of the British Broadcasting Corporation, announced in a deep voice, "This is Windsor Castle. His Royal Highness, Prince Edward." The former King then read his speech to the nation:

> At long last I am able to say a few words of my own.
>
> I have never wanted to withhold anything, but until now it has not been constitutionally possible for me to speak.
>
> A few hours ago I discharged my last duty as King and Emperor, and now that I have been succeeded by my brother, the Duke of York, my first words must be to declare my allegiance to him. This I do with all my heart.
>
> You all know the reasons which have impelled me to renounce the Throne, but I want you to understand that in making up my mind I did not forget the Country or the Empire, which, as Prince of Wales and lately as King, I have for twenty-five years tried to serve.
>
> But you must believe me when I tell you that I have found it impossible to carry the heavy burden of responsibility and to discharge my duties as King, as I wish to do, without the help and support of the woman I love, and I want you to know that the decision I have made has been mine and mine alone. This was a thing I had to judge for myself. The other person most nearly concerned has tried, up to the last, to persuade me to take a different course. I have made this, the most serious decision of my life, only upon the single thought of what would in the end be best for all.
>
> This decision has been made less difficult to me by the sure knowledge that my brother, with his long training in the public affairs of the Country, and with his fine qualities, will be able to take my place forthwith without interruption or injury to the life and progress of the Empire, and he has one matchless blessing, enjoyed by so many of you, and not bestowed on me, a happy home with his wife and children.
>
> During these hard days I have been comforted by my Mother and by my Family.
>
> The Minister of the Crown, and in particular Mr. Baldwin, the Prime Minister, have always treated me with full consideration. There has never been any constitutional difference between me and them and between me and Parliament. Bred in the constitutional tradition by my Father, I should never have allowed any such issue to arise.

Ever since I was Prince of Wales, and later on when I occupied the Throne, I have been treated with the greatest kindness by all classes wherever I have lived or journeyed throughout the Empire. For that I am very grateful.

I now quit public affairs, and I lay down my burden. It may be some time before I return to my native land, but I shall always follow the fortunes of the British race and Empire with profound interest, and if, at any time in the future, I can be found of service to His Majesty in a private station, I shall not fail.

And now we all have a new King.

I wish Him, and you, His people, happiness and prosperity with all my heart.

God bless you all.

God Save The King.[40]

That evening, everyone at Villa Lou Viei gathered around the radio in the drawing room to listen to the King's abdication speech. Wallis sobbed openly as David spoke. When the speech was over, one by one, they fled the room, leaving her alone, curled on the sofa, crying uncontrollably.[41]

After completing his speech, David returned to Royal Lodge to say his goodbyes. His brother George stood crying in a corner of the entrance hall, saying over and over, "It isn't possible! It isn't happening!"[42]

The Princess Royal was in tears as her brother bid her farewell. The only member of the Royal Family who appeared utterly unmoved was Queen Mary. "Edward," Lord Brownlow recalled, "went up to Queen Mary and kissed her on both hands and then on both cheeks. She was as cold as ice. She just looked at him."[43]

The former King returned to the Fort, where the last of his personal luggage was being packed and loaded. At midnight, he finally climbed into his Buick and left his beloved house. Driven by George Ladbrooke, the car raced through the darkness to Portsmouth. They were delayed by the heavy rain, and Ladbrooke had to pull the car to the side of the road several times before he could continue on. Originally, the former King was to sail on the Royal Navy's *Enchantress*, but after realizing the ironic implications of the name, the ship was changed to HMS *Fury*. The car got lost along the docks, and they had to drive back and forth several times before Ladbrooke found the correct berth. Finally, they pulled up to the pier and, joined by Major Ulick Alexander, keeper of the privy purse, and by his new equerry, Sir Piers Legh, David boarded the ship. At two in the morning, in heavy seas and blowing winds, HMS *Fury* slowly steamed out of the harbor toward the open sea.

23

Rat Week

WITH TOUCHING SIMPLICITY," wrote Arthur Bryant of the King's abdication in the *Illustrated London News*, "he made his renunciation, and nothing in his whole brilliant and generous career of service became him like the leaving it."[1]

Not all opinion, however, was as generous. The abdication was a great shock. Only a week earlier, almost no one in England outside of government, aristocratic, and court circles had known who Mrs. Simpson was. A few individuals with friends and relatives on the Continent or in America had read news clippings outlining her story, but the great majority of the King's subjects remained ignorant of the relationship. The feeling of loss and betrayal, therefore, was all the greater when they learned that their beloved King had abandoned them. It was even worse that he had left owing to his desire to be with a twice-divorced woman he could not live without. The lower and working classes on the whole supported the King and would likely have remained loyal to his cause had the issue come to its divisive head; the middle classes, however, opposed the relationship on moral and religious grounds. To them, Wallis, in the words of Caroline Blackwood, "symbolized sex and evil."[2]

The aristocracy and members of the court greeted the abdication with relief. They owed their allegiance not to the sovereign but to the continued existence of the throne; it is no surprise that they readily abandoned the King for his brother. As Harold Nicolson noted on December 9: "What is so tragic is that now the people have got over the first sentimental shock, they *want* the King to abdicate. I mean opinion in the House is now almost wholly anti-King. 'If he can first betray his duty and then betray the woman he loves, there is no good in the man.'"[3]

The American consul in Plymouth reported to the secretary of state that it was not a question of Wallis being an American or even "the inherent distate for divorce" that turned the British people against the marriage. Rather, he declared, "the people here consider the proceedings leading up to the second divorce were too much of a farce for them to endure." It was "the middle class, which includes the dyed-in-the-wool non-conformists and the greater part of the Church of England adherents" who had objected most strongly. Many of the latter "stated openly that it would be quite all right if the King were to follow the example set by some other Kings in the past, and make Mrs. Simpson his mistress. They appeared incapable of realizing the hypocrisy of this view, and find no difficulty in saying, almost in the same breath, that the King must set a moral example for his people."[4]

Public acclaim seemed to fall to Baldwin. After the abdication, Alan Lascelles wrote to the *Times* that "the King had no more loyal and devoted subject than Mr. Baldwin then or at any other time."[5] And Sir Eric Mieville, the private secretary to the Duke of York, recalled: "It is totally unfair and untrue to say that Baldwin had stage managed the whole thing to get rid of the King. A sentimental man, he was just as upset as everyone else. He hated every minute of it."[6]

Abroad, the reaction was mixed, and many believed that the abdication might have been forced on the King. Certainly, this was the view in Germany. On January 2, 1938, Ribbentrop reported to Hitler that "Edward VIII had to abdicate, since it was not certain whether, because of his views, he would cooperate in an anti-German policy."[7] Hermann Goering told his wife that Mrs. Simpson had only been used as a pretext for getting rid of the King.[8] Hitler thought the "real reason for the destruction of the Duke of Windsor was . . . his speech at the old veterans' rally in Berlin, at which he declared that it would be the task of his life to effect a reconciliation between Britain and Germany."[9]

In America, copies of the abdication speech were being sold at a rapid pace, but there was a curious prohibition of sales in England. John Gunther wrote: "It is somewhat shocking . . . that a country which traditionally prides itself on free speech and fair play should submit to the stupid censorship which prevented phonograph records of this speech being bought anywhere in England. Of course, the ruling classes, trying desperately to 'build up' the Duke of York, did everything possible to bury Edward and his memory at once."[10]

Novelist Upton Sinclair was unstinting in his praise for the King: "You have, by one magnificent gesture, done more to dignify womanhood and give woman her rightful place, than many great people have been able to do by long and laborious effort."[11]

America was enraptured by the Romeo and Juliet quality of the story, the romance of a King giving up his throne for love; and the fact that Wallis was an American. Crowds watching newsreels of the participants the week of the abdication at the Embassy Theatre in Times Square in New York City reportedly made their feelings quite clear, as a writer from *Time* magazine noted: "Prince Edward (cheers); Mrs. Simpson (cheers); her first husband Commander Spencer, U.S.N. (boos); her second and present husband Mr. Simpson (cheers and boos); the Archbishop of Canterbury (boos); new Crown Princess Elizabeth (boos); new King George and Queen Elizabeth (boos); Prime Minister Baldwin (prolonged catcalls and boos); King Edward and Mrs. Simpson bathing in Mediterranean (cheers)."[12]

Among those who had known Wallis, reaction to the abdication was also mixed. Chips Channon wrote: "I really consider that she would have been an excellent Queen. . . . She has always shown me friendship, understanding, and even affection, and I have known her do a hundred kindnesses and never a mean act. There is nothing sordid or vulgar in her make-up, but she is modern certainly. . . . She would prefer to be grand, dignified and respectable, but if thwarted she will make the best of whatever position life gives her."[13]

Others were not as supportive. In London, Emerald Cunard and Sir Philip Sassoon, among others, quickly backed away from their former friends; even before the abdication, this disreputable flood began. On December 9, Harold Nicolson noted of Lady Cunard: "She came to Maggie Greville and said, 'Maggie darling, do tell me about this Mrs. Simpson—I have only just met her.' "[14]

In February 1937 the Winston Churchills were present at a dinner party given by Chips Channon. Clementine Churchill, who had disagreed with her husband over support of the King, shared, however, his view of those who now turned their backs on the former sovereign. Chips wrote: "Lord Granard tactlessly attacked the late King and Mrs. Simpson to his neighbour, Clemmie Churchill, who turned on him and asked crushingly, 'If you feel that way, why did you invite Mrs. Simpson to your house and put her on your right?' A long embarrassed pause followed. . . ."[15]

The most famous chronicle of this disassociation was a small poem written by Osbert Sitwell. Called "Rat Week," the verse was a stunning indictment of these former friends and supporters and began:

> Where are the friends of yesterday
> That fawned on Him,
> That flattered Her;
> Where are the friends of yesterday,
> Submitting to His every whim,
> Offering praise of Her as myrhh
> To Him?[16]

Sitwell was no fan of either David's or Wallis's, and the undercurrent of his poem was criticism not only of their friends but ultimately of the pair at the center of the crisis. Copies of the poem were privately printed and circulated with much glee among London society, particularly by Mrs. Ronald Greville, the dedicated enemy of the King and Wallis and great friend of the new King and Queen.

The most hurtful *volte-face* came from the Royal Family itself. When he left England, David carried letters of support and love from many members of his family, including his sister-in-law, the new Queen Elizabeth. Only Queen Mary appeared unmoved, releasing a message to the British people:

> I need not speak to you of the distress which fills a mother's heart when I think that my dear son has deemed it to be his duty to lay down his charge, and that the reign, which had begun with so much hope and promise, has so suddenly ended. I know that you will realize what it has cost him to come to this decision; and that, remembering the years in which he tried so eagerly to serve and help his Country and Empire, you will ever keep a grateful remembrance of him in your hearts. I commend to you his brother, summoned so unexpectedly and in circumstances so painful, to take his place. ... With him I commend my dear daughter-in-law, who will be his Queen.[17]

On Sunday, December 13, the nation gathered in their churches and cathedrals for the first time since the abdication. While most religious figures concentrated their sermons on the future, there were several exceptions where Christian charity was notably absent. The Archbishop of York referred to the "sad, humiliating story" of the King's decision to give up the throne for "another man's wife." Then he added, "A man of honour would have acted differently."[18] The Bishop of Portsmouth, Dr. Frank Patridge, declared: "Events have shown the soundness of the English temperament and its aversion from evil things. Almost universally there was a shudder at the indecency and impropriety of wild conduct that knew no law, of which there had been such plain signs. English people would not stand it. They hate Pharisaism and cannot abide smugness. They have a sense of propriety in great places and in great affairs, and will not tolerate headlong slips into the abyss of shamefulness."[19]

The most virulent denunciation, not surprisingly, came from Cosmo Lang, Archbishop of Canterbury, who had been one of the King's most vocal enemies. The Archbishop declared of the King:

> From God he had received a high and sacred trust. Yet by his own will he has abdicated—he has surrendered the trust. With characteristic frankness he has told us his motive. It was a crav-

ing for private happiness. Strange and sad it must be that for such a motive, however strongly it pressed upon his heart, he should have disappointed hopes so high and abandoned a trust so great. Even more strange and sad is that he should have sought his happiness in a manner inconsistent with the Christian principles of marriage, and within a social circle whose standards and ways of life are alien to all the best instincts and traditions of his people. Let those who belong to this circle know that today they stand rebuked by the judgment of the nation which had loved King Edward.

He ended melodramatically by saying, "The pity of it, O, the pity of it."[20]

Although the public might have been critical of the King's abdication, few thought the Archbishop correct in abusing Edward VIII in such a public manner. His official residence, Lambeth Palace, was flooded with angry letters, all of which took great umbrage at his condemnation of the former King.[21]

The Royal Family, however, appeared to support this very public humiliation, providing some evidence that they were quite out of touch with the general mood of the nation. Queen Mary wrote to the Archbishop immediately, congratulating him on the speech.[22]

Despite the very warm letter she had written to David when he left England, Queen Elizabeth quickly turned on him. Undoubtedly, in this she was influenced by Queen Mary, who remained at the center of the House of Windsor. Queen Elizabeth was particularly supportive of the almost universally condemned speech by Lang. She wrote to Victor Cazalet: "I don't think you need feel the Archbishop failed to express the right thing. *She* [Queen Mary] felt he said exactly what he should and was grateful to him. All the family feels the same. I think the nation vaguely *felt* it, but *he* put the issue clearly and as no one else had the right to do. Nowadays we are inclined to be too vague about the things that matter, and I think it well that for once someone should speak out in plain and direct words, what after all was the truth. . . ."[23]

This reaction became typical for the Royal Family. David's elderly aunt, Queen Maud of Norway, wrote of Wallis: "Wish something could happen to her!" She described Wallis as "one bad woman who has hypnotized him." She concluded: "I hear that every English and French person gets up at Monte Carlo whenever she comes in to a place. Hope she will feel it."[24] And David's great-aunt Princess Louise, Duchess of Argyll, took great delight in repeating a joke to her brother that Wallis must spend lots of time in the bathroom, since it was the "only throne she would ever sit on."[25]

Lady Iris Mountbatten, a great-granddaughter of Queen Victoria, recalled: "The finality with which David ... disappeared out of thoughts and even memories was shocking. I almost expected that when I mentioned him, I would receive the reply, 'Who?' Aunt May [Queen Mary] ... actually seemed unchanged by the great loss of her eldest son. I could see no outward sign that she had been tormented by heartbreak. Her attitude seemed simply to be, 'I do not see how anyone can expect me to understand or accept this.'" Such a severe attitude greatly upset Lady Iris: "I think this was the emotion that shocked me most in those around me, they *did* not, *would* not, *could* not allow themselves to begin to understand or think with compassion. It brought home to me a sense that I had always had, that my family was not motivated by love or human emotions."[26]

Resentment was bound to surface, and the Royal Family was, in the words of a close friend of the present Queen Mother, "in a state of unbelievable shock."[27] The abdication was a terrible ordeal—perhaps not unexpected, but a seeming dismissal of every principle they themselves held dear: loyalty, honor, tradition, and duty. They only seem to have realized the impact of the abdication after it had taken place and by this time simply could not bring themselves to understand or accept David's behavior. And that the cause of such distress should be a twice-divorced American woman only added to the feeling of public disgrace.

The new King appeared haunted by the shadow of his brother. It was not quite true that Bertie was utterly unprepared and ill equipped for his new role. Early in his reign, Edward VIII had begun to initiate his brother into state affairs; Bertie had had access to certain government secret telegrams and papers.[28] As Frances Donaldson points out: "Nor, although one can understand the feelings of the Duke of York on his elevation to the Throne, need one sympathize too greatly with him for his ignorance of state papers, partly because as King he would have a first-class secretariat to instruct and advise him, but even more because the duty 'to advise, to encourage and to warn' is surely one that can be learned only in its performance, not by watching from the sidelines in a state of total discretion."[29]

Instead, the new King was overwhelmed with self-doubt. His insecurity was such that he constantly compared his performance with that of his exiled brother. It is true that George VI suffered by comparison with his more charismatic and charming brother. The new King was plagued with a difficult stutter, which, though he had worked hard to overcome it, still remained a prominent and unwelcome trait. He was shy and known to possess a fierce temper. He was more nervous in public, less intelligent, and less personable than David had been. Brooding about these facts, Bertie would become angry over his accession to the throne, and his resentment grew, eventually to find voice in a series of petty reprisals against his brother and Wallis. In this, he was strongly supported by his wife, who could never forgive either Wallis or David for what she regarded as the unwelcome burden of the throne. Doubting himself, Bertie turned against his brother, and the Queen followed this, naturally overly protective of her husband and herself aware of his shortcomings and doubts.

Despite the furor that preceded it, the actual political impact of the abdication was minimal. The transition between monarchs had gone smoothly. But the real changes brought on by the abdication came not from David himself but from the new King and Queen. Fearing for the stability of the throne and, perhaps more important, their own popularity, George VI and Queen Elizabeth made determined efforts to reinvent the British monarchy in ways which moved the institution not forward but rather back to the days of Queen Victoria. Bertie and Elizabeth carefully crafted public images designed not only to reassure their subjects of their private virtues but also to make direct overtures, with the assistance of the press, to laying claim to the idea that they, and their very photogenic daughters, were the nation's family. The results have pervaded the monarchy throughout the last fifty years; Edward VIII can be said to have been the last British monarch to jealously guard his private life and relationships. Indeed, his brother and sister-in-law, and his niece Elizabeth II, deliberately cultivated press attention in the presentation of idealized family life. When the truth began to seep through this carefully erected façade, the resulting shocks staggered the monarchy in ways and on levels which the abdication had never approached.

Members of the court, following the lead of King George VI, Queen Elizabeth, and Queen Mary, were quick to turn on their former sovereign. "It was nearly impossible to believe how swiftly they cut him loose," recalled a former courtier. "Edward was anathema. Period. One day, I overheard a conversation between Lascelles and another member of the Household. The Coronation of the new King was fast approaching, and my friend, who was no great fan of the former sovereign, casually remarked, 'One can only wonder what a mess we might have had if Edward stayed on.' Lascelles quickly cut him off. 'Wonder on your own time!' he bellowed. "And don't mention him again.' It was shocking how quickly he became a nonperson."[30]

Hector Bolitho was one of the first authors to write about the former King. His book *Edward VIII, His Life and Reign*, appeared in March 1937, just three months after the abdication. A native of New Zealand, he was attached, at the age of twenty-two, to the Prince of Wales's suite when HMS *Renown* brought David to Auckland in 1920 and had written a flattering book called *With the Prince in New Zealand*. Before the abdication, he began writing an official life of the new King and was given access to the Royal Archives at Windsor and the Royal

Family's private correspondence. When the abdication occurred, however, Bolitho quickly rewrote entire sections of his authorized biography according to the general feeling among the court. As Warre Bradley Wells says, "His book about King Edward may therefore be taken to express the views of Court and Church circles."[31]

Halfway through the King's reign, portions of Bolitho's book had been serialized in the magazine *Leisure*, but when the final version appeared, the former King was depicted as "increasingly stubborn and conceited over his popularity";[32] "a distraught, unreasonable man"[33] who was hostage to "his fantastic vanity"[34] and who "had no friends";[35] and "who came to disaster through the slow disintegration of his character."[36] In the portions serialized, Bolitho had written: "The newspapers . . . called him Galahad. He was not made dizzy by this praise . . . indeed, it has been said that he hated the signs of his popularity and sought more and more to escape from compliments and cheers."[37] In the published book the same passage read, "The newspapers . . . called him Galahad. At first he was not made dizzy by this praise. He tried to escape from the flattery and cheers. . . . Although the Prince did all that was asked of him, his modesty was slowly shaken. . . . His slimmest platitude was printed in big letters in the newspapers. It is little wonder that he fell into the harmless conceit which afterwards grew dangerously, so that it destroyed his self-judgment and made him over-assured; which made him lose all capacity of knowing the difference between wild popularity and calm esteem."[38]

Compton Mackenzie was only one of a number of critics of the book. He referred to it as "that tarnished weathercock of a narrative" which "swings true to the veering wind of public opinion."[39] He remarked on "the thoroughness of the *volte face*: it has the gymnastic, nay, the acrobatic precision of a perfect sommersault."[40]

Others who wrote about Edward VIII were a bit more charitable. *The House of Windsor*, by Capt. Eric Acland and E. H. Bartlett, declared that the King had been "a strong man who has weighed carefully every conceivable angle. When the final chapter is written this second king of the house founded by his father will have achieved greatness by having been big enough to have realized his limitations."[41]

Not surprisingly, Alexander Hardinge was chosen by King George VI to continue in his role as principal private secretary; he also received a knighthood two months after the abdication. Alan Lascelles, the King's other main court antagonist, also retained his position as assistant private secretary and, six years later, succeeded Hardinge in the senior post. The second assistant private secretary, Sir Godfrey Thomas, who had been sympathetic to the King, was transferred to the service of the Duke of Gloucester as private secretary.

Some were not quite so fortunate. Lord Perry Brownlow, who,

on the direct orders of Edward VIII, had escorted Wallis to France, held his position as a lord-in-waiting. He was due to go into waiting at Buckingham Palace on December 21 for the new king, George VI. The following day, however, he read in the court circular that the Marquess of Dufferin and Ava had succeeded as lord-in-waiting in his place. The new King had not even bothered to inform him. When he telephoned Buckingham Palace, Brownlow was curtly told that his name could never again be mentioned in the court circular. He demanded to speak with Lord Cromer, the Lord Chamberlain. When he got on the phone, the Lord Chamberlain told him that the new King had been pleased to accept his resignation even though Brownlow had never offered it. "Am I to be turned away, like a dishonest servant with no notice, no warning, no thanks, when all I did was to obey my Master, the late King?" he asked.

"Yes," Cromer replied bluntly, and hung up.[42]

Brownlow remained defiant. At Belton, his great house in Lincolnshire, visitors to one of England's great stately homes were sometimes shocked to wander through the rooms on open days and enter the library, where the desk and tables were absolutely covered with dozens of framed photographs of the Duke and Duchess of Windsor. There were also busts of the former King as well as the only known portrait made during his reign, by Frank Salisbury.[43]

"Are we all on the 'Black List'?" Chips Channon wondered. "Are the Sutherlands, the Marlboroughs, the Stanleys? I cannot believe that it is Queen Elizabeth's doing. She is not so foolish. . . ."[44] But the usually well informed Channon was wrong about the new Queen, who, with Queen Mary, had joined together in a powerful conspiracy to both erase the memory of the former King and his friends and to punish him and his American mistress.

After the abdication, Queen Mary wrote to Prince Paul, the regent of Yugoslavia:

> The other day in my presence Bertie told George he wished him and Marina never to see Lady Cunard again and George said he would not do so. I fear she has *done David a great deal of harm* as there is no doubt that she was great friends with Mrs. S. at one time and gave parties for her. Under the circumstances I feel none of us, in fact people in society, should meet her. I am sure you will agree one should not meet her again after what has happened and I am hoping that George and Marina will no longer see certain people who alas were friends of Mrs. S. and Lady Cunard's and also David's. . . . As you may imagine I feel very strongly on the matter but several people have mentioned to me what harm she has done.[45]

As this letter aptly demonstrates, the old Queen was not above resorting to emotional blackmail to ensure the ostracism of her eldest son's friends. Prince Paul, who had also frequented Lady Cunard's drawing room, certainly took the unsubtle hint, for he joined in the legions of those who now avoided Emerald Cunard at all costs.

Chips Channon wrote of Queen Mary: "Certainly she and the Court group hate Wallis Simpson to the point of hysteria, and are taking up the wrong attitude; why persecute her now that all is over? Why not let the Duke of Windsor, who has given up so much, be happy? They would be better advised to be civil if it is beyond their courage to be cordial."[46] But the elderly Queen, setting the tone which the Royal Family would slavishly follow for decades to come, refused to consider even the slightest concession. A year after the abdication, she declared, in response to a question as to when her eldest son would return to his country, "Not until he comes to my funeral."[47]

24

"The Whole World Against Us and Our Love"

T HE ABDICATION was a great shock to Wallis; but with typical resolution she quickly recovered her composure. Within hours of
listening to the farewell broadcast, she wrote what was to become the
first of many letters which passed between her and the former King:
"My heart is so full of love for you and the agony of not being able to
see you after all you have been through is pathetic. At the moment we
have the whole world against us and our love. . . ."[1]

This set the tone for the correspondence which was to follow. Her
letters reveal a complex character different from her public image. On
paper, she is not the ambitious adventuress depicted by the Royal
Family; rather, a caring, thoughtful, smart woman, missing her lover
and contemplating a future together with him. Occasionally, when
frustrated, her letters transformed themselves into spiteful wails of
mistreatment, which, however justified, do little to endear her. But
overwhelmingly they are filled with thoughts of David. More than
anything else, she appears a woman who, in her own way, loved
David greatly. A gentle side, carefully hidden from the prying eyes of
the public, emerges, lightly admonishing at times, watchful, protective, but undoubtedly filled with genuine affection for the man who
had given up so much to be with her.

After the initial excitement of the abdication, the reporters who
had maintained a twenty-four-hour vigil around the villa gradually
began to fade away. Both Herman and Katherine Rogers insisted that
Wallis remain with them. Mary Burke, her maid, soon arrived with
more of her belongings, and Aunt Bessie, who arrived on December
19, booked herself into a hotel at Cannes to be near her niece.[2]

Every day, stacks of letters arrived in the post. Some were supportive, but most, as she had feared, blamed Wallis for the King's abdication; many even threatened physical violence.[3] Several were filled
with such anger and expressions that Wallis could not read them; at
least one was simply addressed to "King Edward's Whore."[4]

Among the letters was one from Ernest: "I did not have the heart to write before. I have felt somewhat stunned and slightly sick over recent events. I am not, however, going into that, but I want you to believe—I do believe—that you did everything in your power to prevent the final catastrophe. My thoughts have been with you throughout your ordeal, and you may rest assured that no one has felt more deeply for you than I have. For a few pence each day I can keep *au courant* with your doings."[5]

At least once a day, Wallis tried to telephone David in Austria, where he had gone to stay with the Rothschilds. These telephone calls, with their bad connections, proved a terrible strain, and often Wallis was so frustrated that she would slam the receiver down on the telephone on the dining-room table in exasperation. Inevitably, the table shook, and several pieces of Katherine Rogers's coral-handled silver were broken as a result. "She was an angel to put up with me!" Wallis recalled. "I must have been the most exasperating guest in history, what with breaking her spoons and monopolizing her dining room just when dinner was ready to be served." Still, she said, she "lived for" the talks with David during those six months.[6]

Wallis occupied her time by taking walks along the beach or visiting friends. She spent Christmas with author Somerset Maugham in his Villa Mauresque at Cap Ferrat, where she was reunited with her friend Sibyl Colefax. Occasionally, there were run-ins with the press, and once Wallis had to escape from a shop in Cannes through the back door to avoid reporters.[7] On New Year's Day, she and David spoke at length on the telephone; he broke down and sobbed during much of the conversation. She was so touched that she immediately wrote a quick note to comfort him. "Darling sweetheart: I couldn't bear hearing you cry—you who have been through so much and are so brave. My baby it is because I long to be with you so intensely everything becomes so magnified. Darling I love you. Come to me soon."[8]

Her feelings were clearly sincere. But she also worried about their life together. She knew that any slight toward her would rankle her future husband and worried that David, accustomed to his position of power, would suffer during his exile. Wallis was determined that she would protect them both against a Royal Family which had made it painfully obvious that they were to be accorded no place. "One realizes now the impossibility of getting the marriage announced in the Court Circular and of the HRH," she wrote to the Duke on January 3, 1937. "It is all a great pity because I loathe being undignified and also of joining the countless titles that roam around Europe meaning nothing. To set off on our journey with a proper backing would mean so much—but whatever happens we will make something of our lives. . . ."[9] Such letters have often been cited as evidence of Wallis's overwhelming concern not only with obtaining a title for herself but also of her determination to drive a wedge between the two brothers who had shared a throne. Yet it is absurd to think that Wallis wished to further alienate her future husband from his family in England. She knew only too well how he longed to return and live at the Fort. Her letters seem more a commentary on facts and on their likely consequences than an exhortation to battle.

Wallis spent many sleepless nights reflecting on her situation. "My personal folk tale," she wrote, "had gone disastrously awry. Given the circumstances under which it began, I had never been certain what the ending would be, but I had at least been encouraged to believe that it would be reasonably happy. In my darkest moments at the Fort, I had never visualized anything like this—David by his own choice a virtual outcast from the nation over which he had ruled, and each of us condemned to wait in idleness and frustration on our separate islands of exile until my divorce became absolute in early May."[10]

The Duke was just as miserable. Upon arriving in Vienna on December 13, he had been met by Sir Walford Selby, the British ambassador. Dudley Forwood, who had previously attended the Prince of Wales during his skiing holiday at Kitzbühel with Wallis, was also present, and David now asked that he join his staff. Selby temporarily put Forwood in charge of the various royal arrangements, including the Duke's stay at the Rothschilds' Schloss Enzesfeld. Dina Wells Hood, who later acted as the Duke of Windsor's secretary, wrote of Forwood: "He was young, witty, amusing and always immaculately dressed. Though frank and unconventional in conversation, he was almost ultra-conservative and conventional in his attitude toward royalty and to the aristocracy into which he was born."[11] The Honorable John Aird, who had accompanied the Duke, was recalled to England on the new King's orders, and the Duke of Windsor found that he did not get on at all well with his other equerry, Sir Piers Legh. Legh was an older man, not at all sympathetic to the former King or to his relationship with Mrs. Simpson.

David was hopeless in this new world. He had not even brought with him a valet. Baron Eugene Rothschild once entered his room and found the Duke unpacking his clothes, which were draped over chairs, laid out on the bed, and thrown in heaps on the floor. "I'm not very good at this," he admitted with a smile. "You see, I've never done it by myself."[12] When Perry Brownlow arrived at Schloss Enzesfeld, he found David sleeping alone in a room with no fewer than sixteen photographs of Wallis. He was hugging a pillow which had belonged to her and which was sewn with her initials.[13]

Although they spoke to each other every evening by telephone, neither Wallis nor David could risk meeting face-to-face for fear that someone would lodge a protest against her decree nisi and try to prevent the divorce. According to the technical terms of the law, there was nothing to keep the pair apart, but they needed to avoid any potential claims for complaint in the divorce action and the issuance of the decree absolute. A solicitor's clerk, Francis Stephenson, had already gone to the Divorce Registry insisting that the Simpson divorce must not be final and saying that he had some new information. He refused to say whom he represented or just what information he possessed, but his claim sufficiently worried both Wallis and David that they were determined to give no cause for any intervention. Then, just as suddenly as he had lodged the complaint, Stephenson withdrew it, saying, "I was asked to do so."[14]

The faithful and trusted Fruity Metcalfe also arrived at Schloss Enzesfeld the third week of January. He wrote: "Of course he's on the line for hours & hours every day to Cannes. I somehow don't think these talks go so well sometimes. It's only after one of them he ever seems a bit worried and nervous. She seems to be always picking on him and complaining about something that she thinks he hasn't done or ought to do. . . ."[15]

It is difficult to judge these talks. Many observers were often struck by what they perceived to be Wallis's brutal dominance over the Duke; undoubtedly, at times, she could be brittle. But it must be remembered that David himself cherished her for these very reasons: She was the one woman who had not only taken an interest in his life but actively helped guide him, providing him with love, support, and reassurance. Above all else, Wallis provided his strength. Such criticism as she offered was undoubtedly difficult for others to understand. The mixture of emotional security and care with which she framed her arguments was unique to her relationship with David. Then, too, circumstances were difficult: The enforced separation, the discomfort of being a guest, the bad telephone connections, the uncertainty of their future together and particularly of her status as his wife—all of these factors certainly influenced the tone of their conversations. Particularly at this time, David seemed to many to be utterly lost, and it is reasonable to assume that Wallis was attempting to watch over their interests with his blessing. Again, a more positive light is shown in her letters, sentiments which by nature she was reluctant to express in public but which reassured David of her love for him: "Darling—I want to leave here I want to see you touch you I want to run my own house I want to be married and to you," she wrote in February.[16]

David, meanwhile, was fast realizing that he was now an outcast where his family was concerned. He had believed that once the furor over the abdication had passed, he could simply return to England and assume the role of younger brother to the King. If this seems somewhat naive, it should be remembered that in the weeks leading up to the abdication—and even on the day he left England—David had received warm, loving letters from Bertie and Elizabeth assuring him of their support and understanding of his feelings for Wallis. Bertie had made it clear, even when he knew that abdication was the most likely resolution to the crisis, that he believed David would make the right decision where the Crown and Empire were concerned. These letters were undoubtedly genuine, but unfortunately the sentiments expressed within them were not to last. Almost as soon as David had left England, both Bertie and Elizabeth began to turn against the former King, no doubt influenced by Queen Mary. As a result, David felt horrified and deceived when, in exile, he came to understand the strong feeling which now existed against both him and Wallis. He suspected, quite rightly as things turned out, that both Queen Mary and Queen Elizabeth were twisting the arm of the new King. In this, they were supported by the court, those members who had disliked David for fear of his proposed and assumed changes and innovation and who now closed ranks around George VI.

Along with telephoning Wallis every day, the Duke soon developed the habit of ringing his brother, offering him advice in an effort to smooth his transition. These incessant telephone calls, however, quickly annoyed Bertie. Although the former King was simply hoping to assist his brother in his new duties, George VI, already uneasy and insecure, felt certain that in reality David was trying to regain some sort of foothold in the palace. Abruptly, George VI told his brother that the telephone calls would have to stop.

"Are you serious?" David asked, obviously hurt.

"Yes, I'm sorry to say that I am," his brother replied. "The reason must be clear to you."[17]

"My father," Fruity Metcalfe's son David recalls, "was with the Duke when George VI told him not to ring any more. He said he would never forget the look on the Duke's face. He was completely devastated."[18]

The new King was determined, pushed by his wife and his mother, to ensure that his brother never returned to England. He once met with former prime minister David Lloyd George for lunch and discussed David and Wallis.

"She would never dare to come back here," the King declared.

"There you are wrong," the former prime minister said.

"She would have no friends here," said Bertie.

"She has friends," Lloyd George insisted.

"But not you or me?" the King asked anxiously.[19]

Wallis was aware of such animosity. Within a week of the abdication, certain gossips happily occupied themselves by spreading rumors that the Duke and his mistress had gone their separate ways. To counter this, she allowed Herman Rogers to answer some press questions. "There has been no disagreement between Mrs. Simpson and His Royal Highness of any kind," he declared. "Mrs. Simpson is not in a position to make any plans, and did not expect to see His Royal Highness within the next few weeks, and would not express an opinion on the unfairness of the recent comments on the Duke in England by the Church."[20]

In the middle of March, Lord Louis Mountbatten arrived at Schloss Enzesfeld to offer himself to his cousin as supporter, or best man, at the forthcoming wedding; David had been *his* best man when he had married Edwina Ashley in 1922. But David declined the offer, assuming that his brothers, the Dukes of Kent and Gloucester, would themselves attend his wedding and act as supporters.[21]

Wallis spent most of the spring making plans for her life with David. On March 2, she attended her first fashion show in more than a year, to view the new collection of Capt. Edward Molyneux. Thinking ahead to her trousseau, she bought thirteen dresses and outfits. The wedding was very much on the minds of her and David. Both had decided that they would be married in France, and Wallis had discovered a lovely white villa called La Croë at Cap d'Antibes, some five miles from Cannes. Owned by a retired English newspaper executive named Sir Pomeroy Burton, its colonnades and terraces overlooked long green lawns and the Mediterranean beyond.[22]

It was Herman Rogers who eventually proposed an alternative. He was acquainted with a French industrialist named Charles Bedaux, who owned a magnificent old château called Candé, near Tours. It had the advantage of being surrounded by a large, wooded park, a consideration which would guarantee a measure of privacy from the press. Wallis discussed the idea with David, and Herman wrote to Bedaux, advising that they were interested. He bluntly asked if Bedaux had any skeletons in his closet, as the press would certainly turn them up and David and Wallis could not afford to be embarrassed.[23]

Charles Bedaux was a charming French-born American who had made millions all over the world with his time-and-motion studies for improving labor systems. When Hitler came to power in Germany, the Nazi government had closed Bedaux's business office in the country; Bedaux, quite naturally, was greatly anxious to have both the chateau and office reopened. His best friend and most powerful contact in Germany was Dr. Robert Ley, the leader of the Nazi National Labor Front. Bedaux, contrary to decades of sensational and inaccurate press, was not a Nazi; in fact, he advocated a rather peculiar mixture of communism, fascism, and an idealistic approach to the rights of workers. Once Bedaux had assured them that he had nothing to hide,

David consulted his brother, King George VI, who himself recommended the Château de Candé, preferring the idea of the French castle over a villa in the south of France for his brother's wedding. Bedaux's biographer wrote: "There is no way to know what inquiries were made, cursory or otherwise, since British files on the matter are closed until the next century. But it is preposterous to think that the British government did not check out Bedaux. Therefore, they either found something 'on' him or they did not. If the government determined that Bedaux was undesirable and permitted the marriage to take place at Candé, then it must be concluded that they were setting up the unfortunate Duke."[24]

Bedaux was duly informed of the royal decision, and he and his wife began preparations to receive David and Wallis. In Cannes, meanwhile, Wallis was increasingly restless. Although the press had disappeared for a time, with the approaching divorce decree, they were beginning to return, camping out at the gates of the Villa Lou Viei. To avoid them, Wallis decided to move on to Candé. On March 9, accompanied by the Rogerses and twenty-seven pieces of luggage, she left Cannes for Tours.[25]

25

At War With the Royal Family

WALLIS ARRIVED AT CANDÉ during a terrible storm; as she watched from her car, the turrets and gray-stone walls appeared through the pouring rain.[1] Fern Bedaux met her at the massive wooden door. Wallis recalled her as kind and beautiful; she was an American, having grown up in Grand Rapids, and had managed to combine her family money with a vogue for French style and fashion at Candé. She led them into the château, offering tea as she went.

Charles Bedaux had purchased the property in 1927, paying the small sum of $36,500. The château, which had belonged to the Duke del Castillo, stood near the village of Monts in the department of Indre-et-Loire. The original château, dedicated to St. Mattin, was constructed in the 1400s and had been rebuilt with additional wings in 1508. There were large stables; a track, jumps, and bridle paths; a tennis court; swimming pool; and a golf course hidden among the trees.[2]

As Fern Bedaux bid her inside the château, Wallis entered a long hallway lined with nearly two dozen members of the staff; the English butler, V. J. Hale, stood erect and bowed his head slightly as Wallis passed. The footmen wore blue-and-gold jackets and black trousers; everything spoke of the royal world Wallis had fled in England. When tea was finished, Fern Bedaux took Wallis on a tour, leading her through the drawing room, with its oak paneling, high ceiling, and pipe organ at one end; the salon, a smaller, more formal room, with paneled walls and Louis Seize furnishings; the dining room, with a massive beamed ceiling and long refectory table; and by a small guest suite adjoining the main house, where she suggested that the Duke stay upon his arrival; then on to her own bedroom, with cream-colored boiserie and tall windows overlooking the grounds. Herman Rogers, who had slept next door to Wallis every night since her arrival in Cannes with a gun beneath his pillow to guard her against possible attack, took a daybed in an adjoining sitting room, while his wife Katherine was lodged upstairs.[3]

Wallis spent her days wandering through the park and making arrangements for the forthcoming wedding. Under French law, there would be a civil as well as religious service. If Wallis's second marriage had seemed less than regal, this third union was rapidly becoming something altogether different. There was a momentary hitch when a clerk questioned the legality of Wallis's divorce from Ernest; a formal hearing on the matter was held on March 19 in response to the complaint lodged by Francis Stephenson. But the board found no collusion, and Wallis was free to await her decree absolute.

Wallis tried to make the best of the situation; at Candé, she busied herself with preparations for the wedding and planning her trousseau. She could not go to Paris and shop for fear of being hounded by the press; instead, various designers, including Mainbocher, Chanel, and Schiaparelli, submitted original designs to her at Candé. She eventually selected Mainbocher to design the wedding dress; his competitors supplied the trousseau. A total of sixty-six dresses eventually made their way to Candé that spring. Having lived in isolation for nearly six months, Wallis was looking forward to a future which clearly called for a public wardrobe. Among her trousseau was an exotic Schiaparelli waltz dress of white organdy with two red lobsters hand-painted on its skirt; a crepe romain navy blue dinner dress with a polka-dotted silk waist girdle and a matching bolero jacket; a printed crepe dress of violet over a petticoat massed with blue taffeta frills; a white-lace sheath dress with short sleeves and a bateau neck, with red lace roses scattered across the gown; navy blue wool suits with white blouses and gray flannel suits with blue blouses; a black sheath dinner dress embroidered with colored glass flowers; two fitted suits and jackets of light blue tweed; an afternoon ensemble of blue tweed with dolphin buttons and a butterfly on the lapel; blue-fox furs; and a silver-fox knee-length coat from Molyneux.[4]

To keep Wallis company at Candé, David sent the cairn terrier Slipper, or Mr. Loo, which she had left with him at the Fort when she fled England and which he had taken with him to Austria. Wallis was delighted to have her beloved dog back with her, but her happiness at the reunion was short-lived. On the day after the dog arrived at Candé, it was attacked by a snake and died. Wallis was inconsolable.[5]

In late April, Wallis learned that her childhood house at 212 East Biddle Street in Baltimore had been opened as the Mrs. Simpson Museum. Tourists paid to poke their faces around corners and into doors, examining the rooms and climbing the staircases; but none of the original furnishings remained, and the setting was not quite as realistic as people were led to believe. Mrs. W. W. Mathews, who served as guide at the house, explained to journalists that people were clambering into the bathtub for good luck. "Nine out of ten of them get into it, men, women and children. Then they get me to take their pictures. One bride and groom got in, hugged and handed me the camera."[6]

The tourists who flocked to see her childhood home in Baltimore were just one outward sign of the increasing public interest in Wallis's life. Dozens of news reporters camped out day and night before the gates at Candé, hoping to catch a glimpse of the world's most famous woman. One welcome arrival that spring was Cecil Beaton, who had come from London to photograph Wallis. At dinner that evening, he noted: "Wallis sported a new jewel in the form of two huge quills, one set with diamonds, the other with rubies. Her dress shows to advantage an incredibly narrow figure, narrower since the abdication." After Herman and Katherine Rogers went to bed, Beaton and Wallis spoke until dawn. "I was struck by the clarity and vitality of her mind," he said. "When at last I went to bed, I realized she not only had individuality and personality, but was a very strong force as well. She may have limitations, she may be politically ignorant and aesthetically untutored; but she knows a great deal about life."[7]

The main subject of their talk was the abdication, and her feelings for the Duke. Wallis explained that she had been convinced things would have worked themselves out had the King not taken such a drastic step; that when it did occur, it came as a complete surprise and shock. "She obviously has great admiration for his character and vitality and loves him, though I feel she is not *in* love with him. In any case, she has a great responsibility in looking after someone who is temperamentally polar to her, yet relies utterly on her."[8]

On May 3, Wallis was granted her decree absolute and became officially divorced from Ernest. This meant that David could now join her. She immediately rang David, who had by this time left Schloss Enzesfeld and was now staying at a pension in the Austrian village of St. Wolfgang, and told him, "Hurry up!"[9] The next morning, the Duke arrived with Dudley Forwood, who was serving as his equerry. David looked thin and nervous but was clearly delighted to rejoin Wallis; he stepped out of his car and ran up the château steps to take her in his arms.[10]

A week later, on May 11, the former King formally announced his engagement to Wallis, who, a few days prior, had resumed her maiden name and filled out the applications for her marriage license. The timing of the announcement, on the eve of the new King's coronation, was considered inopportune by many, as it diverted attention from London to Candé.

The following day, everyone gathered in the drawing room of the château to listen to the new King's coronation ceremony, which was broadcast for the first time on radio around the world. The former King never said a word, but Wallis could scarcely contain her thoughts.

"All the while the mental image of what might have been and should have been kept forming, disintegrating, and re-forming in my mind."[11]

On May 16, Wallis and David signed their marriage contract, agreeing that their property would be separate and that neither would make any claim on the other's personal possessions in the event of a divorce. When news of this agreement reached London, it took a great many members of the Royal Family and the court by surprise; they had fully expected that Wallis was out to extort everything possible—money, jewels, a title—that she could from the hapless former King. But attitudes were too deeply ingrained for any reasonable analysis, and most continued to assume the worst of Wallis.

With the coronation behind them, David continued to hope that at least some of his family would change their minds and agree to attend his wedding, which was set for June 3, the birthday of his late father, King George V. He reasoned that it was the least he could expect: He was the oldest brother, and this, after all, was his first marriage. Most of all, he wanted George, his favorite brother, to come as his supporter. In one last effort to win this concession, he called Forwood aside one day and said, "You'd better go see Bertie and have a talk with him about Georgie." Forwood duly approached George VI, but the King refused to alter his decision. "I can't have my younger brother there encouraging my older brother to perform an illegal act," he told Forwood.[12] This feeling—that David's marriage was somehow an "illegal act"—was to color the Royal Family's feeling toward Wallis for the rest of her life.

The vast majority of the Royal Family, led by Queen Mary and Queen Elizabeth, continued to believe, even in the face of evidence to the contrary, that Wallis was simply an adventuress. They failed to see that she had tried with all her power to avert the abdication, that she had pleaded and begged and threatened the King, all to no avail. After the abdication, had she not cared about David or possessed a character which impelled her to act nobly, it would have been easy for Wallis to simply abandon him. Had she only wished to be queen, after all, there was nothing left in the game for her. She had not initially wanted a marriage; but now that it was upon her, now that the King had abdicated, she did the honorable thing and determined to spend the rest of her life making happy the man who had given up his entire world to be with her.

Wallis found this humiliation especially difficult. Her sense of shame was increased when she realized that it was she, in the eyes of his family, who had caused the former King's downfall and made him an outcast. It would be inaccurate to say that she did not care for herself, but more important, she knew how much such treatment hurt David. He continued to long for a return to England and, in his simplistic view, could not understand how his family could continue to punish both him and Wallis.

Previously, David had turned down the offer by his cousin Lord Louis Mountbatten to serve as his supporter when he married Wallis. Nevertheless, he fully expected Mountbatten to attend the ceremony. On May 5, however, Mountbatten wrote to David, declining an invitation to the wedding and explaining that those in power had stepped in to prevent the Duke's friends from coming.[13]

At first, it seemed impossible that whatever feelings the Royal Family might continue to harbor against David and Wallis, they would actively step in and block the attendance of the Duke's friends at the wedding. But the desire to punish ran deep. When Sir Ulick Alexander, Edward VIII's keeper of the privy purse, declared that he intended to attend the wedding, he was bluntly informed that if he did so he would lose his post.[14] Other friends, including Lord Brownlow, were threatened with loss of office or position by officials should they attend.[15] Such threats could only have come from the King himself.

There were exceptional difficulties in procuring a minister willing to perform the wedding service. "The Duke," recalled Dudley Forwood, "desperately wanted his marriage to be a highly religious one, and blessed by the Church. . . . You have no idea of the tremendous idealism and dedication with which the Duke approached his marriage. In his mind, it was to be the wedding of all weddings. He felt extraordinarily deeply about the sanctity of marriage."[16]

Finally, the Reverend Robert Anderson Jardine, vicar of St. Paul's, Darlington, an industrial parish near Durham in the northwest of England, wrote a letter to Herman Rogers, offering to marry the couple. He had read an article stating that there would be no religious ceremony for the Duke and was greatly moved at the thought. "I went into the garden," Jardine later explained, "and entered my old army tent in which I used to do much of my preparation work for Sunday. I knelt in prayer of deep earnestness, and rose with the clear conviction that here is a man who needs something; and I must give it to him."[17]

Jardine's offer was indeed courageous. The Church of England still prohibited marriage between divorced persons if a spouse was still living. When they learned of his intention, Jardine's immediate superiors, the Bishop of Durham and the Archbishop of York, simply forbade him to conduct the service. When Jardine refused to acquiesce, the Archbishop of Canterbury threatened him with loss of his religious office.

But Jardine was determined and soon arrived at Candé, where he was warmly welcomed by the Duke. After thanking the minister, David asked, "Why don't they give us a religious ceremony? We are both Christians."

"What could I answer," Jardine wrote. "I am afraid a lump came to my throat at the pathos of this ex-King denied what is the right of every man, king or commoner, the blessing of God on his wedding day. Seeing I did not answer, he went on to tell how they had sought for someone to perform the ceremony and had failed."

"Pardon my language, Jardine," David said, "but you are the only one who had the 'guts' to do this for me."[18] The Duke introduced Wallis and asked Jardine to join them for dinner; when the meal was over, the couple gave him a pair of gold cuff links crested with their joint initials.

As the date for the wedding approached, public interest in the curious ceremony grew, fed by increasing articles in the world press. On May 27, the *Daily Express* declared in an editorial:

Isn't it possible that the Duke of Windsor is being treated with rather too much of a rough edge? As his marriage day draws near, a series of penalties and prohibitions are laid against him and against those who may desire to show him friendship or affection. First, the Church to which he belongs refuses to countenance the wedding in any way. The grounds for this boycott are that the Duke's bride is a woman who has divorced two previous husbands, though on both occasions she was the innocent and injured party. The Church of England, it is true, doesn't look with favour on divorce. But it by no means absolutely excludes divorce. Next, there is the ban placed upon the attendance at the ceremony of the Duke's family, the brothers and sister with whom he grew up, and who have remained in his companionship even after the events of last December. And then there are the friends of his circle who were also members of his personal staff and who now hold offices or posts in the service of the regime which succeeded his own. It has been intimated to these that it would be suitable if they also were among those "unavoidably absent." What justification can there be for such a prohibition of private friendship? Has the Duke ... broken the law in any degree? Never. Did he ever damage even our constitutional usage? No, he did not. So why impose this increasingly severe form of ostracism on those who are about to marry? If it is done to punish Mrs. Warfield it must be pointed that she has not transgressed the laws of the country either. Mrs. Warfield, by a decree of the British Courts of Justice, is fully free to marry, and, of course, is entitled to do so. Plainly it all comes back to the attitude of opposition taken up by the leaders of the Church.[19]

Ironically, on the same day that this plea for reconciliation and justice appeared, David learned of what *Burke's Peerage*, the British bible of social rank, would later call "the most flagrant act of discrimination in the whole history of our dynasty."[20]

26

The King's Wedding Present

On Thursday, 27 May, Sir Alexander Ulick telephoned Candé and told the former King that Walter Monckton was on his way from London with a letter from George VI, containing "not very good news."[1] Monckton arrived later that evening; he took the Duke aside and handed him the letter from his brother. It was then that David learnt that Wallis, on her marriage, would receive the title of Duchess of Windsor, but that, contrary to all custom and practice, she would be denied the usual style of "Her Royal Highness." "This is a nice wedding present," David commented bitterly to Monckton.[2]

No other act on the part of George VI toward his exiled brother and American sister-in-law was to cause so much anger and humiliation as his decision to deprive Wallis of the style of "Her Royal Highness." Although Wallis would later claim that she had not cared about the style, she was deeply hurt, not only for herself but for the sake of David, who was unable to comprehend such a public insult to his wife.

In his letter, the King explained that he had consulted the heads of the Dominion and Empire countries, and that all had advised that they considered that David had lost all royal rank when he abdicated and was no longer entitled to the use of Prince or the style of "His Royal Highness." George VI declared that he did not wish to see his brother go through life as plain Mr. Edward Windsor and would therefore issue letters patent re-creating him His Royal Highness The Prince Edward, the Duke of Windsor. But he also declared that he could not and would not extend this style to Wallis, who would be known simply as the Duchess of Windsor.

Such a decision was utterly contrary to both accepted royal practice and to British common law. A wife automatically took her status from her husband on marriage; the only exception to this was if the wife herself held a higher rank than her spouse— for example, when Edward VIII's sister Mary, the Princess Royal, married Viscount Lascelles, she retained her royal title and the style of "Her Royal Highness" because they superseded those held by her husband.

"Whoever was responsible for withholding from the Duchess the style of Royal Highness ensured her a unique place in history," writes royal authority Marlene Eilers. "No woman before had ever been accorded her husband's title, but been denied his style."[3]

Indeed, all women who have married into the British Royal Family this century—with the sole exception of Wallis— were accorded the title and style held by their husbands. In 1923, Lady Elizabeth Bowes-Lyon married the future George VI. The 28 April edition of the *Times* reported that, "in accordance with the general settled rule, that a wife takes the status of her husband, Lady Elizabeth Bowes-Lyon on her marriage has become Her Royal Highness the Duchess of York."[4]

In 1934, David's brother George, the Duke of Kent, married Princess Marina, who was already a Royal Highness in her own right by birth. A year later, Prince Henry, Duke of Gloucester, married Lady Alice Montagu-Douglas-Scott, who became Her Royal Highness the Duchess of Gloucester; this was the last wedding of a male member of the Royal Family until the Duke of Windsor married Wallis in 1937. Thereafter, the pattern to the present day is absolutely consistent and without exception: in 1961, Edward, Duke of Kent married Miss Katharine Worsley, who became Her Royal Highness The Duchess of Kent; in 1972, Prince Richard of Gloucester, the present Duke, married Miss Birgitte van Deurs, who became Her Royal Highness The Duchess of Gloucester; in 1978, Prince Michael of Kent married Baroness Marie Christine von Reibnitz, who became Her Royal Highness Princess Michael of Kent; in 1981, Charles, Prince of Wales married Lady Diana Spencer, who became Her Royal Highness The Princess of Wales; and, in 1986, Prince Andrew, the Duke of York, married Miss Sarah Ferguson, who became Her Royal Highness The Duchess of York.

Thus, Wallis, on her marriage, should have become Her Royal Highness The Duchess of Windsor. Because it had been agreed to treat the former King as a junior Royal Duke, his wife would have ranked in precedence just behind her two sisters-in-law, the Duchesses of Kent and Gloucester. This is what would have happened, by virtue of hundreds of years of tradition and common law, had George VI not stepped in deliberately to deprive Wallis of the style of Her Royal Highness.

Clearly, there was a great deal of uncertainty over the status of the former King. On the day of his accession, 11 December, 1936, George VI noted: "Lord Wigram & Sir Claude Schuster (as representative of the Lord Chancellor) came to see me...to ask me what my brother King Edward VIII was going to be known as after his abdication. The question was an urgent one, as Sir John Reith (Director of the BBC) was going to introduce him on the air that night as Mr. Edward Windsor. I replied—That is quite wrong. Before going any further I would ask what has he given up on his abdication? S[Schuster] said I am not sure. I said, It would be quite a good thing to find out before coming to me. Now as to his name. I suggest HRH D of W. He cannot be Mr. E. W. as he was born the son of a Duke. That makes him Ld. E. W. anyhow. If he ever comes back to this country, he can stand & be elected to the H of C. Would you like that? S replied No." As D of W he can sit & vote in the H of L. Would you like that? S replied No. Well if he becomes a Royal Duke he cannot speak or vote in the H of L & he is not being deprived of his rank in the Navy, Army, or R. Air Force. This gave Schuster a new lease of life and he went off quite happy."[5]

This indicates the extent of the initial confusion over David's title and style, as well as the desire to quickly move to isolate him from any potential position of power and influence. George VI seemed genuinely unaware of precisely what status his brother had given up. Nevertheless, he ordered that he be introduced that evening by Sir John Reith as His Royal Highness The Prince Edward.

This decision was also confirmed at the new King's Accession Council at St. James's Palace. Speaking to the assembled members of the Privy Council, George VI declared that David "will henceforth be known as His Royal Highness the Duke of Windsor."[6]

David himself had suspected that, due to both the circumstances of his leaving and the antipathy surrounding his relationship with Wallis, when they married, someone might try to use the issue of the title she was due to punish either or both of them for their actions. The day before the Abdication, David himself brought up the subject in a talk with his brother, and the future George VI assured him that Wallis would duly take her place within the Royal Family on her marriage. When the

Princess Marina of Kent, wife of
David's brother George, Duke of
Kent

David as Prince of Wales,
about 1930

David's brother Bertie, Duke of York, and Bertie's wife, Elizabeth, the future King George VI and Queen Elizabeth

David's brother Harry, Duke of Gloucester, with Harry's future wife, Alice

Wallis with the Prince
of Wales at Ascot, 1935
CORBIS/UPI

Aerial view of Fort Belvedere, the country home of the Prince of Wales   CORBIS/UPI

Wallis and David, photographed ashore on the Dalmatian coas during their cruise on Lady Yule's yacht, *Nahlin*, summer 1936. To Wallis's right is her friend Katherine Rogers. COR-BIS/UPI

British Prime Minister Stanley Baldwin, in front, leaving his residence at No. 10 Downing Street CORBIS/UPI

Wallis, photographed by Cecil Beaton in the grounds of the Chateau de Candé, just days before her wedding to the Duke of Windsor, May 1937
PHOTOGRAPH BY CECIL BEATON COURTESY VOGUE, © 1937 THE CONDÉ NAST PUB-
LICATIONS, INC.

HER ROYAL ROMANCE AND LIFE STORY

Mrs. Wallis Simpson

15 CENTS

**THRILLING SECRETS ABOUT THE BEAUTIFUL AMERICAN
WHO HAS WON THE FAVOR OF THE BRITISH KING!**

In November 1936, while the British press continued to maintain its silence about the relationship between King Edward VII and Wallis, American readers were treated to instant "fan" magazines, all disclosing the "secrets" of their affair.

The wedding of the century: The new Duke and Duchess of Windsor, in the Salon at Candé on June 3, 1937. Wallis wears her sapphire blue gown designed by Mainbocher.

Wallis, in her uniform of the Colis de Trianon, handing out gift parcels to French troops, winter 1940
URBAN ARCHIVES, TEMPLE UNIVERSITY, PHILADELPHIA, PENNSYLVANIA

The Duke and Duchess of Windsor meet Adolf Hitler at the Berghof, Berchtesgaden, October 22, 1937.
HULTON-DEUTSCH COLLECTION/CORBIS

Wallis, photographed during the stop in Bermuda on the way to the Bahamas, 1940. She wears her famous flamingo brooch. PHILIP PROCTOR COLLECTION 1950

The Duke of Windsor, with Wallis looking on, is installed as Governor-General of the Bahamas in the Legislative Council Chamber at Nassau, August 29, 1940. HULTON-DEUTSCH COLLECTION/CORBIS

Duke of Windsor later learned of his brother's decision to deprive his wife of the style of Her Royal Highness, therefore, he was justifiably angered. "My brother promised me there would be no trouble over the title!" he declared. "He promised me!"[7]

But George VI had not counted on the formidable opposition he was to face from both his mother and his wife. Both women flatly declared that they would not receive the hated Wallis, and demanded that the new King find a way to deprive her of the style of Her Royal Highness. Queen Mary was particularly vehement that the issue be settled to her satisfaction. Her biographer, James Pope-Hennessy, who had a chance to study her private papers, later admitted that the decision to deny Wallis the style of Her Royal Highness had been made in part "at the insistence of Queen Mary." This seems to have been one of the ways in which she coped with the Abdication—by channeling her anger over her eldest son's decision at the one person she most held responsible and whom she was most in a position to hurt: Wallis. One of the Queen's friends later admitted as much, writing, "HM is still angry with the Duke, & I really think that helps her to bear what she called 'the humiliation' of it all."[8]

Undoubtedly, George VI realized how such a decision to deprive Wallis of what should rightfully have been hers on marriage would deeply hurt his brother. The fact that he discussed the issue prior to the Abdication and agreed that he would not withhold the style indicates both that David was worried about this possibility, and, perhaps more importantly, that Bertie himself saw no reason to interfere in the natural process laid down by tradition and common law.

David, however, underestimated his brother's notoriously weak character, as well as the hold Queen Mary and his wife Elizabeth had over him. As the weeks passed into months, he grew increasingly unsettled at the idea of Wallis taking her place within the Royal Family. Additionally, very few people expected that a marriage between the Duke of Windsor and the often-wed Wallis Warfield Simpson was likely to last. Her track record of keeping her husbands was admittedly bad, whatever the circumstances of her divorces. After consulting with his advisors, George VI explained to Baldwin that this was one reason why he wished to deprive Wallis of the style of Her Royal Highness; according to the King's argument, once a person became a Royal Highness, she kept that style for life, no matter what occurred. Thus, according to the King, were his brother and Wallis to divorce, she would remain Her Royal

Highness Wallis, Duchess of Windsor; even remarriage would not strip her of her right to style herself as a Royal Highness.[9]

The King and his advisors were, in fact, quite mistaken on this issue. The style of Royal Highness was one which came with the marriage, but which belonged to the spouse only for the duration of the union. Because the status and style came with the rank, which in turn came through marriage, both disappeared in the event of divorce. Had David and Wallis divorced, she would have remained simply Wallis, Duchess of Windsor. The recent loss of the style of Her Royal Highness by both the late Diana, Princess of Wales and Sarah, Duchess of York merely indicates that George VI either was unaware of the complexities of the issue, or deliberately misinformed his Prime Minister over the matter.

George VI, Queen Mary and Queen Elizabeth—no doubt along with most of the other members of the Royal Family as well as a good percentage of their subjects—believed Wallis an unsuitable person to bear the style of Royal Highness. The desire, therefore, to protect the image and tradition of the monarchy, is understandable, but the deception and illegal reasoning by which Wallis was to be deprived of the style remain a highly dishonourable episode in the history of the House of Windsor.

It has been argued that the King was legally entitled to withhold the style of "Her Royal Highness" from Wallis. In Great Britain, the sovereign holds a position known as the Fountain of Honours; all titles, awards and peerages thus are said to descend via the Throne through the monarch. Because the sovereign, in this position as Fountain of Honours, held control over such matters, it has been alleged that George VI was thus empowered to deprive his sister-in-law of the style.

However, this is a questionable reading of the situation. The sovereign, as Fountain of Honours, had not had any role in the acquisition of the style of Her Royal Highness on the marriages of Lady Elizabeth Bowes-Lyon to the Duke of York, Lady Alice Montagu-Douglas-Scott to the Duke of Gloucester, Katharine Worsley to the Duke of Kent, nor any of the other royal marriages which took place this century in which such issues were involved. In all of these cases, the style simply followed through common law and tradition, not through any act of the sovereign as the Fountain of Honours. In short, George VI, as Fountain of Honours, had no role unless he deliberately intervened in the issue where Wallis was concerned. The style of Her Royal Highness would simply devolve on her on her marriage through no act of the Throne.

Were the ordinary issuance of the style within the province of the sovereign as the Fountain of Honours, the King certainly would have been aware of this. Thus, he would have been in a position to make a decision without recourse to consultation. This was not the case in the deprivation of the style where Wallis was concerned. Instead, George VI was careful to seek consultation from others and to cloak his decision in a cloud of impromptu legal authority.

The King spent the spring of 1937 trying to find a way in which to deprive Wallis of the style of Royal Highness. To add some form of legitimacy to his decision, he asked Sir John Simon, the Home Secretary, Lord Hailsham, the Lord Chancellor, and Sir Donald Somervell, the Attorney-General, to try to find some legal means on which he could act. These men met repeatedly throughout the winter of 1937, examining documents and working on various schemes.

The Office of the Parliamentary Council was also discreetly advised of the King's wish and asked to seek a solution. At first, the response was uniformly against the King's decision: it was illegal, under British common law, to deny the status of a husband to a wife; not even the sovereign was empowered to alter centuries of accepted custom. But Bertie, pushed by his wife and his mother, was beside himself with agitation over the idea that the hated Wallis Simpson would become Her Royal Highness. He dispatched Lord Wigram to see Granville Ram of the Office of the Parliamentary Council to engage in a little royal arm twisting.

Wigram presented the King's arguments, but Ram offered little hope. When Wigram suggested that custom and the law could be ignored or altered in this special case, Ram told him bluntly that as far as he was concerned, there was nothing the King could legally do to prevent Wallis from becoming Her Royal Highness.[10] "The title seems to me to follow," Ram said, "not from the King's consent, but from the validity of the marriage...I sincerely hope that the Home Secretary's ingenious mind may find some way of reaching a more satisfactory conclusion, but for the life of me, I cannot see how he will ever achieve it."[11]

Wigram duly informed the King of this conversation, but this was clearly not what George VI wished to hear. Once again, Wigram was dispatched to do the King's bidding. This time, he met with Maurice Gwyer, another member of the Parliamentary

Council, and presented the royal arguments. Once again, however, he was met with resistance. "I should have thought myself
that an attempt to deprive the Duke's wife of the title of HRH
would have the most disastrous results," Gwyer declared. "I
have no doubt at all that it would be popularly regarded as an
attempt to strike at the Duke through his wife, and resented
accordingly...It would be impossible to imagine a more public
or deadly slight."[12]

The King refused to give up. During a meeting with the
Minister, he asked Baldwin, "Is she a fit and proper person to
become a Royal Highness after what she has done in this country;
and would the country understand it if she became one automatically on marriage?...I and my family and Queen Mary all
feel that it would be a great mistake to acknowledge Mrs. Simpson as a suitable person to become Royal. The Monarchy has
been degraded quite enough already."[13]

The eventual argument worked out by the Crown Law
Offices was that Edward VIII, on his Abdication, had ceased to
hold royal rank. If George VI could not legally deprive his
brother's wife of her rightful status, they advised, his only
recourse was to deprive his brother of his royal rank and then
restore it with restrictions. The decision was made to draw up
Letters Patent in order to strip the Duke of Windsor of his
birthright. Letters Patent, a declaration from the sovereign in
which certain rights or honours are conferred, were ordinary
used to create titles in the British Peerage. In some cases, they
have been used to create Royal Dukedoms, such as the Dukedom of Windsor.

The Letters Patent drawn up declared that Edward VIII, on
abdicating the British Throne, had lost all royal rank and status.
George VI did not wish his brother to go through life as plain
Mr. Edward Windsor, and therefore decided to re-create him a
Royal Duke entitled to the style of Royal Highness. According
to this document, a previous Letters Patent, issued by George V
in 1917, had restricted the style of Royal Highness to those
Princes in the lineal succession to the Throne; because David
was no longer eligible for the Throne, he therefore fell outside
the bounds of the ordinary requirements, and George VI was
making an exception for the sake of his brother's honour. But in
granting the style of His Royal Highness to the Duke, the Letters Patent also claimed to be able to restrict its use to him and
him alone.

Because a deliberate alteration was being made to the
ordinary course of events by the issuance of Letters Patent to

re-create his brother as a Royal Duke, George VI was constitutionally obliged to seek the advice of his ministers. The King was not empowered to alter royal titles or the succession, according to the Statute of Westminster, without consulting the Dominions. Indeed, this very issue had been the reason why David had not been able to his own accord to marry Wallis morganatically. One suspects the question was allowed to reach this point simply because the King would be required to heed the advice of the Dominions, and George VI, only three months after the Abdication, had little doubt as to their feeling where Wallis was concerned.

The normal procedure involved the King requesting formal consideration and advice on the issuance of the Letters Patent. In this case, however, George VI, unwilling to risk any possible outcome other than the one which he himself wished, had written to the Prime Minister and told him exactly what he wished that opinion to be. This is not idle speculation; Montgomery-Hyde, in his biography of Baldwin, had access to the original letter George VI dispatched to the Prime Minister on the question, a letter which apparently took great care to tell the Cabinet what it was he expected to hear in their report.[14]

Ironically, Baldwin's last Cabinet meeting as Prime Minister, on 26 May, 1937, included discussion and ratification of the King's Letters Patent recreating his brother a Royal Prince and allowing him to withhold the style of Her Royal Highness from Wallis. Two days later, the official announcement appeared in the London Gazette: "Whitehall, May 28, 1937. The King has been pleased by Letters Patent under the Great Seal of the Realm bearing the date the 27th day of May 1937, to declare that the Duke of Windsor shall, notwithstanding his Instrument of Abdication executed on the 10th day of December 1936, and His Majesty's declaration of Abdication Act 1936, whereby effect was given to the said Instrument, be entitled to hold and enjoy for himself only the title, style or attribute of Royal Highness so however that his wife and descendants if any shall not hold the said title, style or attribute."[15]

A day later, the Times repeated the text of the announcement. The accompanying article declared: "Their decision is in keeping with the tradition that a right to the title of Royal Highness and to the recognition accorded to it by custom, at home, throughout the Empire, and elsewhere abroad, is essentially the attribute of a potential successor to the Throne—the Duke of Windsor himself remaining a special exception to the rule. It also accords with such parallels as are to be found in other official practice and should relieve the ceremony which is to take place in France next week from some part of the burden of speculation and discussion that has settled upon it."[16]

This then, was the argument as presented by George VI and his advisors: that David had lost all royal rank on his abdication, and that the King was perfectly entitled to restore this lost rank and also to restrict the use of the style of Royal Highness to the Duke alone. In the years which have since passed, no effort has been made on the part of either George VI or his daughter Elizabeth II, nor the Court, to re-examine this controversial decision.

The case that David never lost his royal rank is absolutely clear. On 5 February, 1864, Queen Victoria had issued Letters Patent which would later substantiate the Duke of Windsor's claims: "The Queen has been pleased by Letters Patent under the Great Seal, to declare Her Royal Will and Pleasure that besides the Children of Sovereigns of these Realms, the Children of the Sons of any Sovereign of Great Britain and Ireland shall have and at all times hold and enjoy the title, style and attribute of 'Royal Highness," with their titular dignity of Prince or Princess prefixed to their respective Christian names[17] ...David was born a Highness in 1894; on 27 May, 1898, he became a Royal Highness, on issuance of Letters Patent from Queen Victoria which gave the style "to the children of the eldest son of a Prince of Wales."

A second Letters Patent, issued by David's father, King George V, in 1917, had declared: "The Children of any Sovereign of the United Kingdom, and the Children of the Sons of any such Sovereign, and the eldest living Son of the eldest Son of the Prince of Wales, shall have and at all times hold and enjoy the style, title or attribute of Royal Highness, with their titular dignity of Prince or Princess prefixed to their respective Christian names, or with their other titles of honour."

These Letters Patent not only confirmed exactly the provisions of those issued by Queen Victoria in 1864, but spelled out in a more explicit fashion the same standards. George V's Letters Patent did nothing to alter or change those issued by his grandmother sixty years earlier.

When David abdicated the Throne, he lost his sovereign status as His Majesty the King. The only way in which his royal rank and style of Royal Highness could be taken away was through the issuance of Special Letters Patent which specifically deprived him of these attributes. Nothing in the Abdication process nor in any of the documents had done this, nor did

King George VI ever issue Letters Patent depriving his brother of his royal rank. He either simply—and wrongly—assumed that he had lost it on abdicating, or even less generously, ignored the facts in his determination to punish David and Wallis. As Philip Thomas stated in *Burke's Peerage*: "The position is that immediately upon his abdication and without any special act of the Prerogative, the former sovereign became, as son of a sovereign and pursuant to Letters Patent of 30 November, 1917, a Prince of the United Kingdom of Great Britain and Ireland, with the qualification of Royal Highness...."[18]

The King's own contention that his brother had lost royal rank on his Abdication was undermined not only by the definitive evidence of both Queen Victoria's and George V's Letters Patent, but also by events more recent. George VI himself had recognized his brother as retaining royal rank at his Accession Council immediately after the abdication, when Edward was referred to as His Royal Highness; in his instructions to Sir John Reith to introduce him before his speech to the nation as His Royal Highness Prince Edward; and in the Letters Patent creating the Dukedom of Windsor, where, before the ratification and issuance, David was referred to as His Royal Highness.

The King and his advisors would also try to claim that because the Duke of Windsor was no longer in the line of succession for the Throne, he did not fall under the provisions of either Queen Victoria's Letters Patent of 1864 or George V's Letters Patent of 1917. But neither of these two Letters Patent in any way dealt with the issue of the succession, or the limiting of titles and styles to those in line for the Throne. No mention was made of any such idea. They only confirmed that all sons and grandsons of sovereigns were entitled to the use of the title of Prince and style of Royal Highness for life without restriction.[19]

The deprivation of the style of Her Royal Highness for Wallis served quite another purpose, as Lady Longford insightfully, and one suspects, accidentally, pointed out in her biography of the present Queen: "Her not being an HRH, however, was the only card the King held: his brother had vowed he would not return to England with Wallis unless she were created HRH. But what if the King, together with his wife and his closest advisors, considered it inadvisable for the Windsors to be let loose on England again during those critical months? It was to the Royal Family's advantage that the Duchess should be denied the title for the very reason that her husband insisted on it: it was the condition of their return from exile."[20] In other words, George VI used the denial of the style of Royal Highness to keep his brother and sister-in-law out of the country—not a very noble use of his position as "Fountain of Honours."

The effect of the King's decision was to make the forthcoming wedding between Wallis and David a morganatic—that is, unequal—marriage. For no other interpretation can be given to a marriage where one partner holds and enjoys a title and style specifically excluded from the other partner. Baldwin had claimed that no such thing as a morganatic marriage existed in England, and used such reasoning to try to block Edward VIII's attempt to contract one with Wallis. "But," writes Michael Thornton, "in the five months since those words had been spoken, morganatic marriage had miraculously become 'known to our law.' For if His Royal Highness The Duke of Windsor, who had been denied such a marriage as King, married a lady whom the British Government intended should be known only as Her Grace The Duchess of Windsor, a morganatic marriage was indisputably what he was getting after all."[21]

George VI acted illegally to deprive Wallis of the style of Royal Highness, and he perpetuated this miscarriage of justice by insisting that he, as Fountain of Honours, held control over such issues. But in the King's Declaration of Abdication, Edward VIII had been careful to declare, "The Royal Marriages Act, 1772, shall not apply to His Majesty after His Abdication." George VI, therefore, was not empowered to interfere in the sharing by the wife of the husband's title and style, which followed from British common law. The King could not act counter to common law, and as the Duke of Windsor fell outside the bounds of the Royal Marriages Act—the only possible example by which his brother might have issued a directive which ran counter to common law—the new King was powerless to restrict use of the style.

David was deeply hurt by this insult to the woman he loved. "The Duke told me once that his brother had denied the Duchess the use of HRH simply as a way to punish her for the Abdication," a former friend declared (personal interview). This is certainly the attitude David was to carry with him for the rest of his life. "I know Bertie," he exclaimed, "I know he couldn't have written this letter on his own. Why in God's name would they do this to me at this time!"[22] George VI himself had met with Monckton the day after the Abdication and acknowledged that his brother kept his royal style and rank; Monckton therefore believed that the King had been influenced by others. "If the King had been left to himself," he wrote, "I feel confident that he would not have assented to this course because he knew the effect it would have on his brother."[23]

Both Wallis and David had little doubt as to who bore ultimate responsibility for the deprivation: the two Queens, Mary and Elizabeth. Wallis, in fact, was frequently to refer to her sister-in-law Elizabeth as "the Dowdy Duchess."[24] The dislike was mutual, and it was Elizabeth, Britain's beloved Queen Mother, who, more than any other person, maintained the ostracism of the Windsors and the vendetta against Wallis. With the passing years, she refused to relent in her determination to punish the Duchess of Windsor. Even when constitutional authorities agreed that her husband had acted illegally, the Queen Mother staunchly held her line, a line her daughter Elizabeth II refused to cross for fear of upsetting her beloved mother.

It was against this divisive background that Wallis and David prepared for their marriage.

27

The Wedding

The arrival of George VI's unwelcome letter cast a grim shadow over the wedding. The Duke immediately appealed to his brother, protesting that his decision was illegal and asking that he reconsider. The day before the wedding, word came from Buckingham Palace that the King refused to alter his decision. Monckton, who received the call, was reluctant to pass this devastating piece of news along. "Duddles," he said to Dudley Forwood, "I've got the unpleasant task of telling His Royal Highness that the Duchess won't be Her Royal Highness."

"Oh, Walter," Forwood replied, "you'll never do it."

"You're right," Monckton admitted, "I won't. Why don't you?" Thus, Forwood shouldered the thankless task of informing the Duke. He pulled David aside and said, "Word has come, Sir, from Buckingham Palace about the Duchess's title. I am afraid, Sir, that she is not to be a Royal Highness."

The Duke, overwhelmed, burst into tears and buried his head in Forwood's shoulder. When he recovered his composure, he asked, "Dudley, will you promise me that you will treat the Duchess as a Royal Highness?"

"Sir," Forwood replied, "she will always be Her Royal Highness to me."[1]

Wallis was determined to ignore the snub, and spent her days preparing for the wedding. Cecil Beaton had come from London and spent an afternoon before the wedding taking photographs of the couple in the park at Candé. Guests continued to arrive; in addition to Wallis's aunt Bessie, the wedding party included Fruity Metcalfe, who was to serve as the Duke's supporter; Fruity's wife, Lady Alexandra Metcalfe; George Allen; Walter Monckton; Randolph Churchill; Baron Eugene de Rothschild and his wife, Kitty; Hugh Lloyd Thomas, first secretary to the British embassy; Lady Walford Selby; Dudley Forwood; and the British consul at Nantes, W. C. Graham and his wife. As expected, no member of the British Royal Family attended.

The day before the wedding was filled with a flurry of activity. Wallis decided that she would like the ceremony conducted in the château's music room, a large room paneled in cream-colored *boiserie*. There was no altar in the château, so a fifteenth-century chest from one of the hallways was determined to be the best substitute. It was placed in a small alcove at one end of the music room; the chest, however, was carved with nude figures, and a mad search took place for some suitable covering. Eventually, Wallis rummaged through her trunks and found an embroidered, cream-colored silk tea cloth and draped it over the offending nudes. Charles Bedaux could only find crucifixes in the château; when Jardine insisted on a Protestant cross, Bedaux dutifully trooped down to the local village and managed to borrow one, which he triumphantly placed at the center of the altar upon his return. George Allen, himself scavenging the château for wedding accessories, set two candlesticks he had taken from the dining room on the altar, only to be spotted by Wallis, who shouted, "Hey, you can't put those up! We want them for the dinner table tonight!"[2]

Somehow, through all of the frenzy and disappointment, Wallis managed to keep her head and her sense of humor. Seeing the intense work going on all over the château, one of the maids declared that it was all too much and that she would never get married. "Oh, it isn't always as bad as this," Wallis replied with a laugh; "only if you're marrying the ex-King of England."[3]

That night, Wallis presided over a celebratory dinner in the château's dining room. The Duke seemed jovial enough, but during the recital which followed, he quickly became bored. He somehow managed to pull Jardine off to one side of the room and spent the next hour questioning the minister at great length as to housing conditions and the welfare of the poor in his district back in England.

Thursday, June 3, 1937, dawned bright and warm at Candé. The sky was cloudless and the sun brilliant, its heat relieved by a gentle breeze sweeping across the park from the surrounding forests. Wallis had been up since dawn, carefully preparing, in her enormous bedroom overlooking the gardens, for what she knew would become one of history's most publicized weddings. As Aunt Bessie assisted, Wallis dressed in the outfit Mainbocher had designed in his Paris studios. Wallis's dress was a simple sheath of blue silk crepe, with a long skirt and a matching long-sleeved, fitted jacket. The color was a pale sapphire; "I named it 'Wallis Blue,'" Mainbocher explained, "a blue of which there was never a sample available to anyone."[4]

The bodice of the jacket draped into a heart shape at the bustline and fell in a series of pleats to the waist. With the jacket, Wallis wore a pair of wrist-length blue-crepe gloves; the left-hand ring finger opened up to allow the placement of the wedding band. Her shoes, by Georgette of Paris, were in a matching blue suede. In place of a veil, Wallis elected to wear a small hat, designed as a halo of pink and blue feathers atop a straw base by Caroline Reboux.[5] To accommodate superstition, Wallis wore a piece of antique lace stitched into her lingerie as something old; a gold coin minted for the coronation of Edward VIII and worn in the heel of her shoe provided something new; Aunt Bessie lent a lace handkerchief as something borrowed; and, of course, her wedding dress itself provided Wallis with the requirement for something blue.

At half-past eleven, escorted by Herman Rogers, Wallis descended the château's grand staircase and made her way to the salon, where the civil ceremony would be held prior to the religious celebration. The salon, a long, dark room dominated by a massive stone fireplace, had been filled with flowers arranged by Constance Spry. Large vases of white and pink peonies stood on either side of the wooden table where the civil documents would be signed; peonies decorated the mantelpiece, and before the open windows were bouquets of white, yellow, and red peonies and lilies. As a tribute to Wallis, someone had also decorated the room with strings of little paper American flags which fluttered crisply in the breeze.

David stood waiting for his bride, smartly attired in a morning suit of striped trousers, gray waistcoat, and black cutaway. Fruity Metcalfe stood to his right, also wearing a morning suit. Herman escorted Wallis to the Duke's side, and the four principals took their seats before the marriage table. The other wedding guests crowded in at the rear of the room, looking on as the mayor of Monts, Charles Mercier—attired in formal dress draped with a red, white, and blue sash edged with gold tassels—began the ceremony.

The civil ceremony was conducted in French; Mercier had been sufficiently worried lest the bride or groom misunderstand him, so he had run them through their paces in several rehearsals. He began: "Conforming to the requirements of the law I will read you Chapter Six of the Civil Code on the respective rights and duties of a married couple." Mercier proceeded to lecture them on their expected behavior, delivering such charges as: "The wife must live with her husband and must follow him to whatever place he deems proper as a residence. The husband must receive her and furnish her with the necessities of life according to his facilities and position."[6]

Mercier carefully led Wallis and David through their vows. With a simple, emphatic *"Oui,"* Wallis became the Duchess of Windsor at 11:47 A.M. Mercier was not one to let such a historic opportunity pass him by; as soon as he concluded the ceremony, he launched into a flowery address in rapid-fire French that was largely lost on both

Wallis and David: "By one of those whims of destiny, it is under the blue sky and among the flowers of the garden of France, in the laughing valley of the Indre, that the most moving of all idylls has just unfolded itself. The illustrious wedding which innumerable hearts will celebrate. . . ."[7]

As the clock struck noon, Wallis and David left the salon for the walk through the château to the music room, where the religious ceremony would take place. The altar blazed with light: Tall candelabra stood on either side of the carved chest, reflecting in the gilded mirror the scene above the cross. Wallis and David entered the room separately. The Duke came first, Fruity Metcalfe at his side, as Marcel Dupree, the organist from Notre Dame in Paris, played Handel's "Wedding March" from *Judas Maccabaeus*. Wallis, escorted once again by Herman Rogers, walked down the aisle to the sound of Dupree's own "Wedding March." Reverend Jardine waited at the altar, standing over two white-satin pillows on low stools upon which the bridal couple knelt for the opening prayer.

Jardine began with the customary address to the bridal couple: "I require and charge you both, as ye will answer at the dreadful day of judgment when the secrets of all hearts shall be disclosed, that if either of you know any impediment why ye may not be lawfully joined together in matrimony, ye do now confess it. For be ye well assured that so many as are coupled together otherwise than God's word doth allow are not joined together by God, neither is their matrimony lawful."

The only French press representative allowed to witness the ceremony, Maurice Schumann, recalled "the slight tremor which ran through the small groups of guests" when Jardine delivered this warning.[8]

Jardine then turned to the Duke: "Edward Albert Christian George Andrew Patrick David, Wilt Thou have this Woman to Thy wedded Wife, to live together after God's Ordinance in the Holy Estate of Matrimony? Wilt Thou love Her, comfort Her, honour and keep Her, in sickness and in health; and, forsaking all others, keep Thee only unto Her, so long as Ye both shall live?"

"I will," David answered.

Turning to Wallis, Jardine asked: "Wallis, Wilt Thou have this Man to Thy wedded Husband, to live together after God's Ordinance in the Holy Estate of Matrimony? Wilt Thou obey Him, and serve Him, love, honour and keep Him, in sickness and in health; and forsaking all others, keep Thee only unto Him, so long as Ye both shall live?"

"I will," Wallis replied clearly.

"Who giveth this Woman to be married to this Man?" Jardine inquired.

Herman Rogers stepped forward slightly, bowed his head, and

returned to his place. Jardine then directed the Duke to take Wallis's right hand in his, and David repeated after the reverend, "I, Edward Albert Christian George Andrew Patrick David, take Thee, Bessie Wallis, to My Wedded Wife, to have and to hold from this day forth, for better, for worse, for richer, for poorer, in sickness and in health, to love and to cherish, till death do Us part, and thereto, I plight Thee My troth."

Wallis repeated her own vows after Jardine's instructions, the same one that the Duke had pledged, with the exception that she also promised to obey. Jardine then brought forth the wedding ring, blessed it, and handed the Duke the band intended for his wife. He repeated after Jardine: "With this ring, I Thee wed, with My Body, I Thee worship, and with all My worldly goods I Thee endow, in the name of the Father, and of the Son, and of the Holy Ghost. Amen."

Wallis and David then knelt before Jardine as the reverend intoned the blessing: "Let us pray. O eternal God, Creator and Preserver of all Mankind, giver of all spiritual grace, the author of everlasting life; send Thy blessing upon these Thy servants, Edward, Duke of Windsor, and Wallis, Duchess of Windsor, that as Isaac and Rebecca lived faithfully together, so these persons may surely perform and keep the vow and covenant betwixt them made, whereof this ring given and received is a token and pledge, and may ever remain in perfect love and peace together and live according to Thy laws, through Jesus Christ our Lord, Amen." As the couple rose, Jardine declared loudly, "Those whom God has joined together, let no man put asunder. Forasmuch as Edward, Duke of Windsor and Wallis Warfield have consented together in Holy Wedlock, and have witnessed the same before God and this company, and thereto have given and pledged their troth either to other, and have declared the same by the giving and receiving of a ring and by joining of hands, I pronounce that they be man and wife together, in the name of the Father, and of the Son, and of the Holy Ghost. Amen."

Lady Alexandra Metcalfe, watching the ceremony from the middle of the music room, later wrote: "It could be nothing but pitiable & tragic to see a King of England of only 6 months ago, an idolized King, married under those circumstances, & yet pathetic as it was, his manner was so simple and dignified & he was so sure of himself in his happiness that it gave something to the sad little service which it is hard to describe. He had tears running down his face. . . . She also could not have done it better."[9]

After the wedding, the new Duke and Duchess of Windsor received their guests in the salon. "If she occasionally showed a glimmer of softness," wrote Lady Alexandra, "took his arm, looked at him as though she loved him one would warm towards her, but her attitude is so correct. The effect is of a woman unmoved by the infatuated love of a younger man. Let's hope that she lets up in private with him otherwise it must be grim."[10]

The wedding luncheon followed in the dining room. The Duke and Duchess and their guests sat down to a rather simple meal of lobster, salad, chicken à la King, and strawberries and cream, washed down with 1921 Lawson champagne. At the end of the meal, Fruity Metcalfe stood and made his formal toast: "Long life and happiness to His Royal Highness, the Duke of Windsor, and his Lady." The sixtier wedding cake, some three feet high, stood on a nearby table. Wallis herself cut the cake, the first piece of which she gave to Aunt Bessie. "Unlike most brides who simply cut through the cake and leave it to others," said Jardine, "the Duchess continued for all of a quarter of an hour cutting pieces for her guests and absent friends. My portion was a fairly large one because the Duchess wished me to take a piece home to my wife and family."[11] These individual pieces of the wedding cake were placed in cardboard boxes covered with white silk and later sent to those friends and family who had been unable to attend, signed on the top by both the Duke and Duchess and tied with white silk ribbons.[12]

After the luncheon, Wallis asked Reverend Jardine to inscribe her prayer book. Jardine went to a nearby table where the book lay, followed by the Duke. "What shall I write—Her Royal Highness, the Duchess of Windsor, or just the Duchess of Windsor?" Jardine asked the Duke.

"Write the Duchess of Windsor," David replied with some hesitation. When Jardine still seemed uncertain, however, David changed his mind and said, "Write Her Royal Highness."[13]

After the cake had been cut, Wallis and Walter Monckton took a short stroll through the garden. Monckton told her how much he sympathized with her position and assured her that he would always try to help both her and the Duke. But he also pointed out how much many people disliked her, believing that she was responsible for the abdication. He warned that for the rest of her life the public would scrutinize her every move to see how she treated the husband who had given up so much to be with her. She replied very simply, "Walter, don't you think I have thought of all that? I think I can make him happy."[14]

Wallis was only too well aware of the truth behind Monckton's words. "If ever there was a marriage that started off inauspiciously, resented and vilified, with many hopes and probably prayers for its failure, it was ours," she later wrote. "If ever the life of two people together was beset with problems—problems, mind you, manufactured by our enemies—it was ours."[15]

"That marriage aged the Duchess overnight," Dudley Forwood recalls. "People always thought she struck the best bargain, but she had to take the place of the Duke's family, his country and his job. What a terrible, terrible responsibility. It was a sacred duty, but she was determined to treat him as he was, a former King of England."[16]

Despite the criticism in certain circles, the world was enraptured, and pictures of the newly married couple were quickly flashed around the world to grace the front pages of newspapers. Predictably, the British Royal Family reacted with less enthusiasm; although both the Duke's brother George VI and his mother telegraphed best wishes, something of Queen Mary's true feelings can be gauged in the entry she made in her diary that day: "Alas! The wedding day in France of David & Mrs. Warfield."[17]

The Duke and Duchess of Windsor, accompanied by two valets, two footmen, two detectives, two dressers, a butler, and three chauffeurs, as well as Dudley Forwood, left Candé late that afternoon in a procession of cars guarded by French gendarmes on motorcycles. There was a brief stop for a small picnic, but when the hampers were opened, it was discovered that someone had neglected to pack the food. The Duke, seeing that the meal would be reduced to some fresh peaches, loudly declared, "If Wallis eats all those peaches, she won't stop going to the loo all night!" The picnic was abandoned.[18]

Late that afternoon, the Windsors and their party arrived in the village of Laroch-Migennes, where they boarded a private *wagon-lits* carriage which had been coupled to the *Simplon-Orient Express* for the journey to Venice. As the Duke and Duchess settled into their compartments, which had been filled with dozens of red and yellow roses, their 266 pieces of luggage were loaded into the baggage car. At six-thirty in the evening, the train steamed out of the station, bound for Italy.[19]

They stopped in Venice to change trains; they had several hours to see the sights, and the new Duke and Duchess enjoyed a gondola ride down the Grand Canal, cheered on by hundreds of applauding spectators and chased by determined photographers. In St. Mark's Square, Wallis fed the pigeons and joined her husband on a tour of the adjacent Doge's Palace. After afternoon tea at the Hotel Excelsior, they boarded a train bound for Vienna.

For the honeymoon, David had arranged to rent Schloss Wasserleonburg, an old castle in Carinthia which belonged to Count Paul Munster, a cousin of the Duke's friend Lord Eric Dudley. At midnight on June 4, the train bearing the Duke and Duchess steamed into the small village of Villach, high in the Austrian Alps, where the local prefect, clad in traditional costume, waited to greet them with a speech. As Wallis stepped from the train, she was presented with a bouquet of red and white roses, and a choir of fifty boys and girls, dressed in colorful peasant costume, burst into song.

The Duke and Duchess were driven in Countess Munster's Mercedes along high Alpine roads, through the forests of fir and pine, and past serene lakes which glowed in the soft moonlight; the road was narrow and filled with curves, which Wallis found unsettling. Just before one in the morning, the car rounded a bend in the drive, and the tower and tall roof of Wasserleonburg came into view. "To come upon the castle so—in the moonlight—was utterly enchanting," Wallis would later declare.[20] As the Duke and Duchess prepared to enter the castle, David stooped down, picked up his wife, and carried her across the threshold, to the applause of the more than two dozen staff and servants who stood gathered in the great hall to greet them upon their arrival.

Wasserleonburg had been built in the fifteenth century around a large cobblestone courtyard. Its arched windows and towers looked out over magnificent views of the surrounding countryside. A high Gothic chapel stood at one end of the small but beautiful garden; beyond lay a swimming pool and tennis courts. Newspaper reporters happily pointed out that the castle was said to be haunted by the ghost of a sixteenth-century woman who had been married six times and [had killed five] of those husbands within Wasserleonburg's walls.[21]

The extent of what exactly it meant to be the wife of the former King of England came as a revelation to Wallis. She later recalled the morning after their wedding in a conversation with author Gore Vidal: "I woke up and there was David standing beside the bed with this innocent smile, saying, 'And now what do we do?' My heart sank. Here was someone whose every day had been arranged for him all his life and now I was the one who was going to take the place of the entire British Government, trying to think up things for him to do. My life's not important. But I think his was. Such a waste, really, for everyone."[22]

Between riding and walking, the Windsors inevitably began to replay the events of the past few months in their minds. Over and over again, they wondered what they might have done differently. Wallis particularly felt responsible for the almost shameful conditions of exile into which her new husband had been forced by his family. "The Duchess wasn't one for emotion," a friend recalled, "but I remember her telling me of the immense weight she felt on marrying the Duke. She was nearly *crushed* by the thought of having to look after him properly. At Wasserleonburg, she confessed, she told the Duke she wanted to walk alone in the forest and actually went out there and sat and cried and cried."[23] Finally, however, Wallis drew herself up to the challenges which lay ahead. She and David realized that they would drive themselves mad if they continued to question every move they had made in the past. For both Wallis and David, it was now the future and their life together that mattered most; they would not look back with regret.

At the beginning of September, while the Windsors were still in residence at Wasserleonburg, David learned that his brother and sister-in-law, the Duke and Duchess of Kent, were on holiday with Prince Paul of Yugoslavia at nearby Brdo in Slovenia. The Duke of Kent wrote to his brother, saying that he would very much like to come and see him for a few days.[24] David, overjoyed at the prospect and convinced that the veneer of family opposition to him and Wallis was about to crack, immediately telephoned his brother and agreed to the meeting.

But as they continued to speak, David gradually began to understand that although she was only a few hours away, his sister-in-law Marina had absolutely no intention of joining her husband, George, on this visit. When David asked why Marina was not coming to Wasserleonburg, he was bluntly informed that Queen Mary had previously warned her not, under any circumstances, to meet the Duchess of Windsor.[25]

Needless to say, David was filled with anger at this deliberate slight and told his brother George that either he and his wife both came or neither was welcome. Unsure of what to do, the Duke of Kent asked his brother the King for advice. Bertie replied that it was important that he visit David even if he had to take Marina with him. In spite of all of the bad feeling which existed between the brothers, Bertie apparently realized that the Royal Family must not completely cut off David.

Marina was reluctant to do as the King wished, but in the end her own feelings mattered little, for Queen Elizabeth and Queen Mary stepped in and repeatedly insisted that Bertie change his instructions.[26] With great reluctance, Bertie folded under this feminine pressure and informed the Kents not to visit the Windsors at Wasserleonburg. When David learned of this, he immediately wrote an understandably angry letter to his mother: "I unfortunately know from George that you and Elizabeth instigated the somewhat sordid and much publicized episode of the failure of the Kents to visit us. . . . I am at a loss to know how to write to you, and further to see how any form of correspondence can give pleasure to either of us under these circumstances. . . . It is a great sorrow and disappointment to me to have my mother thus cast out her eldest son."[27]

The incident with the Kents was just one example of the continuing campaign to marginalize the Windsors taking place in London. In May 1937, George VI had asked the Foreign Office to issue a set of guidelines for the diplomatic corps and Foreign Service staff explaining how the Windsors were to be treated. The official reply by Anthony Eden was that they should be regarded as junior members of the Royal Family on holiday.[28] This raised too many unwelcome possibilities, however, and the still-insecure George VI, pushed by his wife and mother, asked Alexander Hardinge to draft a response to the Foreign Office. The Duke and Duchess of Windsor, the King insisted, must only be entertained privately by ambassadors, never invited to official functions and never asked to stay at an embassy overnight.[29]

Throughout the summer of 1937, however, the King continued to worry that exceptions would be made and that his more accomplished and glamorous brother and sister-in-law would manage to detract from his own position. On September 2, Hardinge wrote to Sir Robert Vansittart, permanent secretary at the Foreign Office, once again stating what Eden had supposedly settled several months before: "The most important point in His Majesty's opinion is that His Royal Highness the Duke of Windsor and the Duchess should not be treated by His Majesty's representatives as having any official status in the countries which they visit."[30]

At the beginning of October, Sir Robert Lindsay, the British ambassador in Washington, D.C., was summoned to Balmoral in Scotland to meet with the King and Queen. He was amazed at the blatant hostility at court toward the Windsors. "The Palace Secretaries are extremist, the Foreign Office still more so," Lindsay noted. "All are seeing ghosts and phantoms everywhere and think there are disasters round every corner."[31]

Lindsay found George VI suspicious of the Duke of Windsor and uncertain as to his own position on the *throne*. He also spoke with Queen Elizabeth—"not a great intellect but she has any amount of 'intelligence du coeur.'" On this occasion, the Queen managed to control her anger, at least toward the Duke. Lindsay noted: "In all she said there was far more grief than indignation and it was all tempered by affection for 'David.' 'He's so changed now, and he used to be so kind to us.' She was backing up everything the men said, but protesting against anything that seemed vindictive. All her feelings were lacerated by what she and the King were being made to go through." However careful the Queen might have been in expressing her feelings about the former King to this unfamiliar diplomat, she had no such restraint when it came to the Duchess. "With all her charity," Lindsay declared, "she had not a word to say for 'that woman.'"[32]

When Lindsay returned to Washington, D.C., he met with the undersecretary of state, Sumner Welles, who reported:

The Ambassador said that before his departure from England he had been summoned to spend a few days with the King and Queen of England. He said that, as I probably knew, the relationship between the present King of England and the Duke of Windsor had been throughout their lives particularly close and that during the present King's earlier years when he suffered from an impediment in his speech, the then Prince of Wales had taken it upon himself to shield and to support his brother and that the present King for that reason had a very natural and particular sense of gratitude and affection for the Duke of Windsor. On the other hand, they both felt that at this time when the new King was in a difficult situation and was trying to win the affection and confidence of his country people, without possessing the popular appeal which the Duke of Windsor possessed, it was singularly unfortunate that the Duke of Windsor was placing himself in a position where he would seem constantly to be courting the limelight. The Ambassador went on to say that he had found on the part of all the governing class in England a very vehement feeling of indignation against the course of the Duke of Windsor based in part on the resentment created by his relinquishment of his responsibilities and in even greater part due to the apparent unfairness of his present attitude with regard to his brother, the King. The Ambassador said that in Court circles and in the Foreign Office and on the part of the heads of political parties, this feeling bordered on the stage of hysteria. . . . The Ambassador expressed the personal opinion that the Duke of Windsor himself is probably not cognizant of the state of feeling in this regard and that it is being exploited without his knowledge. . . . What the British desired he said was to prevent any action on the part of the authorities of the British Government which would permit the Duke of Windsor to appear in the light of a martyr. . . ."[33]

Against this background of political and royal worry over his former position, the Duke of Windsor made what was arguably the worst decision in his postabdication life: in October 1937 he and Wallis embarked on an immensely publicized tour of Nazi Germany, a tour whose associations would continue to haunt both the Duke and Duchess for the rest of their lives.

28

The Visit to Germany

In the fall of 1937 the world stood poised at the edge of an abyss. The ominous signs of growing tensions were everywhere. In Asia, Emperor Hirohito's armies had invaded the Chinese mainland, absorbing the decaying country with little resistance. The Civil War in Spain, pitting Italian and German influence against Russian intervention, upset the delicate peace of Europe. Above all, the world watched with growing unease as Germany continued to rumble with threats. In England, where Baldwin had been replaced as prime minister by Neville Chamberlain, there was a general feeling of unease, although few expected a war to erupt in the future. The mood continued to be, as it had been during the reign of Edward VIII, one of complacent appeasement.

The Duke of Windsor's proposed visit to Germany had been under discussion throughout the summer of 1937. Today, of course, the visit seems almost incredible; in photographs and newsreels the Duke and Duchess appear utterly charmed by their Nazi hosts, and David's glowing praise of the accomplishments of the Third Reich, especially its treatment of workers, rings loudly against the historical record. But the visit must be viewed in the context in which it was made.

At the time the Windsors visited Germany, the Second World War was still two years away. The policy of the British government was one of cooperation and appeasement, and politicians and diplomats regularly made their way not only to Berlin but also to Hitler's private estate at Berchtesgaden for meetings with the Führer. A majority of Europe continued to believe that the Soviet Union was the ultimate enemy, and attempts to negotiate with Hitler would continue until the very outbreak of hostilities in September 1939.

A great deal of mythology and misinformation surrounds the Windsors' trip to Germany. The idea for the visit did not, as has often been asserted, originate with Charles Bedaux. The Duke of Windsor had long been interested in the housing conditions of workers; Germany was then popularly celebrated as boasting model programs for its laboring classes, and David was curious to see for himself the miracles transforming the country. The idea for the visit originated solely with the Duke.

David was also anxious to see Wallis treated with the respect he felt her position demanded, and a ceremonial visit to a friendly country, where they would both be feted and entertained and photographed, seemed an ideal solution. "His Royal Highness," says Sir Dudley Forwood, "wanted to see honour and glory paid to the woman he adored." Wallis, too, realized that her husband longed for something important to do; although he never complained, she knew that he was bored and often longed for the days when his schedule had been filled with engagements that, however banal, had given him some sense of accomplishment. She, however, was a bit more apprehensive of the possible consequences of a German visit. "She didn't want to go," Forwood recalls. "She realized that it might go against them. But His Royal Highness had made up his mind."[1]

Although David was naive in many respects, he was also aware that a visit to Germany was likely to be highly controversial. However, over the past nine months he had also been made accutely aware that he no longer enjoyed any sort of official position or status. He had no intention of doing or saying anything political, nor did he believe, rather impossibly, that either the British or the German governments would be able to interpret such a visit as anything other than that of a private citizen.[2]

Contrary to popular belief, Charles Bedaux opposed the visit to Germany. He advised the Duke of Windsor that the potential controversy resulting from the trip might lead to difficulties in his desire to return one day to England. Nor, according to his biographer, is there any evidence that Bedaux tried to manipulate the visit to gain some business advantage with the Nazis.[3] It is true that Bedaux's business interests in that country had been confiscated, but he was already involved in serious negotiations in the fall of 1937 and had little need of the Duke of Windsor in this respect.

"Kings," wrote Walter Monckton, "not only live in glass-houses, but have constant access to the best advice in every sphere. It was hard to convince people at home how much more difficult it was for the Duke, because of the position he had held and the advice which had been available to him, to keep an even and temperate judgement when responsible ministers never went near him. . . ."[4] David did, in fact, meet with Lord Beaverbrook in Paris prior to the trip and asked his opinion. Beaverbrook was quick to advise against the visit, but David had already made up his mind and refused to reconsider.

Bedaux himself had little hand in arranging the trip. Instead, his friend, Fritz Wiedemann—on the instructions of Hitler himself—had taken charge, working out an exhausting itinerary designed to showcase the best of the Third Reich's accomplishments while at the same time allowing maximum exposure of the celebrated Windsors. All expenses, at the Führer's direct orders, were to be paid out of a special fund from the Reichsbank.

The Duke and Duchess of Windsor arrived aboard the Nord Express at Berlin's Friedrichstrasse station early on the morning of October 11. The entire siding had been decorated with strings of Union Jacks alternating with the Nazi swastika, which fluttered in the cold wind. As a brass band played "God Save the King," the *Nord Express* slowly steamed to a halt, and the Duke and Duchess alighted to cries of *"Heil* Edward!" and *"Hoch* Windsors!"[5] David wore a light gray double-breasted suit with a red carnation in his lapel; Wallis sported a tailored suit in navy blue wool, with a matching navy cape, hat, and shoes.

A line of German officials, headed by Dr. Robert Ley, the leader of the National Labour Front, waited to greet the couple. Ley handed Wallis a box of chocolates with a card which bore the inscription *"Königliche Hoheit"*—"Royal Highness."[6] Although the Nazis had turned out in full force, the British embassy, acting on strict orders from Whitehall in London, had dispatched only a third secretary, Geoffrey Harrison, to welcome the Windsors on behalf of Sir Neville Henderson, the ambassador. With some embarrassment, Harrison quickly handed the Duke a letter from Sir George Ogilvie-Forbes, the British *chargé d'affaires*, saying that Henderson had unexpectedly been called away from Berlin and that the embassy had been instructed to take no official notice of the Windsors' visit. Nor were they to be received at the embassy—a fact which both Wallis and David took as a deliberate humiliation.[7] "Both the Duke and Duchess were very, very hurt at not being extended any sort of regular welcome in Berlin," recalls Forwood.[8]

When the welcoming ceremony had ended, Ley, who was to act as their official host for the duration of the visit, escorted the Duke and Duchess to his waiting black Mercedes and climbed in between them on the rear seat. The driver wore an SS uniform, and four other SS officers, one on each running board, and two armed guards in the front seat added a grim touch. As the car set off, the gathered crowd of several hundred erupted into loud cheers and applause.[9]

The sleek Mercedes raced along Berlin's impressive boulevards at breakneck speed. This so unsettled Wallis that she complained to David later that evening. As the visit progressed and the motorcades continued their dangerous pace, the Duke was forced to tell Ley that either he order his driver to slow down or he and his wife would ride in another car altogether.[10]

The Duke and Duchess were given a spacious suite at the luxurious Kaiserhof Hotel. From their windows, they could look across at Hitler's stunning and massive new Reich Chancellery, its marble walls stretching for hundreds of feet along the avenue. When they arrived at the hotel, the Windsors were welcomed by a specially invited crowd that serenaded them with a bombastic song, composed for the occasion by the Propaganda Ministry on the orders of its head, Josef Goebbels.

The following day, Wallis and David embarked on separate programs. The Duchess was taken to a Nazi Welfare Society department workhouse where she was shown women happily engaged in sewing clothes for the poor. Since her mother, Alice, had done much the same thing in Baltimore, Wallis was able to comment with some interest and knowledge on the products before her; she even tried her hand at communicating in her less-than-perfect German, although the accompanying translator was swift to ensure that no misunderstanding occurred.

While Wallis was thus engaged, David was taken on a tour of the Stock Machine Works at Grünewald. He was impressed by the amenities offered to the workers there, including a restaurant, concert hall, and swimming pool. In fluent German, he spoke with many of those he encountered, questioning them as to their lives, their workday, their pay rates, and their children. That afternoon, David was guest of honor at a free concert given for a thousand workers by the Berlin Labor Front Orchestra during which selections from Wagner and Liszt were played. The concert ended with "Deutschland Ueber Alles," "The Horst Wessel Song," and "God Save the King." Newsreel cameras were rolling as David, a wide smile on his face, was seen to raise his arm in the Nazi salute. Although his apologists have tried to explain this away as misinterpretation of a simple wave, the Duke himself later acknowledged that he had made the offending salute on several occasions during the trip. "There are times when it's necessary to do or say certain things," he told his friend J. Paul Getty, "and then allow them to remain on the record. Wallis and I both have broad shoulders. We can bear the load."[11] As Sir Dudley Forwood rightly points out, "that Nazi salute was no more than the simple courtesy one always extended to one's hosts. If His Royal Highness went to a country where the people rubbed noses in greeting, he would do so. The salute was nothing more than good manners."[12]

That evening, Dr. Ley hosted a party for the Duke and Duchess at his country estate. Among the guests were Joachim von Ribbentrop; SS leader Heinrich Himmler; Rudolf Hess and his wife, Ilse; and Minister of Propaganda Josef Goebbels and his wife, Magda. Goebbels failed to make a favorable impression: Wallis later described him as "a tiny, wispy gnome with an enormous skull. His wife was the prettiest woman I saw in Germany." Together they reminded her of "Beauty and the Beast."[13] Ilse Hess was fascinated by Wallis. She later recalled her as "a lovely, charming, warm and clever woman with a heart of gold and an affection for her husband that she made not the slightest attempt to conceal."[14]

The next morning, Wallis remained at the hotel while her husband set off on a long inspection tour. At Crossensee, he visited the training school of the Death's Head Division of the Elite Squad of the SS. Once the SS band had finished playing "God Save the King," David toured the medieval-style facility, with its thick stone walls, thatched roofs, and tall towers. After lunch, he was driven to the Stargard military airport, where he boarded a twelve-passenger plane that belonged to Ley and made an aerial inspection of a Nazi youth camp along the shores of the Baltic Sea. While David was thus occupied, Wallis toured the former Imperial Palaces at Potsdam.

On October 14, Wallis and David paid a visit to the Berlin War Museum and the Pergamon Museum. That afternoon, they were driven into the countryside to meet with Field Marshal Hermann Goering and his wife, Emmy, at their magnificent country estate, Karinhalle, some forty miles from Berlin. Escorted by Luftwaffe officers, the Windsors' motorcade turned through the long, tall stone piers which marked the entrance to the estate and swept through the forest to the clearing where the house stood. Wallis later recalled how it had appeared out of the rain and mist, a massive baronial house of white stone walls pierced with towers and arcades and topped with a steep thatched roof.[15]

Goering himself was greatly worried over the visit; he was keenly aware that Hitler expected him to do all in his power to favorably influence the Duke toward Germany. Just before the Windsors arrived at Karinhalle, Goering told his wife, "Please make everything nice for them—this visit means a lot to me."[16]

Immaculately dressed in a white uniform covered with medals, Goering stood at the side of his wife, waiting at the front door to greet the Duke and Duchess. The foursome took tea at a round table set up in the hall, an immense room filled with modern furniture. Although a translator was present, the two couples managed on their own: David spoke German to Goering and his wife, while Wallis spoke English and French to Emmy Goering and French with Goering himself. The Duke questioned Goering at length about housing conditions. "He showed himself to be very well informed about the Reichs Government's building program," Emmy Goering recalled, "and talked exhaustively about the plans which he himself had had to improve the social position of the British working man. . . . The Duchess, who was dressed with amazingly simple elegance, pleased me even more than the Duke. I found myself sitting opposite to a real lady and I could not help thinking that this woman would certainly have cut a good figure on the Throne of England."[17]

Wallis asked Emmy Goering to show her around Karinhalle. The house was enormous, with vast rooms hung with Rembrandts and filled with an eclectic mixture of furnishings; the tall windows looked out over magnificent views of the forest beyond. She noted a gymnasium in the basement filled with weights, electric horses, and bars and inspected the servants' rooms, which had the occupant's names painted on the doors. Everything seemed overly picturesque; even the housemaids wore peasant dresses with pleated skirts and smocked blouses. In the barn, the women were joined by the Duke and the field marshal, who delighted in showing his guests an enormous toy train which filled the room.[18]

The only jarring note came when they entered the library. David quickly turned to Wallis and pointed to a large map of Europe which hung above the fireplace. On Goering's map, Germany and Austria had become one country, an ominous sign of the coming *Anschluss.* "Excuse me, Your Excellency *Herr* Field Marshal," David said, pointing at the map, "but that's rather important." According to Sir Dudley Forwood, Goering, rather sheepishly, replied, "It must be, Your Royal Highness." But the Duke would have none of it. He shook his head and said loudly, "Never, never, never."[19] As he and Wallis left, David turned to the Goerings and said in German, "This was the nicest visit of all those we have made in Germany."[20]

The Duke and Duchess paid further visits to Dresden, Nuremberg, Stuttgart, and Munich. Throughout these long days, they were introduced to and escorted by various Nazi officials. The only jarring note was the continued presence of Ley himself, "a rather awful little man," in the words of Forwood.[21] Both Wallis and David found him a boorish, brutal lout; half the time he was with the Windsors, Ley was drunk, a state which only made him more vocal in expressing his admiration of the Third Reich and disapproval of the way in which England had treated the couple. Eventually, word of this behavior reached Hitler, and midway through the visit, Ley was relieved of his duty as official host.[22]

On October 15 the Duke and Duchess went to Essen, where they toured a large coal mine. To the surprise of his hosts, David insisted on climbing some fifteen hundred feet down into the shaft, accompanied by Dudley Forwood, to see for himself the conditions within. Following an afternoon visit to the Krupp's Armaments Factory, the Windsors attended a reception given in their honor by the president of the Rhine province. The next day, they visited Düsseldorf, where they attended an industrial exhibit. Wallis found the display boring, but

David was fascinated. A visit to a miners' hospital followed, where both the Duke and Duchess toured the wards and took time to sit down on the beds of several patients for impromptu chats.

On the twentieth, David's cousin Carl Eduard, Duke of Saxe-Coburg and Gotha, gave a dinner party in their honor at the Grand Hotel in Nuremberg. As the Windsors stood at the head of the receiving line, the hundred guests carefully made their way past the couple. Wallis noticed that each and every lady curtsied to her and called her "Royal Highness," gestures she deeply appreciated.[23]

The highlight of the visit came on October 22, when the Duke and Duchess accepted an invitation from Adolf Hitler to join him for tea at Berchtesgaden. No part of the Windsors' trip to Germany would cause more controversy that this single visit, but it is difficult, in retrospect, to explain why so much ink has been spilled condemning these few hours. Only three days earlier, Edward, Viscount Halifax—the British foreign secretary—had likewise visited Hitler at the express wish of both the British government and King George VI. Chamberlain, desperate to guarantee the future peace of Europe, was willing to negotiate; on his behalf, Halifax told the Führer that England was officially prepared to recognize the preponderance of German interests in Europe. Although nothing came of the visit, it was not the first, nor would it be the last, British attempt to sound out Hitler and actively form some sort of alliance, however uneasy.

The idea for the visit originated with Hitler himself. Neither David nor Wallis had expected to meet him; when he issued the invitation, however, they were honor-bound to accept. Had they refused, their decision would undoubtedly have caused a diplomatic incident. As it was, the Windsors were private citizens; neither brought any agenda to Berchtesgaden. Nor was there anything unusual in such a meeting; high-ranking visitors to Germany were often accorded private audiences with the Führer, which were simply regarded as a matter of courtesy. Under the circumstances, the Duke and Duchess of Windsor had little choice but to honor the Führer's invitation or reason to refuse it.

Hitler dispatched a private train to collect the Duke and Duchess, who were accompanied by Rudolf Hess. When they reached Berchtesgaden, they were joined by Dr. Paul Schmidt, Hitler's personal translator. The Windsors climbed into an open-topped black Mercedes and, escorted by a contingent of SS guards on motorcycles and a host of cars filled with detectives and armed officers, were driven up the mountain at Obersalzburg to Hitler's Berghof.

At the top of the hill, the procession rounded the drive and swung through the gates which marked the entrance court before the Berghof. Hitler, dressed in the brown Nazi Party jacket, black trousers, and black shoes, stood on the steps, waiting to greet them. "His face had a pasty pallor," Wallis recalled, "and under his mustache his lips were fixed in a kind of mirthless grimace. Yet at close quarters he gave one the feeling of great inner force. His hands were long and slim, a musician's hands, and his eyes were truly extraordinary—intense, unblinking, magnetic, burning with the same peculiar fire."[24]

Hitler led the Windsors into the entrance hall, past a huge painting of Chancellor Otto von Bismarck, and into an anteroom. There several tall, well-built young men stepped forward to remove their coats. They were then escorted through a hallway and down three steps into the immense drawing room. One wall was occupied by an enormous picture window with magnificent views of the snow-covered Alps stretching for miles in the distance. Hitler told the Duke he would like to speak with him privately, and Wallis was left with Rudolf Hess in the drawing room to await their return.

David would later recall that the ensuing conversation was utterly banal:

> My ostensible reason for going to Germany was to see for myself what National Socialism was doing in housing and welfare for the workers, and I tried to keep my conversation with the Führer to these subjects, not wishing to be drawn into a discussion of politics. . . . In a roundabout way, he encouraged me to infer that Red Russia was the only enemy, and that it was in Britain's interest and in Europe's too, that Germany be encouraged to strike east and smash Communism forever. . . . I confess frankly that he took me in. I believed him when he implied that he sought no war with England. . . .[25]

The hour-long interview was also recalled by the interpreter, Paul Schmidt:

> Hitler was evidently making an effort to be as amiable as possible towards the Duke, whom he regarded as Germany's friend, having especially in mind a speech the Duke had made some years before, extending the hand of friendship to Germany's ex-servicemen's associations. In these conversations there was, so far as I could see, nothing whatever to indicate whether the Duke of Windsor really sympathised with the ideology and practices of the Third Reich, as Hitler seemed to assume he did. Apart from some appreciative words for the measures taken in Germany in the field of social welfare, the Duke did not discuss political questions. . . .[26]

Finally, the Duke and Hitler returned to the drawing room to join Wallis for tea. David spoke to Hitler in German, although Hitler had ordered Schmidt to translate; several times, the Duke stopped the conversation to correct the translator, saying that he had misinterpreted what he had said. Hitler addressed few words to Wallis. The one chilling remark she did later recall was in answer to her compliment on the splendid architecture she and David had observed. "Our buildings," Hitler declared ominously, "will make more magnificent ruins than the Greeks."[27] After the Windsors had left the Berghof, Hitler turned to Schmidt and announced, "She would have made a good Queen."[28]

The Duke and Duchess were unprepared for the avalanche of criticism which greeted their German visit. They were accused of having been taken in by the Nazis, of swallowing without question the endless propaganda parade of happy workers and beautiful Aryan youth which had greeted them at every stop. Although the Duke was a man of powerful influence, his critics would argue, he had done nothing to discover the ugly reality behind the rumors of concentration camps and imposed brutality. He and Wallis had been used by the very forces which threatened the peace of the world. British MP Herbert Morrison, leader of the London County Council, declared, "The choice before ex-kings is either to fade out of the public eye or be a nuisance. It is a hard choice, perhaps, for one of his temperament, but the Duke of Windsor will be wise to fade."[29]

In retrospect, the Duke's decision to visit Germany, while it may be considered unfortunate for the damage it did to the reputations of him and his wife, cannot be regarded with any political significance. David knew little of the realities of the Nazi regime; in Hitler and the Third Reich he saw—as did so many others at the time—only the admirable economic and patriotic results of their achievements. It is doubtful that he was even aware of Hitler's policies on race. Wallis knew even less than her husband. Both feared Soviet Russia far more than they did any future threat from Germany.

Then, too, Germany was the country of David's heritage; his mother had raised him to speak the language as fluently as a native, and the walls of the royal residences of England were lined with portraits of his Hanoverian ancestors. "The Duke's first country— England—had cut him off," declares a friend. "It was only natural that, in his exile, he would look with misty eyes to the only other country with which he felt a close bond."[30]

Much of the criticism of the Windsors' tour of Germany stemmed from the fact that they were shown only what the Nazis wished them to see; they were not allowed to explore the conditions of those suffering under the Nazi regime, nor did they seem inclined to ask any questions or appear in any context which might have proved controversial. But surely the responsibility for some of this criticism must be laid squarely at the doors of both King George VI and his Foreign Office. Had the British government, acting upon the King's continued wish that his brother be marginalized, not insisted that the Duke be ignored by their own diplomats during his visit and left to misstep on his own without any advice or counsel from the embassy, almost certainly the results of the trip would have been different. At the very least, embassy officials would have been able to ensure that the Duke and Duchess avoided any appearances which might cause offense or lead to misinterpretation.

David himself later admitted that his enthusiasm during the visit had been a mistake. "I acknowledge now that, along with too many other well-meaning people, I let my admiration for the good side of German character dim what was being done to it by the bad," he declared. "I thought that . . . the immediate task . . . of my generation . . . was to prevent another conflict between Germany and the West that could bring down our civilization. . . . I thought that the rest of us could be fence-sitters while the Nazis and the reds slogged it out."[31]

In context, the Windsors' trip to Germany was no more damaging either to British politics, world peace, or their own reputations than any of the numerous visits undertaken in the same period by any number of politicians and diplomats. Certainly it cannot be seen in the same light, for example, as the infamous September 1938 visit by Neville Chamberlain to Hitler at Berchtesgaden, a visit which took place with George VI's full blessing and support. When Chamberlain returned to London with Hitler's signature on the Munich Accord, he went straight to Buckingham Palace, where the King was overjoyed. George VI's endorsement of this policy of appeasement with Hitler climaxed when he and Chamberlain appeared together on the balcony of the palace that evening, triumphantly proclaiming that peace, with the Führer's cooperation, was now at hand. And yet the same voices raised in outrage against the visit of the Duke and Duchess of Windsor to Germany in 1937 have not damned the far more significant overture toward the Third Reich made with the approval of his brother George VI. It is but one example of the Royal Family's relentless circle of protective courtiers ensuring that criticism of the monarch remained buried; the Duke and Duchess of Windsor, alone and without benefit of a press office or public-relations advice, were left to founder on their own before the eyes of the world.

The Windsors had hoped to visit America that fall; after their return from Germany to Paris, they continued to work on the arrangements, which were being negotiated by Charles Bedaux on their behalf.

Bedaux arranged for the Duke and Duchess to travel on the German liner *Bremen* and arrive in New York on November 11. David expressed a wish to meet with President Franklin Roosevelt; tour industrial plants; make several speeches emphasizing the need for peace; and accompany Wallis to visit her relatives as well. At first, everything seemed as if it would go off without any problem. Bedaux received assurances that the president would receive the Duke and Duchess for tea at the White House. George Summerlin, chief of protocol for the U.S. State Department, would welcome the Windsors and remain with them until they left. Two weeks before the proposed tour, David delivered a speech at the Anglo-American Press Association lunch in Paris in which he touched upon both the recent visit to Germany and the forthcoming trip to America:

> Some of the recent misstatements concerning the Duchess and myself have caused us considerable concern and embarrassment, and might well lead to dangerous consequences. . . . Our visit to Germany has been very interesting, and we are now looking forward to our tour of America, and to further opportunities of making a study of the methods which have been adopted in the leading countries of the world in dealing with housing and industrial conditions. . . . I am now a very happily married man, but my wife and I are neither content nor willing to lead a purely inactive life of leisure. We hope and feel that in due course the experience we gain from our travels will enable us, if given fair treatment, to make some contribution, as private individuals, toward the solving of some of the vital problems that beset the world today."[32]

On November 4 the American ambassador in Paris, William Bullitt, wrote to President Roosevelt:

> I talked to the Duke of Windsor and his Duchess for several hours last night. . . . He is much calmer and more self-confident, and seems to be taking serious interest in housing and other problems connected with the life of the industrial workers. Incidentally, he drank almost nothing and is obviously intensely in love with his wife. . . .
>
> I am sorry that Mrs. Roosevelt will be on her speaking tour when the Windsors arrive and I explained to them both, as you ordered, that the tour had been arranged months in advance and could not be cancelled. . . . Incidentally, the Duchess expressed at considerable length, and apparently with sincerity, a deep admiration for Mrs. Roosevelt, and I hope they may meet somewhere sometime while the Windsors are in the United States.[33]

The British government, and most especially Buckingham Palace, was greatly worried over the forthcoming visit of the Windsors to America. By this time, King George VI saw a plot in nearly every move his brother made, and he was convinced that this proposed trip was nothing more than a publicity stunt. Sir Ronald Lindsay, the British ambassador to Washington, D.C., confided as much to the Earl of Crawford, who himself wrote: "The King and Queen are in a state of extreme nervousness about it. . . ."[34]

Lindsay "was staggered by the instructions sent to our Ministers and Ambassadors" regarding the Duke of Windsor and his wife. "They are *forbidden* to put him up in the house, or to give him a dinner, though they may give him a bite of luncheon, or to present him officially to anyone, or to accept invitations from him (except for a bite of luncheon) or to have him met at the station by anyone bigger than a junior secretary."[35]

All of this worry, however, was in vain. Bedaux's connection to the trip resulted in its ruin. American labor regarded both him and his methods as enemies of the working class and feared that his interest was the complete automation of all factories. As soon as word spread that he was behind the planned industrial tours to be undertaken by the Duke and Duchess, a small but highly vocal minority of labor leaders organized demonstrations against Bedaux. Soon strikes and pickets were proposed for any factory or industrial complex which Bedaux would arrange for the Duke to tour.

After much thought, Bedaux withdrew himself from the organization of the tour. From America, he cabled the Duke and Duchess: "Because of the mistaken attack upon me here, I am convinced that your proposed tour will be difficult under my auspices. I respectfully . . . implore you to relieve me completely of all duties in connection with it."[36]

Nothing, however, could halt the damage which had already been done. It soon became apparent that any trip to America would prove a public-relations disaster for the Windsors. To Wallis, who had been greatly looking forward to returning home and to seeing her family again, these developments were a considerable disappointment. Even more, however, she knew how much the visit had meant to her husband; such foreign tours allowed him, however briefly, to relive some of the sense of personal worth he had lost on abdicating the throne.

The decision, however, was made for the Windsors. One day, in the midst of all this planning, Dudley Forwood received a cable saying that George VI wished to speak with him at once. Forwood rang Buckingham Palace and was quickly put through to the King. "Tell David he's not to bloody go to America!" Bertie shouted at the equerry before hanging up the telephone. Forwood went straight to the Duke and informed him that he had just spoken with the King. "His Majesty," Forwood rather diplomatically said, "is highly concerned with your safety if you go to America, and the American Ambassador recommends that you don't go."

"Oh, all right then," the Duke said angrily, "cancel the bloody thing!"[37]

29

Exile in Paris

AT THE END of their honeymoon, the Windsors had settled into a third-floor apartment in Paris's luxurious Hotel Meurice. They chose the Meurice because it offered not only dignity but also privacy. "The service and food were of the highest quality," noted Dina Wells Hood, "the atmosphere affluent, restrained, discreet."[1] The international set flocked to the Ritz, but neither the Duke nor the Duchess had any wish for publicity where their private lives were concerned.

Their suite, consisting of two bedrooms and a sitting room between, overlooked the Tuileries Gardens. The Meurice, however, was only intended as a temporary home: neither the Duke nor the Duchess expected to spend any length of time in exile. Both were still uncertain about what the future held, and with their financial situation not yet settled in the fall of 1937, they were reluctant to make permanent plans.[2] Both assumed that they would return to England and take up residence in the Fort. David had brought few of his belongings with him into exile; most of his things, along with trunks which belonged to Wallis and the furnishings from her London flats, had been placed in storage at Frogmore House, just below Windsor Castle.

For Wallis, the prospect of continued exile was unwelcome. "It was quite clear to me from what she said that she hopes to get back to England," wrote Harold Nicolson. "When I asked her why she didn't get a house of her own somewhere, she said, 'One never knows what may happen. I don't want to spend all my life in exile.'"[3]

Circumstances for a return, however, were not in the Windsors' favor. The feeling against them, especially among the court and the Royal Family, remained as strong as ever. Wallis wrote to Aunt Bessie: "I don't think we will be settled anywhere until the English atmosphere is cleared but the terror of the Duke's return remains—everyone is so afraid that it would upset the King's so-called popularity. If that is so well-established as they all say, what is there to worry about? . . ."[4]

In Paris, the Windsors largely kept to themselves. "The British colony in Paris as a whole were as aloof in their attitude to the Windsors as were their official representatives," recalled Dina Wells Hood. "Intensely interested in the Windsors' doings, they were at the same time inclined to adopt a somewhat disconcerting attitude towards the exiled King and his Duchess. I was struck by this when I was talking one day to the wife of an English official in Paris, whom I met at a friend's house. This lady was discussing the merits of a certain housemaid and I happened to mention that the maid had once been in the service of the Duchess. 'Well, that's no recommendation!' rejoined my compatriot."[5]

This antipathy toward the Duchess often led to embarrassing social situations. No one knew how to treat her: Should women curtsy to her as the wife of a Royal Duke, as would be expected, or should they ignore her, as Buckingham Palace had declared? When Lady Pembroke objected to several women curtsying to the Duchess of Windsor, David angrily told the *Evening Standard* in London, "We are less interested in curtsys than in courtesies."[6]

But Wallis made determined efforts to win over her critics. In November 1937 she accepted an invitation to open a charity sale on behalf of the British Episcopal Church of Christ at Neuilly. When she and David appeared at the bazaar, they were greeted with polite, if somewhat reserved, applause. This was the first occasion since the abdication on which Wallis had come face-to-face with any substantial group of British citizens, and her performance was a resounding success. She toured the numerous booths, happily exchanging small talk with the curious women, and even purchased several of their offerings. To those who had only read about this much-discussed and despised woman, the reality of their encounter with Wallis proved a startling experience. She was warm and friendly, smiled and laughed; although she was undoubtedly nervous, she appeared completely at ease. With the official welcome, Wallis climbed to the podium and delivered her first public speech: "We appreciate the welcome which you have given us. We are glad to be here at your community gathering and wish it every success. In declaring this sale open, I wish to congratulate all those who have worked for it and contributed to it, and I am sure they will meet with a generous response." When the Windsors departed, amid much waving and generous smiles, the applause was deafening.[7]

The beginning of 1938 brought at least some satisfaction when Wallis was named one of the ten best-dressed women in the world, a distinction she was to hold for nearly four decades. The world's press was fascinated with her every move; nothing escaped their notice, from the shade of her dresses to the size of her shoes. When, in April

1938, she changed the style of her hair, it was cause for immediate concern in the world press: "The Duchess of Windsor's famous coiffure,
which launched a thousand imitations the world round is no more.
The Duchess has bobbed her hair," the American artist, Porter
Woodruff, said today in a letter from Paris. "Her long, smooth, soft-
waved tresses knotted at the back of her slim neck have ceased to be
the most distinguishing physical feature of the world's most publicized
woman."[8]

Wallis found such press attention unwelcome and unrelenting.
She explained to Anne Morrow Lindbergh that because she had not
grown up before the public eye, as had her husband, she often felt
unequal to the challenge of coping with such pressures. "She spoke
with some feeling about her not wanting it to *change* her, to get the
best of her," Lindbergh wrote. Wallis complained about the inability
to even shop in ordinary ways any longer: "And you find yourself
doing strange things, like running out the back door" and "going into
a shop for blue ribbon and coming out with black because you were so
flustered."[9]

Wallis rarely spoke to the press in these early years of her marriage to David out of respect for his position and the traditional distance which royalty maintained. But there were occasional exceptions.
To Alice Henning of the *London Sunday Dispatch* she declared in the
spring of 1939:

> The life the Duke and I lead now has no "news value." It is as
> unsensational now as we have always wanted it to be. In many
> ways we live more quietly than the average married couple. . . . I
> expect to take my husband's name and rank, that is all. And I
> expect ordinary graciousness in human relationships. . . . People
> little realize how much we want to avoid excitement and so-
> called glamour. There have been so many pictures of us getting in
> and out of trains that we feel we do not want to get in or out of
> a train again! . . . I could never possibly have the number of hair-
> dressers that are supposed to have attended me on various occa-
> sions. I hate publicity. The dresses I wear and all that. Those are
> not the real things of life. I hope as I grow older I realize it and
> not go about wearing frilly frocks or adopting modes such as the
> one that shows a little bit of petticoat below the dress. I want to
> grow old with dignity, but with fair measure of tolerance towards
> the new generation which I hope to be able to understand.[10]

Despite the unrelenting press attention and public interest in
seemingly every move the Windsors' made, at least one faction was
determined to ignore them: Buckingham Palace and the Foreign Office

continued to insist that the Duke and Duchess be ostracized. In January 1938, the British ambassador in Paris hosted a reception for the president of France. It seemed only natural that the Duke and Duchess of Windsor, as the highest-ranking English couple then in the city, would attend. But when the embassy included their names on the guest list which went to Whitehall, Buckingham Palace immediately objected. King George VI ordered Alan Lascelles to write at once to the embassy, telling them that it would be inappropriate for the Windsors to be asked to attend any official ceremony. "No doubt such decisions could be justified in terms of protocol," writes the Duke's official biographer, Philip Ziegler, "but the situation was not one for which any precedent existed, and it is hard not to feel that a less doctrinaire approach could have been adopted without undue risk to the monarchy."[11]

This was simply a taste of what was to come. In the spring of 1938, George VI and Queen Elizabeth were scheduled to make a state visit to France. It would be cause for endless rumor if the King and Queen, while in Paris, avoided meeting the Duke and Duchess, and David asked the faithful Walter Monckton to try to convince his brother to at least invite him and Wallis to some official reception for the sake of family unity. But when Monckton gently raised the issue, George VI absolutely refused to include his brother or sister-in-law in any part of his visit or even to meet with them privately while in Paris. His rather grim explanation to Monckton was that he worried that by receiving the Windsors their stature might possibly be raised among French society.[12]

When David received word of this stunning decision, he sat down and wrote a pathetic, almost pleading letter to his brother, but the King refused to reconsider his decision. The state visit to France was a great triumph for the King and Queen, who were loudly cheered everywhere they went. But Edouard Daladier, the French premier, was less than won over. After spending a considerable amount of time with the British monarch and his wife, Daladier described the King as a "moron." His impression of the Queen was just as unfavorable. Daladier called her "an excessively ambitious woman who would be ready to sacrifice every other country in the world in order that she might remain Queen Elizabeth of England."[13]

David was deeply hurt and humiliated by what he and Wallis both considered to be continued punishment for the abdication. In despair, he wrote to his mother, asking her frankly what the future held where relations between him and Wallis and the Royal Family were concerned. The Queen replied:

You will remember how miserable I was when you informed me of your intended marriage and abdication and how I implored you not to do so for our sake and for the sake of the country. You did not seem able to take in any point of view but your own. . . . I do not think you have ever realized the shock which the attitude you took up caused your family and the whole Nation. It seemed inconceivable to those who had made such sacrifices during the war that you, as their King, refused a lesser sacrifice. While sympathizing with your distress of mind at the time, I fail to see that your marriage has altered the point of view which we all took up, or that it is possible for you both to come to England for a long time to come. Naturally I am very sorry not to see you, as my feelings to you as your Mother remain the same, and our being parted and the cause of it grieves me beyond words. After all, all my life I have put my Country before anything else, and I simply cannot change now. The feeling about your marriage is far deeper and wider than you seem to realize, and your return to England would only mean division and controversy.[14]

Such a response only fed the Windsors' growing conviction that they would never be welcome again in England, at least not by members of the Duke's own family. The realization that they were doomed to be outcasts for the rest of their lives struck hard at their pride. "The question," wrote Wallis, "was whether we should conduct ourselves like fugitives, always on the run, or put on a show of our own. David was born to be a King; he *had been* a King. In marriage, the palaces were lost; so was the trained staff that smoothed out everything for him. But he still had the mind and character and, yes, the interests of a King; and my duty, as I saw it, was to evoke for him the nearest equivalent to a kingly life that I could produce without a kingdom."[15]

Wallis's first step toward establishing a regular life for her and David was to find some residence other than the temporary rooms they had taken at the Hotel Meurice. She began to search for a house to rent. Both she and David considered the idea of moving to America, but Monckton reminded them that the prohibitive tax rates which existed in England would also apply should the Windsors return to Wallis's homeland. Residence in France seemed an acceptable compromise; the country was cosmopolitan enough to satisfy any future desire for society, there was an established aristocracy, and Paris was close enough to England to make return visits easy when they might become possible.

She wanted to live in Paris itself, while David wished for a country house, where he could indulge his love of gardening. Any house she found in the city lacked enough space to make him happy or too little garden to ensure privacy. Eventually, she found a house in Versailles, the Château de la Maye, which belonged to the widow of French politician Paul Dupuy. The house sat in a large private garden which boasted a swimming pool, tennis courts, and a nine-hole private golf course—a feature which won David over. Wallis asked Dudley Forwood to look into the details, and the equerry managed to sign a six-month lease, which included all of the furniture.[16]

The lease of the house, however, failed to stifle David's desire to return to England. He honestly believed that he and Wallis could be of use to his brother in performing public duties on behalf of the monarchy. His continued hope was spurred on by reports from Monckton that Prime Minister Chamberlain was at least investigating the possibility of a return. On the last weekend in August 1938, Chamberlain and Monckton were both invited to Balmoral to discuss the Duke's return with the King. Monckton was somewhat surprised when George VI invited Queen Elizabeth to join the discussion but said nothing.

Chamberlain explained that the British government had no objection to the return of the Duke and Duchess of Windsor and that, as prime minister, he no longer saw how the former King and his wife could be kept out of the country. He even suggested that the Duke and Duchess of Windsor might be of some assistance to the King, able to take over some of the ceremonial duties which the Royal Family was expected to fulfill. Monckton wrote: "The King himself, though he was not anxious for the Duke to return as early as November 1938 . . . was not fundamentally against the Prime Minister's view. But I think the Queen felt quite plainly that it was undesirable to give the Duke any effective sphere of work. I felt then, as always, that she naturally thought that she must be on her guard because the Duke of Windsor, to whom the other brothers had always looked up, was an attractive, vital creature who might be the rallying point for any who might be critical of the new King who was less superficially endowed with the arts and graces that please."[17]

It was left to Monckton to convey the unfavorable decision that the return of the Windsors was to be delayed for the foreseeable future. As an olive branch, however, he explained that the Duke and Duchess of Gloucester were to stop in Paris on their return from an African trip and that they would like to meet with the Windsors. David's brother Harry and his wife, Alice, would therefore become the first members of the Royal Family to visit him and Wallis since the abdication. David, needless to say, was overjoyed; although he and his brother had never been particularly close, he detected in the move a softening of attitudes on his family's part. Wallis, who had met both of the Gloucesters previously at the Fort, was nervous, fearing that she would "put a foot wrong" and harm her husband. But when the Gloucesters arrived, everything went smoothly. The two couples lunched at the Hotel Meurice, and in the evening the Windsors took the Gloucesters to dine at Larue's in the rue Royal. Both Wallis and David were convinced that the visit at least indicated a willingness on the part of the Royal Family to bridge the differences separating them. Neither would learn the truth: that the visit had not been the idea of King George VI but had taken place at the insistence of the prime minister. Both of the Gloucesters had been unwillingly pushed to make this gesture. "It was Neville Chamberlain's idea, not ours," the Duchess of Gloucester candidly wrote many years later.[18]

When the Gloucesters returned to London, they were greeted with several critical letters expressing indignation that they had met the Duchess of Windsor. Such incidents, though rare, were often used to bolster the perception that the British public stood opposed to the return of the Duke and Duchess. But such propaganda, often repeated, is without merit. A Gallup poll conducted in 1939 revealed that 61 percent of the British public wanted the Windsors to return to England; only 16 percent opposed such a move. The inevitable conclusion is that the only real opposition to the Windsors' return came from the court and the Royal Family.[19]

Nor is it correct to assume that the Duke and Duchess of Windsor were inundated with hate mail and virulent letters opposing their return to England. In fact, most of their mail was positive, as Dina Wells Hood recalled: "Every time an announcement of the Windsors' impending return to England appeared in the press, hundreds of fans wrote to the duke expressing their delight at the good news. They reiterated their disappointment at his abdication, their sorrow at his exile."[20]

Nevertheless, the Windsors remained in exile, and the Royal Family did its best to ignore their existence. One particularly hurtful example came that fall, when David was not invited to attend the unveiling of the memorial to his father in St. George's Chapel, Windsor. David had paid half the cost of the memorial, which was sculpted by Reid Dick, and fully expected, as George V's eldest son, to be present during its dedication. He was beside himself with anger when he learned that the Royal Family had held the ceremony without him. Even more troubling was the way in which he was ignored: not just as a former king but even as a son.

Wallis worried greatly over such humiliations; she tried as best as she could to somehow fill the void in her husband's life, to provide for him both an alternative to the family he had lost, the country he had left, and the throne whose duties had once filled his days.[21] At first, these attempts amounted to little more than idle entertainments. Then, in May 1939, David made his first serious incursion since the abdication into the political arena.

Fred Bate, the head of British and European operations for the

National Broadcasting Company in America, asked David if he would like to make a speech to the United States promoting the idea of world peace. He immediately agreed and decided that he would symbolically deliver it from the battlefields of World War I at Verdun. There was nothing objectionable about the speech, but the timing turned out to be rather unfortunate.

King George VI and Queen Elizabeth had been scheduled to make a tour of the United States beginning in May 1939, at roughly the same time that Bate suggested the Duke should broadcast. Bate had already arranged for David to deliver his speech; a potential conflict seemed averted when Buckingham Palace announced that the King and Queen, due to the worsening international situation, had decided to postpone their American visit. However, on May 2, George VI was advised that the trip to America was vital to the British cause should a European war erupt, and the royal tour, previously canceled, was now back on. On May 5, the King and Queen sailed aboard the *Empress of Australia* for North America.

It was too late for Bate to cancel the speech. The Duke and Duchess of Windsor arrived at Verdun on May 7 and were welcomed in an official ceremony by the mayor. They toured the battlefields that afternoon and spent the rest of the evening working on the speech, which would be delivered on the following day.[22]

Wallis helped David draft the speech. He wanted to emphasize not only the need for peace but the responsibility of the nations of the world to secure that peace for future generations. As a piece of antiwar propaganda, it was effective:

> I am speaking tonight from Verdun, where I have been spending a few days visiting one of the greatest battlefields of the last war. Upon this and other battlefields throughout the world, millions of men suffered and died and, as I talk to you from this historic place, I am deeply conscious of the presence of the great company of the dead; and I am convinced that could they make their voices heard they would be with me in what I am about to say.
>
> For two and a half years I have deliberately kept out of public affairs and I still propose to do so. I speak for no one but myself, without the previous knowledge of any government. I speak simply as a soldier of the last war, whose most earnest prayer is that such cruel and destructive madness shall never again overtake mankind.
>
> I break my self-imposed silence now only because of the manifest danger that we may all be drawing nearer to a repetition of the grim events that happened a quarter of a century ago. The

grave anxieties of the time in which we live compel me to raise my voice in expression of the universal longing to be delivered from the fears that beset us and to return to normal conditions. You and I know that peace is a matter too vital for our happiness to be treated as a political question. We also know that in modern warfare victory will lie only with the powers of evil. Anarchy and chaos are the inevitable results, with consequent misery for us all.

I cannot claim for myself the expert knowledge of a statesman, but I have at least had the good fortune to travel the world and therefore to study human nature. This valuable experience has left me with the profound conviction that there is no land whose people want war. This I believe to be as true of the German nation as it is of the British nation to which I belong, of you in America and of the French nation on whose friendly soil I now reside.

International understanding does not always spring up spontaneously itself. There are times when it has to be deliberately sought and negotiated, and political tension is apt to weaken that spirit of mutual concession in which conflicting claims can best be adjusted. The problems that concern us at this moment are only the reproductions on a larger scale of the jealousies and suspicions of everyday life. In our personal contacts we all strive to live in harmony with our fellowmen. Otherwise modern civilization could never have come into existence.

Are we now going to destroy that civilization by failing to do internationally what we have learned to do individually? In their public utterances the heads of governments are at one in declaring that war would be disastrous to the well-being of their people. Whatever political disagreements may have arisen in the past, the supreme importance of averting war will, I feel confident, impel all those in power to renew their endeavours to bring about a peaceful settlement.

Among measures that I feel might well be adopted to this end is the discouragement of all that harmful propaganda which, from whatever source, tends to poison the minds of the peoples of the world. I personally deplore, for example, the use of such terms as "encirclement" and "aggression." They can only arouse just those dangerous political passions that it should be the aim of us all to subdue.

It is in a larger spirit than that of personal or purely national interest that peace should be preserved. The statesmen who set themselves to restore international security and confidence must act as good citizens of the world and not only as good Frenchmen, Italians, Germans, Americans, or Britons. The benefit to their own nations must be sought through the benefit to the wider community of which we are all members.

In the name of those who fell in the last war I urge all political leaders to be resolute in the discharge of this mission. I appeal to them in the name of the living, whose existence and happiness are in their hands, and I appeal to them especially in the name of the youth of the present day, with all its incalculable potentialities of future service to the human race.

The world has not yet recovered from the effects of the last carnage, which in each and every country decimated my generation. The greatest success that any government could achieve for its own national policies would be nothing in comparison with the triumph of having contributed to save humanity from the terrible fate that threatens it today.

Somehow, I feel that my words tonight will find a sincere echo in all who hear them. It is not for me to put forward concrete proposals; that must be left to those who have the power to guide their nations toward closer understanding.

God grant that they may accomplish that great task before it is too late.[23]

The opinions expressed in the Duke's speech were completely in harmony with both British sentiment at the time and the government's policy of negotiation and appeasement. But no one was prepared to believe that the timing—coming as it did on the heels of his brother's important visit to America—was accidental. Although the evidence is clear that not only did the idea for the speech originate with Bate rather than David and that it had been planned prior to the sudden revival of the royal visit, various writers have attempted to use it against the Windsors. Sarah Bradford, for example, declares: "It is hard not to suspect that there was a decided intent on the part of the Windsors to upstage the King and Queen before they arrived in America and to draw attention to the Duke as an international figure of importance."[24] The truth, of course, was quite different, but few in court circles were willing to believe anything but the worst of the Duke and Duchess.

On May 8 the same day on which David was scheduled to make the speech, the *Daily Express* editorialized: "The decision of the Duke of Windsor to broadcast to the United States today is to be regretted. The moment is unhappily chosen. The King is on his way to America. Any word spoken on the United States at present should come from him. It would have been better for the Duke to wait. It is reported that the Duke will make an appeal for peace in his broadcast. Such an appeal would have been uttered more appropriately after the King's peace mission to the Dominion had been brought to a conclusion."[25] That private citizens were entitled to freely express their views, especially at critical moments in history, seemed to have completely escaped the editors of the *Daily Express*.

But while newspaper editors, members of the court, and the royals were content to criticize the Duke's speech, the majority of his listeners found themselves in wholehearted agreement. Dina Wells Hood recalled the flood of letters which soon arrived in support, "tangible proofs of approval. The broadcast brought a huge fan mail in its wake. Hundreds of people all over the world voiced their admiration of the Duke's gesture. . . ."[26]

30

Two Houses

IN THE SPRING OF 1938, Wallis learned that La Croë, the villa near Cap d'Antibes that she had originally considered a suitable setting for her marriage to the Duke, was available for rent. La Croë was a large house, set in an immaculately landscaped park big enough to ensure their privacy and boasting magnificent views of the Mediterranean. Both she and David enjoyed the surroundings and the warm weather, and so they signed a [ten-year lease] on the estate, at a cost of some 100,000 francs a month (approximately $3,000 U.S.).[1] It was to become their first real home together and also their undoubted favorite.[2]

La Croë offered Wallis a welcome outlet for her creative talents. Few women of the twentieth century have been as well known for their style and taste as the Duchess of Windsor; through lavish surroundings, beautiful clothes, and studied sophistication, Wallis elevated the daily life of both herself and David to a fine art form. Her flair for decoration inspired and drew admiration. "There are not many women," wrote Rebecca West, "who can pick up the keys of a rented house, raddled by long submission to temporary inmates, and make it look as if a family of cheerful good taste had been living there for two or three centuries."[3]

In all of her houses, Wallis set out to fashion and furnish, to the best of her ability and talent, deliberate re-creations of those rooms and atmospheres in which her husband had been raised and lived. He had given up his entire heritage to be with her; now she supervised construction of miniature kingdoms over which they would both rule as king and queen. These houses, like those that David had left behind in England, were powerful statements not only of privilege but also of heritage and instantly both impressed and demanded respect. The Windsors' palaces of exile included splendid rooms in which they could receive and entertain appropriately and were filled with the trappings of royalty: important paintings of titled ancestors; Fabergé boxes

311

and trinkets; family photographs in crested leather frames; and regimental trophies awarded to the Duke through his years of military service. Surfaces of stationery, buttons of liveries, cigarette cases, and crests on picture frames were embossed and crowned with coronets and monograms, further emphasizing the royal associations.

The results were all the more remarkable because Wallis brought little experience to her role of chatelaine. Through sheer effort and the welcome advice of others, she managed to succeed. Her talents lay not only in recognizing what a room needed but in setting aside her own ego and allowing those more skilled than she to craft her own style.

The success of Wallis's first experiments at La Croë became apparent when the Windsors arrived to take up residence at their villa. The twelve-acre estate lay hidden behind a tall stone wall and tall, carefully clipped hedges which completely ringed the grounds on the three sides facing the land. On either side of the entrance gates were small lodges, one of which housed the secretaries and members of the household, the other serving as the house of the concierge, Monsieur Valat, and his family. The gates were always kept locked; a telephone call alerted the lodge at the expected arrival or departure of a car to the estate, and Monsieur Valat always stood ready with his keys to open the gates.[4]

From the entrance gates, visitors could not see the villa; the drive swept in a great curve through the green lawns of the park, shaded by fir, pine, yew, eucalyptus, and cypress trees. A service drive branched off from the main road, leading through the thick groves of trees to the garages and kitchen court; hidden by a screen of flowering shrubs lay the tennis court and vegetable and cutting gardens.[5] At last the trees parted to reveal the tall, gleaming white villa, its windows hung with green shutters and shaded by matching awnings. "It was exquisitely simple and beautifully proportioned," recalled Dina Wells Hood, "and there was about it a certain air of remoteness. It seemed to me a dream-like place, cool, serene and aloof."[6]

Perched at the edge of the sea, La Croë rose three stories above the green lawns and stone terraces. A central portico supported by corinthian columns marked the main entrance to the house; above, a low balustrade rimmed the hipped roof, which was crowned with a small belvedere overlooking the Mediterranean. On the opposite façade, facing the sea, was a semicircular colonnade with ionic columns and enormous blue-and-white-striped awnings.

To advise her in decorating her new house, Wallis called upon the talents of her friend Lady Elsie Mendl. Lady Mendl arrived at La Croë with two assistants: Tony Montgomery, a former apprentice and an authority on antique furniture, and John McMullin, a features editor for *Vogue* and a respected arbiter of international taste and style. With

Wallis, they pored over paint and fabric samples, examined artists' sketches, and planned and replanned the arrangement of furniture. Wallis wished to emulate the sense of light and space beyond the house, and Lady Mendl advised her to paint the rooms in bright colors and use mirrors and the tall windows of the house itself to reflect the sea and sky beyond. Under her guidance, La Croë shone: the gilding of the woodwork, the lacquered screens and consoles, the enormous mirrors and glittering silver, all contributed to the sense of being adrift, creating a luminous prism of sun and sea. Before the Windsors took up residence, central heating and air conditioning were installed, along with an elevator.[7]

La Croë gave Wallis and David a chance to fill the house with their belongings that had been stored in England. The Duke's things from the Fort and York House, along with Wallis's possessions from her London flats, were shipped to the south of France. One afternoon, a long line of moving vans rolled up the drive at La Croë, and for the next few days, Wallis supervised the unpacking and distribution of crates of china, furniture, boxes of books, trunks of clothes, chests of linen, and hundreds of personal souvenirs, photographs, and paintings.[8]

From the portico at La Croë, tall double doors opened to a marble-floored vestibule, which in turn led to a large hall rising two stories. A magnificent marble staircase twisted to a second-floor gallery with wrought-iron railings, resting atop piers of grouped pilasters jutting into the room. The hall was dominated by the Duke's Order of the Garter banner, the ceremonial flag which had hung above his choir stall in St. George's Chapel, Windsor. Below it stood an antique lacquered Dutch chest on which rested a leather guest book.[9]

Directly through a set of mirrored double doors was the salon, an oval room with three tall French doors opening on to a semicircular colonnade. No one ever used the salon at La Croë; it was designed as a very formal space, an extension of the hall, and a means of reaching the terrace. Gilded consoles supported tall mirrors reflecting the shifting sunlight during the day and the glow of candles burning in the carved wall sconces at night, but there was little furniture.[10]

These two rooms served as an immediate and stunning introduction to the splendors of La Croë. There were only three principal rooms on the first floor—a drawing room, a library, and a dining room—but the effect created by their deliberate, almost theatrical decoration could not have been greater. Ceilings rose twenty feet, supported by walls paneled in elegant boiserie and pierced with French doors, which provided welcome breezes from the sea on long summer afternoons. Entire sections of wall were covered in mirrors surrounded by white-and-gold cornices and moldings; doors were also mirrored to provide an even greater sense of light and space. The luxurious effect was heightened by the antique Chinese vases and porcelain bowls kept filled with lavish, towering displays of the Duchess's favorite white arum lilies and orchids.

Wallis decorated the drawing room in shades of white, blue, and yellow, with accents of red and gold. The French doors were hung with yellow-and-light-blue curtains, which echoed the upholstery of the sofas and overstuffed chairs that had been brought from the Fort. Between the French doors stood gilded consoles on which sat two antique Chinese chests in red, gold, and black lacquer. The most significant piece of furniture in the room was the large mahogany desk on which David had signed the Instrument of Abdication, a rather curious piece, laden with memories, which would follow the Windsors to every house in which they lived.[11]

The library, used primarily by the Duke, was dominated by a portrait of Queen Mary, painted in the robes of the Order of the Garter, which hung above the marble fireplace. Two walls were covered with bookshelves of light oak; these were filled with his collection of presentation volumes and military awards and trophies. The sofas and chairs, carpet and curtains, were in red and white, designed by Wallis to provide both sharp and neutral contrasts to the pale beige of the bookshelves. In a far corner of the room stood a Steinway grand piano, used by the Windsors while entertaining.[12]

The dining room, like the other main rooms on the first floor, occupied a corner of the house, with windows on both outside walls. Wallis wanted a space which would dazzle in candlelight. The walls were painted white, with delicate boiserie picked out in blue and gold; the double doors and rounded overdoors were mirrored to reflect the yellow, white, and blue curtains which hung at the French doors. A large Chippendale table occupied the center of the room, surrounded by Empire-style chairs in white and gold. Above the sideboard hung a masterful equestrian portrait, *The Prince of Wales on Forest Witch*, painted by Sir Alfred Munnings.

The Duke and Duchess of Windsor each had a suite of rooms on the second floor. At La Croë, Wallis faithfully duplicated if not the exact surroundings then at least the spirit of David's bedroom at Fort Belvedere. The walls were painted cream, with white mouldings and cornices, which contrasted with the beige-and-scarlet curtains and carpet. The comfortable furniture was upholstered in chocolate and red. Against one wall hung a large damask tapestry in black, scarlet, and gold, showing the arms of a knight of the Order of the Garter.

Wallis's bedroom was decorated in shades of pink and apricot. Most of her furniture was in the fashionable art-deco style, with rounded edges and chrome accents; across her bed lay a heavily tufted satin spread embroidered with her intertwined initials. The most fascinating pieces of furniture were a dressing table and matching chest, painted with trompe l'oeil reminders of her relationship with the Prince of Wales: duplications of his letters to her; an invitation bearing the royal crest; a fan; a pair of long white evening gloves; a lipstick; a jeweled handbag; and a pair of David's golf socks.[13] Her bathroom, in scarlet and black, was dominated by an enormous gilded tub in the shape of a swan.[14]

There were six guest rooms at La Croë, two on the second floor and four on the third. The Rose Room took its name from the color of its decoration; French doors opened to a balcony overlooking the sea. Two antique red-and-gold beds, with a matching bow-fronted chest, gave the Venetian Room its exotic flavor. A staircase and elevator connected to the third-floor guest rooms: the Wedgwood Room, in blue and white; the Toile de Jouy Room, in red and white; the Blue Room, in pale shades of blue and white; and the Directoire, in gray and blue. Wallis kept these rooms filled with fresh flowers, selected especially to match the decoration of the room; towels, linens, even bath soap, were all coordinated to match the decorative scheme.[15]

At the very top of the house was the belvedere, surrounded by the roof terrace. Aside from a wet bar, a closet, and bathroom, the belvedere consisted of one large room which David used as his study. Wallis took particular care over this room and gave it a nautical theme to complement the rest of the house as well as the views of the Mediterranean. The walls and carpet were white, while the curtains at the enormous windows were navy blue, with anchors and rope designs in white. Most of the comfortable, overstuffed furniture was white, edged with navy blue piping. Shelves on two sides of the room held David's family photographs, further military awards, and racing and jumping trophies.[16]

The swimming pool stood at the edge of the sea, reached by a twisting staircase which led from the lawns above to the beach. Burton had cut the pool out of the side of the bluff; it was surrounded by rocks and resembled a natural tide pool. Two small pavilions also stood here, containing dressing rooms shaded by large red-and-white awnings. The red-and-blue-striped sun mattresses, deck chairs, and white lifebuoys were all crested with the Duke's coronet and the intertwined initials WE, for Wallis and Edward.[17]

La Croë also gave Wallis and David an opportunity to reestablish some of the trappings of the world which he had left behind in England. The Duke consulted his tailor in London, who produced the various liveries for the footmen: scarlet coats with gold collars, cuffs, and buttons for formal occasions; black suits with crimson, white, and gold–striped waistcoats and silver buttons for ordinary day and evening wear; and lightweight dress suits of pale gray alpaca for summers at La Croë. The buttons on these liveries were also crested with the Duke's coronet and the intertwined initials. This monogram also began to appear on stationery, note cards, envelopes, linens, and menu cards.[18]

Certain servants remained year-round at La Croë. This number included Monsieur Valat, the concierge, who, with his family, lived in the main gate lodge during the Windsors' residence and in the main house itself during their absence. Valat and his wife had a young son who was crippled and could not obtain any work. When the Duke and Duchess discovered this, they promptly gave him a position as clock winder in the house, for which he was handsomely paid.[19]

The Windsors entertained rather infrequently at La Croë, although there were almost always guests during their stays. More formal parties and receptions were reserved for the city; here, in the country, both Wallis and David relished the sense of freedom and sought to live as informally as possible. Often meals were served on the terrace overlooking the Mediterranean. In the evening, the house was floodlit: Hidden lights shone upon the milky-white façade, against the tall trees that rose into the night sky, and around the riot of colorful flowers and shrubs that filled the gardens. On the terrace, watched over by the gently swaying fronds of the tall palm trees, Wallis and David might host separate tables at dinner, serenaded by music floating through the open French doors from a gramophone in the hall. After dinner, they would dance on the terrace beneath the light of the moon that sparkled over the still waters of the sea beyond.[20]

Occasionally, the Duke and Duchess were entertained by their neighbors. One, the former American actress and hostess Maxine Elliott, lived at a splendid white mansion above Cannes called Château de l'Horizon. Elliott's nephew, Vincent Sheean, recalled dinner with the Duke and Duchess of Windsor as "a strange, surrealiste" experience.[21] On one occasion, the dinner conversation turned, at the Duke's instigation, on the welfare and hygiene of Welsh miners; soon the Duke was busy expounding on the virtues of Germany's treatment of its workers. "The Duchess was so slim and elegant, so suggestive of innumerable fashionable shops, dressmakers, manicurists, and hairdressers that she seemed at the uttermost remove from the pithead of a mine."[22]

They also dined with Somerset Maugham at his Villa Mauresque at Cap Ferrat on August 5, 1938. Fellow guest Harold Nicolson wrote:

> In they came. She, I must say, looks very well for her age. She has done her hair in a different way. It is smoothed off her brow and falls down the back of her neck in ringlets. It gives her a placid and less strained look. . . . There was a pause. "I am sorry

we were a little late," said the Duke, "but Her Royal Highness couldn't drag herself away." He had said it. The three words fell into the circle like three stones in a pool. Her (gasp) Royal (shudder) Highness (and not one eye dared to meet another).[23]

The Duke and Duchess spent Christmas of 1938 at La Croë. "The Duchess took Christmas seriously," recalled Dina Wells Hood. "She loved an old-fashioned festival, with a tree, turkeys, good Christmas fare and lots of presents for everyone."[24] The Windsors traveled from Paris to the Riviera overnight by the famous Blue Train. They booked a set of private compartments, although they took their meals along with the rest of the passengers in the dining car. When the train made occasional stops, David used the opportunity to put their cairn terriers on their leads and take them for short walks along the siding.[25] Upon their arrival at Antibes, the Duke and Duchess would be met by the mayor and a deputation of other officials, who welcomed them, presented Wallis with a bouquet of flowers, and saw them off in a convoy of cars bound for La Croë.

That Christmas, the Duke and Duchess of Windsor were joined by Lord and Lady Brownlow and their two children, the Honorable Caroline and the Honorable Edward Cust; Sir Charles and Lady Mendl; John McMullin; and Wallis's aunt Bessie.[26] They arrived at La Croë to find the hall piled with trunks, boxes, parcels, hundreds of cards, and in their midst, a huge, bare tree which Wallis had selected earlier that week in Paris. John McMullin helped Wallis design the white-and-silver decorations, which everyone helped place on the tree all through Christmas Eve.[27] On Christmas morning, the Windsors and their guests drove to a small Anglican church on the road to Antibes to attend services. Thoughtfully, the Duke and Duchess regularly dispatched welcome checks to the minister to help his parish.[28]

The big event came in the afternoon, when the household and servants assembled in the hall for the presentation of their gifts. For weeks, Wallis had spent long days shopping for gifts: every member of the household or staff, along with their families and anyone who had worked for the Windsors or provided services during the year, received a present, most carefully wrapped by the Duchess herself. The Duke and Duchess stood together before the Christmas tree, receiving each member of the household and staff. They shook hands, smiled and chatted, and Wallis presented them with their gift, which ranged from the useful—household accessories and the newest novels—to the extravagant—alligator-skin wallets and handbags for women, gold cuff links and tie clips for men.[29]

With the Windsors settled in at La Croë, their thoughts turned to a proper Paris house. The lease on the house at Versailles had expired, and they decided not to renew it; instead, Wallis resumed her search for a house in the city itself. Finally, after much negotiation, she and David signed the lease on 24, Boulevard Suchet. Situated at the end of the avenue Henri Martin in the Sixteenth Arrondissement, near the Bois de Boulogne, this was a large, four-story town house surrounded by a small garden and boasting a suite of reception rooms designed for entertaining.[30]

To help decorate the new house, Wallis consulted Stephane Boudin, of Maison Jensen, on the rue Royale. Boudin, who had created Chips Channon's famous blue-and-silver rococo dining room in London, was a short, meticulous little man with immense energy and reserves of talent. Often he would personally scrub woodwork with a wire brush or apply a coat of glaze to achieve the desired effect. He and Wallis spent endless hours hunting for exactly the right furnishings. "Tirelessly," recalled Dina Wells Hood, "she searched for exactly the right furniture, rugs, materials, lamps and *bibelots*. She came to know intimately every antique shop, large and small, in Paris. . . . Tradespeople called . . . at all hours to deliver parcels and to discuss and receive orders. The telephone there too rang incessantly."[31]

If La Croë represented something of the informality of the Fort, the Parisian house was pure Buckingham Palace. It was not a style with which Wallis had much experience; her own tastes at Bryanston Court had run to comfort mixed with a few interesting period pieces. She had shown no inclination to furnish her own rooms with valuable antiques or create stately atmospheres. These things she did for the Duke; at the same time, she began to absorb these tastes as her own, so much so that eventually the Windsor villa in the Bois de Boulogne in Paris was a perfect expression of the woman into which Wallis had transformed herself.

The house at 24, boulevard Suchet stood on a small corner lot overlooking a paved square and surrounded by a tall iron fence and thick hedges. From the boulevard, a short flight of stone steps led to the front door, which in turn opened to the entrance hall. Wallis had wanted a very formal introduction to the house; in the entrance hall, the black-and-white Carrara-marble floor, white columns supporting the ceiling, and tall white caryatids wearing crowns of candles in the mirrored corner alcoves all spoke of the *ancien régime*. A Louis XVI clock, whose face was set within the center of a gilded sunburst, hung above an antique gilt console on which stood the red and gold visitors' books. White Louis XVI stools, with carved legs and green leather seats, stood at intervals around the hall; above, from the center of the ceiling, hung a crystal chandelier; along with the candles atop the caryatids' crowns, it would be lit on the evenings the Windsors entertained.[32]

Just off the entrance hall were several rooms given over to the household, including offices for the secretaries and a sitting room for the detectives who were on constant duty to guard the former King of England and his wife. Wallis took great care with these rooms: in the secretaries' office, for example, she provided comfortable sofas and chairs, a Chippendale dining table, and antique Louis XVI desks for their use.[33]

Glass doors led from the entrance hall to the stair hall. Wallis left this space deliberately restrained to better showcase two exquisite pieces: an antique Japanese screen, which Emperor Hirohito had presented to the then Prince of Wales during a visit to Tokyo in the 1920s; and a tall white-and-gold Louis XVI standing pendulum clock.[34] An elevator rose to the left, while to the right curved the white marble staircase which ascended to the first floor. Alabaster urns atop black marble columns held concealed lighting that glowed against the stark white walls in the evening.

The first floor contained four principal rooms, all of which opened *en suite*: a large drawing room, which occupied the front portion of the house; a salon; a dining room; and a smaller sitting room known as the Banquette Room.

Wallis was at her most assured in the drawing room, which was decorated in the Louis XIV style, with cream-colored boiserie, a black-and-beige Savonnerie carpet, and a Louis XIV chandelier. A large eighteenth-century Venetian screen added a splash of exotic color. A Baroque sofa, with heavily carved and gilded woodwork, along with two matching chairs, was covered in antique red velvet, which Wallis had picked up in a small shop in Paris; the velvet was said to have come originally from a cardinal's robes. Two Regency consoles with marble tops stood between the windows, which were hung with cream and red curtains. Elsewhere, Wallis placed several small Louis XIV chairs and tables in red and black and a Charles II tripod table whose mirrored top was inlaid with a delicate Chinese landscape.[35]

Double doors connected the drawing room to the salon, a smaller, more formal chamber decorated in Louis XVI fashion. Again, the color scheme was neutral: white, gold, pale blue, and yellow. In contrast, the furniture—elaborately carved and gilded chairs and sofas—was upholstered in rich and vibrant brocaded silks, satins, and flowered tapestries. Wallis selected a Savonnerie carpet which drew out these accent colors, as did the pair of lapis-lazuli candelabra which stood above the fireplace—gifts from Queen Mary to her eldest son.[36]

As with the dining room at La Croë, Wallis took great pains with her Paris dining room. The walls were painted cream, with the delicate boiserie picked out in gilt, and pierced by arched windows draped with crimson curtains tied back and hung with enormous gold tasseled cords at two levels. Each window was fitted with matching mirrored shutters on the inside that could be pulled closed to magnify the candlelight on formal occasions—an effect heightened by the immense mirrors that cloaked the doors, stood above the fireplace, and filled an alcove against one wall in which stood the carved and gilded rococo sideboard. In the center of the room, atop the crimson Oriental carpet that covered the shimmering parquet floor, stood the dining table, with intricately carved and gilded legs supporting the black-mirrored top. The table could be extended to seat thirty upon Louis XVI chairs in light pastel blue and gold.[37] Wallis had first encountered the idea for a mirrored tabletop at Lady Cunard's house in London and adopted it at Bryanston Court. She liked the effect it created in candlelight, with the shimmering surfaces of crystal, silver, and jewels reflected in the dusky surface.[38]

The Banquette Room reflected a whimsical side of Wallis's character. The walls were formal, painted white with elegant *boiserie*, but the carpet was a green-and-white lattice pattern, and the furniture was clearly different: Against one wall stood a large green velvet banquette covered with white and green pillows. A sofa and matching chairs, also covered in green velvet, stood facing the antique mantelpiece, dominated by an Italian Renaissance clock depicting two nudes holding aloft a gilded globe. On either side of the fireplace were two small Chinese lacquered chests and two freestanding blackamoors with Venetian turbans, which held lamps. Above the banquette hung a rather severe portrait of Wallis in a blue taffeta ballgown, painted by Drian.[39]

The second floor contained the private apartments of the Duke and Duchess as well as a small suite of rooms for Wallis's personal maid. A large sitting room, decorated with overstuffed modern sofas and chairs covered in bright English chintzes, a Chippendale table, and a crescent-shaped desk used by the Duchess separated the Windsors' rooms. It was used for informal, private entertaining; on occasions when the Duke and Duchess were alone in the evening, they dined here at the small table.[40]

David's bedroom was decorated in cream and beige, with a red carpet and accents. Wallis used a magnificent suite of Empire furniture here; the bed, decorated with ormolu inlays, stood lengthwise against one wall. It was covered with an eiderdown of heavy, cream-colored satin fringed with red and pale gold; before the bed, across the crimson carpet, lay a white bearskin rug. The rest of the pieces in the suite were heavily ornamented with ormolu and black enamel inlays. A gilded mirror, topped with the Prince of Wales's feathers, hung above a chest; an antique bureau stood between the windows and served as David's desk.[41]

Wallis's bedroom was the most theatrical space in the entire house. She and Boudin hung the walls with navy-blue watered silk, pleated at intervals of three inches. The pleating was separated and drawn back over the doors, which were painted white. The windows were hung with heavy, blue satin curtains tied back with white sashes. Across the deep blue carpet lay an oval white-ermine rug above which glittered a rock-crystal chandelier. The bed had been designed by Boudin in the art-deco style: a scroll-patterned headboard, covered in blue satin and piped in white detailing, rose above the white wooden scroll frame. The plush sofa and armchairs were upholstered in navy blue, edged with alternating tassels of white and blue silk. Beside the bed, atop a small table, stood a reading lamp of mother-of-pearl. Across the room, above a white Venetian rococo chest painted in blue with scenes of country life, hung an immense mirror in a white scroll-work frame.[42]

The Duchess's dressing room, in contrast to her bedroom, was white, with a blue carpet, blue and white curtains, and mirrored closet doors. Her dressing table was draped with alternating skirts of white and sapphire-blue lace; atop it stood Wallis's dressing kit in blue and gold, her initials WW in white crystal. Beyond lay her bathroom, with a pink marble floor and a golden bathtub.

For the Windsors, life in Paris soon settled in to a quiet, luxurious routine. In these years before the war, they gave little in the way of lavish entertainments, preferring small dinner parties, and they seldom went out. Occasionally they might take in an evening of dancing or dine with friends in restaurants or nightclubs, but for the most part, they avoided the fashionable cafés where the international set gathered. Believing that they both had a future role to play in the public life of England—and having been severely criticized for their visit to Germany in 1937—the Duke and Duchess avoided publicity, preferring close friends and private dinners to the more extravagant displays which would mark their later lives. The contradiction was noted by more than one visitor: a magnificent house, with beautifully furnished rooms, carefully crafted for entertaining and a couple reluctant to put it to use.

French society continued to be divided over the Windsors. The older, more respectable aristocratic families regarded them snobbishly; although David might be tolerated, Wallis was clearly an object of disdain. Families with fortunes founded in industrial riches, banking, and commerce, however, had no such prejudices and eagerly welcomed the Duke and Duchess on the rare occasions when they ventured out.

Nor did they fare any better among members of the diplomatic corps in Paris. Many European embassies, worried lest they offend British sensibilities, simply ordered important officers to avoid the Duke and Duchess. The few officials who dared break ranks often did so at their own peril. "One of my parents' friends spoke up once on the Duke's behalf at an Embassy reception," recalled an acquaintance of the Duke and Duchess's. "This was just before the visit of a junior member of the Royal Family, and, as usual, no one had tried to include the Duke and Duchess in any official capacity. My father's friend, who had been the sole voice raised in favour of at least some form of public meeting, might as well have been a traitor for the way in which he was treated thereafter. In the end, he was posted back to Whitehall and a potentially brilliant career came to an end behind a desk—and no one can tell me it wasn't because he spoke up on their behalf."[43]

As they would later in their lives, the Windsors turned most of their attention to their collection of dogs. In these days, they favored cairn terriers; one of David's first presents to Wallis, when he was still Prince of Wales, had been the cairn terrier Slipper, or Mr. Loo, and undoubtedly the Windsors associated their new cairns with the lost dog who had been present during their emotional relationship. In Paris, they kept three cairns: Pookie, Detto, and Prisie. As they would later with their pugs, the Duke and Duchess doted on their dogs. Their meals were specially prepared and brought on platters to the Windsors' private apartments, where either Wallis or David would spoon the food into their silver bowls themselves.[44]

The dogs were companions; the Windsors never kept guard dogs. Indeed, they were not needed, for the Duke and Duchess were guarded around the clock. At all times of the day and night, two officers were on guard at 24, boulevard Suchet. Inspector Storrier, who had followed the Duke and Duchess into exile, retired in the summer of 1938; Scotland Yard replaced him with Detective Philip Attfield. His Sûreté partner was Monsieur M. Magnin. The Sûreté also provided uniformed officers to stand regular guard on the sidewalk outside the house in Paris.

As personal detectives, their duties were usually fairly light. They spent the greater part of each day alternating shifts, waiting in their ground-floor sitting room until they were required. Whenever the Duke or the Duchess left their house, they were accompanied not only by regular security forces from the Sûreté but also by one of the private detectives. When they lunched with friends in a restaurant, the detective would patiently wait outside. When Wallis wandered through the Parisian antique shops, she was shadowed by a detective.[45]

The detectives formed only a portion of the household and staff. In the years before the outbreak of the Second World War, more than a dozen men and women worked for the Duke and Duchess. This number included the butler, a chef, and his assistant, a pastry chef, several kitchen boys, a housekeeper, two maids, David's valet, David's equerry; Wallis's lady's maid, two secretaries, and two chauffeurs.

Wallis had been greatly impressed by Hale, the butler employed by Charles Bedaux at Château de Candé; she convinced Fern Bedaux to let her hire him away into their service. Hale was a tall, dignified English expatriate with a detailed knowledge of entertaining and an ability to command respect in a large household.

The Duke and Duchess kept two cars. Both were Buicks, including the one in which Wallis had fled England in December 1936. On its side, in small gold lettering surrounded by a tiny painted diamond frame, were her old initials, WWS; for some reason, she never asked that they be removed. Wallis never learned how to drive; instead, she had a chauffeur, an Englishman named Tony Webster. David had his own chauffeur, Karl Schafranek, whom he had brought with him from Austria. In 1939, Wallis finally replaced her old Buick with a newer model, and the curious initials on its door that spoke of her old life gave way to a coroneted WW.[46]

In time, there would be quite a lot of gossip concerning the lot of the Windsors' servants. But few left their positions, and the turnover in the house on boulevard Suchet was quite low. It is true that the Windsors did not pay competitive wages; in general, household and staff received between 10 and 20 percent less than their colleagues in other establishments. This was not so much an example of the Windsors' oft-discussed tightness, rather, the prevalent attitude in which the Duke himself had been raised. Royal servants were always paid less than their regular counterparts. While Wallis and David were heavily criticized by writers for their perceived lack of largesse, the wages they offered were little different from those paid by David's own brother at Buckingham Palace.

Additionally, if less was paid, there were added incentives for employment in the Windsor household. The Duke and Duchess traveled frequently, and a great many of their staff accompanied them, allowing opportunities to visit countries at no expense. Wallis took great pains with those who worked for her and David. While it is true to say that she was meticulous in her requirements and demanding, she also was quick to recognize a good job done and took a real interest in husbands, wives, and children of the staff. "She was always very kind and generous to the staff," Hale recalled. "Whenever we traveled anywhere, she always made sure we had the best accommodations, the best rooms. The staff always knew what she wanted and we knew what we had to do. And she was quick to compliment."[47]

These servants and staff were governed by the iron rules of royal etiquette which Wallis had imported from her husband's former court. No one sat in either the Duke or Duchess's presence unless invited to do so. Every morning, upon first meeting Wallis or David, a servant or member of the household was expected to bow or curtsy, a procedure followed again in the evening when saying good night. Within the household, the Duke and Duchess were both addressed as "Your Royal

Highness" during their first encounter; thereafter, one could choose to use "Sir" or "Ma'am" in ordinary conversation.

The two members of the household who stood slightly apart from the rest and enjoyed a more intimate relationship with the Windsors were Gertrude Bedford and Dina Wells Hood, private secretaries, respectively, for the Duchess and the Duke. Gertrude Bedford had joined Wallis in April 1937, right after she arrived at Candé. She was married and lived with her husband in a small flat outside Paris, although she always accompanied the Duke and Duchess on their various travels. In the spring of 1939, she was joined by Elizabeth Arnold, who took on many of her duties working for the Duchess while Bedford herself assumed charge of the entire household. In the summer of 1938, Dina Wells Hood joined the Windsor staff as the Duke's private secretary.

These secretaries regularly worked five nine-hour days, with an hour off for lunch. Dina Wells Hood recalled how tradition dictated that she stand while taking dictation for the Duke each morning, often for hours on end. Occasionally, he would offer a chair, but usually she was left to stand—it was simply a part of the royal tradition in which he had been raised.[48]

While Wallis was neat and orderly, her husband seemed to be her exact opposite, especially where his private papers were concerned. Often she would enter his rooms, only to find the former King sitting cross-legged on the floor, surrounded by piles of letters, books, papers, and dispatches. When he read something, he usually tossed it onto the floor; as a result, when he quickly needed to find a certain letter or memo, he had to dig for hours. Wallis tried several times to impose some sort of filing system on him, but to no avail, and it was left to Hood to deal with David's daily debris.[49]

Wallis maintained close contact with every aspect of the running of their house. Each morning, she rose according to a regular schedule no matter how late she and David might have been out the night before. She always remained in her rooms, however; she rarely appeared before eleven unless there was a luncheon or other scheduled engagement. Her first concerns were the menus, which her chef submitted on a daily basis. Sitting in her bed, dressed in her silk-and-lace dressing gown, pen in hand, she would carefully review each and every suggestion, often making notes in the margins. Because the chef spoke only French, Wallis used that language to communicate with him. According to Dina Wells Hood, her comments were "in perfectly grammatical French, which was all the more remarkable because she was somewhat diffident about her French."[50]

Hood recalled her early-morning encounters with the Duchess, when Wallis would summon her for dictation. Clearly, Anna Emory

Warfield's early training had paid off, for Wallis was always perfectly correct. "There was a streak of hardihood in her nature which contrasted oddly with her leisured existence and the luxurious surroundings in which she lived. She never lounged in an armchair or on a sofa. Even if she sat back comfortably, her posture was good. She could sit for long periods on a backless divan without any apparent discomfort. When she sat up in bed in the morning with her breakfast tray or to interview her secretary, she did not lean back among the pillows. She sat upright and unsupported."[51]

Wallis spent the majority of her late mornings and early afternoons inspecting the house, speaking with the servants, consulting with the chef, and arranging flowers. "No detail ever eluded the Duchess's attention," recalled Dina Wells Hood. "Her quick eye noted the precise quality of every material and every fitting—the strength of a cord, the movement of a switch, the finish of a lock."[52] Another time-consuming task was going over the household accounts. Every expenditure was carefully logged in a series of ledgers, following a system the Duke had imported from his days at Buckingham Palace. In the ledgers, expenses were completely broken down so that Wallis could see not only how much food cost from month to month but how much had been spent on milk or cheese. The same sorts of records were kept on cleaning supplies, electricity, laundry, flowers, and wages. "We knew, for instance," wrote Hood, "how much was spent respectively on wines and spirits, on beer, on soft drinks, on mineral waters. We knew not only the cost of fuel in general but the exact amounts expended on coal, charcoal, wood and gas."[53] Only the chef did not have to present itemized bills to her; instead, he presented a monthly account book showing general kitchen expenses.[54]

While Wallis was thus engaged, the housemaids were busy with their work: sweeping, dusting, vacuuming, and polishing. Every afternoon, they reported to Marguerite Moulichon, the Duchess's lady's maid, who had charge of the *lingerie* on the second floor, where all of the household linens were stored. The Windsors' bed linens were all hand-embroidered with coronets and the initials of the Duke and Duchess. All rooms were fitted out with linens to match their color schemes. Bed linens and bath towels were all replaced every day; in the afternoon, sheets were ironed and distributed to the maids, who carried them through the house to their intended destination.[55]

As afternoon turned to evening, the kitchen, situated on the ground floor, was a hive of activity. The Windsors had two chefs during their time at boulevard Suchet: Monsieur Dyot, who had originally worked for the Duke of Alba; and Monsieur Pinaudier, who replaced him when Dyot went to work at the Spanish embassy.

In these years, Wallis favored simple menus when she entertained. Her requirement was that the food be interesting, not exotic. Game was preferred, with woodcock and partridge special favorites. Seafood was also featured prominently on their regular menus: oysters, trout, salmon, and lobster. Occasionally, Wallis would ask for fried chicken, but beef and pork were usually absent from their table. Wallis had a more cultivated palate than her husband; she preferred experimentation and liked to take fresh, simple items and combine or cook them in new ways. David, having been raised on essentially English nursery food, still had a taste for rice pudding, baked apples, and stewed fruits. Neither Wallis nor David drank much, although they maintained well-stocked cellars at both La Croë and the house on boulevard Suchet. With dinner, David enjoyed white Alsatian wines, especially Gewürztraminer and Riesling.[56]

This attention to detail—in decoration, in floral arrangements, in staff, in food—all came together on the nights when the Duke and Duchess entertained. Anne Morrow Lindbergh recalled one such evening she and her husband, Col. Charles Lindbergh, spent at boulevard Suchet, a telling memory of a splendid setting, perfect entertainment, and genial hosts mingled with a sense of forced gaiety and contrived contentment: "The house is rather formal and French: lots of footmen in uniform. We go up the stairs. The Duke and Duchess are in a little room panelled in gold and white, with yellow tulips and dusty black iris arranged beautifully. They come forward very cordially. She looks very thin and rather tired (though incredibly young— smooth skin, lovely complexion, hair beautifully done in waves away from her face) and dressed in a black dress with a gay striped paillette bolero." Anne found the dining room "lovely," with "red and gold curtains and mirrors." After dinner, the ladies retired to "a tiny sitting room ... enchanting ... panelled in a pale blue-grey and white with gay chintz and white lilacs and white calla lilies in vases and a pale pink and pale blue spray of orchids on the mantel." She found time to speak with Wallis for a few minutes alone: "It is a curious thing that one feels with her: that she is building up a face that she thinks is appropriate. ... And yet though this baffles me, it does not make me dislike her. I like her through it, for some reason, partly I think because she is doing it out of defense and because I feel a real person underneath, a person who looks to me (in spite of that lacquered surface) almost tortured underneath in a terrific and rather heroic struggle. But it is such an unnecessary struggle. If they are happy together, as they decidedly seem to be, why make this struggle for a brilliant front? Why try to keep up in this utterly futile world of show?"[57]

31

War

As THE SUMMER OF 1939 wore on, everyone's thoughts turned to the increasing international tensions which seemed to threaten the peace of the world. Both Wallis and David abhorred the very idea of war. As Prince of Wales, the Duke had witnessed first-hand the terrible bloodshed, destruction, and great loss of life the First World War had visited upon his generation. He had also seen how it had torn his family apart over their German relations. Wallis, too, had been seared through experience: Her uncertainties during Win's missions and his brother's tragic death in the First World War had impacted her deeply. She had witnessed the devastation during the conflicts in China; she knew the terrible price which would have to be paid if a war erupted.

On September 1, 1939 the Nazis attacked Poland. Hitler was confident that Great Britain would not challenge his move. Then, after a thirty-six-hour delay, the British government issued an ultimatum, demanding the withdrawal of German troops within two hours. Until the last, David tried to use whatever influence he had left, sending a cable to Hitler, pleading that he not embark on a war. Hitler replied that he had no desire for war, and if one came it would not be his fault.[1] On September 3 the Duke and Duchess of Windsor were staying at La Croë; while hosting a small party at the swimming pool, David was summoned to the telephone. When he reappeared, he informed his wife and guests that the unthinkable had occurred: England had declared war on Germany.[2]

David immediately rang Walter Monckton in London. He offered to return to England at once and place himself fully at the disposal of the King for the duration of the war. Although he hated the thought of war, once it had come, the Duke was determined to utilize his talents to help the British effort. He had a natural ability to sympathize with the common soldier and undoubtedly felt a great sense of loyalty to the country he had left behind.

These talents could have been put to good use in the war. Bryan and Murphy wrote: "Never did the Duke of Windsor have a brighter chance of escaping from the wasteland of his self-centered life, and recovering an honored, useful position, than was offered him by the outbreak of World War II. But through a succession of gaffes and myopic judgments, the chance was repeatedly thrown away. . . ."[3]

Monckton arrived at La Croë on September 7, saying that George VI wished the Duke and Duchess to return to London as soon as possible and that he would dispatch a plane for their trip. He also brought with him news that the Duke was to have his choice of two different posts: regional commissioner of Wales, a civil-defense post; or a member of the British Military Mission attached to the French General Headquarters at Vincennes. He was to inform the King of his decision when he arrived in England.[4]

Fruity Metcalfe happened to be staying with the Windsors at La Croë. David was startled by Monckton's suggestions that Metcalfe accompany the Duke and Duchess on their return to England and that they could stay with him and his wife while in the country. The Duke was not a stupid man: from this, he immediately gathered that George VI had asked Monckton to convey the fact that the Windsors would not be put up in any of the royal residences. Feeling certain that this was only the first of many humiliations he and Wallis would suffer, David refused to return to England. When he confessed his decision to Metcalfe, however, he was surprised at the strength of his friend's objection: "You *only* think of yourselves," Metcalfe told the Duke. "You don't realize that there is at this moment a war going on, that women and children are being bombed and killed while you talk of your PRIDE."[5]

Duly chastised, the Duke and Duchess quickly changed their minds and agreed to return to England. Wallis packed up a few of her most important belongings and, together with David, left La Croë on September 8, accompanied by Fruity Metcalfe and their three cairn terriers. Wallis, however, still refused to fly, and so arrangements were made for the Windsors to sail to England. It took them two days to cross France and arrive at Vichy, where they were to wait for further instruction. After a day had passed, however, with no news from Buckingham Palace, David motored to Paris to consult with the ambassador. After some hurried telephone calls, the Duke was told to proceed to Cherbourg.[6]

On the evening of September 12, the Windsors arrived in the port city, where the British destroyer HMS *Kelly* stood at a dock to convey them across the Channel. Lord Louis Mountbatten and Randolph Churchill both waited aboard. At ten that evening, HMS *Kelly* slowly steamed out of the harbor, following a careful zigzag pattern to avoid potential German submarine fire.[7] They sailed into the unknown; it had been nearly three years since either Wallis or David had set foot in England. Both were uncertain as to the reception they would receive, from the public in general and the Royal Family in particular.

The Royal Family was just as worried about the arrival of the Windsors, especially the Duchess. "What are we going to do about Mrs. S.?" Queen Elizabeth asked Queen Mary.[8] It is possible to gather something of the continuing animosity that the two Queens harbored against Wallis from their reference, two years after she had married David, to her as "Mrs. S." Even in private, they refused to relent and acknowledge between themselves that Wallis had become a member of their family. The Duchess was soon to discover how far this hatred of both her and her husband was to be carried.

Winston Churchill had by this time been returned to the post of First Lord of the Admiralty, a position he had previously held during the last war. A great friend of the Duke's, he was embarrassed that the Royal Family had refused to make any arrangements for the Windsors. To lend the return of the former King some kind of dignity, Churchill arranged for a naval guard of honor to greet the Windsors when they landed at Portsmouth. As they descended the gangway, Wallis and David were saluted by the Royal Marine Band, which played the first six bars of the national anthem. The Duke, who had been accustomed to receiving the entire salute as king, was startled by this abbreviated version and turned to the Duchess to remark on the contrast.[9]

No arrangements of any kind had been made for the Duke and Duchess of Windsor; when they arrived in Portsmouth, they did not even have a place to stay. Wallis, particularly, was angry at this treatment of her husband. She had absolutely no doubt that the Royal Family had decided intentionally to ignore their presence as far as was possible even though they had come at the King's request. On their first night back in England, therefore, the Duke and Duchess stayed at Admiralty House, the guests of Adm. Sir William James, commander in chief at Portsmouth, and his wife, who, although they were gracious, could not conceal their curiosity about the Duchess.[10]

The next day, the Duke and Duchess moved on to South Hatfield House in Ashdown Forest to stay with the Metcalfes. Two days before, Lady Alexandra Metcalfe had phoned Buckingham Palace and asked if the Windsors would be accommodated by the Royal Family either in London or in the country. She was told they would not. She then asked if the palace would at least dispatch a car for the couple's use while in the country; this was also refused.[11] "I do think the family might have done something," Lady Alexandra wrote with some anger in her diary. "He might not even exist. . . ."[12]

Lady Alexandra herself went to pick up the Duke and Duchess, while her chauffeur followed with a Ford van to carry their luggage.

Her daughter, Linda Mortimer, recalls that their house "was suddenly surrounded by lots of police. We had heard stories that people were waiting to throw acid in the Duchess's face, and I was quite worried that my mother would be mixed up with her and have it chucked at her instead. So I was quite relieved when they all returned safely."[13]

The Metcalfe children—David, the Duke's godson, and the twin girls, Linda and Davina—were in a privileged position to observe the Duke and Duchess away from the glare of the cameras. David Metcalfe was struck by "how extraordinarily nice they both were, how they both took lots of trouble to be nice to us."[14] And his sister Linda recalls "games of croquet on the lawns, lots of laughs and lots of fun. The Duchess was always very relaxed, and very sweet to us children."[15] During the time they stayed, the Windsors and the Metcalfes would sit down to cards, and the sound of their games could be heard throughout the house. "The Duchess always dominated the room," Metcalfe says. "She made a tremendous din, but she was always very exciting, very amusing, full of noise and fun. Everyone always thinks, Oh my God, what a horrible decision he made, but if he ever regretted it, I don't know when it would have been. She was everything to him, everything, and you could see that from the way they acted together."[16]

The next day, September 14, the Duke went to Buckingham Palace to meet with his brother. This was a rather strained meeting, and both men carefully avoided the main subjects of contention between them. David declared that he had decided to take the job of regional commissioner of Wales, as he wished to remain in England, and thought that his talents would prove more useful in that sphere.[17] He also knew that the post in Wales might keep Wallis near, while the job in France would involve long separations. Bertie seemed to suggest that the job in France would involve more excitement but said little else, and the Duke left the palace believing that he would receive the post in Wales.

By that evening, however, Bertie had changed his mind about the Welsh appointment. The return of the former King had received a great deal of coverage in the national press, and he was loudly cheered on several occasions when he was recognized. David had little doubt that word of this had reached the King, who, both jealous of his brother's popularity and insecure about his own position, wished to avoid the chance of setting a rival up in Wales.[18]

Without bothering to inform his brother that the choice had been taken away from him, the King had Alexander Hardinge write a letter to the secretary of state for war, Leslie Hore-Belisha: "The conclusion reached by His Majesty is that His Royal Highness would be most suitably employed as a member of the Military Mission to France, of which General Howard-Vyse is the head."[19] Hore-Belisha was also told, untruthfully, that the Duke knew of this decision.

On the morning of September 15, David arrived at the War Office to meet with Hore-Belisha and Field Marshal Sir Edmund Ironside, then chief of the Imperial General Staff. When Hore-Belisha began to speak to the Duke about his new post in France, David was startled; his brother had given him no indication that his request to assume the position in Wales would be denied. But rather than object, according to Hore-Belisha, David listened patiently as his new job was explained to him: He was to be assigned to the British Military Mission in France and was to report to Vincennes as soon as possible. There was another problem, however: as former King, he still retained his former military ranks of admiral of the fleet, field marshal of the army, and marshal of the Royal Air Force. David agreed to waive his ranks and accepted the lower rank of major general to avoid a conflict. As a small concession, Fruity Metcalfe was allowed to be posted to the Duke as his personal aide-de-camp.[20] The Duke declared that the Duchess had decided to turn over and finance La Croë as a convalescent home for British officers.[21] His last request was that he be able to visit his former military commands and take the Duchess with him. All of this was done with a far better spirit of reconciliation and selflessness than his brother had shown. The Duke even expressed his appreciation to Hore-Belisha for his understanding.[22]

On the morning of September 16, Hore-Belisha was summoned to Buckingham Palace. The King expressed grave doubts about allowing the Duchess to accompany her husband on the tour of commands. He was determined that the former King should not remain anywhere in England and paced up and down the room during this interview, quite agitated. Hore-Belisha had to leave for a midday cabinet meeting but was again unexpectedly summoned to the palace that afternoon to listen while the King continued to express his uncertainties. Bertie declared that all his predecessors had succeeded to the throne on the death of its previous occupant. "Mine is not only alive, but very much so," he declared. He ended by saying he thought it best for the Duke to leave the country and go to Paris at once.[23]

One afternoon during their stay in England, the Duke and Duchess returned to Fort Belvedere. They found the lawns overgrown and choked with weeds and the gardens fallen into decay. The swimming pool below the battlements was filled with debris, while the house itself stood silent, shuttered and wrapped in a veil of solitude, slowly falling into disrepair from being abandoned. They left filled with sad memories of what had once been.[24]

Aside from his one meeting with Bertie at Buckingham Palace, David saw no member of his family. The day before he and Wallis arrived, Queen Mary had come up to London from Badminton House in Gloucestershire, where she was staying for the duration of the war, to meet with George VI. The elderly Queen was fearful lest Bertie, under the emotional pressure of the moment, relent and agree to receive Wallis. Queen Mary herself, who had not seen her eldest son in nearly three years, expressed no desire to meet with him again while he was in London; indeed, she deliberately returned to Gloucestershire before he arrived. When the Duke of Kent declared that he intended to visit David while his brother was in London, he was forbidden by Bertie from doing so.

The reaction of the Royal Family left an indelible impression on the Duke and Duchess of Windsor. The way in which they had been ignored was hurtful and humiliating. It was not that the Royal Family was too busy with the war to extend the courtesies expected; through the six years of conflict, the Royal Family never failed to dispatch at least a junior member to meet a visiting royal or important dignitary or ensure that appropriate arrangements for their comfort had been made. The Windsors were the exceptions, the only two people deliberately snubbed in such blatant ways. Michael Bloch writes of the Duke: "He was determined not to expose himself to such treatment when he next returned home. It is important to remember this when considering his attitude nine months later."[25]

The Windsors left England aboard the destroyer *Express* on September 29. The crossing to Cherbourg was rough, and Wallis was happy to be back on land. Wallis returned to Paris, while David immediately went to Nogent-sur-Marne, near French General Headquarters at Vincennes, to report to the commander, Maj. Gen. Sir Richard Howard-Vyse.

Along their German borders, the French had built a series of expensive forts—the famous Maginot Line—connected by underground trains and equipped with such luxuries as sun-ray rooms and movie theaters. The Maginot Line was popularly believed to be the last word in defense; the French, convinced that it guaranteed their victory in any conflict, were lulled into dangerous complacency. The French command, led by Gen. Maurice Gustave Gamelin, was ill prepared for a twentieth-century conflict. They believed in playing a careful, drawn-out game of attrition, one which was undoubtedly to prolong the war and result in millions of unnecessary casualties.

The first seven months of the war saw little military action. The French had more than a hundred divisions in readiness, while the German Army on the Western front was incomplete. Their Siegfried Line was punctured with enormous, unfinished gaps. Only twenty-five reserve divisions, with enough ammunition for only three days' battle, stood poised along the border. The Luftwaffe had yet to stockpile any substantial amount of bombs. Had the French attacked in force when the war erupted, they could undoubtedly have reached the

Rhine within a few weeks and very possibly won the war. But Gamelin kept his huge army inactive, waiting for the Germans to move. He remained at his headquarters in a French château, without radio or telephone, sending important dispatches by motorcycle.

Gamelin was notoriously uncooperative with the British command. No member of the British command had been allowed to visit the French defenses, including the all-important Maginot Line. There is substantial evidence that the British command at Vincennes used the Duke of Windsor to spy on the French General Staff, who at that time were renowned for their secrecy. He managed to tour French defenses, question officers, and make reports, all without Gamelin suspecting a thing. At Vincennes, the value of this information was appreciated; but when forwarded to London, it was largely ignored, simply because it had come from the Duke, who was thought by both the King and certain members of the government to be incapable of faithfully reporting what he had seen.[26]

It has often been alleged that the Duke of Windsor, while in his post with the British command, was responsible for leaking secrets to the Axis powers. Specifically, the German minister to The Hague, Count Julius von Zech-Burkersroda, reported in a memo to Berlin that the Duke was unhappy in his role and that he freely and indiscreetly talked of confidential plans. But there seems to be absolutely no evidence to support such a conclusion; certainly, at times, the Duke may have spoken without thought, and it is impossible to say that the wrong ears may not have picked up carelessly divulged details. But there is nothing to substantiate the recent, popular assertions that the Duke was a traitor. All of his loyalties remained with England.

Undoubtedly, there were times when David was intensely frustrated. His brother the Duke of Gloucester once came to visit the French military headquarters; as the two brothers were leaving, the Duke of Windsor inadvertently, and without intent, walked out first, thus receiving the salute of the staff, which had been meant for the Duke of Gloucester. A few days later, he was formally reprimanded by the British Military Staff for having taken the salute intended for his brother.[27]

"In that one respect," Wallis later wrote, "we had two wars to deal with—the big and still leisurely war, in which everybody was caught up, and the little cold war with the Palace, in which no quarter was given. ... It seemed to me tragic that this unique gift, humbly proffered, was never really called upon, out of fear, I judged, that it might once more shine brightly, too brightly."[28]

Wallis, meanwhile, was engaged in her own war work. After several months in a small flat at Versailles, she finally decided to return to Paris. She was accompanied by Maj. Gray Phillips of the Black Watch

Regiment, an old friend of the Duke's, who now took over the position of comptroller of their household. Because the Windsors had been at La Croë for the summer, the house on boulevard Suchet had been closed for the season: When Wallis and Phillips arrived, the carpets were rolled and lying against the walls, dust covers remained on the furniture, and the chandeliers had been taken down and stood on the bare floors for fear that any bombardment would bring them crashing down. Wallis decided to open only those rooms which they would need for daily use: the kitchen, bedrooms, bathrooms, the second-floor sitting room, and the dining room.

Most of the windows remained shuttered; across those that were opened Wallis stretched tape to prevent breakage and heavy black curtains to disguise light.[29] These quickly proved a necessity, as Paris was often subject to air raids. Wallis stubbornly refused to go to any shelter. "I suffer from claustrophobia," she explained. "Anyway, if you are at war, you must accept your chances. Being killed by a bomb is something like being killed in an automobile accident if you are a careful driver. A sort of act of God. It is unpredictable and there isn't much you can do about it."[30]

Wishing to make herself useful, Wallis became honorary president of the French relief organization *Colis de Trianon*, which was controlled by her friend Elsie, Lady Mendl. She wrote to her friend Sibyl Colefax, "The British have not asked me to help them—so time and money have gone to the French."[31] Every morning, she dressed in her khaki uniform of mid-length skirt, jacket, and jaunty military-style cap and reported to work. The organization distributed kits to French troops containing knitted sweaters, socks, gloves, toiletries, soap, and cigarettes. These articles were collected and packed by Wallis and other volunteers, then delivered to the front.[32] Wallis learned to knit in order to help supply some of the items herself and dipped into her bank accounts for those provisions which could not be made. Among her other projects, she lent her financial support to a soup kitchen for the poor in Montmartre.[33]

She also joined the *Section Sanitaire* of the French Red Cross and volunteered herself and her Buick for frequent and dangerous delivery missions to the front. Several times a week, Wallis would collect plasma, boxes of bandages, and cartons of cigarettes, load them into her car, and accompanied by a driver, set off for the field hospitals behind the Maginot Line, making stops at each. She was usually gone by seven in the morning and almost never returned to Paris until long after night had fallen. In between supply drops, she often visited soldiers in the field hospitals, asking if there were any supplies or favors they needed.[34] This was dangerous work: On at least one occasion, unexpected hostilities forced her to remain just behind the line for the night; from her makeshift bed she could hear the booming guns of enemy artillery.[35]

On the days when she was not carrying out these duties with the French Red Cross, Wallis continued to work for Lady Mendl. She continued to fund projects from her personal fortune: Through her efforts, soldiers' recreation centers in France were supplied with gramophones and records.[36] Wallis may have been anathema to the Royal Family and the court back in England, but the French were quick to recognize her generosity and invaluable contribution, and she won many fans among the soldiers. A certain Captain Colliere, commander of the First Battalion of the 423rd Regiment of Pioneers, wrote to Wallis asking for a signed photograph to hang in their mess. She duly sent the picture and asked if there was anything else she could do. She was somewhat surprised when Colliere requested a regimental banner in Wallis blue, but she had one made up at her own expense in a shop on the rue de Rennes and dispatched to hang alongside the photograph.[37]

Their respective work kept the Duke and Duchess of Windsor apart until the spring of 1940. They telephoned each other when possible and wrote letters, but David's leaves of absence were rare. It was often impossible to coordinate their schedules; Wallis might be at the front when the Duke returned to Paris.

The spring of 1940 came early in Paris; Wallis noted that the flowers were out, the chestnut trees lining the avenues were in bloom, and the sun was warm.[38] The war seemed distant, unreal. It was all a mirage. For nine months the French army had remained silent, sitting behind their Maginot Line, waiting for Germany to direct an attack. French and British troops had massed along the frontiers of Belgium and Holland, expecting the Nazis to eventually march from the north across the Belgian plain.

Then, on May 10, two diverse events occurred which were to profoundly affect the outcome of the war: In London, Winston Churchill became prime minister of Great Britain; and in the Ardennes Forest, Panzer divisions invaded Luxembourg, while the planes of the Luftwaffe dropped hundreds of paratroopers into Holland. The Nazis moved swiftly west, bypassing the dreaded Maginot Line; within a week, they had circumvented the Allied forces and breached the front. The French, with no reserves and no backup defenses, were quickly on the run.

Within the space of a week, half of France had fallen to the Germans. Nazi troops were crossing the Loire and quickly gaining ground in Bordeaux, where the last government of the Third Republic huddled in fear. On May 15, David suddenly appeared at their house in Paris and told Wallis that she must leave immediately. She was rather reluctant to do as he wished, believing that such an act would be interpreted as cowardice, but David insisted.[39] The wives of all British diplomats and officials were already being evacuated from the capital, and so she finally consented.

Wallis left Paris on the following day; Major Phillips remained at the house on boulevard Suchet, expecting that the British command would be relocated to Paris and that the Duke himself would soon return to take up residence. A long line of cars, horns blaring and worried refugees hanging from their windows, jammed the roadways out of Paris. The Duke and Duchess initially decided to go only as far as Blois in the Loire Valley. When they arrived at a hotel there, however, they were told that there was no room for them. As it was too late to leave that evening, the manager eventually found two cots, which he set up for them in his own sitting room.[40]

David decided that Wallis should go to Biarritz; after making the arrangements, he returned to his post with the French Military Mission, and she continued on, this time to a room at the Hotel du Palais, where she remained for a week.[41] A few days into her stay, David telephoned and told her that Paris was about to fall and that she must leave France altogether. He explained that he would join her shortly. At the time, David was still accompanied by Fruity Metcalfe, who continued to serve as an unpaid aide-de-camp. One morning, Metcalfe went to call on the Duke, only, in the words of his son David, "to find that the Duke had buggered off to get the Duchess, without bothering to inform him he was even leaving. My father was terribly upset and betrayed, but the Duke didn't give a shit about anyone but the Duchess." Not until after the war would the two men resume their friendship.[42]

It has often been alleged that the Duke of Windsor deserted his post to join Wallis. This is simply not true. When he appealed to Maj. Gen. Howard-Vyse for leave, his commanding officer told the Duke that the British expected to evacuate at any moment and that he was free to go. Thus, David, without formally resigning his post, was directed to leave it by his superior officer.[43]

The Duke and Duchess arrived at La Croë on May 29. The Duke immediately attached himself to the French command at Nice and spent his days undertaking reviews and inspections.[44] By the second week of June, Italy had entered the war; from La Croë, the Windsors could hear the sounds of gunfire in the distance as the French bombed Genoa. Wallis later wrote with some dismay about how the French resistance had simply fallen away. After a few weeks, there was no opposition to the German invasion; this left the Duke and Duchess with little doubt as to the necessity of leaving the country.[45]

The British consul at Nice, Maj. Hugh Dodds, also joined in urging the Duke and Duchess to leave with him for Spain. On June 19 a caravan of four automobiles drew up before the white portico of La Croë. The Duke and Duchess of Windsor climbed into their Buick, accompanied by their three cairn terriers and driven by George Ladbrook; Major Dodds, accompanied by his vice-consul, followed in a Bentley with diplomatic number plates; a Citroen, towing a trailer of luggage, held Capt. George Wood, his wife, Rosa, her maid, and their dog; and a hired van, containing the luggage of the Duke and Duchess, also carried Wallis's lady's maid, Mademoiselle Moulichon.[46] As the sad procession slowly turned down the drive, Wallis turned back to look on La Croë one last time, convinced she would never return. It was her forty-fourth birthday.[47]

The journey to Spain was fraught with danger. Neither the Duke nor the Duchess possessed any diplomatic papers, and there remained the threat that David might be arrested as a serving Allied officer the moment he crossed into neutral soil. All along the route, the Windsors encountered hundreds of refugees, all fleeing the country. Under the most trying of circumstances, Wallis managed to maintain her composure, as Rosa Wood later recalled:

I thought of Wallis and how so many people believed she cared only for clothes and jewels, and how they always pictured her against backgrounds of castles, with maids, couturiers, and hairdressers. I saw her in mud and dirt, sleeping in cars, eating sardines out of tins, I saw when we were held up for hours before we could go south, when we had to sit all night in the lobbies of little hotels. I saw her when we had no place to wash, much less do any of the things women like to do to make themselves look nicer. I saw her awaken at four o'clock in the morning and come out in the drizzle and help the Duke and my husband to arrange things on the lorry, when we didn't know where we were going or whether we were walking into traps or whether we would be bombed. Never once did I see her cross or hear her complain or even falter except at the sight of the sufferings of others."[48]

At the Spanish border, they encountered another problem: The officials refused to let the Duke and Duchess into their country until they obtained permission from their authorities. Wallis and David had to wait for the Spanish ambassador to intervene before they were finally granted asylum. By midnight, after a twenty-hour drive, they finally reached Barcelona.

32

The Plot to Kidnap
the Windsors

On their first morning in Barcelona, the Duke and Duchess went to the British consulate general and dispatched a cable to the Foreign Office in London, alerting them to their arrival and saying that they would shortly be on their way to Madrid.[1] They spent a quiet two days here before moving on to the Spanish capital, arriving on June 23, David's forty-sixth birthday. The British ambassador in Madrid at the time happened to be Sir Samuel Hoare, the Duke's old friend, and he entertained them at the embassy and made certain that they were lodged in comfort at the Ritz Hotel. The Windsors had nothing to do but wait for some form of transportation to be arranged so that they might presumably return to England.

At first, Hoare had received instructions that the Windsors should be sent immediately to Lisbon, from where they could be safely evacuated to England. But David's brother the Duke of Kent had also been expected in Lisbon to celebrate the eight hundredth anniversary of Portuguese independence; Buckingham Palace and the Foreign Office believed that it was undesirable that the two brothers should meet, for Wallis would undoubtedly be present and thus come face-to-face with another member of the Royal Family. Hoare was duly informed that the Windsors would have to wait while other arrangements were made on their behalf and handed the Duke a cable from Churchill informing him that the cabinet would shortly meet to discuss the details of his return. In response, David cabled Churchill the following day, thanking him but adding that he was not certain if his return to England would be best. He feared that his presence might cause undue embarrassment to the Royal Family and offered to take up some foreign post in the empire should this be the case.[2]

Hoare telegraphed Churchill that the Duke was ready and willing to leave as soon as possible but that he was "most anxious" to know if there was to be a job in England when he returned. "He does not want to appear to be returning as a refugee with nothing to do. I hope you can help him with a friendly answer as soon as possible. I have told him that if he fails to return to England within a few days, all sorts of mischievous rumors will circulate about him."[3]

Churchill was in something of a difficult position. He had only been prime minister a few weeks, and due to his previous support of the Duke during the abdication, George VI was deeply suspicious of his loyalties. His first moves were therefore cautious. He informally suggested that Buckingham Palace might find a useful position for the Duke, where he could utilize his talents for the war effort. But this was not what George VI wished. On his orders, Hardinge replied to this inquiry by saying that the King doubted that the Duke, "as an ex-King," could "perform any useful service in this country."[4]

The Windsors, rather than being evacuated quickly, as they were certainly willing to be, were left to sit in Madrid. Thus, the continued desire to isolate Wallis was to lead to one of the most peculiar and controversial episodes in the lives of the Duke and Duchess.

On June 23 the Windsors were perfectly eager and ready to return to London. Wallis was particularly desperate to leave; she knew how anxious her husband was to be back in England and join in the war effort. She also believed that if they returned, their myriad difficulties with the Royal Family might be more easily dispelled. If they worked hard and proved how willing they were to cooperate, she saw no reason why the Royal Family's vendetta should continue. Significantly, too, Churchill, who had always maintained a warm and supportive friendship with the Duke, was now in power on Downing Street; with such a strong and important ally, it only seemed natural that concessions might eventually come.

The news that the Windsors were to be kept waiting in Madrid rather than move on to Lisbon, however, made the Duke reconsider his original plans. He had not forgotten how he and Wallis had been treated on their last visit to England; the humiliation of his family's deliberate snub had struck him hard. While his own family was incapable of understanding it, the simple truth was that in their desire to continually punish and isolate Wallis, they repeatedly antagonized David in the one area in which he remained most sensitive: his wife. He took every affront to her twice as hard as any slight to himself. Now he was determined that when the time came, Wallis would be treated with the dignity she deserved as the wife of the former king of England.

David was realistic enough to know that there was little he could do to change attitudes within his family; but the public, which rightly interpreted the treatment of the Windsors over the last three years as a series of deliberate humiliations, might be convinced otherwise should some public display of reconciliation take place. He wrote to Churchill, saying that he and Wallis would not return to England unless the King and Queen consented to receive them at Buckingham Palace and his wife was granted the style of Her Royal Highness, gestures the Duke believed would end press speculation over the continued breach with the Royal Family. He also wanted to know what sort of job he might be given and what salary he might expect.

Wallis tried to intervene, but on this point she was powerless; David would not yield where he felt her honor and dignity were at stake. Years later, the Duke recalled that Churchill's "personal advice to me was not to quibble about terms, but to come home and wait patiently while he 'worked things out.' But I could not in honour take this line. The year before, while we had been in England, the presence of the Duchess at my side had never been acknowledged, even perfunctorily. Before going back I wanted an assurance that simple courtesies would be forthcoming. Winston could not manage this. From a distance, what I insisted on may look to be of small value. But the perspectives of my life had changed, and the matter loomed mighty large for me."[5]

Hoare did his best to change the Duke's mind. On June 29 he reported to Churchill that David was now willing to give up most of his demands. The request, Hoare wrote, now "boiled down to both of them being received only once for quite a short meeting by the King and Queen, and notice of this fact appearing in the Court Circular." He pointed out that this need be a "once only" meeting of "a quarter of an hour" and expressed his hope that the King would agree to such a minimal request.[6]

In London, John Colville recorded: "The Prime Minister talked with Beaverbrook, and later with Alec Hardinge, who came to tea. They discussed the position of the Duke of Windsor who is . . . trying to impose conditions, financial and otherwise, about his return to this country. It is incredible to haggle in such a way at this time, and Winston proposes to send him a very stiff telegram pointing out that he is a soldier under orders and must obey. The King approves and says he will hear of no conditions, about the Duchess or otherwise."[7]

Contrary to what has often been asserted, Wallis herself had no part in his imposition of conditions; she tried in vain to convince David to take Churchill at his word and agree to return at once. Needless to say, the Duke has been roundly criticized for his actions, which seem especially petty at a time of war. But this view is mitigated somewhat by an understanding of just how vehemently the Royal Family and Foreign Office were obsessed with the same issues at the same time of crisis. When the Duke and Duchess first arrived in Spain, the Foreign Office notified Hoare that a flying boat would be sent to Portugal to collect them. "Please invite Their Royal Highnesses to proceed to Lisbon," it added.[8]

This telegram drew a swift reaction from Buckingham Palace. On George VI's orders, Hardinge wrote to the Foreign Office, indicating the King's "extreme displeasure" that the Duke and Duchess had been referred to as "Their Royal Highnesses." "This appellation was false and utterly impermissible. His Majesty's express wish . . . was that steps be taken to ensure that such an official error never occur again."[9] If nothing else, this indicates that the King was just as guilty of carrying on a petty battle over the question of Wallis's style during a national emergency.

The British ambassador to Portugal, Sir Walford Selby, arranged for the Duke and Duchess to stay at the house of a banker with the exotic name of Dr. Ricardo de Espirito Santo e Silva, a man with the unfortunate reputation of being a Nazi sympathizer. The Windsors' new residence, a large pink stucco house surrounded by colonnades and commanding a magnificent view of the beach, was near Cascais, on the coast of Portugal. This was to be only a temporary stop; when they arrived, Selby greeted them, then informed them that they would be able to leave the following morning.[10] But David immediately objected, pulling the ambassador aside and telling him that he would not return until he had heard from either Buckingham Palace or No. 10 Downing Street about both his own position and that of his wife.

In response, Selby handed the Duke a cable from Churchill, effectively ordering that he return to England at once: "Your Royal Highness has taken active military rank, and refusal to obey direct orders of competent military authority would create a serious situation. I hope it will not be necessary for such orders to be sent. I most strongly urge immediate compliance with wishes of the Government."[11]

"What followed now seems fantastic and perhaps even a little silly," Wallis later wrote. "But David's pride was engaged, and he was deadly serious." "I won't have them push us into a bottom drawer," the Duke exclaimed. "It must be the two of us together—man and wife with the same position."[12] Wallis tried to talk him out of this stubborn position, but with no success; although she wielded considerable power and influence over her husband, there was one area in which he refused to relent: the treatment of his wife. Wallis was too keenly aware that as humiliated as she felt by the continued snub, it affected David even more.

The dilemma was resolved on the following day. On July 4 a cable arrived from Churchill announcing the Duke of Windsor's appointment as governor-general and commander in chief of the Bahamas. He added: "Personally I feel sure it is the best option in the grievous situation in which we stand. At any rate, I have done my best."[13]

David was gracious in his response: "I am sure you have done your best for me in a difficult situation. I am sending Major Phillips to England tomorrow and will appreciate your receiving him personally to explain some details."[14]

Privately, neither Wallis nor David was thrilled with the appointment. To Aunt Bessie, Wallis complained: "The St. Helena of 1940 is a nice spot."[15] There was little doubt that the appointment was meant as a punishment. The colonial secretary, Lord Lloyd, dined with Sir Ronald Storrs, who noted: "G. [Lloyd George] told me that the Windsor appointment in the Bahamas is the King's own idea, to keep him at all costs out of England."[16] The appointment, harsh as it was, failed to please Queen Elizabeth, who later wrote to Lord Lloyd that she thought the Bahamas was too good for the Windsors and that Wallis was wholly unfit to be the wife of a governor-general.[17]

The great irony, of course, was that George VI, in his desire to marginalize his brother, had ensured that David and Wallis would have to spend the entire war in the public eye. Rather than letting the Duke busy himself in some obscure military post in Wales or England, where David would have no contact with the public and Wallis no opportunity to appear in the public eye, Bertie's insecurity drove him to make his brother the symbolic representative of the Crown in some faraway outpost in the empire. Undoubtedly, the repercussions of this decision were lost on the King and Queen, who presumed that the Windsors would now be safely out of harm's way.

While all of this was taking place, more diplomatic intrigue was under way. On June 23, the same afternoon that the Windsors arrived in Madrid, the German ambassador to Spain, Eberhard von Stohrer, sent a confidential cable to the Nazi foreign minister, Joachim von Ribbentrop, requesting "advice with regard to the treatment of the duke and duchess of Windsor." Stohrer declared that he had received "certain impressions . . . that we might perhaps be interested in detaining the Duke of Windsor here and possibly establishing contact with him."[18] This was to set into motion a chain of events as intricate and filled with intrigue as any spy thriller.

The reply came promptly: "Is it possible in the first place to detain the Duke and Duchess of Windsor for a couple of weeks in Spain before they are granted an exit visa? It would be necessary in all events to be sure that it did not appear in any way that the suggestion came from Germany."[19]

Unfortunately, that summer, the Windsors spoke freely and somewhat carelessly about the conduct of the war, sentiments which only encouraged the Germans to believe they might cooperate. On July 2, for example, American ambassador Alexander Weddell reported to the U.S. State Department:

In a conversation last night with one of the Embassy staff the Duke of Windsor declared that the most important thing now to be done was to end the war before thousands more were killed or maimed to save the faces of a few politicians. With regard to the defeat of France he stated that stories that the French troops would not fight were not true. They had fought magnificently, but the organization behind them was totally inadequate. In the past 10 years Germany had totally reorganized the order of its society in preparation for this war. Countries which were unwilling to accept such a reorganization of society and its concomitant sacrifices should direct their policies accordingly and thereby avoid dangerous adventures. He stated that this applied not merely to Europe, but to the United States also. The Duchess put the same thing somewhat more directly by declaring that France had lost because it was internally diseased and that a country which was not in condition to fight a war should never have declared war. . . . These observations have their value in reflecting the views of an element in England, possibly a growing one who find in Windsor and his circle a group who are realists in world politics and who hope to come into their own in event of peace."[20]

The British government formally announced the Duke of Windsor's appointment to the governor-generalship of the Bahamas on July 9. Neither the Duke nor Duchess made much secret of their displeasure over the situation, and surrounded as they were by spies, this news leaked back rather quickly to Berlin. From his ambassador Baron Oswald von Hoyningen-Huene in Lisbon, Joachim von Ribbentrop soon received a further report on the Windsors: "As Spaniards from among those around the Duke of Windsor have informed us confidentially on visits to the Legation, the designation of the Duke as Governor of the Bahama Islands is intended to keep him far away from England, since his return would bring with it very strong encouragement to English friends of peace." The report speculated on the Duke's state of mind and contained one of the most damning assertions ever made against him: "He is convinced that if he had remained on the Throne war would have been avoided, and he characterizes himself as a firm supporter of a peaceful arrangement with Germany. The Duke definitely believes that continued severe bombing would make England ready for peace."[21]

It is this last line which has become rather infamous. The difficulty with assuming the face value of the remark, however, is somewhat more complex. First, it was not attributed to the Duke as a direct quote—a fact which seems to have escaped those critics who have seized upon it as proof of his supposed treachery. Assuming for the moment that the sentiment, if not the remark itself, is correct, one would be advised to consider not only the context in which it may have been made but also the source through which it became known.

The Duke, as Weddell's account makes perfectly clear, continued to believe, despite his active participation in the war, that the conflict might somehow reach a negotiated peace. Undoubtedly, at times he expressed this desire in terms easily misinterpreted. Because David was, as Weddell also noted, a realist, it is not difficult to imagine that he may indeed have made some vague remark regarding England's ability to survive a prolonged bombing campaign. That the Duke would have expressed himself in terms which suggested he supported a bombing campaign, however, is exceptionally unlikely. This becomes even more probable when one considers not only the fact that any communication with Ribbentrop was prone to optimistic expression; Hitler hoped that the Duke might prove amenable to German overtures, and Hoyningen-Huene, career diplomat that he was, undoubtedly would have been clever enough to shade his reports to reflect his efforts in the most favorable light imaginable. Michael Bloch points out that the Duke of Windsor's "every utterance was liable to be picked up and repeated and exploited for enemy purposes."[22]

The Germans swung into action. Ribbentrop reported:

In our opinion, haste is accordingly required. From here it would seem best if close Spanish friends of the Duke would privately invite him, and of course his wife, for a short one- or two-week visit to Spain on pretexts which would seem plausible both to him, to the Portuguese, and to the English agents. That would mean, therefore, that the Duke and Duchess, as well as the English and the Portuguese, must believe that Windsor in any event is going to come back there. . . . After their return to Spain, the Duke and his wife must be persuaded or compelled to remain on Spanish territory. For the event of the latter alternative we must reach an agreement with the Spanish Government to the effect that by reasons of the obligations of neutrality the Duke will be interned, since the Duke as an English officer and a member of the English Expeditionary Force must be treated as a military fugitive who has crossed the frontier. . . . At any rate, at a suitable occasion in Spain the Duke must be informed that Germany wants peace with the English people, that the Churchill clique stands in the way of it, and that it would be a good thing to hold himself in readiness for further developments. Germany is determined to force England to peace by every means of power and upon this happening would be prepared to accommodate any desire expressed by the Duke, especially with a view to the assumption of the English Throne by the Duke and Duchess. If the Duke should have other plans, but be prepared to cooperate in the establishment of good relations between Germany and England, we would likewise be prepared to assure him and his wife of a subsistence which would permit him, either as a private citizen or in some other position, to lead a life suitable for a King."[23]

This report contained a brief outline of the plot. On July 11, Ribbentrop conveyed further details to Gestapo counterespionage chief Walter Schellenberg:

> The crux of the matter is that, since his abdication, the Duke has been under strict surveillance by the British Secret Service. We know what his feelings are: it's almost as if he were their prisoner. Every attempt that he's made to free himself, however discreet he may have been, has failed. And we know from our reports that he still entertains the same sympathetic feelings toward Germany, and that given the right circumstances he wouldn't be averse to escaping from his present environment—the whole thing's getting on his nerves.
>
> We've had word that he has even spoken about living in Spain and that if he did go there he'd be ready to be friends with Germany again as he was before. The Führer thinks this attitude is extremely important, and we thought that you with your Western outlook might be the most suitable person to make some sort of exploratory contact with the Duke—as the representative, of course, of the Head of the German State. The Führer feels that if the atmosphere seems propitious you might perhaps make the Duke some material offer. Now we should be prepared to deposit in Switzerland for his own use a sum of fifty million Swiss francs—if he were ready to make some official gesture dissociating himself from the maneuvers of the British Royal Family. The Führer would, of course, prefer him to live in Switzerland, though any other neutral country would do so long as it's not outside the economic or political influence of the German Reich.
>
> If the British Secret Service should try to frustrate the Duke in some such arrangement, then the Führer orders that you are to circumvent the British plans, even at the risk of your life, and, if need be, by the use of force.
>
> Whatever happens, the Duke of Windsor must be brought safely to the country of his choice. Hitler attaches the greatest

importance to this operation, and he has come to the conclusion after serious consideration that if the Duke should prove hesitant, he himself would have no objection to your helping the Duke to reach the right decision by coercion—even by threats or force if the circumstances make it advisable. But it will also be your responsibility to make sure at the same time that the Duke and his wife are not exposed to any personal danger.

Now, in the near future the Duke expects to have an invitation to hunt with some Spanish friends. This hunt should offer an excellent opportunity for you to establish contact with him. From that point he can immediately be brought into another country. All the necessary means for you to carry out this assignment will be at your disposal. Last night I discussed the whole matter again thoroughly with the Führer and we have agreed to give you a completely free hand. But he demands that you let him see daily reports on the progress of the affair."[24]

Schellenberg asked for further details about his possible use of force. "Well," Ribbentrop answered, "the Führer feels that force should be used primarily against the British Secret Service—against the Duke only insofar as his hesitation might be based on a fear psychosis which forceful action on our part would help him overcome."[25]

Obviously, if the use of force against the Windsors was being discussed, the Duke could not have known in advance of such plans. Nor would it seem, from this discussion, that the Nazis expected him to be fully cooperative; had he been vocally sympathetic to the Nazis, as critics have alleged, the Germans would certainly have known this, with their well-placed spies, and realized that there was no need to prepare for possible arm-twisting. Ribbentrop also explained that the "fifty million Swiss francs by no means represents the absolute minimum. The Führer is quite prepared to go to a higher figure." Hitler himself discussed the ideas on the telephone with Ribbentrop and said, "Schellenberg should particularly bear in mind the importance of the Duchess's attitude and try as hard as possible to get her support. She has great influence over the Duke."[26]

Schellenberg hurried to Madrid, where he met with German ambassador Stohrer. Stohrer himself reported that he had talked with Spanish interior minister Ramón Serrano Suner, a brother-in-law of Generalissimo Francisco Franco, and asked for his and Franco's personal support in the Windsor project. Franco arranged to send the Marques de Estella, Miguel Primo de Rivera, a friend of the Duke's, as an agent to Portugal.[27] Rivera would personally invite the Duke and Duchess to a hunting trip in Spain.

Next, Schellenberg traveled to Lisbon and recruited a Japanese friend to get precise information about the Windsor residence in Cascais. He wanted to know how many entrances it contained, how many floors, where windows stood, and other details which would make his job easier. "Within two days, I had drawn a close net of informants round the Duke's residence," said Schellenberg. "I had even managed to replace the Portuguese police guard with my own people. I was also able to place informants among the servants, so that within five days I knew of every incident that took place in the house and every word spoken at the dinner table."[28]

By the middle of July, Rivera had arrived at Cascais and called on the Windsors. "His designation as Governor of the Bahamas was made known in a very cool and categorical letter from Churchill with the instruction that he should leave for his post immediately without fail," Rivera reported back to his superiors. "Churchill has threatened W. with arraignment before a court martial in case he did not accept the post (this appears to have been communicated orally only to the Duke)."[29]

Rivera next reported that the Duke had received a postponement, since he was awaiting some of his effects and objects from his house in Paris. He further transmitted to Ribbentrop:

> The Duke expressed himself very freely. In Portugal he felt almost like a prisoner. He was surrounded by agents, etc. Politically he was more and more distant from the King and the present English Government. The Duke and Duchess have less fear of the King, who was quite foolish, than of the shrewd Queen who was intriguing skillfully against the Duke and particularly against the Duchess. . . .
>
> The Duke was considering making a public statement and thereby disavowing present English policy and breaking with his brother. . . .
>
> The Duke and Duchess were extremely interested in the secret communication which the Minister of Interior promised to make to the Duke. . . . The Duke and Duchess said they very much desired to return to Spain and expressed thanks for the offer of hospitality. The Duke's fear that in Spain he would be treated as a prisoner was dispelled by the confidential emissary, who in response to an inquiry declared that the Spanish Government would certainly agree to permit the Duke and Duchess to take up their residence in southern Spain (which the Duke seemed to prefer), perhaps in Granada or Malaga, etc.[30]

Schellenberg, in the meantime, tried to exert his final influence:

I therefore arranged for a high Portuguese police official to tell the Duke that the Portuguese guard would have to be strengthened because they had information that the Duke was being watched. . . . That same night I staged an incident in the garden of the Duke's villa; stones were thrown at the windows, and as a result an intensive search of the whole house was made by the Portuguese guard which caused a considerable disturbance. I then started rumours among the servants at the villa that the British Secret Service had been behind the incident. They had orders to make the Duke's stay as uncomfortable as possible and thus make him readier to leave. . . .[31]

Schellenberg also had a note inserted in a bouquet of flowers which was delivered to the Duchess: "Beware of the machinations of the British Secret Service—a Portuguese friend who has your interests at heart."[32]

In addition, Schellenberg informed the police and the Duke, through mutual friends, that the British Secret Service intended to plant a bomb on the ship the Windsors would take to sail to the Bahamas, explode it before their arrival, and blame it on the Germans. He hoped this news would help persuade the Duke to accept the overtures being made on behalf of the Germans. Rivera repeatedly urged the Duke not to accept the British government's offer of a ship to leave; the Germans were desperate to keep him in Portugal, where they could more easily kidnap him and take him to Spain.

Schellenberg had one last measure. He planned to have shots fired at the Duchess's bedroom window; he eventually decided against this, "since the psychological effect would only have been to increase her desire to depart."[33] Instead, he contented himself by dispatching another note, warning that the British Secret Service was planning to assassinate them the moment they left Portugal.

Ultimately, desperation drove the Germans to make more direct overtures. Rivera directly confronted the Windsors:

When he [Rivera] gave the Duke advice not to go to the Bahamas, but to return to Spain, since the Duke was likely yet to be called upon to play an important role in English policy and possibly to ascend the English Throne, both the Duke and Duchess gave evidence of astonishment. Both appeared to be completely enmeshed in conventional ways of thinking, for they replied that according to the English constitution this would not be possible after the abdication.

When the confidential emissary then expressed his expectation that the course of the war might bring about changes even in the English constitution, the Duchess especially became very pensive."[34]

It is clear from this report that neither of the Windsors was aware of the German machinations until Rivera specifically informed them of the possibilities. Their surprise that they might somehow be given power in England alone proved that they were not conspiring against the government there. This was not the response Rivera and the Germans had been hoping for, and it propelled the plot into dangerous territory. "The Führer orders that an abduction is to be organized at once," Ribbentrop cabled Schellenberg.[35] Using a second confidential emissary, this time a woman, Schellenberg outlined his plan for the Duke and Duchess: They would set out officially for a summer vacation in the mountains at a place providing the opportunity for hunting near the Spanish frontier. Schellenberg would send forces to guarantee safety on the Portuguese side, while Rivera would wait on the Spanish side. As soon as they arrived, both would be taken hostage.[36]

David later admitted that he had had discussions with Nazi emissaries but added "At no time did I ever entertain any thought of complying with such suggestions, which I treated with the contempt they deserved."[37] Unfortunately, his responses were too easily misinterpreted; he still had no taste for the war and made little secret of the fact, statements which the Germans seized upon as evidence of his willingness to cooperate. David never entered into serious negotiations with Rivera or any of Hitler's agents, and the Germans were forced to resort to terrorist tactics and kidnap plots to win him over. If anything, the Duke of Windsor was guilty of bad judgment in speaking too freely. But there is no reliable evidence that he acted in any manner which could be termed traitorous.

While all of this was taking place, David's attention was devoted to a new battle with the Foreign Office in London. He wished to make his own arrangements for him and Wallis to travel to the Bahamas, allowing for a short stop in America. This caused a considerable flap in the British Foreign Office and a flurry of messages between the prime minister and the British ambassador to the United States, Lord Lothian: "The more I think of it the more I am convinced that it is very undesirable that His Royal Highness should come to the United States at all en route to the Bahamas. . . . If he visits New York there will inevitably be a great deal of publicity, much of which will be of an icy character and which will have a most unfortunate effect at the present juncture."[38]

When the British government refused to grant the Duke his preferred transport, he cabled Churchill: "Have been messed about quite long enough and detect in Colonial Office attitude very much same hands at work as in my last job. Strongly urge you to support arrangements I have made as otherwise will have to reconsider my position."[39]

Officially, the British used the excuse that the Duke, as a British officer, could not travel on a neutral American ship for fear of violating America's Neutrality Act. David was not pleased. "Regarding not landing in the United States at this juncture, I take it to mean that this only applies until after the events of November. May I therefore have confirmation that it is not to be the policy of His Majesty's Government that I should not set foot on American soil during my term of office in the Bahamas? Otherwise I could not feel justified in representing the King in a British Colony so geographically close to the United States if I was to be prevented from ever going to that country."[40] Churchill agreed that the Duke could visit America at any time with the proper notification.

Churchill sent Monckton to persuade the Duke and Duchess to leave at once. They, in turn, told him what Rivera had said about a possible kidnapping and murder by the British Secret Service. Monckton confronted Rivera and said that if he could produce evidence he would ask the Duke not to leave. Rivera said he would need at least ten days, but Monckton would not be put off. Several Scotland Yard detectives were dispatched, one to travel with them and one to meet them in Nassau. Finally, Monckton told the Duke and Duchess that Churchill had learned that there was indeed a kidnapping plot but that it was of German origin.

On August 1 the Duke and Duchess boarded the American Export Lines ship the *Excalibur* bound for Bermuda, where they could switch ships and travel on to the Bahamas. Carefully packed into the holds were fifty-two pieces of their luggage, a portable sewing machine, a set of golf clubs for the Duke, four baskets of old Madeira and port wine, and a 1940 limousine with a trailer. Wallis, attired in a light blue linen dress and dark sunglasses, stood on deck next to David, who wore a gray pin-striped suit and light straw hat. Between them, yapping with excitement, were their three cairn terriers. Amid a flash of press lightbulbs and the blare of the ship's horn, the Windsors, smiling and waving to the crowd that had gathered alongside the dock, left Portugal for the unknown of their wartime home in the Bahamas.[41]

33

The Bahamas

T HE VOYAGE TO BERMUDA took a week. Along with the Duke and Duchess, the *Excalibur's* passengers included Maj. Gray Phillips; George and Rosa Wood; and Marguerite Moulichon, the Duchess's lady's maid. Wallis and David shared an ordinary cabin, nine-by-sixteen feet, with twin beds, a desk, and two chairs. As a concession to their special status, however, they were given a small, private deck on which they ordinarily took their meals. They ate very little; neither Wallis nor David took breakfast, and the Duke boiled his own water to make tea on a hot plate which had been brought in for his use. Aurelio Gonzalaz, one of the *Excalibur's* stewards, recalled that the Windsors constantly referred to each other as "darling"; they spent their evenings strolling about the decks arm in arm.[1]

At half-past two on the afternoon of August 8, the *Excalibur* anchored in the harbor off Hamilton, Bermuda; a tender pulled alongside, and the Duke and Duchess slowly descended the ladder and boarded the small vessel. Swiftly, it brought them to the dock of the Royal Yacht Club, where some thirty-five hundred people waited. As the Windsors stepped ashore, they were greeted with a military salute from a guard of honor and the cheers of the gathered crowd. Wallis wore a crepe dress, a matching coat in royal blue with accents of pink, elbow-length white gloves, and white shoes. Atop her head was a small cap composed of cascades of white beads. The governor-general, Sir Denis Bernard, greeted them warmly; however, as they made their way down the receiving line, none of the women present curtsied to the Duchess.[2]

The Windsors were forced to wait a week in Hamilton before they could transfer to another ship. They spent their time shopping, swimming, and touring several of the local hospitals. In Hamilton, the Windsors gave their first joint press conference. The Duchess, asked about the war, declared, "When you live in this war, you get used to anything. You never know anything, and it's not knowing that's the worst. When you're told to move, you move and move very quickly."[3]

On Sunday morning, they attended services at the Anglican Cathedral. The *New York Times* noted: "The couple went by carriage through the crowded street. The Duke, hatless, responded by smiling and waving to the throng, but the Duchess in the carriage behind, for the first time unquestionably stole the show. She looked and smiled her best and was the object of another of those unpredictable but plainly sincere bursts of applause to which Bermudians have rarely given way."[4]

Frank Giles, one of Bernard's aides-de-camp, had been prepared to discount the Duchess of Windsor. Instead, he was impressed, as he later recalled:

> She is a very clever woman &, like all clever women, contrives to hide her real feelings behind what is in her case a highly polished exterior. I have never known a woman to have so much of what the French would call 'le style.' She is not extrinsically beautiful or handsome, but she has a good complexion, regular features & a beautiful figure, for him who likes very small waists. To her, herself, though, & not to nature, goes the palm for her appearance, for it is an article whose beauty has been fashioned by human and not divine hands which confronts us. She is, of course, beautifully dressed—and this does not mean just extravagantly dressed—with a canny sense of fitness, with knowledge of how to avoid the bizarre but strike the original. The coiffure is superb and judging from the number of times she summoned the hairdresser to the house, must—and quite rightly so—be her chief pride. . . . She has good legs and ankles and she moves well—not self-consciously, but with obvious attention to appearance. More than all the charm of her physical appearance, though, is her manner: she has, to an infinite degree, that great gift of making you feel that you are the very person whom she has been waiting all her life to meet. With old & young & clever & stupid alike she exercises this charm, and during the week she was here, I never saw anyone who could resist the spell—they were all delighted and intrigued. . . . She does not talk much unless she sees you want to talk & she is always quiet and dignified & composed. . . . She is never anything but stately, & when she had to wave to the crowds on her arrival & subsequently whenever we drove through the town, she did it with an ease and charm and grace which suggested she had been at it all her life.[5]

Finally, after taking a zigzag route to avoid any lurking German U-boats, the liner *Lady Somers*, carrying the Windsors, arrived in Nassau on the morning of August 17. The Bahamas, encompassing some twenty-nine islands and hundreds of coral reefs and cays, was home to a population of just over seventy thousand. Of this number, 80 percent were black or of mixed race. For the most part, they were poorly educated, often deliberately kept economically dependent on the handful of wealthy white merchants known as the Bay Street Boys. Their stranglehold on the economic and social life of the country had been tacitly endorsed by every previous governor-general, and no attempt had been made to break their agricultural and commercial monopolies. The problems of trade, social improvement, and race relations all contributed to make the Bahamas one of the most difficult and political of all colonial governorships in the empire. "It was regarded as a kind of punishment station in the Colonial Service," writes Michael Bloch, "combining a minimum of importance with a maximum of frustration."[6]

The frustrations the Windsors were to face had already been increased even before their arrival. On George VI's orders, the lord chamberlain had issued a telegram to all Bahamas officials: "You are no doubt aware that a lady when presented to HRH The Duke of Windsor should make a half-curtsey. The Duchess of Windsor is not entitled to this. The Duke should be addressed as 'Your Royal Highness' and the Duchess as 'Your Grace.'"[7] For the Duke and Duchess, it would become just another incident in the constant battle waged against them by Buckingham Palace. "Such were the concerns of certain officials during what Winston Churchill called 'their finest hour,'" comments respected historian Kenneth Rose.[8]

In the brilliant sunshine of that August morning, Wallis and David stood on the bridge of the *Lady Somers*, watching as the island of New Providence and its main city and Bahama's capital, Nassau, came into view. Wallis wore a pink-and-blue print dress, a navy blue silk coat, and a white cap stitched with pearls; at her side, the Duke was already beginning to sweat in his major general's heavy khaki uniform. The sky above them was cloudless; by nine A.M., the temperature already stood at just under a hundred degrees, and the intense humidity was something on which neither of the Windsors had counted.[9]

Sixteen thousand of New Providence's twenty thousand inhabitants had turned out to greet the Windsors.[10] Prince George Wharf, where they alighted, was decked with bunting and hundreds of Union Jacks as well as American flags in honor of the Duchess. Waiting to greet them were a guard of honor and the Bahamian Executive Council, their wives, and members of their staffs.

The Duke and Duchess were escorted on foot across Rawson Square, past the bright, whitewashed, and pastel-painted buildings hung with flags, to the Legislative Building, where they were met by the president of the Legislative Council and the speaker of the House of Assembly. Here David, suffering from the heat and sweating despite his tropical uniform, was to take the oath of office.[11] The Duke sat on a throne beneath a crimson velvet canopy embroidered with a golden crown. Wallis sat in her own chair, on a special platform one step below David; the wife of an ordinary governor-general would normally have sat in the audience, and the local authorities had spent a great deal of time trying to find a compromise for this woman who, though married to the former king and a Royal Duke, was not, on orders of the Foreign Office, to be regarded as royal herself. It is not known what, if any comment, this last measure aroused among the Foreign Office or from Buckingham Palace.

Lt. Col. R. A. Erskine-Lindop, commissioner of police of the Bahamas, read the commission of office; then the chief justice, Sir Oscar Daly, administered the sacred oath, during which the Duke of Windsor swore allegiance to his brother. In his speech, David declared, "How delighted I am that the Duchess is with me to share the pleasure of my first visit to these islands."[12] Afterward, Wallis and David stood patiently in the intense, suffocating heat, shaking hands with all of those present. They then walked to the balcony overlooking Rawson Square, where they were loudly cheered by the gathered crowd as the national anthem was played.

After the official welcome, they were driven to their new home, Government House, high on the hill above Nassau. Tall hedges of purple bougainvillea and low stone walls enclosed the ten-acre garden, shaded by enormous palm trees. From the terrace, where a swimming pool offered welcome relief from the humid heat, the view stretched over downtown Nassau and on to the Caribbean. The house itself, a large, plantation-style building dominated by a tall, columned portico and surrounded by wide verandas, had been built in 1801. There were seven bedrooms, six bathrooms, and twenty-four other rooms, including a grand ballroom. Tall French windows and jalousied doors opened to the gardens and terraces.[13]

As the Duke and Duchess looked more closely, however, their initially favorable impression was replaced by shock. The swimming pool was cracked and filled with debris; the stones in the garden walks were loose and uneven. Within the house, the situation was even worse. Wives of various Nassau officials had filled its rooms with their cast-off antiques—huge, battered mahogany dressers and sagging sofas and chairs from the turn of the century. At one time, all of the interior rooms had been painted with industrial blue enamel; although the rooms were filled with fresh flowers, nothing could disguise the threadbare carpets, peeling paint, smell of mold, or falling plaster. In the kitchen, even in the hundred-plus-degree days of summer, all cooking was done on an old woodstove. There was no laundry room; all washing was carried to a small stream which ran through the garden and was beaten on rocks.

Wallis and David stayed barely a week. One morning, while Wallis was working at her desk, a piece of the ceiling broke and crashed down next to her chair.[14] Immediately, the Duke called in the Bahamian director of public works and ordered a full inspection. The results came as no great surprise: Government House was riddled with termites and unstable and was, in the opinion of the surveyors, unsafe for habitation.[15] It would have to be completely renovated.

David cabled Lord Lloyd, the colonial secretary, proposing that he and the Duchess leave for his ranch in Canada for several months until Government House could be redone. The secretary replied that "it would not only inevitably create a sense of disappointment but also possibly some misgiving and anxiety among the public as well" if the Duke left so soon after arriving. He suggested he postpone his departure for at least several months. He added: "There is of course no reason why, if the Duchess feels the heat, she should not go away for a few weeks."[16] This rather heavy-handed hint that the Duchess was welcome to leave was, however, ignored; if the Duke remained, so would the Duchess, and the matter was dropped.

While the renovations were under way, the Duke and Duchess stayed with Frederick Sigrist and his wife and, later, with Sir Harry and Lady Oakes at their house in Westbourne. From here, Wallis supervised the work at Government House. To assist in the decorative changes, she hired her Baltimore friend Mrs. Winthrop Bradley and American architect Sidney Neil. The Bahamian legislature voted five thousand dollars for structural repairs, rewiring, and new plumbing; this was less than half the cost of the eventual renovation, however, and the Duke and Duchess of Windsor themselves paid the difference out of their own income.[17]

The exterior of Government House was repainted a pale pink. The water damage and flaking plaster inside were repaired, and the old wicker furniture was taken away. The drawing room was filled with bright chintz-covered sofas and chairs; over the fireplace hung Gerald Brockhurst's famous portrait of the Duchess. The library was lightened through use of an imported French wallpaper and more chintz; soft green wall-to-wall carpet replaced the dark colors of the Oriental rug in the dining room. The Duke and Duchess had adjoining suites on the second floor overlooking the Caribbean. Wallis had four rooms: a bedroom, a dressing room, a bathroom, and a study–sitting room built into one of the porches. Again, as in her house in Paris, the rooms were decorated in her favorite shade of blue, with white accents. Across the hall were the Duke's rooms, with lime-colored walls, rattan and bamboo furniture, and bold English chintz fabrics.

The Windsors eventually settled into Government House. They had brought with them a number of members of their household, including Maj. Gray Phillips, who served as comptroller and doubled as the Duke's private secretary; George Wood, who served as aide-de-camp, and his wife, Rosa; and Capt. Vyvian Drury, Maj. Gen. Howard-Vyse's brother-in-law, who acted as equerry. Contrary to the orders which had gone out from the Foreign Office, this trusted staff always addressed both the Duke and Duchess in exactly the same manner, as "Your Royal Highness," and extended bows and curtsies. The native Bahamian staff at Government House was soon told that they, too, should follow suit; any deviation from the expected pattern was cause for a severe reprimand.

The difficult climate in Nassau was an element which neither Wallis nor David had anticipated. The intense heat and humidity bred all manner of unwelcome intruders: Sitting in the garden, Wallis might be startled to suddenly gaze down and find a lizard crawling over her legs. In the evening, when the heat from the sunset was at its worst in the house, they could not open the windows; if they did, the rooms would quickly fill with thousands of mosquitoes. At night—despite the thousands of dollars spent on renovations—cockroaches scurried across the floors. Even for Wallis, who had grown up accustomed to the temperatures and insects of Baltimore, the combination was nearly too much to bear. "All my life I've disliked hot weather," she told a reporter, "and coming to Nassau has been like taking a permanent slimming cure."[18]

Inevitably, disillusion and frustration over the situation spilled onto the pages of Wallis's letters to Aunt Bessie. "The heat is *awful*. I long for some air that isn't caused by electric fans. . . . I hate this place more each day. . . ." On one occasion, she referred to Nassau as "this dump." And again she wrote: "We both hate it and the locals are petty-minded, the visitors common and uninteresting. . . ."[19] Although they made no secret of their feelings in private or in personal letters, neither Wallis nor David ever publicly complained of the Nassau appointment; no matter how disgruntled they might have been, they were always careful to put a good face on the situation for the public.

The Windsors had few friends in Nassau. One, Alastair Mackintosh, happened to have been a friend of the Duke for many years. He had retired to Nassau while his two children attended boarding school in Canada. Shortly after arriving in the Bahamas, Wallis dispatched a note to Mackintosh: "The Duke and I know how much you will be missing the children, so please come and stay with us at once."[20]

Such a direct approach was typical for the Duchess; she had many acquaintances but few longtime friends and consequently valued those relationships which had managed to survive not only the passage of time but also the trials of her somewhat peculiar life. Another of her friends in Nassau, Cora Mallory Munson, was the widow of the president of the Munson Steamship Line. One day she happened to be at home, finishing her daily cleaning, when Wallis arrived unexpectedly. "When she called on me in Nassau and found me finishing my housework," Munson recalled, "she just snatched up a duster and began working away alongside me like any other American housewife."[21]

But for the most part the Windsors kept largely to themselves. The struggles both had undergone had drawn Wallis closer to David. Her devotion was witnessed by many, including Hearst newspaper reporter Adela Rogers St. John. Once, when St. John was interviewing Wallis, the Duchess telephoned for the Duke to join them. "Then I saw an expression I liked best of anything about her," St. John later wrote. "Her face was simply a little brighter, her mouth was amused, but in her eyes there was a light, an expectation of happiness."[22] At a party, St. John noticed how the Duchess was careful to watch after her husband, making sure that he remained comfortable and the center of attention. "David, darling, tell your wonderful story," she might say, launching the Duke into a lengthy memory which would hold his audience spellbound.[23]

Nassau was a far cry from the Europe left behind by the Duke and Duchess. Here there was no sign of the devastating war. The streets were filled with American tourists, enjoying the warm sunshine and sandy beaches. In an effort to temper some of this misplaced gaiety, the Duchess announced that she and the Duke would give small dinner parties but not the regular balls and receptions which had been standard before the war.[24]

The Duke found that he had inherited a politically volatile situation in the Bahamas. Agriculturally, the country was decades behind its North American neighbors; to improve the commercial situation, the Duke formed an economic committee, designed to import modern ideas and technology along with Western investment. Unfortunately, nearly all his efforts to reform the antiquated laws governing his new home met with considerable resistance. Hugo Vickers noted insightfully: "A Royal Prince, whose first rule of behaviour had previously been to stand outside politics, now had to carry out government policy, however unwelcome to sections of the local population, and to take public criticism for it."[25] Never was this more true than with his attempts at race reconciliation.

The Duke and Duchess, like many people of their social backgrounds, harbored certain color prejudices from birth. David had never been exposed to such intimate relations with blacks before; all of his previous dealings with them had been merely social. Their attitudes were no different from those of the rest of the Royal Family; Queen Elizabeth, the present Queen Mother, is known to still possess color prejudices, and in an overwhelmingly diverse commonwealth, only the Prince of Wales has seen fit to appoint a black member to his household.

David was confronted with a majority population which was largely poor, ill educated, and none too willing to believe the word of the latest occupant of Government House. Wallis, having been raised in Baltimore, where color barriers ran deep, and with more exposure to blacks in her childhood, was a bit more tolerant, but certainly neither could be considered free of prejudice. But the attitudes of the Duke and Duchess, as Michael Bloch points out, were "considerably more enlightened" in their dealings with the native blacks "than the majority of Bahamian whites, or either of his predecessors."[26]

Unfortunately, in trying to institute economic and limited social reform to benefit the black population, David faced the nearly impenetrable barriers erected by the Bay Street Boys. As a result, the Duke was roundly denounced as inefficient; his most vocal critic was Etienne Dupuch, the mixed-race proprietor and editor of the *Tribune*, one of two daily newspapers in Nassau. As a pious Catholic, Dupuch believed that both the Duke and Duchess were living in open adultery. At the same time, he was violently opposed to the social and economic establishment, both in the Bahamas and in England, which he considered corrupt and immoral. In consequence, he disliked the Windsors on both counts. Dupuch did all he could to present the Duke and Duchess in the worst possible light, and their time in Nassau often found them at the center of a storm directly created by Dupuch's overly earnest agenda.

The Duke's first, tentative steps toward reform were welcomed with much enthusiasm, at least by the Americans. In October 1940, David opened the Bahamian legislature with his first throne speech. He promised to improve agricultural developments, lower unemployment, and raise wages. Many of his specific reforms were aimed at the primarily black population of the out islands surrounding New Providence.[27] The American consul in Nassau, John Dye, reported to the State Department: "The speech is one of the most sensible and business-like that has been delivered by a Governor for many years. . . . It may be true that he and his Duchess were sent out here to get rid of them, so to speak, but he is taking his job seriously and is showing a keen interest in the welfare of the Bahamas."[28] A short time later, Dye wrote: "The Duke accompanied by the Duchess every day visits some place of Government activity. The Duchess is active in Red Cross work and both are becoming popular with all classes of the population with the exception of a few die-hard English."[29]

Since arriving in Nassau, the Duke had expressed his wish, as had all his predecessors, to call upon the president of the United States as a courtesy. Franklin Roosevelt was willing enough to receive the Duke, but the Foreign Office, to whom David had to formally apply for permission to leave the Bahamas, refused to grant him the necessary leave. Their explanation was that with the presidential elections in the fall of 1940, the visit of the Duke might be interpreted as partisan support and interference in American politics. David realized that this was an excuse but for the moment did nothing. But after the reelection of Roosevelt there was no longer any reason for the Foreign Office to prevent the visit. Yet when the Duke tried to arrange it, he was told there were difficulties and was refused permission once again.

In December 1940, President Roosevelt set off on a Caribbean visit aboard the presidential cruiser *Tuscaloosa*. He asked Lord Lothian, the British ambassador to the United States, to inquire whether the Duke and Duchess would like to meet with him during his trip. But Lothian, alarmed at the idea, immediately contacted the Foreign Office in London, which wished that no such meeting should take place and ordered the ambassador not to mention the prospect to the Duke of Windsor. Thus, the wish of the American president was deliberately ignored by those who feared that the Duke of Windsor might once again appear in the public spotlight.

There the matter might have rested but for an unexpected illness on Wallis's part. That December she fell violently ill with an impacted wisdom tooth; the dentist she consulted in Nassau advised immediate surgery but recommended that she go to Miami to have the operation.[30] This time, David's request to travel to the United States was immediately approved: The Foreign Office, alerted that the president was on his way to the Caribbean, had been worried that despite Lothian's failure to deliver Roosevelt's direct request, somehow a meeting with the Duke would be arranged during his cruise. The Duchess's illness fortuitously offered a resolution: With the Windsors out of the country and occupied in Miami, there would be no opportunity for them to meet with the president.

Arrangements were quickly made. Regular passenger service had been canceled between Nassau and Miami, and the Windsors instead traveled as guests of Swedish industrialist Axel Wenner-Gren aboard his yacht the *Southern Cross*. This later proved to be something of an inopportune choice, as Wenner-Gren was widely suspected of harboring Nazi sympathies. At the time, however, the Windsors knew very little about Wenner-Gren or his connections in Europe, and the seriousness of Wallis's illness dictated an immediate departure.

They arrived in Miami on the morning of December 10; some twelve thousand people lined the docks, waiting to welcome the world's most famous husband and wife. Wallis was in terrible pain, but she smiled and waved to those who had gathered to greet her and David. Another ten thousand curious spectators stood along the route from the dock to St. Francis Hospital, cheering and applauding loudly as the Windsors' motorcade passed. Upon arriving at the hospital, Wallis was quickly examined; Dr. Horace Cartee discovered that the impacted molar was abscessed and had infected the entire lower right jaw. At one that afternoon, he operated and removed the molar, but the accompanying infection meant that Wallis had to remain in the hospital for several days.

On December 12, while Wallis was still in the hospital, David received two pieces of news: Lord Lothian, the British ambassador to the United States, had died suddenly; and President Roosevelt, hearing that the Duke was in Miami, asked if he would be willing to fly to Eleuthera for the day to join him aboard the *Tuscaloosa*. The two ideas mingled in David's mind, and he briefly entertained the thought that he might somehow manage to overcome the intense prejudice of Buckingham Palace and the Foreign Office against both him and Wallis and win an appointment as Lothian's replacement. The position was promising: Not only would it remove the Duke and Duchess from Nassau, but it was politically more important and offered David a larger scope for meaningful work. He also realized that Wallis, an American, would be a natural asset in the post. In the end, the meeting with Roosevelt was a success, but the Duke's aspirations toward a post in Washington were not to be: Lord Halifax was soon appointed as the new ambassador.

Wallis was finally discharged from the hospital on December 17, and the Windsors returned to Nassau in time for their first Christmas. Although still recovering, Wallis threw herself wholeheartedly into the preparations. She had decided to devote their celebrations to the underprivileged children of Nassau. Christmas trees were erected for several schools in Government House. At the celebratory luncheon, Wallis made the rounds, shaking hands and congratulating the mothers whose children had been evacuated during the war for their bravery. As they would do each year during the Duke's governor-generalship in the Bahamas, the Windsors purchased presents for hundreds of children from their private fortune and delighted in their distribution. David happily got down on his hands and knees, playing with the boys and their train sets, while Wallis played tea with the girls and spoke with their new dolls, just as her own mother had once done when she was young.[31]

34

The Visit to America

I N APRIL 1941, the Windsors again went to Miami, this time to meet with Sir Edward Peacock, the Duke's financial adviser. They left Nassau on April 16, passengers aboard the liner *SS Berkshire,* and arrived two days later in Miami, where the mayor and a crowd of two thousand waited to welcome them. From Miami they drove to Palm Beach, where they stayed at the Everglades Club. The following afternoon, David met privately with Peacock, while Wallis shopped along fashionable Worth Avenue for summer clothes. On April 20, the Windsors hosted a cocktail party for three hundred; the next afternoon, they visited the British War Relief Headquarters. They could not arrange for any regular transport back to Nassau; in desperation, Wallis agreed to accept the offer of a private plane made by their friend Harold Vanderbilt. She was loath to do so. On April 22, tightly clutching David's hand, she settled into her seat on the small plane for her first air trip. She kept her eyes closed for almost the entire hour, only opening them when David told her that she should look out the window at the view.[1]

They returned to America for a much longer tour that fall. This was to be Wallis's triumphant homecoming, and plans were made to visit not only the president at the White House but Baltimore, New York City, Chicago, and the Duke's E. P. Ranch in Alberta, Canada. They arrived in Miami on September 23; as was typical with nearly all of their American visits, they were greeted by a large crowd, this time some five thousand people who lined the roads to cheer them on.[2] David inspected the university RAF cadets, who were then undergoing flight training with American and British instructors; the following day, the Duke and Duchess boarded a private train provided for their use by their friend Robert Young, president of the New York Central Railroad. Their private Pullman car had adjoining bedrooms, a private dining room, a sitting room, and a bathroom. Other cars were coupled to the train, including a baggage compartment to hold their 146 pieces of luggage. Also on board were their three cairn terriers.

The Windsors first visited Washington, D.C., where a crowd of over ten thousand well-wishers waited to greet their arrival at Union Station. This stood in stark contrast to the small group of minor officials from the British embassy that had come to receive them. The British ambassador, Lord Halifax, was nowhere to be seen; he was, in fact, away from the city, having absented himself, as he often would when the Windsors visited the American capital. However, Charles Peake, Halifax's secretary, recalled that even the ambassador found many of the harsh directives against the Windsors too much to accept: "It is a pity that the Royal Family cannot behave with common decency to him. Distance, frigidity one expects, and is no more than he deserved. But civility (which costs nothing) might certainly be given and if given would deprive him of one well merited grievance."[3]

A planned luncheon at the White House was canceled due to the serious illness of Eleanor Roosevelt's brother; instead, the Duke met with the president privately for several hours. That evening, the Windsors attended a dinner party at the British embassy, and, the following day, Wallis accompanied David to the National Press Club, where the Duke gave a speech to a joint meeting of the National Press Club and the National Women's Press Club. The Associated Press reported: "Washingtonians received the famous pair with enthusiasm. Everywhere they went, peering, cheering, crowds gathered. Government clerks hung precariously from the windows and building ledges to see them; pretty girls showered the Duke with confetti; police battled crowds in corridors when the Duke entered Government buildings."[4]

From Washington, D.C., the Windsors journeyed by rail across America, stopping for a few hours in Chicago. Thousands of people crowded the railway station, hoping for a glimpse of the couple. David duly appeared, smiling and waving, but Wallis, who was suffering from a painful eye infection, remained hidden away. Finally, however, the repeated chants of her name won her over, and she walked out onto the rear platform of the train, smiling while the audience erupted in cheers.[5]

The route taken by the Windsors from Washington, D.C., to Alberta, Canada, had been dictated by the Foreign Office, which wished at all costs to avoid their presence in any large Canadian city where they might elicit precisely the sorts of favorable demonstrations taking place in America. As a result, the trip took a few days longer than necessary. David was particularly keen on showing Wallis his E. P. Ranch, nestled near the Pekisko Hills town of High River in Alberta. He had purchased the ranch in 1919; over the years, he had sunk a considerable fortune into the ranch, practicing stockbreeding and other agricultural endeavors. He always lost money, but David was loath to sell the property. Wallis found the setting—with its distant, snow-capped mountains, fields, and forests—attractive, but she had little liking for either the ranch itself or her time there. The ranch house, a long, low building with rooms tacked on over the years as needed, was too rustic for her tastes; nor did she have any interest in riding or hiking.[6]

While the Windsors were in Canada, they learned that a powerful storm had swept through the out islands of the Bahamas, leaving hundreds of families homeless. Wallis immediately sent cables to the Red Cross and the Daughters of the British Empire, saying that she was confident of their ability to deal effectively with the crisis. "I only wish I was there to help you in your work," she added. "Let me know if there is anything I can do or that you need."[7] There was indeed little Wallis could do from Canada, and any return trip to the Bahamas would take nearly two weeks; if relief was needed, she and the Duke would undoubtedly have been more effective securing foreign aid in Washington, D.C., than in Nassau.

The emotional highlight of the trip was Wallis's return to Baltimore. She herself was very nervous at the idea, declaring, "That's going to be quite an experience for me."[8] The Windsors spent two private days with her uncle Henry M. Warfield and his wife Rebecca, at Salona Farms, north of the city, where Wallis had often gone for summers as a child. They arrived at the quiet country siding of Timonium aboard their private train on October 11. Wallis rushed from the train to embrace her uncle, whom she had not seen for eight years, and kissed her cousin Anita Lewis, who stood by her father's side.[9] Although it was a private visit, five thousand people had gathered around the tracks, hoping to catch a glimpse of the historic moment. "With a gesture that spoke more loudly than her words," wrote Inez Robb of the meeting between uncle and niece, "drowned out by huzzahs of the crowd, she presented to her uncle and her cousin the man who gave up his heritage to be her husband. The Duke seemed almost boyishly eager that the general like him. . . ."[10] Having been rejected by his own family, David now looked to that of his wife for support and companionship.

October 13 was the day of the public welcome. After lunch the Duke and Duchess and General and Mrs. Warfield left Salona Farms by car; at the city limits they were met by a police escort on motorcycles and were taken to city hall. Wallis wore a simple white dress, edged in black, with a sable wrap. Offices and shops were practically deserted. A crowd estimated at 200,000 lined the city streets, applauding and waving American flags and Union Jacks.[11] "The crowds cheered like fans at a football game to greet its most famous daughter," the Associated Press reported.[12] "This is *her* party," one woman remarked. "It must be wonderful to have this many people waiting to take a look at you."[13] There had been nothing quite like it before in Baltimore.

The Duke and Duchess rode in an open car with the mayor, Howard W. Jackson. At city hall, Jackson declared: "Until the day of victory comes, and come it must, and always after that, we hope both of you will continue to regard Baltimore as another home, where you will always find peace and happiness."[14] There was a reception at the Baltimore Country Club for eight hundred specially invited guests that afternoon. When one of her former teachers, Miss Ada O'Donnell, appeared, Wallis recognized her at once and ran from the receiving line to embrace her.[15]

The next few days were divided between Baltimore and Washington, D.C., between public duties and private recreation. The Duke met with Lord Halifax, who by this time had returned to the capital and who, three days later, hosted a luncheon for the Windsors at the British embassy. Wallis spent much of her time at Salona Farms with Aunt Bessie. There were joint visits to the American Red Cross, the British War Relief Society; and the British Seaman's Institute. In the midst of the visit, she was taken ill with a recurrence of her old stomach trouble. Doctors found a perforated duodenal ulcer, which they advised required an immediate operation, but Wallis refused to interrupt the schedule.[16]

From Baltimore, the Windsors traveled to New York City, where, at the Waldorf Towers, they booked a twenty-eighth-floor suite overlooking Park Avenue. During their stay, Wallis had arranged for Mainbocher to come to the suite and fit her for some new clothes. Unfortunately, he also spoke with the press, and rumor magnified the amount of Wallis's simple order. She was angry enough to grant a rare interview: "I haven't been in a shop since May 1940, before I left Paris. I'm trying to collect money for a third clinic, but I hope you don't mind if I buy one or two dresses." According to one press report, she had purchased thirty-four new hats during the visit to America; Wallis quickly corrected this, saying the actual number was five. "Since I am actually shopping for a year, I don't think anyone could consider this outrageous." She did enjoy shopping in New York, but she also worked hard at persuading the city's department stores to purchase Bahamian coral jewelry, usually handcrafted by the poorer residents of the out islands, to sell to their customers.[17]

The Windsors, like other famous visitors to New York, received a ticker-tape parade through lower Manhattan. But most of their time was spent on serious pursuits. Wallis visited Inwood House on West Fifteenth Street, a home for unmarried mothers. She toured the wards, spoke to the expectant mothers about birth control and its advantages, and played with the babies "like a social worker rather than a socialite," in the words of Michael Pye.[18] Together with David, she inspected fifteen mobile army hospital units. The pair later visited Bundles for Britain's main office, where the Duke purchased a lapel pin for five dollars despite protests that he was being too generous.[19] There was a tour of the Royal Air Force Benevolent Fund offices, followed by a luncheon, after which the Windsors visited the Seaman's Church Institute. As Wallis walked past a group of sailors playing darts, one of them called out, "Have a shot, Duchess!" With a laugh, Wallis protested that she had never played before, but she agreed to try. Her first shot landed near the bull's-eye, but her next two missed the board altogether. Nonetheless, she was loudly cheered by the delighted sailors.[20]

Together the Windsors toured the Brooklyn Naval Yard and visited several housing projects for the poor on the East Side of the city. On Halloween, Wallis organized a party for underprivileged children. They also returned to Washington, D.C., where they met again with the president. After talking with the first lady, Wallis decided to write a cookbook, *Some Favorite Southern Recipes of the Duchess of Windsor*, whose proceeds would all be donated to war-relief agencies; Mrs. Roosevelt was to provide the introduction. All the while, Wallis tried to do what she could for those charities most desperately in need of assistance. "I'm not nearly so interested in clothes as people think," she said. "I'd rather talk about Red Cross work and infant welfare."[21]

On the whole, the visit was a great success. There was a certain limited amount of criticism of the trip for what some writers took as frivolous expenditure on the part of the Duke and Duchess, but as Michael Bloch points out, a press survey found that the unfavorable reaction represented no more than 4 percent of the actual coverage. The vast majority of their time, and the concentration of their energies, had been focused on visiting hospitals, touring war-relief facilities, and raising funds for Bahamian charities. Nevertheless, the British Press Service report on the visit inaccurately declared: "The general impression created was that of a rich and carefree couple, travelling with all the pre-war accoutrement of royalty, and with no thought either of the sufferings of their own people or of the fact that the world is at war."[22]

As much as Wallis had not wanted the war, she was genuinely moved when, following the Japanese attack on American forces at Pearl Harbor, the country of her birth finally entered into the hostilities. But America's entry into the war also brought with it new worries. Early in 1942 there were rumors of German U-boats in the Caribbean; several shipwrecked crews did indeed wash ashore or were rescued and brought to Nassau, where Wallis supervised their care.[23] The concerns for the Windsors' safety—with unwelcome memories of the German kidnapping plot—were such that a company of Cameron

Highlanders was dispatched to build a barbed-wire fence around Government House and to post sentries.[24]

Throughout 1941, following passage of the Lend-Lease Act in the U.S. Congress, American forces were dispatched to Nassau to construct a large airfield for use by American and British Air Force troops. Eventually called Windsor Field, it provided a boost to the local economy, which, due to the onset of the war, had slowed considerably with the drop-off of tourism. But the imported American workers were paid a higher wage than the mainly black Bahamanian workers, and by the late spring of 1942, an undercurrent of hostility began to grow over the situation.[25] Six months earlier, the Duke had proposed that workers' wages be raised by eighty cents an hour; nothing, however, came of the plan when the legislature refused to consider the idea.[26]

On May 28, 1942, the Duke and Duchess sailed to Miami on a small private cruiser they had purchased called the *Gemini*. The Duke had certain business with the U.S. naval authorities regarding supplies to the Bahamas. Afterward, the Windsors traveled to Washington, D.C., where they stayed with Lord and Lady Halifax at the British embassy. On June 1 they dined at the White House with the Roosevelts; during the dinner, David was handed an urgent cable: Discontented Bahamanian workers, upset over the wage disparity, were rioting in the streets of Nassau. The president immediately put the secretary of the navy's private airplane at the Duke's disposal so that he might quickly return home.[27] Wallis would remain behind until the situation had calmed down.

David returned to demonstrations in the streets, marches, and looting. He immediately called out the troops to restore order. His first concern, once the rioting had been quieted, was to resolve the problem which had led to the outburst in the first place. He tried to impose a 25 percent increase in wages for Nassau workers along with a free midday meal. Once again, however, his proposals were met with resistance at the hands of the Bay Street Boys, who exerted near total control over the legislature. David eventually managed to win meager concessions, which, though they fell far short of what he himself had proposed, proved acceptable to the rioters.

As soon as things had calmed down, David returned to Washington to collect Wallis. However, only a few days after their return, a devastating fire broke out in the center of Nassau. The Duke and Duchess rushed from Government House to the scene, and both quickly took charge: David stood in the middle of the street, amid the soot and rubble raining down all around him, directing firefighters and helping drag hoses to distant hydrants. "He seemed what he always should have been: prince-hero, battling odds, silhouetted against rising fire."[28] Meanwhile, Wallis had run to Red Cross headquarters, which lay in the line of the fire; she organized a group of workers, and together they managed to haul most of the fittings and supplies from the building before it, too, caught fire and was destroyed.[29] All night long, the Windsors and hundreds of others desperately battled the flames; finally, when morning came, David ordered the neighboring buildings dynamited to stop the spread. His scheme worked. By afternoon, four city blocks lay smoldering in ruins, but the fire was out.[30] Although the cause was believed to be arson, the fire was never formally tied to the previous riots.

Scarcely a month after the Nassau riots and the fire, David faced a personal tragedy. On August 25, 1942, word arrived in the Bahamas that the Duke's youngest brother, George, Duke of Kent, had died in a plane crash. David dearly loved his younger brother, and this news devastated him. He immediately dispatched a letter to his sister-in-law Princess Marina, George's widow, but somehow—whether accidentally or not—the letter was lost in transit; Marina, convinced that the Windsors had deliberately ignored her loss, refused to forgive them for what she believed a heartless snub. The Duke and Duchess had hoped that with George's death "there would be a drawing together of the family, a softening of all hearts. But even these shared sorrows proved not enough."[31]

35

The Duchess's War Work

THE WINDSORS," wrote Frances Donaldson, "have to be judged on their record in Nassau because on this they must rest all their claims to a job of world importance, many of their complaints against the Royal Family and the government of England, the belief that they were treated with spite and jealousy because of his superior gifts, and the grievance that his years of training were thrown away."[1] Using these criteria, it is difficult to condemn the Windsors' time in Nassau. There were, admittedly, certain missteps, mainly on David's part; in fairness, however, he faced an uncooperative legislature and a notoriously volatile political, economic, and social situation. More than anything else, the Windsors showed that they were capable of performing to royal standards; they might continue to harbor a grudge against the King and dislike their temporary home, but in public they managed to convey genuine interest in, and enthusiasm for, the people of the Bahamas. Above all, Wallis's time in the Bahamas witnessed an incredible transformation in her; far from the popular image of her as decadent adventuress, which the Royal Family continued to promote, she became, in fact, an ideal governor-general's wife.

Nevertheless, the Windsors' image suffered from their time in the Bahamas in comparison with the Royal Family back in England. This was not because the Duke and Duchess were any less dedicated to the war effort or worked any less hard than George VI or Queen Elizabeth; however, the Royal Family was surrounded by advisers, cosseted and protected, the beneficiaries of an intense publicity campaign designed to showcase their efforts. The Windsors, on the other hand, operated almost entirely beyond the bounds of the royal system. As a result, few knew or appreciated the very real differences they made during their time in Nassau.

Then, too, the Royal Family continued to make very deliberate efforts to undermine all that the Duke and Duchess did. To assist the British relief efforts, David dispatched a large sum of money to London to establish a canteen for bombing victims. His only request, not unnaturally, was that it be called "the Duke and Duchess of Windsor's Canteen." Buckingham Palace immediately objected, however. The King was still convinced that his brother was trying to undermine his position on the throne and seek publicity for himself. David was told, therefore, that so naming the canteen would not be acceptable to the palace. It is a measure of David's dedication to the war effort and his ability to ignore the petty annoyances which continued to plague him that he agreed without comment and sent the money, anyway. The canteen duly opened, but not one of the refugees knew that their former monarch had funded their relief.[2]

Two completely different legends surrounding the Royal Family and the Windsors themselves need to be exploded, for both directly affected the perception of the Duke and Duchess. In London, during the war, a great mythology arose about the Royal Family. Scenes of the King and Queen visiting bombed districts, digging victory gardens, or knitting for soldiers became legendary, ensuring the devotion of their subjects, who were thereby assured that neither George VI nor Elizabeth, not to mention either of their two daughters, enjoyed any extra privileges during the time of national crisis because of their positions. The Windsors, on the other hand, were—and continue to be—unfairly castigated for what has been termed their conspicuous consumption during the war.

When discussing the Duchess during the war, for example, Frances Donaldson, one of the more balanced writers on the subject, fell into the trap of bearing the animosity of the Royal Family and court in her biography of the Duke. Of Wallis, she wrote: "The Duchess was the more unpopular. Her pre-occupation with her appearance, her jewelry and her clothes was unsuitable to the role of Governor's wife on a small group of islands. It may or may not have been true that she visited Miami every week to have her hair done or that while she was in Nassau her purchases from New York averaged a hundred dresses a year at an average of $250 a dress, but these things were said in the American Press and were generally believed."[3]

The fact is, however, that the Duchess of Windsor was not unpopular at all during her tenure in the Bahamas. Here Donaldson is guilty of condemnation based on demonstrably false facts; it would have been an easy matter to add that the stories in the newspapers concerning the Duchess were largely favorable or that the assertions she traveled to Miami to have her hair done or purchased hundreds of dresses in New York were inaccurate. In repeating the charges and leaving them unanswered, she has done no more than any number of writers before or since; unfortunately, the damage to Wallis's reputation as a result is almost impossible to overcome.

Both Wallis and David were acutely conscious of the dichotomy between the press they received and the coverage extended to the King and Queen. They were also aware, unlike the majority of the British public, that the oft-repeated stories concerning privations at Buckingham Palace during the war were not quite accurate. It was true that Buckingham Palace had been bombed; but of course only a small portion of its six hundred rooms had been damaged, and unlike the vast majority of those whose homes were destroyed in the blitz, the King had five other houses untouched by the ravages of war. Queen Elizabeth's oft-repeated statement "I'm glad we've been bombed. It makes me feel I can look the East End in the face" was thus something of an exercise in good public relations.[4] It is true that the Royal Family was issued ration books; but they also owned thousands of acres of farmland and agricultural concerns, which kept their table stocked with fresh beef, game, and vegetables. Life at Buckingham Palace and Windsor Castle carried on as luxuriously as before; George VI even continued to order special toilet paper from America throughout the hostilities, sent by courier courtesy of the British embassy in Washington, D.C.[5]

Most irritating to Wallis were the inaccurate stories concerning her rumored extravagance where clothing was concerned. In fact, the Duchess spent far less on clothes and purchased fewer items than her rival Queen Elizabeth. Ordinary clothing rations in England during the war began at sixty-six coupons per person; as the war progressed, the number was reduced to forty-eight. In contrast to this, the Queen, like all other members of the Royal Family, received 1,277 clothing coupons a year—a fact which the public never learned.[6] When Wallis appeared at a hospital tour or charity benefit, her choice of clothing was subject to criticism: The British press maintained that the Duchess cared too much about her appearance, that she dressed inappropriately for such duties during a time of war. But Queen Elizabeth, touring the East End of London and meeting those who had lost everything they owned, was always immaculately turned out, with coats and matching dress, suede shoes and gloves, diamond brooches and her famous halolike hats. "If the poor people had come to see me *they* would have put on their best clothes," Elizabeth declared.[7] The Queen, with the immense publicity resources of Buckingham Palace behind her, managed to become celebrated for such remarks; Wallis, on the other hand, who dressed for such occasions in a much more sedate fashion, was subject to criticism. The double standard hurt, but there was little she could do to fight against the establishment in England. Instead, she turned her attentions to the job before her, and in examining her work, the second legend—that of the frivolous Windsors—can finally be put to rest as well.

Wallis readily assumed those traditional duties associated with the wife of the governor-general. She became president of both the Bahamian Red Cross and the Nassau chapter of the Daughters of the British Empire. She involved herself with charity work, hospitals, and schools and lent her name and presence to benefits that raised money for the underprivileged. But she also went beyond the ordinary boundaries that previous governor-generals' wives had followed. Wallis had always been a woman of action, and this was never more true than during her tenure in Government House. Nor did she approach her new work cynically: No one who worked with her during these years had any doubt as to her sincerity. Given her anomalous position, made even more uncomfortable by the continued animosity of the Royal Family, Wallis was not required to do anything in her role as governor-general's wife; that she did so—and did so well—is to her credit.

The scope of her work was all the more impressive because Wallis deliberately chose to involve herself in the most difficult and least fashionable problems: infant welfare, unwed mothers, education, and health care, and nearly all of her efforts were directed toward assisting the native Bahamian black population. Given her strong southern heritage and ingrained color prejudices, this was remarkable. Even more so was the extent of her actual work. "The Duchess of Windsor, American-born, is the only person known who has practised philanthropy, at least in the interests of health for the poor Negros," declared a contemporary report by the Rockefeller Foundation.[8]

"No one has any idea how hard she worked," recalls one friend from the Bahamas. "With the Duchess, it wasn't just raising money— she did plenty of that—but she went beyond what other Governors' wives had done. She got in, rolled up her sleeves and worked. I'll never forget her returning to Government House one night. She had been away for twelve hours, first at one hospital, then a school, a clinic, a canteen. Her energy was palpable, contagious. She walked in and immediately began planning what to do the next day."[9]

One of her first works was founding the Bahamas Assistance Fund, designed to improve the health care and education of the mainly black population of the out islands. The Bahamian legislature, not surprisingly, proved uncooperative in granting funds, and so the Duke of Windsor signed over the income from one of the charitable trusts he had founded when Prince of Wales.[10] It became one of Wallis's pet projects and one to which she devoted her not inconsiderable talents as an organizer.

The Duchess's involvement with child-welfare agencies was deliberate, for it fulfilled in her a maternal urge which otherwise had no outlet. "The one thing missing in our lives was a child," she would later tell one friend.[11] Although Wallis was not a particularly motherly figure—her streak of independence and sophisticated tastes meant that her patience with children was limited to carefully controlled periods of exposure—it is clear that she had moments when she actively sought to fill the void through her social work.

Both she and David delighted in entertaining both children and soldiers at Government House. For Christmas, 1942, she and David decided that they would not give each other presents and instead spend that money on soldiers and children. They went to Miami on a shopping spree. Wallis purchased Kodak cameras, shaving kits, diaries, billfolds, and pipes for the soldiers and toys for the children. She and the Duke provided hams and turkeys for all the troops and gave a number of dinner parties and dances on their return, during which the men were presented with their gifts and took their turns dancing with the Duchess.[12]

This work also provided Wallis with an important sense of fulfillment. Previously her achievements had amounted to little more than taking care of her husbands and decorating houses. Now she could put her energies to productive use and, perhaps more important, experience the satisfaction of actually seeing results which directly affected the lives of others. The vast difference between providing a comfortable bedroom for David and potentially saving the lives of hundreds of children was not lost on her; Wallis, in both her head and heart, engaged in something she knew to be important. For perhaps the first time in her life, she threw herself into her work for others.

Wallis tried to involve herself in projects already under way when possible, for she felt it better to fund a proven program than risk important dollars on the unknown. She met and befriended Alice Hill Jones, a native black nurse who had for some time been working in local hospitals, trying to lower infant-mortality rates. Jones paid frequent visits to outlying communities, and Wallis soon learned that she had to use public transportation to reach her destinations; one day shortly thereafter, Wallis showed up unannounced at Jones's house, with a brand-new four-door Plymouth sedan, the Duchess's gift to help in her work.[13]

Shortly after, Wallis began to pay regular visits to the weekly clinics held by Jones at Western High School. According to Jones, the Duchess was "awfully distressed to see what a terrible problem we had to deal with and how bad the facilities were. There and then she said she was going to set up a proper clinic, and that very night she rang America to arrange it all."[14] Jones quickly had a string of permanent clinics, courtesy of the Duchess of Windsor and the money of her husband's friend Axel Wenner-Gren. But Wallis's involvement did not stop here, for she continued to involve herself actively in Jones's work.

Every week, on Wednesday afternoons, Wallis personally assisted in Jones's clinics. Her approach was direct, hands-on. She helped Jones weigh and wash babies, change their diapers, feed them, and rock them to sleep. She also poured hundreds of her own dollars into obtaining proper supplies. "My heart sinks when I see the doctor write out the prescription for an undernourished case—milk, cod-liver oil, and fruit juice—because we can't cope with it," she declared. "But one day we will."[15] Her commitment, financial and personal, made the difference, and soon the clinics were operating at a level of care at least comparable to similar institutions in America. "In her class and her time," writes Michael Pye, "she could hardly have hoped for such achievement; when the chance was offered, she took it brilliantly."[16]

Her work also extended to adult education as well. Through her hospital work, Wallis became aware of the difficulties facing the native Bahamian population, particularly in the area of sexually transmitted disease. The syphilis rate among blacks was extraordinarily high; due to the nature of the disease, no one—least of all the wife of any previous governor-general—had done anything to try to improve the situation. There was no mechanism in place in the Bahamian public-health system to deal with the epidemic, nor was anyone inclined to tackle such a sensitive subject—no one, that is, until the Duchess of Windsor came along. With no assistance—practical or financial—forthcoming from the Bahamian legislature, Wallis once again utilized her private resources, founding a clinic for those suffering from venereal disease.[17]

What Wallis did was extraordinary. Not only did she break the stringent color barriers which existed in the Bahamas at the time, but she took on the most controversial and unfashionable social causes as well. She became the first governor-general's wife to have such intimate contact with the native black children. She also broke taboos which still existed in the British Royal Family. At the same time that Wallis was thus engaged in her war work, her dedicated enemy, Queen Elizabeth, was making her reputation touring the bombed slums of East End London; the approaches of the two women, however, could not have been more different. The Queen, richly attired, maintained a careful distance; the gloves she habitually wore rarely came off, and she certainly never took on such unpopular projects as the Duchess. The smiling face of the Queen, with her steely determination, was featured around the world in photographs and newsreels; such public displays led Hitler to once describe her as the most dangerous woman in Europe. Wallis, on the other hand, rarely carried out any of her work in the public eye; she certainly never publicized—in ways which the Royal Family, with their advisers, actively sought to do—her work as an example of her personal sacrifice and devotion to the war effort. She saw what needed doing and did it without concern for the consequences to her reputation.

"She very much resembled a 1940s version of the late Princess of Wales," recalled one friend from the Bahamas. "The Duchess managed to do exactly those same sorts of things for which Diana became so famous—breaking the barriers of social stigma where disease was concerned, taking off the gloves, and meeting people face to face, on their level, touching them person to person. The contrast to the Royal Family could not have been more great; but they continued to demonize her, ignoring her work. And the Duchess, bless her, never cared—she wasn't in it for the glory. She *wanted* to make a difference."[18]

This human touch—previously dormant—came to fruition during the war years. Wallis had a genuine ability to mix easily with those people she met, whether simple workers or members of European aristocracy. Once, during a visit to the Valley Forge Army Hospital in Pennsylvania, Wallis was asked to help distribute some fifteen hundred roses to wounded soldiers. To help speed the process along, one man from each ward was to receive the bouquets on behalf of his fellow patients during a special presentation ceremony in the recreation room. The selected soldiers were called to the platform one by one; Wallis went through several of these presentations, listening to their stories of battle and injury, before she decided that the wounded deserved better. She declared that she would personally hand-deliver the remaining flowers—with nearly a thousand left! The remainder of the afternoon's engagements were canceled so that Wallis and David could walk from ward to ward, from bed to bed, handing out flowers and taking time to chat with each man about his experiences. There were no newsreel cameras there; it was a spontaneous gesture from her heart, one of many such incidents that for the most part went unnoticed, especially in the British press.[19]

In late summer of 1942, Windsor Field was completed, and some four thousand RAF troops arrived in Nassau to share coastal watch patrols with members of the U.S. Army Air Force, which was already present. As a result, there were hundreds of soldiers wandering the streets. Although incidents were few, Wallis was quick to recognize the urgent need for some form of canteen or recreation center to keep them occupied. With her customary energy, she undertook several plans to establish organizations for the soldiers in Nassau.

She founded a canteen for the black members of the Bahamian Defense Force. Of necessity, the institute was segregated; it would have been impossible—with both the American and British armed forces segregated—for Wallis to do otherwise. But she took as much care over the club as any of her other endeavors, personally selecting the games and furnishings and visiting from time to time to engage the soldiers in conversation.[20]

Wallis also managed to take over the lease of an unused wing of the Royal Victoria Hotel in downtown Nassau. Here she created a hostel for the survivors of wartime shipwrecks off the Bahamian coast—an all-too-frequent occurrence. With each new wreck, Wallis was ready: She would rush from Government House to the hotel, welcome the survivors, find out what they needed, and try to make them comfortable.[21]

To accommodate the RAF and U.S. troops, Wallis, as president of the Daughters of the British Empire, took over the Masonic Building on Nassau's downtown Bay Street. She helped fit out the building and arrange the entertainments: There were weekly dinners, movies, and dances for the troops, many of which Wallis herself directly presided over.[22] But perhaps Wallis's most accomplished achievement—and certainly the one that consumed her greatest energy—was the founding of the Bahamian Club on Nassau's West Bay Street.

The Bahamian Club resulted from the severe overcrowding of the other recreational facilities designed for the troops. Wallis approached her friend Frederick Sigrist and asked if he would be willing to lend his newly purchased Bahamian Club, a large, ungainly building which had formerly housed a casino populated largely by tourists and the rich white inhabitants of Nassau. Once the club was fully outfitted, Wallis devoted herself to its operation wholeheartedly. Every morning, she reported for work at the club to personally assist in the kitchen making breakfast. The sight of the Duchess of Windsor standing behind the large stoves, asking how the men wanted their eggs, was something which none of the soldiers ever forgot. Wallis happily posed for photographs, gave out autographs, and chatted with the men as she continued her work.[23] According to military censors, the subject of meeting the Duchess and being served by her was the most common topic in all letters from military personnel stationed in Nassau.[24]

This work now filled Wallis's days. With mornings spent at the Bahamian Club, she devoted her afternoons to the Red Cross and the infant-welfare clinics. In the evenings, she arranged dinners, receptions, and dances to benefit her charities and to entertain the troops. Even this was not enough, and she continued to push herself harder and harder. Wallis started a needlepoint class for a hundred black women in an effort to promote Bahamian crafts. She became director of the Dundas Civic Center, which trained young Bahamians for employment and provided job-placement assistance. She raised money for the local YWCA and the Nassau Garden Club and funded, out of her own pocket, a local program which delivered hot meals to shut-ins throughout the Nassau area. "I never worked harder in my life," she declared. "I never felt better used." She said that she was exhausted by all the work but exhilarated as well. "I have to keep busy. I couldn't stay here if I didn't."[25]

Wallis found great satisfaction in her work. Despite her occasional critical comments about the Bahamas, she responded with useful action, and action of a very royal kind, as a letter she wrote to a friend in 1943 makes clear:

> I can't wait for your visit—at last some relief from the daily grind! If you can bring any new records I know the men would appreciate it—we keep playing the same old songs over and over—they don't complain but you can only listen to the same noise and pretend to like it for so long! We try to do what we can—keeping spirits up—it's hard, I must say, but necessary and I feel as tho' in some way we at least make a difference. When I go to bed at night I worry and wonder what the next day will bring—but the challenge is great, we have a great responsibility, and anything to keep our minds off this damn place helps as you can imagine! When this war is over I shall feel like I actually accomplished loads, which is better than sitting here hating our life.[26]

It is a measure of the continued discrimination against Wallis that, despite her years of service, George VI repeatedly refused to offer her any award in his annual New Year's Honours Lists. The Duchess of Windsor, as a result, must rank as the only wife of a governor-general who served during the war, not to mention the founder and patron of any number of successful charities, to be so deliberately ignored. The Duke himself suggested on several occasions that even the merest recognition of her war work would be appreciated, but Buckingham Palace refused to alter their position.

David also tried, once again, to convince his brother to create Wallis a Royal Highness. On November 10, 1942, when he submitted the colony's New Year's Honours List to London, the Duke wrote to Churchill, asking him to suggest that the King do so in recognition of her two years of public service.[27] Churchill did submit the matter to the King, and George VI replied to the prime minister on December 8. He wrote that he did not feel he could "alter a decision which I made with considerable reluctance." He declared that there were many people in England and the empire "to whom it would be most distasteful to have to do honor to the Duchess as a member of our family." He had consulted the family over the issue of the style of Royal Highness and wrote that, regarding his decision to withhold it, they "share these views." He ended by declaring that his refusal to grant Wallis the style of Royal Highness was for the good of both the Royal Family and the country.[28] Thus, Wallis was once again denied not only what had rightfully been hers upon marriage to David but the most simple expression of gratitude for the services she had rendered in the Bahamas.

36

Shady Friendships, Murder, and Treachery

O<small>N THE NIGHT OF J</small>ULY 7, 1943, the Windsors' friend Sir Harry Oakes was murdered in his bed in the Bahamas. The resulting investigation—and the scandal it caused—hung like another shadow over the Duke and Duchess for the rest of their lives. But the Oakes murder was just one of many peculiar incidents involving questionable friendships, suspected money trading, and ties to the Nazis that clouded the last two years of the Duke's time as governor-general.

Many of the allegations were easier to believe due to the well-known associations the Windsors had enjoyed with those suspected of harboring Nazi sympathies. As Hugo Vickers rightly points out, it was only expected that the Duke, in his position as governor-general, "should meet most of the rich and powerful men circulating in the area. But in dealing with these characters, the duke of Windsor, who all his early life had been protected by courtiers and other advisers, was somewhat ill equipped. He was not much helped by the Foreign Office in London, which showed itself to be ambivalent about him. Old rumors about his supposed pro-German leanings as well as his now-reduced status made British officials less than open when it came to briefing him about their suspicions concerning his acquaintances. The Duke of Windsor had not been left in safe waters, as had been hoped, but dropped in a sea of sharks."[1]

Then, too, the Duke sometimes misspoke. In the March 12, 1941, issue of *Liberty* magazine, an interview with the Duke by Fulton Oursler was published which caused considerable consternation. The actual interview itself was fairly innocuous, and David had only given it on the advice of President Roosevelt's press secretary. But one implication it contained was that it was better to leave Hitler alone to lead the German people and that in the best interests of everyone and to spare as many lives as possible, a peace should be negotiated at once. Although the Duke himself later protested that the interview had contained many inaccuracies, this sentiment was something he had certainly expressed before. When Churchill got wind of it, he was indignant: he cabled the Duke, chastising him for his "defeatist" talk and asking him to refrain from further interviews.[2]

In May 1943 the Duke asked that the Duchess's letters, like his, be exempt from censorship due to shared diplomatic status. He was told this would not be possible; he did not know the contents of the vicious report, filed by Adolf Berle, coordinator of intelligence, who noted:

I believe that the Duchess of Windsor should emphatically be denied exemption from censorship. Quite aside from the shadowy reports about the activities of this family, it is to be recalled that both the Duke and Duchess of Windsor were in contact with Mr. James Mooney of General Motors, who attempted to act as mediator of a negotiated peace in the early winter of 1940; that they have maintained correspondence with Bedaux, now in prison under charges of trading with the enemy and possibly of treasonous correspondence with the enemy; that they have been in constant contact with Axel Wenner-Gren, presently on our blacklist for suspicious activity, etc. The Duke of Windsor has been finding many excuses to attend to "private business" in the United States, which he is doing at present.[3]

As noted in this report, Charles Bedaux, the man who had invited Wallis and Edward to stay at Candé and use it for their wedding and who had arranged their controversial trip to Germany in 1937 was arrested and charged with treason in 1943. Bedaux had always been a man of rather peculiar politics. He had continued to play a dangerous game of appeasing both his Nazi friends and his American business interests, a charade which was bound to catch up with him one day. His close ties with the Nazi industrial leadership immediately marked him as a man of questionable character to those with suspicious minds. No evidence of treason against Bedaux was ever discovered, but the vindication came too late for him. Unable to continue his imprisonment any longer, the wealthy industrialist committed suicide in his Miami jail cell. His name was later cleared of any wrongdoing, and the French government posthumously awarded him their *Legion d'honneur* in the 1960s.

The other associate marked out in Berle's report was Axel Wenner-Gren, the Swedish multimillionaire industrialist and friend of Bedaux. Like Bedaux, he does not seem to have had any real political affiliations; his concerns were chiefly financial. He lived aboard his immense yacht, the *Southern Cross*, which he kept moored off the Bahamas. The United States, as in the case of Bedaux, wrongly assumed—and on the basis of very little evidence—that Wenner-Gren was a Nazi sympathizer. A State Department report declared:

> The most recent information I have regarding Mr. Wenner-Gren indicates that he is in constant and close touch with the Duke of Windsor and that both of them are seeing a great deal of prominent and influential American businessmen, particularly from the mid-Western states, where a strictly commercial point of view would appear to prevail in business circles with regard to relations between the United States and Germany. There would appear to be certain indications that Wenner-Gren, as well as the Duke of Windsor, is stressing the need for a negotiated peace at this time on account of the advantages which this would present to American business interests. This angle, I think, should be closely observed. . . .[4]

The relationship between the Duke and Duchess of Windsor and Axel Wenner-Gren was a constant source of tension. He had contributed large sums of money to the Duchess's charities in Nassau and had always been willing to lend the couple his yacht if needed. When he sought permission to purchase a small island, London appealed to the U.S. State Department for advice. State Department officials replied that they did not think it wise to allow someone with such close ties to the Nazis to do so; the Duke of Windsor somehow learned of this and demanded that the U.S. government tell him precisely what evidence it had against Wenner-Gren. The State Department was forced to admit that it had no proof, but fell back on innuendo, declaring that "his links with high Germans are very intimate and suspicious."[5]

One area of particular concern was Wenner-Gren's connection with the Mexican Banco Continental, of which he was a partner. The bank was rumored to have Nazi connections and widely believed to be used as a conduit for illegal money trading. The Windsors were thought to have engaged in such trading practices during the war, arranged by Wenner-Gren through his bank. On July 21, 1942, a secret State Department memorandum reported:

> Axel Wenner-Gren is supposed to have according to my information the following sums of money on deposit and now all frozen:

London	$50 millions.
Bahamas	$2,500,000.
United States	$32 millions.

| Mexico | $2 millions. |
| Norway | $32 millions. |

It is understood that the deposits of $2,500,000 in the Bahamas were made at the express request and in part for the benefit of the Duke of Windsor ... he is a very close friend of the Duke.[6]

It should be noted that this report rests on the unverified surmise of an unidentified American agent. The evidence in support of the allegation, therefore, is entirely circumstantial. Even so, it is important to point out that were the allegations accurate, the Windsors were not the only important Britons to engage in illegal trading. In fact, no less a person than Winston Churchill was actively involved in illegal money trading during the war, also on the behalf of the Duke and Duchess. On April 7, 1941, he dispatched the following message to the United States:

Mr. Winston Churchill presents his compliments to His Excellency the United States Ambassador and, with reference to Mr. Achilles' letter of 1st March to Sir George Warner of the Foreign Office concerning the property in Paris of His Royal Highness the Duke of Windsor, has the honour to request that the United States Embassy in Paris may be asked to be so good as to make the following payments on behalf of the Duke of Windsor, from British funds at their disposal, the payments to be shown as separate items in their account with the Foreign Office:

1. Rent of 55,000 Francs for the current year, but not to continue the purchase option.

Renew the insurance, costing 10,000 Francs.

Pay back wages to Fernand Lelorrain at the rate of 2000 Francs monthly for January, February and March, 1941, plus 30 Francs daily for food for the whole period. It should be explained to Lelorrain that this latter rate is the rate paid to the servants at La Croë, His Royal Highness's house at Antibes.

Continue to pay Lelorrain monthly, upon presenting himself, his 1000 Francs, plus 30 Francs a day for food.

2. The Duke of Windsor would also be grateful if the United States Embassy could enquire the situation regarding his possessions in the Banque de France and pay 15,000 Francs for the current year's rent of his strong room there, which expired last November.

3. Mr. Churchill would be obliged if an expression of His Royal Highness's appreciation could be conveyed to the United

States Embassy in Paris for the able assistance they are giving to his affairs.[7]

The Banque de France was, in fact, controlled by the occupying Germans. Thus, although the money went toward preserving existing property, according to the simple facts, Churchill was guilty of trading with the enemy in much the same terms that the Windsors have been alleged to have been. Whatever the truth behind the allegations, the Windsors have been subject to an immense amount of negative publicity over the money issue.

These allegations, friendships with supposed Nazi sympathizers, and other rumored indiscretions were damaging enough, but the Windsors could never entirely escape—no matter how little evidence existed to the contrary—from the suspicion that both harbored pro-German tendencies. The incident in Spain and Portugal in 1940, coupled with letters and German dispatches, was to lead to the most damaging allegation of all: that the Windsors had been traitors and that the Duke had collaborated with the Nazis with the idea of regaining his abdicated throne.

In October 1945 a number of German Foreign Office archives detailing the Nazi plot to win the Duke of Windsor over as a supporter were discovered hidden in an isolated castle. There were dozens of cables which mentioned the Windsors, including much correspondence regarding his possible pro-Nazi attitude and discussion of placing him on the British throne again once the war had ended. However, in 1957, when the papers were published in the *Documents on German Foreign Policy*, volume 10 included a statement from the British Foreign Office that the Duke "never wavered in his loyalty to the British cause. . . . The German records are necessarily a much-tainted source. The only firm evidence is of what the Germans were trying to do in this matter and how completely they failed."[8]

Around the same time in 1945, King George VI ordered that certain documents be retrieved from Germany and dispatched Anthony Blunt, the British art historian later exposed as a Soviet spy, and Owen Morshead, librarian at Windsor Castle. Officially, they were sent to retrieve correspondence between Queen Victoria and her eldest daughter, Empress Friedrich of Germany, but suspicious minds have since speculated that the real purpose of their mission was to find and destroy any papers which implicated the Duke of Windsor in treasonous activities. No such papers are known to have been found, and Edward VIII's official biographer, Philip Ziegler, clearly indicates that the Blunt-Morshead mission had nothing to do with the Duke of Windsor. Despite the rather dubious efforts of later writers, no reliable evidence has ever come to light to indicate either the alleged treason of the Duke or that the Blunt-Morshead mission concerned the retrieval and suppression of such evidence.[9]

Undoubtedly, however, it was the murder of Sir Harry Oakes which most adversely affected the Windsors' time in Nassau. Oakes had made a fortune in Canada when he discovered the world's second-largest gold vein; he spent time in England and America and finally settled in Nassau when he retired. He and his wife lived in splendor in their house, Westbourne, where he was killed.

Oakes was a rather big, somewhat crude man with a brash, boisterous personality. His Australian wife, Eunice, was a complete contrast, while their daughter Nancy would eventually marry the renowned playboy Alfred de Marigny. Oakes's business partner in Nassau was Harold Christie, a volatile former rumrunner who had bootlegged alcohol during the Depression. In time, Christie became the leading real-estate developer in the Bahamas.

The Windsors were quite close to the Oakes family, but both had mixed feelings about the ever-present Marigny. Ironically, both apparently harbored suspicions that he was involved in some undefined but illegal business practices. Meeting Wallis, Marigny recalled: "I could understand how a frail and effeminate little man like the Duke could have lost his heart and his throne over her. She had the charm of a femme fatale, and a serene control that made her irresistible. I had a glimmer through her eyes of the warmth and passion that she disguised so well under her cool appearance."[10]

There was a great deal of tension between Oakes and his future son-in-law, but this was nothing compared to the disastrous relations which quickly developed between him and Harold Christie, his former business partner. Oakes discovered that Christie had sold land for a new RAF base behind his back to an American syndicate and cut him out of the deal. Oakes therefore began to make preparations to call in Christie's numerous loans and to repossess his only fully owned asset, the island of Lyford Cay.

On the evening of July 7, Oakes gave a small party at Westbourne, whose guests included Christie. When a storm blew up, Christie announced that he would stay the night, for he did not want to drive home; he had also stayed over the previous evening. Before going to bed, he dismissed the two night watchmen, saying that he would see to looking after the house. That night, as the storm broke, there were wild bursts of thunder rattling the windows and lightning flashing across the tropical sky. The noise was such that no one heard the commotion in Oakes's bedroom. The next morning, Harry Oakes was found dead in his bed; his head had been crushed by repeated blows from a blunt instrument, he had been stabbed, and the body afterward was set on fire.

At Government House, the Duke of Windsor was awakened by Maj. Gray Phillips and told of the murder. Immediately, the Duke consulted with the Nassau attorney general and chief of police; there seemed to be few clues, and the Duke, with the approval of the Nassau authorities, telephoned the Miami Police Department and asked that Capt. Edward Melchen, who had been assigned to act as his bodyguard on his most recent visit there, assist on the case. Ordinarily, a colonial governor would have consulted Scotland Yard, and the Duke was roundly criticized for his failure to follow procedure. What little evidence Melchen gathered seemed to point to de Marigny, who was eventually brought to trial for the crime but found not guilty. Officially, the crime remains unsolved, but those who knew Oakes had little doubt that Harold Christie had in fact hired an assassin to kill the man who had threatened to ruin him financially. Years later, at a party, Lady Mosley recalled hearing Lord Beaverbrook stroll up to Christie and say in a loud voice, "Come on, Harold, tell us how you murdered Harry Oakes." Christie merely smiled and said nothing, seemingly confirming with his silence his part in the crime.[11]

In August 1944 the Duke and Duchess visited Palm Beach and Newport, Rhode Island, where they stayed with their friend Robert Young. For some time Wallis had been working at her charity concerns for upwards of eighteen hours a day, six days a week. Not only was she exhausted, but her stomach ulcers, which had long been a source of constant pain, had begun to bother her again. For some time, she simply ignored the symptoms, but during their visit to the United States, the pain became so bad that she agreed to see a specialist in New York. The doctors diagnosed appendicitis, and Wallis was admitted to Roosevelt Hospital. During the surgery, her stomach was also examined; doctors noted several suspicious tumorlike growths. When a biopsy showed cancer, the malignancies were removed.[12] The operations were deemed successful, and on September 11 a crowd of five hundred cheering schoolchildren greeted the Duchess as the Duke escorted her from the hospital.[13]

Upon their return to Nassau, the Duke's thoughts turned increasingly to the day when he might leave his post in the Bahamas. He hoped that he might gain another assignment closer to home. But when he cabled Churchill with such a request, the prime minister replied with the less-than-satisfactory offer of the governor-generalship of Bermuda. "David," Wallis wrote, "could see that this would only be exchanging one military backwater for another. Bitterly disappointed, he declined the Bermuda offer and decided to finish out his war service where he was."[14]

On her own, Wallis tried to repair relations between her husband

and his family. When the Archbishop of Canterbury appointed Rev. John Dauglish, the Bishop of Nassau, to a post in London, Wallis took advantage of the fact to send a letter to Queen Mary, the first she had ever written, in which she suggested that the Queen might speak to Dauglish if she wished to learn about David's life. The Bishop of Nassau was indeed summoned to Marlborough House, where he met with Queen Mary. She questioned him at length about the Duke's job, but when the Bishop spoke glowingly of the work which Wallis had undertaken, the Queen made no comment. However, a few weeks later, Queen Mary wrote a rare letter to her son and ended with "I send a kind message to your wife," the first time she had taken care to note the fact that her eldest son had a wife of almost six years. "Now what do you suppose has come over Mama?" the Duke asked upon reading the letter, unaware of his wife's intervention.[15]

By the winter of 1944 everyone had begun to realize that the war was coming to an end. The Duke, feeling that he could do nothing further with his post, formally resigned on March 15, 1945. The resignation took effect on April 30, the day on which Hitler shot himself.

The Duke had been planning for his resignation since October of the previous year. Now he had one last detail to worry over. He had written to Churchill:

> Were the King and Queen to behave normally to the Duchess and myself when we pass by England, and invite us merely to tea at one of their residences, a formality which as a matter of fact is prescribed by Court protocol in the case of Colonial Governors and their wives, it would avoid any division of feeling being manifested. . . . It could never be a very happy meeting, but on the other hand it would be quite painless, and would have the merit of silencing, once and for all, those malicious circles who delight in keeping open an eight-year-old wound that should have been healed officially, if not privately, ages ago.[16]

It was, after all, a simple request, and only the courtesy dictated by tradition, but the Duke felt so uncertain of his brother's ability to be civil where Wallis was concerned that he raised the issue directly with the prime minister. In the end, the Duke was right to be worried. Churchill tried to intercede with the King on the Duke's behalf; it took three months before he eventually replied in the negative. The prime minister had pleaded with the King for just one meeting with the Duke and Duchess. Gen. Charles de Gaulle had added his voice, along with Princess Alice, countess of Athlone, and the Duchess of Beaufort.[17] But all to no avail: neither the King's wife nor his mother would agree to receive Wallis, and George VI was far too weak to stand up to the women who had dominated his life. "I do not see any prospect of removing this difficulty," Churchill wrote. "I have not concealed my regret that this should be so."[18] Thereafter, both the Duke and Duchess would refer to Queen Elizabeth as "that fat Scotch cook"; to Wallis, she became "the Dowdy Duchess" and "the Monster of Glamis."[19]

After four and a half years, the Duke and Duchess of Windsor left Nassau on May 3, 1945. They were showered with gifts, including a silver box presented to Wallis by the ladies of the Red Cross and a silver salver from the officers of the Royal Air Force, whom she had hosted at her canteen.[20] The Windsors left with their futures once again unsettled. "We're right back where we were in 1938," the Duke told Inez Robb. "When we were married, we rented a couple of houses in which to sit down and think. We wanted to find out where we wanted to live, and what we wanted to do." "Then we were caught up in the War," the Duchess added. "We're not really thinking of buying a house anywhere at the moment," the Duke continued. "It's very difficult to know where to settle now."[21]

37

Postwar Wanderings

THE DUKE AND DUCHESS of Windsor could not arrange transport of their possessions from Nassau until September; they remained in New York until their affairs could be sorted out. Finally, they sailed aboard the troop ship *Argentina*, landing at Le Havre on September 22. With them they brought a seventeen-year-old Bahamian named Sydney Johnson, who was to remain in their employ until shortly after David's death.

When they returned to Paris, the Windsors found that their house at 24, boulevard Suchet had been carefully looked after, guarded first by the U.S. embassy staff, then by the Swiss legation. Throughout, the French caretaker had remained in the house, ensuring that it stayed in good condition. Originally, the Windsors had taken the house on an extended lease, with an option to buy; by the spring of 1946, however, they had waited too long and were told that the house had already been sold. The Duke and Duchess were given six months to vacate the property; because most of their things were already packed, it only took a short time to store them and take a suite in the Ritz Hotel.[1]

Paris was a city still under seige; there were frequent power cuts, ration cards, and black marketeers roaming through the streets. The Windsors managed to survive reasonably well. Wallis still gave dinner parties, although, as she noted in a letter to Aunt Bessie, the menu was often peculiar: hot dogs shipped in from the U.S., ham mousse made from tinned ham rations, canned vegetables, and black-market caviar.[2]

"My husband and I joined the Windsors one evening in Paris," an acquaintance recalls. "It was the most curious thing I ever saw. Halfway through dinner, a footman came in, carrying a bowl piled high with baked beans. Another followed with some form of meatloaf. There we were, in this very swank room, dressed to the nines, eating beans and hamburger. The Duchess explained the menu away with a short laugh and a high-pitched 'Y'all understand that my menus have suffered a bit!' "³

In December they received permission from the U.S. Army, which still controlled the area, to return to La Croë. The Italian Army had occupied the property during the war but had quartered their troops in the garages rather than billet them in the main house. The entire garden and surrounding area, however, had been dug in, and over two dozen land mines had been planted about by German troops, all of which had to be removed. But the Duke and Duchess found life at La Croë far different than it had been before the war. Most of their friends on the Riviera had gone, the lush golf courses the Duke had so enjoyed had been neglected, and tourists had replaced the former elements of society. In 1949, at David's wish, Wallis reluctantly agreed to sell La Croë.⁴

During their first months back in Europe, David—unaccompanied by Wallis—returned to England on several occasions. In October he paid a private visit to his mother at Marlborough House. He arrived at Hendon Airfield aboard an RAF transport; no member of the Royal Family or anyone from the household had come to meet him. Word of the visit had leaked out, however, and crowds pushed around the gates at Marlborough House, shouting, "Good old Edward!" and "You must come back!"⁵ There was a family dinner of sorts that evening: The King attended, but Queen Elizabeth, along with the Duchess of Kent, purposely remained away. David returned to London in January; he met the King at Buckingham Palace to ask if he might be granted a special role as a roving British ambassador to the United States, a position which would complement, not replace, the official ambassador in Washington, D.C. He met with several officials, but nothing came of the proposal; both the King and the government rejected it.

David returned to France, clearly frustrated at the prospect of spending the rest of his life without a meaningful job. One of the Windsors' friends, Susan Mary Alsop, recalled: "I never saw a man so bored. He said to me, 'You know what my day was today? . . . I got up late and then I went with the Duchess and watched her buy a hat, and then on the way home I had the car drop me off in the Bois to watch some of your [American] soldiers playing football and then I had planned to take a walk, but it was so cold that I could hardly bear it. In fact I was afraid that I would be struck with cold in the way people are struck with heat so I came straight home. . . . When I got home the Duchess was having her French lesson so I had no one to talk to. . . .' "⁶

Wallis tried to step into the void. "I was frightened in his first years of idleness after the war," she recalled. "I realized that I had to take the place of the King's boxes—the red dispatch cases that used to bring him his daily business of state from Whitehall."[7] Their feeling for each other was stronger than ever; Noël Coward, who saw them soon after their return to Europe, wrote: "He loves her so much, and at long last I am beginning to believe that she loves him."[8] But, she once commented sadly to a friend, "You have no idea how hard it is to live out a great romance!"[9]

That December marked the tenth anniversary of the abdication. "Ten years have passed, but not the romance," the Duke told a reporter, smiling at the Duchess. "It's gone on and on." "I'm afraid a great deal of wishful thinking went into the predictions that our marriage wouldn't last," added the Duchess. "Now, we're just a happy middle-aged couple," David declared.[10]

When Harold Nicolson met the Windsors shortly after their return to Europe, he noted that the Duke "has stopped calling his wife 'Her Royal Highness.' He calls her 'the Duchess.' I notice also that people do not bow as they used to, and treat him less as a royalty than they did when he had recently been King." Nicolson found Wallis

> much improved. That taut, predatory look has gone; she has softened. I have a talk with her alone. She says that they do not know where to live. They would like to live in England, but that is difficult. He retains his old love for Fort Belvedere. "We are tired of wandering," she says. "We are not as young as we were. We want to settle down and grow our own trees." He likes gardening, but it is no fun, gardening in other people's gardens. Where can they live? They are sick of islands (after Nassau), otherwise they might go to the Channel Islands. They are sick of France. He likes America, but that can never be a home. He wants a job to do. "You see," she says, "he was born to be a salesman. He would be an admirable representative of Rolls-Royce. But an ex-King cannot start selling motor-cars." I feel really sorry for them. She was so simple and sincere.[11]

In October 1946, Wallis and David returned to England together on a private visit for the first time since the outbreak of the war. Since no invitation was forthcoming from the Royal Family, they stayed with the Earl and Countess of Dudley at their house, Ednam Lodge, at Sunningdale, Berkshire, near Windsor Castle. The Duchess brought with her a large jewel box, roughly the size of an overnight suitcase, which was normally placed beneath her maid's bed at night. On October 16 the Duke and Duchess went to London for the evening. Wallis had moved the jewel box into her own bedroom and apparently forgot that it was there.

At six that evening, the regular detective who accompanied the

Windsors joined the rest of the staff at Ednam Lodge for dinner in the kitchen. During this time, thieves hurled a rope through the open window of Lady Dudley's daughter's bedroom, climbed into the house, found Wallis's jewel case, and left Ednam Lodge, all without causing the slightest commotion. Shortly after seven, the Duchess's maid went into her bedroom and noted the missing box. The police were quickly rung up, and the entire house was thrown into a panic. The Windsors immediately returned from London, followed by the Dudleys. R. M. Howe, assistant commissioner of Scotland Yard's Criminal Investigatory Division, and Chief Inspector J. R. Capstick were dispatched to Ednam Lodge to investigate. They were joined by Deputy Comdr. W. R. Rawlings and Detective Sergeant Monk, along with fingerprint expert Superintendent Cherrill, who was already at work examining the windowsills and doors of the house.[12]

A caddie from a nearby course reported that he had found a number of earrings scattered around the green; a more extensive search by the staff members at Ednam Lodge discovered a Fabergé box abandoned on a windowsill. Within a few hours of the crime, it became apparent that the job had been carried out by professionals.

Wallis insisted that all of the Dudleys' staff be questioned, a reasonable enough request. But Lady Dudley found the entire episode extremely distasteful. She later wrote that Wallis now showed

> an unpleasant and to me unexpected side of her character. . . . She wanted all the servants put through a kind of third degree, but I would have none of this, all of them except for one kitchen maid being old and devoted staff of long standing. By the following night the Duke was both determined with worry and near to tears. The Duchess started the next day with a grim face and wearing on her dress about the only jewel that remained to her. Just before we all went out for a little stroll she said, "David, put this brooch in a safe place." On our return he could not remember where he had put it! He thought the most likely place was the room he was using for sorting the papers he had fetched from Windsor. There ensued a frantic search, but to no avail. When it was time for bed the Duchess and Eric went upstairs; it had been a grim day. The Duke said he was going to continue the search although he looked grey with worry and exhaustion. I was desperately sorry for him, and anyhow I would have stayed to help him in his search, hoping at least to find this one remaining jewel to which the Duchess appeared so attached. We stayed up most of the night; he obviously feared to go up to bed empty-handed. I made endless cups of black coffee while the Duke went through his papers, which he seemed convinced was the likeliest place.

At about 5 A.M. by some miracle we found it, under a china ornament. Never have I seen a man so relieved. He was still ashen in
the face but he rushed upstairs.[13]

This peculiar spectacle—the former King of England crawling around
on his hands and knees through the middle of the night searching for
a missing jewel—has inevitably been used to cast Wallis in the worst
possible light. However, it must be pointed out that at no time did
Wallis ask David to search, nor did she make any scene over the incident. The perceived gravity of the situation appears to have come
entirely from the Duke himself.

The robbery, however, had clearly unnerved Wallis. On the following day, the Duke and Duchess gave an interview to the press
about the theft. When the Duchess was repeatedly questioned by a
persistent reporter as to the type of jewels missing, she suddenly
snapped from the strain and angrily declared, "A fool would know
that with tweeds or other daytime clothes one wears gold, and that
with evening clothes one wears platinum."[14]

The outburst was a rare display of emotion, but Wallis quickly
recovered her composure. The letter she wrote to the Dudleys on
November 26 was gracious, never mentioned the theft, and proved
that Wallis had mastered the royal art of ignoring unpleasantnesses:

> Dear Laura and Eric: The Duke and I find it impossible to express
> our Thanks and sincere gratitude for our visit to the Lodge—
> everything has been <u>so</u> perfect—the staff couldn't have been
> better and they all have taken endless Trouble to please and we
> have been most comfortable and happy—I hope we have not
> been too much Trouble and worry to you both—if there is any-
> thing we can do for you in New York please cable. . . . Once again
> a million thanks and affectionate greetings from Wallis Windsor.[15]

For the next few years, the Duke and Duchess of Windsor lived a
restless existence. They moved between Paris, New York, and Palm
Beach, from hotel to hotel, mansion to mansion, aboard the Cunard
liners. During the first years after the war, they favored the *Queen Elizabeth*; when Capt. Harry Grattidge transferred command to her sister
ship the *Queen Mary*, the Windsors also switched their allegiance. In
these years, it was the Duke and Duchess of Windsor, more than any
other couple, who seemed best to epitomize the sleek glamour and
international chic of the famous vessels.

Life at sea for the Windsors followed a regular pattern. Aboard
the *Queen Mary*, they always booked the same main-deck suite, M58,

consisting of a Honduras mahogany–paneled bedroom decorated with art-deco motifs, a sitting room, and a bathroom. Before the Windsors arrived, the chief steward would be dispatched to their cabin to replace the standard Cunard linens with the Duchess's own Porthault sheets and bath towels.[16]

Each morning, David rose early and quietly slipped into the restaurant, where he sat in silence and watched as the tables were set for first service under the command of the second steward. Following a visit to the ship's barber, he returned to the cabin, by which time Wallis would have arisen and already dressed.[17] They spent the majority of their time alone, sitting on the sun deck, reading and sipping tea; only occasionally, when they discovered friends onboard, did they socialize during the day. In the evening, at nine, they regularly dined in the Verandah Grill, an elegant restaurant and lounge overlooking the aft deck and decorated with an enormous art-deco mural of a circus painted by Doris Zinkeisen.[18]

The Windsors were very fond of Grattidge, and he, in turn, found the Duke and Duchess thoughtful and polite. One day, when the Windsors were sitting on the sun deck reading, the captain approached with a question. David was so engrossed in his book that he did not see Grattidge. " 'Dear,' said the Duchess, touching him gently on the arm. 'Dear . . .' That is typical of the Duchess of Windsor, as I found her. She never raises her voice, never intrudes her personality. Few women better convey the impression of a loyal and unobtrusive wife."[19]

The Windsors' closest American friends were Robert and Anita Young, whom they often visited at their Newport, Rhode Island, cottage, Fairholme, perched along the famous Cliff Walk on the edge of the Atlantic. As a favor to their friends, the Windsors were the guests of honor at the grand April 17, 1948 reopening of Young's Greenbrier Hotel in White Sulphur Springs, West Virginia; ironically, both the Duke and Duchess had stayed at the resort before, David during one of his tours of America as Prince of Wales and Wallis on her honeymoon with Win Spencer. When the Windsors arrived, they joined the Youngs and fellow guests Prince and Princess Hohenlohe; Lady Hartington, the former Kathleen Kennedy; the Anthony Biddle Dukes; the Winston Guests; Bing Crosby; and William Randolph Hearst.[20] The guests dined on turtle soup, stuffed lemon sole with Maine lobster, grilled filet mignon, and baked Alaska for dessert.[21]

"They were always very gracious, very charming, and utterly themselves," recalls a fellow guest. "I never saw anything other than love and affection between them, and they seemed genuinely in love. You can act all you want, but the little gestures—the look in his eye when she was across the room, the way she took his arm and led him to meet someone important—those things were natural. When they danced with the other guests, they were always looking around, making sure that the other was having a good time as well."[22]

The Duke and Duchess enjoyed their time at the Greenbrier. Thereafter they would often come in the spring on their annual holiday, staying in the Presidential Suite, an immense wing which included a living room, study, library, office, dining room, service kitchen, seven bedrooms, and seven bathrooms. Wallis and David made a point of competing in the annual Anniversary Ball's Viennese waltz contest, much to the delight of the other couples.[23]

Also that month, the Windsors accepted an invitation from Joseph E. Davies, the former U.S. ambassador to the Soviet Union, and his wife, heiress Marjorie Merriweather Post, to join them aboard their luxurious yacht for a Caribbean cruise. Wallis enthusiastically wrote that she and her husband "have never had such a thrilling invitation! I can't think of anything the Duke and myself would rather do than have a trip with you and Mr. Davies on the *Sea Cloud*. Nassau, of course, would be charming, but we must be frank and say we are tempted by your suggestion of Cuba as we have never been there."[24]

Wallis liked Marjorie Post; both were strong, stylish women with an eye for collecting beautiful antiques and decorating their lavish homes exquisitely. Once, in New York, the Duchess was having lunch at the Louis XVI Restaurant and spotted Marjorie Post at a table with her granddaughter, Marjorie Durant, who had recently been involved in something of a disgrace and had been taken out of her grandmother's will. Wallis came over and joined the two for coffee. "She asks me a few questions," recalled Durant, "and I start telling her about myself—about school, about swimming. When I go to the ladies' room she tells my grandmother what a wonderful wholesome girl I am, how fresh and American, how she wished she had a young relative like me. I don't know whether my grandmother had told her about the trouble I was giving then, but whether she did or not, she got back nothing but compliments for me. And do you know what? That coffee chat saved my god-damned neck. The Duchess turned my grandmother around. I was back in with Grandma, I was back in the will—everything."[25]

These new friendships helped replace the loss of others. In May 1949, Wallis's closest friend, Katherine Rogers, died. A year later, Herman Rogers married Lucy Wann, widow of Air Vice Marshal Archie Wann. Their wedding took place at Cannes, and the Duke and Duchess acted as witnesses. Wallis was not particularly enamored of the new wife at first and missed her old friend. But when invited on the honeymoon yacht trip, she warmed to Lucy and chatted amiably with her.[26]

A year later, on May 29, 1950, Wallis's first husband, Win Spencer, died in San Diego at the age of sixty-one. His career in the U.S. Navy had not progressed as far as he had wished, and he died a commander, retired. He left a fourth wife, Lillian Phillips Spencer, and a history of tangled, violent relationships.

At least one important friendship had resumed: that of the Duke and Duchess with the Metcalfes. Throughout the war, Wallis had continued to write to Lady Alexandra: "Our Men have fallen out but that doesn't mean that we have to as well," she said in one letter. But Lady Alexandra left her letters unanswered, uncertain what to do or say and more than a little angry at the way her husband had been treated in France by the Duke. The Duke himself had written during the war, and Fruity, according to his son David, "had wished to answer, but my mother felt rather strongly about it and put her foot down." Then, one day, Walter Monckton, on the Duke's behalf, asked Fruity Metcalfe to come to London; David was visiting his mother at Marlborough House and had expressed some regret to Monckton over the breach with Metcalfe, saying that he wished they could meet. When Fruity walked into the drawing room at Marlborough House, he found the Duke of Windsor standing there. David held out his arms and simply said, "Fruity!" and the two men embraced. Without any apology, the rift was over.[27]

The void in the lives of the Duke and Duchess became glaringly apparent with the end of the war. David might have stepped in and performed some useful function in England had his family relented in their campaign against him and the Duchess. But the years following the war proved just as damaging to the already fragile relations between the Windsors and the Royal Family.

The Windsors had spent the spring of 1947 in America; on May 10, however, they sailed back to Europe aboard the *Queen Elizabeth* so that the Duke would be able to attend his mother's eightieth birthday celebrations on the twenty-sixth. When they arrived in London, however, David was deeply hurt to discover that neither he nor Wallis had been invited; when he rang to ask why, he was bluntly informed that neither he nor his wife would be welcome at the official functions. David paid a private visit to his mother at Marlborough House, but although both he and Wallis were still in London on Queen Mary's birthday, no invitations to the Buckingham Palace luncheon were forthcoming.

On July 9, 1947, Buckingham Palace announced the engagement of Princess Elizabeth to Lt. Philip Mountbatten, son of Prince and Princess Andrew of Greece. The wedding was set for November. The Duke made it plain that he would not attend without the Duchess. "His attitude is proper, and will be shared by many people," editorialized the *London Evening Standard*, "for any such discrimination against the Duchess would be outrageous. What has the Duchess done that she should be held up to ridicule in this way? As the wife of the bride's uncle, if for no other reason, the Duchess should be accorded the dignity of an invitation to her niece's marriage."[28] In fact, there was never any question as to the Duke's receiving an invitation. Queen Elizabeth flatly declared that she would not attend her own daughter's wedding if he came.[29] On October 13, David's secretary announced to the press that neither the Duke nor the Duchess had received any invitation to the forthcoming wedding.

Certain members of the Royal Family, however, felt that this ostracism was the last straw. In protest at the lack of an invitation for her brother and sister-in-law, Mary, the Princess Royal, deliberately stayed away from the ceremony. To the public, it was simply announced that she was ill; but privately her protest was made quite clear, although it failed to have any effect on Buckingham Palace's continued war against the Windsors.[30] At least Wallis enjoyed a bittersweet triumph when, three weeks after the future Elizabeth II's wedding, Wallis was named the world's best-dressed woman; neither Queen Mary, Queen Elizabeth, nor Princess Elizabeth had received enough votes to qualify.[31]

In April 1949 the *London Evening Standard* declared that it was time for the Royal Family to receive Wallis. "Throughout the twelve years of her marriage to the Duke this American lady has behaved with dignity," it declared. It argued that Wallis was the innocent party in both of her divorces and added that the palace ban on receiving and entertaining divorced persons, which had been used as a formal excuse against such a reconciliation, had recently been relaxed. The paper pointed out that the week before, Princess Elizabeth and Prince Philip had entertained Sir Laurence and Lady Olivier, although both had been named as co-respondents in divorces from their former partners. "So it is hardly consistent that the Duchess of Windsor should be excluded from the courtesies extended to those who have been divorced," the editors declared.[32]

Such public sentiments prompted David once again to raise the issue of granting to Wallis the style of Royal Highness. A decade earlier, the respected judicial authority Sir William Jowitt had studied the dilemma and advised the Duke that there was no legal justification for the continued withholding of the style of Royal Highness from the Duchess. Now Jowitt was the crown's most senior legal adviser and the head of the English judiciary. But any hopes David had were dashed when he had a meeting with Jowitt in London in 1949. Jowitt did not deny that he believed in what he had said a decade before, but he now insisted that he was powerless to do anything to change it. As a part of the court establishment, he was loath to risk his career by

e Duke and Duchess of Windsor with one of their cairn terriers, about 1950   CORBIS/UPI

(*Above*) Photographers and reporters awaiting an appearance by the Duke and Duchess of Windsor, during their visit to her uncle Henry Warfield, at his country house, Salona Farm, outside of Baltimore, October 11, 1941
HULTON-DEUTSCH COLLECTION/CORBIS

(*Left*) The Duke and Duchess of Windsor at the Greenbrier, White Sulphur Springs, West Virginia, about 1950
© THE GREENBRIER HOTEL

rial view of the Mill, showing the collection of buildings. The old Millhouse is near the ter of the photograph, with the long wing extending to the right; below that, the barn ens on to the Duke's garden. COLLECTION OF JOHN WIENEMAN

e entrance to the Mill COLLECTION OF JOHN WIENEMAN

(*Above and below*) The Duke and Duchess of Windsor in the early 1960s   CORBIS/UPI

The Duchess of
Windsor in a publici-
ty photograph for
her dress pattern
series URBAN
ARCHIVES, TEMPLE
UNIVERSITY,
PHILADELPHIA,
PENNSYLVANIA

The Duke of
Windsor, accompa-
nied by his wife,
leaves the London
clinic after undergo-
ing his retina opera-
tion, March 1965.
HULTON-DEUTSCH
COLLECTION/CORBIS

The Duke and Duchess of Windsor with President and Mrs. Richard Nixon, April 4, 197
CORBIS/UPI

The Duchess of Windsor on the steps of the Windsor Villa in the Bois de Boulogne with
the Duke of Edinburgh, Queen Elizabeth II, and Charles, the Prince of Wales, following
their visit to the dying Duke of Windsor, May 18, 1972 CORBIS/UPI

e funeral of the Duke of Windsor, St. George's Chapel, Windsor, June 5, 1972. Queen
zabeth II is followed by the Duchess of Windsor, the Queen Mother (*partially obscured*),
Duke of Edinburgh, and King Olav of Norway. HULTON-DEUTSCH COLLECTION/CORBIS

e auction of the Windsors' furniture and accessories set new records at Sotheby's in
37. ©1997 SOTHEBY'S, INC.

The Duchess of Windsor BACHRACH PHOTOGRAPHY

supporting the Duke; instead, he declared that it was a political question for the King, prime minister, and the government.[33]

David waited some six months after his meeting with Jowitt to raise the issue with the King. George VI's letter in reply was highly revealing. He declared that it had been "a very great shock" to learn that his brother wished to marry Wallis and that everything which followed had been a great strain. David's departure had left "a most ghastly void," which he seemed unable to understand or appreciate, in both the Royal Family and in the country and empire. Somewhat presumptuously, George VI insisted that in abdicating David had in fact accepted the view that his wife was unfit to be queen; it therefore followed, Bertie said, that she was equally unfit to be both his wife now and a member of the Royal Family forever. If he reversed his decision to deny Wallis the style of Royal Highness, he declared, it "wouldn't make sense of the past."[34]

38

The Death of the King

AT THE BEGINNING OF 1951, Wallis fell ill. A number of malignant tumors were found in her uterus, and the doctors decided to perform a full hysterectomy.[1] She entered the Harkness Pavilion in New York City on February 20, registering under the name of Mary Walters to throw off inquisitive news reporters, but inevitably word quickly spread and the hospital was surrounded by the press. The operation was performed by Dr. Henry Wisdom Cave, president of the American College of Surgeons, and a gynecologist, Dr. Benjamin P. Watson, a fellow of the Royal College of Surgeons in Edinburgh. Both physicians, in a short statement to the press, declared that the Duchess had undergone "a minor operative procedure and her condition is satisfactory."[2] On this occasion, David received an inquiry from his mother, asking after Wallis's health: "I feel so sorry for your great anxiety about your wife, and am thankful that so far you are able to send a fair account so we must hope the improvement will continue. Do write me a short account of what has really happened."[3]

The Windsors remained in New York to celebrate the publication of the Duke's memoir, *A King's Story*. It was not uncommon for exiled royals to write their memoirs, but from the very beginning, the Duke of Windsor's book promised to be controversial. He would be writing not about long-dead relatives and distant cousins who peopled royal courts filled with celebrations but of those very much alive: his mother, his brother the King, Queen Elizabeth, and others. Nor would the centerpiece of the book—the abdication—be a subject any of the principals would be happy to dredge up once again. But David also saw the book as a chance to set out his version of the abdication crisis and also to present a sympathetic portrait of the woman who became his wife. Wallis, too, encouraged him in his endeavors; not only would she welcome a different view of both her and her role in the abdication, but perhaps more important, the writing of a book would help fill the Duke's long, somewhat empty days.

To help him write his memoirs, David hired an accomplished journalist, Charles J. V. Murphy. Murphy, an editor for *Time-Life* and contributor to *Life* magazine, found working with the Duke nearly impossible. David often spoke for hours as Murphy took notes, then later changed his mind, believing that he had revealed too much. Some days, David was filled with enthusiasm for the project; on others, he seemed distant and uncooperative. Wallis, too, had little idea of what was involved in the production of a book and constantly interrupted her husband's sessions with Murphy.[4] Nor were the Windsors any more impressed with Murphy; after spending several months with the writer, both the Duke and Duchess found him arrogant, demanding, and inflexible. Under these strained circumstances, it is not surprising that Murphy and the Windsors barely managed to maintain a working relationship and produce the book at all.[5]

In April 1951, *A King's Story* was finally published. In a review in the *New Statesman*, the historian Noel Annan wrote that "reflections of inconceivable banality succeed descriptions of Court life so bizarre that the characters seem permanently to be playing charades. . . ."[6] But the book, in addition to presenting David's point of view, also brought with it welcome royalty checks, and the extra money would prove useful to the Windsors in the next few years.[7]

The writing of the book and the presentation of an alternative view of the abdication stirred up old and painful memories and made the Windsors acutely aware of their continued slights at the hands of the Royal Family. American journalist C. L. Sulzberger and his wife, Marina, dining with the Duke and Duchess one evening, were, in his words, "treated to an extraordinary conversation." He wrote:

In essence, it comprised a tragic lament about the British Royal Family. The Duchess kept insisting she would never go back to England because "the Duke," as she always calls her husband, had been treated so shabbily. . . . The Duke was furious over the following incident. He had prepared a lengthy speech designed to boost his book of memoirs. The thing was recorded for a publishers' dinner but Buckingham Palace ordered it stopped on the grounds that it was no time to make such a speech because of the King's illness. On the afternoon before the speech was to have been delivered, Princesses Elizabeth and Margaret went to the races. Both the Duke and Duchess kept repeating that the two "nieces" had gone "to the races," while at the same time, the speech was banned because of King George's illness. The Duchess said: "Why don't you play them your record?" The Duke protested: "Oh, no, no, I can't." Then we were escorted downstairs where they kept a long-playing phonograph. The

Duke's speech said he now "knew why Job said, 'I wish my enemies had written a book.'" It was a great honour for him because
"it is the first time in fifteen years that I have spoken in England,
which, in spite of everything, is my country and my home." The
speech continued: A lot of people had been nasty about the book,
there had been criticism, but he didn't see why, just because he is
an ex-king, he wasn't allowed to write. He brought in a lot of
examples of English rulers who had written books—Charles II,
Henry VIII, and Queen Victoria. The speech ends with the
remark: "My book is not a novel, but it is a romance, and all I
can say is that I hope it can end like most fairy tales—'and they
lived happily ever after.'" The speech was very pleasant but we
were told he had never been allowed to make it. The Duchess
kept saying, "What nonsense! What hypocrisy! What jealousy!
When I think that that very day, the girls went to the races and
the Duke of Gloucester went to a dinner party!"[8]

The Windsors' bitterness was tempered somewhat by the illness
of George VI. Beginning in 1947, Bertie's health became increasingly
fragile. Suffering from constant cramps in his legs, he sought medical advice, and doctors discovered arteriosclerosis; at one point,
it was feared that his left leg might develop gangrene and have to
be amputated.

For the next few years, Bertie's health fluctuated wildly, his recur-
rent circulatory problems exacerbated by his incessant smoking. In
March 1949 a portion of his right lung had to be removed. In August
1951, while at Balmoral, the King developed a chill and sore throat. In
September, at the insistence of his doctors, he traveled to London for a
detailed examination; on September 15, a bronchoscopy was performed
at Buckingham Palace to remove tissue from his lungs. Shortly thereafter, it was discovered that he had a malignant growth which necessi-
tated the removal of his entire left lung. Bertie was only informed of the
need for the operation but not the cause of his ailment. Queen Elizabeth, however, knew the truth: Bertie had cancer. On September 23, the
left lung was removed, along with certain nerves in his larynx which
prevented the King from speaking above a loud whisper.

The Queen was told that the King had little more than a year to
live. The removal of the lung might increase his chances, but the cancer
was already spreading throughout his body. In December he underwent a second bronchoscopy, which left him greatly weakened and
unable to make a scheduled tour of Africa; in his place, he sent his
eldest daughter, Princess Elizabeth, and her husband, Prince Philip.
On January 31, 1952, George VI, looking gaunt and frail, stood bare-
headed beside the Queen and Princess Margaret on the tarmac at

Heathrow Airport, watching as Elizabeth and Philip boarded an airplane and left for Africa in his place. Six days later, in the early-morning hours of February 6, George VI died in his sleep at Sandringham House in Norfolk.

Queen Elizabeth had always been a firm, unforgiving enemy of the Duchess of Windsor; the premature death of her husband cemented a near-hysterical hatred against Wallis which nothing has erased. "It is quite simple, the Queen Mother believes that Mrs. Simpson shortened her husband's life and she has never been able to forgive her," said one friend of the Royal Family. "The interesting thing is that she never openly blames her brother-in-law the Duke of Windsor."[9] This conviction—absolute, unwavering—would cloud any future hope the Windsors might have had of gaining the acceptance of the Royal Family. That the King's death had been brought on by his heavy smoking seemed not to matter at all; to Queen Elizabeth, Wallis had killed her husband, and she would refuse to listen to any contrary point of view.

The Duke and Duchess of Windsor were in New York, staying in their suite at the Waldorf Towers, when they learned of the King's death. David immediately made plans to return to London. Before he even had a chance to ask, he was told that Wallis would not be welcome to attend the funeral; none of the three queens—David's mother, Queen Mary, his sister-in-law, Queen Elizabeth; his niece, Queen Elizabeth II—would receive the Duchess of Windsor. On the evening of the following day, February 7, they held a press conference in the Verandah Grill on the sun deck of the Cunard liner *Queen Mary*. The surrounding circus murals, according to one reporter, made for "the most macabre setting in which British Royalty can ever have appeared. For audience, there was a crowd of gum-chewing reporters, photographers and film cameramen."[10]

David, who wore a black armband, read from a prepared statement: "This voyage, upon which I am embarking aboard the *Queen Mary* tonight is indeed sad—and it is all the sadder for me because I am undertaking it alone. The Duchess is remaining here to await my return. I am sailing for Great Britain for the funeral of a dear brother, and to comfort Her Majesty, my mother, in the overwhelming sorrow which has overtaken my family and the Commonwealth of British Nations. . . . the late King and I were very close. . . . King George VI steadily maintained the highest standards of constitutional monarchy. And these same attributes will, I am sure, descend to his daughter, the new Queen."[11] The Duchess, wearing a black sealskin bolero over a black costume, with a black fur cap perched on the side of her head, stood in silence behind the grand piano. Journalist Kenneth Hord noted that she "repeatedly . . . glanced at [the Duke] in compassion."[12]

David stayed at Marlborough House. At the funeral, he walked behind his brother's coffin, next to the Duke of Edinburgh, the Duke of Kent, and the Duke of Gloucester. It has often been said that Wallis used the occasion to try to force concessions from her husband's family at their weakest moment; in fact, Wallis, fully aware that David was returning to a volatile situation, was worried that he would take advantage of his presence to press that she be granted the style of Royal Highness. She wrote: "Now that the door has been opened a crack try and get your foot in, in the hope of making it open even wider in the future because that is the best for WE. . . . I should also say how difficult things have been for us and that also we have gone out of our way to keep our way of life dignified which has not been easy due to the expense of running a correct house in keeping with your position as a brother of the King of England. And leave it there. *Do not mention or ask for anything regarding recognition of me.* I am sure you can win her over to a more friendly attitude."[13]

Nevertheless, on February 26, Chips Channon was asked to host a luncheon party at which the Duke of Windsor, Queen Elizabeth II, and the Duke of Edinburgh would be present. The meeting, requested by David himself, against the advice of Wallis, was to discuss the possibility of a proper job for himself, formal recognition of his wife and the official granting of the style of Royal Highness, and his financial settlement with his late brother. On the first request, the Queen was polite but evasive; the Duke asked about a potential ambassadorship or perhaps another colonial post. It says much for the boredom which had consumed his life that David, having lived through four years of misery in the Bahamas, was once again willing to accept a post not likely to be more impressive because it brought with it responsibilities and authority. Elizabeth II consulted with Winston Churchill on this issue, and the prime minister apparently informed her that he thought it inadvisable to grant the Duke such a position.

On the second issue—that of receiving Wallis and granting her the style of Royal Highness—there was no hesitation on the Queen's part in providing a negative answer. Elizabeth II had been raised largely in an environment surrounded by prejudices against the Duchess; by the time she came to the throne, it is scarcely surprising, therefore, that she had inherited most of her mother's and grandmother's virulent views toward Wallis. It has often been said that the Queen made such decisions out of respect for her grandmother and mother and that while Queen Mary and Queen Elizabeth were still alive, she would not force them into an uncomfortable situation; this is true, but perhaps the most important factor was the Queen's belief that by doing what her father had so strenuously refused to do, she would dishonor his memory. Her devotion to George VI would ensure that Wallis would never be granted the style of Royal Highness.

The Duke's financial settlement also proved a tricky question. He had, since 1938, received some £21,000 a year, a sum granted to him only after much family tension. At first, Elizabeth II informed her uncle that his agreement with the Crown had only been with her father; when George VI died, the obligations to pay had also come to a stop. The Duke was on his own. David immediately protested this decision. He asked George Allen, his London solicitor, to intervene; Allen met with the Queen's legal representative and eventually managed to convince the new sovereign that the agreement should be continued. But the payment of the annual £21,000, for all intents, remained contingent on the Duke's continued absence from England. When he inquired about moving back to Fort Belvedere, he was told that doing so would mean that his payments from the Crown would automatically fall under the category of taxable income.[14]

Such continued ostracism on the part of the Royal Family was difficult for certain members to understand. David's nephew, the earl of Harewood, later recalled: "It was hard for the younger amongst us not to stand in amazement at the moral contradiction between the elevation of a code of duty on the one hand, and on the other the denial of central Christian virtues—forgiveness, understanding, family tenderness."[15] Nor was David any more favorably impressed by the battle he had had to wage to keep his financial settlement. In anger, he wrote to Wallis: "It's hell to be even this much dependent on these ice-veined bitches, important for WE as it is."[16]

A year later, the same tense family scenes would be repeated. On March 6, 1953, David, along with his sister Mary, the Princess Royal—who happened to be visiting him and Wallis in New York—sailed from America to Southampton upon learning that their mother was dying. Once again, there was no question of Wallis's joining him, and she remained at the Waldorf Towers in New York. There, on March 24, she learned that Queen Mary had died. Her reaction was a curious one: Upon hearing the news, she immediately burst into tears. For the rest of her life, she would keep a small photograph of the Queen on a table in her bedroom in Paris.[17]

Queen Mary had never wavered from her belief that Wallis was simply an adventuress, unworthy of her son and a royal title and style. She had never bothered, in the sixteen years of their marriage, to address a single letter to her daughter-in-law. Her Christmas cards, regularly dispatched from Marlborough House, were pointedly inscribed: "To David."[18] But Wallis, according to one intimate friend, was "haunted by the idea that she had forever come between mother and son." More than anyone, she knew how much the Duke had loved and revered his mother: "He spent his entire life trying to win her approval," she commented sadly. "Now, it is too late."[19] She had always hoped that despite the numerous indications to the contrary, David, at least, would be accepted back into his family.

If David had hoped that his mother's death would help lessen some of the antipathy toward him among the Royal Family, he was mistaken. He attended Queen Mary's funeral but was told he would not be welcome at the family dinner which followed at Windsor.[20] The experience left him bitter, filled with unhappy reflections on how he had been treated. He wrote to Wallis: "My sadness was mixed with incredulity that any mother could have been so hard and cruel towards her eldest son for so many years and yet so demanding at the end without relenting a scrap. I'm afraid the fluids in her veins have always been as icy cold as they now are in death."[21]

The Duke and Duchess of Windsor did not attend the coronation of Queen Elizabeth II that spring. It was not simply a matter of David's refusing to join the celebrations if Wallis was not invited, for he himself was deliberately excluded as well. Traditionally, of course, a king or queen followed to the throne upon the death of his or her predecessor; it was therefore considered somewhat unlucky that any former sovereign, with the exception of a consort, should be present during a coronation. The Duke knew that such an exclusion could only be advanced on the idea that one Crowned sovereign did not attend the coronation of another. Edward VIII, of course, had never been Crowned and thus fell beyond the bounds of convention. Even though a coronation traditionally brought together the scattered aunts, uncles, cousins, nieces, and nephews, which constituted the entire Royal Family—a gathering which should automatically have included the Duke and Duchess of Windsor, as aunt and uncle of the new Queen—Queen Elizabeth II flatly declared that she did not wish for her uncle to be issued an invitation; neither he nor Wallis was welcome.[22] On June 2, 1953, London and the world celebrated the start of a new reign filled with promise and hope; however, for the Windsors, this new Elizabethan age would bring no relief from the royal vendetta.

39

The Last Two Houses

For sixteen years, since that cold December day when David had abdicated, Wallis knew that his most heartfelt desire was to return home to England to live. Pathetically, he had hoped against hope that someday his family would relent. When his brother died, David briefly thought that his niece would halt the Royal Family's war against him and his wife. Then, in 1953, Buckingham Palace announced that it was selling the lease on Fort Belvedere; David was informed that he would not be allowed to purchase it.[1] With this, it finally became clear that the new Queen would be just as unforgiving as her father where the Windsors were concerned. They finally abandoned their years of leases and temporary housing and began a serious hunt for a house in France to purchase.

From 1949 to 1953 the Duke and Duchess had lived in a rented house at 85, rue de la Faisanderie, in Paris. This was not as large as their house at 24, boulevard Suchet, nor did it possess a suitable garden. The salon was of an adequate size, but Wallis found the dining room too small for entertaining. They continued to remain in residence, but Wallis began to search for a new house in Paris.

It was by accident that she happened upon the house at 4, route du Champ d'Entrainement, in the fashionable Bois de Boulogne, only fifteen minutes by car from the center of Paris. A moderate-sized villa, it had been occupied immediately after the war by President Charles de Gaulle. The two acres of landscaped gardens, surrounded by tall hedges and an iron railing, promised privacy. Perhaps most important, the price was right: the French government agreed to let the Windsors take up residence for a token rent of fifty dollars (U.S.) a year; they signed the lease, and Wallis immediately set to work transforming the house into a miniature palace.[2]

Situated near the Porte de Madrid in the Neuilly District, the Windsors' new house had been built in the 1880s by architect Gabriel-Jean Antoine Davioud.[3] The massive iron gate, topped with gilded iron spikes and ducal coronets, was flanked by two tall stone posts that marked the entrance to the property. A small lodge, in the same style as the main house, stood here as well, providing accommodation for the concierge and his family. The crushed-gravel drive swept in a careful arc across the manicured, rolled lawns, past the immense oak and chestnut trees and clumps of colorful rhododendron bushes, to the columned portico of the main house. The Windsor Villa, as it came to be called, was an eclectic mixture of Third Empire architecture, mansard roofs, ornate stonework, and elaborate window grilles. From the exterior, it was a rather grand house, but there was only a handful of rooms within, allowing Wallis to entertain in the style she wished but comfortable enough for the Windsors to feel that they were, at last, home.

As in her house on boulevard Suchet, Wallis again called on the talents of Stephane Boudin, who by this time had perfected his skills as an interior designer. His approach to the Windsor Villa was more refined, and also much more lush, than his work at boulevard Suchet. Wallis, too, had changed: Her tastes and experiences had been honed through several decorating projects, and she brought to their new house very definite ideas she wished to see carried out. As a result, the house in the Bois de Boulogne became a true collaborative effort between Duchess and designer.

"It is hard to believe that there can ever have been an interior more surpassingly clean—where crystal was more genuinely scintillating and porcelain more luminous, or where wood and leather, polished to the consistency of precious stone, could more truthfully be said to shine," wrote author Valentine Lawford of the Windsor Villa.[4] The sense of luxurious indulgence was immediate upon entering the house. From the front doors, a small vestibule opened to the foyer, rising two stories and circled by a second-floor gallery with an iron-and-bronze decorative railing. Wallis wanted a very grand, very formal introduction to the house, and Boudin provided his idea of a re-created Italian palazzo in the rococo style. The walls were painted in shades of antiqued yellow, apricot-and-green scagliola, or imitation marble, with gilded moldings, heavily veined greenish-blue pilasters, and touches of scarlet rubbed into corners and daubed on walls to add a richer, deeper hue. Above the cornice, a trompe l'oeil balustrade circled a painted blue sky filled with white clouds and free-flying birds.[5]

The most prominent feature of the foyer was the Duke's Order of the Garter banner, from his time as Prince of Wales, hanging from the second-floor gallery. Opposite the front door, on either side of the entrance to the drawing room, were eighteenth-century, Regency-style consoles resting on immense gilded eagles; above them hung octagonal, gilded mirrors. Enormous banks of white orchids and arum lilies, in crystal and porcelain vases, stood at intervals around the room, illuminated by concealed spotlights, which cast a seductive, subdued glow over the jewel-toned walls. A sedan chair stood in one corner opposite a colorful antique Chinese screen. In the center of the foyer, on a mahogany-and-ormolu desk, stood the Windsors' guest books and the red leather dispatch box marked simply: "The King." There were further echoes of this royal heritage: Boudin had designed the wall sconces, carved in wood and brightly painted and gilded, to resemble the royal coat-of arms, with the motto of the Prince of Wales, *Dieu et mon Droit*, picked out in scarlet and gold; above hung a glass-and-ormolu Louis XV–style four-light lantern, surmounted by gilded Prince of Wales feathers, which had formerly been in Fort Belvedere.[6]

The drawing room occupied the center of the garden side of the house. Previously, Boudin had created his famous dining room for the London house of Chips Channon, modeled after François Cuvillies's blue-and-silver rococo salon in the Amalienburg Pavilion at Nymphenburg Palace in Munich. At the Windsor Villa, he continued to draw from this inspiration, although this version was muted in its flamboyant detail. The walls were painted a pale blue, with moldings of braiding and tassels, as well as cornices, picked out in antiqued silver. Three French doors opened onto the terrace and garden beyond; between them stood silver Italian neoclassical-style consoles by Jansen, along with Empire-style painted fauteuils and matching stools.[7] The parquet floor was covered with a specially woven Aubusson carpet of pale blue with a motif of intertwined flowers and trelliswork enclosing the Prince of Wales's feathers, worked in silver thread.[8] In one corner stood a black Steinway baby-grand piano; against the long wall opposite the French doors were sofas and armchairs in blue and silver, also by Jansen; the rest of the furniture—tables, chairs, consoles—was French Louis XV and XVI. Two enormous paintings hung on either side of the door to the foyer: Sir William Llewellyn's portrait of Queen Mary in Garter Robes, painted in 1919, always hung to the left of the door; and at various times, Etienne Drian's stern portrait of the Duchess in her blue taffeta gown ("It was my Scarlett O'Hara dress," the Duchess had remarked with a laugh to a friend[9]) or a portrait of the Duke in his Garter Robes by Sir James Gunn hung to the right. "On every table," wrote Lawford, "console, commode, and *gueridon*, are equally priceless objects and bibelots; a profusion of gold, enamel, porcelain and vermeil—seal cases, snuff boxes, Augsburg and Chinese and Meissen birds. And there is a phenomenal array of Meissen pugs—pugs on cushions, pugs on stools, pugs scratching themselves behind the ears, pugs asleep, pugs on the *qui-vive*."[10] This assortment rested on small outlines of felt, carefully cut to shape and placed to prevent scratching; wax had been melted onto the tables in their outlines to hold them in place in case they were jostled. "We have collected a few things," Wallis remarked to one visitor.[11] With due irony, Lawford noted that Wallis's "collector's eye is by now as sure and discerning as her Royal mother-in-law's ever was."[12]

On the left side of the drawing room, double doors opened to the dining room, lit by two tall windows overlooking the gardens. When the Windsors leased the house, they also purchased the music room *boiserie* from the Château de Dampierre-sur-Aube, which was disassembled and later used on the walls of the new dining room in the Bois. Boudin painted the paneling a deep blue, then had workers scrub away at it with wire brushes to antique it; finally, glaze was rubbed into the paneling to create an authentic look. Above the paneling were painted Chinese scenes of exotic gardens, bridges, waterfalls, and distant pavilions.[13] From the center of the ceiling, painted in a trompe l'oeil scene of ribbons, flowers, sky, and birds, hung a chandelier of foliage and shell design. The rear wall contained a mirrored alcove in which stood a console; to either side were doors to the pantry; above were two tiny loges, which Wallis and Boudin decorated with old musical instruments. "The quarters must have been extremely cramped," Wallis wrote "and I am sure that if the musicians were not dwarfs to begin with, they certainly must have learned how to perform in the pretzel position."[14] The table here was new, but the Windsors used their old suite of French dining chairs from their house on boulevard Suchet, now painted deep blue and covered with light blue upholstery.

To the right of the drawing room was the library, with light yellow walls and French doors opening to the garden. The room boasted the only fireplace on the first floor, a red-marble mantel above which hung, against a mirrored background, Gerald Brockhurst's portrait of the Duchess. "She looks like Joan Crawford!" a guest was heard to exclaim upon seeing the painting one night.[15] (Wallis, in fact, was never entirely pleased with any of her numerous portraits; she admired the portrait Salvador Dali painted of her friend Mrs. Winston Guest and also liked the work of Pietro Annigoni but never seemed to have the time to commission either artist.[16]) The interiors of the four bookcases were painted bright crimson to match the scarlet tones of the carpet and the reds in the mantelpiece.[17] Against the rear wall, in an alcove, Boudin placed a large banquette upholstered in yellow silk, later replaced with a simple couch. Above this hung Sir Alfred Munnings famous painting *The Prince of Wales on Forest Witch.*

A splendid marble staircase curved up from the left-hand side of the foyer to the open gallery which circled the space on the second floor; there was also an elevator hidden behind a door near the downstairs secretaries' office behind the library. On the upstairs landing, display cabinets held the Duke's collection of glassware, including many commemorative objects connected to his aborted coronation in 1937.

The Duke and Duchess each had a suite of rooms on the second floor, separated by a small boudoir that overlooked the garden. This room, just above the drawing room, was paneled in pale peach–colored *boiserie*, with accents of white and yellow. The curtains on the two windows were of yellow-and-white taffeta, while the sofa and overstuffed chairs were upholstered in bright yellows, peach, and apricots, with leopard-print pillows used as exotic accents.[18] The boudoir served as the Windsors' main sitting room. Here they met each morning, took tea in the afternoon, and ate dinner on trays while watching the corner television set if they had no guests. The small tables were absolutely crammed with books, magazines, photographs, and souvenirs. In one corner stood an eighteenth-century japanned secretary in green, gold, and black lacquer which Wallis used as a writing desk.

The Duke's bedroom was connected by a large, open doorway to his study, a small alcove lined with shelves holding his collection of biographies and books of history. As she had done at La Croë, Wallis virtually re-created the bedroom he had used at Fort Belvedere, with the same beige walls, white moldings, brown carpets, and hanging banner with the Prince of Wales's monogram and motto above his bed. His leather-topped desk was crowded with photographs of the Duchess, while military prints hung on the walls. The Duke's dressing room, filled with row upon row of his famous plaid and checked suits, connected to his black-and-white-marble bathroom. David preferred his shower to the actual tub, which he used instead for storage of his papers—documents, letters, photos, and old scrapbooks. The Duchess once took a visiting Diana Vreeland into the bathroom and showed her the mess in the tub. "It was piled with papers, papers, pa-pers, PAPERS!" recalled Vreeland. "Bills, little things to do with golf." "Isn't this terrible?" Wallis said with a laugh. "Look at this heap!"[19]

Wallis's own suite of rooms was on the opposite side of the boudoir, directly above the library and secretaries' office. The walls of her bedroom were covered in pale blue silk moiré, with moldings antiqued and finished in pale gray; against one wall stood an alcove in which rested her bed, covered in a matching blue satin eiderdown. At the foot of the bed stood a small French sofa piled with pillows. Many of them were silk screens of the Windsors' favorite pugs; others were embroidered with the Duchess's frequent sayings, including, "You Can Never Be Too Rich or Too Thin."[20] Friends also contributed to this menagerie: Actress Sylvia Sidney stitched a pug pillow in petit point for her friend that Wallis kept at the foot of her bed until her death.[21] On either side of the bed, small shelves held Wallis's collection of books, a Russian icon in a silver frame, and a number of Wedgwood medallions depicting members of various European royal families. Wallis's kneehole dressing table, also covered in blue silk moiré, featured a glass top sprinkled with photographs of David. The rest of the furnishings—a Victorian-style plush chaise-longue and overstuffed slipper chairs—were done by Jansen in white cotton with white and blue bullion fringe and piping.

A door on the left side of the bed led to Wallis's dressing room, a long, narrow space lined with closets whose doors were mirrored. The end of the room, before the window, widened into an oval whose white walls rose to a shallow dome, resting on slim columns and whose ceiling had been painted with a trompe l'oeil sky.[22] Two red George III japanned étagères filled with various souvenirs, photographs, and pieces of porcelain stood in the corners. This, in turn, led to Wallis's bathroom, a piece of pure fantasy designed by Boudin to resemble the interior of a tent. The sloped ceiling was painted in alternating white-and-blue trompe l'oeil striped cloth, which continued down the walls in hanging tassels and strings of blue, white, and yellow lilacs, the work of theatrical designer Dimitri Bouchene. The wall above the bathtub was covered with a large mirror against which hung Cecil Beaton's gouache of Wallis, done during his visit to her flat at Cumberland Terrace in London in 1936.

The villa in Paris satisfied the Duchess. It proved a welcome outlet for her talents and gave her an admirable setting in which to conduct her and the Duke's life in a proper style. But the Duke still longed for a house in the country surrounded by a garden in which he could happily toil. In June 1952 they discovered that their friend, painter Etienne Drian, had put his country estate up for sale; one day the Duke and Duchess drove the forty miles from Paris to the small village of Gif-sur-Yvette, situated in the Chevreuse Valley, and eagerly inspected the property. Called the Moulin de la Tuilerie, or the Mill, the estate consisted of twenty-six acres, sliced in half by the River Merantaise. Four stone buildings, including an old, medieval millhouse, had been converted by Drian into lodgings. Wallis immediately fell in love with "this enchanting spot."[23] She and David paid several further visits to the property before making their decision: in July the Duke paid $80,000 for the estate.[24] It was to be the only house the Duke and Duchess ever owned outright during their marriage.

The actual millhouse was the largest of the existing buildings; although the nearly two foot thick stone walls and low, beamed ceilings lent great character, Wallis was also determined to install modern conveniences; the cobbled courtyard was dug up, and a new septic system was buried beneath the stones. Other buildings—the old barn, servants' quarters, and farm buildings—were modernized. Steel girders and support beams, trusses, and arches were carefully inserted between walls and floors, adding support and reinforcement. The Windsors hired a builder from Châteaufort and engaged local craftsmen to carry out the project.[25]

The Mill stood secluded behind high stone walls and a massive oak gate. A narrow drive ran parallel to a long, two-storied stone building which housed both the gatekeeper and rooms for guests and opened to the large, cobbled courtyard at the center of the complex. The walls of the buildings were overgrown with wisteria, honeysuckle, and ivy; old roses climbed lattice arbors to the steeply pitched slate roofs; and stone terraces sloped from French doors to the rolling green lawns and river beyond.

Wallis asked Nancy Lancaster and John Fowler to assist both her and Stephane Boudin in decorating the Mill. Most of the furnishings came from storage, where they had been waiting for use since the Windsors sold La Croë; Nancy Lancaster was disheartened to see so many pieces by Syrie Maugham, but the Duchess was sentimentally attached and insisted on using them.[26] Because most of the ceilings in the Mill were so low, Wallis decided to paint nearly all of the rooms white; to counter this effect, Wallis deliberately choose extravagant accents. "I wanted to have a fling with rich bright colors," she declared. "In the past I'd always leaned to soft pastels but The Mill was my chance to do something different."[27] Work on the Mill progressed quickly, and by the spring of 1953 the Windsors were able to take up residence in their new home. Contrary to what has often been written, Nancy Lancaster recalled that the Windsors "not only paid on the dot, but we each had the most marvelous personal letters of appreciation."[28]

From the cobbled courtyard, a massive oak door opened to the lower story of the millhouse. A small entrance hall was filled with reminders of the Windsors' lives: A red-and-gold Louis XV chest from Wallis's Bryanston Court flat stood against one wall; above this hung the gilded sunburst clock from the vestibule of the house on boulevard Suchet in Paris. Two old Irish leather chairs stood to either side, originally from David's apartments at York House, St. James's Palace.[29]

Thick posts, supporting the beamed ceiling, separated the entrance hall from the big hall, which Wallis considered her favorite room—"so cheery and comfortable," she called it.[30] The floor here was original, composed of sixteenth-century gravestones. The uneven surface was covered with a red, black, and white carpet sewn with floral motifs. A large, open fireplace stood against one wall; ranged around it were comfortable overstuffed sofas and chairs covered with bright English chintz. French doors, curtained in a matching chintz fabric, opened to the courtyard beyond.

On one side of the big hall were the pantry and the kitchen, with the dining room on the other. Wallis wanted something whimsical in this last room, and she eventually asked John Fowler to paint the white walls with trompe l'oeil trelliswork, vines, and bullrushes. To accent these touches, the windows were curtained in green-and-cream-colored taffeta, and the Italian table and chairs were painted in green as well; the floor was covered with rush matting to add to the illusion of dining out of doors. In the corners stood tall metal cranes, peculiar pieces Wallis had discovered in an antique shop on the Left Bank and instinctively purchased without the vaguest idea of how she would use them. At the Mill, she decided they would make perfect lamps and had them painted green, wired for electricity, and set against her make-believe garden on the walls.[31]

A narrow wooden staircase rose from a corner of the big hall to the drawing room. The largest room in the millhouse, it rose one and a half stories to an open, arched, and beamed ceiling whose white color only seemed to increase its height. Because the millhouse itself was built against the side of a hill, the second floor facing the courtyard was actually at garden level at the rear. French doors opened to a large stone terrace overlooking the river and gardens. The drawing room was dominated by the massive fireplace which stood against one wall, above which hung an elaborate ten-foot-high Baroque mirror. The furnishings were an eclectic mixture of English chintzes and French antiques in bright yellows, reds, greens, and blues; in one corner stood a grand piano. White was the only cohesive color in the entire room: The carpet was a bold tartan pattern, the curtains a bright mixture of yellow and red, and the odd corner under the eaves had been painted by Drian in a colorful trompe l'oeil screen.[32] Through a low door was a room the Windsors called the Bahamas Bar, a nook adorned with souvenirs from their days in Nassau.[33] On one wall hung a replica of the old mill wheel, emblazoned with the slogan "I'm not the Miller's Daughter, but I've Been Through the Mill."[34]

David's bedroom was perched beneath the eaves of the roof. The only way Wallis could find enough space for both his bedroom as well as a dressing room and bathroom was to place them one above the other; to reach the bedroom, one had to walk through his bathroom, which also doubled as his dressing room. To disguise this fact, all of the fixtures were concealed beneath retractable tops or behind sliding doors. A staircase in the corner of the room connected with the Duke's bedroom, where he slept on a simple bed hidden behind a screen. The walls of the staircase and bedroom were hung with prints showing uniforms of the Grenadier Guards Regiment; the military motif was carried on in the drum table David had brought with him from Fort Belvedere.[35] From his dormer windows, David enjoyed feeding the pigeons that congregated on the slate roof outside.[36]

Wallis's bedroom was contained in a long wing which stretched at an angle to the drawing room and enclosed one side of the upper terrace. Like the Duke's room, it was tucked away under the eaves; a window at the far end of the room overlooked the millstream. The colors here were yellow, pink, blue, and green, repeated in the striped taffeta curtains and the harlequin bedspread. One personal touch was her grandmother Anna Emory Warfield's rocking chair, set at the side of the fireplace; another reminder of days past were the chest of drawers and dressing table from La Croë, painted with souvenirs of Wallis's life and love affair with the Prince of Wales.[37]

Across the courtyard was the old barn, which Wallis converted into a study for David. This enormous room, forty feet long and half as high, boasted two massive fireplaces against either short wall that could each take five-foot logs. Above one hung a huge map of the world showing the travels of the Duke when Prince of Wales. Scattered across the green carpet were overstuffed sofas and chairs in green and red velvet and corduroy. Drums from the Grenadier Guards Regiment were used as sidetables, and stacked with framed photographs of the Royal Family. Tall French doors along the rear opened to the walled garden; before them stood the abdication desk, piled with photographs, books, and souvenirs. Bookshelves held regimental trophies and awards, presentation swords, foreign orders and decorations, and other regalia from David's days as Prince of Wales and king.[38] "This room represents the Duke's life," Wallis told visiting author James Pope-Hennessy.[39]

An open breezeway at the side of the barn contained a small, rustic fountain crowned with a half shell. Wallis stacked clay pots filled with flowers along the flagstone walls and over the rough, cobbled floor to brighten the space, which led to a covered porch. Here she created an outdoor dining area, with brightly painted green furniture scattered across the flagstone floor. The open windows and doors were hung with bright yellow sailcloth awnings to protect the diners from wind and rain.[40]

At the other end of the old barn, Wallis converted the former cattle stalls into guest rooms, which she called *Les Celibataires*, or the bachelors' quarters. Beyond the stone walls, covered with flowering purple clematis and honeysuckle, were two oddly shaped rooms. One was a five-sided chamber, painted white, with a green daybed and prints of the coronation of George IV hung on the walls. The other was done in black-and-white floral wallpaper, with peach-colored furnishings. Other guests could be accommodated in a small, converted farm building across the cobbled courtyard. Only a single room wide, this building held two guest rooms separated by a small sitting room and a bathroom.[41] "There was so much furniture in those little rooms," recalls Fruity Metcalfe's daughter Linda Mortimer, "that you had to snake round it to get from one side of the room to the other. It wasn't terribly convenient not being in the Mill itself; one had to cross the courtyard for dinner, which could be difficult at times. Rain made the cobbles unsteady, and Lady Monckton always had to have a footman dispatched to help her so that she wouldn't slip."[42]

The gardens and grounds at the Mill were David's particular pleasure. The estate nestled along the banks of the two smaller branches of the River Merantaise, surrounded by the sheltering belt of forest along the valley walls, with open vistas across the pastures to the steeple of the local church in the distance. Crumbling stone walls marked out what had once been a formal garden, and David quickly imagined that he could do here what he had once done at Fort Belvedere, creating herbaceous borders and rock gardens next to the stream.

David asked noted landscape architect Russell Page to help him lay out the gardens. Together they envisioned a series of informal flower gardens, alternating with stretches of lawn trimmed with colorful borders and surrounded by a rock garden as the floor of the valley began to rise into the hills. In what had formerly been a chicken run, he created a series of water pools, bricked walks, and flagged terraces surrounded by lush plantings of dahlias, sweet peas, delphinium, and roses. To one side, along a low hill, he installed a rock garden with a splashing cascade which spilled over a slope planted with Alpine flowers. The borders were planted with chrysanthemums, asters, and other flowers. An Alsatian gardener assisted the Duke in the construction and upkeep.[43] David wrote that he could "garden as one should, in old clothes, with one's hands, among familiar plants."[44] Here, in these tranquil surroundings, the Windsors spent the happiest years of their marriage, living not as Duke and Duchess but as middle-aged husband and wife.

40

A Woman of Style

MY HUSBAND gave up everything for me," Wallis once told Elsa Maxwell. "I am not a beautiful woman. I'm nothing to look at, so the only thing I can do is dress better than anyone else. If everyone looks at me when I enter a room, my husband can feel proud of me. That's my chief responsibility."[1]

The Duchess of Windsor was one of the twentieth century's most stylish and elegant women. Along with Jacqueline Kennedy Onassis and Diana, Princess of Wales, she became one of the most celebrated fashion icons of her age. Wallis was named to the world's best-dressed list for over four decades, a singular accomplishment equaled by no other woman. "She elevated sobriety to an art form," declared the French magazine *Elle* upon her death in 1986.[2]

She had always stood apart from members of her husband's family, and nowhere was this more evident than in her appearance. Wallis took pride in knowing that she set styles, was named to best-dressed lists, and maintained her figure into her seventies, accomplishments which stood in great contrast to her sister-in-law Queen Elizabeth the Queen Mother. "She has the most *awful* taste," Wallis confided to a friend. "With her shape, it's no wonder she wears those hanging tents and frumpy hats—she has to do something to distract attention. Every time I see pictures of her, I have to laugh—I think it can't get worse—but then it does."[3]

Wallis had always taken great care with her appearance. Even as a girl, when her friends sported brand-new store-bought fashions and she had been forced to wear handmade dresses, Wallis was always immaculately turned out. It was a trait she carefully nursed throughout her life. Lady Diana Cooper, writing of Wallis in the 1930s, declared: "She was always correctly dressed, never funny, never slouchy, never don't care, always right and wearing pearls."[4]

"The royalty stuff is very demanding on clothes," Wallis confessed to her aunt Bessie in the midst of her relationship with the

Prince of Wales.[5] Even on Ernest's limited income, she managed to cultivate a certain elegant chic, restrained yet exotic, from which she rarely deviated. Though she inevitably favored the simplest of clothes, they were always of the best materials, of the most flattering cut, and somehow worn with a self-confidence which made them all the more attractive. "I began with my own personal ideas about style," the Duchess told Fleur Cowles in 1966. "I've never again felt correct in anything but the severe look I developed then."[6]

This look, adopted during her time in London, followed the fashion trends of the day: slinky gowns of lamé, crepe, and satin, cut on the bias and draped seductively around her petite frame, emphasizing her waiflike figure. In the thirties, her favorite designers were Mainbocher and Schiaparelli. Mainbocher produced plain, almost austere clothes that served as admirable backgrounds to Wallis's dazzling collection of jewels. She also favored clean lines for another reason: Wallis knew that with her angular face and boyish figure, plain clothing was likely to complement rather than contrast. "In my opinion," she wrote, "there is only one important rule about clothes: it is that they should be so simple and unobtrusive as to seem unimportant. Simplicity of line, relieved from plainness by richness of fabric and elegance of detail, is my golden rule."[7]

The impression was almost always favorable. In June 1944, *American Mercury* magazine reported:

> The Duchess gives the impression of terrific neatness, not a hair out of place, not a line awry. Her nose never shines. Her slip never shows. She looks like a period room done by a furniture house, a room in which nobody lives comfortably. Figuratively speaking, there are no ashes on her rugs, no papers lying around, no blinds askew. To give a real picture of the Duchess, I must describe her clothes. In them—it sounds harsh, but it is true—a large part of her personality resides. And she spares no effort to put it there. She has lost none of her flair for style. It has become one of her prime passions. She is proud to be called the best-dressed woman in the world. It is a profession with her. She enjoys setting the style. She has launched many fashions. The vogue for high-necked evening gowns, for example, may be traced directly to her—she wears them because of her flat-chested and boyish figure.[8]

Throughout her forty years in the public eye, Wallis continually kept up with the latest fashion trends and designers. In the 1950s, once the Windsors had comfortably settled in Paris, the Duchess turned to

Christian Dior, Balenciaga, and Chanel. Hubert de Givenchy became a favorite in the sixties, as did Marc Bohan at Dior, Valentino, Madame Grès, and Emilio Pucci, with his vibrant, colorful prints. Some of these fashions worked well on Wallis, while others—notably the full-skirted New Look dresses from Dior in the mid-1950s—did not. But Wallis never gave up her taste for experimentation, whether it led to a brief dalliance with pants suits in the late 1950s or miniskirts in the 1960s.

Wallis usually devoted several weeks each spring and fall to the Paris couture collections. "It takes me a while to come to final decisions," she explained. "I return to the various showings at least three and often four times, and therefore, I have the advantage of seeing not only the clothes but sharply contrasting audiences."[9]

There were also frequent visits to her favorite designers. Wallis would spend hours at the couture houses; her chef usually packed a small hamper, which contained the Duchess's lunch: fried chicken, soup in a thermos, and a few sandwiches. Occasionally, if she ran into a friend, she would open the hamper and share her meal between showings or fittings.[10]

"It was somehow always an event when she came to the salon," recalled Hubert de Givenchy. "But not a solemn occasion, because she was always smiling and joking."[11] Once she arrived, Wallis reviewed designs, suggesting alternatives, and shared ideas. "My favourite couturier simply can't start with a blank board each time," she explained. "The individuals he dresses must regularly inspire his first ideas. I nearly always recognize the dress designed with me in mind."[12]

Wallis was not a difficult client, as Mainbocher recalled: "She has always been a joy to fit. She can take a longer fitting at one sitting than most. She has fabulous energy and concentrates on what she's doing. She's cooperative. She stands so quietly. She doesn't intrude until the fitters finish their work. Then she says what she wants. With so many women their reactions can't wait, and it disconcerts the fitters. She's also a joy because she takes time to choose, sometimes seeing a collection twice. And she has a fabulous figure, because she's not that scrawny. She's what is known as false-thin—slim, but not with a starvation body."[13]

Each season, Wallis would select perhaps two or three day suits, two or three day dresses, and several evening gowns. But her rumored extravagance where clothing was concerned is something of a canard: She rarely ordered more than a dozen items each season, alternating her favorite houses according to that year's collection. Nor did Wallis ever ask for discounts; designers often cut their prices for her, recognizing that publicity from dressing the Duchess of Windsor was worth far more than any income lost. In return, Wallis was always appreciative, dispatching thank-you letters and cards to both designers and staff, along with gold cuff links, tie pins, brooches, and bracelets on holidays.[14]

Wallis favored blue and black color schemes; occasionally, she wore gray or beige and, for dramatic impact, brilliant reds. In summer, she preferred pale pastels, especially blues, yellows, and lilacs. She disliked tweeds, which she considered too heavy to be comfortable. For a country look, she adopted her husband's favored tartan patterns: Dior made several long skirts for her in the Royal Family's Balmoral tartan, Stuart dress tartan, and Stuart old tartan.[15] For day wear on the beach and when on the Riviera, she preferred matching bathing gowns and suits, along with colorful wraps, and always coordinated shoes and bathing cap. Wallis rarely wore shorts; instead, there were simple print summer dresses, light, sleeveless designs in pastels, with matching jackets.[16]

"You have to wear black, aging or not" she told Fleur Cowles, "because when the little black dress is right, there is nothing else to wear in its place."[17] But Wallis's idea of black stretched to include white trims, gold braiding and scallops, and exotic hints of the Far East in Mandarin-inspired detailing. She often picked designs from the *pret à porter* collections and took her chances; occasionally, this resulted in some uncomfortable moments, as when the Duchess, elegantly attired in a blue-and-white-striped Givenchy sheath dress entered a party only to discover eight other women also wearing the same outfit. But Wallis merely laughed and made the women form a conga line through the room and be photographed together.[18]

Wallis often wore favorite items from her wardrobe. "You can wear a dress that's twenty years old," she explained, "but it must be immaculate. And it cannot have a wrinkle. You must always look like you just stepped out of a bandbox."[19] She told one fashion writer that her Dior cape was three years old, "and what's more you're going to see it for three years more. Prices are frightful in Paris. You have to buy less and wear them longer and more often."[20] One of her maids, packing for a trip to Palm Beach, informed the Duchess, "Madame, some of these evening dresses have gone to Palm Beach with you three times." But Wallis answered, "I hope nobody will remember."[21] No one did, as columnist Suzy Knickerbocker noted: "Everyone in Palm Beach is saying that it is hard to remember when the Duchess of Windsor has ever looked so marvelous. She's a smash in everything she wears, be it her flowered paper dress or the pale blue caftan from Balenciaga. . . ."[22]

Wallis usually went through her wardrobe twice a year, selecting gowns and outfits she no longer wanted. Some were passed along to friends or members of the household or staff, while others were donated to charities in Paris.[23] In the 1960s, Diana Vreeland managed to convince Wallis to donate many of her gowns to the Costume Institute at the Metropolitan Museum of Art in New York City; over the next decade, dozens of suits and dresses made their way to New York, including the Duchess's wedding dress by Mainbocher.

It was with her accessories that Wallis managed to refine the simplest of dresses. She was always immaculately turned out, as her friend Aline, countess of Romanones, recalled: "She always carried an extra pair of white gloves, 'One pair to go, one pair to come back.' Her shoes were always shined underneath, on the instep and inside the heel, which can be seen when you cross your legs."[24]

Behind the mirrored doors of Wallis's dressing room were long, narrow drawers filled with rows of day and evening gloves in doeskin, brushed cotton, and kid leather, often made by Balenciaga or purchased by the Duchess at Saks Fifth Avenue during her trips to New York City.[25] There were shelves of evening bags in leather, velvet, and suede in every conceivable color, pattern, and design, often adorned with gold monograms or ducal coronets.[26] She had hundreds of chiffon, silk, and mousseline scarves, made by Chanel, Hermès, Givenchy, and Marc Bohan for Dior. These were hand-painted with exotic patterns and colors, bore animal prints, or were embellished with her cipher of intertwined Ws. Wallis wore them draped around her neck or shoulders, occasionally slung diagonally across her bodice or twisted around ropes of pearls which were tied around her neck.[27] Although she rarely used them, Wallis had a number of parasols, most in light pastel colors with bone, ivory, or carved wooden handles. Likewise, her fans were either practical, simple items or exotic, hand-painted antiques or plumes of ostrich feathers used for costume balls.

There were belts in leather or suede; sashes of velvet and chiffon; and, later, jeweled belts made by New York designer Kenneth Jay Lane. Wallis had dozens of shoes from which to choose, ranging from suede and leather to satins, velvet, and crocodile skin. She favored designs made by Roger Vivier for Dior, usually with court heels so that she would not tower over her husband.[28] There were also furs, usually purchased from Dior and Maximilian. Although she owned long coats of mink, beaver, fox, and ermine, Wallis disliked their weight and instead favored sable or mink wraps.[29]

The Duchess's elaborate coiffures, created by Alexandre of Paris, were designed to accommodate a variety of hats. Wallis disliked large hats; occasionally, she would sport a wide-brimmed picture hat to match a summer dress, but her tastes veered more to pillboxes and bonnets designed by Chanel, Dior, and Givenchy. She absolutely abhorred the sorts of elaborate concoctions sported by her archrival Queen Elizabeth the Queen Mother, referring to them as "Cookie's latest flower basket."[30]

Wallis's lingerie was always of the finest quality and design. Her nightgowns and dressing gowns were in crepe de chine, fine silk, and sheer satins; the necklines were occasionally adorned with lace or finely embroidered, intertwined Ws. Inevitably, this evening wear was in peach, pale pink, or pastel blue; at night, entering her bedroom, Wallis would find her lingerie neatly folded and tucked in a quilted case covered with lace and embroidered with her cipher.[31]

While the Duke and Duchess shared a passion for clothing, their interests did not extend to the other's wardrobe. Once, when Fleur Cowles tried to include the Duke in a conversation she was having with the Duchess about her clothes, Wallis interrupted. "Oh, the Duke isn't interested in women's fashions. He never even notices what I've got on!"

"Quite right!" David responded, "but I do often think of my mother. Fashion held no interest for her. *She* never changed how she looked."[32]

Eventually, Wallis channeled some of her interest and energy into creating her own dress-pattern service, which was syndicated in America, along with a series of articles entitled "How to Be Well-Dressed." "I've done two or three hundred patterns so far," Wallis explained, "and I love doing them. I usually take my ideas from the clothes I wish I *could* wear—so as not to put every other woman in round high necks and the severe lines I insist on for myself."[33] The Duchess's dress designs were indicative of her own tastes; she seems to have had more than a passing interest in the actual design, fashion always having been something of a hobby since her schooldays. She designed a cocktail dress; an afternoon dress, which she recommended in red; a cardigan suit in tweed; and several day dresses, coats, and an evening dress of simple lines.

With her clothes, Wallis wore her magnificent collection of jewelry. While other royal women could boast pieces in greater number and of far more value than the Duchess of Windsor, perhaps no other woman in the twentieth century possessed such a diverse display of antique and modern, of the priceless worn with costume jewelry. Her eye was impeccable: Wallis preferred to let her jewels dominate rather than her clothing, and she possessed the enviable talent of being able to wear contrasting pieces at the same time, and in abundance, without appearing vulgar.

She began with little: a few simple rings, a string of pearls inherited from her Warfield grandmother, and some necklaces and bracelets. At the time of her presentation at court in 1931, she had to make do with the simulated aquamarine-and-diamond cross which hung around her neck; within five years, she would possess nearly a half million dollars' worth of lavish jewels, bestowed upon her by the Prince of Wales.

The love story of the Duke and Duchess of Windsor was also told through her jewels, with inscriptions, trinkets, and charms to remind her of significant dates and events in their romance. Nearly all her important jewels bore romantic engravings written by David. For her birthday in 1936, for example, the then King presented Wallis with a massive diamond-and-ruby tasseled necklace from Van Cleef & Arpels in Paris; on the reverse of the clasp was inscribed: "My Wallis from her David 19.vi.36"[34]

Many of the jewels in this period reflected the taste for art deco, with sleek platinum settings and pavé diamonds combined with brilliant rubies, sapphires, or emeralds to create stunning pieces. She also experimented with diverse materials. One of her most famous suites of jewels was made of an almost mauve-colored chalcedony, a necklace, bracelets, and earrings created by Suzanne Belperron and adorned with sapphires and diamonds. Wallis loved these jewels and continued to wear them until her final illness in the mid-1970s.

Van Cleef & Arpels created a number of her important pieces in the 1930s, including the sapphire-and-diamond bracelet she wore on the day she and David were married. The reverse bore the inscription "For our Contract 18-V-37."[35]

In 1940 the Duke presented her with her first flamingo brooch, composed of rubies, diamonds, and sapphires. To celebrate their return to Paris at the end of the war, he gave her an 18-carat-gold bib necklace set with diamonds, rubies, and emeralds, which he had purchased from Cartier, a rather enormous piece which she rarely wore.[36] In 1946 he gave her a spectacular jeweled brooch in the form of a bird with a long, sweeping tail composed of 322 brilliants that Cartier had made specially for her. Its centerpiece was a cabochon sapphire of 64.80 carats. The piece had been created by breaking up three diamond rings, eight brooches, and two pairs of earrings.[37]

This piece, and many others, were among those stolen during the October 1946 robbery of the Duchess's jewels. Precisely what was stolen has never been entirely clear. Lady Dudley, later Laura, Duchess of Marlborough, recalled: "The Duchess's jewel case was no ordinary affair. It was a trunk in which she had many of HRH's fantastic collection of Fabergé boxes and a great many uncut emeralds which I believe belonged to Queen Alexandra. The Duchess liked jewels very much, though this is rather an understatement as she was continually having them re-set, mostly in Paris. One of these priceless baubles had only just reached her, a vast sapphire which she had had converted into a bird of paradise by Van Cleef & Arpels."[38]

Another missing piece was a platinum-and-diamond tiara, the Duke's wedding gift to his wife. It was made by Cartier in Paris in 1937, and David had originally intended that Wallis would wear it on their wedding day; like every other royal bride, he expected that the occasion, as a royal wedding, would call for the formality of a tiara. But Buckingham Palace apparently objected to the idea, and the tiara—worn thereafter only for a series of photographs—was never seen again.

One of the great mysteries is the presence and provenance of the Duchess's emeralds. Throughout the last sixty years, it has frequently been alleged that David presented Wallis with some portion of the British crown jewels or that emeralds which had belonged to his grandmother Queen Alexandra had ended up in the Duchess of Windsor's collection. When Princess Alexandra of Denmark came to England in 1863 to marry Albert Edward, the Prince of Wales, she supposedly brought with her a number of priceless, uncut emeralds. When she died in 1925, she was thought to have left them to her grandson David, expecting that one day they would adorn his wife, whom she assumed would also be Queen of England. David, of course, was popularly thought to have given them to Wallis, and the British Royal Family, understandably, was said to be furious.

In truth, David never gave Wallis any portion of what are considered to be the crown jewels, nor did she receive any pieces which composed the private collection of the British Royal Family. American author Leslie Field, who produced an authorized account of Elizabeth II's personal collection of jewelry, flatly declares that Wallis at no time possessed any pieces which had belonged to either the Crown or to Queen Alexandra.[39]

Suzy Menkes, who produced an authoritative study of the jewelry belonging to all members of the British Royal Family, has also pointed out that Queen Alexandra's famous emeralds, if they existed at all, were more likely to have been private gifts to her from either her sister Empress Marie Feodorovna of Russia or from Indian princes and not part of her dowry.[40] She also believes that David, having been showered with many gifts of jewelry during his tour of India as Prince of Wales, would have possessed privately any number of uncut gems or pieces which could be broken apart and reset to form new pieces for Wallis.[41]

The most likely explanation for the confusion also comes from Menkes, who writes that Queen Alexandra left a number of emerald pieces to her daughter Princess Victoria, who in turn sold them to Garrard's Jewelers in London. Garrard's sold the emeralds to Cartier in Paris, where David, by an amazing coincidence, happened upon them and purchased them for Wallis.[42] The only emerald known to have been stolen from the Duchess of Windsor in 1946 was a 7.81-carat solitaire set in a small ring.[43]

The theft of the Duchess of Windsor's jewels made headlines; not surprisingly, there was much speculation among certain members of the court that the Windsors had arranged the entire thing themselves for insurance purposes. This preposterous idea is easily corrected, however, for at the same time as Wallis's jewels went missing, a very sophisticated ring of thieves was obviously operating around London. On October 25, just a week after the Windsor robbery, thieves broke into the London home of Lady Hartington, the former Kathleen Kennedy, and stole some $40,000 worth of jewels. Another $3,200 worth of gems were stolen from an apartment in St. James's Palace belonging to Lady Legh, wife of the Duke's former equerry Sir Piers Legh; a few days later, jewels worth an estimated $20,000 were taken from an aristocratic London household. Scotland Yard detectives had little doubt that all the cases were connected but were never able to find any concrete evidence.[44] In 1960 a man named Richard Dunphie finally confessed to the crimes, saying that he and three accomplices had been responsible for the string of thefts.[45]

After the theft, the Duke quickly set about replenishing his wife's collection. In 1947 he purchased an amethyst, gold, and turquoise bib necklace from Cartier. In February 1948, Wallis saw a pair of brilliant canary-yellow diamonds. "I can't think of anything I would rather have than these two diamonds," she told jeweler Harry Winston. The two diamonds, weighing 92.48 carats and encased in fine gold wire, were soon among the Duchess's favorite pieces.[46] She called them her "very ripe pears."[47]

Other favorite pieces were her famous Prince of Wales's feathers brooch and her flamingo brooch, purchased from Cartier to replace the stolen bird of paradise brooch. In 1948 she received her first panther, a brooch designed by Jeanne Toussaint for Cartier consisting of a cabochon emerald of 116.74 carats, atop which stretched a golden panther. The following year, David presented her with a second panther, this one of diamonds flecked with sapphires and perched on top of a cabochon sapphire of 152.35 carats.[48] There was also a panther bracelet with an articulated body of pavé-set diamonds flecked with onyx spots.[49]

In the 1950s, Wallis began to experiment with more exotic designs. She liked the very modern pieces of Fulco di Verdura, which mixed precious gems with natural shells against extensive gold backgrounds. She also began to wear smaller brooches in the shape of frogs or various other jeweled animals, a taste which eventually led her to costume jewelry in the 1960s.

"I hate to admit it," Wallis said in 1966, "but I am absolutely fascinated by fake jewelry at the moment. It is so good."[50] One of Wallis's most fruitful associations came when Diana Vreeland introduced her to Kenneth Jay Lane, a smart young designer in New York City. Lane created several dozen pieces for the Duchess, including serpent bracelets, jeweled belts, earrings, brooches, and necklaces, all with colorful enamels, enormous stones, and expansive gold.[51]

Of all the magnificent jewels in Wallis's collection, there was one piece she favored above all others: her bracelet hung with tiny jeweled crosses. The diamond bracelet, purchased by the then Prince of Wales from Cartier in 1935, was hung with nine crosses of aquamarine, amethyst, emeralds, baguette diamonds, rubies, yellow sapphires, blue sapphires, and platinum. On the back of each cross was an inscription representing a significant date in their relationship, including: "Our Marriage Cross Wallis 3.VI.37 David"; "God Save the King for Wallis, 16.VII.36" after the attempt on his life in London; and, significantly, "WE Are Too 25-XI-34," following the Duke of Kent's wedding. It says much that she chose to wear this bracelet, her most personal piece of jewelry, at her wedding to David.

41

Life in Paris

In THEIR TWO HOUSES, Wallis and David lived in a curious kind of limbo. They were considered royalty but were also excluded from much of that privileged world. "You and the Duke have none of the advantages of royalty and all of its disadvantages," their friend Duff Cooper once told Wallis.[1]

The one advantage they did share was the privileged style of life the Windsors led in their luxurious houses. Perhaps no other couple in the twentieth century have so exemplified style and refined living as did the Duke and Duchess of Windsor. The actions of their lives were simple enough, but played out against this background of miniature palaces and country kingdoms Wallis had created, they took on a kind of enchanted quality which seemed alluring in its unique splendor.

Each morning, Wallis regularly rose between eight and nine; she rarely slept later even if she and David had been out the night before. Her first act each morning was to weigh herself on a set of scales she kept in a corner of her bathroom; Wallis was always terribly conscious of her appearance, and if she had gained any weight, she would order her chef to restrict her diet. She took breakfast in her bedroom, brought to her on a wicker tray by one of the maids. She spent most of the morning sitting in bed, reading. She spent at least an hour catching up on the latest news; the Windsors took nine daily newspapers, two American, three French, and four English, which Wallis usually read in bed.[2] Inevitably, there were also stacks of magazines: *Life, Time, Newsweek, Vogue, Harper's Bazaar,* and *Elle* from America; *Realités, Paris Match,* and *L'Oeil* from France; and a few English titles such as *Country Life.*[3]

Wallis was a great letter writer; her collection of stationery, ranging from formal vellum crested with her intertwined initials to pastels and shocking pinks with "Wallis" engraved in bold, modern print, was stocked at her desk in the boudoir.[4] Her personal mail was answered in her sloping longhand, while business letters and inquiries from the public were largely dealt with by the secretary. She often received

unsolicited mail from those around the world who wrote to her, sometimes expressing criticism, more often admiration and sorrow that she
and the Duke had been cut off by the Royal Family. She was especially
careful that these letters received answers. "If someone takes the trouble to write," she declared, "he deserves an answer."[5] Madame Janine
Metz (née Spaner), who worked as the Windsors' social secretary for
nearly ten years, recalls: "She received a lot of fan mail, so that very
often I stayed late to sort through, organize, and answer it. Many,
many letters requested autographs, and so Their Royal Highnesses had
prepared cards, with their crest, and they both signed them before they
were sent out. We never used a stamp—they always insisted on signing these themselves." Nearly all of the mail was positive: "In the ten
years I was with Their Royal Highnesses," Madame Metz says, "there
were only a few negative letters; everyone was very, very nice."[6]

The Windsors rarely saw each other in the mornings. Occasionally, they would meet for a light breakfast in the boudoir, but more
often than not, he remained in his bedroom, reading the papers, showering and shaving, and eating the inevitable meal of smoked haddock
and stewed peaches which was brought up to him every morning.[7]

The relative silence of the morning was often broken by the barking and snuffling of the Windsors' dogs. By the middle of the 1950s,
pugs had replaced the cairn terriers the Duke and Duchess had formerly favored. The pugs were small enough to be trusted in the magnificent rooms and traveled well; both the Duke and Duchess also
valued their intelligence and loyalty and doted on them. The first, Dis-
raeli, was soon joined by Imp, Ginseng, Trooper, Davy Crockett, and
later, Black Diamond. The dogs ruled the Windsors' lives and accompanied them everywhere they went. Linda Mortimer recalls a visit the
Windsors and their dogs paid to her and her husband: "The pugs had
the run of the house, and were yapping and racing about for hours.
The Duke and I went upstairs and found a mess on the floor. He was
rather shamefaced about it, but we both looked at each other and
laughed, at the same time lunging forward to scoop it off the carpet
and almost knocking our heads together."

"Oh, no, Sir!" Mortimer said. "Let me do that."

"No, no," David replied. "I always pick up after our dogs. I'm
sorry for this, they don't normally do this."

"Of course not," Mortimer answered, although, as she says, "I
suspected that they did it rather regularly."[8]

The Duke and Duchess usually went their separate ways before
afternoon. "I married the Duke for better and for worse, but not for
lunch," Wallis once joked.[9] Occasionally, they might host a luncheon in
Paris, dining on the terrace if the weather was nice; but for the most
part David was content to work there when the weather permitted, his

papers piled atop the glass-topped wrought-iron table which stood beneath the awning. He himself often disappeared to join his friends for the usual afternoon of golf. His favorite courses, at St. Cloud, La Boulie, and St. Germain, were all only a few minutes' drive from the house in the Bois de Boulogne.

In Paris, Wallis spent her afternoons visiting the rich multitude of Parisian shops. "I adore to shop," she declared. "All my friends know I'd rather shop than eat."[10] "She was tireless," recalls a friend. "By three in the afternoon I was ready to give in, but not the Duchess—she would keep on going until someone reminded her that the Duke would be waiting back home for her."[11] She continued to haunt the antique stores along the Left Bank, searching for the occasional piece to add to the house in the Bois de Boulogne or to the Mill. She often met friends for lunch in some quiet restaurant, attended the latest showings of the Paris designers' collections, or visited them at their houses for long games of bridge. Once a week she would go to the Elizabeth Arden Salon in the Place Vendôme to have her hair and makeup done. Although she did not usually tip, Wallis always dispatched valuable gifts for all the salon girls on holidays. Very often these were much more valuable than any number of accumulated tips: gold-and-diamond pins in the shape of the Prince of Wales's feathers or gold cuff links, for the men, stamped with her husband's crest.[12]

Wallis usually returned home in time for tea with David at five. This was a large meal, in the English manner, with sandwiches, toast, jam, cake, cookies, and petit fours served in the boudoir or on the terrace. Wallis added several of her favorite southern recipes to the meal, including Cajun shrimp, blocks of cheese wrapped in bacon and broiled—"so tiny they dissolved in your mouth instantly," the Countess of Romanones recalled—and pieces of crisp bacon covered with melted brown sugar.[13] Although she joined her husband, Wallis almost never took tea, nor did she serve it, letting David act as host.[14] A silver bowl served as the repository for the Duke's half-consumed cups of tea; he was constantly filling his cup, sipping a bit, then emptying it when it became cool. "Iced tea is all right, but if there's anything I hate it's cold hot tea," he explained.[15] Throughout, David smoked his pipe. Each day, he smoked a tin of pipe tobacco, two packs of cigarettes, and every night he had two cigars after dinner. "He smoked relentlessly," remembered the Countess of Romanones, "the only thing he did which infuriated the Duchess."[16]

If there were no guests for dinner and no invitations to spend the evening out, the Duke and Duchess happily adopted their own version of informal dining. David showered and shaved again, changed into a velvet smoking jacket, black tie, and his velvet house slippers, and joined Wallis, attired in a long caftan and adorned with jewels, on the terrace in nice weather or in the boudoir, where they ate on trays before the television.[17] "I like quiz programs," Wallis explained, "but of course everything is in French—Westerns, Bob Hope, Frank Sinatra—everything. It's an absolute scream."[18] On Sunday evenings, when the servants were off, she usually crept down to the basement kitchen and fixed their dinner herself. Her tastes were simple. She wished for American conveniences, like frozen cakes. "I keep remembering the name Sara Lee," she said with a smile. "They were such good cakes. I wish there was some way to get them to Paris."[19] The couple usually remained together for several hours, often climbing into Wallis's bed to read and talk; the Countess of Romanones remembers, while a guest of the Windsors, returning at four in the morning to the villa and hearing the Windsors giggling and telling jokes in Wallis's bedroom.[20]

To maintain this miniature kingdom and ensure its smooth operation required several dozen servants and staff. In overall charge of the house was Georges Sanegre, who, with his wife, Ophelia, personally saw to most of the details of the Windsors' lives. Georges occasionally called on the Duke's valet Sydney Johnson, the faithful and devoted Bahamian servant the Windsors had brought with them from Nassau, to assist him as an underbutler during large parties. Several footmen helped during the Windsors' parties and ran errands when necessary. Anne, the housekeeper, had charge of a staff of four housemaids. Wallis had two lady's maids, Victoria Margiers and Maria Costa. In charge of the kitchens during these years were several men: the Frenchman René Legros was replaced by Jean Pierre Auge, who, in turn, was replaced by Lucien Massey. Massey and the Duchess got on very well, and she ensured that he had the staff he required to operate the kitchens, including several kitchen boys, a pastry chef, and several assistant chefs. Wallis also had a private secretary, Denise Hivet, a former TWA stewardess, while from the early 1960s, John Utter, a retired American Foreign Service officer, served as the Duke's private secretary. In 1961, Janine Spaner assumed the position formerly held by Hivet and began a ten-year term of employment with the Windsors.

Two chauffeurs, Ronald Marchant and David Boyer, had charge of the garage and the Windsors' four motorcars; later, Gregorio Martin would largely assume these duties. There was a Humber sedan; a Buick sedan; a Buick station wagon with "the Duke of Windsor" in metal letters on both front doors; and a Cadillac limousine, which, on the Duke's orders, had been slightly modified to provide more privacy between driver and passengers. Boyer and his French wife, Germaine, lived in the gatehouse at the villa, and she also served as the switchboard operator. Four gardeners, who had charge of the lawns and the greenhouses, completed the outside staff at the Bois de Boulogne.[21]

One of the most pervasive allegations made against the Duke and Duchess is that they mistreated their servants. "In my days of living abroad," says Letitia Baldrige, "I knew many of her staff, and she did not treat them particularly well."[22] However, aside from a few minor complaints and the occasional misunderstanding, the vast majority of those formerly in the employ of the Windsors seem to have had no humiliating experiences, nor had they been the victims of angry outbursts. Significantly—and as could be expected—the tales of mistreatment emanated from those who parted company with the Duke and Duchess on less than friendly terms. "I never saw her rude to her butler, Georges," recalls C. Z. Guest, "or to her personal maid, or the chef, or anybody. Of course not."[23] And Janine Metz recalls: "I never heard either one of Their Royal Highnesses speak badly to their staff, and I was close with them for ten years. The Duchess was always extremely nice to everyone, and I never heard her say a bad word about anyone in the Household. They created a family-like ambiance, and they were always interested in what was going on with their [servants'] private lives."[24]

However, Wallis was exacting in the cleanliness she demanded. "The Duchess knows everything about cleaning every kind of fabric, exactly what removed every kind of spot," Ophelia Sanegre told the Countess of Romanones. "She has taught us just what kind of iron to use for pressing every material, and we have marvelous equipment. We rarely send anything out to a dry cleaner."[25] Even her money went through these same intense procedures: Paper money for the Duchess, at the Duke's insistence, was either ordered new and crisp from a bank or wash cleaned and ironed by the housemaids; coins were always washed.[26]

Each evening, just before dinner was served, two maids could be found carrying bedsheets through the halls by their corners; the bed linens, having just been ironed, were destined for the rooms of the Duke and Duchess. Wallis could not stand wrinkles in her bed and insisted that it be made as near to the evening as possible. Once the bed was made, a plastic sheet was spread atop the satin eiderdown so that the pugs could climb onto the bed with Wallis; there she would feed them the hand-baked dog biscuits prepared fresh each day by her chef.[27] Usually the pugs slept on the bed with her, although the Duke's favorite might disappear through the boudoir to his own spot at the foot of his master's bed.[28]

The Duke and Duchess rarely entertained guests overnight in Paris. Two of the most frequent visitors, however, were the dashing Spanish Count Luis Romanones and his beautiful American-born wife, Aline. Wallis had taken an immense liking to the younger Countess, who helped fill the place a daughter might have taken as the Duchess grew older. In addition, their shared American heritage drew the two women together, as did their somewhat sharp senses of humor.

There were only two guest rooms at the Windsor villa in Paris, tucked away beneath the eaves of the mansard roof on the third floor. "I wish we could do better for you, but it's all we have," Wallis explained once. "That's why we never have houseguests." The two small bedrooms were separated by a large bathroom. The Porthault sheets and pillowcases matched the colors used on the walls, curtains and in the carpets, as did the flowers arranged in crystal and porcelain vases, which were refreshed every day. Guests' suitcases or trunks would be unpacked by members of the Windsor staff if the guest did not bring his or her own valet or maid. Suits, tuxedos, dresses, and gowns were hung in closets, aligned with matching shoes and accessories; clothing to be worn that evening would be taken away, to be pressed, laundered, and returned before dinner.[29]

Nothing in the guest rooms had been left to chance. A small tray held a Thermos of cold water, a plate of ginger cookies freshly made by the chef, decanters of whiskey, gin, and sherry, a small ice bucket, and a selection of soft drinks. A large blue folder awaited each guest. Within was the proposed agenda for the guest's visit, including dinners and luncheon invitations which had been accepted, along with seating arrangements and short biographies of guests invited to these occasions.[30]

In the bathroom, care had also been taken for the guests' comfort. Toilet paper was always removed from the roll and cut with scissors in lengths of two squares, folded, and piled on a small tray near the toilet. A perfume burner incensed the room "with the most marvelous scent." In the evening, baths were drawn by the maid or valet, temperatures measured, the surface sprinkled with Elizabeth Arden's Fluffy Milk Bath or the guest's choice of six different bath oils.[31] The medicine cabinets were stocked with aspirin, laxatives, remedies for upset stomachs, bandages, mouthwash, toothpastes, and other needs. Every night, a maid or valet laid out the toothbrush and squeezed toothpaste on it so that it stood waiting by the time the guests retired.[32]

The efficiency of the staff was truly put to the test on those occasions when the Windsors entertained. No invitation in Paris in the 1950s and 1960s was as sought out as the stiff vellum card bidding a guest to dine at the villa in the Bois de Boulogne. Wallis worked closely with her chef, Lucien Massey, who joined the household when in his late twenties and who proved amenable to her desire to try fresh ideas and create inspired meals. Nothing at a Windsor dinner party was left to chance. Menus were planned weeks in advance, and even the food on each plate was color coordinated, designed to match the selected china service as well as the linens.

Wallis and her butler, Georges Sanegre, would visit the basement storerooms to select the china and crystal. In setting her tables, Wallis benefited immensely from the royal heritage her husband brought with him. Few wives could preside over dinner parties at which her guests dined off china which had belonged to generations of sovereigns. The storerooms were a showcase of fine china and porcelain: There was a Royal Copenhagen service from the turn of the century; services from Limoges, the Nymphenburg works, Royal Doulton, Staffordshire bone china, services which had belonged to George IV and Queen Alexandra, and most famous of all, the Meissen "Flying Tiger" service of Elector Friedrich Augustus of Saxony. Wallis also enjoyed the more fanciful pieces of eighteenth- and nineteenth-century porcelain, including serving dishes designed to resemble frogs, cockerels, and other wildlife. The crystal was engraved with the Windsors' double monogram "WE," along with the ducal coronet, designed to match the silver menu holders and crested napkin rings.

Many afternoons, Alexandre, of the rue du Faubourg Saint-Honoré, would come to the villa to set Wallis's hair; if he was unavailable, he would dispatch his pupil Edouard Orengin. "Alexandre understands my hair," she once told a visitor.[33] Once a week, she had it washed at Elizabeth Arden. "Her hair was rich and full and long, and her wonderful skin was a major beauty asset," the Countess of Romanones recalled. Wallis once declared, "Aline, the most important thing is to take care of your face. The other end you sit on. My mother used to tell me that."

Three times a week, a manicurist from Elizabeth Arden came to do her nails, and on the evenings when the Windsors were giving a party, a consultant arrived to do her makeup as well. Wallis thought her eyelashes were too thin and wore very discreet false lashes. Some afternoons, she might lie down for a massage, but she never napped.[34] Clad in a silk dressing gown covered in Oriental designs, Wallis would inspect the house in the early evening, checking that the tables were properly set, that ashtrays had been put out on the tables in the drawing room, and that the flowers had all been placed according to her instructions.

Wallis worked hard at creating interesting guest lists. "She liked people to be expressive," remembered the Countess of Romanones, "to have a sense of humour, to be attractive and extroverted. For her dinner parties she looked for outstanding people—the best novelist of the moment, or whatever scientist or musician or explorer happened to be interesting at a given time. The Duke liked political people, military personalities, and sportsmen"[35] An amazing cross-section of writers, artists, actors, and society members formed the Windsors' favored circle. In these years, guests were likely to include Baron Frederic de Cabrol and his wife, Daisy; Prince and Princess von Bismarck; Prince and Princess Felix Youssoupov; Sir Oswald and Lady Mosley; Grace, Lady Dudley; Princess Ghislaine de Polignac; the Count and Countess of Romanones; the Winston Guests; Vicomtesse de Ribes; and Gerald Van der Kemp, curator of Versailles and the man who helped shape Wallis's interest in French art and furniture.

Dinner guests were asked to arrive promptly at quarter-past eight. As their cars pulled up before the portico, two footmen, clad in their formal scarlet-and-gold liveries, descended the steps and ran to either side of the vehicle to quickly open the doors, ensuring that no one had to slide across a seat.[36] They entered the foyer, where the butler bid them to sign the leather guest book that lay open on the table at the center of the room. The yellow scagliola walls glowed in the soft candlelight; along the staircase and upon the consoles, enormous arrangements of white arum lilies and orchids, draped with trailing ivy, stood at intervals. As guests handed their coats and hats to a waiting footmen, they stepped carefully, dodging the circling, yapping pugs. "Watch out! Watch out!" she would cry to unwary guests as the pugs swarmed around. "He'll get your stockings. He doesn't mean to, but he likes to climb all over people."[37] "Oh my God, those damn dogs!" a friend recalls. "They were the absolute worst animals in the world! All over the place, snorting and rubbing up against you and leaving spit and snot on your clothes. They ruined one of my really gorgeous gowns—the Duchess saw it happen and came over and scolded the damn dog, and of course dispatched a check for the dress—but it made one always on edge in their house."[38]

From the foyer, guests entered the drawing room. "Walking through that house was a sensuous experience," the Countess of Romanones recalled, "because every room had its own perfume burner with its own distinct perfume."[39] The Windsors waited in the drawing room, greeting their guests as they entered. The impression upon first meeting could be indelible. Noted author and historian James Pope-Hennessy wrote that Wallis was

> one of the very oddest women I have ever seen. . . . I should say she was on the whole a stupid woman, with a small petty brain, immense goodwill (*une femme de bonne volonté*) and a stern power of concentration. . . . I should therefore be tempted to classify her simply as An American Woman *par excellence,* were it not for the suspicion that she is not a woman at all. She is, to look at, phenomenal. She is flat and angular, and could have been designed for a medieval playing card. The shoulders are small and high; the head very, very large, almost monumental; the expression is either anticipatory (signalling to one, "I know this is going to be loads of fun, don't yew?") or appreciative—the great giglamp smile, the wide, wide open eyes, which are so very large and pale and veined, the painted lips and the cannibal teeth. . . . She is

wildly good-natured and friendly; but with both of them one somehow feels that so much enthusiasm might suddenly gell up and one would be in the limbo reserved for the many, many people who have treated them badly or turned out a disappointment. . . . Her high smooth flat forehead is cloven by a deep single vertical line of concentration. Her neck makes her age apparent, a tendency to wattles. Her jawbone is alarming, and from the back you can plainly see it jutting beyond the neck on each side.[40]

Footmen moved in and out of the drawing room carrying silver trays bearing cocktails. Guests who had previously been invited were surprised to be handed their favorite sherry, martini, champagne, or highball; Wallis, with her careful attention to detail, always noted what her guests preferred and made certain that this drink greeted them on their return.[41] Guests were served two cocktails, never more; Wallis would tolerate no excessive drinking among her guests. "I remember one night," says a friend, "when the Duchess and I found [a very prominent French aristocrat] hiding outside on the terrace, flask in hand, sipping away! We had all gone into the dining room and there was this obvious hole where he should have been, so we went looking. It was the most embarrassing moment—I doubt he was ever asked back."[42] At the end of forty-five minutes, the doors of the dining room were opened, and Georges appeared, announcing in a loud voice, "*Son Altesse Royale, diner est servé!*"

For dinners, Wallis preferred two round tables of ten or twelve to one larger table. She was also careful about placing those with a tendency to dominate the conversation together at tables, wishing to spare her guests. Beside each place at dinner was a menu handwritten by the butler Georges.[43] Occasionally, there were arrangements of flowers, but Wallis liked to keep everything on her table below the level of her guests' eyes to help ease conversation and eye contact. To provide more direct, flattering uplight, candles were deliberately low as well.[44]

Particular care was taken with the arrangement and presentation of food. "I imagine," Wallis wrote, "one of the most important features about food, assuming the quality and preparation are there, is the way it is presented. An attractive ambiance can work magic with an appetite."[45] She spent many hours planning her menus with her chef. "You don't get any original food if you don't work with a cook," she explained.[46] "The worst mistake a hostess can make is to stand pat on the old reliables," she declared. "A good menu can be repeated only with new people; if friends can say, 'Well, we're going to the Dots for dinner tonight. It'll be roast beef, as usual,' this is, to my way of thinking, death."[47]

At her table, beside her dinner plate, Wallis kept the small gold notebook inscribed with the poem "King's Cross," which she had given to the King in the spring of 1936. The staff called it her "grumble book." In it, she noted any ideas she might have for the next dinner party as well as any comments on service or presentation: "Too hot," "Too Cold," and "Cigars handed at wrong time."[48]

Wallis usually took one table; the Duke, the other. Her famous quick wit was at its best—sharp, sparkling, entertaining. "I just love your pansies," a guest complimented once. Without a thought, Wallis shot back: "In the garden or at my table?"[49] She expected the same energy from her guests. "Nobody has the right to come to a party and sit there like a piece of furniture," she told the Countess of Romanones. "You're invited to contribute to the party. ... I resent intelligent, worldly people who won't make an effort. They're just parasites, relaxing while other people entertain them."[50]

For a first-time guest, these surroundings, the expectations, and the exalted diners could be intimidating. Fearful of a faux pas, guests often said nothing; only later would they learn that by doing so they had guaranteed they would not receive a second invitation. "I was completely reserved and proper when I dined with the Windsors," recalls a former guest. "I said nothing controversial, joined in the conversation, ate all my food, didn't drink too much and left before overstaying my welcome. But I never received another invitation either. Later, I heard that the Duchess thought I was a bore! I thought that was pretty ruthless."[51] Even more wearing on the nerves was the fear that one might accidentally break something priceless. Wallis, however, was always prepared for the worst. Hearing the sound of breaking glass or porcelain, she would simply shrug and say, "Now forget this and get on. If you don't, you'll break three more things and I don't want that."[52]

After dinner, the Duchess and the ladies retired to the drawing room and library, leaving the Duke to preside over cigars and port. Within forty-five minutes, both groups had assembled together again, usually grouped around the baby-grand piano in a corner of the drawing room, singing popular songs. Like his niece Princess Margaret, the Duke loved to lead his guests, although, according to at least one guest, Elsa Maxwell, "he had no voice at all." He liked show tunes, and his favorites included the score from the musical *Oklahoma!* which he sang at the top of his lungs and distinctly off-key.[53] Occasionally, he hauled out the record player. "Georges, where's the gramophone," the Duke would yell over his guests. Georges would duly appear with a very old, very battered portable machine on which the Duke would play more show tunes, records of Churchill's speeches, and music from his youth. A few couples might dance or stroll on the terrace if the weather was warm.[54]

While David was thus employed, Wallis held court on a corner sofa, laughing, exchanging the latest gossip or racy joke, or played bridge with her guests. Once, in the middle of a game, she famously declared, when asked why she had failed to support a fellow player with the three Kings in her hand during a no-trump bid, "My Kings don't take tricks. They only abdicate."[55] Writer Gore Vidal described her "flapper's wisecracking charm."[56] When asked why she and David never had any children, she shrugged and laughed. "The Duke is not heir-conditioned."[57]

Inevitably, such evenings showcased the talents of the Windsors' servants, who were known to be among the best trained in Paris. Their demanding routine was duly rewarded every year at Christmas. "Since the Windsors had no family of their own," the Countess of Romanones recalled, "they derived an enormous amount of pleasure from a big Christmas celebration for their servants."[58] Wallis regularly purchased hundreds of presents for those in her service; not only the men and women who worked in the house but those who worked on the grounds, those at the Mill, their husbands and wives, and their children, all received gifts from the Duke and Duchess. These gifts varied from year to year and according to the recipient's position and length of service, but male members of the household typically received leather wallets, watches, gold cuff links, and shaving kits, while the women were given small pieces of jewelry, cashmere sweaters, leather purses, or in the years immediately following the Second World War, nylon hosiery Wallis had brought back from the United States. Their children always received toys and books, and the Duke and Duchess favored anything from Walt Disney.[59]

In addition, the Duke and Duchess gave all of the household and staff an extra month's pay each December and threw an enormous party and dinner for them in the villa in Paris. It was a chance for the Duke and Duchess to relax and enjoy themselves as well; they hired caterers, brought in a band, and happily danced with their servants in the candlelit foyer of the villa. "No one who ever spent their Christmas with Their Royal Highnesses," recalled a former staff member, "had any doubt as to their happiness. It was infectious, and both took a great delight in the children, who, although warned by their parents to be on their best behaviour, inevitably wound up racing through the rooms. Once, a boy playing with some tin soldiers accidentally knocked over the vase which was serving as his castle. It broke of course and he burst into tears. But the Duchess took his hand, helped him clean up the pieces, and spent the rest of the afternoon playing soldiers with him on the Grand Staircase."[60]

42

American Adventures

EACH YEAR, in the midst of the bleak Parisian winter, the Duke and Duchess of Windsor abandoned the chill winds and sleet of the French capital and sailed to America. Until the end of the 1950s, they always booked passage on the *Queen Mary*, where they had become well-known and respected additions to the valued Cunard client list. As the years passed, the Windsors became more comfortable in mixing with other passengers and even joined in the last-night dances, trading partners with anyone bold enough to approach and ask for a turn on the floor.

From the middle of the 1950s onward, the Duke and Duchess switched their allegiance to the *SS United States,* the proud, sleek flagship of the United States Line and holder of the coveted Blue Riband for fastest Atlantic crossing by any ship. The decision was primarily financial; unlike Cunard Lines, which charged the Windsors the full price for the suites aboard the *Queen Elizabeth* and *Queen Mary,* the United States Line allowed the Duke and Duchess to occupy a special suite of rooms, whose ordinary cost would have been $1,200, and pay only the regular first-class passage of $340.[1] In return, the Duke and Duchess agreed to attend at least several of the onboard functions during the voyage, pose for the ship's photographer, and hold a small end-of-voyage press conference in the tourist lounge.

The Windsors always occupied cabins U87, U89, and U91, known as the "Duck Suite."[2] This consisted of two bedrooms, with a sitting room between; for the valet and maid, they took inside cabins nearby, and a third cabin was always booked to serve as a wardrobe and linen room. As on all of their voyages, the ship's linens in their suite were always replaced prior to sailing by the Duchess's maid, who also supervised the placement of the framed photographs, bits of porcelain, and other souvenirs with which they traveled.[3] "They were always very easy to travel with by my standards," recalled Comdr. Leroy

Alexanderon, captain of the ship. "They never made any special demands and it was a feather in our cap to have them."[4]

The Windsors' favored first destination was Palm Beach, where, in the warm tropical climate, they could relax and forget the harsh weather they had left behind in Europe. They often stayed at the Everglades Club, in a special suite set aside for their use. Inevitably, upon their arrival, they were greeted with large, cheering crowds, and Wallis and Edward would make appearances on their balcony and wave to the sea of faces that greeted them with rounds of applause. Their arrival usually marked the start of the Palm Beach social season, during which the Duke and Duchess were guests of honor at the massive balls given in the extravagant Biltmore Hotel and the Breakers.[5]

In the afternoon, Wallis often disappeared to shop, while David played golf with friends. Occasionally, there were less expected adventures. Wallis was forever curious about life in the country she had left behind and tried to keep abreast of the latest changes. In Florida, she often ventured into supermarkets—an exotic discovery which was unknown in Paris. After exploring the aisles, she would purchase slices of meat, salami, smoked cheese, and crackers from the startled attendants, return with her prizes to the Duke, and share an impromptu picnic in their car alongside the ocean.[6]

After Palm Beach it was off to New York, where the Duke and Duchess moved into their regular suite, 28H, in the Waldorf Towers. In 1948 they had shipped many of their own furnishings, pictures, souvenirs, and housewares to the hotel, and these helped fill the drawing room, dining room, bedrooms, study, and guest rooms that constituted the apartment. The Waldorf Towers, atop the Waldorf-Astoria Hotel but with its own, discrete entrance and aristocratic patrons was the ideal base for the Windsors in the city.

One of the most persistent allegations made against the Windsors is that they avoided paying their bills, sought out discounts, accepted questionable gifts, and never tipped. The Duke and Duchess, living on investments and on the annual allowance of £21,000 David received from the Royal Family, were never as wealthy as many imagined. The Duke had never had to deal with money; as Prince of Wales and as king, he had had an equerry to take care of his financial concerns. He therefore had little practical experience and constantly worried over his economic affairs. Wallis, too, having been raised in genteel poverty and reminded at nearly every turn of the importance of money, was careful with her expenditures.

But, these factors aside, the Windsors never avoided their financial obligations. In New York, for example, bills were regularly sent to their suite in the Waldorf Towers, where the Duke himself would carefully make out the checks and send them off to his creditors.[7] They occasionally accepted special rates, but these were the exceptions rather than the rule. "I would like to state here once and for all time: the Duke and I pay our bills!" Wallis wrote in February 1961. "Oddly enough, the slanderous gossip that we do not has only recently reached my ears, and I was completely bowled over by it."[8]

The arrival of the Duke and Duchess of Windsor in New York would be cause for immediate excitement in the society columns as hostesses vied with each other for the couple's presence at their parties. Wallis and David themselves took the lead at least once or twice; with the assistance of society lion Elsa Maxwell, Wallis managed to found a permanent event, the Windsor Ball, which was designed to raise money for a number of charities under the Duchess's patronage.

The alliance with Maxwell was a curious one. Both she and Wallis were strong, independent, stubborn women, and inevitably they clashed repeatedly when one trod on the other's ego. If Wallis offended certain refined sensibilities with her brash charm and wit, Maxwell was something altogether different. She made the Duchess of Windsor appear to be a paragon of good breeding. Diana Vreeland called Maxwell an "*enormous* mountain of a woman. . . . Elsa wasn't a vulgar woman. This is hard to explain to someone who never knew her, because she *looked* vulgar. You see pictures of her where she looks like a cook on her night out."[9]

The first Windsor Ball took place in the Grand Ballroom of the Waldorf-Astoria on January 5, 1953. In addition to the work Elsa Maxwell did, Wallis asked Cecil Beaton to design the decorations, which included coral-pink ornaments, tables covered with pink satin cloths and draped with pink satin bows, and banks of pink carnations and tea roses. The ball, given to raise money for the Hospitalized Veterans Music Service, was attended by a host of famous guests: John F. Kennedy dined at a table near Salvador Dali, while Ethel Merman and Beatrice Lillie provided the entertainment. Wallis was escorted by Prince Serge Obolensky, while the Duke presided at a nearby table over a meal of channel sole, filet mignon, and pasta. After the dinner, Wallis disappeared; she changed into a $1,200 white-and-coral taffeta gown and, to the strains of the specially composed "Windsor Waltz," led a string of society beauties, all modeling the latest Parisian fashions, onto the dance floor.[10]

The evening was a great success, but Wallis and Maxwell found working with each other exceedingly difficult. A year later, when Maxwell organized another charity event, she pointedly neglected to invite the Duchess of Windsor. Instead, she declared that *her* event would include *four* Duchesses—the Duchess of Argyll, the Duchess de Brissac, the Duchess of Alba, and the Duchess of Sera.

When Wallis was asked about these choices, she remarked caustically to the press, "It would take four ordinary duchesses to make one Duchess of Windsor."[11]

Maxwell retaliated by writing her memoirs and speaking most ungenerously of her former friend to the press: "I no longer see the Duchess of Windsor. She has become so completely engrossed in herself and in her pursuit of pleasure that she neither knows nor cares what others are thinking or feeling. Had she been more conscientious about her position in history, she would not have to search so constantly for excitement and amusement. She would have found peace within herself. . . . It's my considered opinion that many of the things she has done in this search, largely because of the high-handed, selfish way in which she has done them, have contributed to her final frustration—the fact that the Windsors' prestige is not what it was—what it used to be."[12]

"Elsa was just horrible about the Duchess," recalls a friend. "She used to delight in spreading any kind of malicious gossip she heard, and with her damn big mouth, it went a long way. I don't think she ever really wanted to hurt Wallis, but she sure didn't help her cause, either. No one had much sympathy when she complained that the Duchess wouldn't see her any more."[13]

But Maxwell got her ultimate revenge on the Duchess in 1957. The Duke and Duchess were the guests of honor at the April in Paris Ball at the Waldorf-Astoria and as usual were the focus of everyone's attentions. Maxwell, who arrived late, brought with her possibly the only ammunition which could detract from the glow of the Windsors: She entered the ballroom between the arms of playwright Arthur Miller and his new wife, actress Marilyn Monroe. The result could not have been greater had Maxwell herself choreographed it. The press, which had concentrated on the Windsors all evening, made a mad dash across the floor, camera bulbs flashing, to capture the arrival of the famous actress, leaving Wallis literally in the dark.[14]

In New York the Duke and Duchess often stayed with the Winston Guests. Guest, wealthy heir and renowned polo expert, was married to the beautiful Lucy Douglass Cochrane, known to her friends as C.Z. Like Aline, the Countess of Romanones, C. Z. Guest was to become both a confidante to Wallis and also something of a substitute daughter. Wallis and David enjoyed their time at Templeton, the Guests' Long Island Georgian mansion, "considered to be one of the most palatial of the North Shore residences."[15]

"There is so much garbage written about the Duke and Duchess," says C. Z. Guest, "that I don't even bother to read it any longer. It's just god-damned nonsense, people trying to dig up scandals. But I saw them, they stayed with Winston and [me], and they were perfectly charming and gracious and easy to get along with. Just two very nice people. And they were always perfect guests."[16]

Nevertheless, it was, in fact, one of these Long Island friendships which was to lead the Duchess of Windsor into one of the most sordid affairs of her later life. During the fall of 1955 the Windsors were visiting New York as usual; Edith Baker, widow of the president of the First National City Bank, had arranged to give a party in their honor at her house, Viking's Cove, in Locust Valley, on the evening of October 29. At the last minute, however, the Duke felt ill, and C. Z. Guest suggested that a twenty-four-year-old bachelor and polo player named Michael Butler escort the Duchess in his place. Wallis, not wishing to let her hostess down, agreed and duly appeared dressed in a tight, floor-length navy blue gown.[17]

Also present that evening were thirty-five-year-old sportsman and racehorse owner William Woodward Jr. and his wife, Ann. Wallis had met the couple several times before, both in New York and in Paris, where she had shown Ann the villa in the Bois de Boulogne. The Woodward marriage was known to be unstable; Woodward, egged on by his imperious mother, Elsie, did little to make the less privileged Ann feel welcome in their elevated social circles and never let her forget her own humble beginnings. In Paris, Wallis had witnessed how uncomfortable Ann seemed to be and deliberately tried to compliment her in front of Woodward.[18]

This evening, Ann spoke pointedly of reports of a local burglar loose on Long Island. When the Baker party broke up, the Woodwards returned to their own house in Oyster Bay. What happened next has never been determined with any certainty. Just after two that morning, the local police received an emergency call from a hysterical Ann Woodward, saying that she had just killed her husband. When police arrived, they found Woodward's naked body, facedown on the bedroom floor, shot through the temple. Above him, perched jauntily on an armchair, was a pillow which Ann Woodward had copied from one Wallis had shown to her in Paris: "Never Complain, Never Explain."

Ann Woodward declared that she had been getting ready for bed when she heard her dog barking; fearing that the burglar was trying to break in, she grabbed a loaded hunting rifle which she had previously stood next to her bed and walked toward the closed door. When it suddenly flung open, she fired, killing her husband instantly. The next day, police arrived at the Waldorf Towers to question Wallis, who had danced the previous evening with Woodward several times and also spoken to his wife. She knew very little, and at the grand-jury hearing, which was set up to investigate the shooting, her evidence, such as it was, was not even presented. Ann Woodward was cleared of any guilt in the death of her husband; but suspicion that it had not been an accident continued to linger on. In particular, author Truman Capote hinted heavily that his infamously "unwritten" book *Answered Prayers* would detail the truth of Ann Woodward's guilt. It is difficult to say what effect this had on Ann Woodward, but she found herself whispered about, suspected of any number of offenses, and ostracized by many of her former friends. She eventually committed suicide. The story later became the subject of Dominick Dunne's fictionalized treatment *The Two Mrs. Grenvilles.* "How sordid that business was," Wallis commented to a friend. "And poor Ann. I know what it's like to be ostracized for no reason."[19]

June 1957 marked the Windsors' twentieth wedding anniversary. The state of their marriage had long been fodder for international gossip columns, with rumors of imminent breakups, rifts, adultery, and other such allegations rounding out the insatiable press interest. Although friends of the Duke and Duchess would later insist that the marriage had been without any friction, this is not quite correct. The truth lies somewhere between these two extreme views.

The Duke and Duchess were both stubborn, strong-willed individuals who, each in their own way, had had to learn to adapt themselves to the other. To the Duke, this meant grateful submission to the more dominant Duchess, allowing her to take on a sort of perpetual mother-nanny role which many outsiders found startling. The Duchess, too, had learned to adapt: in many ways, her role was the more difficult, for she had to accept the Duke's overwhelming love for her, a proposition which bound her with certain restrictions and meant the loss of much of her own personality to his.

Writing in 1961, Wallis said:

I am well aware that there are still some people in the world who go on hoping our marriage will break up. And to them I say, Give up hope, because David and I are happy and have been happy for twenty-four years, and that's the way it will continue to be. ... For my part, I have given my husband every ounce of my affection, something he had never had a great deal of in his bachelor life. Notice, I use the word "affection." I believe it is an element apart from love, the deep bond one assumes as a part of marriage. You may know the phrase "tender loving care;" it means much the same thing. It means doing the things that uphold a man's confidence in himself, creating an atmosphere of warmth and interest, of taking his mind off his worries.[20]

This, of course, was the ideal, but occasionally the veneer of tender care cracked. In this, there was nothing unusual about the Windsors, who, like any other couple, had their share of disagreements and quarrels. Temperamentally and in practice, Wallis and David were two very different people, and inevitably there were clashes of both will and temperament. Fleur Cowles, meeting with the Duke and Duchess, recalled "how coolly she responded to his insistent attention."[21]

Although Wallis had loved David, it is clear from both her letters and from what she told friends that she had never intended to marry him. Her affair with the Prince of Wales was just that—a passing infatuation which opened many otherwise closed doors. But when David became king, the rules of the game had suddenly changed. There is no denying the attraction that possibly being married to the king held for Wallis; but at the same time her goal had never been marriage. And yet throughout these months her feelings for him grew deeper and more certain. Although she was always willing to give him up for the sake of England, she wanted nonetheless to remain at his side.

In the aftermath of the abdication, Wallis had faced a personal dilemma: how to reconcile her fierce independence with the Duke's overwhelming, obsessive love. She was largely successful in this, but there were certainly times when the constant struggle became too much. Wallis had been cast into a role she had not wanted: She had no taste for public life, had not been raised to guard her every action or thought, and had not learned to hide her feelings, as had her husband. Many times, and in many ways, the Duke simply smothered his wife with his attentions, so much so that they threatened to consume her own identity completely. Petty disagreements and bursts of temper—natural in all marriages—were amplified in the case of the Windsors, much of whose lives were lived in public, and Wallis's frustration sometimes erupted before witnesses eager to believe the very worst.

The Windsors' occasional losses of temper or bitter words, sometimes witnessed in public, were almost gleefully seized upon by those already predisposed—either through aristocratic snobbery or political and social ambition—to expect nothing less from Wallis. But it would be wrong to characterize the Windsors' marriage as a series of petty quarrels. The close friends of the Duke and Duchess and those who worked for them for many years contradict the popular image of a constantly bickering couple. Helen Rich, a Palm Beach friend of the Windsors, told author Denis Brian, "They were always pleasant. If she humiliated him, or told him off in public, I never was on the scene, thank God. . . . She was too smart for that. She was not stupid, you know. She knew perfectly well that they were being observed every minute from all directions."[22] "All of their arguments were just little things," says another intimate. "Nothing that one wouldn't see elsewhere a hundred other times. But because it was the Duke and Duchess of Windsor, everyone blew it out of all proportion. Theirs was the love story of the century, and any crack in that fairy tale assumed the very worst interpretation immediately."[23]

The Duchess, too, suffered in comparison with the Duke's very public, almost fawning displays of affection over his wife. Wallis had never been given to great shows of emotion, and this lack of feeling was often wrongly interpreted as both coolness and outright hostility toward her husband. But her true feelings are a bit easier to gauge in the private letters she wrote to her husband during this same period. "Darling," she said in one, "I love you so very much and miss you every minute."[24] Leaving New York to join David after being apart several weeks, she wrote, "Never will I be away from you so long again. Can't wait for Friday. . . . I love you more and more . . . your Wallis."[25] "We've never had a real spat," she told a reporter. "I give him most of the credit there. I think we'd laugh first anyway."[26]

"She was wonderful to him," C. Z. Guest recalled. "She adored him. They were very, very happy."[27] This deep affection came out occasionally for all to witness: during a game of gin rummy, one of her partners declared, "You've thrown away three kings!"

"But I kept the best one, didn't I?" Wallis replied with a soft smile and nod toward her husband.[28]

Throughout the thirty-five years of the Windsors' marriage, there was only one serious public breach between the Duke and Duchess. During a party at Delmonico's Hotel in the late 1940s, Wallis first encountered James Paul Donahue Jr. Donahue was the son of Jessie Woolworth Donahue, daughter of billionaire Frank Woolworth and cousin of the famous heiress Barbara Hutton. Donahue's childhood had been an unhappy one: His father committed suicide in 1931, allegedly as the result of a homosexual liaison gone wrong, and his mother Jessie was an overpowering, domineering woman. When his grandfather, Frank W. Woolworth, died in 1919, Donahue, known to his friends as Jimmy, inherited the substantial sum of $15 million in cash and Woolworth stock.

Donahue was in his early thirties, of medium height, slightly full in the face, with a receding hairline and piercing blue eyes. He was renowned for his biting, often vicious wit and practical jokes. Donahue was also a notorious homosexual. "Jimmy made no bones about the fact that he was a homosexual," recalls the Countess of Romanones. "Everyone knew about his pursuit of men—it happened all the time, and he never tried to hide it from either the Duke or the Duchess."[29] Any number of sordid tales surround Donahue: orgies at his mother's Palm Beach estate, call boys and bribes of police, and even the accidental castration of one of his lovers. He was also heavily involved in drugs. "He was an *awful* character," recalls one of the Duchess's friends, "and he was always drunk or stoned out of his mind. He popped pills, snorted cocaine—God knows what all. The Duchess can't have been so naive that she didn't know—we all knew what he was doing."[30]

The Duke of Windsor was not known for his love of homosexuals. He referred to them as "those fellers who fly in over the transom." As he said this, he would make little flapping gestures with his hands. "I won't have 'em in my house!"[31] Donahue, however, was a notable exception; he was not only befriended by Wallis, but the Duke himself welcomed him into their circle. "There's been such a lot of nonsense about the Duke and Jimmy not getting along," recalls the countess of Romanones, "but I never saw it. I doubt he enjoyed Jimmy's company as much as did the Duchess, but there was never any animosity between them that I witnessed."[32]

Donahue came along at a time when David was busy working on his memoirs and Wallis was left largely on her own. Although she sometimes bristled at the Duke's constant attentions, she quickly found that she missed them when he was consumed with his own affairs. Donahue managed to successfully slip into the role of escort; while David remained in Paris working away or returned home early on evenings out, Wallis and Donahue would travel to New York and celebrate with friends all night.

Wallis enjoyed Donahue's biting humor and his vigor. His money—and the luxuries it helped supply—was another welcome asset. Donahue was also of a different cut than the Duke. "Perhaps she was looking for someone to help her plan her parties and enjoy life with," said one friend. "He made her life exciting, and his money made it unpredictable. The Duke's unceasing adoration simply wore her out at times, and she needed to break free now and then. Donahue gave her that chance."[33] There was another element to the relationship: with David, Wallis was always the responsible party, the one who made the plans, who did the entertaining, who ensured that her husband was happy; Donahue took on much of these same functions for the Duchess, and Wallis was ready and willing to sit back and let someone else take charge for once.

Inevitably, tongues wagged, and speculation as to the exact nature of the relationship between Wallis and Donahue was a source of endless gossip. Despite Donahue's well-known homosexuality, people assumed that he and Wallis were lovers. Donahue himself did nothing to dispel this belief and even amplified it with stories of his own. "She's marvelous!" he allegedly declared. "She's the best cock sucker I've ever known!"[34] Those who knew Donahue well were acutely aware that this was "just the sort of goddamned rubbish he was likely to spew," in the words of one of the Duchess's friends. "Everyone knew he lied and lied and lied—nobody believed a word he said."[35] But to those who were unaware of Donahue's propensity to distort the truth, such tales only fueled the ceaseless gossip alleging that he and Wallis were conducting a scandalous affair right under the Duke's nose.

More and more, on their evenings out together, David began to disappear earlier, leaving his wife and Donahue with their friends. "I think it was simply because he didn't like to be out late," says the Countess of Romanones, "whereas Jimmy and the Duchess loved to stay out all night."[36] Wallis herself made light of the growing concern. "*Really*, David!" she once exclaimed. "What could possibly be more harmless? Everybody knows what Jimmy is! Why, his friends call me the Queen of the Fairies!"[37]

In the fall of 1950, the Duchess, according to the usual schedule she and her husband followed, sailed to New York for an annual two-month holiday in America. The Duke, who was busy working on his memoirs, was left behind in Paris at the insistence of his collaborator, Charles Murphy. Over the next few weeks, as the Duke followed press reports of his wife's adventures with Donahue in New York nightclubs, he became increasingly concerned; finally, he abruptly told Murphy he had to go to America and sailed aboard the *Queen Elizabeth*.

While he was at sea, on December 4, Walter Winchell reported in his column in the *New York Daily Mirror* that "the Duke and Duchess thing is now a front" and hinted that a divorce was imminent. The press was out in force to witness the reunion of the Duke and Duchess when the ship docked on December 6, 1950. "The Duke," wrote Louis Sobol in the *New York Journal-American* on December 7, 1950, "threw his arms around the Duchess . . . seven times they kissed." The *New York Times* noted that the Windsors "embraced for the benefit of the camera men. . . . The couple denied published reports that they are estranged. . . ."[38]

The Windsors had been reunited, but this public display did not mean that Donahue had disappeared from the scene. Indeed, David simply joined his wife and her friend on their nightly round of New York's fashionable clubs: El Morocco, the Colony, the Stork Club, and Le Pavillon. Unfortunately, the Donahue story was only replaced in society columns by rumors of a new infatuation on the part of the Duchess. On January 24, Louella Parsons's syndicated column declared: "From New York comes word that Russell Nype, Manhattan's new rave—he's with Ethel Merman in 'Call Me Madam'—is the Duchess of Windsor's favorite dancing partner. She and the Duke, who are admirers of his, are reported giving a big party at the St. Regis, where he's booked for a midnight stint after the show."[39]

Five days later, *Newsweek* reported that the Windsors had attended the American National Theatre and Academy Ball, where the Duke had stayed all of ten minutes for photographs before leaving.

Wallis had remained and danced until dawn with Cecil Beaton, who acted as her escort. This did nothing to convince the columnists that the most famous marriage of the century was not about to collapse.[40]

The heavy hints angered Wallis. Columnist Louis Sobol wrote in the *New York Journal-American* on January 31, 1951: "The Duchess of Windsor has been telling friends: 'We no longer care about rumors. We used to be sensitive, but not any more.' Nevertheless the rumors have been growing—and among those spreading them are the so-called 'friends.'"[41]

Now it was Donahue and Nype who took center stage in the latest controversies. On February 19, 1951, Walter Winchell wrote in his column in the *New York Daily Mirror*:

> The Duchess of Windsor and Mrs. Vincent Astor clashed in a furious scene. ... Jimmy Donahue made a reservation at the Maisonette (in the St. Regis), and when they didn't arrive by 12:30 showtime the table was peddled. ... A few moments later James ankled in with Her Grace. ... A table was offered on the floor ringside, but it was spurned. ... She stalked out in a swivet. ... A few nights later (at a Plaza charity affair) Mrs. Astor danced by Mrs. Windsor's table. ... The latter got up, grabbed Minnie's best arm and said, "Minnie, you owe me an apology, and I feel it should be a public one". ... Minnie said she didn't know what she was talking about. ... To which the Duchess responded: "I was insulted in that basement saloon your husband runs". ... The diatribe continued with another demand for an apology. ... Minnie looked at her coldly and meow'd "My dear woman, why don't you act your age?" and then floated away. ... The noblewoman started after Minnie, but Russell Nype ... pleaded with the husbandless woman to sit down. To which, in her most regal tone, she barked, "Shaddup!"[42]

Nype was quickly pursued by the press, eager for any revelation about his relationship with the Duchess of Windsor. According to the *New York Journal-American* of October 19, Nype declared that he was merely the Duchess's mascot and that she had nicknamed him "Harvey." "What," he asked a reporter, "could there be romantic between a middle-aged Duchess and a young man who reminds her of an invisible rabbit?"[43]

In the fall of 1951, attention was focused back on Donahue. A painful incident took place of which much has been made. In his October 15, 1951, column in the *New York Journal-American*, Cholly Knickerbocker reported: "The Duchess of Windsor was recently at Chez

Florence, one of Paris' most frequented nite spots, with Jimmy Donahue. He ordered an enormous bunch of red roses for her. At the time she was waving a large feather fan. She put it on the table and said to the girl with the flowers: 'Put the flowers on the fan. Isn't it amazing? The Donahue roses on the Prince of Wales's feathers!' "[44]

David had also been present and reportedly took his wife's gesture as an insult. In retrospect, Wallis's action appears to have been nothing more than an offhand remark and attempt at a joke; she certainly had not meant to provide her enemies with ammunition. But the result was the same, and gossips once again speculated that the Windsor marriage was on the rocks.

In the *American Weekly* on December 9, 1951, Elsa Maxwell wrote in a story headlined "Will the Windsors Ever Separate?": "It is natural for people to gossip—even when they see the Windsors apart on a single occasion. But remember this man gave up his Throne for the woman he loved. She loved him enough to give him up if necessary. . . . Will the Duke and Duchess of Windsor ever separate? No, never!"[45]

In the end, of course it was Donahue whom Wallis gave up. By the middle of the 1950s, the friendship had begun to sour. The Countess of Romanones recalled: "The Duchess and Jimmy were very simpatico, and I don't think people really remember his great charm, how funny and witty he was. But he was also daring, and one heard more stories about him as time went on. I don't think he really ever used either of them consciously, but it was impossible not to know that he was involved with them. Eventually the Duchess became upset, because she heard stories, and he began to be rude to the Duke. A few times I saw him be rude to the Duchess, and she said nothing, I think, because she was so shocked. But her attitude changed."[46]

The end came during a dinner in Baden Baden. The Duke and Duchess and Donahue were sitting together at a table in the Windsors' hotel suite. According to what Wallis later told one of her friends, Donahue had been drinking and began to belittle the Duke, saying that the Duke only kept Donahue around to pay the bills. Wallis told him that he was drunk and to be quiet. In response, Donahue violently kicked her beneath the table, and she screamed out in pain. David immediately rushed to her side and helped her to a nearby sofa: Donahue had drawn blood, which was streaming through a hole in Wallis's stocking down her leg. David rang for a maid and asked for towels and antiseptic and himself knelt down and bandaged his wife's leg. After he had looked after his wife, the Duke screamed, "We've had all we can take of you, Jimmy! Get the hell out of here!"[47] Donahue duly slunk away, and the Windsors never saw him again. On December 6, 1966, his mother found him dead, the victim of an overdose of sleeping pills.

The end of the Donahue affair marked the beginning of a period of relative calm in the lives of the Windsors. In the spring of 1956, the Duchess released her memoirs, *The Heart Has Its Reasons,* to great success. Like her husband, she needed a ghostwriter with whom to work. She first turned to Charles Murphy, who had helped the Duke. Then, after a series of heated arguments, Murphy was abruptly fired from the project. Wallis had previously read and enjoyed a book by Cleveland Amory and thought he might prove a good choice. During one of their visits to New York, Wallis contacted him and asked for a meeting at the Waldorf Towers to discuss the project. Amory agreed to begin work on the project, which he proposed to call, as a play on the Duchess's lack of the style of Royal Highness, "Untitled." But when Amory shared this suggestion, "there was dead silence. I was not surprised."[48]

"The trouble, Amory," the Duke said, "is that the HRH, H-her R-royal H-highness, which the D-duchess did not r-receive, is not a t-title, it's an ap-appellation. Could you do anything with the word ap-appellation?" "It was my turn for a long silence," Amory recalled. "I did think of unappellated, but frankly the more I thought about it the more I was sure it would not fly."[49]

Amory believed he would have a certain degree of freedom in working on the book; Wallis, however, had no wish to embarrass her husband by dredging up many past, painful incidents, and she therefore directed that certain topics were not to be pursued. When Amory began research, he would often find that Wallis cut him off, saying that she could not be completely candid for the Duke's sake.[50] These restrictions eventually got to Amory, and he abruptly quit the project. To the press, he angrily declared that he had no desire to help write a book which would make the Duchess of Windsor look like "Rebecca of Sunnybrook Farm."[51]

A third ghostwriter, Kennett L. Rawson, lasted scarcely more than a few weeks. In the end, Wallis returned to Murphy. The book was well received, although, predictably, certain segments of society were prepared to give it as little attention as possible. The *Times* (London) review was remarkably concise: "*The Heart Has Its Reasons* carries the memoirs of the Duchess of Windsor from her childhood in Baltimore to the present day."[52]

The Heart Has Its Reasons sold fairly well, and Wallis emerged in a much more sympathetic light. On September 28, 1956, she and David participated in one of the aspects of being a published author which she found less pleasing: a live interview with Edward R. Murrow from their suite in the Waldorf Towers. The majority of the interview was fairly innocuous, with Wallis, clad in a mid-calf satin dress with a full skirt, discussing flower arranging and demonstrating the game of jacks. But Murrow caught the Windsors off guard when he asked them about the abdication. "Do you two ever have occasion to discuss what might have been?" he asked. David's hesitant reply was awkward and uncomfortable. He shifted uneasily on the sofa and averted his eyes, while Wallis sat forward, looked at him, then away. "Um . . . Mr. Murrow," the Duke stumbled, ". . . I . . . I . . . I think you must be referring to . . . um . . . to the . . . to the . . . to the events of nineteen hundred . . . to the crucial events in my life and our life of nineteen hundred and thirty-six, and are wondering whether they have ever preoccupied our minds since that time. Well now, the answer is most emphatically, No. We both feel that there is no more wasteful or foolish or frustrating exercise than trying to penetrate the fiction of what might have been."[53] Although he had recovered his composure, it was evident that neither of the Windsors relished the idea of discussing the abdication, particularly on live television. The Duke later confessed to a friend that the question had taken him aback; in any other setting, he would have answered promptly, but he was aware that his every word was being broadcast live to millions of homes in the United States.[54] It was the last live television interview the Windsors ever gave.

Two years later, Wallis was greatly saddened to learn that Ernest Simpson had died of cancer in London on November 30, 1958. In the fall of 1937 he had married Mary Kirk Raffray, who had divorced her husband, Jacques. Together, the Simpsons had a son, Henry, born in 1939; during the war he was evacuated to the United States along with thousands of other children. Mary discovered that she had cancer but continued to work as a Red Cross volunteer until her illness forced her into hospital. She died in October 1941. Ernest himself had maintained infrequent contact with Wallis, but they had spoken occasionally, and as she later told a friend, she felt "miserable about the trouble I had caused him back then."[55] Wallis sent an enormous bunch of white chrysanthemums to his funeral; attached was a card on which she had written simply, "From the Duchess of Windsor."

Increasingly, the Windsors spent more and more of each year in America. David had always enjoyed his visits there, and Wallis had found a new purpose in her life through her charity work there. One of the greatest canards about the Duke and Duchess is that they lived an aimless existence, attending frivolous party after frivolous party. In particular, they have been roundly condemned by British critics who assert that, unlike members of the Royal Family in England, who carried out public duties and undertook charity work, the Windsors did nothing to earn their keep and cared only about themselves.

This is simply not true, although as the establishment line promoted both by the Royal Family and by members of the court it is certainly the most prevalent attitude. In fact, the lives the Duke and

Duchess of Windsor led were little different from those of any British duke or duchess: presiding over grand houses, supervising their estates and financial concerns, and hosting the odd charity event.

The Windsors did not undertake regular duties in the same way as members of the British Royal Family, but this was through no fault of their own. Both Wallis and David had wished to fulfill such obligations, and the Duke had repeatedly tried to win permission to pursue some sort of semiofficial role in which he could make himself useful. Wallis also repeatedly offered her services to various charities, asking that she be allowed to come and address envelopes, make telephone calls, or assist with fund-raising. On several occasions, however, she was told that her presence might create an unwelcome distraction: because she had been denied the style of Royal Highness, none of the ladies would know how to treat her and would worry over whether they should curtsy or address her as "Your Royal Highness" or "Your Grace."[56]

The truth is that George VI denied the Windsors' requests to perform any useful public duties. The Duke himself told his private secretary, John Utter, that the King, and Queen Elizabeth II after him, had both asked the Windsors not to pursue any projects or charity work likely to attract public attention. The Windsors were free to attend parties, dinners, and receptions but were informed that it was in the best interests of the Royal Family if their profile in Europe was not too high.[57]

The Windsors reluctantly agreed to do as Buckingham Palace wished. They lent their financial support, albeit anonymously, to several French charities. "Everything was done quietly, under cover," recalls Janine Metz. "They sent regular checks to a private foundation in France dedicated to rescuing animals from slaughterhouses, and there were other gifts to cancer research."[58]

In America, however, Wallis was less fearful of retribution from London. She had demonstrated during her time in the Bahamas that she was fully capable of performing under pressure; she was, however, in her sixties when most of her work took place in the United States, and it is not surprising that she often chose to sponsor events or appear as guest of honor at fund-raisers. Among their concerns, the Windsors sponsored a clinic for rehabilitation of the handicapped in New York City and later set up a branch of the same organization in Paris. Wallis also served as patron of a number of other charities, including the Heart of America Charity Ball; Cancer Care U.S.; the April in Paris Ball; and the Hospital for Special Surgery in New York.[59]

Because she sought out no publicity for herself, according to the dictates laid down by Buckingham Palace, these endeavors rarely received any press attention. Few knew that Wallis did more than accompany her husband to parties. But a considerable majority of the affairs she and David attended were charitable, and invitations were accepted simply because it was a way of helping raise funds. In England, members of the Royal Family undertook two kinds of engagements: public duties, such as hospital openings, tree plantings, and factory inspections, and social duties, appearing at charity premieres or events. Thus, the Windsors, restricted by Buckingham Palace from undertaking the first, were doing no more than the rest of their family in concentrating on the second.

In August 1964, Wallis's aunt Bessie celebrated her hundredth birthday with a party at Wakefield Manor outside Baltimore, but the Duke and Duchess were unable to attend due to health problems. That November, Bessie died. Wallis was in the hospital in New York at the time, having just undergone foot surgery, and her doctors would not allow her to attend the funeral; David went in her place. The press, and unfortunately some of the Duchess's own family, made much of her absence, ignoring the fact that her doctors had forbidden her to leave her bed.

On the day she was released from the hospital, Wallis—still in great pain and scarcely able to walk—kept a prior engagement. Norbert, her French hairdresser in New York City, was celebrating the grand opening of his new salon and had previously asked the Duchess if she would attend as his guest of honor. Everyone had expected that she would cancel after her operation, but according to Janine Metz, she felt "very strongly that she had made a promise and that her presence would help ensure his success." Her feet were still bandaged, and she could not wear shoes; instead, she put on a pair of the Duke's velvet bedroom slippers and, hobbling on a pair of canes, duly appeared to wish Norbert well. The next day, however, several fashion editors wrote that her appearance in slippers was less than dignified, criticism which hurt Wallis very much.[60]

Just a few days after this, David himself fell ill; doctors discovered that he had an aneurysm in an artery that threatened to burst and kill him. Ten days after Aunt Bessie's death, the Windsors—Wallis still hobbling uncomfortably on a cane—traveled to Houston, Texas, where the Duke entered Methodist Hospital for an operation. On December 16, the swollen section of artery—the size of a small grapefruit—was cut away by Dr. Michael DeBakey, assisted by the Duke's personal physician, Dr. Arthur Antanucci, and replaced with four inches of knitted Dacron tubing. The operation was a success, and the Windsors were able to leave Houston in a few weeks.[61]

In 1965 producer Jack Le Vien released his documentary *A King's Story,* based on the Duke's memoirs and filmed with the cooperation of the Windsors, who allowed him and his assistant, Linda Mortimer—Fruity Metcalfe's daughter—unprecedented access to their private archives. The film was a fairly straightforward portrait of the King's reign and abdication, with glimpses of his life with Wallis in Paris and at the Mill. The result was a rather curious collection of old newsreels, coupled with stock footage of dancing natives in Africa to demonstrate the numerous cultures the Duke had experienced and interviews with Wallis and David at the Mill. During the premiere, David burst into tears watching the old footage of himself as king. Cecil Wilson, writing his review in the *London Daily Mirror*, declared: "However you viewed the Abdication at the time, it still stirs the heart to see the ex-King sitting at his desk re-enacting in old age his farewell broadcast to the nation between shots of his early idolatry. Even more stirring is the final garden glimpse of this Romeo and Juliet turned Darby and Joan walking into the distance arm in arm to the closing words of the broadcast."[62]

In June 1967 the Windsors marked their thirtieth wedding anniversary. To commemorate the occasion, the Duke and Duchess collaborated on a syndicated newspaper article entitled "The Duke's Formula for a Happy Marriage," a collection of tongue-in-cheek reflections which revealed a rare glimpse of the couple's shared humor, not to mention the level of comfort they had reached with each other and their lives before they met. Among other things, David advised:

> Don't ask questions. If you got the right answer, it might hurt. If you didn't, it surely would. If she absentmindedly calls you Ernest or Winfield, don't comment; at least she has your role fixed in her thoughts. . . . Don't let marriage interfere with old customs. Step out to an occasional nightclub, but with your wife, just to keep in practice. This will make her feel that whatever pleasure you used to have in such frivolities were incomplete until you met her. If she shows an inclination to go with you to your tailor, ignore it. This is a major encroachment upon your freedom. A minor menace is the selection of your ties, socks and pyjamas. There is nothing you can do about this. . . . Always praise the way she wears her hair. If possible, like it. She will wear it that way anyway.

And Wallis wrote: "Be first to decide any question, no matter how trivial. After you've made the decision, ask your husband what he thinks. All men like to be deferred to. . . . Praise any little accomplishments he may have, such as skirling bagpipes. At least you know where he is when he is playing. Tell him how strong he is, and praise him for his character. But suggest that all decisions be mutual. . . . Make him think this love, the only real one of your life, will last forever."[63]

43

The Windsors and the Royal Family

THE WINDSORS had hoped that the reign of the Duke's young niece, Elizabeth II, would begin a period of reconciliation between themselves and the Royal Family, however slight; but there was no lowering of the drawbridges that, in David's words to Wallis, had gone up after the abdication many years earlier. What little gestures came from Buckingham Palace trickled out over a period of twenty years, leaving a bitter taste among the Windsors, their friends, and a large portion of the British public as well.

Shortly after Elizabeth II's coronation, in November 1953, the Duke and Duchess made their first joint visit to London in many years. Although the occasion was a purely private one, word eventually leaked out, and wherever they went, the Windsors were greeted by cheering crowds. One evening, they attended a production of Agatha Christie's *Witness for the Prosecution* at the Winter Garden Theatre. They had asked Sir Peter Saunders, director of the theater, to keep their arrival a secret; but to reach their box, Wallis and David had to walk past the crowded stalls, and soon everyone in the theater recognized them. Within minutes, the crowd was on its feet, applauding their entrance into their box. Surprised and touched, the Windsors moved to the front of the box to acknowledge the ovation. When they left the theater, a cheering throng of people surrounded their car. "Certainly, in my mind," Saunders later wrote, "there was no doubt about the feeling of the people of England towards this couple."[1]

Despite the warm welcome they had received from the British public they had encountered, the Duke and Duchess were cautious in their visits to London over the next few years for fear of their presence creating tension. When they did return, inevitably the reception was much the same, with cries of "God Bless the Duchess!" and "Don't go away again!"[2]

The Windsors—perhaps more than most people—watched with interest and not a little resentment as the scandal over Princess Margaret's affair with a divorced group captain, Peter Townsend, broke with a vengeance unequaled in the British press since the abdication. The crisis which followed has been aptly described by Sarah Bradford as the result of "the moral straightjacket into which the Royal family was to be confined, trapped by an image of its own creation."[3]

Townsend, sixteen years Margaret's senior, had been equerry to her father, George VI. The King genuinely liked Townsend, who was married with two sons, and promoted him, in 1950, to the position of deputy master of the royal household. In 1951, Townsend divorced his wife, citing her in a divorce action; the following year, the Queen Mother appointed him to the position of comptroller of her own household at Clarence House.

Although Margaret had first encountered Townsend in her youth, by her twenty-first birthday, in 1951, she was deeply in love with the dashing group captain, and she made no secret among her family that she wished to marry him. The Queen Mother and Margaret's sister Queen Elizabeth II were openly supportive but noncommittal; behind Margaret's back, however, they were well aware of the crisis which would break should Margaret follow her heart.

Elizabeth II, as supreme governor of the Church of England, could not sanction her sister's marriage to a divorced man. If Margaret wished to marry, therefore, she would have to relinquish royal status, her succession rights to the throne, and her official civil-list income. When consulted, the cabinet advised against the marriage. Townsend was packed off to Brussels, and Margaret was asked to wait and rather duplicitously told by her mother, her sister the Queen, and others that when she was twenty-five, in 1955 she could marry without the sovereign's consent.

Townsend returned to England in October 1955; the following day, he was at Clarence House, where Margaret lived with her mother. For the next three weeks, the question of the Margaret-Townsend relationship filled the headlines of newspapers around the world. Even though she could now marry without her sister's permission, Margaret was told that if she did, she would still require the government's permission to keep her royal status and civil-list income; on October 18 the cabinet, presided over, ironically, by the divorced prime minister, Anthony Eden, voted to advise against the marriage. If Margaret wished to marry Townsend now, she would almost certainly have to follow her uncle into exile. In the end, Margaret announced that she would not marry Townsend. Her personal sacrifice to the idealistic view which the Royal Family had carefully cultivated over the last half century would, in the end, be futile. Her rather sad life which followed the Townsend affair, with her failed marriage, very public divorce, and bitter feelings over the thwarted relationship, marked Margaret as one of the most visible reminders of the hypocrisy of the court establishment.

The other, more lasting legacy of the Margaret-Townsend affair was to have a fateful influence on the Royal Family to the present day. Sarah Bradford has called it "the first example of the dangers of the family policy, initiated by Queen Elizabeth, of 'ostriching,' of ignoring a potentially dangerous situation until it became explosive, of 'non-interference' and 'non-confrontation.' "[4] The Duke and Duchess of Windsor, and more recently, Diana, Princess of Wales, were to provide ample evidence of this disastrous trait of ignoring crises, circumstances, and changing public opinion.

On May 6, 1960, Princess Margaret was married to Antony Armstrong-Jones in Westminster Abbey. Neither the Duke nor the Duchess was invited to attend the ceremony, nor were they asked to the wedding of Edward, Duke of Kent, to Katharine Worsley in York Minster on June 8, 1961 or that of Princess Alexandra of Kent to the Honorable Angus Ogilvy on April 24, 1963. On this last occasion, Wallis suffered an additional, needless humiliation: in the souvenir wedding program approved by the Lord Chamberlain's Office, the Duchess of Windsor was the only member of the family not included in the Royal Family tree; all other wives—even nonroyal wives of distant nephews—were listed.[5]

As time passed, the Windsors became more vocal in their displeasure over these continued slights. "I was treated bloody shabbily," David declared to author James Pope-Hennessy.[6] Wallis went further. In February 1961, *McCall's* magazine in America began publication of a regular column written by the Duchess of Windsor, with the assistance of Etta Wanger. She chose the first installment to break her silence on the way her husband had been treated by his family:

It suddenly occurred to me how ridiculous it is to go on behind a family designed, government manufactured curtain of asbestos that protects the British Commonwealth from dangerous us. . . . I wish to make it clear at the outset, however, that none of this is written with venom or bitterness, although twenty-four years of persecution, even in small ways, are more than enough to break anybody's spirit. . . . My husband has been punished, like a small boy who gets a spanking every day of his life for a single transgression. . . . I think the monarchy's lack of dignity toward him then, and occasionally now, has been resented. . . . When World War II came, this man, with his unparalleled knowledge, trained in the affairs of state, with a lifetime's experience behind him, was first given an insignificant military post. Eventually, he was

put "out of harm's way" with an appointment of little consequence—the governorship of the Bahamas. . . . His hurt has been
deep.[7]

In December 1963 the Duchess gave an interview to Susan
Barnes. She asked if Wallis thought she would ever be granted the style
of Royal Highness. "Never!" she answered. "I don't mind. There are a
great many things I have had to learn not to give any importance to.
. . . I don't know, but I think the refusal to give me equal rank with my
husband may have been done to make things difficult for us. It *is* difficult—because people are puzzled about what to do with me. At parties. At any time. They don't understand being married to Mr. Smith
and being called Mrs. Jones. And I know it hurts my husband. . . . I
know that he has been hurt very deeply. . . . I don't mind for myself.
I've lived without this title for twenty-five years. And I'm still married
to this man!"[8]

The Countess of Romanones remembers that the Duke and
Duchess "were very careful about what they would say" about the
Royal Family. "They rarely mentioned what he had left behind in
England, or his family there. It was as if the Royal Family didn't exist.
I'm sure the Royal Family felt the same way. I know it hurt the Duke
and Duchess very much. He took it very hard. I only recall one or two
times when he seemed very upset about his family when the subject
came up. She was upset for his sake."[9]

In 1964, Elizabeth II gave birth to her fourth child, Prince
Edward. One of the Duchess's friends apparently asked if he had been
named in honor of his great uncle, a question which elicited a very
frank response from Wallis:

> No doubt it would be nice if the cracks were that wide, but don't
> count on it. In the very, very unlikely event that Lilibet [the
> Queen] had wanted to honour David, Cookie [the Queen Mother]
> would have stepped in and ranted and hollered her little tulled
> and flowered head off! Now *that* would be well-worth seeing
> (and I for one would pay the price!) but fear of poor little US runs
> too deep! No, I'm afraid that for us, it goes on and on. I wish for
> David's sake, of course, that it didn't, but by now, what's the
> point? The years of damage have already been done, and we're
> both too old now to care—it's too late to make any difference. It's
> just the odd letter or Christmas Card for us.[10]

In February 1965 the Windsors traveled to London so that David
could have surgery on a detached retina. During his stay in the
London Clinic, Wallis took a room near his; between visits to the

doctor, they took a suite at Claridge's Hotel. The public, confronted by their aged former King and his elderly wife holding each other's hands as they entered the hotel amid the flashing of cameras, began to question why the Windsors had not been invited to stay at Buckingham Palace. Indeed, during their stay in London, the press, sensing the public mood, created much sympathy for the Duke and Duchess, hinting broadly that the time had come for a reconciliation between the Royal Family and "a blind old man and the woman who had been his wife for nearly thirty years."[11]

In the six weeks that the Duke and Duchess were in London, Queen Elizabeth II visited them twice, meetings which were largely regarded as welcome gestures on the part of the sovereign. The Queen, however, originally had no intention of visiting her ailing uncle at all; only after her private secretary, Sir Michael Adeane, along with Walter Monckton's widow, Alexandra, and several others intervened did Elizabeth II agree to the visits. Certain members of the court pointed out that the reaction of the press—already strongly sentimental in favor of the Windsors—would be vehement if the Queen failed to make this simple gesture. Dowager Viscountess Monckton of Brenchley informed Buckingham Palace, on behalf of the Duke, that he would be greatly appreciative if his niece could find the time to pay him a short visit while he was in the hospital.[12] "Poor David practically had to beg to see her," Wallis told a friend.[13]

The first visit came on the evening of Monday, March 15. The Queen, escorted by Adeane, arrived at the London Clinic and went directly to the third-floor suite of her uncle and aunt. This was the first time Wallis had come face-to-face with Elizabeth since that spring afternoon in 1936 at Royal Lodge, when the ten-year-old girl had tugged at her governess's hand and asked who her uncle David's friend was. As the Queen entered, Wallis dropped a deep curtsy. Elizabeth II stayed for a half hour. Before she left, the Duke asked if he might come to Buckingham Palace to walk in the gardens during his stay in London. Apparently, the Queen agreed, but not without delivering another humiliation: The Duke might come to the palace, provided he be accompanied by a valet and not the Duchess.[14]

There were two more important questions the Duke asked his niece. In 1957 he had purchased a large burial plot in the Green Mount Cemetery in Baltimore, where many of Wallis's relatives were interred. Although he had wished to be buried at Windsor, David, after so many years of continued ostracism, was not convinced that he would be allowed to return even in death. Now he asked his niece if he and his wife would be granted permission to be buried in the Royal Family's private burial plot in Frogmore Gardens, below Windsor Castle and near the grave of his beloved brother George, Duke of Kent. His second request was that both he and Wallis would be allowed to have their funeral services in St. George's Chapel, Windsor. Elizabeth II declared that she would look into the matter and left the clinic.[15]

Incredibly, it took Elizabeth II ten days to consent to this simple, almost pathetic request. On her second visit to the Duke, this time at Claridge's Hotel on March 25, the Queen informed David that both he and Wallis would be allowed funeral services at St. George's Chapel and burial at Frogmore. Apparently, this was done with great reluctance; Elizabeth II was none too keen about having Wallis honored by a funeral in St. George's Chapel and permanently buried so close to Windsor Castle, but the publicity surrounding the burial of a former King of England in America was thought the greater of the two evils.[16]

Once Elizabeth II had relented, the Windsors received visits from David's sister Mary, the Princess Royal; Princess Marina, Duchess of Kent; and her daughter, Princess Alexandra. The meeting with Marina was particularly moving. Since the death of her husband in 1942, she had never forgiven David for his failure to send a letter of condolence; she did not know that one had been dispatched but lost. When she entered the suite at Claridge's, Wallis curtsied, but Marina swept her into her arms, and the two embraced. Although they had been friendly in the years before the abdication, they had not met since. Marina bent down next to the chair where her brother-in-law sat and, in tears, kissed him. The three spent the next hour discussing their lives and seem to have come to a genuine understanding. "It was one of the most touching moments," Wallis later told a friend. "It meant so much to David, because George had meant so much to him."[17] Before she left, Marina promised that her children would now visit their aunt and uncle in Paris regularly.[18] The only notable absentee was Queen Elizabeth the Queen Mother, who, although she sent flowers, refused to visit the Windsors.

On March 28, while the Windsors were in London, David's sister Mary died at the age of sixty-five. Alone among the Royal Family, she had been forgiving and had not forgotten her brother or his wife, often visiting them in New York. David was too ill to travel to Harewood House in Yorkshire for the funeral; instead, on April 1, the Duke and Duchess attended a memorial service at Westminster Abbey along with twenty-five hundred invited mourners. David, looking frail and his eyes guarded by dark glasses, was helped by Wallis, clad in a black coat and hat, down the aisle of the transept; seeing them, the congregation rose spontaneously in silent respect. It was the first time the Windsors had ever appeared together at an official function in England.

True to her word, Princess Marina ensured that her children did begin to include their aging aunt and uncle in their lives. Young Prince

Michael, the most studious of the children and the one most imbued with a sense of family history, began what was to become a rather ironic association. The Duke and Duchess of Kent visited as well. Princess Alexandra, the Duke of Kent's sister, and her husband, Angus Ogilvy, after obtaining permission from Buckingham Palace, also visited the Duke and Duchess at their Paris villa.[19] Each year, Alexandra duly dispatched a Christmas card to "Uncle David and Wallace." The Princess cannot have been ignorant of the spelling of her most famous aunt's Christian name, and one can only conclude that such a transcription reflected a continued feeling of unease over familial acceptance, whether conscious or not.[20]

There were also visits from the Earl of Harewood, son of Mary, the Princess Royal. He spent an afternoon with his aunt and uncle at the Mill and recalls that it was "highly enjoyable."[21] Ironically, it was the Earl of Harewood who would provide the next marital scandal in the Royal Family, twelve years after the Princess Margaret–Peter Townsend affair.

In January 1967 it was announced that the Earl was being sued for divorce by his wife, the former Marion Stein, on the grounds of his adultery. The woman in question was a beautiful, vivacious Australian, Patricia Tuckwell, who formerly had been a violinist with the Sydney Symphony Orchestra. Tuckwell, who had already had one marriage, began sharing a London house with the Earl in 1965, a year after she bore their son, Mark. The Earl issued an admirably honest statement admitting the adultery and acknowledging both his son and his intention to marry Tuckwell when he was free. In July 1967, with Elizabeth II's permission, as required by the Royal Marriages Act, the Earl and Tuckwell were wed in America.

In 1967 the Duke and Duchess were invited to attend the dedication of a memorial plaque to Queen Mary on the wall outside her former residence, Marlborough House, in London. Queen Elizabeth the Queen Mother, who, as one of Queen Mary's four daughters-in-law, would attend the ceremony, was at first adamant that if Wallis was invited she would not attend. An official in the Queen's household told a close friend of the Windsors' that the Queen Mother "was absolutely vitriolic in her hatred of the duchess and that she had got it into her head that her husband died an early death because of the Duchess."[22] Because the Duke was one of only two surviving children (the only other now being his brother Harry, Duke of Gloucester), it would have been a blatant snub were he to be missing from the ceremony honoring his mother. And he himself had made it quite clear that he would not attend unless Wallis was also invited. Finally, after much concerted effort, the Queen Mother relented. The public, however, knew very little of the palace politics and greeted the ceremony as the final gesture of reconciliation on the part of the Royal Family. As William Hickey noted in the *Daily Express*: "The poignancy of the Duchess's meeting with the members of her husband's family will be heightened by her encounter, for the first time since 1936, with her sister-in-law, the Queen Mother."[23]

The Windsors arrived in Southampton aboard the SS *United States* and were met by Lord Mountbatten; the Duke and Duchess had celebrated their thirtieth wedding anniversary a few days before, and Mountbatten wished them well. A number of reporters waited to capture the moment, shouting questions and firing off cameras. One television reporter asked about "disagreements with the Royal Family," but David cut him short and graciously said, "We know nothing at all about them."[24] (Asked where and how he would like to spend the remaining years of his life, the Duke turned to the Duchess, smiled, and answered, "Together."[25] As they left the dock, there were cries of "Good old Teddie!"[26])

The Duke and Duchess were to spend the night with Mountbatten at his nearby house, Broadlands, just outside the village of Romsey. In the village itself and along the road to the house, hundreds of people had gathered to cheer the couple on.[27] John Barrat, Mountbatten's private secretary, later recalled: "The staff were in a great twitter—should they curtsy or bow to her? I asked Lord Mountbatten and he said that, although he would not insist, he felt it would be polite if we accorded her the same niceties that we did the Duke, so we all inclined our heads to her."[28]

The Windsors were not asked to stay in any of the royal residences as guests of the sovereign, so they once again booked a suite at Claridge's Hotel in London. When they arrived there, a crowd numbering into the hundreds surrounded the main entrance, applauding as they stepped from their car. Both responded with smiles of genuine feeling. They took lunch with the Duke and Duchess of Gloucester at York House, a somewhat strained occasion due to Prince Harry's increasing illness; not only was he hard of hearing, but his memory was failing as well, and conversation was difficult between the two brothers.

The following day, Wednesday, June 7, 1967, dawned bright and clear. A crowd of nearly five thousand waited outside the walls of Marlborough House and into the yard of St. James's Palace across the roadway.[29] The Duke and Duchess of Windsor were among the first members of the Royal Family to arrive for the ceremony; when their limousine slowly pulled up the roadway, the crowd erupted in loud cheers.[30]

Wallis emerged from the car first, dressed in a deep-blue coat with a knee-length hemline by her favorite designer, Givenchy. A small, matching pillbox hat was perched atop her carefully arranged hair, and a white mink muffler was draped around her shoulders and neck. Her entire appearance was one of elegance and sophistication. The contrast with the other ladies of the Royal Family could not have been greater; Wallis looked, in Diana Mosley's words, "like the denizen of another planet."[31] The Duke followed, dressed in a dark suit; additional cars contained the Gloucesters and their children; Marina, Duchess of Kent and her children; and other members of the Royal Family.

Another cheer announced the arrival of the Queen Mother. She wore a loose lilac coat and one of her unmistakable, enormous, halolike hats. The Windsors stood at the head of the line. Elizabeth reached out a gloved hand to the Duke, who bowed his head and kissed it gallantly; as he rose, she turned her head to receive a kiss on the cheek. All eyes were on the Queen Mother as she reached Wallis. The Duchess of Windsor did not curtsy to her sister-in-law, as custom dictated; the two enemies shook hands but exchanged no kiss. "How nice to see you," Elizabeth said simply to Wallis before quickly moving on down the line.[32]

A few minutes later, the Queen and the Duke of Edinburgh arrived from Buckingham Palace. Elizabeth II seemed to take little notice of the Duke and Duchess of Windsor, giving a short, almost dismissive nod as she walked past them. The Duke bowed as his niece passed, and Wallis dropped into a very brief curtsy—so brief, in fact, that it escaped many people, including the reporter for the *Daily Mail*, who, on the following day, noted that "the Duchess of Windsor bowed slightly from the waist."[33] This in itself was an indication of how much press attention was being paid to the issue of a simple curtsy, but the correspondent for the *Daily Mail* was not the only person so preoccupied with the question. At the very moment the Queen passed the Windsors, author Michael Thornton has since pointed out, the Queen Mother bent forward slightly and turned her head, presumably to see if Wallis would pay her daughter the honor she had pointedly denied to her only minutes before.[34]

A short memorial service, conducted by Dr. Robert Stopford, the bishop of London, followed in which Wallis stood silent and correct as one of the two women who were most responsible for her years of public humiliation and private distress was praised as a model of virtue and duty. At the end, the Queen unveiled a plaque that showed Queen Mary in profile. When the Queen and Duke of Edinburgh departed, Wallis again dropped a deep curtsy, very prominent this time. As the Queen Mother returned down the line toward her limousine, she stopped before the Duke and Duchess of Windsor and exchanged a few brief words. When she said goodbye, David again kissed her, and Wallis shook her hand but did not curtsy. "I do hope we meet again," the Queen Mother declared. "When?" Wallis asked pointedly. The exchange took the Queen Mother by surprise, and she left quickly and without further comment.[35]

That afternoon, the Queen, the Duke of Edinburgh, the Queen Mother, and the Duchess of Gloucester attended the derby at Epsom Downs; the Windsors were not invited to join the royal party. Instead, they drove to Kensington Palace and took lunch with Princess Marina and her family.[36]

The day had come to an end, and the public at large was gratified that the Royal Family had seemingly embraced—to some extent, at least—the Duke and Duchess of Windsor. But the Royal Family and court would have one last insult to direct at the Windsors. On the following day, the court circular, the official list of royal engagements approved by the lord chamberlain, appeared in several newspapers, including the *Times* and the *Daily Telegraph*: It described the ceremony at Marlborough House and listed the presence of the Queen; the Duke of Edinburgh; the Queen Mother; the Duke and Duchess of Gloucester; Princess Marina, Duchess of Kent; the Duke and Duchess of Kent; and Prince Michael of Kent. Of the Duke and Duchess of Windsor, there was no mention whatsoever.[37] When the press picked up on the omission, the Lord Chamberlain's Office declared that it had been an unfortunate oversight but pointed out that the court circular listed only those members of the Royal Family who undertook active engagements; the Duke and Duchess of Windsor, it was said, were not members of the Royal Family and were thus not entitled to be listed. This rather petty piece of backpedaling, however, was quickly shown up to be inaccurate; just a year later, when Princess Marina died, the Duke of Windsor was duly listed in the court circular as having attended her funeral.

This last humiliation of the Windsors, coming as it did in the midst of what was believed to have been a generous gesture on the part of the Royal Family, did much to spark renewed public debate on the status of the Duke and Duchess. That fall, *Burke's Peerage,* the great British arbiter of titles and styles, publicly declared that George VI had been wrong to deny Wallis the style of Royal Highness. The publication argued that not only had the King acted illegally in depriving her of what should rightfully have been hers but that he had had absolutely no justification in arguing that the Duke of Windsor had lost his royal status upon his abdication. They urged that "steps should be taken without further delay to right this the most flagrant act of discrimination in the whole history of our dynasty. To do so does not require an Act of Parliament for the matter is solely within the Royal Prerogative, and all that is necessary is the issues of Letters Patent revoking those of 27th May, 1937."[38]

The Windsors themselves had no doubt about the identity of the architect of their continued humiliation. For thirty years Queen Elizabeth the Queen Mother had remained their most implacable enemy, complaining to anyone who would listen about the evils of the Duke and, most especially, the Duchess. "My husband would be alive today if it hadn't been for that woman," she once told Lady Diana Cooper.[39] To the Queen Mother, Wallis was "the woman who killed my husband."[40]

It is well known that the Duke and Duchess of Windsor, in private, often expressed their strong feelings about the Queen Mother; less well known is that the Queen Mother was just as virulent in her condemnation of the Windsors. Behind the friendly veneer and set smile, her iron will, which had kept the Duke and Duchess in a state of perpetual punishment, never softened, infecting generation after generation. When Prince Charles was asked about his great aunt the Duchess of Windsor—whom he had never met—he declared, "She's a dreadful woman." He was asked why he said this. His chilling reply left no doubt about the source of his animosity: "I know because my grandmother says she was."[41]

44

Declining Years

I CAN'T *STAND* PEOPLE MY AGE!" Wallis once declared to her friend Aline, the Countess of Romanones. "Old people like me are such bores, the way they forget things."[1] However, by the end of the 1960s, despite her best efforts, the Duchess of Windsor could no longer disguise the fact that she was rapidly aging.

For many years, Wallis had prided herself on keeping up with the latest fashions and newest trends: The photographs of her dancing the twist in a miniskirt in her late sixties turned many heads. Nor was her youthful appearance confined to fashion and dance. In 1961 cosmetic surgeon Dr. Daniel Shorell was rumored to have treated a well-known royal lady. The press bluntly asked if his patient was the Duchess of Windsor. "Let us say I know her very well," he answered. "Beyond that, I don't think I'd like to go." He admitted that the patient was not "a member of the royal family by lineage." He also explained that he had operated to "reduce redundancy of the neck, and to improve the jowls."[2]

But Wallis could not prevent the inevitable. Her face was gently lined now, her graying hair carefully dyed each week. Moreover, although she could manage her appearance, there was nothing she could do about her health. In 1968 she began to suffer from short memory lapses. At first, they were nothing serious, and she dismissed them as no more than troublesome instances of normal aging. But as her moods increasingly changed, David was concerned enough to call in the doctors, who diagnosed arteriosclerosis. There was little the doctors could do; the disease, which had already began to interefere with the supply of blood to the Duchess's brain, would only progress with the passage of time.[3]

The changes were gradual, but members of the household in Paris noticed small things: occasional bursts of temper and regular orders not given by the Duchess, all of which seemed to indicate that something was amiss.[4] Certainly there seems to have been nothing quite as dramatic as the incidents alleged by John Utter, who not only claimed that the Windsors were alcoholics but that "the sound of their drunken bickering was unbearable."[5] The evidence from the Windsors' friends and former staff members contradicts Utter's assertions; if the secretary witnessed anything of the sort, undoubtedly it was symptomatic of the Duchess's increasing illness. "I do not think the Duchess had a problem with alcohol," says Janine Metz. "The problem is that she did not eat, and when she ate, she ate very little. When she drank the smallest quantity it immediately affected her. I never saw that the Duke had a problem. If he had a problem, I would have known."[6]

Cecil Beaton, on a visit to the Windsors, noted how rapidly time had caught up with the Duke and Duchess:

She seems to have suddenly aged, to have become a little old woman. Her figure and legs are as trim as ever, and she is as energetic as she always was, putting servants and things to rights. But Wallis had the sad, haunted eyes of the ill. In the hospital they had found that she had something wrong with her liver and that condition made her depressed. When she got up to fetch something, she said: "Don't look at me. I haven't even had the coiffeur come out to do my hair," and her hair did appear somewhat straggly. This again gave her a rather pathetic look. She loves rich food and drink but she is now on a strict diet and must not drink any alcohol. Wallis tottered to a sofa against the light in a small overcrowded drawing room. Masses of royal souvenirs, gold boxes, sealing wax, stamps and seals; small pictures, a great array of flowers in obelisk-shaped baskets. These had been sent up from The Mill, which will be sold now [that] the Duke is not able to bend down for his gardening. . . . "Well, you see, we're old! It's awful how many years have gone by and one doesn't have them back!" . . . The Duchess leaning forward on tiny legs, looked rather blind, and when an enormous bouquet of white flowers and plants arrived, she did not seem able to see it. She leant myopically towards it and asked, "What's that? A tuberose? An arum lily?" The man corrected her—"An auratum"—"Ah yes, will you tell them how beautifully they have done them." I watched her try to open the card. . . . "Who is it from?" asked the Duke. "Don't be so full of curiosity," said his wife trying to read without glasses. . . . The two old people, very bent, but full of spirit and still both dandies, stood at the door as I went off. . . .[7]

The Windsors' dealings with the Royal Family were still limited and always tinged with questionable intentions and fears of humiliation. In 1969, Prince Charles was invested as Prince of Wales in a ceremony closely based on the 1911 proceedings which had been instigated by George V for David. Neither of the Windsors attended the ceremony. Shortly thereafter, the Duke declined an invitation from the Queen to join the Royal Family at the dedication of a new Order of the Garter window in St. George's Chapel, Windsor. "Although you did not include Wallis by name in the invitation . . ." he wrote, "I presume that you would have expected her to accompany me. You see, after more than thirty years of happy married life, I do not like to attend such occasions alone."[8]

In January 1970 the Duke and Duchess granted an interview to the BBC's Kenneth Harris. During the interview, which aired on British television to an audience of some 12 million, the Windsors displayed a natural understanding and empathy, finishing each other's sentences and making jokes which helped dispel rumors that their relationship was cold and uncomfortable.

For the interview, Wallis appeared in good health, showing no sign of her illness. She declared that if she were a young woman she would like to be the head of an advertising agency; she also confided that the Duke had two bad habits—smoking, which she abhorred, and his golf, which, she complained, "keeps him away from me." When asked about the latest trends, the Duke replied: "Now, the Duchess and I are a little past the age of being what they call with it, but don't for one minute imagine that we weren't with it when we were younger. In fact I was so much with it that this was one of the big criticisms that was levelled against me by the older generation." And the Duchess spoke of loneliness: "There is no problem for a man alone, but it is different for women who are widows. Who is going to take her out to dinner? How much time is she going to spend sitting alone unless she is going to entertain a great deal; and then most of her friends are probably widows too, you see. Then the great manhunt has to go on to get someone to come to dinner and sit next to these people."[9]

In April of that year the Windsors, during a visit to Washington, D.C., attended a state dinner given in their honor at the White House by President Richard Nixon. To most people, it was a visit of the stars of the century's most romantic story, two elderly people whose marriage had survived adversity for more than three decades. To the British government, however, it was simply another occasion for worry. If anyone believed that the vendetta against the Windsors on the part of the Royal Family and the government had come to an end, they simply had to learn of the orders which the Foreign Office in London fired off to the British embassy. The Duchess, they warned, was not to be addressed as Her Royal Highness; in no instance was she to be curtsied to, and the ambassador was directed to personally inform the United States' chief of protocol that these requests must be followed by the Nixons during the state dinner. "This heavy-handed advice did not go down well in Washington," writes Kenneth Harris, "and even the British took exception to it. The Ambassador's wife said afterwards, 'I curtsied anyway—and I called the Duchess Your Royal Highness.' "[10]

The dinner took place on April 4. The Windsors, who were staying down Pennsylvania Avenue at Blair House, arrived in a limousine under the North Portico; President and Mrs. Nixon stood on the steps, waiting to greet them. David, dressed in white tie and tails, leaned heavily on a cane as he exited the car; Wallis, dressed in a white-silk crepe gown by Givenchy adorned with medallions and a belt of colored metallic beads, took his hand and helped him climb the stairs, where they stood side by side with the Nixons and posed for photographs.[11]

One hundred and six invited guests waited within to greet the Duke and Duchess. Several of Wallis's relatives, including the Mustins, had received invitations and greeted her warmly as they passed through the receiving line. Other guests included President Theodore Roosevelt's daughter Alice Roosevelt Longworth, Col. and Mrs. Charles Lindbergh, the Winston Guests, Fred Astaire, and Arnold Palmer. According to Marie Smith, writing in the *Washington Post*, "the Duchess looked decades younger than her 73 years." The Windsors sat with the Nixons at the head of an E-shaped table in the State Dining Room. The menu included Le Saumon Froid Windsor, a mousse of sole and shrimp molded in the form of a royal crest and surrounded by cold salmon; and a strawberry dessert called Le Soufflé Duchesse. Throughout the meal, observers noted that the Duke and Duchess could be seen holding hands, whispering to each other and exchanging jokes. They seemed perfectly comfortable and at ease. At the end of the meal, when toasts were being exchanged, David said, "I have had the good fortune to have a wonderful American girl consent to marry me. I have had thirty years of loving care, devotion, and companionship—something I have cherished above all else."[12]

At the end of the dinner, a second group of invited guests arrived for drinks and entertainment in the East Room. Among them were George and Barbara Bush. The future first lady later recalled "being surprised by how tiny the Duke and Duchess were and how charming she was."[13] Bobby Short played piano and sang many of the Windsors' favorite songs; David could be seen tapping his cane in time with the music. Afterward, a group of high school and college students known as the Young Saints performed traditional American hymns and Negro spirituals. At the end of the evening, the Duke and Duchess climbed to the stage and thanked each of the performers before returning to Blair House just before midnight.

In these last years, Lord Mountbatten became a frequent—if not altogether welcome—visitor to the Windsor Villa in the Bois de Boulogne. Wallis had never particularly cared for him, and even David by now was angry at the way he seemed to inspect the house, examining papers and souvenirs. "Who are you going to leave that to?" he would ask the Duke, pointing at some object. "I think that should go to Charles." "How dare he!" David declared after one such visit. "He even tells me what *he* wants left to him!"[14]

Mountbatten, to his credit, had quietly been suggesting to Prince Charles that the time had come for a new generation of the Royal Family to make overtures toward the Windsors. This provoked the Prince's curiosity, and he approached his grandmother the Queen Mother with the idea. Jonathan Dimbleby, in his authorized biography of the Prince, writes, however, that "it was immediately apparent to him how difficult she would find it to be reconciled with the man whom she held responsible for consigning her husband to an early grave."[15]

On October 3, 1970, Prince Charles, who happened to be shooting near Paris with British ambassador Sir Christopher Soames and his son Nicholas, decided he wanted to visit the Duke and Duchess. Although Soames objected that both the Queen and the Queen Mother would strenuously object, Charles was adamant. There was a large dinner party already taking place in the house in the Bois de Boulogne when the Prince of Wales arrived, and he was immediately uncomfortable with the gathered company. "The Duchess appeared from among a host of the most dreadful American guests I have ever seen," he later wrote. He clearly disliked Wallis, whom he described as "flitting to and fro like a strange bat. She looks incredible for her age and obviously has her face lifted every day. Consequently she can't really speak except by clenching her teeth all the time and not moving any facial muscles. She struck me as a hard woman—totally unsympathetic and somewhat superficial. Very little warmth of the true kind; only that brilliant hostess type of charm but without feeling. . . ." He spent most of his time in a corner of the drawing room with the Duke, chatting about his role as Prince of Wales. "The whole thing," Charles declared "seemed so tragic—the existence, the people, and the atmosphere— that I was relieved to escape it after 45 minutes and drive round Paris by night."[16]

One of the last parties the Duke and Duchess attended was given by Guy de Rothschild at Château Ferrières-en-Brie on December 2, 1971. The Windsors joined Prince Rainier and Princess Grace of

Monaco, Elizabeth Taylor and Richard Burton, Audrey Hepburn, Brigitte Bardot, Cecil Beaton, and a hundred other celebrities in a lavish costume ball which began at half-past ten and broke up at seven the next morning. Burton recalled that during the dinner Wallis seemed hopelessly lost. "She had an enormous feather in her hair which she got into everything, the soup, the gravy, the ice-cream, and at every vivacious turn of her head it smacked Guy sharply in the eyes or the mouth and at one time threatened to get stuck in Guy's false mustache which was glued on."[17]

A few days later, at a dinner at the villa, Burton noted sadly: "It is she who is now nearly completely ga-ga. It was a sad and painful evening and needs a long time to write about. . . . He is physically falling apart, his left eye completely closed and a tremendous limp and walks with a stick. Her memory has gone completely and then comes back vividly in flashes."[18]

"I told him to stop smoking all those cigarettes," the Duchess said sadly in 1972. "We had some friends who had died of throat cancer. He said he started smoking a lot when he was traveling around as Prince of Wales making so many speeches. He was always nervous about making speeches and that's why he smoked so much. He did cut down. He started smoking half-cigarettes in a holder. But I guess it was still too much; it all added up."[19]

In late summer of 1971, David began to lose his voice. That fall, doctors discovered a small tumor in his throat; a biopsy was taken on November 17, and the tumor proved not only malignant but also inoperable. He immediately began forty-one days of cobalt treatments, which left him terribly weak.[20]

At first, it seemed the cobalt treatments had worked and the cancer had gone into remission; then, in February 1972, David entered the American Hospital in Neuilly in Paris for a routine hernia operation, during the course of which his blood work indicated something was wrong. Dr. Jean Thin, who for several years had been treating the Duke and Duchess in cooperation with Dr. Arthur Antonucci in New York, found that the cancer had returned. Under French medical-ethics law, Thin was prevented from disclosing the terminal nature of the illness. But as his time in the hospital increased and he underwent further treatments, Thin felt that the Duke instinctively realized he was dying.[21]

During the Duke's stay in the hospital, the Duchess sat with him every afternoon. Oonagh Shanley, the Irish nurse on duty, recalled that Wallis was "full of affection for HRH. They remained as lovers—hand in hand!" When she had gone, she remembered, "the Duke was lonely. He could not bear to be separated from his Wallis another night."[22]

Shanley was "pleasantly surprised" at the relaxed nature of her first meeting with the Windsors.[23] Above all else, they seemed to her simply two people very much in love. She was delighted, therefore, to be asked to accompany them back to their villa and act as live-in nurse to the Duke during his illness.

On the afternoon that David was released from the American Hospital and returned home, he found the entire staff of the villa lining the portico, waiting to welcome him back. Oonagh Shanley was shown to her room on the third floor—the red, gold, and black Napoleon suite. Before leaving her, Wallis invited Shanley to join her and the Duke for dinner in the evenings if she had no other plans. She was to live with the Windsors until David's death. She later recalled: "The Duke and Duchess were in love, and their interaction was like a young couple in love. There was a real togetherness about them, and a harmony which must have been there *always* because such virtues don't suddenly come into being."[24]

The following day, after the Windsors had brunch in the boudoir, Shanley went to see if the Duke had eaten well. When she entered the room, the Duchess stood up and handed Shanley a small wrapped box; inside was a diamond floral brooch. "Oonagh," she said, "we want you to have this brooch, the smallest carnation in the world, and designed by the Duke. It's his favourite flower, and it is to thank you for bringing David home safely."[25]

David was stoic. Shanley remembered that he "was so courageous and never complained, always keeping his spirits up, never wanting the Duchess to worry about him. She was not fully aware of the gravity of his illness."[26] The ravages of the illness, however, soon became more and more apparent. "He was very, very thin," Dr. Thin remembered.[27] Wallis later told the Countess of Romanones: "He pretended up to the last minute that he was in no danger, and I did the same. I think we both knew the other knew. How strange it was, trying to fool ourselves, to save the other from suffering."[28]

On May 10 David suffered cardiac arrest. Oonagh Shanley had taken the evening off to dine in the Latin Quarter. Wallis had already retired when she returned to the villa near midnight. "When I took over from the nurse who replaced me," Shanley recalled, "I found the Duke agitated (she was French and perhaps a bit shy and the Duke was not relaxed I believe the whole afternoon). And then he collapsed. I was absolutely alone and had no one to help. I raced upstairs for my nursing bag, grabbed an ampule of IV cortisone and mercifully got into a vein in his ankle—I did a very light cardiac massage and prayed quietly. What a relief when the cocktail worked, and slowly he returned to life." She quickly telephoned Dr. Thin and returned to the Duke's side, holding his hand and soothing him until Thin arrived.

"He ordered coramine," she remembers, "and promised to come back in the morning with Dr. [François] Jaquin to install an intravaneous drip with saline/glucose, vitamins and cardiac remedies to improve and maintain better heart function."[29]

Wallis was surprised the next morning to find that her husband was now connected to a drip; no one told her what had happened, wishing to spare her any additional worry. "I knew something was wrong, terribly wrong," she later told a friend, "but I didn't want to upset David by asking questions."[30] It was Thin who explained—without disclosing the cardiac arrest—that the Duke's condition was grave; according to the doctor, the Duchess quickly guessed that her husband had but a few weeks to live.[31]

Elizabeth II and the Duke of Edinburgh were scheduled to visit Paris in the middle of May in connection with the British government's decision to join the Common Market. A short time before, Lady Monckton had visited the Windsors and been shocked at the Duke's condition. Upon her return to London, she telephoned Buckingham Palace and informed Sir Martin Charteris, the Queen's private secretary, that the former King was dying. This news sent the palace into a frenzy: If the Duke died before the Queen's visit to Paris, undoubtedly it would have to be postponed. If he should die during her visit, the timing would be considered most unfortunate. Charteris contacted Sir Christopher Soames, the British ambassador in Paris, and asked that he consult Dr. Thin. Thin, however, could say little. There was no indication as to whether the Duke's condition would worsen or improve over the next few weeks.[32]

Presuming that the Duke would linger on for at least a few weeks, it was suggested that the Queen pay a private visit to her uncle. Apparently, this idea was received with something less than enthusiasm: Elizabeth II dreaded personal confrontations and the more unpleasant realities of life, and the thought of coming face-to-face with her dying, exiled uncle and his despised wife left her uneasy. "I think," remembers a close relative of the Royal Family, "that there was a certain element of guilt in her reluctance as well. For years, she had bowed to the wishes of her mother and refused to grant the Windsors any concessions; now, it was too late."[33]

The Queen, the Duke of Edinburgh, and Prince Charles arrived at Orly Airport on May 15. A visit to the Duke and Duchess was announced for May 18. When the Queen's private secretary was asked if Elizabeth II realized how ill her uncle was, Charteris replied, "You know he's dying. I know he's dying. But *we* don't know he's dying."[34] This rather cold, official line would unfortunately characterize the brief royal visit to the Windsor Villa.

In the three days leading up to the visit, Soames telephoned Dr.

Thin each evening at six to check on the Duke's progress. For several days David had been unable to swallow "any significant amount of fluids" and instead was on a glucose drip. On May 17, in a raspy voice, David told both Thin and Shanley that he wanted the drip unhooked for the Queen's visit. Although both protested, he was adamant, and the drips were duly unhooked except for one painkiller that was left in place for the night. "He was not in excruciating pain, and received only small doses of sedatives," Thin recalled.[35] Contrary to several accounts, David received no blood transfusions prior to the Queen's visit.[36]

On the afternoon of the eighteenth Wallis, in a short-sleeved Dior dress of deep blue crepe, stood on the steps of the villa, watching as the limousines bearing the Queen and her entourage slowly pulled up the drive. As Elizabeth II stepped out of her car, Wallis sank into a deep but rather awkward curtsy; she later confessed to a friend that her legs had almost given out beneath her.[37] She repeated the honor to the Duke of Edinburgh and to the Prince of Wales before leading the Royal trio inside. The Queen, her husband, and her eldest son all seemed distinctly uncomfortable, and Wallis later recalled that Elizabeth in particular had behaved coldly toward her. "She was not at all warm to his wife of thirty-five years," she told the Countess of Romanones.[38]

They all took tea in the drawing room. Peculiarly, neither the Queen, her husband, or their son asked the Duchess about the state of the Duke's health. "It was as if they were pretending that David was perfectly well," she declared later.[39] After fifteen minutes, Wallis led the Queen up the staircase and into the boudoir, where David sat in a wheelchair. Although Thin had advised him to remain in bed, David had insisted on receiving his sovereign with proper respect. He had struggled into a blue polo neck and blazer he himself had selected that morning. It was obvious that he was gravely ill: The blazer hung loose on his already-small frame, his face was deeply lined, and his eyes were dark and circled.

When Wallis entered the boudoir with Elizabeth, David rose and kissed the Queen. Wallis would later tell the Countess of Romanones: "The Queen's face showed no compassion, no appreciation for his effort, his respect. Her manner as much as stated that she had not intended to honour him with a visit, but that she was simply covering appearances by coming here because he was dying and it was known that she was in Paris."[40] Oonagh Shanley, however, recalled that the Queen chatted amiably with her uncle, who could barely speak above a whisper. Then Wallis brought the Duke of Edinburgh and the Prince of Wales to the boudoir. David began to question Prince Charles about his life in the Royal Navy, but his conversation was interrupted by a fit of uncontrollable coughing, and he motioned for Oonagh Shanley to wheel him away. The Queen was completely silent, and all rose and left the boudoir.[41]

It was soon apparent to Wallis that the Queen had no intention of remaining. She escorted Elizabeth, the Duke, and Prince Charles to the front door of the villa and stood on the steps while photographers captured the moment for the following day's papers. Wallis, perhaps overcome, glanced down momentarily. The visit, so pregnant with meaning, had come too late. The Queen smiled, and the Duke of Edinburgh—rather inappropriately but not untypically—tried to make casual, joking remarks which Wallis found offensive and callous.[42] As the royal party left, Wallis carefully curtsied once again to each one; she remained standing on the steps of her house, alone, watching as the limousines swept down the drive and disappeared from view. The entire visit was over in thirty minutes.

45

The Duke's Death

THE DAY AFTER the royal visit, according to Oonagh Shanley, the Duke of Windsor seemed to improve slightly. "He was at peace within himself," she recalls. Wallis joined him for lunch, and he ate more than usual. After this, she left him so that he might rest. He lay down for a nap, but when he awoke early that evening, he felt worse; he grew steadily weaker and was scarcely able to eat anything.[1]

Thursday, May 25, marked the first time that David was unable to leave his bed. His temperature rose and fell, making him delirious at times. Wallis spent the majority of the day with him, occasionally returning to her own bedroom to rest for a few minutes. Finally, at midnight, she retired, leaving Oonagh Shanley to watch over him.

Just after three that morning, Shanley heard "a sickening thud and crash that suddenly shattered the silence. It came from the bathroom and as I leapt up and went in there it happened again, this time followed by a rasping croak, and I realized that some night creature was hitting against the window." David seemed to be much worse. Fearing that he would not survive the night, she woke Wallis's maid Giselle and prepared to ring Dr. Thin.

Throughout, a loud squawking from beyond the bedroom windows shattered the silence of the night. "What on earth are those birds making that horrible noise?" Shanley asked the maid.

"Oh, it's the *corbeaux*," she answered, a reply which Shanley interpreted to mean ravens, "though I've *never* heard them in the night before." She paused a few seconds before adding thoughtfully, "But then, they're Royal Birds, aren't they?"

"She said it matter-of-factly," Shanley recalled, "but I glanced at her in astonishment. I suddenly realized she meant the huge, shiny black ravens I'd often seen in the garden and then all the ominous legends, learned in childhood, came to my thoughts. The fatal ravens consecrated to the Danish war god, the ravens in *Macbeth* croaking their warning of Royal death. . . . I simply looked at the Royal Coat of Arms pinned to the wall above the bed, and the face of the man who'd once been a king, and thought, 'Some things don't change. The ravens have come for him.'"[2]

On Friday, deeply worried about the Duke, Wallis immediately telephoned New York and asked Dr. Arthur Antonucci, their American physician, to come to Paris at once. Antonucci dropped his schedule and caught the next plane, arriving in Paris late that afternoon. But after a careful examination of the Duke and review of his medical progress with Thin and Shanley, he took Wallis aside and sadly told her that there was nothing he could do.

From this moment on, Wallis rarely left her husband's side. Both Thin and Shanley, who witnessed her sitting quietly at the side of David's bed, holding his hand and whispering to him, saw and heard the struggle in her voice and actions to remain composed. Once, when she had disappeared temporarily, Shanley heard the Duke mutter, "England not far away. . . . The Waste . . . the waste."[3]

Wallis spent most of Saturday with the Duke. She remained with him until eleven that night, when he said to her, "Darling, go to bed and rest. Oonagh will look after me." Reluctantly, Wallis, overcome with exhaustion, allowed Giselle to lead her to her bedroom.[4]

Late that night, Sydney Johnson, David's valet, joined Shanley in his bedroom. Together, the two of them prayed. David's favorite pug, Black Diamond, lay at the foot of his master's bed; usually, when Dr. Thin approached, the dog raised its head and growled. This time, however, the dog simply turned its head away. "See," Thin said to Shanley. "The dog knows what's happening!"[5]

David's end, according to Oonagh Shanley, was entirely peaceful. According to the nurse, he died in his sleep, quietly, at 2:20 A.M., on Sunday, May 28. Later, Sydney Johnson would say that the Duke's last words had been "Mama, Mama, Mama, Mama."[6] But, according to Shanley, the story is apocryphal: Johnson was not present when the Duke died.

As soon as David died, Shanley left him, walking through the boudoir to the Duchess's bedroom, where she woke Wallis and brought her back to his side. Wallis leaned down and kissed his forehead, then cupped his face in her hands and said quietly, "My David, my David. . . . You look so lovely."[7]

Wallis, in the words of Shanley, was "devastated." The man who had given up his entire life to be with her was now gone; she lay on her bed, sobbing until exhaustion crept over her and she lapsed into an uneasy sleep.[8]

The official announcement came from Buckingham Palace: "It is announced with deep regret that His Royal Highness The Duke of Windsor has died at his home in Paris at 2:25 A.M., Sunday, 28 May,

1972." The text of a telegram from the Queen to the Duchess was also released to the press: "I know that my people will always remember him with gratitude and great affection and that his services to them in peace and war will never be forgotten. I am so glad that I was able to see him in Paris ten days ago."[9] Wallis, according to one friend, was deeply hurt that there was no personal telegram, no expression of grief or any mention at all of her own loss.[10] This, however, was by careful design. The telegram, writes Ben Pimlott, was "the product of much drafting."[11]

Tributes poured in from all over the world, and even the British newspapers were careful to mention the support which Wallis had given to David throughout their marriage. The *Daily Mail* commented in an editorial: "We cherish the memory of that most charming and most English of Englishmen whose love for a woman lost him his crown . . . but not the affection of his people."[12] And the *Guardian* noted that the Duke "was most fortunate in a long life in marrying a woman of admirable warmth and character."[13]

That Sunday was a busy day at the Windsor Villa. Early that morning, the French coroner arrived to certify the death. Sydney Johnson had carefully washed David's body and laid him out in his bed; a Union Jack covered him to his neck, and the entire bed was surrounded with banks of white lilies, roses, chrysanthemums, and orchids.[14] Here he would remain until he was taken back to England; there was no autopsy.[15]

Maurice Schumann, the French foreign minister, arrived at the villa to officially express the condolences of his government; exiled King Umberto of Italy also paid his respects that day, braving the crowd of press photographers and reporters that thronged around the tall, wrought-iron gate to the estate. Crowds also congregated at the British embassy on rue du Faubourg, where a condolence book had been set out for mourners to sign; by the end of the afternoon, over three hundred people had passed through the line to record their names in the book.

Another visitor to the villa that morning was designer Hubert de Givenchy, whom Wallis had asked to come and fit her for a mourning dress, coat, and hat. "It was the only time I ever saw her in bedroom slippers," he told author Suzy Menkes, "with no make-up and her hair in a mess. She called me over to Neuilly and stood in her dressing room with her face completely overwhelmed with grief, and said, 'You must make me a black dress and coat for the Duke's funeral. Can you do it?' I replied 'Of course' and we worked on it all night. She never forgot. That's when she started to call me Hubert."[16]

The expressions of condolence and grief in Paris, indeed, pouring in from around the world, stood in stark contrast to the utter silence from Buckingham Palace. The day after David died, Monday, May 29, Harry Middleton of the BBC rang up Lord Mountbatten and asked if he would broadcast a tribute to the former King. "I refused," Mountbatten recorded in his diary, "as this was against all precedent; I pointed out that I had not done anything of that sort for George VI when he died and he also had been a great friend. Middleton then made the point that the Royal Family had not paid any adequate tribute to the former King Edward VIII, certainly nothing comparable to the tributes paid by other Heads of States, like President Nixon and President Pompidou, and that it would be taken very much amiss by the public as a whole and the many great admirers of the former King if none of the family said anything about him at all." Mountbatten rang Buckingham Palace to obtain official approval and found that Sir Martin Charteris, the Queen's private secretary, opposed the idea of a tribute to the Duke. Only after Mountbatten pointed out the concerns Middleton had voiced about the public perception of the Royal Family's surprising lack of grief did Charteris agree to speak to the Queen. Even so, Elizabeth II was reluctant to allow Mountbatten to broadcast any tribute to her late uncle. Only after "considerable thought" did she approve the idea, and then only if Mountbatten was careful not to praise him too highly.[17]

This was not the only questionable response from Buckingham Palace. Later that afternoon, they announced simply: "The Duchess of Windsor has accepted the Queen's invitation to stay at Buckingham Palace." This rather uncomplicated sentence, however, hid a half day's worth of animated discussions between John Utter in Paris, Sir Martin Charteris, and Lord Maclean, the Lord Chamberlain, during which the very issuance of the invitation was debated. Utter—and the Duchess—clearly expected that this simple courtesy would be extended as a matter of form; but the same reluctance which caused the Queen to warn Mountbatten that he must not speak too highly of the Duke also gave rise to speculation about Wallis's presence in the palace. Eventually, it was decided that if the invitation was not issued, a major scandal would erupt over such a public humiliation, but Utter had had to work long and hard to convince the palace of this.[18]

The announcement from the palace—although perfectly natural under other circumstances—was so out of the ordinary where the Duke and Duchess of Windsor were concerned that reporters asked why, after so many years of being forced to take a suite at Claridge's Hotel when in London, the Duchess was now being accommodated by the Queen. "For this occasion, and for obvious human reasons, protocol has been waived," the palace press office declared in response.[19] There was no official explanation of exactly what "protocol" was being waived; certainly it was customary for other members of the Royal

Family and their close relatives to be accommodated in Buckingham Palace during funeral ceremonies. As a result, the invitation was viewed rather cynically in the press. Leslie Pine, former editor of *Burke's Peerage*, commented: "I welcome it. But the invitation should have been extended to both of them before the Duke's death."[20] And the *London Evening News* declared: "How ironic it is that the first occasion since the Abdication on which she will have been welcomed to the Palace will be for her husband's burial. Would this visit not be an appropriate time for her to be accorded the courtesy title of Her Royal Highness on which the Duke had set his heart?"[21] But there would be no offer of a royal style forthcoming; Queen Elizabeth II would never have gone against the policy set down by her father, particularly not while her mother was alive.

On Wednesday, May 31, David's body was returned to England. That afternoon, Wallis, clad in a simple black dress, stood in silence on the steps of her villa, surrounded by members of the household and staff, watching as the body of her husband, now encased in a simple coffin of English oak, was carried through the front door and to the waiting hearse. The lid of the coffin was covered with the Duke's standard; a simple cross of red and white carnations and gladioli rested atop the standard, with a card reading "From Wallis."

Wallis was overwhelmed with grief and decided to temporarily remain in Paris. Overcome with the enormity of her loss and the strain, she collapsed from exhaustion The hearse, accompanied by a motorcycle escort, an air marshal, and three vice-marshals, drove to Le Bourget Airport, where a plane from the Queen's flight waited to take the Duke back to England. At the end of the short, hour-long flight, the plane landed at RAF Benson, where the Duke and Duchess of Kent met the coffin. As it was unloaded from the plane, a band played the first six bars of the national anthem. That night, the Duke's body lay in the RAF Chapel. On the following day, however, he went home, to Windsor.

David's coffin first rested in the Albert Memorial Chapel before being moved into the adjacent St. George's Chapel, where he was to lie in state. At eleven o'clock on Friday morning, the public was admitted for their first glimpse of the coffin. It lay on a catafalque at the center of a dais carpeted in the same blue as the sash of the Order of the Garter. The Duke's personal standard was draped carefully over the edges of the coffin. Six tall candlesticks stood around the dais; the mourning candles, of unbleached orange wax, burned all day and night. On the tier below were officers of the Household Cavalry and the Brigade of Guards standing a guard of honour, four men at a time.[22]

Wallis, meanwhile, continued to remain secluded in Paris. Not only was she devastated at the death of her husband, but the idea of joining his family for the funeral was almost too much for her to consider. She had always been an outsider among them, never welcome, and now, at the time of her greatest grief, she had no wish to put herself through what she clearly believed would be a terrible ordeal. The Royal Family, too, was worried. Originally, Wallis had been scheduled to accompany her husband's body on its return to England. Her decision to remain in Paris, therefore, came as a surprise. Lord Mountbatten himself noted that there was some discussion as to whether the Duchess would attend her husband's funeral.[23] It was clearly in the best interests of the Royal Family that she do so: Her absence, particularly after years of very public ostracism, would only be interpreted as the final humiliation. There was a great sense of relief when Buckingham Palace received a telephone call asking if a plane could be sent for the Duchess to bring her to England.

Wallis flew from Paris to London aboard an airplane from the Queen's flight on Friday, June 2. She was accompanied by her friend Lady Grace Dudley; Mary Churchill Soames, the wife of the British ambassador in Paris, Sir Christopher Soames; Dr. Arthur Antonucci; Brig. Douglas Greenacre, equerry to Elizabeth II; the Duke's secretary, John Utter; and Alexandre, Wallis's hairdresser. The latter had telephoned and asked if the Duchess wished him to join her to do her hair during her stay in England; at first, Wallis said no. "But then I thought, Yes, of course," she later told the Countess of Romanones. "The last thing David would want was for me not to look my best."[24]

Lord Mountbatten had come to greet her. Wallis was a bit surprised at this and wondered why Prince Charles had not been dispatched instead. "I helped Wallis down the ladder as she was very frail and nervous," Mountbatten recalled.[25] The television cameras captured her descent: a tiny, bent figure in black, clutching the rails and stepping carefully onto the tarmac. It was a startling image: Here was the woman the Royal Family had so feared, so loathed, that she and her husband had been punished for thirty-six years. The contrast between the popular misconception and the stark reality could not have been greater.

Wallis and Mountbatten rode together in a Rolls-Royce to London. As they drove, Wallis began to express her fear that the Royal Family would treat her coldly; she was especially worried about the reception she would receive from the Queen Mother, who she knew had continued to blame her for her husband's death. But Mountbatten tried to reassure her, saying, "Your sister-in-law will receive you with open arms—she is so deeply sorry for you in your present grief and remembers what she felt like when her own husband died."[26] Ironically, the next morning, Wallis received the first official recognition by the Royal Family and court of her existence during her entire marriage to the Duke. The court circular read: "Buckingham Palace, 2 June. By

Command of The Queen, Admiral of the Fleet the Earl Mountbatten of Burma was present at Heathrow Airport-London this morning and, on behalf of Her Majesty, greeted the Duchess of Windsor upon arrival in this country in an aircraft of The Queen's Flight."[27]

Despite this concession, the four days Wallis spent at Buckingham Palace were remarkable for both the cold demeanor of the Royal Family toward her and the subtle ways in which this elderly widow was subjected to petty humiliations. Important visitors to the palace used the main entrance; members of the diplomatic corps, the ambassador's entrance; and members of the Royal Family, the private entrance in the garden, hidden from public view by a long, one-story wall pierced with an arch. Wallis, upon arriving at the palace, used none of them. Instead, her Rolls-Royce pulled up before the doorway into the privy-purse corridor, used by members of the household and other court officials. No member of the Royal Family waited to greet her; an official led her through long, crimson-carpeted corridors to the suite she was to occupy at the front of the palace, overlooking the Mall. When Wallis had settled in to her rooms, an official arrived and informed her that the Queen would receive her. This stiff, rather formal summons seemed to Wallis a bit cold; as a matter of courtesy to a grieving widow, she had thought that the Queen might come to her.[28] Instead, Elizabeth received her aunt in her private sitting room. She told Wallis that if there was anything she wished, it would be arranged for her. "They were polite to me," Wallis recalled, "polite and kind, especially the Queen. Royalty is always polite and kind. But they were cold. David always said they were cold."[29]

Ben Pimlott, Elizabeth II's most recent biographer, recalls a conversation with a former courtier who was present at the palace when the Duchess came to stay: "The Queen didn't want to have much to do with Wallis. Dinner was given in the Chinese Room—with anybody else, it would have been in the Queen's own dining room. She preferred to go down to where Wallis was set up. It was okay—everybody behaved decently. Charles was there, and helpful. But there was certainly no outpouring of love between the Queen and the Duchess of Windsor, or vice versa."[30]

Wallis felt lost. She tried to make conversation but found that for the most part her efforts went unrewarded. The Prince of Wales later noted rather ungenerously of his grieving great-aunt that she had "prattled away" during the dinner.[31] "In all the time I was there," Wallis later told the Countess of Romanones, "no one in the family offered me any real sympathy whatsoever." Still, she was resolute. "They were going to continue to hate me no matter what I did, but at least I wasn't going to let them see David's wife without every shred of dignity I could muster."[32]

The Queen herself, who had often played with her uncle David as a child, was not overwhelmed with grief at his passing. As with her instructions to Mountbatten regarding his BBC tribute, she was determined that the Duke be accorded precisely the respect and privileges due him, but no more. According to her private secretary, the Duke "had been a threat. The Queen wanted to play things down."[33] "The general principle was to err," writes Ben Pimlott of the funeral and its attendant ceremonial, "but only a little, on the side of magnanimity."[34] As the recent funeral of Diana, Princess of Wales, confirmed, this would not be the only occasion on which the Queen misjudged the extent of public grief and sympathy.

By the end of Saturday afternoon, when the Duke's lying in state came to an end, some sixty thousand people had paid their respects, silently shuffling through St. George's Chapel, Windsor. Many—especially those in their fifties and sixties—recalled the reign of Edward VIII with favorable nostalgia. "He should have stayed on," said one woman, interviewed while waiting in line. "The wife he wanted would have just slipped into the background. We wouldn't have cared at all. She's a lovely woman." "They should have accepted her," declared another, while a third added sadly, "We love our Royal Family. But that Duchess should not have been snubbed all these years. If I were her, I would never have agreed to go to the palace now. I would have said, Thank you, and then gone off to Claridge's Hotel."[35]

Such sentiments were more prevelant than either Buckingham Palace or Queen Elizabeth II wished to believe. The criticism among the public, reported in the newspapers and repeated on nightly television broadcasts, drove Labour MP Ian Mikardo to declare: "In a generation from now, when we have quietly got rid of the monarchy, people will see the events of this week as the beginning of the end of the court and all the mumbo jumbo that goes with it. . . . When he was alive Edward Windsor was savaged and his wife was condemned by the court, the established church and the government. Now, with sickening hypocrisy, they are all falling over themselves to show to the corpse the charity they denied to the man."[36]

Trooping the colors had previously been scheduled for Saturday, June 3, and there was some question as to whether the Queen would cancel the ceremony. It has often been written that she instead dedicated it to her uncle, wearing a black armband on the left sleeve of her crimson uniform as a tribute. The armband was indeed in place, but the suggestion to make the occasion a tribute to the late Duke did not come from the Queen. When it was initially suggested that she cancel the ceremony out of respect for her dead uncle, Elizabeth flatly declared that she thought this too much and asked her advisers to work out some compromise. It was her private secretary, Sir Martin

Charteris, who proposed that the Queen wear a black armband and that a piper's lament be played to provide a suitable atmosphere.[37]

As the Queen and her procession rode out from Buckingham Palace, Wallis was caught by a photographer looking from a curtained window of her suite, dressed in black, a string of immensely large pearls around her neck, her eyes haunted by sadness. The trooping passed off without incident: There was a roll of black-draped drums, a minute's silence, and the playing of a bagpipe lament, "Flowers of the Forest," by the massed bands of the Irish and Scots Guards. Upon her return to Buckingham Palace, the Queen came to the Duchess's suite and informed her that the rest of the family would be leaving for Windsor Castle; Wallis could join them if she wished. After years of rejection during the Duke's life, this sudden attempt at thoughtfulness and familial embrace in his death, as Wallis later confessed to a friend, seemed hypocritical. She admitted privately that she had no desire to put herself through the strain, and so she remained at Buckingham Palace—alone.[38]

That afternoon, the Queen, the Duke of Edinburgh, and Princess Anne visited St. George's Chapel and stood with heads bowed in silent tribute for six minutes. Later that evening, after the chapel had been closed to the public, Wallis came from London, escorted by Lord Mountbatten and Prince Charles. She walked alone through the austere chapel, her footsteps echoing against the stone floor as she passed the tombs of King George V and Queen Mary and approached the catafalque in the center of the nave. The arc lights in the arches shone down upon the royal standard, mingling with the soft light from the setting sun filtering in through the tall windows above. Mountbatten recalled that she stood looking at the coffin and said "in the saddest imaginable voice: 'He was my entire life. I can't begin to think what I am going to do without him, he gave up so much for me, and now he has gone. I always hoped that I would die before him.'"[39] The Prince of Wales later wrote that his widowed aunt had declared, "He gave up so much for so little," and pointed at herself with what he termed "a strange grin."[40] The emotion of the moment was overwhelming. As she stood before her husband's coffin, Wallis repeated over and over, "Thirty-five years . . . thirty-five years. . . ."[41] It would have been their thirty-fifth wedding anniversary.

Monday, June 5, was to be the day of the Duke of Windsor's funeral. In London, a motion had been introduced in the House of Commons "that a Humble Address be presented to Her Majesty on the death of His Royal Highness the Duke of Windsor, expressing the deep sympathy which this House extends to Her Majesty and to all members of his Family on their grievous loss, and recording grateful remembrance of his devoted service to his Country and to the British Empire."[42] After the motion was read into the record, Prime Minister Edward Heath spoke, paying tribute to "the wife for whose love King Edward was content to give up his patrimony and who has repaid his devotion with an equal loyalty, companionship and love. His death is, above all, her loss, and to her the House will wish to extend its profound sympathy."[43]

This set off a storm of controversy; the seemingly simple issue of including the Duchess of Windsor by name in the motion expressing sympathy on the death of her husband reawakened old animosities and conservative fears. Incredibly, a debate arose over the propriety of mentioning the Duchess by name. The Democratic Unionist member for North Antrim, the Reverend Ian Paisley, fearing the worst, intervened: "Surely, today, when this matter is brought before the House, specific mention should have been made in the Motion of the person who will miss the Duke most."[44] But the speaker replied, "That is not a matter of order for the Chair."[45]

Harold Wilson, the opposition leader, rose in tribute to the Duke's "gracious lady, the Duchess of Windsor. . . . We all welcome the fact that she has felt able to be in Britain to hear and sense the feelings of our people, and we are all appreciative of the dignity she has shown, not only in these tragic days but over all the years. We hope that she will feel free at any time to come among and freely communicate with the people whom her husband, Prince of Wales, King and Duke, lived to serve."[46]

Jeremy Thorpe, the controversial Liberal leader, declared: "I would have hoped that it might have been possible to mention his widow by name in the Motion which we shall pass, for not only does our sympathy go out to his family but in particular it goes out to his widow whose sadness has been shared by many in this country and whose composure and dignity have won our deep respect."[47] Even Willie Hamilton, the staunchly antimonarchist MP, said: "No woman could have behaved with more dignity and grace in the face of the humiliations and indignities piled on her by the Government, the House and by Our Government over the last thirty-six years."[48] In the face of such overwhelming support, the motion was rewritten to include the extension of the government's sympathy to "Her Grace the Duchess of Windsor."

That morning, alone in her suite at Buckingham Palace, Wallis dressed in the simple black dress, black coat, and plain black pillbox hat with a waist-length veil which Hubert de Givenchy had created for her in Paris. She wore a pair of pearl-studded earrings which David had liked. A few minutes after ten, Wallis climbed into the waiting

Rolls-Royce in the palace quadrangle and began the forty-minute drive to Windsor Castle; it was the last time she would ever set foot in Buckingham Palace.

It was a fine, warm, clear summer day; as the Rolls-Royce bearing the Duchess of Windsor drove up the hill and through the Henry VIII Gate of Windsor Castle, the bell in the Curfew Tower, overlooking Eton, the Thames, and the Berkshire countryside beyond, tolled once each minute, its mournful sound breaking the reverential hush of the gathered crowd. The Duke's coffin had been taken to the Albert Memorial Chapel for the formal procession into St. George's Chapel. Wallis stepped from her car and discreetly slipped through a side entrance to join the other members of the Royal Family. She found that the Queen, the Duke of Edinburgh, the Queen Mother, the Prince of Wales, and Princess Anne had not yet arrived from their private apartments in the upper ward of the Castle. Another notable absentee, and one who was not waiting to make his appearance, was the Earl of Harewood, eldest son of David's sister Mary, the Princess Royal. He had not been invited, although his younger brother Gerald Lascelles was present. At first, Harewood thought there must have been a mistake and rang the Lord Chamberlain; only then was he bluntly told that he would not be welcome. His absence was duly noted in the British newspapers. "The charitable theory of oversight," wrote the *Sunday Times* a week later, "is unconvincing since the Earl's younger brother, Gerald Lascelles, was invited and attended. . . . That, as a divorced person, he should be barred from the funeral of an uncle who married at such deliberate cost a divorced person, is a ludicrous persistence of Abdication attitudes, bordering on the unbelievable. Yet no other official explanation was offered."[49]

Just before eleven, the Queen, her husband, mother, and two eldest children arrived from the upper ward. Wallis, despite her grief, was struck by the appearance of her archenemy the Queen Mother. She later told the Countess of Romanones: "How she was dressed! What would I look like in that dress and hat? I really must copy that outfit. It looked as if she had just opened some old trunk and pulled out a few rags and draped them on herself. And that eternal bag hanging on her arm. . . . She wore a black hat with the brim rolled up, just plopped on her head, and a white plastic arrow sticking up through it. I thought how David would have laughed."[50]

With the Queen and the Queen Mother, Wallis led the women of the Royal Family, walking from the Albert Memorial Chapel and into St. George's Chapel. As she entered the nave, a sea of unknown faces turned to stare at her, watching as she purposefully made her way through the congregation to the choir, where the Queen directed her to a seat in the carved stalls; sunlight blazed through the enormous stained-glass window above the altar, mingling with the soft glow from the choir lamps and the flickering flames of the tall candles. Ahead of her, standing in the center of the nave, was a catafalque draped in deep blue cloth, waiting to receive her husband's coffin.

The sudden quiet of the curfew bell signaled the start of the funeral. The constable of Windsor Castle led the procession of the Military Knights of Windsor, a collection of uncertain-looking elderly men holding their plumed caps beneath their arms. The somber, almost hushed tones of the choir's anthem "I Am the Resurrection and the Life," sung at all royal funerals, filled the chapel as the white-robed men and boys moved slowly down the aisle, followed by the clergy: the Dean of Windsor, the Very Reverend Launcelot Fleming, preceded Dr. Michael Ramsey, the Archbishop of Canterbury, attired in a tall white miter and black-and-gold cope. The soaring melodies of the choir drowned out the click-clack of their footsteps as eight scarlet-coated members of the Prince of Wales's Company, First Battalion, Welsh Guards, bore the Duke's coffin down the nave and into the choir. The Duke of Edinburgh, David's cousin King Olav of Norway, Lord Mountbatten, and the Prince of Wales led the male members of the Royal Family as they followed the coffin through the chapel to the catafalque on which it was carefully placed.

"I could not believe what was happening," Wallis later recalled sadly. "I had held him in my arms as he died, but I could not really believe that I would never see him again. Then I saw the flowers, white callas, which I had ordered, on top of his bier, which was covered with his flag, and I wanted to weep. But I said to myself that I was going to be as brave and as tough as those English. I wasn't going to let them show me up in any way. They had been so cruel to my husband for so many years, to that wonderful, kind, good, patriotic man, and I maintained the same expression that they all bore, they who didn't care."[51]

Despite her best efforts, however, Wallis was often overwhelmed during the service, appearing confused and lost; several times, the Queen had to help her find her place in the order of service. At the end, after the hymns, proclamations, and prayers, four state trumpeters of the Household Cavalry sounded last post and reveille, echoing off the Gothic arches and fan vaults of the ceiling above. Within an hour, it had all come to an end.

Wallis exited to brilliant sunshine. At some point, the Queen began to walk ahead of the Duchess, assuming the role of chief mourner, and Wallis reached out for her, bending forward to ask some question. Behind her came the Queen Mother, who took Wallis's arm and began to point out the floral tributes which lay banked around the walls of the chapel. They climbed into waiting limousines which quickly sped them through the lower ward and on to the upper ward and the private apartments of the castle.

Invited guests—friends and family members—also began arriving in the upper ward after the service; Elizabeth II had disappeared into the private drawing room. Lord Mountbatten found her peeking through the door toward the Green Drawing Room, where the rest of the guests were assembling. In answer to his puzzled expression, she explained that she was trying to avoid everyone until the last minute. Soon Wallis appeared, and the Queen took her to the Green Drawing Room for the after-funeral reception. She did not remain with her widowed aunt, however; instead, she asked Lord Mountbatten to look after Wallis, and he immediately led her to a sofa, where they could rest.[52] At one point, the Queen Mother came over and sat down on the sofa beside Wallis. "I know how you feel," she said. "I've been through it myself."[53]

The Queen had arranged for a luncheon to which forty guests had been invited. Wallis recognized only a few faces and felt distinctly uncomfortable. "I sat next to the Duke of Edinburgh," Wallis told the Countess of Romanones, "who I had always imagined would be better, kinder, perhaps more human than the others, but you know, Aline, he is just a four-flusher. Not he, or anyone else, offered me any solicitude or sympathy whatsoever."[54] During the luncheon, seated between Prince Philip and Lord Mountbatten, Wallis was bombarded with questions: What did she intend to do with David's papers? With his royal souvenirs? Did she think she might return to America now to live? This was all too much for her. "Don't worry," she said, "I shan't be coming back here, if that's what you're thinking."[55]

The Duke's burial at Frogmore, sheltered among the trees below the castle, took place immediately after the luncheon. David was interred near the corner of the royal burial ground, next to a long, low hedge which separated the royal burial ground from the gravel paths leading to Queen Victoria's mausoleum and, farther along, Frogmore House, where he had spent his childhood summers. The spot was tranquil but seemed much too small to accommodate both Wallis and David. Seeing the size of the plot, Wallis turned to the Archbishop of Canterbury and said, "I realize that I'm a very thin, small woman, but I do not think that even I could fit into that miserable little narrow piece of ground." The Archbishop, somewhat startled by this piece of conversation, replied rather brusquely, "I don't see that there's much that can be done about it. You'll fit, all right." But Wallis was adamant that the hedge should be moved to provide more room. "After all, I'm not a hedge-hog, you know," she said. This unexpected burst of her famous quick wit left the Archbishop speechless; finally, Ramsey promised that he would see to it that the hedge was moved back. In the end, Wallis's concerns proved correct, and the hedge indeed had to be moved before her own grave could be dug.[56]

As soon as her husband was buried, Wallis declared that she wished to return to Paris. "Throughout her four days in Britain," writes Michael Thornton, "Wallis had imposed herself on the Royal Family to the smallest extent possible. She had politely declined to attend the trooping-the-color ceremony. She had opted out of the family weekend at Windsor, and she was now relieving them of her presence at the earliest opportunity. She had shown throughout a dignified reticence of which they had never thought her capable."[57]

No member of the Royal Family accompanied her to the airport; instead, the Queen's lady-in-waiting, the Honorable Mary Morrison, and Lord Maclean, the Lord Chamberlain, traveled with her the few miles from Windsor to Heathrow. Lord Mountbatten, hearing that Wallis was to leave at once, had wished to stay with her but decided against trying to do so for fear of upsetting the Queen. "In retrospect," he wrote in his diary, "I think it was a mistake as quite a number of the papers commented that no member of the family had gone to see her off at the airport."[58] The scene was poignant in its simplicity: Wallis, still clad in Givenchy's mourning coat, hat, and veil, walked resolutely across the tarmac and slowly climbed the steps of the airplane. She never once faltered or paused to turn and look back. Within minutes, the plane from the Queen's flight was in the air. Just after six that evening, the wheels of her car crunched along the gravel drive of her house in the Bois de Boulogne, and Wallis, alone now, entered the empty Villa, silent but for the incessant, lonely whine of Black Diamond, David's favorite pug.

46

Wallis Alone

At the age of 76, Wallis was alone. Life in her magnificent villa in the Bois de Boulogne became an ordeal. Reminders of her life with David stared at her from every room: paintings of him on the walls, his favorite chair, his pipes, the last book he had been reading, and everywhere, photographs of them together. For thirty-six years, she had devoted herself to the Duke; if at times his attentions had seemed fawning and she had attempted, in subtle ways, to break free, Wallis had always enjoyed and relished her central role. In turn, she took care of her husband: planned parties and meals to make him happy, receptions to keep him entertained, built her days around her time with him. Now that he was gone, the enormity of the void was immense. "I think," recalls the Countess of Romanones, "that the Duke was more in love with the Duchess than the Duchess with him, but by the time he was dying, she had begun to realize how much in love with him she was. He meant more to her than anyone."[1]

Whether consciously or not, Wallis mirrored the Duke's great-grandmother Queen Victoria, who mourned her beloved husband Prince Albert until the day she joined him in their mausoleum. Everything in the Windsor villa remained exactly as it had been on the last day of the Duke's life. His bottles of cologne and shaving lotion, tube of toothpaste, and other toilet articles were perched along the top of his sink and in his medicine cabinet in the bathroom, and his clothes hung in his closets. Each night, before she herself went to bed, Wallis slipped into his dark, shuttered bedroom and whispered, "Goodnight, David."[2]

She had her servants, her friends, but no one else. Relations with her own, scattered family back in America had long since evaporated through infrequent contact and simple distance. "I wish I knew them, I wish there was someone who cared for me," she told the Countess of Romanones. "But too much time has passed, it's been too long."[3]

In the first few months after the Duke's death, Wallis had to force herself to deal with the Duke's financial legacy. She was doubly lucky where the French government was concerned: Wallis was not asked to pay death duties, which at the time would have taken upwards of two-thirds of the estate; and she was reassured that she could remain in the villa in the Bois de Boulogne for the remainder of her life for the token rent she and the Duke had paid.

Another welcome, if rather sad, financial development came a year after the Duke's death when the Mill was finally sold for nearly a million dollars. Although Wallis had loved the rambling old Country estate, it had always been the Duke's retreat more than hers; now that he was gone, she had no desire to return to the poignant memories which pervaded every building and corner of her husband's garden.[4] Before she agreed to the final sale, however, Wallis imposed one term: the graves of their dogs, buried on the hillside above the stream, had to be preserved.

"It would never have occurred to the Duke to have done anything about his possessions," says David Metcalfe, son of Edward's great friend Fruity Metcalfe.[5] Indeed, Wallis now faced the formidable prospect of determining what should become of the Duke's papers, his possessions, his souvenirs, and one day, the contents of the villa in Paris. A few personal gifts were made to those whom the Duke had known well; but for the most part Wallis put off making any permanent decisions. She had never had any understanding of finances; even as a girl, mathematics had been the one subject in school which had eluded her grasp. The Duke had always told her that they were not terribly wealthy; her surprise at discovering the extent of his estate was tempered by her fear that a careless move or sudden financial crisis might wipe her out entirely. These financial uncertainties were to increasingly trouble her existence and eventually make Wallis susceptible to the ominous warnings of those around her.

For a few months, at least, Wallis experienced a bit of a thaw in her relations with the Royal Family. After the Duke's death, the Prince of Wales wrote her a warm letter praising the great-uncle he had never known. "It can't have been much more than a simple courtesy on his part," says one friend of the Duchess, "because, during the Duke's life, he had not bothered to see him for any more than an hour or two, but to Wallis, it meant so much. It was the first significant crack in the wall of ice which had separated her from his family."[6]

In return, Wallis tastefully but subtly reminded the Royal Family that although the Duke had died, she remained very much alive. In August 1972 her nephew Prince William of Gloucester, son of the Duke's brother Harry and his wife, Alice, was killed in an airplane accident. Although she did not receive an invitation to the funeral, Wallis dispatched a large spray of white lilies, accompanied by a card with the simple inscription "With love from the Duchess of Windsor."[7]

The British press had been rife with speculation over Wallis's future at the time of the Duke's death; for several months they continued to debate the abdication and the degree of punishment which David and Wallis had been made to endure. In September 1972, *Debrett's Peerage* and its editor, Patrick Montague-Smith, expressed doubt regarding the validity of the decision to withhold the style of Royal Highness from Wallis at the time of her marriage. Once again, their arguments rested on the idea that George VI had not been entitled to strip his brother of royal rank in the first place and that the letters patent of May 1937 were therefore illegal. "It is doubtful how knowledgeable the British and Commonwealth Ministers of the Crown were on constitutional and legal issues," the journal declared; "whether they consulted eminent authorities for advice before the May statement was issued; or if they did so, whether they took the advice which was offered."[8]

There was temporary hope, at least on Wallis's part, that attitudes were changing. In addition to the letter sent by the Prince of Wales, there were now frequent visits by Lord Mountbatten. On July 11, 1973, Elizabeth II dispatched a plane from the Queen's flight to collect the Duchess and bring her back to England. Mountbatten and the Duke of Kent met her at the airport and escorted her to Frogmore so that she could visit her husband's grave. By this time, the Portland stone slab had been put in place, and Wallis placed flowers next to it before joining the Queen for tea at Windsor Castle. That afternoon, she returned to Paris. The press was never informed of this meeting, the last time the Duchess would ever visit England.

But relations with the Royal Family soon turned formal. There were subtle incidents, small in themselves, which amounted, as Wallis told a friend, to little more than deliberate humiliations. Before the Duke's death, for example, the annual Christmas card from the Queen had always been signed—as were all cards from the Royal Family, "Fondest love, Lilibet." Now, following the Duke's death, they came with the very formal inscription "Elizabeth R"—the same signature reserved for officials.[9]

On May 29, Buckingham Palace had announced the engagement of Princess Anne to Lt. Mark Phillips. Wallis happened to be on holiday at Cap Ferrat in the South of France when a reporter broke the news to her. "Oh, how wonderful!" Wallis declared. "I have been reading all the rumours in the papers, but you cannot believe everything you read. This is wonderful. I have never met the young man, but of course I know Princess Anne very well." She wished the couple "all the happiness in the world."[10] But Wallis was not invited to attend Anne's wedding that November in Westminster Abbey.

Alone among the Royal Family, Lord Mountbatten continued to

make friendly overtures and pay the Duchess regular visits. Wallis, however, found little comfort in these visits, which she described to the Countess of Romanones: "It was awful," she declared after one visit. "He wanted me to make out a will right there and then, giving everything to David's family, and, of course, some to himself. He had it all worked out, just where everything should go. Well, I did my best to stick up for my rights. After all, I do want to be fair, and what should go to the Royal Family will go. But they did David out of properties which were his own."[11]

Linda Mortimer happened to visit Wallis shortly after one of Mountbatten's appearances. She found the Duchess "very angry. She said she had been thinking of leaving most of her things to Prince Charles, and some younger members of the Royal Family." Mountbatten, however, had swept through the villa, "picking up boxes and swords and trinkets," saying, "This belongs to the Royal Collection." Wallis was so irritated by this behavior that she told Linda she had changed her mind about leaving anything to the Royal Family. "Oh, please don't do that," Linda exclaimed. "That's just the way Mountbatten is. He's never been known for his tact." But Wallis was adamant.[12]

Mountbatten himself found Wallis often confused and agitated—symptoms, no doubt, not only of her increasing ill health but of her anxiety over his visits. On February 8, 1973, he noted: "She came to me quite radiant and obviously pleased to see me and said, 'Have you seen David yet?' This shook me. However I said, 'How nice that you feel he is so close. I share your feelings that he is very close to us now. Isn't it sad to think that he is now actually dead and gone?' She sadly shook her head and said, 'Yes, I suppose he has gone, but I feel he is always with me and I can keep close touch with him.' "[13]

Mountbatten seemed most concerned with convincing Wallis to turn over the Duke's papers, military insignia, and other royal mementos to the Royal Family. Some of these items were duly returned, and Mountbatten noted in his diary that he had thanked the Duchess for doing so.[14] Mountbatten also suggested that the Duchess might set up a charitable foundation to administer the Duke's estate and endow certain charities with gifts. Knowing that Wallis had taken a liking to the Prince of Wales, he even suggested that Prince Charles be the chairman.[15]

At first, Wallis seemed amenable to this idea, but whatever initial enthusiasm she felt for the project was tempered by both her growing realization that the Royal Family was not interested in her as much as they were her possessions and, perhaps more important, by the continued, overly effusive involvement of Mountbatten in the scheme. She had never really grown to trust him, and his behavior after the Duke's death simply reaffirmed her deeply held suspicions that he was determined to wrest her money and belongings from her. In December 1974 she finally wrote to Mountbatten: "As to the depositions in my will, I confirm to you once more that everything has been taken care of according to David's and my wishes, and I believe that everyone will be satisfied. There is therefore no need of your contacting my advisor in Switzerland. It is always a pleasure to see you, but I must tell you that when you leave me I am always terribly depressed by your reminding me of David's death and my own, and I should be grateful if you would not mention this any more."[16] His frequent visits and overtures to Wallis about the Duke's estate so disturbed her that eventually Dr. Jean Thin asked Mountbatten not to come to the villa any longer, as her blood pressure increased dramatically when he did so.[17]

In the first months after the Duke's death, Wallis led a quiet life. Gradually, she began to find her feet again, although the great void in her life caused by her husband's death could never be filled. She found herself concerned with little things: After nearly forty years of her carefully coiffured hairstyle, Wallis returned to parting it in the middle and having it combed straight. "I'm putting my hair back to the Mrs. Simpson days," she told Ralph G. Martin with a smile.[18] There were small dinner parties for a few guests, and she occasionally went out to dine in restaurants in Paris. When the son and daughter-in-law of her friends the Count and Countess of Romanones visited, Wallis took them to Maxim's, where, to their surprise, she proceeded to order a hamburger; even after so many years spent in Europe, her taste for things American had never completely disappeared.[19]

Before the Duke's death, the Windsors had maintained over thirty staff and servants. Now Wallis began the inevitable task of thinning out what seemed an excessive number of retainers for one woman. A few were let go simply because their positions with the Duke no longer existed; but Wallis tried to keep others who had worked for her husband, like his secretary, John Utter, and the faithful Sydney Johnson. Georges Sanegre and his wife, Ophelia, continued to supervise the running of the household, while Utter was assisted by Johanna Schutz, a young woman who acted as secretary to the Duchess.

Utter and Schutz made an odd pair, and Wallis had never been overly fond of either of them. She found Utter abusive of his position and suspected that he disliked her as much as she did him. "Utter was a two-faced, if not a multifaced, man," recalls Janine Metz, who worked closely with him during her tenure in the Windsor household. "He rarely gave you a straight answer. Her Royal Highness was quite annoyed with him and his way of doing things. He often did things thinking she did not know, and did them behind her back. The Duchess disliked him, and asked that I convey instructions to him so that she would not have to, which made him even more mad. 'Can't she tell me that herself?' he would ask me."[20]

There had apparently been some talk within the Windsor household of firing Utter from his post. Wallis herself told Janine Metz that the Duke had considered letting Utter go because he knew that his behavior upset her.[21] Even Linda Mortimer, who liked Utter and recalls him as "absolutely charming," admits that "the Duchess used to say some rather spikey things about John."[22]

Johanna Schutz, on the other hand, apparently behaved imperiously before Wallis. Shortly after the Duke's death, Wallis expressed her displeasure to the Countess of Romanones, saying that she had every intention of dismissing her secretary.[23] But other matters intervened, and Wallis found that she was not, in the words of Janine Metz, "mistress in her own house."[24]

It is impossible to know precisely what role Schutz played in the deteriorating relations between Wallis and several members of her staff or if she had a hand in the controversial firing of Sydney Johnson. Johnson, the Bahamian native who had served the Windsors with loyalty and devotion since the age of fourteen, had recently lost his wife, and it fell to him to look after their three children. At the end of his regular shift in the Windsor Villa, he returned to his home to care for his children. One day, he apparently asked if he might leave early, as he had been unable to find anyone to watch them that afternoon. According to Johnson, Wallis declared that if he left early, he should not come back again.[25] Johnson had no choice: he left, and his thirty-two years of employment came to an abrupt end.

The story of Johnson's termination has been repeated often, but several circumstances which might have led to this disagreeable outcome have been overlooked. The Duchess had never approved of Johnson's marriage to a white woman, and he was rather hurt that his wife had failed to find a place at his side in the Windsor household. "I cannot tell you how devoted and loyal Sydney was," says Janine Metz, "but he was very unhappy with the Duchess's attitudes about his marriage." Thereafter, Johnson occasionally spoke bitterly of the Duchess, and it is possible that this was used against him.[26] Wallis, increasingly forgetful of her actions and reliant on others for correct information, seems to have acted in haste, with unfortunate results. Erractic behavior of this sort was to gradually overtake the Duchess as the years passed.[27]

In April 1974, Wallis made her first visit to the United States since the Duke's death. She traveled aboard the Italian ocean liner *Rafaello* with Johanna Schutz, arriving in New York City on April 9 to a flood of curious reporters. "I don't go out as much and I'm much lonelier," she told them. She said that she had no plans to return to England; the

Royal Family "made a fuss at the time of the abdication, but I don't think they would make a fuss now. I get on well with the Royal Family."[28] She returned to the Waldorf Towers; but in her widowhood she had exchanged the lavish suite she and the Duke had once occupied for a much smaller set of rooms. Wallis was reunited with friends, went out to dinner in the city, and took in several plays on Broadway, her arrivals and departures always greeted with much interest and enthusiasm.

"When the Duchess was in New York," recalls Janine Metz, "I rang to speak with her, but Schutz had left orders at the Waldorf to transfer no calls at all to the suite. I asked the operator to put me through, but she said, 'I'm sorry Mrs. Metz, it breaks my heart, but if I connect you with the apartment and Miss Schutz hears of it, I run the risk of losing my job.'" Eventually, Madame Metz managed to visit the Duchess, but she found Schutz an unwelcome presence. "She was not nice to the Duchess," she says. "She spoke to the Duchess in a way that would have blown your ears off! Schutz would tell the Duchess, 'You sit on this little stool and don't move,' and the Duchess would comply, completely lost."[29]

Princess Margaret and her husband, Lord Snowdon, happened to be staying at the Waldorf Towers when the Duchess arrived. This was an unforeseen embarrassment; Margaret, like her sister the Queen, had been raised by her mother to despise the woman they all held responsible for George VI's premature death. The press, on learning of the two royal guests, wondered if they would meet, speculation which may have forced the issue, for Margaret and Snowdon duly called upon Wallis in her suite, where they spent fifteen minutes asking after her health and her life. Wallis, according to what Margaret would later say, seemed depressed and lonely. Back in her own suite, however, she decided to sign a photograph of herself and dispatch it to her lonely aunt. "Just to cheer her up," she declared later.[30]

Such "hollow gestures," in the words of one of the Duchess's American friends, brought little comfort.[31] It is true that Wallis had become increasingly depressed, a condition no doubt accelerated not only by her loneliness for the Duke but by her deteriorating health. Her arteriosclerosis made her forgetful, which frustrated the once-vibrant Duchess, and this frustration, along with the sudden changes in mood which sometimes accompanied the forgetting, made her seem volatile on occasion. Her greatest worry, however, was her physical health, which, in the years immediately following David's death, steadily declined.

At the end of 1972, while walking across the drawing room floor in the villa in Paris, Wallis accidentally caught the heel of her shoe at the edge of the carpet and took a nasty spill, breaking her hip. Dr. Thin placed her in the American Hospital in Paris so that she could be properly cared for. There the nurses reportedly found her "very senile." One nurse recalled: "She was very confused. She would ask the same question forty times and still not seem to understand the answer. We attached a button to her nightdress to turn off the light but she just couldn't find it, as hard as she tried. They had to put sideboards on her bed because she kept trying to climb out at night. I remember her saying once that if it wasn't for her, Elizabeth wouldn't have been Queen."[32]

Her recovery was slow, and just on the point of being mobile, she suffered a setback which left little doubt that her state of mind was rapidly failing. One day, she asked the nurse attending her, "Can you do the Charleston?"

"No, Ma'am," the nurse replied. "I never learned."

"You should," Wallis answered. "It's fun and it's easy. Watch!" She then climbed out of her bed, and before the nurse could stop her, tried to demonstrate the dance; in the process, she fell and rebroke her hip, lengthening her stay in the hospital.[33]

She had scarcely been out of the hospital for more than a few months when, in August 1973, she suffered another setback. Lady Grace Dudley had invited her friend to join her on holiday at the Hotel du Palais in Biarritz. One evening, as Wallis prepared to take her bath, she tripped on the raised edge of the sunken bathtub and fell hard against it, cracking several ribs. Once again, she was back in the hospital for a month while doctors made certain she was properly healed.

These physical ailments, coupled with her loneliness and illness, only worsened Wallis's emotional state. She rarely ate and even then had to force her food down. She had never been much of a drinker; but Wallis had always been able to handle her alcohol well. Now, however, her friends worried that she was perhaps drinking a bit too much, a concern refuted by her physician, Jean Thin. Because she was more forgetful, however, she often drank on an empty stomach, and this, coupled with her illness and interaction with medications (the Duchess was given regular doses of Valium), undoubtedly heightened the effect on her. Thin, worried greatly about these difficulties and how the alcohol was affecting Wallis's high blood pressure, finally advised that all alcohol be removed from the villa.[34]

Her friend Diana Vreeland was startled, during a visit she made to the Duchess in Paris, to find her once-vibrant friend confused and unsteady. She recalled: "The Duchess looked too beautiful, standing in the garden, dressed in a turquoise djellaba embroidered in black pearls and white pearls—marvelous—and wearing all her sapphires. She was so affectionate, a loving sort of friend—very rare, you know. . . . So we were talking after dinner, the two of us. And then suddenly she took hold of my wrist, gazed off into the distance, and said, 'Diana, I keep telling him he must not abdicate. *He must not abdicate.* No, no, no! No, no, no, I say!' Then, suddenly, after this little mental journey back more than thirty-five years, her mind snapped back to the present; she looked back at me, and we went on talking as we had been before."[35]

John Utter, whom Wallis had never liked, was fired in the fall of 1975. Wallis discovered that he had apparently worked out some sort of private arrangement with Lord Mountbatten on behalf of the British Royal Family and had secretly been handing over the Duke's papers and other objects for return to England.[36] Utter received no pension for his years of service, a circumstance which undoubtedly contributed to the bitter attitude he adopted toward his time with the Duke and Duchess and tainted the inflammatory interviews he often gave before his death in 1980.

Throughout the fall of 1975, Wallis was increasingly unwell; her old stomach ulcers, which had long bothered her, began bleeding, and Dr. Thin ordered her into the American Hospital once again. During the course of this hospital stay, Thin also discovered that Wallis was suffering from Crohn's disease, a debilitating illness which caused intense intestinal discomfort and frequent vomiting.[37] "From then on," recalled her friend Lady Mosley, "[she] was never quite well again. At times she seemed to be on the point of recovery, but it always eluded her, and her many friends could do little to help."[38]

Wallis was indeed unwell when she was released. Her senility increased dramatically; although there were often periods when she was perfectly well, her outbursts of temper and lapses of memory became more frequent. Physically, Crohn's disease left her unable to leave her bed for long periods of time; when she did venture out, inevitably her weakness caused her to stumble and fall. She refused to eat and consequently became dangerously thin. In February 1976 she was back in the American Hospital, suffering from a near-total physical collapse.[39]

For a time after her release from the hospital that spring, Wallis seemed to improve. She occasionally dined out in Paris with a friend and gave a few dinner parties at the villa. In May two newspaper photographers with telephoto lenses managed to climb the walls of the villa and photograph Wallis as she was carried onto the terrace wearing a dark print dress, a white shawl, and a string of pearls. Unaware of their presence, she sat in the sunshine, reading. The next day, the photographs appeared, and Maître Suzanne Blum, the Duchess's French lawyer, sued for invasion of privacy, litigation which eventually forced the defendants to pay Wallis damages of 80,000 francs.

In 1976, former U.S. first lady Jacqueline Kennedy Onassis, who had taken a position as an editor of the American publishing house

Viking, wrote to Wallis asking if she would be willing to collaborate on a second volume of her memoirs. She even offered to fly to Paris to meet Wallis and discuss the idea. Wallis was still capable of determining her own future, and Onassis received a reply stating that the Duchess had no desire to discuss her life with any publisher.[40]

That fall, Wallis's condition deteriorated once again. In October 1976, Queen Elizabeth the Queen Mother visited Paris. There had been some discussion that she might call on her sister-in-law; but the visit, if ever planned, failed to take place. It has been said that Dr. Thin, worried about his patient's condition, had Johanna Schutz ring the British embassy and cancel the meeting; instead, the Queen Mother sent a bouquet of white and red roses, along with a card which read: "In Friendship. Elizabeth."[41] Thin, however, contradicts this story, saying that he was never consulted over the Duchess's condition, nor did he or Schutz advise that such a visit be canceled.[42]

As Wallis continued her deterioration, Johanna Schutz prevented the Duchess's friends from calling on her. She was now in almost total control of Wallis's day-to-day life. "Everyone thought Johanna Schutz very difficult," says Linda Mortimer. "She got rather too big for her breeches, and the Duchess always used to say that she didn't like her at all." Mortimer's repeated calls to the Windsor Villa were not put through to the Duchess: Schutz told her that the Duchess was unwell; that she was out; that she could not speak at the moment. When she finally did manage to reach the Duchess, Wallis asked, "Linda, why don't you come to see me? I heard you were in Paris. Have you forgotten me also?"

"No, Duchess," Mortimer replied, "I haven't forgotten you, but it is impossible to get through to you."

"Well," Wallis said in a rather hushed, almost conspiratorial tone of voice, "if you happen to ring between one and two on Tuesdays, you might get put through to me."[43]

One day, the Countess of Romanones received a telephone call from the Duchess asking her to come visit her in Paris. She made the arrangements to fly to France and rang the Windsor villa to ask if a car would, as was customary, meet her at the airport. The Countess was told, however, that she should not come, as the Duchess was unwell and unable to receive visitors. For the next year, although she tried to reach Wallis by telephone numerous times, the Countess could never get her calls put through.[44]

Metz encountered the same difficulties in Paris as she had in New York. "I would try to ring, but not be put through to Her Royal Highness. Georges would say, with seeming great sadness, 'It is better that you don't see Her Royal Highness, and it is better that you remember her as she was.'" Nevertheless, Metz, on her visits to Paris, would ring the villa and arrange to meet Georges and his wife, Ophelia. She always found the house sadly quiet. The old butler and his wife might ask her to join them in the pantry for tea but absolutely refused to let her slip up the staircase to see the Duchess. "Georges apologized to me, but said he was under orders, and that he might lose his job if he let me see Her Royal Highness."[45]

The veil of secrecy about life in the Windsor villa, and the Duchess herself, drew higher and higher. In April 1978, Maître Suzanne Blum fired Schutz, and Wallis's friends temporarily found their access to her much easier.

Janine Metz managed to reach the Duchess, and Wallis quickly asked her to come around for dinner. Just before they were to sit down, Wallis looked around the room in desperation. "Oh," she said, "the Duke is so late. He must have been detained somewhere, but it is strange not to have him call." She soon forgot this momentary lapse and embarked on a somewhat confused conversation. "She seemed to forget what she said two minutes after she had said it," Metz recalls sadly.

At the end of their evening, a maid appeared to help escort Wallis to her bedroom and assist her, but the Duchess turned around and said, "You can go. Madame Metz will take care of me." Janine Metz helped Wallis undress and change into her lingerie, then attended to her evening toilette, cleaning her face with lotion and brushing out her long hair. "Her skin was pink and fresh, and she was truly at peace," Metz recalls. She helped Wallis into bed and found that she was "like a feather, there was nothing much left of her." They spoke for several minutes. Finally, Wallis took Madame Metz's hand in hers and said, "You know, Janine, you are the only one I trust totally. Please stay with me." Madame Metz switched off the lights and sat in the darkened room, watching as the Duchess quickly fell asleep. After several hours, however, she had to leave and crept out of the room. "To this day," she says, "I feel very remorseful that I simply didn't stay the whole night."[46]

On February 23, 1979, Wallis was back in the American Hospital for the removal of an intestinal blockage. Three months later, a bacterial infection forced her return. The situation turned out to be much more serious than first expected, and Dr. Thin was forced to keep the Duchess under hospital care for four months. On September 14, she was finally released. News reporters, camped out at the hospital entrance, caught her exit: a rather sad, frail old woman, a shawl draped around her bent shoulders, her step slow and uncertain. When she saw their cameras, Wallis stopped for a moment, smiled, and raised her hand in an unsteady wave before entering her car. This was the last glimpse the public would ever have of the Duchess of Windsor.

47

Last Years

Two years after the Duke of Windsor's death in 1974, Frances Donaldson's much-anticipated biography *Edward VIII* was published to great critical acclaim. However, Maître Suzanne Blum, the Duchess's French lawyer, was greatly upset with the result; she was angry that although Donaldson had begun the book during the Duke's lifetime, she had apparently made no attempt to consult either David or Wallis. The Windsors' friends were, for the most part, also neglected, and as a result, Donaldson had relied heavily on English sources. Not surprisingly, this biography thus tended to reflect the views of the Royal Family and the court.

Blum claimed that "it would take a 400 page book" to answer the inaccuracies she alleged in Donaldson's biography.[1] The situation did not improve a few years later when, in May 1978, Verity Lambert, director of drama at Thames TV, approached Blum and informed her that Simon Raven would be writing a television script based on Donaldson's book. Blum immediately tried to intervene; if she could not halt production, she insisted that she have full script approval. Thames TV, however, was unwilling to comply with her demands, and the series, *Edward and Mrs. Simpson,* duly aired to large audiences that fall in England, with Cynthia Harris as Wallis, Edward Fox as Edward, and Dame Peggy Ashcroft as Queen Mary. According to Verity Lambert, Maître Blum's very public objections only created more interest in the series. "We could never have bought such publicity," he declared.[2]

Blum, however, was not finished. On November 20, 1978—after two episodes of the series had already aired on British TV—she released a press statement which declared that the series was "largely and essentially a fable based on an incorrect or distorted interpretation of the facts." To Blum, every hour included a "wave of calumnies." To counter these alleged inaccuracies, she announced that a famous—but unnamed—French historian would soon publish the couples' private papers and letters.[3]

"People," Blum declared, "will be amazed to discover how seriously they have been fooled. Mrs. Simpson, the Duchess of Windsor, has been portrayed as a cheap adventuress, determined to get hold of the Duke of Windsor, determined to marry the King and destroy the King. The reverse is true. She was the reluctant partner. What has particularly distressed her—and myself—has been the allegation that she was Edward's mistress. This was quite untrue. The King did not want a mistress, and if he had, no doubt he would not have abdicated. He wanted a wife and the support of this one woman for the rest of his life."[4]

The enormous publicity over the Thames TV series was the first time most people heard of Maître Suzanne Blum. As much as the Duchess of Windsor herself, Blum remains a figure of great controversy: Was she a loyal and dedicated servant to the Duchess in her failing years, devoted to preserving both Wallis's life and her memory; or was she something far more sinister—a malevolent force in the Duchess's life, separating her from her few remaining friends, instructing that Wallis be kept alive by any means necessary, and presiding over the questionable dispersal of the Windsor estate?

Suzanne Blumel had been born in 1898, in the tiny provincial French village of Niort. She was an unusual young woman, gifted, headstrong, and determined to overcome any prejudices attached both to her sex and to her Jewish heritage. Exceptionally intelligent, she graduated from the University of Poitiers in 1921; that same year, she married lawyer Paul Weill, who later worked as the Paris representative of the London firm of Allen and Overy, the Duke of Windsor's solicitors.

At the outbreak of the Second World War, she had fled occupied Paris and studied law at Columbia University in New York City. In her exile, she spent much of her time and energy trying to win the release of former French premier Léon Blum, a great friend of her brother's who had been imprisoned for alleged treachery in the fall of the Third Republic. At the end of the war, she and her husband returned to France, where, having legally changed her name to Suzanne Blum, she took on the formal legal title of maître, or master, and began her illustrious career. Her list of famous clients included Rita Hayworth, Charlie Chaplin, Jack Warner, Darryl F. Zanuck, and Walt Disney. When her first husband died, Blum was married to Gen. Georges Spillmann, a distinguished soldier and noted Arabic scholar.

Blum, according to one reporter, was "a woman of incisive manner and sharp brains. Diminutive, she still dominates by her presence. Her face is unlined, her complexion excellent and her features bear evidence of her once having been a considerable beauty—and she manages to look elegant, even in her lawyer's robes."[5]

In 1979, Blum asked Michael Bloch to write several books on the Duke and Duchess of Windsor. His view of the lawyer, whom he considered a close friend, is entirely favorable: "The Maître was an extraordinary personality, who throughout her long career had taken the causes of her clients to heart, and she felt strongly that the Windsors had been mistreated and maligned and that it was her duty to protect their interests and reputation staunchly. She was a chivalrous woman of great ability and it was easy to understand why the Duchess so valued her."[6]

The formidable quality was not imagined; whether she was challenging British television or suing reporters and photographers for invasion of the Duchess's privacy, few who came into contact with Maître Blum were left with any doubt as to her strength of will. Many of those who knew the Duchess well have nothing but praise for Blum. According to Dr. Jean Thin, she has been made into "a grotesque character" by writers. "I got on perfectly well with Madame Blum."[7] And the Countess of Romanones says: "She was a marvelous woman, very badly treated by writers and other people. She protected the Duchess and never resisted my attempts to see the Duchess."[8]

Others, however, found her less pleasant. Mrs. Linda Mortimer dealt with Blum on several occasions, trying to win permission to visit the Duchess. "I think she was a perfectly dreadful woman," she says. She recalls that during the few times she was allowed to visit the Windsor Villa, many valuable objects—the Duchess's collection of gold boxes, pieces of Fabergé, important paintings, and even the wedding present from Linda's parents to the Windsors—were missing. Because Blum was firmly in control of the villa, Mortimer has little doubt that she was responsible for the disposal of the items.[9] In fact, as Michael Bloch has confirmed, Blum found such sales a financial necessity. Although the Duchess's estate was substantial, there was not much in the way of liquid assets, and the medical expenses for Wallis's care as well as the maintenance of the villa and its staff required currency which could not otherwise be obtained.[10]

More than one writer has commented on the similarities between the Duchess of Windsor and her French lawyer: Both were strong women, of independent spirit, who have been largely overshadowed by negative publicity. In truth, Blum appears to have been genuinely devoted to the Windsors, especially the Duchess. "She was very forceful," admits Michael Bloch, "and perhaps became a little too adamant in her protection, but she was only doing what she thought to be the proper thing."[11] Unfortunately, many of the painful incidents involving friends of the Duchess being denied visits seem to have come about at the hands of Johanna Schutz rather than Blum. For a time after Schutz's firing, the lawyer did indeed allow the Duchess's friends to visit; Wallis's illness in 1979, however, effectively put an end to these occasions, as Dr. Thin advised Blum that it was unwise to excite the Duchess in any way.[12]

By 1980, Wallis had deteriorated to a pitiable state. Shortly after the Duke's death, she had spoken with the Countess of Romanones, reminding her that her own aunt Bessie had lived to be a hundred years old. "Do you suppose I'll live that long, Aline?" she asked sadly. "I hope not."[13] Now, midway through her ninth decade of life, she found herself scarcely able to move. Circulatory problems meant she could no longer use her hands or feet, and she had to be carried through the house. She was still awakened each morning, bathed, and dressed by the nurse on duty; her long hair was carefully combed out and styled into a bun at the rear of her head. Once the most celebrated hostess of her age, Wallis—who had planned and presided over elegant dinner parties—was now spoon-fed by her nurse.[14] She spent most of her days in a wheelchair, alone. Occasionally, she might ask the nurse to take her to the window and open it so that she could hear the birds singing in the garden beyond.[15]

Although her periods of lucidity were fewer now, she had not completely lost her sense of reason. "She was not in a coma," recalls Dr. Thin, "and had moments of awareness which to anyone of her vitality and love of life must have been unendurable."[16] Once, as a little girl, she had been terrified of being left alone, abandoned to the dark night; now she was condemned to this twilight existence, carefully nursed and provided with the best medical care. Having expressed her dread of living to an old age, Wallis now endured the tragic, inescapable fate that she was powerless to prevent.

Throughout, the Duchess's friends continued to phone the villa and beg to be allowed to visit. Inevitably, however, Georges would sadly report that the Duchess was unwell and unable to receive callers. He kept her friends at bay by order of Blum. "Maître Blum," says Dr. Thin, "knew better than to expose her friend the Duchess in her decline, to the curiosity of visitors who had no other motivation than gossip. Maître Blum knew how the Duchess was keen of preserving her 'look,' and how much she would have hated to be exposed unwillingly when she was no more her real self. I believe that, especially at the end of her life, the Duchess preferred being protected from unwanted visits. Maître Blum protected the Duchess, and as long as the Duchess expressed her feelings, she relied gratefully on Maître Blum's protection."[17]

Thin himself had warned that visits were not advisable. "The sudden increase of the Duchess's blood pressure after being exposed to emotional stress was a fact that became more and more threatening," Thin says. "Some visitors caused these variations more than others."[18]

Wallis's friends, however, were not so easily put off. Diana, Lady Mosley; Madame Janine Metz; Princess Ghislaine de Polignac; Aline, Countess of Romanones; and Mrs. Linda Mortimer all repeatedly phoned the villa, begging to be connected with the Duchess, only to be told that she was unwell.[19] Eventually, however, Blum relented and allowed the Countess of Romanones to pay several visits. "I rather suspect," says Linda Mortimer, "that Maître Blum let Aline visit in an attempt to placate the rest of us."[20]

It had been several years since Aline Romanones had visited Wallis in Paris; the first thing the Countess noticed was the overwhelming silence of the villa. Previously, the yapping of the dogs had echoed through the rooms; now the pugs had all gone. She found Wallis sitting in a wheelchair in the boudoir, dressed in a vividly embroidered blue silk brocade dressing gown, clear-eyed and coherent. Her hair had been arranged, makeup applied to her features, and she wore a favorite sapphire necklace to match the color of the dressing gown.[21]

A few months later, the Countess returned to the villa. She was shocked by Wallis's appearance. Her hair, which had formerly been dyed and set, was now completely white; unbound, it fell around her shoulders. She wore no makeup and no jewels. "Who are you, my dear?" Wallis asked when she entered the room. The Duchess turned her head toward the window. "Look at the way the sun is lighting the trees," she said softly. "You can see so many different colors. Tell David to come in. He wouldn't want to miss this."[22]

Wallis's decline from this point on was rapid. By the time the Countess next visited, the Duchess had gone completely blind. She lay in her bed, her long white hair now brushed into a neat ponytail. The Countess thought her skin looked "surprisingly fresh." She held out her hand in greeting, but Wallis could not see it, nor could she communicate with her friend.[23]

Janine Metz was one of the last of these women to visit the Duchess. Through sheer determination and repeated telephone calls and letters, she won permission to come within the carefully guarded doors of the villa. Wallis lay in bed. "She was like a little bird," Metz recalls, "all shrivelled up. I came up very close to the bed, bent down, and kissed her. She seemed to have no idea who I was, or even that I was in the room." Metz leaned over her, reached out and took one of Wallis's hands in hers, and whispered, "I am Janine. I am here with you." She pressed the Duchess's hand, and Wallis pressed back, her only way of communicating.[24]

By the beginning of 1984, Wallis was completely paralyzed. Her inability to swallow meant that the daily feedings by the nurses had stopped, replaced with an intravaneous drip which would sustain the

Duchess for the last two years of her life. Dr. Thin regularly visited the villa to examine the Duchess. Daily, the nurses changed her drip, cleaned and washed Wallis, swabbed her gums, ears, and nose, massaged her arms and legs, and turned her to prevent bedsores. Contrary to some reports, Thin says, "her colour remained normal. She was not cyanosed, nor sun-tanned, nor pigmented by Addison's disease."[25]

Only one man outside the narrow circle controlled by Maître Blum managed to penetrate the thick veil of secrecy covering the Duchess's last years. Once each week, the iron gates to the Windsor villa parted to allow Rev. Jim Leo, of the American Cathedral in Paris, entrance. In the cool, brooding house, he would ascend the marble staircase to the second floor, walk through the boudoir, still piled with books and papers, and quietly open the door to the Duchess's bedroom. The once-vibrant blue silk on the walls had faded, washed by the sunlight that spilled through the windows. Here, surrounded by photographs of the Windsors from their happier days, Leo prayed before the silent, curled figure that lay on the bed before him, the centerpiece of the twentieth century's most famous romance, unable to speak to, see, or comprehend the world which had passed her by.

Wallis died on April 24, 1986, of heart failure arising from a recent bout with pneumonia. She was just two months short of her ninetieth birthday. "Death," Rev. Jim Leo told the press, "came round the corner as a very gentle friend, and she was content, she was happy."[26] Her body was washed and carefully laid out on her bed; as with her husband, no autopsy was performed on the Duchess.[27] Georges Sanegre supervised as the frail body, clad in a simple black dress, was gently placed in the plain oak coffin when it arrived at the villa.[28] Her only adornment was a jeweled belt, one of several Wallis had purchased in the 1960s from designer Kenneth Jay Lane.[29]

On Sunday, April 27, the lord chamberlain, on Queen Elizabeth II's instructions, flew to Paris to collect the Duchess's body and return with it to England for burial alongside the Duke at Frogmore. Georges and Ophelia Sanegre, along with the remaining staff, stood on the steps of the villa, watching in silence as the coffin, covered with a spray of white lilies, was carried from the house and placed in a waiting hearse. Within two hours, the plane had landed at RAF Benson, and Wallis entered, for the last time, the country which had rejected her fifty years before.

Prince Richard, Duke of Gloucester, waited to escort the body to Windsor. With television lenses and cameras trained on the plane, the coffin was unloaded and, carried by eight members of the Royal Air Force, placed in the hearse. A motorcycle policeman led the small motorcade as it left the base, followed by a limousine carrying the

Duke of Gloucester and, finally, the hearse. Small crowds of curious onlookers had gathered around the streets in Windsor, watching in silence as the cars sped through the town and disappeared into the castle. Eight members of the Welsh Guards carried Wallis's coffin up the steps to the west door of St. George's Chapel, through the chapel itself, and on into the adjacent Albert Memorial Chapel, where it would lie until her funeral.

Wallis's funeral took place at three-thirty in the afternoon on Tuesday, April 29, at St. George's Chapel. One hundred seventy-five guests received invitations, including the Duchess's friends Lady Mosley, the Countess of Romanones, the Duke and Duchess of Marlborough, Lady Alexandra Metcalfe, and Grace, Lady Dudley. Wallis's country of birth was represented by U.S. ambassador to the Court of St. James's Charles Price. Each guest received a simple two-page program whose white cover bore the inscription "Funeral of the Duchess of Windsor" as well as a black cross.

The constable of Windsor Castle, marshal of the RAF Sir John Grandy, and the Military Knights of Windsor Castle formed the guard of honor that accompanied Wallis's coffin as eight Welsh Guardsmen, attired in scarlet tunics, bore it upon their shoulders down the nave of St. George's Chapel and into the choir aisle. Wallis's body rested on the same catafalque before the high altar that had borne her husband's coffin fourteen years earlier. Atop the simple coffin was a wreath of yellow and white madonna lilies from the queen.

Sixteen members of the Royal Family attended Wallis's funeral. The Queen was accompanied by her husband, the Duke of Edinburgh. The Prince of Wales wore formal mourning clothes, while his wife, Diana, Princess of Wales, in the words of Lady Mosley, "looked too beautifully lovely" in her simple black dress, coat, and hat. The Queen Mother, who had despised her sister-in-law for half a century, appeared unusually serene.[30]

The service began with the choir intoning "I Am the Resurrection and the Life," the anthem which traditionally opens all royal funerals. This was followed by Psalm 90, a blessing, and then a prayer, read by Dr. Michael Mann, the dean of Windsor. At the conclusion of the lesson, taken from 2 Corinthians, the choir sang "Thou Wilt Keep Him in Perfect Peace." A number of prayers followed, ending with the words of the dean of Windsor: "O Father of all, we pray to Thee for those whom we love, but see no longer. Grant them Thy peace; let light perpetual shine upon them; and in Thy loving wisdom and Almighty power work in them the good purpose of Thy perfect will; through Jesus Christ Our Lord, Amen. Almighty God, Father of all mercies and giver of all comfort: Deal graciously, we pray Thee, with those who mourn; that casting every care on Thee, they may know the consolation of Thy love; through Jesus Christ our Lord, Amen." The congregation sang the hymn "Lead Us, Heavenly Father, Lead Us" before the Archbishop of Canterbury pronounced a final blessing and prayed for Wallis. At the conclusion of the service, to the organ music of Sir Edward Elgar's *Enigma Variations,* Wallis's coffin was carried out of the chapel into the bright afternoon sunlight. The service, which had lasted just twenty-eight minutes, was undoubtedly unique: Not once was the name of the deceased—in any form—mentioned during her own funeral. "It was the most impersonal funeral service I have ever been to," says Linda Mortimer.[31]

The coffin was lifted into a hearse and, with the Royal Family and the few remaining members of the Duchess's household following, driven down the hill to Frogmore, where she was to be laid to rest beside the Duke. A simple service was conducted by Rev. Jim Leo at the graveside before the coffin was lowered into the ground. The Princess of Wales was seen to wipe tears from her eyes as she mourned this outcast member of the Royal Family whom she had never met, and Prince Charles appeared deeply moved.[32] At least one source reports that Queen Elizabeth herself momentarily broke down and cried.[33] "If the Queen wept," says one of the Duchess's friends who attended the funeral, "they were tears of guilt, not grief."[34]

After the funeral, as the late-April sunshine slowly faded from the sky, Lady Mosley wandered through the Horseshoe Cloister, which encircled the steps leading to the west door of St. George's Chapel, examining the "masses" of flowers which had been arranged there.[35] One wreath, from the Duke and Duchess of Kent, had a handwritten note attached reading: "Eddie and Katharine." Another arrangement bore a card rather formally inscribed "From Her Royal Highness Princess Alice, Duchess of Gloucester and Their Royal Highnesses the Duke and Duchess of Gloucester." There were floral tributes from Wallis's friends as well as hundreds of bouquets and arrangements, large and small, from people who had never known the Duchess but who had been moved by the story of her life. "The Heart Has Its Reasons" read one card tied to a wreath, while a second was dedicated simply "To a Gracious Lady." Of all the wreaths, perhaps the most poignant bore a note reading "From RAF Unit III 1942–1945 Now Nassau Association." Below the inscription was a poem that paid tribute to Wallis's work in the Bahamas:

> Gentle treasures of memories fall,
> Heartfelt remembrances from us all,
> rest in peace our dear Duchess. . . .[36]

Epilogue

W HEN THE DUCHESS DIED IN 1986," writes Piers
Brendon, "there were curious manifestations of public grief, sternly
discouraged by the Palace, which to the last had denied her the
coveted title HRH, and gave her a very private funeral indeed. It was
the culmination of fifty years' vindictiveness, something which the
royal image-makers had difficulty in reconciling with the saccharine
benevolence they attributed to the Queen Mother. But somehow they
managed to incorporate the Duchess into the beatific myth. The nation
liked the notion of royal happy families."[1]

That myth, however, was soon shattered. Within a week of
Wallis's death, Maître Blum authorized publication of the Windsors'
private correspondence. Consisting mainly of letters between Wallis
and David written between 1934 and 1937, it would form the centerpiece of a book to be edited by author Michael Bloch, who had previously published two works on the Windsors. The private battles Wallis
and David had waged with the Royal Family were exposed to public
scrutiny, as were the affectionate feelings the couple had shared.

In death, as in the last years of her life, Wallis was still guarded by
Blum. In 1973 the Duchess had signed over her personal power of attorney to the French lawyer.[2] In 1975, before her health went into its final
decline, Wallis gave most of her private papers to Blum, along with permission to publish them in an effort to present her and David's side of
their story. It is not clear if Wallis realized that her private love letters
were to be included in this agreement, and her mental state at the time
was already rapidly deteriorating. It is known that Blum certainly
began to read through the papers, for she was able to discuss their contents at the time of the production of *Edward and Mrs. Simpson*.[3]

Wallis also made a new will, under the direction of Blum, in 1975,
in which she appointed the Pasteur Institute in France her principal
beneficiary. The Pasteur Institute, a respected medical-research foundation, seems a somewhat curious choice, and Michael Bloch confirms

that it was chosen largely on the advice of Blum.[4] The Duchess, however, had always supported cancer research, and it seems likely that her decision was reached with this thought in mind. Then, too, it was, as Michael Bloch has pointed out, a way of expressing her gratitude to France for the years of low rent on the villa in the Bois de Boulogne as well as her continued tax-free status.[5]

On March 30, 1973, Wallis had signed an agreement giving the French government nearly 140 important pieces of furniture and works of art from the Windsor villa. This had come about at the suggestion of her friend Gerald van der Kemp, curator at Versailles and the man who had helped craft her appreciation and knowledge of French antiques. The pieces, which were transferred to the government following her death, included all of the Louis XVI furniture, estimated in 1973 at £750,000; several of her gold boxes, estimated at £25,000 each, which are now in the collection of the Musée du Louvre; a Stubbs painting which had hung in the library, formerly in the collection of the Curzon family, which went to Versailles; and some important pieces of eighteenth-century porcelain, which were donated to the National Ceramics Museum.[6]

In the late 1970s, Blum began quietly selling pieces of furniture, porcelain, and works of art from the Windsor villa to help pay for Wallis's medical expenses. A few were placed on the open auction market, while others were offered to several of the Windsors' friends. Nathan and Joanne Cummings, for example, purchased the table from the dining room, along with silver pieces and the famous Meissen Flying Tiger dinner service. By this time, Wallis, lying upstairs and completely helpless, was no longer able to visit the first floor and had no idea that the rooms below were slowly being stripped of their grand fittings.

The remaining collections in the villa, upon Wallis's death, became entangled in the disposition of her estate. Her principal beneficiary, the Pasteur Institute, had no use for them, and plans were made to auction off the furniture, paintings, and porcelain. It was at this point, in the summer of 1986, that Mohammed al Fayed, Egyptian-born owner of the Ritz Hotel in Paris as well as fabled Harrod's department store in London, stepped in and purchased the contents of the villa outright.

Al Fayed also managed, through the generous offer of Paris mayor Jacques Chirac, to obtain a fifty-year lease of the Windsor villa at a nominal cost. The lease, however, came with a condition: He was to restore the house completely, as it had been in the Windsors' time, at his own considerable expense. "I am in love with the Windsors' love story," he said in an interview.[7] He declared his intention of creating a museum dedicated to the Duke and Duchess, using the contents which he had purchased from Wallis's estate. It was to be a permanent memorial to the royal couple that had lived within its walls.

With the villa under restoration and the majority of the contents purchased by Al Fayed, thoughts turned to the only other item left in Wallis's estate: her fabled collection of jewelry. David had always expressed the wish that Wallis's jewels—inscribed with so many private tokens of affection—be broken up after her death so that no other woman could wear them.[8] But neither David nor Wallis had made any such provision for their dispersal. After the Duke's death, designer Hardy Amies asked the Duchess if she would be willing to leave a piece of her jewelry to the Victoria and Albert Museum in London. "I guess I could spare a leopard," she offered. Not realizing that she meant one of her famous jeweled panther bracelets by Jeanne Touissant for Cartier, Amies politely declined. Only later did he realize his mistake.[9]

At one time, Wallis had considered leaving the pieces to Prince Charles, hoping that his future wife might wear them. But Lord Mountbatten's aggressive campaign for furniture, porcelain, boxes, swords, and paintings had left Wallis bitter. Lady Monckton, visiting Wallis in the early 1970s, suggested another course of action: "Princess Alexandra and the Duchess of Kent are loyal, hard-working girls, both of them," she told Wallis, "and they haven't many jewels. Unless you've made other plans, you might remember them."[10]

Wallis did indeed leave a few pieces of her jewelry to Princess Alexandra; Katharine, the Duchess of Kent; and Marie Christine, Princess Michael of Kent. A few other pieces were left to Aline, Countess of Romanones, and to the Baronne de Cabrol.[11] It was left to Blum to determine the fate of the remaining pieces. Rather than break them up and sell the stones, she decided that they would bring more intact at auction; as all of the money would go to the Pasteur Institute, it was hoped that this deviation from the Duke of Windsor's wishes would, in the end, prove of greater benefit.

Blum cannot have anticipated the worldwide interest in the auction of Wallis's jewels. Sotheby's, in charge of the sale, printed an initial fifteen thousand catalogs; when these quickly sold out, they were forced to republish.[12] When the public exhibition opened in Sotheby's Manhattan showrooms in March 1987, the lines to view the fabled jewels grew so long that people were repeatedly turned away. Police were eventually called out to monitor the situation, and viewing was limited to fifteen minutes in order to move the massive crowds through the building.[13] The exhibit also traveled to Palm Beach, Monaco, and Geneva, where the actual auction would take place; a London exhibition was deliberately avoided, as Sotheby's officials felt it would somehow be disrespectful to the Royal Family.[14]

The auction, held beneath a large red-and-white-striped marquee erected in the gardens of the Hotel Beau Rivage, along the shore of Lake Geneva, began precisely at nine on the evening of April 2. Fifteen hundred people filled the tent, among them Prince Serge of Yugoslavia; Prince Dimitri of Yugoslavia; Princess Firyal of Jordan; the Princess of Naples; Infanta Beatriz of Spain; Baroness Thyssen-Bornemisza; and Wallis's friends Aline, Countess of Romanones and Grace, Lady Dudley. Another seven hundred people watched the auction on closed-circuit television in the hotel's ballroom, and satellite links provided coverage to New York and London. Over 250 journalists, fashion experts, and television reporters surrounded the tent and hotel, their arc lights and flashbulbs providing a certain theatrical touch.[15]

There were to be two sessions. Nicholas Rayner, Sotheby's Geneva jewelry expert, began the auction with a ruby-and-sapphire-bead clip. The estimate was 7,000 francs; it sold for 65,000 francs, the first sign that the Duchess of Windsor's jewels would likely break all previous auction records. One by one, piece by piece, Wallis's collection was dispersed: pearls to Japan, diamonds to New York, amethysts to Los Angeles. Actress Elizabeth Taylor, who had previously admired the large diamond-and-platinum Prince of Wales's feathers brooch, purchased it for $567,000. Other pieces went to fashion designer Calvin Klein and Hollywood divorce lawyer Marvin Mitchelson. With each lot, the level of excitement grew. "People," wrote author Dominick Dunne, "realized that they were present at an event, engaged in the heady adventure of watching rich people acting rich, participating in a rite available only to them, the spending of big money, without a moment's hesitation or consideration. . . . Powdered bosoms heaved in fiscal excitement at big bucks spent. Each time the bidding got into the million-dollar range, for one of the ten or so world-class stones in the collection, the tension resembled the frenzy at a cockfight."[16] At the end of the two days, the auction had raised $50,281,887, more than seven times its presale estimates. The money was welcome at the Pasteur Institute, which it used to fund AIDS research.

Perhaps it was fortunate that Maître Suzanne Blum, who had so zealously guarded their legacy and relentlessly defended the Duke and Duchess in what seemed to be the eternal campaign waged against them by the British Royal Family, died in January 1994, before what one of the Windsors' friends has termed "the Royal Family's final revenge."[17] In 1996, British and American television premiered a new documentary on Wallis and David, a two-hour look at their lives after the abdication. In keeping with the general tone of both books and television specials following Wallis's death, this program was highly critical in tone; but it had one distinction which set it apart from all other media attention: *Edward on Edward* had been written and produced by Prince Edward, Queen Elizabeth II's youngest son.

Aside from a few brief comments scattered over the years in memoirs and the occasional interview, this program was the first attempt by any member of the Royal Family to address the legacy of the Duke and Duchess. Coming from Elizabeth II's son and the Queen Mother's grandson, it was presumed to carry some form of royal approval as well as to convey their true feelings about the Windsors. Prince Edward interviewed many of the Windsors' friends, along with diplomats, those involved in the Nazi plot in Spain and Portugal in 1940, and former members of the household in Paris.

Others, however, were wary of participating in any film on the Windsors produced by a member of the very family which had never forgiven either the Duke or the Duchess for what some choose to perceive as their offenses. Several of the Windsors' acquaintances refused to cooperate, while others required many reassurances. Janine Metz at first declined Prince Edward's request. The Prince, however, made several overtures to the former secretary, declaring that it would be "the film of reconciliation" between his family and the Duke and Duchess and assuring her that what she said would be faithfully reproduced in the final version. With some trepidation, Metz finally acquiesced and submitted to the filmed interviews, which would be pieced together, along with new footage and old newsreels, to form the documentary.[18]

Janine Metz was one of the specially invited audience who attended the American premiere at the Museum of Television and Radio in New York City in June 1996. Many of the Americans who had participated in the film were there as well, along with Prince Edward himself, who had come from London for the event. After thanking the audience, Edward settled in to watch the documentary along with his guests.

A few weeks earlier, in an article in *Hello!* designed to coincide with the British television premiere, the Prince had inadvertently given a taste of what was to come. "People," he declared of the Duke and Duchess, "would enthuse about him, but could say little about her. She was a much more difficult character to understand or get close to. Perhaps contrary to expectations, she seems to have been a much more reserved and secretive person. Then again, she might have been a bit superficial—fun, quick-witted, gossipy, with no real personality."[19] This rather unsubtle suggestion would set the tone for the documentary which followed.

If there was any lingering doubt that this was to be the Royal Family's view of the Duke and Duchess's story, it was quickly put to rest. In the opening sentences of the program, Prince Edward spoke of the "appalling shock" which David had "inflicted upon his family." He proceeded to add that there were still many "who cannot forgive him or her for that," shifting the blame for the abdication crisis toward Wallis, in complete contradiction of the historical record.

The Prince's commentary was emphatic as to the effects of the abdication. He declared that it had brought David "into conflict with everyone from the government to the man in the streets," again ignoring the historical divide in public opinion at the time. He was particularly hard on the Duchess: "Wallis is often depicted as hard, ambitious and grasping," he announced. "There were other, much worse descriptions flying around as well." Edward himself apparently felt no need to correct these assumptions or present alternatives to them, leaving these "much worse descriptions" to the imaginations of his viewers. Tales of the Windsors' frivolous style of life, their obsession with money, and their sordid friendships were repeated with little or no attempt to present an alternative view. Wallis's relationship with Jimmy Donahue was declared outright to have been an affair, and John Richardson was allowed to repeat stories from Donahue himself without any warning that the Woolworth heir had been an acknowledged liar. Worst of all was Edward's treatment of the Nazi plot to kidnap the Windsors: Speaking of the Duke's requests that Wallis be received and that he be given a proper job, he says, in absolute opposition to the written record, that "it is quite possible that the Duchess was behind much of it."[20] Few of those interviewed spoke favorably of the Duke and Duchess, and those who did were reduced to brief appearances. In contradiction to what Prince Edward had promised, Janine Metz found that virtually none of her serious comments about the life of the Windsors, their charity work and her correction of the rumors surrounding them—the very reasons she had agreed to cooperate with the Prince—had been used.

At the end of the premiere, Metz felt so betrayed that she quickly exited the theater. Prince Edward spotted her and asked, "How did you like the film?"

"I feel sick at what I've just seen and heard," she told him. She began to explain how disappointed she was in the treatment of the Windsors when John Richardson approached. He began to put his arm around her shoulder, but Madame Metz pushed him away. "How dare you come to me after saying the lies that you said!" she declared.

Meanwhile, Prince Edward continued to stand in silence. He appeared utterly confused and stared pointedly at the floor as Metz walked away. "I don't think anyone had ever spoken to him before with such frankness," she says. A short time later, he approached the former secretary once again, asking why she was so upset.

"That film was a lie from the beginning to the end!" she told him.

She felt particularly betrayed that the gossip about the Windsors seeking discounts and not paying their bills—rumors which she had carefully corrected in the portions of her interview which had been edited out—had been given such prominence in a film which she had been told was to correct the misconceptions. The Prince tried to object, but Madame Metz was clearly angry and, as she says, "filled with great sorrow at how he had betrayed the Duke and Duchess." "Of course," she said to Edward, "you couldn't do anything else because of your family."[21]

Prince Edward's cameras would, ironically, be among the last to capture the restored interior of the Windsor Villa in Paris. Mohammed al Fayed had taken great pains to faithfully copy everything as it had been during the Windsors' lives. He managed to repurchase many of the pieces which Blum had sold and even successfully bid on the Duke's ceremonial swords and military souvenirs which had been auctioned off along with Wallis's jewels in Geneva in April 1987. Al Fayed transformed the former secretaries' office on the first floor into a small Windsor museum, with glass shelves and display cases holding personal memorabilia, including letters, their scrapbooks, and some of the hundreds of photographs and papers which had been discovered beneath the mahogany cover of the Duke's bathtub. An additional two museum rooms were created in the basement to display the royal souvenirs.[22]

Al Fayed decided he wished to live in the Windsor Villa, and so the attic story was converted into a small flat. The restoration was complete, and cataloging of the collection well under way, but al Fayed did little to encourage visits to the house. Although he encouraged and welcomed celebrity visits, he proved less amenable to those with a genuine interest in the Duke and Duchess. Erna Bringe, a member of the Duke and Duchess of Windsor Society in America, recalls: "I did have his approval at one time to visit the house, but I had to find ten others willing to pay the price to stay at the Paris Ritz in order to make it worth his while."[23]

For those who did gain admittance, al Fayed had published a small souvenir booklet describing the restoration of the house and the collection within. "It is certain," he declared confidently, "that future generations will come here to inspect the souvenirs of the most famous love story of the 20th century, in the way that tourists go to Verona to speculate on the exact position of the balcony under which Romeo professed his love for Juliet. If we had not acted swiftly the furniture, the works of art, the effects and personal objects of the Duke and Duchess would have disappeared to the four corners of the globe."[24]

Despite his assurances that his Windsor museum would survive for "future generations," al Fayed, in 1997, made the startling announcement that, in September, Sotheby's would auction off the entire contents of the restored villa. "I think time for me to enjoy the house," he explained in an interview, "because it's difficult with five kids just to live in a museum. . . . I think its time for me, for the whole world to enjoy, you know, I think everyone can have a souvenir from the love story of the century, its nice to restruct all that and just bring it back to life for people and for future generations." Christiane Sherwen, in charge of the Windsor archive al Fayed had assembled, added: "What do you do? The place is too small to be a museum and you cannot have people passing through and so, as with all human things, it's going to be dispersed. . . . One would maybe like to keep it together, but it's not a real proposition."[25]

These rather peculiar explanations raised more than a few eyebrows. Mohammed al Fayed certainly did not need the money which the sale of the Windsor possessions would bring; nor was his declaration that his children needed additional space any more convincing. Al Fayed was wealthy enough to purchase five separate villas in Paris for his children if they felt cramped. If he truly adored the Windsor villa as a structure, it would have been a simple matter to transfer its carefully accumulated contents to a regular museum or even to found a permanent memorial to the Duke and Duchess where their belongings could be enjoyed by the public and utilized by historians for decades to come. "How much nicer it would have been for the entire collection to have been preserved," wrote editor Ingrid Seward in *Majesty* magazine, "not in the house in Paris, but in a museum in London with a fee-paying public being granted access to a piece of living history."[26]

But the Windsor auction, scheduled to begin in New York the third week of September 1997, did not take place as planned. On August 31, just after midnight, the Mercedes carrying Diana, Princess of Wales; Dodi, Mohammed al Fayed's son; bodyguard Trevor Rees-Jones; and driver Henri Paul veered out of control and smashed into one of the concrete support piers in the Place de l'Alma tunnel in Paris. Paul, whose body was later found to contain nearly three times the legal limit of alcohol—along with a mixture of antidepressants and other drugs—was killed instantly, his spinal cord severed by the column of the steering wheel. Dodi Fayed, seated on the left rear, also died on impact. Rees-Jones, the only passenger in the car wearing a seat belt, was severely injured and his face lacerated. Seated immediately behind him, Diana suffered a ruptured pulmonary artery but despite her internal injuries was not killed. Although the French paramedics were on the scene within a few minutes, the Princess did not arrive at La Pitie-Salpêtrière Hospital until some ninety minutes had elapsed, during which time her internal injuries went untreated. At four that morning, she was officially pronounced dead.

The week that followed was akin to the assassination of U.S.

president John F. Kennedy in 1963; for the first time in many people's lives, the world seemingly ground to a halt at the death of this one woman. The reaction of the Queen and the British Royal Family was widely criticized; while London—indeed, the world—shared in an outpouring of grief, Elizabeth II and her family remained cloistered at Balmoral Castle in Scotland, where Prince Charles had been staying with his and Diana's two sons, Prince William and Prince Harry.

At the time of the Duke of Windsor's death in 1972, the public demonstrations of grief had caught the Royal Family off guard. David, as an exiled former king and outcast member of the Royal Family, had fallen beyond the concerns of his British relatives, who had ignored him in life and now attempted to do much the same in his death. Several times—notably the BBC memorial broadcast with Lord Mountbatten and the trooping the color ceremony, among others—Elizabeth II had to be advised to make small concessions to public sympathy. To a lesser extent, this had been the case at Wallis's death, when the public interest in the Duchess and sympathy for her again took the Royal Family by surprise.

Now, in September 1997, the familiar pattern once again repeated itself, this time with far more serious results. To the Royal Family, Diana—even in death—remained an outsider, the divorced wife of the heir to the throne, having lost her rank and the style of Her Royal Highness. In life, they had marginalized her and attempted to isolate her from public support and affection; in death, they fully expected that she would be treated in the same fashion. Aside from a brief statement released by Buckingham Palace the day Diana died, there was utter silence from the Royal Family for three days. The rest of the world was unanimous in praising the late Princess, but her former family said nothing. The public, overwhelmed at the loss of arguably the most popular member of the Royal Family in the entire century, demanded more. In an increasingly hostile atmosphere, the Queen agreed to return to London.

As defenders of the Royal Family pointed out, no one—not any member of the government or the public on the street—had any right to dictate how the Queen and her family should mourn the late Princess. However, the Queen's most important constitutional role is that of continued stability; it is she who forms the focal point of national rejoicing, and she has traditionally led the nation in times of crisis, providing a moral and reassuring center removed from the transient political arena. Over the past thirty years of her reign, Elizabeth II had carefully cultivated the media to display her family in the best possible light, asking them to share family holidays and celebrations; now, in a time of national mourning, she was subject to the same forces which had helped craft her very popularity.

Upon the advice of senior palace officials and Prime Minister Tony Blair, Elizabeth II did something unprecedented: She agreed to address the nation on live television. Her five-minute speech recalling Diana, if somewhat impersonal and bearing all the hallmarks of careful scripting, did much to silence the criticism which had resulted in headlines, such as the *Daily Express's* banner "Show Us You Care," in several London papers. Diana's funeral, on Saturday, September 6, also witnessed another unique move: Amid controversy that the royal standard atop Buckingham Palace was the only flag in the country not at half staff, once the Queen left the palace for Westminster Abbey, it was changed to a Union Jack, which was duly lowered, a tribute to the late Princess. The Royal Family's famous stiff upper lip, firmly in place during Diana's funeral, stood in stark contrast to the scene less than three months later when the Queen and other members of her family were seen to wipe away tears as they watched the Royal Yacht HMS *Britannia* decommissioned, a show of feeling which caused considerable comment in the press.

In New York City, news of the fatal car crash in Paris brought last-minute preparations for the Windsor auction at Sotheby's to a halt. No one knew if they should continue with their plans. Finally, on September 3, Diana Brooks, chief executive officer of Sotheby's, made the announcement: "Following the deaths of Diana, Princess of Wales, and his eldest son, Mr. Dodi Fayed, Mr. Mohammed al Fayed has consulted with Sotheby's and together we have decided that it would be appropriate to postpone the auction of Property from the Collection of the The Duke and Duchess of Windsor."[27] The auction, it was announced, would take place sometime in 1998, when it could be rescheduled to accommodate both al Fayed and the already-booked showrooms at Sotheby's in Manhattan; proceeds from the sale would now go to the newly formed Dodi Fayed International Charitable Foundation.

The Windsor auction was eventually rescheduled for the third and fourth weeks of February 1998. Richard Appelbaum Associates of New York was hired to completely transform two floors of Sotheby's Manhattan showrooms into a re-created Windsor Villa in the Bois de Boulogne. Enormous blown-up photographs of the hall, the drawing room, the dining room, the library, the boudoir, and both the Duke's and the Duchess's bedrooms were suspended from the tall ceilings, providing a surreal backdrop for the pieces of furniture, paintings, and porcelains which had seemingly leaped from the second into the third dimension.[28]

The fame of the love story of the century, now coupled with the links through the al Fayed family to the late Princess of Wales, lent an extraordinary interest to the auction. Just after half-past six on the evening of Thursday, February 19, Diana Brooks ascended the podium in the main auction room and announced the start of the sale. The first lot, a miniature, hand-colored oval portrait of David as a baby, sold to Memphis, Tennessee, designer Pat Kerr for some $24,000; Sotheby's original estimate had been $2,000–$3,000. This inflated bidding quickly set the tone for the two weeks which were to follow, an increasing spiral of excitement and desire to own a piece of the Windsors' lives.

Perhaps not surprisingly, over half the lots went to Americans, who had always appeared more interested in, and accepting of, the Windsors. Benjamin Yim of San Francisco spent $29,000 to purchase a piece of the Windsors' wedding cake, still contained in its neatly wrapped white silk box and bearing David's and Wallis's signatures. The Duke's morning suit, which he had worn at his wedding, sold for $27,000; Wallis's blue-velvet Christian Dior "Lahore" evening gown brought $26,450; and the red-leather dispatch box emblazoned with "The King" went for $65,000.

Designer Tommy Hilfiger purchased many of the furnishings from the villa for use in his new house in Connecticut. Pat Kerr, who had won the first bid, also purchased the album of the Windsors' wedding as well as additional items and clothing; eight months before, she had also purchased four of the gowns auctioned by Diana, Princess of Wales. The famous Gerald Brockhurst portrait of Wallis was purchased by the National Portrait Gallery in London for $107,000; the Munnings equestrian painting of David as Prince of Wales sold for $2,312,000; and the two sketches Cecil Beaton had made of Wallis in 1936 at Cumberland Terrace and which had hung in her bathroom were sold for over $310,000.

Perhaps the two pieces which drew the biggest interest were the abdication desk and the Duke's Garter banner. There was a great deal of criticism that these items—historically associated with the history of the Royal Family—were not returned to their collection. But it is difficult to believe that the Royal Family would have wished to add the abdication desk, which eventually brought $415,000, to any of their palaces. Ironically, in 1986, Mohammed al Fayed had given Prince Charles a private tour of the Windsor Villa and offered him the choice of any objects he desired. He had had no interest in the family albums or the Garter banner or any other souvenirs of his great-uncle's life.[29]

Many of the Windsors' friends and intimates were horrified at the auction. "It was shocking," says David Metcalfe. "The Duke would have been horrified at the auction. Nothing there had any great value, but it had a lot of sentimental value. I am sure he would have wanted most of it returned to the Royal Family."[30] Metcalfe's sister Linda Mortimer called the auction "an absolute disgrace. It should never have happened. The Duchess had so much style and dignity and grace, and she would have been appalled by the sale."[31] And Janine Metz adds: "The Duke and Duchess were such private people. They would have died of sorrow at this sale."[32]

The auction at Sotheby's arguably closed the last chapter in the love story of the century: The Duke and Duchess were dead, their possessions scattered to the corners of the globe and their correspondence published. The tangible reminders of their life together have nearly vanished. La Croë still stands on a slope above the Mediterranean, half-hidden in an overgrown garden, its windows open to the sky, its rooms burned-out shells. The Paris villa, emptied of its contents, not only retains poignant memories of the Windsors but is now inexorably linked, through Mohammed al Fayed, with the tragic death of the most famous of royal outcasts, Diana, Princess of Wales. Buried side by side at Frogmore, beneath immense slabs of Portland stone, Wallis and David belong to history.

A few miles away, ringed by thick clumps of azalea and rhododendron and guarded by groves of fir and pine, stands Fort Belvedere. For many years abandoned by the crown, it has been brilliantly restored to its former glory. For twenty years, Wallis and David fought for permission to return to the Fort, where their romance had first played itself out; ironically, in death, they rest in the same idyllic stretch of Berkshire countryside.

"I would hesitate," Wallis wrote in her memoirs, "to call the Fort mine in the way that women sometimes feel that they have an emotional claim to a setting where they came to share profound love." Nevertheless, even after many years of exile in France, she declared that "a part of me remains in the vicinity." After she was gone, Wallis warned, she would return to Fort Belvedere, "a pale and anonymous phantom," flitting in and out of "the shadows along the Cedar Walk," high above the tranquil stretch of Virginia Water in Windsor Great Park.[33] In death, Wallis, Duchess of Windsor, would remain forever with the family that in life had rejected her.

Acknowledgments

ALTHOUGH I HAD MADE a private decision to undertake this book at some future date while I was living in London in 1996, impetus was given to the project by Allan J. Wilson, my editor at Birch Lane Press. During the course of long telephone conversations between London and New York, he persuaded me to seriously consider this as my next endeavor. It was an enormous decision, but throughout the process Allan carefully steered the book from idea to fruition. Had it not been for his diligence, I would certainly have stalled for several years. Now I'm glad I listened to his advice. Throughout the publication of my previous three books, Allan has always been a constant source of encouragement and wisdom, and I owe him an immense debt for whatever success I have enjoyed.

In helping me master the often overwhelming struggle to bring this book in on deadline, I also must thank my second editor, Francine Hornberger. Francine went out on a limb for me, sensing the desperation in my five A.M. telephone calls as the due date approached. She has facilitated the quick and easy completion of this book, always with understanding and patience.

I also must thank my U.K. editor at Aurum Press, Sheila Murphy. Sheila has been an amazing source of support and information over the past two years, gathering together names, addresses, and telephone numbers, conducting interviews on my behalf, and rounding up assorted articles and reviews which were particularly important. As always, it was a great pleasure to work with her, and I consider myself lucky to have her in my corner.

This task has been made much easier through the generous cooperation and assistance of many people who had no stake in the project: William Aergraf, Robert Anderson, Elizabeth Argol, Joyce Behncke, Steve Cash, Mike Champion, Jane Corrier, Ron Darrow, Robert Dishaw, Hillary Donner, Ross Duden, Fred Exbery, Diane Farner, Nick Fenton, Malcolm Ford, Michel Frank, Ted Garrison, Jay Gendol, Kathryn Glennie, Michael Horton, Beth Hughes, Mary Anne Hugheson, David Ingersoll, Cary James, Alex Joyce, Ruth Judas, Dee Kapethorne, Patty Kerrigan, David Kramer, Mary Lawrence, Tim Loder, Connie Mason, Bill Mathews, Natasha McDermott, Cynthia Melin, Bill Nelson, Vanessa Nerome, Drew Pearson, James Polomis, Kathy Rierdon, Greg Ritchie, Mark Robards, Bob Samson, Kay Smithson, Chris Sorrel, Joe Spitz, Monica Tapert, Jay Tennant, Dawn Terrance, Vivica Tremayne, Corey Urbach, Edd Vick, Russ Vorshon, Phil Wamsher, Brodie Williamson, Mick Woelk, and Craig Wranner all have my thanks.

My friends have been particularly supportive, never failing to forgive me for disappearing from their lives for nearly two years. I would like to especially thank Sharlene Aadland, Daniel Briere, Liz and Andy Eaton, Laura Enstone, Jake Gariepy,

Nils Hanson, Barbara and Paul Harper, Gretchen Haskin, Kathy Hoefler, DeeAnn Hoff, Dianne Holme, Jeff Hooks, Brien Horan, Chuck and Eileen Knaus, Angela Manning, Cecelia Manning, Mark Manning, Grant Michael Menzies, Denis Meslans, Russ Minugh, Steve O'Donnell, Sue and Ken Ottinger, Marina and Dick Schweitzer, Anne Shawyer, Caroline Shawyer, and Alexei Urmanov for their patience.

My parents, Roger and Helena King, once again lent their invaluable support—emotional, practical, and financial. Their generous understanding of my admittedly peculiar career has undoubtedly enabled me to achieve whatever I have managed thus far.

A great many people have submitted to interviews, answered my queries, provided me with valuable information, and assisted with the completion of this book. While some of those interviewed for this book requested anonymity, and others, while allowing me to mention their contributions, wished that specific information not be attributed, an ovewhelming majority deserve my public thanks: John Abbott, Joss Abercrombie, John Adams, Derek Adler, Jane Admonson, Nancy Keyes Adrian, Edward J. Alberts, Mary Aldridge, Jason Alexandrov, Morgan Balb, Letitia Baldridge, Elenya Baskin, Jeremy Bates, Peter Bawmer-Kitt, Jonathon Becker, William Beddoe, Gudrun Beker, Kathleen Belmond, Virginia Belushi, Enid Bennett, Charles Bickford, Horst Bierbicher, Norman Bishop, Ashley Black, Arnell Bledsoe, Bernard Blessert, Michael Bloch, Dirk Blum, Ann Bogart, Christopher Bonascelli, Anthony Bonar, Timothy Booth, Victor Boyle, Bruce Brackford, Alex Bradbury, Michael Brandon, Neville Brauner, Ian Briely-Curtis, Piers Brompton, Wilifrid Brody, Alistair Brown, Michele Brumfield, Michael Burgess, Robert Burton, Niall Byrd-Jones, Carol Byron, Wallace Calder, Lee Campbell, Katherine Cannon, Princess M. Cantacuzene, Alexander Carnovatsky, Rachel Carr, Lynn Carroll, Mathew Carroll, Noah Carter, Dame Barbara Cartland, Tristan Cassell, Jean-Pierre Cassidy, Ekaterina Cedvenska, Dolores Celi, Josephine Cervi, Edward Chapman, Nikolai Chessiakov, Anna Churchill, Francisco di Ciardi, Mary Clark, Stanley Clarke, Rupert Clarke-Davies, David Cobb, Gregoire Coghian, Constance Cole, Jennifer Collins, William Connick, Dr. Robert Conte, Russell Conway, Elise Corbett, Mara Courdant, Isabel Cross, Antoinette Curnett, Robert Cutler, Cyril Daily, Cynthia Dale, Blythe Damon, Danielle Daste, Jean David, Lisa Davidson, Marc Davis, Brandon Dee, Rosanna Degemark, Jaime Degrassie, Marguerite Delemedicos, Mylene Demazaris, Charles Dennis, Lorraine Deruddre, Judi Derricks, Gustav Dietrich, Andre Di Fiore, Reginald Dillan, Marlene Dinsdale, Angelica Domergue, Sarah Donovan-Smith, Eric Douglas, Claudia Duke, Allison Eastland, Denholm Edwards, Archie Elron, Stephen Emerwood, George Ewing, Douglas Fabares, Anthony Franklin Farmer, Peter Farrell, Evelina Feraco, Verna Ferrer, James Fields, Nigel Fisher, Jack Fleming, Bridget Flynn-Wood, Paul Ford, Sir Dudley Forwood, Michael Foster, Arthur Franklin, Noel Fraser, Mona Frye, Joachim Fuchs, Morgan Gage, Philippe Galland, Allen Ganz, Mikhail Gastrinski, Rita Geddes, John Gilbert, Paul Gilbert, Etienne Glessner, Jakub Goetzka, Ruth Gorman, Harold Gould, Maurice Grandforth, Dolores Gray, Lola Griest, Hugh Gros, C. Z. Guest, James Gunston, Patrick Gunther, Wick Gwynne, Charles Hall, Trevor Hallick, Carl Halperin, Linda Hamilton, Gordon Hardwood, the earl of Harewood, Dan Hatcher, Signe Hesketh, Sachiko Hessigawa, Christianne Hodges, Niaomi Holiday, Leslie Hope, Donald Howard, Nancy Howard, Thomas Hoyt, Elizabeth Hume, Martha Hutchinson, Izumia Igawa, Freda Ivory, Uta Jacobs, Dorothea Jenks, Claudia Jenner, Joseph Johnson, Johannes Jokovic, Edward Jones, Erland Kanaly, Larisa Kandansky, Yuri Kazurinsky, Howard Keyes-Burns, Susan Kennedy, Ian King, Klaus Knopper, Elias Kosleck, Alexei Kruschen, Peter Kurth, Eleanor Lamb, Julius Lamoux, Kenneth Jay

Lane, Rex Leclerc, Mitchell Lee, Barbara Lehr, Paul Lenz, Tisa Liddy, Richard Lithgow, Jeremy Lloyd, Greer Lockhart, Christopher Loomis, Paulina Lopez, Andreas Lowitsch, Anne Luce, William Luce, Diego St. Muriez del Mancino, Joe Mansfield, Kenneth Marquand, Adele Marshuk, Jared Martin, Lee Mathews, Axel Mattsauch, Marc McCormack, Elaine McCoy, Malcolm McKay, Brian McNair, Donald Meija, Dominique de Menil, Haines Menzies, John Merrill, David Metcalfe, Joanna Miles, Lydia Miller, James Mills, Paul Minet, Ann Mitchell, Felix Molina, Robert Montgomery-Smith, Deborah Moore, Nathan Morley, Eugenia Morris, Linda Mortimer, Helena Morwalk, the Hon. Lady Mosley, Shirley Munroe, Hildegard Muti, Claudine Neill, Kenneth Newley, Birgil Niklas, Jens Nilsson, Nathalia Noble, Simon Oberon, Arthur O'Brien, Eleanor Dana O'Connell, Una O'Connor, Ian Page, Daniel Paget, Michael Parsons, Robert Parsons, Julia Payne, J. Michael Penny, Werner Petersen, Sarah Pickering, Robin Piguet, Marisa Pinuette, Jean Pollan, Tyrone Pritchard, Philip Proctor, Vsevevold Ptskiawalskaya, Maggie Pugilise, Michael Quinn, Colin Rafferty, Anna Rathbone, Rosita Ratzinberger, Duncan Redgrave, Kate Reid, Fiona Reilly, Astrid Rentschler, Irene Richards, Werner Rigg, Chris Roberts, Eve Roberts, May Rogers, Andrew Rohm, Yvonne Roman, Aline, Countess of Romanones, Norman Rowe, Sidney Rubin, Sir Steven Runciman, Harold Russell, Sheila Ryan, Margot Ryder, Therese Salvador, Colm Sassoon, Pamela Savage, Maximilian Scott, Linda Seale, Jacques Sezer, Oonagh Shanley-Toffolo, James Shawn, Elizabeth Sheperd, Christiane Sherwen, Frank Simpson, Russell Simpson, Lila Smith, Samantha Smith, Victor Snyder, Josef Stein, William Stephens, Charles Stevens-King, Leo Stone, George Stowe, Raymond St. Spiner, Marilyn Swezey, Dirk Taylor, John Terry, Marthe Thimmon, Dr. Jean Thin, Scott Thompson, Mari-Claire Tooms, Cordelia Tracey, Constance Trevor, Desmond Underwood, Anne Van de Castle, Luca Venora, Alex Vincent, Eric Wagner, Victoria Wallach, Fred Walston, Ruth Warner, Sam Wayne, Max Weber, Norbert Weiss, Mae Welles, Benjamin White, Cara Wilding, Mike Williams, Terry Williams, Penny Wilson, Norman Wise, Sue Woolmans, Karl Wyatt, Keenan Yorke, Audrey Young, and Georgi Zubkov.

I would also especially like to thank Madame Janine Metz, whose dedication and loyalty to the Duke and Duchess of Windsor were an inspiration to continue my pursuit of the truth.

The majority of this book was written over the course of eighteen very intense months, between the hours of midnight and six A.M. While I find my "Jack the Ripper hours," in the words of my friend Lisa Davidson, the most productive, they are also the most lonely. For whatever contributions they have made to keeping me entertained and charging ahead, I would like to thank Dario Argento, Rupert Everett, Penelope Keith, Christopher Lee, Paul Rudd, and Barbara Steele.

Lucia Bequaert, of Rainy Day Books in Fitzwilliam, New Hampshire, gave this project an immense jump start by putting me in touch with many people whose assistance I came to value greatly. In addition, she sought out obscure titles and kept an eye out for material I might otherwise overlook. I highly recommend her incredible selection of royal titles.

Candace Metz-Longinette-Gahring has proved invaluable in this project, willingly sacrificing her own time to help organize my research, provide me with a considerable amount of material, and cheer me along. Her great skill with the written word helped formulate my thoughts into meaningful paragraphs. I look forward to the day when she decides to share her own royal endeavors with the rest of us.

Marlene Eilers once again provided thoughtful analysis and expert advice on matters far beyond my comprehension. Over the last ten years and through all of my books Marlene has proved herself a true friend and ardent specialist in European royal genealogy. Although she and I disagree over some of the interpretations contained within, this book undoubtedly owes a great debt to her consistent support.

John Wieneman shared his vast collection along with his copious knowledge and valuable photographs of the Duke and Duchess of Windsor. Always a pest, I undoubtedly asked too many questions amid too many deadlines, but he was always quick to respond and offer assistance. It was indeed fortunate that we happened to cross paths or this book would be something less than it is now.

Susanne Meslans again rescued me over and over again during what I can only describe as a torturous year. Whether searching for obscure books when I could not make it to the library, hauling them back and forth for me, or setting aside her own intense schedule to step in and offer advice on the manuscript, she never failed to provide inspiration and assistance. I keep trying to convince her to write her book on the Souls; maybe one day she will.

Finally, it is a great pleasure to acknowledge the contributions of Erna Bringe. It would be impossible to describe my debt to her. For the last eighteen months, she has provided me with weekly packages of material on the Duke and Duchess, read and extracted pieces on them from her personal library, made telephone calls, secured photographs, arranged permissions, sat in her local library and done research on my behalf, and even provided me with delicious cookies to keep me going. Her constant support, through letters, telephone calls, and our E-mail correspondence, has kept my head on track when the project threatened to overwhelm me. If not for Erna, this book simply would not exist. I am convinced that from somewhere Wallis is smiling on Erna.

Source Notes

I N MY SOURCE NOTES, Wallis's book *The Heart Has Its Reasons* is cited as WW; David's book, *A King's Story* is cited as David; Philip Ziegler's authorized biography of David, *King Edward VIII*, is cited as Ziegler, with all other titles cited by the same author delineated according to individual title; and the auction catalogs from Sotheby's are cited as Sotheby's, *Private* or *Public Collection*.

Introduction
1. International News Service article, 21 February 1956.
2. WW, vii.

Prologue
1. Bradford, *Elizabeth*, 456.
2. Sarah Ferguson, 199.
3. Hugo Vickers in *Hello!* 23 August 1997, 26.
4. Private information.

The quotation from Wallis's commonplace books (at the beginning of the book) is quoted in Bloch, *Letters*, 343.

Chapter 1
1. WW, 5–6.
2. *New York Herald Tribune*, 13 December 1936; *New York Daily News*, 2 December 1936.
3. Martin, 15–16; Wilson, 26.
4. Wilson, 26.
5. Thornton, 14.
6. Martin, 18.
7. WW, 4.
8. Ibid., 4.

9. Bocca, *Woman Who Would Be Queen*, 14; *London Sunday Chronicle*, 7 December 1936.
10. Culver, Francis, and William R. Marye, *Southern Spectator*, March 1937.
11. Martin, 16.
12. WW, 4.
13. Ibid., 4.
14. Ibid., 5–6.
15. The cottage burned to the ground on 1 July 1942. *Baltimore Evening Sun*, 2 July 1942.
16. See Higham, 14.
17. Bloch, *Duchess*, 13.
18. Information from Dr. Jean Thin to author.
19. Thornton, 21.
20. WW, 4–5.
21. WW, 5.

Chapter 2
1. WW, 8.
2. Ibid., 8.
3. Ibid., 7.
4. Ibid., 10.
5. Gordon, 71.

521

6. Amory, *Who Killed Society?* 235.
7. Ibid.
8. WW, vii.
9. Ibid., 8.
10. Ibid., 11.
11. Ibid., 4.
12. Ibid., 6.
13. Ibid., 9.
14. Ibid., 9.
15. Ibid., 10.
16. Ibid., 10.
17. Ibid., 9.
18. Ibid., 12.
19. Ibid., 13–14.
20. Ibid., 16.
21. Ibid., 13.
22. Ibid., 13.
23. Ibid., 15.
24. Ibid., 15.
25. *Baltimore News-Post*, 4 February 1957.
26. WW, 16–17.
27. Ibid., 20–21.
28. Amory, *Who Killed Society?* 235.
29. WW, 19.
30. Ibid., 19.
31. Ibid., 20.
32. Ibid., 15–16.
33. Bove, 243.
34. Donaldson, 157.
35. WW, 18–19.
36. Ibid., 24.
37. Bryan and Murphy, 18.
38. WW, 25.
39. Ibid., 25.
40. Ibid., 25–26.
41. Ibid., 26.

Chapter 3
1. WW, 27.
2. Ibid., viii, 28.
3. *New York Evening-Journal*, 6 February 1937.
4. WW, 30.
5. Wilson, 33; WW, 31.
6. WW, 31.
7. Ibid., 32.
8. Ibid., viii.
9. St. John, *Honeycomb*, 490.
10. *The Sunday People*, London, 29 April 1973.
11. Ibid.

12. *Baltimore News-Post*, 1 October 1936.
13. WW, 36.
14. Quoted in Martin, 33.
15. WW, 37.
16. Wilson, 49–50.
17. WW, 38–39.
18. Ibid., 39.
19. Ibid., 38.
20. Ibid., 39–40.
21. Ibid., 40; Beirne, 286–89.
22. Ibid., 41.
23. *Baltimore News-Post*, 30 September 1936.
24. WW, 42.
25. *Baltimore News-Post*, 21 November 1936.
26. *Baltimore Sun*, 8 December 1936.
27. *The Sunday People*, London, 29 April 1973.
28. *Baltimore News-Post*, 1 October 1936.
29. *Baltimore News-Post*, 8 February 1957.
30. Brody, 65.
31. WW, 44.

Chapter 4
1. WW, 47.
2. Ibid., 47.
3. Ibid., 48.
4. Ibid., 48.
5. Ibid., 49.
6. Ibid., 46.
7. Ibid., 49.
8. Ibid., 50.
9. Ibid., 51.
10. Ibid., 51.
11. Ibid., 51.
12. Ibid., 51.
13. Ibid., 52.
14. Ibid., 52.
15. Ibid., 52.
16. Ibid., 52.
17. Ibid., 52.
18. Ibid., 53.
19. Ibid., 53–54.
20. Ibid., 54.
21. Ibid., 54.
22. Ibid., 54.
23. *Baltimore News-Post*, 1 October 1936.

24. WW, 55.
25. *Baltimore News-Post,* 16 September 1916.
26. Wilson, 61.
27. WW, 55.
28. Ibid., 56.
29. Ibid., 56.
30. Ibid., 56.
31. Beirne, 120.
32. WW, 56.
33. Ibid., 56.
34. Ibid., 61.
35. Ibid., 61–62.

Chapter 5
1. WW, 63.
2. Ibid., 63.
3. Ibid., 64–65.
4. Ibid., 65.
5. Ibid., 65.
6. Ibid., 66.
7. Ibid., 67.
8. Ibid., 66–67.
9. Ibid., 67–68.
10. Ibid., 68.
11. Ibid., 68.
12. Ibid., 69.
13. Ibid., 70.
14. Ibid., 71.
15. Ibid., 71.
16. Ibid., 71.
17. Ibid., 71–72.
18. Bryan and Murphy, 25.
19. WW, 72.
20. Ibid., 73–74.
21. Ibid., 73.
22. Private Information.
23. WW, 75.
24. Ibid., 75–76.
25. Ibid., 76.
26. Ibid., 76.
27. Ibid., 77–78.
28. Ibid., 51.
29. Ibid., 79.
30. Ibid., 80.
31. Ibid., 80.
32. Ibid., 86.
33. Ibid., 87–88.
34. Ibid., 89.
35. Ibid., 89.
36. Ibid., 90.
37. Ibid., 82.

Chapter 6
1. WW, 93.
2. Higham, 44–45.
3. WW, 93.
4. Ibid., 94.
5. Cole, 31.
6. Ibid., 28.
7. WW, 94.
8. This sequence of events differs slightly from that given by Wallis, between pages 94–95 in her book, and is based on information given to me privately in an interview with one of the Duchess's friends.
9. Higham, 48–49.
10. Information from the Countess of Romanones to author.
11. Parker, *King of Fools,* 4.
12. Ziegler, 195.
13. Higham, 49.
14. Ibid., 52.
15. WW, 95.
16. Private information.
17. Cole, 40.
18. WW, 96–97.
19. Ibid., 96–99.
20. *The Sunday People,* London, 6 May 1973.
21. WW, 101–102.
22. Ibid., 102.
23. Fowler, 190.
24. WW, 103.
25. Abend, 96–97.
26. WW, 104.
27. Ibid., 104–105.
28. WW, 108–109.
29. Ibid., 109–110.
30. Bryan and Murphy, 38.
31. WW, 112.

Chapter 7
1. WW, 113.
2. Information from Dame Barbara Cartland to author.
3. Amory, *Who Killed Society?* 238.
4. WW, 119.
5. Ibid., 123.
6. Bryan and Murphy, 42.
7. *Baltimore News,* 28 October 1927.
8. Bryan and Murphy, 42; WW, 124–26.
9. Bryan and Murphy, 42; WW, 126.

10. Quoted in Martin, 130–31.
11. Associated Press article, 17 October 1936.
12. Bloch, *Letters*, 20–21.
13. WW, 127.
14. Ibid., 127.
15. Ibid., 128.
16. Ibid., 128–29.
17. Ibid., 131.
18. Information from Dame Barbara Cartland to author.
19. WW, 133.
20. Ibid., 134.
21. Ibid., 136.
22. Bloch, *Letters*, 24.
23. WW, 135–36.
24. Ibid., 137.
25. Information from Dame Barbara Cartland to author.
26. WW, 138–40.
27. Ibid., 140–41.
28. Ibid., 141–42.
29. Ibid., 144.
30. Ibid., 145.
31. Ibid., 145–46.
32. Ibid., 147.
33. Ibid., 146–47.
34. Ibid., 149.
35. Ibid., 149–50.
36. Beaton, *Self Portrait*, 47.
37. Goldsmith, 153.
38. Bloch, *Letters*, 46.
39. For further information, see Mooney, *Evelyn Nesbit and Stanford White: Love and Death in the Gilded Age.*
40. Vanderbilt and Furness, 287–88.

Chapter 8
1. Bradford, *Reluctant King*, 10.
2. Cited, Pope-Hennessy, *Queen Mary*, 32.
3. Pope-Hennessy, *Queen Mary*, 77.
4. Ibid., 230.
5. David, 27.
6. Pope-Hennessy, *Queen Mary*, 242.
7. Cited, Pope-Hennessy, *Queen Mary*, 262.
8. Ibid.
9. Ibid., 426.
10. *Hansard's Parliamentary Debates*, 28 June 1894.

11. Duff, *Queen Mary*, 127.
12. Cited, Pope-Hennessy, *Queen Mary*, 391.
13. Quoted, Pope-Hennessy, *Queen Mary*, 299.
14. Donaldson, 25.
15. Rose, *King George V*, 58.
16. Pope-Hennessy, *A Lonely Business*, 219.
17. David, 28.
18. Ibid., 26.
19. Churchill, *Lord Derby*, 159.
20. See Donaldson, 22–24, for further discussion of this infamous quotation.
21. Lees-Milne, 230, 235.
22. Pope-Hennessy, *A Lonely Business*, 214.
23. Gore, 368.
24. David, 28.
25. Pope-Hennessy, *Queen Mary*, 391.
26. David, 11.
27. Ibid., 13.
28. Parkhurst, 24–25.
29. Nicolson, *George V*, 86–87.
30. David, 9.
31. Quoted, Bradford, *Elizabeth*, 15.
32. Cited, Ziegler, 26.
33. *New Yorker*, 3 October 1941.
34. David, 62.
35. Ibid., 81.
36. Getty, 81.
37. Ziegler, 51.
38. David, 111.
39. Bolitho, *Edward VIII*, 72.
40. Pope-Hennessy, *Queen Mary*, 514.
41. Quoted in Brendon and Whitehead, *The Windsors*, 29.
42. Most famously, on 21 April 1917, H. G. Wells, in a letter which appeared in the *Times*, declared that the time had come to rid England of "the ancient trappings of throne and sceptre." He said the country was struggling under the influence of "an alien and uninspiring court." Hearing this, George V fumed, "I may be uninspiring, but I'll be damned if I'm alien." Nicolson, *George V*, 403.
43. Nicolson, *George V*, 405.

44. At the same time, the German names and titles held by other royal relatives were also relinquished. The Battenbergs became Mountbattens, with the creation of the earldom of Milford Haven for the head of the family; another Battenberg, Prince Alexander, was created Marquess of Carisbrooke. Queen Mary's two brothers jettisoned Teck in favor of their maternal grandmother's family name of Cambridge, one becoming Marquess of Cambridge, the other the Earl of Athlone.
45. *New York Times*, 29 May 1972.
46. Ziegler, *Mountbatten*, 54.
47. David, 138.
48. *New York Times*, 14 January 1970.
49. Prince Christopher of Greece, 165.
50. Bolitho, *Edward VIII*, 75.
51. Bradford, *Reluctant King*, 95.
52. Hart-Davis, xi.
53. Ziegler, 142.
54. Quoted, Middlemas, *George VI*, 201.
55. Wheeler-Bennett, *King George VI*, 151.
56. Airlie, 166.
57. Thornton, 46.
58. Bryan and Murphy, 70.
59. Hatch, 124.
60. Leighton, 370.
61. Rose, *King George V*, 303.
62. Pope-Hennessy, *Queen Mary*, 521–22.
63. Airlie, 163.
64. Behrman, 100–101.
65. Hart-Davis, 88.
66. Ibid., 109.
67. Asquith, *Diaries*, 421.
68. Vanderbilt and Furness, 274–75.
69. Ibid., 279.

Chapter 9
1. WW, 154.
2. Ibid., 155.
3. Ibid., 155.
4. Ibid., 156.
5. Ibid., 157.
6. Ibid., 157.
7. Ibid., 157–58.
8. Ibid., 158.
9. David, 257.
10. Vanderbilt and Furness, 288.
11. WW, 158–59.
12. Ibid., 159.
13. Ibid., 161.
14. Ibid., 162.
15. Ibid., 162.
16. Ibid., 162.
17. Ibid., 163.
18. Ibid., 164.
19. Ibid., 164.
20. See Vanderbilt and Furness, 265–66.
21. Private information.
22. WW, 169.
23. Ibid., 171.
24. David, 237.
25. WW, 169–71.
26. Cooper, *Light of Common Day*, 162.
27. WW, 171.
28. Ibid., 171.
29. Ibid., 171–72.
30. Ibid., 172–73.
31. Ibid., 173.
32. Ibid., 173–74.
33. Ibid., 174.
34. Ibid., 175.
35. Ibid., 176.
36. Edwards, "Fort Belvedere," in *Architectural Digest*, 180.
37. WW, 176–77.
38. Bloch, *Letters*, 86.
39. WW, 178.

Chapter 10
1. WW, 179.
2. Bloch, *Letters*, 91.
3. Ibid., 95.
4. WW, 179.
5. Ibid., 180.
6. Lockhart, *Diaries*, 264.
7. Ibid., 215.
8. WW, 182.
9. Vanderbilt and Furness, 306.
10. Ibid., 306.
11. Thornton, 65.
12. WW, 181–83.
13. Ibid., 183.
14. Bryan and Murphy, 106.
15. Bloch, *Letters*, 114.

16. Ibid., 116.
17. Vanderbilt and Furness, 311.
18. Ibid., 296.
19. WW, 184.
20. Ibid., 184.
21. Vanderbilt and Furness, 312.
22. Ibid., 313.
23. Donaldson, 170.
24. Ziegler, 198–99. Neither Thelma nor Freda was mentioned by the Duke in his memoirs. Freda died in 1983, having, for the most part, maintained her silence.
25. Bloch, *Letters*, 119.
26. WW, 191–92.
27. *Time*, 14 December 1936.
28. Interview with Sir Dudley Forwood.
29. Bloch, *Letters*, 120–21.
30. Ibid., 122–23.
31. London *Observer Review*, 24 June 1973.
32. WW, 184–85.
33. Ibid., 185.
34. Ibid., 188.
35. Ibid., 187.
36. Ibid., 187.
37. Ibid., 190.
38. Ibid., 191.
39. Bloch, *Letters*, 129.
40. Lowndes, 141–42.
41. Airlie, 200.
42. Ibid., 200.
43. WW, 192.

Chapter 11
1. Bloch, *Letters*, 133.
2. WW, 198.
3. *Time*, 9 November 1936.
4. WW, 198–99.
5. Ibid., 200–201.
6. Interview with Sir Dudley Forwood.
7. Ibid.
8. WW, 201.
9. Interview with Sir Dudley Forwood.
10. Warwick, 81.
11. Ibid., 83.
12. Donaldson, 181.
13. One of David's friends later told author Ralph G. Martin, "To put it bluntly he had the smallest pecker I have ever seen. Can you imagine what this did to him? Here are all these beautiful women all over the world, all ready and willing to go to bed with the Prince Charming of the world, all of them expecting the most eventful romantic night of their lives. And the ones who made it with him, can you imagine their disappointment? And can you imagine how he felt?"(Martin, 149) And Wallis herself is supposed to have told Adela Rogers St. John that all of the sons of George V "have small penis complexes."(Birmingham, Duchess of, 59)
14. Private information.
15. Other tales have ranged from the mild to the truly extraordinary. Several of those interviewed for this book have accused David of having a foot fetish, an infantile fetish, and even of having talked Wallis into donning a strap-on dildo so that she might have intercourse with him. Such wild gossip, spread with much fervor among the aristocracy and members of the court, is, needless to say, entirely without support.
16. Edwards, *Matriarch*, 359.
17. Ziegler, 205.
18. Ibid., 203.
19. Bryan and Murphy, 361.
20. See Bloch, *The Duchess of Windsor*, 229, for details; also 19, where Bloch suggests that it is possible she suffered from *vaginismus*, whereby psychologically she produced the inability to have intercourse.
21. Private information.
22. Information from Dr. Jean Thin to author.
23. Martin, 150.
24. Private information.
25. WW, 204–205.
26. Information from Sir Steven Runcimann to author.

27. Knighted in 1957, Chips died the following year.
28. Channon, 33.
29. Ibid., 41.
30. Ibid., 23.
31. Rose, *Who's Who in the Royal House of Windsor*, 55.
32. Duff died in 1954; Diana, in 1986, a month after Wallis.
33. Masters, 88.
34. Ibid., 106.
35. Everett, 66.
36. Channon, 29.
37. Ibid., 34.
38. Sibyl Colefax died in 1950.
39. Beaton, *Self Portrait*, 47.
40. Mosley, *My Life*, 76. Emerald Cunard died in 1948.
41. Ibid., 75.
42. Acton, 220.
43. Cooper, *Light of Common Day*, 215.
44. WW, 208.
45. *Philadelphia Evening Bulletin*, 31 May 1937.
46. Cross, 85.
47. Fest, 436.
48. Goering, 70.
49. Donaldson, 207.
50. Quoted, Martin, 171–72.

Chapter 12
1. Watson, 24.
2. WW, 206–208.
3. Christopher of Greece, 162.
4. Airlie, 197.
5. Thornton, 74–75.
6. Morrow, *Queen Mother*, 81.
7. Gilbert, vol. 5, 810.
8. Channon, 45.
9. David, 258.
10. Birkenhead, 126.
11. WW, 209.
12. Beaton, *Self Portrait*, 47.
13. Associated Press article, 25 November 1935.
14. Channon, 57.
15. Lowndes, 143–46.
16. David, 261.
17. Airlie, 197.
18. Cited, Bradford, *Reluctant King*, 154.
19. WW, 210.

20. Cited, Watson, 27.
21. Donaldson, 190.
22. Watson, 28.
23. WW, 210.
24. Ibid., 210.

Chapter 13
1. Attlee, 85.
2. WW, 211.
3. David, 267.
4. WW, 212.
5. David, 268.
6. WW, 212.
7. Channon, 71.
8. Ziegler, 214.
9. Lindbergh, 12–13.
10. Inglis, 2.
11. WW, 212–13.
12. Templewood, 223.
13. Birkenhead, 127.
14. *New York Daily News*, 12 December 1966.
15. David, 280.
16. WW, 214–15.
17. David, 282.
18. Donaldson, 320–21.
19. Channon, 60.
20. Hardinge, 55.
21. Hart-Davis, 50.
22. Crawford, *Crawford Papers*, 569.
23. Bloch, *Reign*, 19.
24. Peacocke, 236.
25. Inglis, 72.
26. Jones, 69.
27. Stevenson, 309.
28. Wheeler-Bennett, *Nemesis*, 354.
29. *Documents on Germany Foreign Policy, 1918–1945*, ser. C, vol. 4, 1962, 1024–25.
30. Ribbentrop, 61.
31. *Documents on German Foreign Policy, 1918–1945*, ser. C, vol. 4, 1962, document no. 531.
32. *London Daily Express*, 30 October 1962.
33. Hesse, 21–23.
34. Donaldson, 215.
35. *Documents on German Foreign Policy, 1918–1945*, ser. C, vol. 7, 1966, document no. 77.
36. Speer, 72.
37. Higham, 154–55.

Chapter 14
1. WW, 213.
2. Leslie, 199.
3. Cumming, 167.
4. Quoted in Lacey, *Majesty*, 103.
5. Bloch, *Letters*, 190.
6. Channon, 76.
7. Crawford, 566.
8. WW, 213.
9. Airlie, 197–98.
10. Alice of Gloucester, 113.
11. Cooper, *Light of Common Day*, 163.
12. Morrow, *The Queen*, 19.
13. Bloch, *Letters*, 202.
14. Bryan and Murphy, 153.
15. Birkenhead, 128.
16. Private information.
17. Bryan and Murphy, 157–58.
18. Sotheby's, *Public Collection*, 36. This same gold case would later become famous as the one which Wallis kept by her side at the dinner table, her "Grumble Book," in which she noted any suggestions or corrections for her cook or staff.
19. Hardinge, 91.
20. Ibid., 91.
21. WW, 215–16.
22. Ibid., 215–16.
23. Ibid., 216.
24. Crawford, *Little Princesses*, 72.
25. Ibid., 72.
26. WW, 216.
27. Bloch, *Letters*, 211–14.
28. Channon, 78.
29. Lindbergh, 94.
30. WW, 216.
31. Ibid., 217.
32. Ibid., 217.
33. Thornton, 52–55.
34. Hardinge, 97–98.
35. Airlie, 198.
36. Nicolson, *Diaries*, 261–62.
37. Birkenhead, 123–24.
38. Nicolson, *Diaries*, 263–64.
39. Lockhart, *Diaries*, 346; Nicolson, *Diaries*, 263–64.
40. Lockhart, *Diaries*, 346.
41. Channon, 89.
42. Quoted in *Visitor*, San Diego, October–December 1992.
43. Hardinge, 102–103.
44. Ibid., 103.
45. In April 1938 when he was released from prison, McMahon wrote to the Duke and apologized for the attempt. David, hearing that he was having a difficult time getting employment, sent him a substantial check and a note from himself and Wallis, wishing him well. (Charles A. Smith, "Edward Lends Aid to his Menacer." *Philadelphia Evening Bulletin Weekly*, 4 April 1938.)
46. Channon, 93.
47. Lockhart, *Diaries*, 350.
48. Thornton, 103.
49. Warwick, 95.
50. Inglis, 47.
51. *Times* (London), 22 July 1936.
52. Bryan and Murphy, 193–94.

Chapter 15
1. Bryan and Murphy, 198.
2. WW, 220.
3. Cooper, *Light of Common Day*, 178.
4. Ibid., 183.
5. Ibid., 177.
6. Ziegler, *Diana Cooper*, 178.
7. Pryce-Jones, 108.
8. WW, 221.
9. Maxwell, 295–96.
10. Thornton, 108.
11. Sitwell, 57.
12. *Cavalcade*, 15 August 1936.
13. WW, 227.
14. Bloch, *Letters*, 234–35.
15. Vidal, 206.
16. *Aberdeen Evening Express*, 23 September 1936.
17. Thornton, 110–111.
18. Bryan and Murphy, 214.
19. Private information.
20. Smith, *Lord Mountbatten*, 52.
21. WW, 229.
22. Private information.
23. Quoted, Thornton, 113.
24. See Thornton, 133, for further information.
25. Private information.
26. Bradford, *Reluctant King*, 172.

Chapter 16
1. Wright, *Strange History*, 187.
2. Mansbridge, 282.
3. Associated Press article, 21 October 1936.
4. St. John, *Honeycomb*, 434.
5. Beaton, *Self Portrait*, 49.
6. *London Observer Review*, 24 June 1973.
7. Beaton, *Self Portrait*, 48.
8. Ibid., 48.
9. Bloch, *Letters*, 240–41.
10. Beaton, *Self Portrait*, 305.
11. Cumming, 167.
12. WW, 230.
13. *Time*, 9 November 1936.
14. Testimony from *Simpson v. Simpson* and attendant court proceedings is drawn from Montgomery-Hyde, 456–58; Associated Press articles dated 27 October 1936; and the *New York Times*, 28 October 1936.
15. United Press International article, 28 October 1936.
16. Quoted in "Mrs. Wallis Simpson," *Modern Romance*, 10.
17. *New York Journal-American*, 26 October 1936.
18. Quoted, Donaldson, 247.
19. Inglis, 192–93.
20. Mitford, 103.
21. Quoted, Montgomery-Hyde, *Baldwin*, 570.
22. Nicolson, *Diaries*, 276–77.

Chapter 17
1. Beaverbrook, 30–31.
2. Hardinge, 117.
3. Bryan and Murphy, 225–26.
4. David, 319.
5. Ibid., 319.
6. Airlie, 201.
7. Wrench, 343.
8. Channon, 97.
9. Quoted, Ziegler, *Mountbatten*, 93.
10. Beaverbrook, 34–35.
11. Cited in H. Montgomery-Hyde, "The Windsors and the Londonderrys."
12. WW, 233.
13. Birkenhead, 132–33.

14. Ibid., 126–27.
15. Templewood, 218–19.
16. Hardinge, 131.
17. *Times* (London), 29 November 1955.
18. Wrench, 339.
19. Ibid., 339.
20. Ibid., 342.
21. *Times* (London), 29 November 1955.
22. Beaverbrook, 99.
23. Middlemas and Barnes, 987–88.
24. Ibid., 991.
25. Ibid., 991–92.
26. Nicolson, *Diaries*, 279.
27. Lockhart, *Diaries*, 360.
28. Nicolson, *Diaries*, 279.
29. Private information.
30. WW, 236.
31. Ibid., 236.
32. Ibid., 236.
33. Ibid., 236.
34. Ibid., 236.
35. Ibid., 237.

Chapter 18
1. Donaldson, 263.
2. Birmingham, 97.
3. Lockhart, *Cosmo Gordon Lang*, 398.
4. David, 330.
5. Middlemas and Barnes, 994.
6. *Hansard's Parliamentary Debates*, 10 December 1936.
7. Jones, *Ponsonby*, 217.
8. *Hansard's Parliamentary Debates*, 10 December 1936.
9. David, 333.
10. Middlemas and Barnes, 995.
11. Wheeler-Bennett, *King George VI*, 281.
12. Alice of Gloucester, 114.
13. Bryan and Murphy, 220.
14. David, 334.
15. Airlie, 198.
16. Bloch, *Reign*, 87.
17. Pope-Hennessy, *Queen Mary*, 577.
18. Ibid., 576.
19. David, 339–40.
20. Duff, 201.
21. Hardinge, 116; Middlemas and Barnes, 987.

22. David in *Sunday Express,* (London), 10 June 1962.
23. WW, 238.
24. Channon, 104.
25. *Newsweek,* 26 November 1936.
26. *Times* (London), 20 November 1936.
27. Quoted, Martin, 220.
28. Channon, 255.

Chapter 19
1. The exact date of the luncheon meeting remains something of a mystery. Michael Thornton places it two days after the King's return from Wales, on November 21. This date is also what Beaverbrook himself recalled. Michael Bloch, who had access to unpublished documents in the Windsor Archive in Paris, suggests that it occurred on November 18 or 19. Chips Channon wrote about the luncheon in his diary on November 23 and reported that it had taken place a few days earlier. Wallis herself declared in her memoirs that the meeting had taken place on November 19, the same day on which the King returned, and there seems little reason to question her memory in this respect.
2. WW, 238–39.
3. Ibid., 240.
4. As is the present Duke of Edinburgh, Prince Philip, consort of Queen Elizabeth II.
5. Incidentally, Mary became a Royal Highness not through the issuance of special letters patent, but through accepted custom on her marriage. Such, however, would not be the case when Wallis married David.
6. Hough, *The Mountbattens,* 8.
7. Brook-Shepherd, 109–111.
8. Taylor, 10.
9. Rhodes, 416.
10. Quoted in Donaldson, 275.
11. Rhodes, 417.

12. Birkenhead, 125.
13. Ibid., 137.
14. Attlee, 123.
15. David, 343.
16. WW, 240–41.
17. *Sunday Times* (London), 24 April 1966.
18. Taylor, 370.
19. Beaverbrook, 50–51.
20. Channon, 109–110.
21. Nicolson, *Diaries,* 280.
22. Macleod, 197.
23. Montgomery-Hyde, *Baldwin,* 568.
24. David, 346.
25. Channon, 110.
26. Nicolson, *Diaries,* 280.
27. Montgomery-Hyde, *Baldwin,* 477.
28. Ziegler, 256.
29. Leighton, 378.
30. Ibid., 378.
31. *New York Herald Tribune,* 28 November 1936.
32. Associated Press article, 17 December 1936.
33. *Baltimore News-Post,* 9 December 1936.
34. WW, 242.
35. Colville, 716.
36. WW, 242.

Chapter 20
1. WW, 242.
2. Ibid., 242.
3. Ibid., 242–43.
4. David, 340.
5. WW, 243.
6. Ibid., 243.
7. Bloch, *Letters,* 254–55.
8. *Times* (London), 3 December 1936.
9. Freemantle, 178.
10. David, 353.
11. Quoted in Young, *Baldwin,* 137.
12. WW, 244.
13. *Washington Star,* 17 December 1936.
14. Ibid.
15. WW, 244.
16. Ibid., 244.
17. Ibid., 244.
18. Ibid., 244–45.
19. Ibid., 245.
20. Crawford, *Crawford Papers,* 573.

21. Channon, 114.
22. Lockhart, *Diaries,* 359.
23. *Times* (London) 3 December 1936.
24. *London Daily Telegraph,* 3 December 1936.
25. *London Daily Express,* 3 December 1936.
26. *London Daily Mail,* 3 December 1936.
27. WW, 245.
28. Ibid., 246.
29. Ibid., 246.
30. Birkenhead, 141.
31. WW, 246–47.
32. Ziegler, 269.
33. WW, 248.
34. Ibid., 248.
35. Ibid., 249–50.
36. Ibid., 250.
37. Ibid., 250–51.
38. Ibid., 252.
39. Ibid., 252.
40. Vreeland, 97–98.
41. WW, 252–53.
42. Ibid., 253–54.
43. Martin, 252.
44. Vreeland, 98.
45. WW, 256.
46. Ibid., 257–58.
47. Ibid., 259.
48. Ibid., 290.

Chapter 21

1. WW, 261.
2. Bloch, *Letters,* 261–62.
3. Churchill, *Gathering Storm,* 218.
4. Young, 239–40.
5. *Time,* 7 November 1936.
6. Quoted, De-la-Noy, 35–36.
7. David, 365.
8. Wheeler-Bennett, *King George VI,* 285.
9. Channon, 117.
10. *Hansard's Parliamentary Debates,* 4 December 1936.
11. Beaverbrook, 78.
12. Martin, 296.
13. Taylor, 370–71.
14. Interestingly, almost precisely this same path had been taken by the mistress of the present Prince of Wales, who, trying to ingratiate

herself with a largely hostile public in anticipation of a larger role in the Prince's life, took on a visible role in a charity and planned to make appearances with the Prince before this was cut short by the death of Diana, Princess of Wales.
15. Birkenhead, 145.
16. David, 379.
17. Nicolson, *Diaries,* 282–83.
18. David, 381–82.
19. Ibid., 385–86.
20. Crawford, *Crawford Papers,* 573.
21. *New York Times,* 6 December 1936.
22. *London Daily Herald,* 6 December 1936.
23. *Literary Digest,* 12 December 1936.
24. *New York Times,* 7 December 1936.
25. Channon, 120.
26. Information from Dame Barbara Cartland to author.
27. Cross, 164–65.
28. *Time,* 14 December 1936.

Chapter 22

1. *Hansard's Parliamentary Debates,* 7 December 1936.
2. Nicolson, *Diaries,* 282.
3. *Times* (London), 8 December 1936.
4. Nicolson, *Diaries,* 282.
5. Cited, Bradford, *Reluctant King,* 192.
6. Wheeler-Bennett, *King George VI,* 285.
7. *Times* (London), 8 December 1936.
8. Birkenhead, 149.
9. Ibid., 149–50.
10. Ibid., 150.
11. Cited, Pope-Hennessy, *Queen Mary,* 579.
12. Quoted, Pope-Hennessy, *Queen Mary,* 579.
13. *Daily Telegraph* (London), 21 April 1984.
14. WW, 262.
15. Birkenhead, 147.
16. WW, 263.
17. Washington *Herald,* 8 December 1936.
18. Birkenhead, 146.
19. WW, 264.

20. Ibid., 264–65.
21. Ibid., 266.
22. Ibid., 267.
23. Ibid., 268.
24. Middlemas and Barnes, 1013.
25. WW, 267–68.
26. *New York Times*, 22 January 1939.
27. Private information.
28. WW, 267.
29. Ibid., 269.
30. Nicolson, *Diaries*, 285.
31. *Hansard's Parliamentary Debates*, 10 December 1936.
32. Nicolson, *Diaries*, 285.
33. *Hansard's Parliamentary Debates*, 10 December 1936.
34. Nicolson, *Diaries*, 285–86.
35. Bloch, *File*, 44–45.
36. Bloch, *File*, 46. This figure is equivalent to roughly $40 million or £25 million in 1998 rates.
37. Bloch, *File*, 47.
38. Birkenhead, 151–52.
39. Sitwell, 76.
40. *New York Times*, 12 December 1936.
41. WW, 269.
42. David, 412.
43. Vreeland, 99.

Chapter 23
1. *Illustrated London News*, 19 December 1936.
2. Blackwood, 3.
3. Nicolson, *Diaries*, 283–84.
4. National Archives, Washington, D.C.: U.S. State Department file 841.001, VIII/77, 11 December 1936.
5. *Times* (London), 23 December 1936.
6. Birkenhead, 160.
7. Quoted, Donaldson, 217.
8. Mosley, *Goering*, 265–66.
9. Hitler, 551.
10. Gunther, 305.
11. *New York Evening Journal*, 12 December 1936.
12. *Time*, 21 December 1936.
13. Channon, 67–68.
14. Nicolson, *Diaries*, 283.
15. Channon, 146.

16. Sitwell, 58–60.
17. Laird, 154.
18. *Washington Herald*, 26 December 1936.
19. Quoted in Mackenzie, 541.
20. Lockhart, *Cosmo Gordon Lang*, 405.
21. Bryan and Murphy, 321.
22. Ziegler, 293.
23. Rhodes, *Cazalet*, 188–89.
24. Longford, *Darling Loosy*, 309.
25. Van der Kiste, *Edward VII's Children*, 176.
26. Quoted, Warwick, 125–26.
27. Private information.
28. Cited, Bradford, *Reluctant King*, 157.
29. Donaldson, 129.
30. Private information.
31. Wells, 7.
32. Bolitho, *Edward VIII*, 237.
33. Ibid., 267.
34. Ibid., 237.
35. Ibid., 260.
36. Ibid., 284.
37. Quoted, Mackenzie, 136.
38. Ibid., 136–37.
39. Mackenzie, 151.
40. Ibid., 149.
41. Acland, *House of Windsor*, v.
42. Channon, 131.
43. Ironically, there was some discussion in 1980 that Charles, Prince of Wales, might purchase Belton House as his country estate. Instead, he selected Highgrove House in Gloucestershire.
44. Channon, 131.
45. *Times Literary Supplement* (London), 4 January 1980.
46. Channon, 158.
47. Ibid., 237.

Chapter 24
1. Bloch, *Letters*, 273.
2. WW, 270.
3. Ibid., 270–71.
4. Bryan and Murphy, 350.
5. WW, 273.
6. Bryan and Murphy, 352.
7. WW, 277.
8. Bloch, *Letters*, 287.

9. Ibid., 287–88.
10. WW, 278.
11. Hood, 53.
12. *American Weekly*, 9 December 1956.
13. Martin, 306.
14. *New York Times*, 19 September 1949.
15. Quoted, Donaldson, 311.
16. Bloch, *Letters*, 303–304.
17. David in the *New York Sunday News*, 11 December 1966.
18. Interview with David Metcalfe.
19. Stevenson, 327.
20. *Baltimore News-Post*, 18 December 1936.
21. Donaldson, 316.
22. WW, 281.
23. Ibid., 282.
24. Christy, 141.
25. WW, 282.

Chapter 25
1. WW, 283.
2. Christy, 66–67.
3. WW, 282–83.
4. Details culled from Associated Press article dated 21 March 1937; Associated Press article dated 7 May 1937; Associated Press article dated 21 May 1937; Associated Press article dated 3 June 1937; and Martin, 325.
5. WW, 286.
6. Associated Press article, 14 October 1937.
7. Beaton, *Wandering Years*, 51.
8. Ibid., 52.
9. *New York Times*, 3 May 1937.
10. WW, 288.
11. Ibid., 288–89.
12. Interview with Sir Dudley Forwood.
13. Bloch, *War*, 18.
14. Ibid., 338.
15. Ziegler, 308.
16. *New York Journal-American*, 3 June 1962.
17. Jardine, 54.
18. Ibid., 72.
19. *London Daily Express*, 27 May 1937.

20. Thomas, *Burke's Peerage*, 1967, xxi–xxiii.

Chapter 26
1. WW. 290.
2. Birkenhead, 166.
3. Eilers, 62.
4. *Times* (London), 28 April 1923.
5. Wheeler-Bennett, *King George VI*, 294–95.
6. Wheeler-Bennett, *King George VI*, 288.
7. Bryan and Murphy, 341.
8. Pope-Hennessy, *Queen Mary*, 581–82.
9. *Times* (London), 20 September, 1972.
10. Ziegler, 285.
11. Ziegler, 285.
12. Ziegler, 286.
13. Ziegler, 286.
14. Montgomery-Hyde, *Baldwin*, 518.
15. *London Gazette*, 28 May, 1937.
16. *Times* (London), 29 May, 1937.
17. Bocca, *She Might Have Been Queen*, 153; Bryan and Murphy, 411.
18. Thomas, *Burke's Peerage* As author Michael Thornton points out, p.149, were Queen Elizabeth II to abdicate the Throne in favour of the Prince of Wales, she would automatically revert to the last title and style held prior to her accession, i.e., Her Royal Highness The Princess Elizabeth, Duchess of Edinburgh.
19. wIn 1978, in fact, when Prince Michael of Kent married his wife Marie-Christine, he was forced to renounce his place in the line of succession for the Throne as she was Roman Catholic and such a union contravened the Act of Settlement. But he kept the style of Royal Highness and his wife is Her Royal Highness Princess Michael of Kent. Supporters of George VI have tried to argue that Michael's marriage, unlike that of the Duke of Windsor, fell within the provisions of the Royal Marriages Act and was thus in a

different category; however, with reference to the issue of the provisions contained in the two Letters Patent in question–which have nothing at all to do with the Royal Marriages Act or indeed any marriage–it is clear that no use of the lineal succession argument was made in Prince Michael's case. Thus the lineal argument was selectively applied only to the Duke of Windsor, and then only to prevent Wallis from enjoying the style of Her Royal Highness.

20. Longford, *Elizabeth R*, 76.
21. Thornton, 151.
22. WW, 290.
23. Birkenhead, 166.
24 St. John, *Honeycomb*, 439, 527.

Chapter 27
1. Interview with Sir Dudley Forwood.
2. Beaton, *Wandering Years*, 310.
3. Ibid., 307.
4. Lee, 156.
5. Menkes, *Style*, 106–107; Lee, 156.
6. Thomas, *Pageant of Romance*, 127.
7. Associated Press article, 3 June 1937.
8. *Times* (London), 29 May 1972.
9. Quoted, Donaldson, 347.
10. Ibid., 347.
11. Jardine, 91.
12. Sotheby's, *Public Collection*, 44.
13. Jardine, 88. Jardine later tried to capitalize on his brief notoriety; he and his wife moved to Los Angeles, where he opened the Windsor Cathedral, a small chapel over which he presided. This venture, however, did not prosper, and Jardine died in 1950.
14. Birkenhead, 162.
15. *McCall's*, June 1961.
16. Interview with Sir Dudley Forwood.
17. Pope-Hennessy, *Queen Mary*, 586.

18. Interview with Sir Dudley Forwood.
19. Bryan and Murphy, 376; Martin, 338; Associated Press article, dated 3 June 1937; interview with Sir Dudley Forwood.
20. Bryan and Murphy, 377.
21. *Philadelphia Evening Bulletin*, 2 June 1937.
22. Vidal, 206.
23. Private information.
24. Cited, Ziegler, 327.
25. Ibid., 327.
26. Ibid., 327.
27. Ibid., 328.
28. Ibid., 329.
29. Ibid., 329.
30. PRO/FO file 954/33 ff. 36–38.
31. Cited, Crawford, *Crawford Papers*, 619.
32. Ibid., 618.
33. National Archives, Washington, D.C.: U.S. Department of State file FW033.4111, Memorandum of Confidential Conversation, dated 2 November 1937.

Chapter 28
1. Interview with Sir Dudley Forwood.
2. WW, 295.
3. Christy, 155.
4. Birkenhead, 168.
5. Associated Press article, dated 12 October 1937.
6. Christy, 164–65.
7. WW, 295–96.
8. Interview with Sir Dudley Forwood.
9. Associated Press article, dated 12 October 1937; Bryan and Murphy, 390.
10. Bryan and Murphy, 390.
11. Getty, 84.
12. Interview with Sir Dudley Forwood.
13. WW, 299.
14. Cited, Ziegler, 338.
15. WW, 297.
16. Goering, 88.
17. Ibid., 89.

18. WW, 297–98; Goering, 89.
19. Interview with Sir Dudley Forwood.
20. Goering, 89.
21. Interview with Sir Dudley Forwood.
22. WW, 296.
23. Private information.
24. WW, 300.
25. David in *New York Daily News*, 13 December 1966.
26. Schmidt, 75.
27. Bullitt, 230.
28. Schmidt, 75.
29. *Forward*, 13 November 1937.
30. Private information.
31. David in *New York Daily News*, 13 December 1966.
32. *New York Herald Tribune*, 28 October 1937.
33. Bullitt, 230.
34. Crawford, *Crawford Papers*, 582.
35. Quoted, Crawford, *Crawford Papers*, 617.
36. Associated Press article, dated 5 November 1937.
37. Interview with Sir Dudley Forwood.

Chapter 29
1. Hood, 42.
2. WW, 304.
3. Nicolson, *Diaries*, 351–52.
4. Bloch, *File*, 131.
5. Hood, 99.
6. *London Evening Standard*, 12 December 1938.
7. *New York Times*, 20 November 1937.
8. *Philadelphia Inquirer*, 21 April 1938.
9. Lindbergh, 494.
10. *London Sunday Dispatch*, 12 March 1939.
11. Ziegler, 329.
12. Cited, Ziegler, 330.
13. Bullitt, 310.
14. Quoted, Pope-Hennessy, *Queen Mary*, 575.
15. Bryan and Murphy, 404.
16. WW, 301.
17. Birkenhead, 169.

18. Alice of Gloucester, 117.
19. Ziegler, 324.
20. Hood, 66.
21. WW, 307.
22. Hood, 83–84.
23. *New York Times*, 9 May 1939.
24. Bradford, *Reluctant King*, 286.
25. *London Daily Express*, 8 May 1939.
26. Hood, 87.

Chapter 30
1. Bryan and Murphy, 407.
2. WW, 301.
3. Rebecca West, "Uneasy Lies the Head." *Sunday Telegraph*, 16 December 1979.
4. Hood, 48.
5. Bryan and Murphy, 406.
6. Hood, 49.
7. Bryan and Murphy, 406–07.
8. WW, 302–04.
9. Hood, 49.
10. Ibid., 49.
11. Ibid., 50.
12. Hood, 50; Bryan and Murphy, 408–09.
13. Maxwell, 302; Hood, 50–51.
14. Bryan and Murphy, 409.
15. Hood, 132–33.
16. Ibid., 60–61.
17. Ibid., 130.
18. Ibid., 118–19.
19. Ibid., 89–90.
20. Ibid., 60.
21, Sheean, 61.
22. Ibid., 65.
23. Nicolson, *Diaries*, 351–52.
24. Hood, 45.
25. Ibid., 47.
26. Ibid., 51.
27. Ibid., 55.
28. Ibid., 56.
29. Ibid., 56.
30. WW, 307–308.
31. Hood, 41.
32. Ibid., 68–69.
33. Ibid., 77.
34. Ibid., 69.
35. Ibid., 70.
36. Ibid., 69.
37. Sotheby's, *Public Collection*, 48–49.

38. Hood, 95.
39. Sotheby's, *Public Collection*, 49; Hood, 70.
40. Hood, 72.
41. Ibid., 75.
42. Ibid., 75.
43. Private information.
44. Hood, 74.
45. Ibid., 43–44.
46. Ibid., 44–45.
47. Martin, 357.
48. Hood, 37.
49. Ibid., 37.
50. Ibid., 106.
51. Ibid., 110–111.
52. Ibid., 109.
53. Ibid., 106–107.
54. Ibid., 108.
55. Sotheby's, *Public Collection*, 205–209.
56. Hood, 91–92.
57. Lindbergh, 491–95.

Chapter 31
1. Birkenhead, 170.
2. WW, 311.
3. Bryan and Murphy, 429.
4. WW, 311–12.
5. Quoted, Donaldson, 369–70.
6. WW, 313.
7. Ibid., 314.
8. Cited, Ziegler, 348.
9. WW, 315; Bryan and Murphy, 434.
10. Ibid., 316.
11. Bloch, *File*, 144.
12. Quoted, Donaldson, 373.
13. Interview with Linda Mortimer.
14. Interview with David Metcalfe.
15. Interview with Linda Mortimer.
16. Interview with David Metcalfe.
17. WW, 316.
18. Ibid., 317.
19. Wheeler-Bennett, *King George VI*, 417.
20. WW, 317–18.
21. Minney, 237.
22. Ibid., 239.
23. Ibid., 238.
24. Ibid., 317.
25. Bloch, *File*, 146–47.
26. See Bloch, *File*, pp. 147–48, for further information.

27. WW, 321.
28. Ibid., 321.
29. Ibid., 320.
30. *Baltimore American*, 24 December 1939.
31. Bloch, *File*, 151.
32. WW, 319.
33. Bloch, *War*, 44.
34. WW, 320.
35. Bryan and Murphy, 448.
36. Bloch, *War*, 59.
37. Ibid., 59.
38. Shirer, 604; WW, 321.
39. WW, 322.
40. Ibid., 322–23.
41. Ibid., 323.
42. Interview with David Metcalfe.
43. Ziegler, 358–59.
44. Bloch, *War*, 68–69.
45. WW, 324–25.
46. Bocca, *She Might Have Been Queen*, 189–90.
47. WW, 326.
48. St. John, *The Windsors' Own Story*, Part 11, 17 November 1940, King Features Syndicate, Inc.

Chapter 32
1. Bloch, *Willi*, 23.
2. Cited, Ziegler, 364.
3. PRO/FO file 800/326 ff.196.
4. Quoted, Gilbert, *Finest Hours*, 614.
5. David in *New York Daily News*, 13 December 1966.
6. Gilbert, *Finest Hours*, 614.
7. Colville, 176–77.
8. PRO/FO file 800/326 ff.195
9. Bloch, *War*, 75; PRO/FO file 800/326 ff.195.
10. WW, 332.
11. Quoted, Gilbert, *Finest Hour*, of series *Winston Churchill*, 694.
12. WW, 333.
13. PRO/FO file 371/24249 ff.148, 556, No. 479.
14. Ibid., No. 369.
15. Bloch, *File*, 162–63.
16. Quoted, Thornton, 207.
17. Charmley, *Lord Lloyd*, 248.
18. *Documents on German Foreign Policy, 1918–1945*, ser. D, vol. X, no. 2051.

19. *Documents on German Foreign Policy, 1918–1945,* ser. D, vol. X, 9, no. 6.
20. National Archives, Washington, D.C.: U.S. State Department Document, Telegram to Secretary of State Hull, FRUS 740.0011 1939/4357 European War.
21. *Documents on German Foreign Policy, 1918–1945,* ser. D, vol. X, no. 1023.
22. Bloch, *Willi,* 60.
23. *Documents on German Foreign Policy, 1918–1945,* ser. D., vol. X, B15/B002549-51.
24. Hagen, 129–30.
25. Ibid., 130.
26. Hagen, 131.
27. *Documents on German Foreign Policy, 1918–1945,* ser. D, vol. X, no. 2331, 199.
28. Hagen, 138.
29. *Documents on German Foreign Policy, 1918–1945,* ser. D, vol. X, no. 2384, 223.
30. *Documents on German Foreign Policy, 1918–1945,* ser. D, vol. X, no. 211, 2474, 227.
31. Hagen, 138.
32. Ibid., 138.
33. *Documents on German Foreign Policy, 1918–1945,* ser. D, vol. X, no. 808, 401.
34. *Documents on German Foreign Policy, 1918–1945,* ser. D, vol. X, no. 290, 2495, 290.
35. Hagen, 139.
36. *Documents on German Foreign Policy, 1918–1945,* ser. D, vol. X, no. 2520, 317–318.
37. *Washington Post,* 1 August 1940.
38. PRO/FO file 371/24249 ff.149, no. 485.
39. PRO/FO file 371/24249 ff.149
40. PRO/FO file 371/24249 ff.184, no. 485.
41. WW, 336; Associated Press article, dated 2 August 1940.

Chapter 323
1. Associated Press article, dated 10 August 1940.

2. Associated Press article, dated 8 August 1940.
3. *New York Times,* 9 August 1940.
4. *New York Times,* 12 August 1940.
5. Quoted, Donaldson, 404–405.
6. Bloch, *War,* 96.
7. Quoted, Bloch, *File,* 84.
8. Rose, *Who's Who in the Royal House of Windsor,* 81.
9. Bloch, *War,* 119.
10. Ibid, 119.
11. WW, 337.
12. *New York Times,* 17 August 1940.
13. WW, 337.
14. Private information.
15. Bloch, *War,* 125.
16. PRO/FO file 371/24249, ff. 193.
17. WW, 338.
18. United Press International article, dated 5 September 1940.
19. Bloch, *File,* 175.
20. Cited, Ziegler, 382.
21. Grattidge, 264.
22. St. John, *Honeycomb,* 584.
23. Quoted, Birmingham, 241.
24. WW, 338–39.
25. Vickers, *Private World of the Duke and Duchess of Windsor,* 180.
26. Bloch, *War,* 138.
27. Pye, 100–101.
28. National Archives, Washington, D.C.: U.S. State Department file 844E/001/60.
29. Ibid.
30. Bloch, *War,* 165.
31. Pye, 75; private information.

Chapter 34
1. Bloch, *War,* 191.
2. Pye, 115.
3. Roberts, 291.
4. Associated Press article, dated 26 September 1941.
5. Associated Press article, dated 27 September 1941.
6. Evans, *Prince Charming Goes West,* 74–78. Eventually, the Duke and Duchess decided to sell the ranch in Canada, since they went infrequently and had failed to find oil there. Col. Douglas Kennedy, who had managed it

since 1956, put it on the market in November 1961. A number of Hereford and Galloway cattle, eight hundred hogs, and a team of Welsh ponies were offered along with the four thousand acres. There was also a large stable of Clydesdale and thoroughbred horses, as well as imported collies and German shepherds. The estimated sale price was $300,000.

7. Quoted, Pye, 118.
8. *Baltimore News-Post,* 10 October 1941.
9. Associated Press article, dated 11 October 1941.
10. *Baltimore American,* 12 October 1941.
11. Beirne, 122–23.
12. Associated Press article, dated 14 October 1941.
13. *Baltimore Sun,* 14 October 1941.
14. Associated Press article, dated 13 October 1941.
15. Beirne, 123–24; *Baltimore Sun,* 14 October 1941.
16. Bloch, *War,* 216.
17. Pye, 121.
18. Ibid., 120.
19. *New York Times,* 23 October 1941.
20. Ibid.
21. Quoted, Pye, 120.
22. Quoted, Bloch, *War,* 222.
23. WW, 339.
24. Ibid., 340.
25. Ibid., 339.
26. *Philadelphia Evening Post,* 16 July 1941.
27. WW, 340–41.
28. Pye, 177.
29. WW, 342.
30. Pye, 176–77.
31. WW, 344.

Chapter 35
1. Donaldson, 407–408.
2. Bloch, *War,* 148.
3. Donaldson, 408.
4. Shew, 76.
5. Brendon and Whitehead, 111–113.
6. Ibid.

7. Longford, *Queen Mother,* 86.
8. National Archives, Washington, D.C.: U.S. State Department file 844E/12.5, ff.12/6.
9. Private information.
10. Bloch, *War,* 190.
11. Private information.
12. Pye, 194–95.
13. Bloch, *War,* 183.
14. Quoted, Bloch, *War,* 183.
15. Quoted, Pye, 138.
16. Pye, 188.
17. Ibid., 138–39.
18. Private information.
19. *Philadelphia Evening Bulletin,* 9 June 1943.
20. Pye, 188–89.
21. Ibid., 189.
22. Ibid., 189.
23. WW, 344–45.
24. Pye, 189–90.
25. *New York Post,* 5 June 1943.
26. Letter of the duchess of Windsor, in private collection.
27. Quoted, Bloch, *File,* 84–85.
28. Quoted, Howarth, 143.

Chapter 36
1. Vickers, *Private World of the Duke and Duchess of Windsor,* 185.
2. Cited, Ziegler, 396.
3. National Archives, Washington, D.C.: U.S. State Department file 811.711/4039, dated 18 June 1943.
4. National Archives, Washington, D.C.: U.S. State Department file 800.20211/W G/44 1/2, dated 25 January 1941.
5. Quoted, Pye, 114.
6. National Archives, Washington, D.C.: U.S. State Department file RG 59/2682K/1940–1944.
7. National Archives, Washington, D.C.: U.S. State Department file 70032L, no. X1937/188/503.
8. *Documents on German Foreign Policy, 1918–1945,* ser. C, vol. X, introductory statement.
9. See Costello, chapter 17, for a full examination of the incident.
10. De Marginy, 28.
11. Mosley, *The Duchess of Windsor,* 167

12. Bloch, *File*, 211–12; Bryan and Murphy, 476; Ziegler, 427.
13. Associated Press article, dated 11 September 1944.
14. WW, 347.
15. Ibid., 348.
16. Quoted, Bloch, *File*, 86.
17. Bloch, *War*, 338.
18. Quoted, Thornton, 227.
19. Bryan and Murphy, 439.
20. WW, 349–50.
21. *New York Daily Mirror*, 8 December 1946.

Chapter 37
1. WW, 353.
2. Bloch, *File*, 223.
3. Private information.
4. WW, 354.
5. Bryan and Murphy, 487.
6. Alsop, 55.
7. Bryan and Murphy, 491.
8. Payn and Morley, 54, 61.
9. Bryan and Murphy, 491.
10. *New York Daily Mirror*, 8 December 1946.
11. Nicolson, *Diaries*, 98–99.
12. *Times* (London), 18 October 1946.
13. Laura, Duchess of Marlborough, 104–105.
14. *London Evening Standard*, 17 October 1946.
15. Letter of the Duchess of Windsor, in private collection.
16. Steele, 130.
17. Grattidge, 257.
18. Steele, 84–87.
19. Grattidge, 258.
20. Matthew, 279.
21. Information from Dr. Robert Conte to author.
22. Private information.
23. Olcott, 65.
24. Wright, 177.
25. Ibid., 187.
26. Bryan and Murphy, 559–60. Herman Rogers died in October 1957.
27. Interview with David Metcalfe.
28. *London Evening Standard*, 2 September 1947.
29. Private information.

30. Cited, Bradford, *Reluctant King*, 424, and also confirmed to me privately by one of the Duchess's friends.
31. Associated Press article, dated 26 December 1947.
32. *London Evening Standard*, 25 April 1949.
33. See Bloch, *File*, 89–90 for details.
34. Quoted, Bloch, *File*, 91–92.

Chapter 38
1. Personal information.
2. Associated Press article, dated 22 February 1951.
3. Quoted, Pope-Hennessy, *Queen Mary*, 614. A few weeks before the Duke's death in 1972, the Duchess told nurse Oonagh Shanley that a year after their marriage, in the summer of 1938, she had undergone a hysterectomy. Shanley's veracity is without question, but considering the evidence to the contrary, one must wonder why Wallis would put forth a story which she must have known could be disproved in the future.
4. Bryan and Murphy, 496–97.
5. See Bloch, *File*, chap. 9, for details.
6. *New Statesman*, 29 September 1951.
7. The Duke was indeed fortunate, where his family was concerned, that they appeared to take no notice of his book, for they were capable of treating other sets of royal memoirs with lasting contempt. Marion Crawford, the Scottish governess who had worked for the King and Queen for seventeen years, retired from service in 1947—the same year that her former charge, Princess Elizabeth, was married—and herself wed Maj. George Buthlay. The pair had been given a grace-and-favor house, Nottingham Cottage, Kensington Palace, along with numerous gifts from the Royal Family, including a dinner

service from Queen Mary, a coffee set from Princess Elizabeth, and table lamps from Princess Margaret. Crawford, as a reward for her services as royal governess, was created a commander of the Royal Victorian Order in 1949 (an interesting point, this: George VI felt Crawford's years as his children's governess more deserving of an honor than the four years his sister-in-law the Duchess of Windsor spent in public service in the Bahamas). Both Crawford and her husband had retired on modest pensions; needing some extra money, the former governess sold her memoirs; serialization of her book *The Little Princesses,* began in 1950. The contents were slavishly loyal and innocent, no more revealing than the authorized books written two decades earlier by Lady Cynthia Asquith, but Crawford had apparently broken a confidentiality agreement. Queen Elizabeth was horrified: within weeks, the Buthlays were ordered out of their home. Although Crawford went on to write four more books on the royals, she became a taboo subject within the Royal Family and household. When she died in 1987, not one member of the Royal Family even bothered to send flowers (Bradford, *Reluctant King,* 133).
8. Sulzberger, 690–91.
9. Morrow, *Queen Mother,* 79.
10. *London Daily Mirror,* 8 February 1952.
11. *New York Times,* 8 February 1952.
12. *London Daily Mirror,* 8 February 1952.
13. Bloch, *File,* 261–62.
14. Ibid., 66.
15. Harewood, 17.
16. Bloch, *File,* 264–65.
17. Higham, 417.
18. Sotheby's, *Public Collection,* 96–97.

19. Private information.
20. Channon, 576.
21. Bloch, *File,* 277.
22. See Bradford, *Elizabeth,* 183–84.

Chapter 39
1. Bloch, *File,* 102; personal information.
2. WW, 354.
3. "A Love Affair With Style," in *Town and Country,* 163.
4. Lawford, 183.
5. Cornforth, *The Duke and Duchess of Windsor in Paris,* 122.
6. Vickers, *Private World of the Duke and Duchess of Windsor,* 9.
7. Sotheby's, *Public Collection,* 255.
8. Ibid., 270.
9. Personal information.
10. Lawford, 184.
11. Curtis, 280.
12. Lawford, 184.
13. Menkes, *Style,* 23.
14. *McCall's,* April 1961.
15. Personal information.
16. *McCall's,* May 1961.
17. Cornforth, *The Duke and Duchess of Windsor in Paris,* 124.
18. Ibid., 125.
19. Vreeland, 89.
20. Romanones, *Dancing,* 181.
21. Information from Sylvia Sidney to Allan Wilson.
22. Cornforth, *The Duke and Duchess of Windsor in Paris,* 125.
23. Wallis, "Our First Real Home," in *Woman's Home Companion,* 30.
24. WW, 354; Bryan and Murphy, 521.
25. Wallis, "Our First Real Home," in *Woman's Home Companion,* 33.
26. Becker, 315–16.
27. Wallis, "Our First Real Home," in *Woman's Home Companion,* 36.
28. Becker, 316.
29. Wallis, "Our First Real Home," in *Woman's Home Companion,* 30.
30. Ibid., 31.
31. Ibid., 29.
32. Ibid., 32.
33. Ibid., 33.
34. Pope-Hennessy, *Lonely Business,* 209.

35. Wallis, "Our First Real Home," in *Woman's Home Companion,* 36.
36. Ibid., 57.
37. Ibid., 34–5.
38. WW, 355.
39. Pope-Hennessy, *Lonely Business,* 210.
40. Wallis, "Our First Real Home," in *Woman's Home Companion,* 28.
41. Ibid., 27.
42. Interview with Linda Mortimer.
43. WW, 355.
44. David, "My Garden," in *Life,* 62.

Chapter 40
1. Maxwell, 301.
2. *Elle,* French edition, May 1986.
3. Private information.
4. Cooper, *Light of Common Day,* 161.
5. Bloch, *Letters,* 113.
6. *Harper's Bazaar,* May 1966.
7. WW, second photograph insert caption.
8. *American Mercury,* June 1944.
9. *McCall's,* March 1961.
10. Menkes, *Style,* 132.
11. Ibid., 134.
12. *Harper's Bazaar,* May 1966.
13. Associated Press article, dated 3 June 1962.
14. Menkes, *Style,* 138–39.
15. Sotheby's, *Private Collection,* 192–94.
16. Hood, 102–103.
17. *Harper's Bazaar,* May 1966.
18. Menkes, *Style,* 139.
19. Romanones, "The Dear Romance," in *Vanity Fair,* 75.
20. *Women's Wear Daily,* 17 March 1967.
21. *Time,* 8 April 1966.
22. Suzy Knickerbocker, in *Palm Beach Post,* 6 April 1967.
23. Menkes, *Style,* 138.
24. Romanones, "The Dear Romance," in *Vanity Fair,* 75.
25. Sotheby's, *Private Collection,* 124.
26. Ibid., 130–32.
27. Ibid., 120, 134.
28. Ibid., 150.
29. Ibid., 184; Hood, 103.
30. Personal Information.

31. Sotheby's, *Private Collection,* 224–25.
32. Cowles, *She Made Friends and Kept Them,* 230.
33. *Harper's Bazaar,* May 1966.
34. Menkes, *The Royal Jewels,* 88.
35. Culme, 138.
36. Ibid., 176.
37. Menkes, *The Royal Jewels,* 85.
38. Bryan and Murphy, 546.
39. Field, 86–87.
40. Menkes, *The Royal Jewels,* 89.
41. Ibid., 93.
42. Ibid., 95.
43. Ibid., 83–4.
44. Associated Press article, dated 26 October 1946.
45. Menkes, *Style,* 193.
46. Sotheby's, *Jewels of the Duchess of Windsor,* 91.
47. Romanones, *Dancing,* 8.
48. Nadelhoffer, 230.
49. Menkes, *Style,* 152.
50. *Harper's Bazaar,* May 1966.
51. Lane, 89.

Chapter 41
1. WW, 357.
2. *McCall's,* October 1961.
3. Curtis, 281.
4. Sotheby's, *Private Collection,* 298.
5. Curtis, 280.
6. Interview with Janine Metz.
7. Romanones, "The Dear Romance," in *Vanity Fair,* 118.
8. Interview with Linda Mortimer.
9. Menkes, *Style,* 31.
10. Wallis, "Our First Real Home," in *Women's Home Companion,* 36.
11. Private information.
12. Birmingham, 269.
13. Romanones, "The Dear Romance," in *Vanity Fair,* 73.
14. Ibid., 176.
15. Ibid., 177.
16. Romanones, "The Dear Romance," in *Vanity Fair,* 73.
17. Ibid., 119.
18. Curtis, 281.
19. Ibid., 280.

20. Romanones, "The Dear Romance," in *Vanity Fair*, 119.
21. Bryan and Murphy, 525.
22. Information from Letitia Baldridge to author.
23. Brian, 220.
24. Interview with Janine Metz.
25. Romanones, "The Dear Romance," in *Vanity Fair*, 75.
26. Bry, 126.
27. Ibid, 131.
28. Romanones, "The Dear Romance," in *Vanity Fair*, 75–80.
29. Ibid., 74.
30. Ibid., 75.
31. Ibid., 74.
32. Menkes, *Style*, 66.
33. Curtis, 280.
34. Romanones, "The Dear Romance," in *Vanity Fair*, 74.
35. Ibid., 75.
36. Ibid., 80.
37. Curtis, 279.
38. Private information.
39. Romanones, "The Dear Romance," in *Vanity Fair*, 80.
40. Pope-Hennessy, *Lonely Business*, 211.
41. Menkes, *Style*, 13.
42. Private information.
43. Romanones, "The Dear Romance," in *Vanity Fair*, 80.
44. *McCall's*, April 1961.
45. Ibid.
46. Curtis, 280.
47. *McCall's*, April 1961.
48. Hood, 109–110.
49. Menkes, *Style*, 31.
50. Romanones, "The Dear Romance," in *Vanity Fair*, 80.
51. Private information.
52. Alan Fisher, in "The Windsors: The Sale of a Lifetime." Channel 4 Television Production, 20 February 1998, produced by Stephen Leahy, hosted by Angela Rippon.
53. Maxwell, 303.
54. Romanones, "The Dear Romance," in *Vanity Fair*, 80.
55. Maxwell, 301.
56. Vidal, 205.

57. Lockhart, *Diaries*, 411–12.
58. Romanones, *Dancing*, 161.
59. Bryan and Murphy, 526; private information.
60. Private information.

Chapter 42
1. Miller, *United States*, 138, 141.
2. Ibid., 136.
3. Ibid., 142.
4. Ibid., 136.
5. Murray, 65.
6. Wallis, "My Personal Cookbook," in *American Weekly*, 2 November 1958.
7. Interview with Janine Metz.
8. *McCall's*, February 1961.
9. Vreeland, 152.
10. *New York Times*, 6 January 1953.
11. Maxwell, 308–309.
12. *American Weekly*, 18 December 1955.
13. Private information.
14. United Press article, dated 12 April 1957.
15. Randall, 179.
16. Interview with C. Z. Guest.
17. Braudy, 253–57.
18. Ibid., 209.
19. Private information.
20. *McCall's*, June 1961.
21. Cowles, *She Made Friends and Kept Them*, 228.
22. Brian, 218–19.
23. Private information.
24. Bloch, *File*, 291.
25. Ibid., 364.
26. Associated Press article, dated 4 October 1956.
27. Brian, 219
28. Birmingham, 227.
29. Interview with Aline, Countess of Romanones.
30. Private information.
31. Bryan and Murphy, 501.
32. Interview with Aline, Countess of Romanones.
33. Private information.
34. Quoted, Birmingham, 264.
35. Private information.
36. Interview with Aline, Countess of Romanones.

37. Bryan and Murphy, 503.
38. *New York Times,* 7 December 1950.
39. Brody, 32.
40. *Newsweek,* 29 January 1951.
41. *New York Journal-American,* 31 January 1951.
42. *New York Daily Mirror,* 19 February 1951.
43. *New York Journal-American,* 19 October 1951.
44. *New York Journal-American,* 15 October 1951.
45. *American Weekly,* 9 December 1951.
46. Interview with Aline, Countess of Romanones.
47. Private information.
48. Amory, *Best Cat,* 119.
49. Ibid., 120.
50. Private information.
51. Associated Press article, dated 5 October 1955.
52. *Times* (London), 27 September 1956.
53. CBS Television Broadcast, "Person to Person," air date 28 September 1956.
54. Private information.
55. Ibid.
56. Interview with Janine Metz.
57. Ibid.
58. Ibid.
59. *New York Times,* 1 June 1966.
60. Interview with Janine Metz.
61. Associated Press article, dated 17 December 1964.
62. *London Daily Mail,* 4 May 1965.
63. Women's News Service story, dated 4 June 1967.

Chapter 43
1. Cited, Thornton, 301.
2. Associated Press article, dated 13 November 1956.
3. Bradford, Elizabeth, 211.
4. Ibid., 193.
5. The official souvenir programs were approved by the Office of the Lord Chamberlain in all details relating to the Royal Family.

6. Pope-Hennessy, *Lonely Business,* 218.
7. *McCall's,* February 1961.
8. *London Sunday Express,* 8 December 1963.
9. Interview with Aline, Countess of Romanones.
10. Letter of the Duchess of Windsor, in private collection.
11. Cathcart, *Queen Mother,* 129.
12. Bryan and Murphy, 528.
13. Private information.
14. Bloch, *Duchess,* 209.
15. See Thornton, 292, for further details.
16. Private information.
17. Ibid.
18. Whiting, 181.
19. Thornton, 295.
20. James, 121.
21. Information from the Earl of Harewood to author.
22. Interview with Linda Mortimer.
23. *London Daily Express,* 6 June 1967.
24. Quoted, Thornton, 300.
25. *London Daily Mirror,* 6 June 1967.
26. Evans, *Mountbatten Years,* 88.
27. Ibid., 88.
28. Barratt, 105.
29. Thornton, 1.
30. *Times* (London), 8 June 1967.
31. Mosley, *Duchess of Windsor,* 191.
32. *London Daily Express,* 13 February 1979.
33. *London Daily Mail,* 8 June 1967.
34. Thornton, 7.
35. *London Daily Express,* 13 February 1979.
36. Thornton, 7.
37. *Times* (London), 8 June 1967; *London Daily Telegraph,* 8 June 1967.
38. Thomas, *Burke's Peerage,* xxiii.
39. Birmingham, 289.
40. Talbot, 164.
41. Flamini, 38.

Chapter 44
1. Romanones, "The Dear Romance," in *Vanity Fair,* 75.
2. *London Daily Mail,* 19 June 1961.
3. Private information.

4. Ibid.
5. Pryce-Jones, 110.
6. Interview with Janine Metz.
7. Beaton, *Self Portrait*, 405–407.
8. Cited, Ziegler, 479.
9. Kenneth Harris interview, BBC Television.
10. Harris, *The Queen*, 195.
11. Sotheby's, *Private Collection*, 215.
12. *Washington Post*, 6 April 1970.
13. Bush, 77.
14. Quoted, Ziegler, *Mountbatten*, 679.
15. Dimbleby, 178.
16. Ibid., 178–79.
17. Bragg, 471.
18. Ibid., 474.
19. *London Sunday Express*, 2 December 1972.
20. Bryan and Murphy, 580.
21. Interview with Dr. Jean Thin.
22. Interview with Oonagh Shanley.
23. Ibid.
24. Ibid.
25. Ibid.
26. Ibid.
27. Interview with Dr. Jean Thin.
28. Romanones, "The Dear Romance," in *Vanity Fair*, 64.
29. Interview with Oonagh Shanley.
30. Private information.
31. Interview with Dr. Jean Thin.
32. Bryan and Murphy, 583.
33. Private information.
34. *London Evening Standard*, 30 May 1972.
35. Interview with Dr. Jean Thin.
36. Interviews with Dr. Jean Thin and Oonagh Shanley.
37. Private information.
38. Romanones, "The Dear Romance," in *Vanity Fair*, 66.
39. Private information.
40. Romanones, "The Dear Romance," in *Vanity Fair*, 66.
41. Interviews with Dr. Jean Thin and Oonagh Shanley; private information.
42. Private information.

Chapter 45
1. Interview with Oonagh Shanley.

2. Joan Reeder, "The End of a King's Story," In *Woman*, London, 5 July 1980.
3. Shanley, in *Hello!* 58.
4. Interview with Oonagh Shanley.
5. Bryan and Murphy, 585.
6. Menkes, *Style*, 196.
7. Interview with Oonagh Shanley.
8. Ibid.
9. *Times* (London), 29 May 1972.
10. Private information.
11. Pimlott, 408.
12. *London Daily Mail*, 29 May 1972.
13. *The Guardian* (London), 29 May 1972.
14. United Press International article, dated 29 May 1972.
15. Interview with Dr. Jean Thin.
16. Menkes, *Style*, 128.
17. Ziegler, *Shore to Shore*, 250–51.
18. Private information.
19. *London Daily Express*, 29 May 1972.
20. *London Daily Mail*, 29 May 1972.
21. *London Evening News*, 29 May 1972.
22. Bryan and Murphy, 586–87.
23. Ziegler, *Shore to Shore*, 251.
24. Romanones, "The Dear Romance," in *Vanity Fair*, 66.
25. Ziegler, *Shore to Shore*, 252.
26. Ibid., 253.
27. *Times* (London), 3 June 1973; and *London Daily Telegraph*, 3 June 1972.
28. Private information.
29. Bryan and Murphy, 587.
30. Pimlott, 408–09.
31. Dimbleby, 179.
32. Romanones, "The Dear Romance," in *Vanity Fair*, 66.
33. Pimlott, 408.
34. Ibid.
35. *London Sunday Bulletin*, 4 June 1972.
36. Ibid.
37. Pimlott, 408; and personal information.
38. Private information.
39. Ziegler, *Shore to Shore*, 253–54.
40. Dimbleby, 180.
41. *London Sunday Express*, 4 June 1972.

42. *Hansard's Parliamentary Debates,* 5 June 1972.
43. Ibid.
44. Ibid.
45. Ibid.
46. Ibid.
47. Ibid.
48. Ibid.
49. *Sunday Times* (London), 11 June 1972.
50. Romanones, "The Dear Romance," in *Vanity Fair,* 67.
51. Ibid., 67.
52. Ziegler, *Shore to Shore,* 254.
53. Bryan and Murphy, 555.
54. Romanones, "The Dear Romance," in *Vanity Fair,* 67.
55. Bloch, *Duchess,* 216.
56. Romanones, "The Dear Romance," in *Vanity Fair,* 67.
57. Thornton, 330.
58. Ziegler, *Shore to Shore,* 255.

Chapter 46
1. Interview with Aline, Countess of Romanones.
2. Bryan and Murphy, 563.
3. Interview with Aline, Countess of Romanones.
4. Martin, 12.
5. Interview with David Metcalfe.
6. Private information.
7. *London News of the World,* 3 September 1972.
8. Cited, Thornton, 389.
9. Ibid., 418.
10. *Times* (London), 30 May 1973.
11. Romanones, "The Dear Romance," in *Vanity Fair,* 68.
12. Interview with Linda Mortimer.
13. Ziegler, *Shore to Shore,* 259.
14. Ibid., 259–60.
15. Bryan and Murphy, 596–97.
16. Quoted, Ziegler, *Mountbatten,* 681.
17. Interview with Dr. Jean Thin.
18. Martin, 9.
19. Romanones, "The Dear Romance," in *Vanity Fair,* 199.
20. Interview with Janine Metz.
21. Ibid.
22. Private information.

23. Romanones, "The Dear Romance," in *Vanity Fair,* 66.
24. Interview with Janine Metz.
25. Bryan and Murphy, 585.
26. Interview with Janine Metz.
27. Sydney Johnson died in 1990, having returned to the Windsor Villa, after Wallis's death, in the employ of Mohammed al-Fayed.
28. *New York Times,* 10 April 1974.
29. Interview with Janine Metz.
30. Aronson, Margaret, 250.
31. Private information.
32. Martin, 496–97.
33. Bryan and Murphy, 566.
34. Interview with Dr. Jean Thin.
35. Vreeland, 90–91.
36. Bloch, *Duchess,* 222; interview with Janine Metz.
37. Interview with Dr. Jean Thin.
38. Mosley, *Duchess of Windsor,* 209.
39. Interview with Dr. Jean Thin.
40. Anderson, 312.
41. Thornton, 354.
42. Interview with Dr. Jean Thin.
43. Interview with Linda Mortimer.
44. Romanones, "The Dear Romance," in *Vanity Fair,* 121.
45. Interview with Janine Metz.
46. Ibid.

Chapter 47
1. Pryce-Jones, 38.
2. Pryce-Jones, 38. This was not the first production featuring the story of the Duke and Duchess of Windsor, nor would it be the last. American television had been the first to produce a one-hour drama, *The Woman I Love,* starring Richard Chamberlain as the Duke and Faye Dunaway as Wallis. In the fall of 1972, the play *Crown Matrimonial* opened in London at the Theatre Royal, Haymarket. Written by Royce Ryton, it starred Wendy Hiller as Queen Mary, Peter Barkworth as Edward VIII, and Andrew Ray as the Duke of York. Wallis did not appear as a character in the play, but her archrival the Duchess of York did,

played by Amanda Reiss. In October 1973 actress Phyllis Calvert took over the role of Queen Mary, while actor John Frasier assumed that of the King. Interestingly, both Andrew Ray and Amanda Reiss would reprise their roles as the Duke and Duchess of York in the Thames TV series *Edward and Mrs. Simpson*, reflecting something of a career association with the royals for Ray, who, as a child, had appeared as "Wheeler," the boy in the film *The Mudlark*. In 1978 a play called *The Woman I Love* by Dan Sutherland opened at the Churchill Theatre, Bromley, Kent, starring Martin Jarvis as David, Holly Palance as Wallis, Ellen Pollock as Queen Mary, and Robert Beatty as Lord Beaverbrook. The last production before Wallis's death in which she was featured was the 1983 film *To Catch a King*, based on the Windsors' experiences in Portugal in 1940 and starring John Standing and Barbara Parkins as the Duke and Duchess. In April 1988, Jane Seymour and Anthony Andrews played Wallis and David in the CBS Television production *The Woman He Loved*, written by Tony Award–winning playwright William Luce. The program aired to good reviews and won for its time period.

3. Pryce-Jones, 38.
4. Ibid., 38.
5. *London Evening Standard*, 8 October 1976.
6. Bloch, *Duchess*, 225.
7. Interview with Dr. Jean Thin.
8. Interview with Aline, Countess of Romanones.
9. Interview with Linda Mortimer.
10. Interview with Michael Bloch.
11. Ibid.
12. Interview with Dr. Jean Thin.
13. Romanones, "The Dear Romance," in *Vanity Fair*, 73.

14. Interview with Dr. Jean Thin.
15. Romanones, "The Dear Romance," in *Vanity Fair*, 73.
16. Interview with Dr. Jean Thin.
17. Ibid.
18. Ibid.
19. Information from Diana, Lady Mosley, and interviews with Janine Metz; Aline, Countess of Romanones; and Linda Mortimer.
20. Interview with Linda Mortimer.
21. Romanones, "The Dear Romance," in *Vanity Fair*, 122.
22. Ibid.
23. Ibid.
24. Interview with Janine Metz.
25. Interview with Dr. Jean Thin.
26. Jim Leo to press, on CBS Television Evening News, 24 April 1986.
27. Interview with Dr. Jean Thin.
28. Georges Sanegre died in 1989.
29. Information from Kenneth Jay Lane to author.
30. Information from Diana, Lady Mosley to author.
31. Interview with Linda Mortimer.
32. Private information.
33. Bradford, *Elizabeth*, 417.
34. Private information.
35. Information from Diana, Lady Mosley to author.
36. Warwick, 170.

Epilogue
1. Brendon, *Our Own Dear Queen*, 135.
2. Bloch, *Duchess*, 221.
3. Ibid., 222.
4. Interview with Michael Bloch.
5. Bloch, *Duchess*, 22.
6. Menkes, *Style*, 198.
7. "A Love Affair with Style," in *Town and Country*, 163.
8. Culme, 10.
9. Menkes, *Royal Jewels*, 100.
10. Morrow, *Queen Mother*, 80.
11. Menkes, *Royal Jewels*, 101.
12. Culme, 11.
13. Ibid., 11.
14. Dunne, 223.
15. Culme, 7.

16. Dunne, 226.
17. Private information.
18. Interview with Janine Metz.
19. "Edward on Edward," in *Hello!* 46.
20. *Edward on Edward*, 1996, Ardent Productions.
21. Interview with Janine Metz.
22. Vickers, *Private World of the Duke and Duchess of Windsor*, 10.
23. Erna Bringe to author, 12 August 1997.
24. Al-Fayed Windsor Villa booklet, in private collection.
25. *Edward and Mrs Simpson: Going Going Gone*, BBC Television, produced and hosted by Desmond Wilcox, 1997.
26. Ingrid Seward, editor in chief's letter, *Majesty*, September 1997, 4.
27. Letter of 3 September 1997, from Diana Brooks of Sotheby's.
28. *New York Times*, 12 February 1998; Lacey, *Bidding for Class*, 306.
29. Menkes, *Style*, 200–201.
30. Interview with David Metcalfe.
31. Interview with Linda Mortimer.
32. Interview with Janine Metz.
33. WW, 178.

Bibliography

Aarons, Slim. *A Wonderful Time: An Intimate Portrait of the Good Life*. New York: Harper & Row, 1974.

Abend, Hallett. *My Life in China, 1926–1941*. New York: Harcourt, Brace, 1943.

Acland, Eric, and Ernest H. Bartlett. *Long Live the King: George V — King and Emperor, Prince and Sovereign — Edward VIII*. Toronto: John C. Winston, 1936.

_____. *The House of Windsor: George V to George VI*. Chicago: John C. Winston, 1937.

Acton, Harold. *Memoirs of an Aesthete*. London: Methuen, 1948.

Allen, Peter. *The Crown and the Swastika: Hitler, Hess and the Duke of Windsor*. London: Robert Hale, 1983.

Alsop, Susan Mary. *To Marietta From Paris, 1945–1960*. London: Weidenfeld & Nicolson, 1976.

Amory, Cleveland. *The Last Resorts*. New York: Harper & Brothers, 1952.

_____. *Who Killed Society?* New York: Harper & Brothers, 1960.

_____. *The Best Cat Ever*. Boston: Little, Brown, 1993.

Anderson, Christopher. *Jackie After Jack*. New York: William Morrow, 1998.

Aronson, Theo. *Royal Family: Years of Transition*. London: John Murray, 1983.

_____. *Crowns in Conflict: The Triumph and the Tragedy of European Monarchy, 1910–1918*. Manchester, N.H.: Salem House, 1986.

_____. *The King in Love*. New York: Harper & Row, 1988.

_____. *The Royal Family at War*. London: John Murray, 1993.

_____. *Princess Margaret: A Biography*. London: Michael O'Mara Books, 1997.

Aslet, Clive. *The Last Country Houses*. New Haven, Conn.: Yale University Press, 1982.

Asquith, Lady Cynthia. *The Duchess of York*. London: Hutchinson, 1927.

_____. *Her Majesty the Queen: An Entirely New and Complete Biography, Written with the Approval of Her Majesty*. New York: Dutton, 1937.

_____. *Diaries, 1915–1918*. New York: Knopf, 1969.

Attlee, Clement R. *As It Happened*. New York: Viking, 1954.

Baldry, A. L. *Royal Palaces*. London: The Studio, 1935.

Balmain, Pierre. *My Years and Seasons*. New York: Doubleday, 1965.

Barratt, John, with Jean Ritchie. *With the Greatest Respect: The Private Lives of Earl Mountbatten and Prince & Princess Michael of Kent*. London: Sidgwick & Jackson, 1991.

Barrymaine, Norman. *The Peter Townsend Story*. New York: Dutton, 1958.

Beaton, Cecil. *The Wandering Years*. Boston: Little, Brown, 1961.

_____. *Self Portrait With Friends: The Selected Diaries of Cecil Beaton, 1926–1974*. London: Weidenfeld & Nicolson, 1979.

Beaverbrook, William Maxwell Aitken. *The Abdication of King Edward VIII.* Edited by A. J. P. Taylor. New York: Atheneum, 1966.

Becker, Robert. *Nancy Lancaster: Her Life, Her World, Her Art.* New York: Knopf, 1996.

Behrman, S. N. *Portrait of Max: An Intimate Memoir of Sir Max Beerbohm.* New York: Random House, 1960.

Beirne, Francis F. *The Amiable Baltimoreans.* New York: Dutton, 1951.

Bennett, Daphne. *Queen Victoria's Children.* New York: St. Martin's Press, 1980.

Bentley-Cranch, Dana. *Edward VII: Image of an Era, 1841–1910.* London: Her Majesty's Stationery Office, 1992.

Birkenhead, F. W. F. S. *Walter Monckton: The Life of Viscount Monckton of Brenchley.* London: Weidenfeld & Nicolson, 1969.

Blackwood, Caroline. *The Last of the Duchess.* New York: Pantheon, 1995.

Bloch, Michael. *The Duke of Windsor's War: From Europe to the Bahamas, 1939–1945.* New York: Coward-McCann, 1983.

_____. *Operation Willi: The Nazi Plot to Kidnap the Duke of Windsor, July 1940.* New York: Weidenfeld & Nicolson, 1984.

_____. *Wallis and Edward: Letters 1931–1937.* New York: Summit Books, 1986.

_____. *The Secret File of the Duke of Windsor.* New York: Harper & Row, 1988.

_____. *The Reign & Abdication of Edward VIII.* London: Bantam, 1990.

_____. *The Duchess of Windsor.* London: Weidenfeld & Nicolson, 1996.

Blume, Mary. *Côte d'Azur: Inventing the French Riviera.* London: Thames and Hudson, 1992.

Bocca, Geoffrey. *The Woman Who Would Be Queen.* New York: Rinehart, 1954.

_____. *The Life and Death of Sir Harry Oakes.* Garden City, N.Y.: Doubleday, 1959.

Bolitho, Hector. *King Edward VIII: His Life and Reign.* London: Eyre and Spottiswoode, 1937.

_____. *Royal Progress: One Hundred Years of British Monarchy.* London: B. T. Batsford, 1937.

_____. *King George VI.* New York: Lippincott, 1938.

_____. *A Century of British Monarchy.* London: Longmans, Green, 1951.

Bove, Charles. *A Paris Surgeon's Story.* Boston: Little, Brown, 1956.

Bradford, Sarah. *The Reluctant King: The Life & Reign of George VI, 1895–1952.* New York: St. Martin's Press, 1989.

_____. *Elizabeth: A Biography of Britain's Queen.* New York: Farrar, Straus & Giroux, 1996.

Bragg, Melvyn. *Richard Burton: A Life.* Boston: Little, Brown, 1988.

Brandon, Ruth. *The Dollar Princesses: Sagas of Upward Nobility, 1870–1914.* New York: Knopf, 1980.

Braudy, Susan. *This Crazy Thing Called Love.* New York: Knopf, 1992.

Brendon, Piers. *Our Own Dear Queen.* London: Secker & Warburg, 1986.

Brendon, Piers, and Phillip Whitehead. *The Windsors: A Dynasty Revealed.* London: Hodder & Stoughton, 1994.

Brian, Denis. *Fair Game: What Biographers Don't Tell You.* Amherst, N.Y.: Prometheus, 1994.

Brinnin, J. Malcolm. *The Sway of the Grand Saloon.* New York: Delacorte Press, 1971.

_____. *Beau Voyage: Life Aboard the Last Great Ships.* New York: Congdon & Lattes, 1981.

Brody, Ilse. *Gone With the Windsors.* Philadelphia: John C. Winston, 1953.

Brook-Shepherd, Gordon. *Victims at Sarajevo: The Romance and Tragedy of Franz Ferdinand and Sophie.* London: Harvill Press, 1984.

Brown, Ivor. *Balmoral: The History of a Home.* London: Collins, 1955.

Brown, Michelle. *Rituals of Royalty.* London: Sidgwick & Jackson, 1983.

Bryan, J., and Charles J. V. Murphy. *The Windsor Story.* New York: William Morrow, 1979.

Bullitt, Orville H., ed. *For the President: Personal and Secret. Correspondence Between Franklin D. Roosevelt and William C. Bullitt.* Boston: Houghton Mifflin, 1972.

Bush, Barbara. *A Memoir.* New York: Scribners, 1994.

Campbell, Judith. *Royalty on Horseback.* Garden City, New York: Doubleday, 1974.

Carlton, Charles. *Royal Mistresses.* London: Routledge, 1990.

Cathcart, Helen. *Sandringham: The Story of a Royal Home.* London: W. H. Allen, 1964.

_____. *The Queen Mother.* London: W. H. Allen, 1965.

_____. *Anne and the Princesses Royal.* London: W. H. Allen, 1973.

Channon, Sir Henry. *Chips: The Diaries of Sir Henry Channon.* Edited by Robert Rhodes James. London: Weidenfeld & Nicolson, 1967.

Charmley, John. *Duff Cooper: The Authorized Biography.* London: Weidenfeld & Nicolson, 1986.

_____. *Lord Lloyd and the Decline of the British Empire.* New York: St. Martin's Press, 1987.

Chisholm, Anne, and Michael Davie. *Lord Beaverbrook: A Life.* New York: Knopf, 1993.

Christy, Jim. *The Price of Power: A Biography of Charles Eugene Bedaux.* Garden City, N.Y.: Doubleday, 1984.

Churchill, Randolph. *Lord Derby, King of Lancashire.* London: Heinemann, 1959.

Churchill, Winston S. *The Gathering Storm* (vol. 1, *Second World War*). Boston: Houghton Mifflin, 1948.

_____. *Their Finest Hours* (vol. 2, *Second World War*). Boston: Houghton Mifflin, 1949.

Cole, Bernard D. *Gunboats and Marines: The United States Navy in China, 1925–1928.* Newark: University of Delaware Press, 1983.

Collier, Richard. *The Rainbow People.* New York: Dood, Mead, 1984.

Cologni, Franco, and Eric Nussbaum. *Platinum by Cartier: Triumphs of the Jewelers' Art.* New York: Abrams, 1995.

Colville, John. *The Fringes of Power: 10 Downing Street Diaries 1939–1955.* New York: Norton, 1985.

Cooke, Alistair. *Six Men.* New York: Knopf, 1977.

Cooke, Ann Kirk, and Elizabeth Lightfoot. *The Other Mrs. Simpson: Postscript to the Love Story of the Century.* New York: Vantage Press, 1977.

Cooper, Duff. *Old Men Forget.* London: Rupert Hart-Davis, 1954.

Cooper, Lady Diana. *The Light of Common Day.* London: Rupert Hart-Davis, 1959.

Cooper, Artemis. *The Diana Cooper Scrapbook.* London: Hamish Hamilton, 1987.

Cornforth, John. *The Inspiration of the Past.* London: Penguin, 1985.

Costello, John. *Mask of Treachery.* New York: William Morrow, 1988.

Cowles, Fleur. *She Made Friends and Kept Them: An Anecdotal Memoir.* New York: HarperCollins, 1996.

Cowles, Virginia. *Gay Monarch: The Life and Pleasures of Edward VII.* New York: Harper & Brothers, 1956.

Crawford, David Lindsay. *The Crawford Papers: The Journals of David Lindsay, Twenty-seventh Earl of Crawford and Tenth Earl of Balcarres 1871–1940 During the Years 1892–1940.* Edited by John Vincent. Manchester, Eng.: Manchester University Press, 1984.

Crawford, Marion. *The Little Princesses.* New York: Harcourt, Brace, 1950.

Cross, Colin. *The Fascists in Britain.* London: Barrie and Rockliff, 1961.

Culme, John, and Nicholas Rayner. *The Jewels of the Duchess of Windsor.* London: Thames and Hudson, 1987.

Cumming, Valerie. *Royal Dress.* New York: Holmes & Meier, 1989.

Curtis, Charlotte. *The Rich and Other Atrocities.* New York: Harper & Row, 1976.

Day, J. Wentworth. *HRH Princess Marina, Duchess of Kent.* London: Robert Hale, 1962.

De-la-Noy, Michael. *The Queen Behind the Throne.* London: Hutchinson, 1994.

De Marginy, Alfred. *A Conspiracy of Crowns.* London: Transworld, 1988.

Dimbleby, Jonathan. *The Prince of Wales.* New York: William Morrow, 1994.

Domville-Fife, Charles W. *King Edward VIII.* London: Rankin Brothers, 1937.

Donaldson, Frances. *Edward VIII.* New York: Lippincott, 1974.

Donzel, Catherine, Alexis Gregory, and Marc Walter. *Grand American Hotels.* New York: Vendome Press, 1989.

Duff, David. *George & Elizabeth: A Royal Marriage.* London: Collins, 1983.

_____. *Queen Mary.* London: Collins, 1985.

Duncan, Andrew. *The Reality of Monarchy.* London: Heinemann, 1970.

Dunne, Dominick. *The Mansions of Limbo.* New York: Crown, 1991.

Edgar, Donald. *The Queen's Children.* London: Arthur Barker, 1978.

Edwards, Anne. *Matriarch: Queen Mary and the House of Windsor.* New York: William Morrow, 1984.

_____. *Royal Sisters.* New York: William Morrow, 1990.

Eilers, Marlene A. *Queen Victoria's Descendants.* Baltimore: Genealogical Publishing Co., 1987.

Evans, Simon. *Prince Charming Goes West: The Story of the E. P. Ranch.* Calgary, Can.: University of Calgary Press, 1993.

Evans, William. *My Mountbatten Years: In the Service of Lord Louis.* London: Headline, 1989.

Everett, Susanne. *London: The Glamour Years, 1919–1939.* New York: Gallery Books, 1985.

Fabb, John. *Royal Tours of the British Empire, 1860–1927.* London: Batsford, 1989.

Fest, Joachim. *Hitler.* New York: Harcourt Brace Jovanovich, 1973.

Field, Leslie. *The Queen's Jewels: The Personal Collection of Elizabeth II.* New York: Abrams, 1987.

Fisher, Graham and Heather. *Monarchy and the Royal Family.* London: Robert Hale, 1979.

Fisher, Richard B. *Syrie Maugham.* London: Duckworth, 1978.

Flamini, Roland. *Sovereign: Elizabeth II and the Windsor Dynasty.* New York: Delacorte Press, 1991.

Ford, Colin, ed. *Happy and Glorious: Six Reigns of Royal Photography.* London: Angus & Robertson, 1977.

Foss, Arthur. *The Dukes of Britain.* London: Herbert Press, 1986.

Fowler, Marion. *The Way She Looks Tonight.* New York: St. Martin's Press, 1996.

Fremantle, Anne. *Three Cornered Heart.* New York: Viking, 1970

Fulford, Roger. *Hanover to Windsor.* London: Batsford, 1960.

Garrett, Richard. *Mrs. Simpson.* New York: St. Martin's Press, 1979.

Getty, J. Paul. *As I See It.* Englewood Cliffs, N.J.: Prentice-Hall, 1976.

Gilbert, Martin. *Winston Churchill.* 22 vols. London: Heinemann, 1966–1993.

Girouard, Mark. *Windsor: The Most Romantic Castle.* London: Hodder & Stoughton, 1993.

Gloucester, Princess Alice, Duchess of. *The Memoirs of Princess Alice, Duchess of Gloucester.* London: Collins, 1983.

Goering, Emmy. *My Life With Goering.* London: David Bruce & Watson, 1972.

Golby, J. M., and A. W. Purdue. *The Monarchy and the British People.* Portland, Oreg.: Areopagitica Press, 1988.

Goldsmith, Barbara. *Little Gloria . . . Happy At Last.* New York: Knopf, 1980.

Gordon, Elizabeth Gordon Biddle. *Days of Now and Then*. Philadelphia: Dorrance, 1945.

Gore, Sir John. *King George V: A Personal Memoir*. London: John Murray, 1941.

Graeme, Bruce. *A Century of Buckingham Palace*. London: Hutchinson, 1937.

Grattidge, Harry. *Captain of the Queens*. New York: Dutton, 1956.

Graves, Robert, and Alan Hodge. *The Long Week-End: A Social History of Great Britain, 1918–1939*. New York: Norton, 1963.

Greece, Prince Christopher of. *Memoirs*. London: Right Book Club, 1938.

Gunther, John. *Inside Europe*. New York: Harper & Brothers, 1940.

Hagen, Lewis, ed. and trans. *The Schellenberg Memoirs*. London: Deutsch, 1956.

"*Hail and Farewell: The Passing of King George V.*" London: Times Publishing Co., 1936.

Hall, Michael. *Buckingham Palace: The Palace and Its Royal Residents in Photographs.* London: Salamander Books, 1995.

Hall, Phillip. *Royal Fortune: Tax, Money & The Monarchy*. London: Bloomsbury, 1992.

Hall, Trevor. *Royal Canada: A History of Royal Visits to Canada Since 1786*. Godalming, Eng.: Archive, 1989.

Hall, Unity. *Philip: The Man Behind the Monarchy*. New York: St. Martin's Press, 1987.

Hamilton, Willie. *My Queen and I*. London: Quartet Books, 1975.

Hardinge, Helen. *Loyal to Three Kings*. London: Kimber, 1967.

Harewood, George, Earl of. *The Tongs and the Bones*. London: Weidenfeld & Nicolson, 1981.

Harris, John, Geoffrey de Bellaigue, and Oliver Millar. *Buckingham Palace*. New York: Viking, 1968.

Harris, Kenneth. *The Queen*. New York: St. Martin's Press, 1994.

Harris, Marion. *The Queen's Windsor*. Bourne End, Eng.: Kensal House, 1985.

Hart-Davis, Duff, ed. *In Royal Service: The Letters and Journals of Sir Alan Lascelles, Volume II, 1920–1936*. London: Hamish Hamilton, 1989.

Hatch, Alden. *The Mountbattens*. New York: Random House, 1965.

Heald, Tim, and Mayo Mohs. *H.R.H. The Man Who Will Be King*. New York: Arbor House, 1979.

Healey, Edna. *The Queen's House: A Social History of Buckingham Palace*. London: Michael Joseph, 1997.

Hepworth, Philip. *Royal Sandringham*. Norwich: Wensum Books, 1978.

Hesse, Fritz. *Hitler and the English*. Edited and translated by F. A. Voigt. London: Allen Wingate, 1954.

Hibbert, Christopher. *The Court at Windsor: A Domestic History*. London: Longmans, Green, 1964.

_____. *Edward: The Uncrowned King*. New York: St. Martin's Press, 1972.

_____. *The Royal Victorians*. New York: Lippincott, 1976.

_____. *The Court of St. James's*. New York: William Morrow, 1980.

Higham, Charles. *The Duchess of Windsor: The Secret Life*. New York: McGraw-Hill, 1988.

Highsmith, Carol M., and Ted Landphair. *Embassies of Washington*. Washington, D.C.: National Trust for Historic Preservation, 1992.

Hitler, Adolf. *Hitler's Secret Conversations*. Introduction by Hugh Trevor-Roper. New York: Farrar, Straus & Young, 1953.

Hoare, Philip. *Serious Pleasures: The Life of Stephen Tennant*. London: Hamish Hamilton, 1990.

Holden, Anthony. *Prince Charles*. New York: Atheneum, 1979.

_____. *The Tarnished Crown*. New York: Random House, 1993.

Hood, Dina Wells. *Working for the Windsors*. London: Allen Wingate, 1957.

Hough, Richard. *The Mountbattens*. New York: Dutton, 1975.
_____. *Born Royal: The Lives and Loves of the Young Windsors*. New York: Bantam, 1988.
Howarth, Patrick. *George VI*. London: Hutchinson, 1987.
Inglis, Brian. *Abdication*. London: Hodder & Stoughton, 1966.
James, Paul. *Princess Alexandra*. London: Weidenfeld & Nicolson, 1992.
Jardine, H. A. *At Long Last*. New York: Murray and Dore, 1943.
Jones, Raymond A. *Arthur Ponsonby: The Politics of Life*. London: Hutchinson, 1989.
Jones, Thomas. *A Diary With Letters, 1931–1950*. London: Oxford University Press, 1954.
Judd, Denis. *The House of Windsor*. London: Macdonald, 1973.
_____. *The Royal Victorians*. New York: St. Martin's Press, 1975.
_____. *King George VI*. New York: Franklin Watts, 1983.
Junor, Penny. *Charles*. New York: St. Martin's Press, 1987.
Keay, Douglas. *The Queen*. New York: St. Martin's Press, 1991.
Kidd, Charles, and Patrick Montague-Smith. *Debrett's Book of Royal Children*. New York: William Morrow, 1982.
King, Stella. *Princess Marina: Her Life and Times*. London: London House & Maxwell, 1969.
Kinross, John Patrick Douglas Balfour. *The Windsor Years*. New York: Viking, 1967.
Krotz, Larry. *A Manitoba Album: Royal Visits*. Winnipeg, Can.: Turnstone Press, 1984.
Lacey, Robert. *Majesty: Elizabeth II and the House of Windsor*. New York: Harcourt Brace Jovanovich, 1977.
_____. *Sotheby's: Bidding for Class*. Boston: Little, Brown, 1998.
Laird, Dorothy. *Queen Elizabeth*. London: Hodder, 1966.
Lane, Kenneth Jay. *Faking It*. New York: Abrams, 1996.
Lane, Peter. *The Queen Mother*. London: Robert Hale, 1979.
_____. *Princess Michael of Kent*. Manchester, N.H.: Salem House, 1986.
Latham, Caroline, and Jeannie Sakol. *The Royals*. New York: Congdon & Weed, 1987.
Lawford, Valentine. *Vogue's Book of Houses, Gardens, People*. New York: Viking, 1968.
Lee, Sarah Tomerlin, ed. *American Fashion*. New York: New York Times Book Co., 1975.
Lees-Milne, James. *Harold Nicolson*. London: Hutchinson, 1981.
Leighton, Isabel, ed. *The Aspirin Age 1919–1941*. New York: Simon & Schuster, 1949.
Leslie, Anita. *The Marlborough House Set*. New York: Doubleday, 1973.
Lesley, Cole. *The Life of Noël Coward*. London: Jonathan Cape, 1976.
Lindbergh, Anne Morrow. *The Flower and the Nettle: Diaries and Letters, 1936–1939*. New York: Harcourt Brace Jovanovich, 1976.
Liversidge, Douglas. *The Mountbattens*. London: Arthur Barker, 1978.
Lockhart, J. G. *Cosmo Gordon Lang*. London: Hodder & Stoughton, 1949.
Lockhart, Robert Bruce. *The Diaries of Sir Robert Bruce Lockhart, 1915–1965*. Edited by Kenneth Young. 2 vols. London: Macmillan, 1973.
Lockridge, Norman. *Lese Majesty: The Private Lives of the Duke and Duchess of Windsor*. New York: Boar's Head Books, 1952.
Longford, Elizabeth. *Queen Victoria: Born to Succeed*. New York: Harper & Row, 1964.
_____. *The Royal House of Windsor*. London: Weidenfeld and Nicolson, 1974.
_____. *The Queen Mother*. London: Weidenfeld & Nicolson, 1981.
_____. *Elizabeth R*. London: Weidenfeld & Nicolson, 1983.
_____, ed. *Darling Loosy*. London: Weidenfeld & Nicolson, 1991.
_____. *Royal Throne: The Future of the Monarchy*. London: Hodder & Stoughton, 1993.
Lord, Walter. *The Good Years*. New York: Harper, 1960.

Lowndes, Susan, ed. *Diaries and Letters of Marie Belloc Lowndes, 1911–1947*. London: Chatto & Windus, 1971.

Lundberg, Ferdinand. *The Rich and the Super Rich*. New York: Lyle Stuart, 1968.

MacKay, Robert, Anthony Baker, and Carol A. Traynor. *Long Island Country Houses and Their Architects, 1860–1940*. New York: Norton, 1997.

Mackenzie, Compton. *The Windsor Tapestry*. New York: Frederick A. Stokes, 1938.

———. *The Queen's House: A History of Buckingham Palace*. London: Hutchinson, 1953.

Mackworth-Young, Robin. *The History & Treasures of Windsor Castle*. London: Pitkin Pictorials, 1994.

Macleod, Ian. *Neville Chamberlain*. London: Frederick Muller, 1961.

Maddocks, Melvin. *The Great Liners*. Alexandria, Virginia: Time-Life Books, 1982.

Magnus, Philip. *King Edward the Seventh*. London: John Murray, 1964.

Maine, Basil. *Edward VIII—Duke of Windsor*. London: Hutchinson, 1937.

Manchester, William. *The Last Lion: Winston Spencer Churchill. Alone: 1932–1940*. Boston: Little, Brown, 1988.

Mansbridge, Michael. *John Nash: A Complete Catalogue*. New York: Rizzoli, 1991.

Marchant, William. *The Privilege of His Company: Noël Coward Remembered*. New York: Bobbs-Merrill, 1975.

Marlborough, Laura, Duchess of. *Laughter From a Cloud*. London: Weidenfeld & Nicolson, 1980.

Martin, Ralph G. *The Woman He Loved*. New York: Simon & Schuster, 1973.

Masters, Brian. *Great Hostesses*. London: Constable, 1982.

Matthew, Christopher. *A Different World: Stories of Great Hotels*. New York: Paddington Press, 1976.

Maxtone-Graham, John. *The Only Way to Cross*. New York: Macmillan, 1972.

Maxwell, Elsa. *R.S.V.P. Elsa Maxwell's Own Story*. Boston: Little, Brown, 1954.

Menkes, Suzy. *The Windsor Style*. London: Grafton Books, 1987.

———. *The Royal Jewels*. New York: Contemporary Books, 1989.

Middlemas, Keith. *The Life and Times of George VI*. London: Weidenfeld & Nicolson, 1974.

Middlemas, Keith, and John Barnes. *Baldwin: A Biography*. London: Weidenfeld & Nicolson, 1969.

Miller, Hope Ridings. *Great Houses of Washington, D.C.* New York: Clarkson N. Potter, 1969.

Miller, William H. *SS United States: The Story of America's Greatest Ocean Liner*. New York: Norton, 1991.

Minney, R. J. *The Private Papers of Hore-Belisha*. London: Collins, 1960.

Mitchell, Henry. *Washington: Houses of the Capital*. New York: Viking, 1982.

Mitford, Jessica. *Hons and Rebels*. London: Gollancz, 1960.

Montague-Smith, Patrick, and Hugh Montgomery-Massingberd. *The Country Life Book of Royal Palaces, Castles and Homes*. London: Country Life Books, 1981.

Montgomery-Hyde, H. *Norman Birkett*. London: Hamish Hamilton, 1964.

———. *Baldwin*. London: Hamish Hamilton, 1978.

Montgomery-Massingberd, Hugh. *Blenheim Revisited*. London: Bodley Head, 1985.

Mooney, Michael Macdonald. *Evelyn Nesbit and Stanford White: Love and Death in the Gilded Age*. New York: William Morrow, 1976.

Morshead, Owen. *Windsor Castle*. London: Phaidon Press, 1957.

Morrow, Anne. *The Queen*. New York: William Morrow, 1983.

———. *The Queen Mother*. London: Granada, 1984.

Mortimer, Penelope. *Queen Elizabeth: A Portrait of the Queen Mother*. New York: St. Martin's Press, 1986.

Morton, Andrew. *Inside Buckingham Palace*. New York: Summit Books, 1991.

_____. *Diana: Her True Story*. London: Michael O'Mara Books, 1992.

Morton, Frederic. *The Rothschilds: A Family Portrait*. New York: Atheneum, 1961.

Mosley, Lady Diana. *A Life of Contrasts*. London: Hamish Hamilton, 1977.

_____. *The Duchess of Windsor*. London: Sidgwick & Jackson, 1980.

Mosley, Leonard. *The Reich Marshal: A Biography of Hermann Goering*. New York: Doubleday, 1974.

Mosley, Oswald. *My Life*. London: Thomas Nelson, 1968.

Murat, Laure. *The Splendour of France: Great Chateaux, Mansions and Country Houses*. New York: Rizzoli, 1991.

Murphy, Sophia. *The Mitford Family Album*. London: Sidgwick & Jackson, 1985.

Murray, Mrs. John T., ed. *Palm Beach Entertains*. Tampa, Fla.: Junior League of Palm Beach, Inc., 1976.

Nadelhoffer, Hans. *Cartier: Jewelers Extraordinary*. New York: Abrams, 1984.

Nares, Gordon. *Royal Homes*. London: Country Life, 1953.

Nash, Roy. *Buckingham Palace: The Place and the People*. London: Macdonald Futura, 1980.

Nicolson, Harold. *King George V*. London: Constable, 1952.

_____. *Diaries & Letters, 1930–1939*. Edited by Nigel Nicolson. New York: Atheneum, 1966.

Ogden, Christopher. *Life of the Party: The Biography of Pamela Digby Churchill Hayward Harriman*. New York: Warner Books, 1994.

Olcott, William. *The Greenbrier Heritage*. White Sulphur Springs, W.V.: Arndt, Preston, Chapin, Lamb & Keen, 1967.

Packard, Jerrold M. *The Queen and Her Court*. New York: Scribners, 1981.

Palmer, Lilli. *Change Lobsters and Dance*. New York: Warner Books, 1976.

Parker, John. *King of Fools*. London: Macdonald Futura, 1988.

Parkhurst, Genevieve. *A King in the Making*. London: G. P. Putnam's Sons, 1925.

Patterson, Jerry E. *The Best Families: The Town and Country Social Directory 1846–1996*. New York: Abrams, 1996.

Payn, Graham, and Sheridan Morley, eds. *The Noël Coward Diaries*. Boston: Little, Brown, 1982.

Peacocke, Marguerite. *The Story of Buckingham Palace*. London: Odhams Press, 1952.

Pearce, David. *The Great Houses of London*. New York: Vendome Press, 1986.

Pearson, Hesketh. *The Marrying Americans*. New York: Coward McCann, 1961.

Pimlott, Ben. *The Queen: A Biography of Elizabeth II*. New York: John Wiley, 1997.

Plumb, Barbara. *Horst Interiors*. Boston: Bulfinch Press, 1993.

Plumb, J. H., and Huw Wheldon. *Royal Heritage: The Treasures of the British Crown*. New York: Harcourt Brace Jovanovich, 1977.

_____. *Royal Heritage: The Reign of Elizabeth II*. London: Peerage Books, 1984.

Plumptre, George. *Royal Gardens*. London: Collins, 1981.

Ponsonby, Frederick. *Recollections of Three Reigns*. New York: Dutton, 1952.

Pool, James, and Suzanne Pool. *Who Financed Hitler: The Secret Funding of Hitler's Rise to Power, 1919–1933*. New York: Dial Press, 1978.

Pool, James. *Hitler and His Secret Partners*. New York: Pocket Books, 1997.

Pope-Hennessy, James. *Queen Mary*. London: George Allen and Unwin, 1959.

_____. *A Lonely Business*. Edited by Peter Quennell. London: Weidenfeld and Nicolson, 1981.

The Prince of Wales' Eastern Book: A Pictorial Record of the Voyages of HMS Renown, 1921–1922. London: Hodder and Stoughton, 1922.

Property From the Collection of the Duke & Duchess of Windsor. 3 vols. New York: Sotheby's, 1997.

Pye, Michael. *The King Over the Water*. London: Hutchinson, 1981.

Pye, Anne Briscoe, and Nancy Shea. *The Navy Wife.* New York: Harper & Brothers, 1942.

Ramsthorn, Alice. *Yves Saint Laurent: A Biography.* New York: Doubleday, 1996.

Randall, Monica. *The Mansions of Long Island's Gold Coast.* New York: Rizzoli, 1987.

Rhodes, Robert James. *Memoirs of a Conservative.* London: Weidenfeld & Nicolson, 1969.

_____. *Victor Cazalet.* London: Hamish Hamilton, 1976.

Ribbentrop, Joachim von. *The Ribbentrop Memoirs.* London: Weidenfeld & Nicolson, 1954.

Roberts, A. *The Holy Fox: A Biography of Lord Halifax.* London: Hutchinson, 1991.

Robinson, John Martin. *Buckingham Palace: A Short History.* London: Michael Joseph, 1995.

Romanones, Aline, Countess of. *The Spy Went Dancing.* New York: G. P. Putnam's Sons, 1990.

Rose, Kenneth. *King George V.* New York: Knopf, 1984.

_____. Rose, Kenneth. *Who's Who in the Royal House of Windsor.* New York: Crescent Books, 1985.

Rowse, A. L. *Royal Homes Illustrated.* London: Odhams Press, 1952.

Sailsbury, Marjorie Cecil. *The Gardens of Queen Elizabeth the Queen Mother.* London: Penguin, 1988.

Sancton, Thomas, and Scott MacLeod. *Death of a Princess: The Investigation.* New York: St. Martin's Press, 1998.

Schellenberg, Walter. *Hitler's Secret Service.* New York: Harper & Row, 1956.

Schmidt, Paul. *Hitler's Interpreter.* London: Heinemann, 1951.

Shaum, John H. Jr., and William H. Flayhart III. *Majesty at Sea: The Four Stackers.* New York: Norton, 1981.

Sheean, Vincent. *Between the Thunder and the Sun.* New York: Random House, 1943.

Shew, Betty Spencer. *Queen Elizabeth, the Queen Mother.* London: Macdonald, 1955.

Shewell-Cooper, W. E. *The Royal Gardeners: King George VI and His Queen.* London: Cassell, 1952.

Shirer, William L. *The Collapse of the Third Republic: An Inquiry into the Fall of France in 1940.* New York: Simon & Schuster, 1969.

Simon, Kate. *Fifth Avenue: A Very Social History.* New York: Harcourt Brace Jovanovich, 1978.

Sitwell, Osbert. *Rat Week: An Essay on the Abdication.* London: Michael Joseph, 1984.

_____. *Queen Mary and Others.* London: Michael Joseph, 1974.

Smart, Ted, and David Gibbon. *Royal Family Album.* Text by Don Coolican. London: Colour Library, 1978.

Smith, Charles. *Lord Mountbatten: His Butler's Story.* New York: Stein & Day, 1980.

Smith, Jane S. *Elsie de Wolfe: A Life in the High Style.* New York: Atheneum, 1982.

Smith, Sally Bedell. *Reflected Glory: The Life of Pamela Churchill Harriman.* New York: Simon & Schuster, 1996.

Snowman, A. Kenneth, ed. *The Master Jewelers.* New York: Abrams, 1990.

Speer, Albert. *Inside the Third Reich.* New York: Macmillan, 1970.

Spoto, Donald. *The Decline and Fall of the House of Windsor.* New York: Simon & Schuster, 1995.

Stannard, Martin. *Evelyn Waugh: The Early Years 1903–1939.* New York: Norton, 1987.

Stasz, Clarice. *The Vanderbilt Women.* New York: St. Martin's Press, 1991.

Steele, James. *Queen Mary.* London: Phaidon Press, 1995.

Stefanidis, John. *Rooms: Design and Decoration.* New York: Rizzoli, 1988.

Stevenson, Frances. *Lloyd-George: A Diary.* London: Hutchinson, 1971.

St. John, Adela Rogers. *The Honeycomb.* New York: Doubleday, 1969.

Strachey, Lytton. *Queen Victoria*. New York: Harcourt, Brace, 1921.

Strong, Roy. *Cecil Beaton: The Royal Portraits*. New York: Simon & Schuster, 1988.

_____. *Royal Gardens*. New York: Pocket Books, 1992.

Sullivan, Mark. *Our Times: The United States, 1900–1925, III: Pre-War America*. New York: Scribners, 1930.

Sulzberger, C. L. *A Long Row of Candles: Memoirs and Diaries, 1934–1954*. New York: Macmillan, 1969.

Sutherland, Douglas, and Anthony Purdy. *The Royal Homes & Gardens: A Private View*. London: Leslie Frewin, 1966.

Swallow, Robert W. *Sidelights on Peking Life*. Peking: China Booksellers, 1927.

Sykes, Christopher. *Nancy: The Life of Lady Astor*. London: Collins, 1972.

_____. *Private Palaces: Life in the Great London Houses*. New York: Viking, 1986.

Talbot, Godfrey. *The Country Life Book of Queen Elizabeth the Queen Mother*. London: Country Life Books, 1978.

Tapert, Annette, and Diana Edkins. *The Power of Style: The Women Who Defined the Art of Living Well*. New York: Crown, 1994.

Taylor, A. J. P. *Beaverbrook*. New York: Simon & Schuster, 1972.

Templewood, Viscount. *Nine Troubled Years*. London: Collins, 1954.

Thomas, Gwynne. *King Pawn or Black Knight?* Edinburgh: Mainstream, 1995.

Thomas, Lowell. *Pageant of Romance*. New York: P. F. Collier & Son, 1943.

Thorndike, Joseph J. Jr., *The Very Rich: A History of Wealth*. New York: American Heritage, 1976.

Thornton, Michael. *Royal Feud*. New York: Simon & Schuster, 1985.

Tinniswood, Adrian. *Belton House*. London: National Trust, 1992.

Tomlinson, Richard. *Divine Right: The Inglorious Survival of British Royalty*. London: Little, Brown, 1994.

Townsend, Peter. *The Last Emperor*. New York: Simon & Schuster, 1976.

Townsend, W. and L. *The Biography of HRH the Prince of Wales*. London: Albert E. Marriott, 1929.

Van der Kiste, John. *Childhood at Court, 1819–1914*. London: Alan Sutton, 1995.

_____. *Edward VII's Children*. London: Alan Sutton, 1989.

Vanderbilt, Gloria, and Thelma Furness. *Double Exposure: A Twin Autobiography*. New York: David McKay, 1958.

Vanderbilt II, Arthur T. *Fortune's Children: The Fall of the House of Vanderbilt*. New York: William Morrow, 1989.

Vickers, Hugo. *Cecil Beaton*. London: Weidenfeld & Nicolson, 1985.

_____. *The Private World of the Duke and Duchess of Windsor*. London: Harrods, 1995.

Vidal, Gore. *Palimpsest*. New York: Random House, 1995.

Vreeland, Diana. *D.V.* New York: Knopf, 1984.

Wall, Robert. *Ocean Liners*. Secaucus, N.J.: Chartwell Books, 1977.

Wallace, Ann, and Gabrielle Taylor. *Royal Mothers: From Eleanor of Aquitaine to Princess Diana*. London: Piatkus, 1986.

Warwick, Christopher. *Abdication*. London: Sidgwick & Jackson, 1986.

Waterson, Merlin, ed. *The Country House Remembered: Recollections of Life Between the Wars*. London: Routledge and Kegan Paul, 1985.

Waugh, Evelyn. *The Letters of Evelyn Waugh*. Edited by Mark Amory. London: Weidenfeld & Nicolson, 1980.

Weitz, John. *Hitler's Diplomat: The Life and Times of Joachim von Ribbentrop*. New York: Ticknor & Fields, 1992.

Welfare, Simon, and Alastair Bruce. *Days of Majesty*. New York: Cross River Press, 1993.

Wells, Warre Bradley. *Why Edward Went: Crown, Clique and Church*. New York: Robert M. McBride, 1937.

West, J. B. *Upstairs at the White House*. New York: Coward, McCann & Geoghegan, 1973.

Wheeler-Bennett, John W. *The Nemesis of Power: The German Army in Politics, 1918–1945*. New York: Macmillian, 1953.

_____. *King George VI: His Life and Reign*. London: Macmillan, 1958.

The White House: An Historic Guide. Washington D.C.: White House Historical Association, 1962, 1971 editions.

White, J. Lincoln. *The Abdication of Edward VIII: A Record With all the Published Documents*. London: George Routledge & Sons, 1937.

Whiting, Audrey. *The Kents*. London: Hutchinson, 1985.

Whittle, Tyler. *Victoria and Albert at Home*. London: Routledge and Kegan Paul, 1980.

Williams, Neville. *The Royal Residences of Great Britain*. New York: Macmillan, 1960.

Wilson, Edwina H. [Aileen Winslow]. *Her Name Was Wallis Warfield: The Life Story of Mrs. Ernest Simpson*. New York: Dutton, 1936.

Winchester, Simon. *Their Noble Lordships: Class and Power in Modern Britain*. New York: Random House, 1982.

Windsor, Edward, Duke of. *A Family Album*. London: Cassell, 1960.

Windsor, Wallis, Duchess of. *The Heart Has Its Reasons*. London: Michael Joseph, 1956.

Wrench, Evelyn. *Geoffrey Dawson and Our Times*. London: Hutchinson, 1955.

Wright, Patricia. *The Strange History of Buckingham Palace*. London: Sutton, 1996.

Wright, William. *Heiress: The Rich Life of Marjorie Merriweather Post*. Washington, D.C.: New Republic Books, 1978.

York, Sarah, Duchess of, with Jeff Coplon. *My Story*. New York: Simon & Schuster, 1996.

Young, G. M. *Stanley Baldwin*. London: Rupert Hart-Davis, 1952.

Yugoslavia, Queen Alexandra of. *Prince Philip: A Family Portrait*. New York: Bobbs-Merrill, 1960.

Ziegler, Philip. *Crown & People*. New York: Knopf, 1978.

_____. *Diana Cooper*. London: Hamish Hamilton, 1981.

_____. *Mountbatten: A Biography*. New York: Knopf, 1985.

_____, ed. *The Diaries of Lord Louis Mountbatten, 1920–1922, Tours with the Prince of Wales*. London: Collins, 1987.

_____, ed. *From Shore to Shore: The Tour Diaries of Earl Mountbatten of Burma, 1953–1979*. London: Collins, 1989.

_____. *King Edward VIII*. New York: Knopf, 1991.

Documents

Documents on German Foreign Policy. London: Her Majesty's Stationary Office, 1957–1966.

Hansard's Parliamentary Debates; referenced by date in source notes.

U.S. State Department Files, in the U.S. National Archives, Washington, D.C., referenced by date in source notes.

Periodicals and Journals

"A Love Affair With Style." *Town and Country*, April 1988.

Bry, Charlene. "End of an Era." *People*, 22 December 1986.

Cornforth, John. "The Duke and Duchess of Windsor in Paris." *Country Life*, 25 June 1987.

Cowles, Fleur. "The Duchess of Windsor Talks Clothes With Fleur Cowles." *Harper's Bazaar*, May 1966.

"Edward Windsor Presents a Television Documentary About the Great Uncle He Never Knew." *Hello!* 13 April 1996.

Edwards, Anne. "Fort Belvedere: Inside the Private Realm of Edward VIII and Wallis Simpson." *Architectural Digest*, December 1991.

Montgomery-Hyde, H. "The Windsors and the Londonderrys." *Harpers & Queens*, July 1980.

"Mrs Wallis Simpson: Her Royal Romance and Life Story." *Modern Romance*, 1936.

Oursler, Fulton, Jr. "Secret Treason." *American Heritage*, December 1991.

Pryce-Jones, David. "TV Tale of Two Windsors." *New York Times Magazine*, 18 March 1979.

Romanones, Aline. "The Dear Romance." *Vanity Fair*. June 1986.

Rozsnyai, Susan. "On the 24th Anniversary of the Duke of Windsor's Death." Oonagh Shanley: The Woman Who Was with Him to the End, Tells Her Story for the First Time." *Hello!* 1 June 1996.

St. John, Adela Rogers. "Windsors Own Story." King Features Syndicate, Inc., November 1940.

Seward, Ingrid. "A King's Ransom." *Majesty*, September 1997.

Thomas, Philip M. "The Duchess of Windsor: Her Position Reappraised." *Burke's Peerage*, 104th ed. 1967.

Visitor, October–December 1992.

Watson, Francis. "The Death of George V." *History Today*, December 1986.

Webster, Jonathan. "Madame Metz—Social Secretary to the Duchess—Speaks Publicly for the First Time About Their Very Special Relationship." *Hello!* 21 February 1998.

Windsor, Edward, Duke of. "My Garden." *Life*, 16 July 1956.

Windsor, Wallis, Duchess of. "Our First Real Home." *Woman's Home Companion*, October and November 1954.

_____. "Our Life Today." *Look*, 30 October 1956.

_____. "My Personal Cookbook." *American Weekly*, 2 and 16 November 1958.

Index